WAGE AND SALARY ADMINISTRATION

SECOND
EDITION

HERBERT G. ZOLLITSCH, M.S., Ph.D.

Personnel Consultant
and Professor of Industrial Management.
College of Business Administration
Marquette University

ADOLPH LANGSNER, M.E., M.B.A.

Former Management Consultant,
Lecturer at Northwestern University,
and Factory Manager, Eugene Dietzgen Company

P31

PUBLISHED BY

SOUTH-WESTERN PUBLISHING CO.

Cincinnati • Chicago • Dallas • New Rochelle, N.Y. • Burlingame, Calif.

DEDICATED TO THE MEMORY

of

ADOLPH LANGSNER

Gentleman — Thinker — Doer

A Pioneer in the Field of Adequate and Equitable Compensation

Library of Congress Catalog Card Number: 76-94053

2 3 4 5 6 K 4 3 2 1

Printed in the United States of America

preface

Since the first edition of this book was published, the field of compensation has continued to be as dynamic as technological and social progress. There have been advancements in compensation theories, criteria, assumptions, laws, techniques, and research. The revised edition, therefore, is intended to update the text so that it incorporates the most recent compensation progress and the many helpful suggestions that have been received by readers and users of the first edition. In this way, the revised text should prove even more practical and worthwhile than the first edition.

The basic aim of this book is to present to students of wage and salary administration the philosophy and fundamental guiding principles that are essential for establishing and maintaining adequate and equitable compensation for all employees in an enterprise. The book is intended as a textbook for undergraduate and graduate college students. In addition, practitioners in industrial engineering and wage and salary administration, and others interested in gaining an insight into the various activities, principles, and techniques of compensation should find the book resourceful.

Fundamentally, we believe that sound wage and salary administration attempts to attract competent employees, retain them in the company, inspire employees to do their best, and reward everyone according to merit and accomplishment. The various parts of this book are intended to show how these objectives may be accomplished.

Throughout the textbook we have attempted to present a philosophy of successful compensation based on fair treatment for the employee, the employer, and the customer. The practice of fair play is involved in every decision, principle, procedure, or technique. Emphasis has been placed on the philosophy of why certain procedures must be strictly followed, together with the practices that have been tested and proven successful.

It has long been recognized that the satisfactory compensation of employees in an enterprise involves more than the application of a single technique. Successful wage and salary administration requires the coordinating of the many facets of compensation under the direction of an executive in personnel management. The sequence of the chapters in this book have been arranged to guide the reader through the development of the various areas in wage and salary administration so as to show how the principles, fundamentals, procedures, and current practices are coordinated and utilized in building a solid foundation and a stable compensation structure.

Part One, *Introduction and Background*, contains two chapters that inform the reader about the present scope of the field of wage and salary administration and the historical events that preceded present-day activities. Students who have completed courses in personnel administration, industrial management, labor problems, or other courses relating to the subject of compensation, may find that they are already acquainted with the background and present scope of the field of wage and salary administration. If such is the case, these chapters may be omitted or read as a review prior to covering the second part of the book.

In Part Two, *The Framework of Wage and Salary Administration*, discussions are devoted to identifying the role that wage and salary administration plays in an enterprise and what the essentials are for its successful accomplishment.

In Part Three, *Fundamentals of Job Evaluation*, the chapters are devoted to the theory, principles, procedures, and methods involved in analyzing and rating jobs to establish clear job differentials as well as to price the jobs. Full consideration is given to the relationship between jobs and positions in the total compensation picture. Our objective is to discuss "why" certain techniques and methods are necessary and, at the same time, to explain "how" they are applied.

Part Four, *Fundamentals of Employee Evaluation*, contains three chapters which emphasize the effect that the employee and his performance have in determining wage differentials for the same job and for the total compensation. The theory and practice of establishing job standards and employee performance are fully discussed, since employee evaluation serves as the basis for granting monetary rewards according to individual merit and provides an incentive for an employee to work up to his capacity.

Part Five, *Basic Systems and Plans of Compensating Employees*, contains chapters that identify the various methods used to pay employees. These chapters also describe the influence that the behavior sciences have had on compensation. Special treatment is given to individual, group, and plant-wide incentives that are available to employers for stimulating employees to perform to the limit of their capacities.

Part Six, *Supplementary Plans of Compensating Employees*, identifies the importance and use of supplementary compensations in the overall compensating structure.

Part Seven, *Managerial Compensation*, comprises chapters that show how the principles, procedures, practices, and theory of compensation apply to foremen, supervisors, professionals, and executives in an enterprise.

Part Eight, *Wage and Salary Administrative Controls*, identifies the various controls and activities that need to be integrated into remuneration activities if an already equitable wage and salary compensation program is to be adequately maintained.

All chapters are followed by thought-provoking review questions, research or seminar questions, practical experience assignments, and realistic case problems that are intended to stimulate the student's interest in the subject matter as well as to acquaint him with practical problems and how to cope with them. The practical experience assignments represent a teaching aid designed to give the student real insight into supervisory and administrative problems. These assignments are actual day-to-day problems and experiences that will provide the students with opportunities to develop judgment and to gain mature viewpoints. These teaching aids are intended to coordinate effectively the theory with the practice.

Since "One picture is worth 10,000 words," we believe that the illustrations, tables, and figures contained in this book are an immensely valuable means of clarifying discussions to give the reader a better understanding and grasp of the subject. An effort has been made to bring the tables and figures as up-to-date as possible. However, the reader should bear in mind that some tables and figures are introduced for illustrative and comparison purposes only.

We believe that the best textbooks are the result of suggestions and constructive criticism offered by those who use the books. We will therefore gratefully welcome any comments, advice, suggestions, or ideas that the readers may have on how this book may be improved.

During the revision of this book, Mr. Langsner passed away on September 15, 1967. The book is thus dedicated to his memory.

The authors are grateful to the many companies and publishers which were very responsive to our requests for permission to quote and to reprint some of their original materials. The wholehearted cooperation we have received from these organizations and their personnel is greatly appreciated.

It is impossible to enumerate all the many persons, commercial and manufacturing enterprises, and publishers to whom we are indebted for their cooperation. Painstaking care has been used throughout the book to give due credit and to acknowledge the permissions to quote or reproduce authentic material. However, we wish to extend our appreciation to the following individuals, who are not cited elsewhere, for their part in the preparation of the book.

To our wives, Donna T. Zollitsch and Lucy S. Langsner, we are indebted for their continued patience and understanding during the revision of the book.

To Messrs. James Moriarty, Culter-Hammer, Inc., Milwaukee; Bert L. Metzger, Profit Sharing Research Foundation, Chicago; Michael Smith, First Wisconsin Bank, Milwaukee; James H. Landree and Neal Meitler of A-C Electronics Division of General Motors, Inc.; Louis Seiberlick, Manpower, Inc., Milwaukee; and to Professors Walter Korek, St. Norbert's College; B. Lewis Keeling, Bucks County Community College; Clement Nouri and Stewart Scrimshaw of Marquette University our thanks for having read parts of the manuscript and for offering constructive criticism.

To Professors Eugene S. Booker, Western Michigan University; Elmer H. Burack, Illinois Institute of Technology; John E. Burns, De Paul University; Ralph C. Davis, Ohio State University; Carl O. Mann, University of Toledo; Franklin G. Moore, University of Michigan; Ralph S. Novak, Northern Illinois University; Everett Refior, Wisconsin State College at Whitewater, Wisconsin; James Schaefer, University of Wisconsin at Milwaukee; Frederick R. Shedd, Michigan State University; Warren C. Waterhouse, Bowling Green State University; Joseph P. Schwitter, Kent State University; Joseph W. Towle, Washington University; Joseph Atwood, Lloyd Doney, Howard Healy, and Richard Kaimann of Marquette University; Messrs. Roland Hennarichs, Caterpillar Tractor Co.; Robert De Satnick of Booz, Allen, & Hamilton, Inc.; John P. Malloy, Modern Machine Works; Edwin E. Ross, Milwaukee Employers Assn.; Harvey Gittler, American Radiator and Standard Sanitary Corp., New York; Nicholas Fostar, Albert Raymond and Associates, as well as to many former students who occupy important managerial positions, we are grateful for their interest and constructive comments that were helpful in revising this edition.

Our thanks to Sandy Lukaszek Gorecki, Carole Mickle, Jeanne Blasky Batcheor, and Dolores Rewolinski for their assistance in typing and proofreading and to former students John Becker, Dave Brandel, James Schreier, and Kelly Kornely for having performed a number of tasks essential to the manuscript.

While it is a pleasure to make the above-mentioned acknowledgments, it is understood, of course, that the authors assume full responsibility for the views, philosophies, and possible shortcomings in this book.

Herbert G. Zollitsch
Adolph Langsner

contents

part one • Introduction and background

part two • The framework of wage and salary administration

part three • *Fundamentals of job evaluation*

part four • *Fundamentals of employee evaluation*

part five • Basic systems and plans of compensating employees

part six • *Supplementary plans of compensating employees*

part seven • *Managerial compensation*

part eight • *Wage and salary administrative controls*

chapter 1

THE FIELD OF WAGE AND SALARY ADMINISTRATION

For the past seventy years there have been great technological advances in the United States. We have progressed from the horse and buggy era to the space age. With these developments has come a new concept of human values that recognizes employees as the important factor in our technological progress. The principal difference between one business firm and another — or between the success and the failure of an enterprise — is people. Today's emphasis upon people is revolutionizing socioeconomic and political thinking and is developing new and better methods of compensating employees.

The economic greatness of the United States is due to many factors, of which mass production, purchasing power, and consumption have played a major role. This means that the wages and salaries that employees earn are vital to their standard of living and to the socioeconomic well-being of society as a whole. Employees are anxious to have satisfactory jobs, steady incomes, and social prestige. Employers are interested in keeping production costs low enough to compete in the open market and to be able to earn sufficient profits to pay adequate dividends for invested capital. The customer is interested in effective production so as to obtain more high-quality products and services at the lowest prices. The vast majority of the consuming public is against prolonged disputes between employees and employers that disrupt a normal satisfying life and a

1

WAGE AND SALARY ADMINISTRATION

WHAT it is known by:	For WHOM:	Payments may be made in MEDIA of:	Total compensation may depend upon such FACTORS as:
Compensation or Remuneration or Wages, Salaries, and Fringes	Factory workers Clerical help Supervisors Sales Administrative Technical Professional Executives (all employees)	Cash Paychecks Bonuses Profit sharing Stock options Pensions Insurance Vacations Holidays Awards Rest periods Lunches Services	Skill Effort Responsibility Working conditions } of Job Supply and demand (Motivation Performance) of Employee Productivity (Profitability Costs Type Location) of Industry Cost of living Going wages Laws Traditions Customers) of Community Collective bargaining

FIGURE 1.1   GENERAL NATURE OF WAGE AND SALARY ADMINISTRATION

smooth-functioning national economy. Thus, employees, employers, customers, and the general public are all affected by the well-being of our national economy. All have a vital interest and a part in the establishment of a sound and equitable wage and salary program and its administration. The purpose of this first chapter is to present an overall framework of what is involved in the field of wage and salary administration.

What is wage and salary administration?

Wage and salary administration may be thought of as the planning, organizing, and controlling of those activities that relate to the direct and indirect payments made to employees for the work they perform or the services they render. A more accurate and all-inclusive term to describe such activities would be the word "compensation." However, the business world has been slow to accept this term; therefore, we shall consider the more commonly used expression of "wage and salary administration" as synonymous with the word "compensation." Remuneration is occasionally used as a substitute term for either compensation or wage and salary administration.

Nature of Wage and Salary Administration

In analyzing the definition of wage and salary administration, it should be made clear that the reference to employees is all inclusive (from the janitor to the president). This means that compensation concerns operating workers in the factory, clerical personnel in the offices, first-line supervisors, junior and senior executives, salesmen, and professional, administrative, and technical personnel. The reference to direct and indirect payments means that all forms of remuneration — cash, bonuses, profit sharing, pensions, insurance, vacations, holidays, rest periods, stock options, and awards — come under the purview of wage and salary administration.

To compensate employees adequately and equitably there are a host of factors to be considered. Some of the more common factors that usually have a bearing on how large a wage or salary the employee receives are as follows: the skill, effort, responsibility, and working conditions of the job; the supply, motivation, and performance of the employee; the productivity, profitability, costs, and type of industry; the cost of living, area wages, legislation, traditions, and customer reactions of the community; and the relationship between the union and management in collective bargaining.

It is easy to see that the subject of wage and salary administration contains a vast number of diverse factors that have to be dealt with in some meaningful fashion if employee compensation is to be successful. The general nature of wage and salary administration is summarized in Figure 1.1.

Common Misconceptions About Wage and Salary Administration

It is generally assumed that workers are adequately and equitably compensated and that there is a definite relationship between compensation and production based on the maxim, "a fair day's pay for a fair day's work." As discussed later, however, the complex problem of what constitutes "fair" to both employer and employee is not always satisfactorily solved. Apparently, neither employers nor employees realize the full significance of establishing practical criteria (standard values) for jobs, wages, and salaries that can be agreed upon by both parties. If they did, millions of man-hours would not be lost because of strikes, work interferences, and other misunderstandings.

It is often taken for granted that production is now maintained at the highest possible level by means of employer-employee agreements. However, we find management maintaining that production pace-setting and labor-compensating matters are management's prerogative. Labor, on the other hand, insists on workers' rights to bargain, and demands a "just wage" and a fair share for the extra efforts that increase output. Inevitably, productivity is not kept at a maximum while the two forces pull in opposite directions.

Similarly, it appears — superficially at least — that the wage and salary agreements between employers and employees are satisfactory. Nevertheless, both sides generally harbor distrust. Some employers tend to keep wages as low as possible in order to reduce costs, while employees often conspire to prolong their jobs by restricting production.

Adherence to the underlying principles of job standardization and the fundamentals of compensation will create a friendlier understanding between management and labor. Agreements and adjustments can be made only if standards are established. Then, by logical comparison, each wage criterion may be weighed. Furthermore, wage and salary criteria are unreliable unless job categories and the values of each job class in comparison with other job classes are considered.

General goals of wage and salary administration

In order for the various facets of compensation to be handled in a logical, meaningful, and systematic manner, it is necessary to identify the overall goals that are being attempted in the field of wage and salary administration. The student, or remuneration practitioner, may quickly become confused by the vast number of goals to be achieved by this field. For this reason, only the global goals will be described at this time to obtain a firm grasp of the "big picture." The more specific objectives will be reserved for Chapter 3, "The Role of the Wage and Salary Administrator in an Enterprise," because the administrator is charged with carrying out these objectives.

The management of any enterprise should be vitally interested in its employees because employees are the most important ingredient in the makeup of a firm and thus are the key to the company's success. If employees are to make an enterprise successful, the relationship between the managers and the employees should be at least a satisfactory one, if not an ideal or a perfect one. Managements need to foster a cooperative relationship to stimulate employees to be efficient and to work up to their capabilities. The company, therefore, needs to do whatever is necessary to secure competent employees and to see that they are given the opportunity to develop and perform according to their greatest efficiency. Thus, the general objectives of wage and salary administration are intended to assist these overall management goals.

The following are the major goals of compensation:

To Motivate Employees to Optimum Job Performance

It is common knowledge that very few employees in any enterprise are performing as well as they are capable. Industrial engineers generally believe that the average employee is only performing about one half of what he could perform without any danger to his health. Therefore, managements are anxious to find ways and means of encouraging the employees to improve their efficiency.

Wage and salary administration is considered one of the key departments or vehicles for motivating employees. This may be accomplished by offering various financial and nonfinancial wage incentives to create a desire on the part of the employee to be more efficient and productive. If employees are to be spurred on to work up to their capabilities, they must receive their fair share of the rewards of the increased productivity and efficiency of the company.

To Control Employee Costs

If an enterprise is to be competitive in its field, the various costs it incurs have to be justified. One of the largest costs in a company is the compensation of its employees. Wages and salaries of all employees from the sweeper to the president have to be controlled. This may be done by developing compensation policies and procedures that make the various employee costs equitable and keep them in balance with their value to the enterprise. If a company is to offer job security to its employees, it must be financially successful. This means that there must be a proper balance between expenditures and their results.

To Provide a Basis for the Effective Hiring, Utilization, and Promotion of Employees

If an enterprise hopes to attract, hire, develop, promote, and utilize competent employees, it needs reliable information upon which to base its decisions. Wage and salary administration provides staff assistance in analyzing jobs and establishing job performance standards useful as a basis for evaluating the

WAGE AND SALARY ADMINISTRATION		
WHAT it attempts to do (AIMS)	**HOW it attempts to do this** (METHODS)	**WHY it is done** (JUSTIFICATION)
1. Motivate employees to optimum job performance	By offering various incentives to make the employee want to be more efficient and productive	To increase productivity for greater profits, higher wages, and lower selling prices
2. Control employee costs	By establishing policies, methods, and procedures for making costs competitive, consistent, and commensurate with their contribution	To establish a favorable balance between the various employee costs so the returns to the company, investors, employees, and customers are adequate to give the company security and respectability
3. Provide a basis for the effective hiring, utilization, and promotion of employees	By establishing job standards and evaluating employee performance	To make more efficient use of employees and to create greater employee job satisfaction
4. Promote harmonious employee-employer relations	By paying a fair day's pay for a fair day's work (equity)	To be a satisfactory company to work for and to reduce compensation grievances and strikes

FIGURE 1.2   GENERAL OBJECTIVES OF WAGE AND SALARY ADMINISTRATION

employee and in making these decisions. Employee performance, therefore, should be periodically evaluated and communicated to the employee so that his performance can be efficiently utilized and he may be satisfied with the type of work to which he is assigned.

To Promote Employee Cooperation Through Harmonious Employer-Employee Relations

Sound personnel management has established that most employees are more likely to cooperate with management directives when relations between the employee and the employer are on a pleasant basis. Since many union-management disagreements come from compensation matters, good wage and salary administration can do much to promote harmonious union-management relations. This is done by attempting to determine what a fair day's work is and then to pay a fair day's wage. If this goal is never attempted, the company is not likely to have a high reputation among employees or in the community, nor to be considered a good place in which to work. Unless this relationship goal is satisfactorily reached, a company may be plagued with wage and salary grievances and labor strife. The record shows that in the state of New Jersey, disputes surrounding wages and related issues accounted for at least half of all work stoppages in every year of the 12-year period 1952 through 1963.[1]

The above four considerations represent the global aims of compensation. These should give the student a picture of the "forest" before attempting to examine the "trees" or subgoals. The general objectives of wage and salary administration are summarized in Figure 1.2.

Once it is made clear what is being attempted in the field of compensation, it is then appropriate to identify the activities that have to be performed to accomplish the objectives. These activities are discussed in the section below.

Major wage and salary activities

Every company, large or small, has to provide systematic and coordinated activities that serve as a sound foundation for compensating employees in an equitable and adequate manner. The following major activities are typical of those carried on in the field of wage and salary administration.

Development and Communication of Wage and Salary Policies and Plans

Compensation policies and plans, whether formal or informal, establish the goals, working framework, and guidelines to administer a remuneration program. They also serve as criteria for evaluating how successful or unsuccessful

---

[1]Institute of Management and Labor Relations, *Work Stoppages in New Jersey 1952–1963*, Work Stoppage Series No. 2 (New Brunswick: Rutgers — The State University, 1965), p. 9.

the program has been. After policies and plans have been carefully formulated, they need to be disseminated to all employees involved so there will be no doubts about management's intentions or suspicions of its integrity. This phase of compensation is fully treated in Chapter 4.

Analysis of All Company Jobs

Analyzing the jobs in the company provides the factual basis for arriving at a host of decisions that are important to both management and the union. Facts are needed to prepare job descriptions and job specifications that are used to evaluate, classify, and code jobs for company use. These facts are instrumental in determining the value of each job to the company. Facts are also instrumental in establishing job performance standards as a basis for evaluating employees. Such facts provide reasonable men with the rationale for arriving at solutions to problems arising out of collective bargaining. Chapters 11 and 12 are devoted to the methods and techniques of analyzing jobs and preparing job descriptions and specifications.

Evaluation and Classification of Jobs

One of the major problems of compensation is to appraise jobs; that is, how to find their order of importance to the company. Fundamental to this is a knowledge of how the various jobs in the company differ. Job evaluation techniques provide a means of comparing jobs according to their skill, effort, responsibility, and working conditions, and arriving at a designated overall value of each position. The jobs can then be classified into similar groups and a starting wage assigned to each. Chapters 6 through 13 discuss the fundamentals of evaluating and classifying jobs.

Pricing Jobs

This means deciding upon the starting wage or salary for each job in the company. This decision is a difficult one because a beginning wage has to be high enough to attract capable employees and low enough to keep the company from losing money. Many factors influence the starting wage for each job. Among these are the wages other companies are paying for comparable jobs, the collective bargaining position of union and management, the traditional relationships among jobs, the cost of living, and the minimum wage laws. Usually wage surveys play an important part in determining starting wages. Unless jobs are priced according to a systematic and consistent procedure, several comparable jobs might be priced at various levels, thus causing resentment by the respective holders of these jobs. Eliminating wage inequities by pricing jobs fairly is another major problem of wage and salary administration. Chapter 13 is devoted to the subject of pricing jobs within a company.

Establishing Compensation Structures

This activity consists of plotting the results of job evaluation on graph paper so that the whole picture of the company wage structure can be viewed for analysis. Such a graph or job scattergram allows the company to compare its wage structure with other community wage structures. Such comparisons are helpful in appraising equitability and competitiveness, and in formulating future company policies.

Separate wage structures may be developed for such job groups as factory workers, clerical employees, managerial personnel, and sales, administrative, professional, and technical employees. Wage structures are also instrumental in determining internal wage equitability as well as establishing a pay range for each job. Maximum pay rates for each job need to be established that will serve as a strong incentive for each employee to advance himself. Chapter 13 discusses the determination of pay ranges and wage structures.

Determining Performance Standards for Jobs and Methods of Payment

Various job performance standards need to be established because they affect several aspects of compensation. They assist in determining what a fair day's work is, what constitutes success or failure on a job, and what rewards and methods of payment may be appropriate to the employee's job performance. Chapter 15 is devoted to these topics.

Employee Evaluation

Appraising employees is an essential activity if an employee is to be paid a fair day's pay for a fair day's work. Only through periodic evaluation is it possible to reward employees for exceptional contributions or for extra effort put forth in maintaining the highest quantity and quality of production. After the various job performance standards are established for the various degrees of job success, the employee's performance can be appraised by comparing his results with the job standards. Thus, the basis for adequate compensation commensurate with performance has been established. Chapters 14 through 16 deal with the fundamentals of employee evaluation.

Motivation of Employees

Stimulating employees to work up to their capabilities has always been a management function. A wage and salary program utilizes financial and non-financial incentives to motivate employees to greater performance. The number of powerful incentives available to management are many. The more common forms include bonuses, profit sharing, stock options, suggestion awards, extended vacations, and pensions. Incentives may be of the individual, group, or plant-wide types. How to control supplementary compensation (fringe benefits) and to use incentives properly are probably the greatest problems facing wage and salary administrators today. Contemporary and past methods of motivating employees through incentives and supplementary compensations (fringes) are dealt with in Chapters 17 through 21.

Administering and Maintaining a Compensation Program

This activity involves the housekeeping duties that go with any management program. In compensation it consists of adjusting wages and salaries according to the fluctuations of the labor market. It includes keeping track of remuneration records and granting pay raises based on seniority, merit, etc. Assuming that the previously discussed compensation activities have been carried out effectively and the wage and salary program has achieved an equitable status, it is necessary to see that this condition is maintained. Procedures have to be established to control costs and to assure that the program is coordinated, competitive, consistent, fair, and soundly conceived and perpetuated. The purpose of Chapter 26 is to treat the mechanics of maintaining an equitable program.

These major activities of wage and salary administration represent not only the main areas around which the field is composed but also the major problems encountered. The major activities of wage and salary administration are summarized in Figure 1.3.

Importance of wage and salary administration

Wage and salary administration should be conducted in such a manner that it will benefit the enterprise, the employees, and indirectly the public. We shall now point out its effect on each of these groups.

Importance to the Public

On a national scale, compensation costs constitute upwards of 70 percent of the total cost of a product. According to United States government statistics, wages and salaries represent 54 percent of the total value of all the goods and services produced in the United States (Gross National Product).[2] However, these statistics on wages and salaries do not include supplementary compensations (fringes) which, according to the United States Chamber of Commerce, average at least 26.6 percent of payrolls.[3] Neither do the wage and salary figures include those of farmers or proprietors. Thus, when all forms of compensation are considered, they are estimated to be at least 70 percent of the Gross National Product (GNP).

---

[2]U.S. Bureau of the Census, *Statistical Abstract of the United States* (89th ed.; Washington: U.S. Government Printing Office, 1968), pp. 312 and 317.
[3]Chamber of Commerce of the United States, *Employee Benefits 1967* (1968), p. 5.

WAGE AND SALARY ACTIVITIES

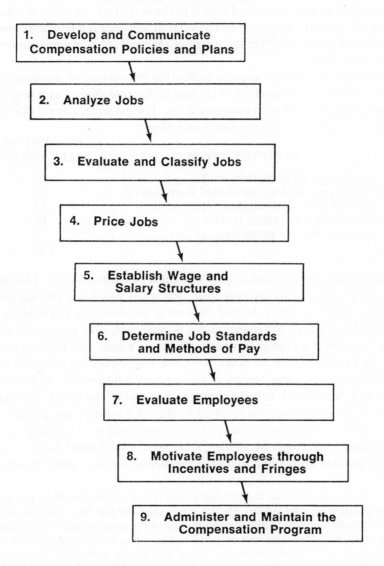

FIGURE 1.3 SUMMARY OF THE MAJOR ACTIVITIES OF WAGE AND SALARY ADMINISTRATION

When an average American buys an average American product — be it a suit of clothes, a car, or an appliance — very little of the price he pays for the product is for the actual, tangible materials out of which the product is made. More than three fourths of the purchase price goes to pay the men and women who transformed the raw materials into the finished product, transported the product to the market place, and sold it to the consumer. In other words, what we are *really* buying when we spend a dollar at the store is a few cents' worth of materials and more than 75 cents' worth of *time and effort* of some employee or group of employees.[4]

Too often the public does not realize the importance of compensation in relation to the cost of a product. This may be because *direct* wages may appear as a small percentage of total company costs. For example, assume that the five basic costs of all businesses are stated as follows:

COMPANY COSTS	PERCENT OF SALES DOLLAR
1. Equipment (depreciation, etc.)...................	6
2. Goods and services (purchased from others).....	44
3. Labor (wages and salaries)....................	33
4. Government payments (taxes)...................	10
5. Profits (return to investors)....................	7
	100

It appears that compensation is only one third of the total cost. This may be true as far as direct costs are concerned, but when goods and services are purchased, does not the largest share of this cost go for the direct and indirect wages that the supplier pays? When equipment is purchased, does not a good share of the purchase price go for commissions, bonuses, wages, and indirect benefits? When the company pays its taxes, does not this money go primarily for the wages, salaries, and fringe benefits of those people who provide the government services and benefits for us? In short, an analysis of the direct, indirect, and supplementary compensations involved in the total price of any product is the "lion's share" and must be justified or the customer may not be getting true value for his money. Mr. Roger M. Blough, Chairman of the United States Steel Corporation, pointed up the importance of compensation costs when he said:

> If you took all of the products that are made in America, put them in one huge pile, and added up the price tags on the lot, upwards of three quarters of this total value would represent the employment costs that were incurred all along the line of production. The remaining quarter or less would cover not only the basic cost of all the raw materials but would also pay for the rental of property, the interest on debt, and the dividends that pay for use of all of the tools of production that were employed in the manufacture of these products.[5]

---

[4]Roger M. Blough, "A Tale of Two Cities" (From a speech published by Employee Relations, Inc., New York, 1958), p. 8.

[5]Roger M. Blough, "Price and the Public Interests" (From a speech to the Detroit Economic Club, September 15, 1958). See *U.S. Steel Quarterly*, Vol. XII, No. 4 (November, 1958), p. 7.

Importance to the Company

Wage and salary administration is important to the company because compensation costs are the largest costs of production. To be competitive, a company needs to keep its labor costs in balance with the results that labor produces. When wages and salaries are not administered properly, the company is likely to be plagued with grievances on these matters. Very few companies, or employees, can afford the costs of strikes resulting from such wage disagreements. If an employer hopes to attract and hold high-grade employees, his wages, salaries, and supplementary compensations (fringes) have to be adequate. When the company's compensation structure becomes obsolete or inadequate, the employer can expect to experience such problems as lower morale, higher labor turnover, absenteeism, increased unit costs, and lower quality and quantity of work.

Importance to the Employee

Compensation is considered one of the primary incentives for an employee to be productive and to develop himself. To the employee it represents his standard of living. It may offer him security, status, and the chance to satisfy his basic needs. Most employees are interested in learning about the different facets of wage and salary administration. They want to know the starting wage of a job and the maximum possible for it. They want to know which are the better paying jobs in the company. They want to know whether they are being compensated fairly and how well. They want to know how to get pay raises. In short, wage and salary matters are of keen interest to the employee because they greatly affect him and his family's standing in the community.

Differences between wages and salaries

The term "wage" is commonly used to denote payment for job performance or services rendered, and is also used as a general term to indicate the different types of remuneration such as salaries, piece rates, bonuses, and premiums. In line with our discussion, wages refer to compensations paid to workers hired on an hourly basis and who are paid for the actual time spent on a job. Wages also mean the aggregate earnings of an hourly worker for a given period of time calculated by multiplying the number of hours worked times the hourly base-rate. The term "salary" refers to the remuneration of executives, supervisors, office employees, and salesmen hired on a basis other than an hourly rate, such as weekly, biweekly, semimonthly, monthly, or annually. Since part of a Roman soldier's pay was in salt, the word salary is said to have come from the word salt, or sal, which means pay.

It is significant to note that there are two hierarchies in the compensation structure. For example, in a factory or in a workshop, there is the wage hierarchy that is confined to the ability and skill of the worker or the evaluated job. In the salary hierarchy, the differentials conform to the position and function at the organizational level. These characteristics are sometimes used in reference to "blue-collar workers" and "white-collar workers" respectively.

Because of the two hierarchies, some companies have separate wage and salary programs. Therefore, in some companies where a large variety of jobs exist and both group structures differ considerably, there is a "wage administrator" and a "salary administrator." Furthermore, the wage group, as such, is usually union organized, which means that all base rates are bargained for, with periodic contract renewals for the entire group. On the other hand, the salaried group, especially those at the exempt level — that is, those employees exempt from overtime compensation and not subject to seniority regulations according to the Fair Labor Standards Act —, remains aloof from joining unions and generally prefers to deal with the employer individually regarding salary rates.

Most companies (large, medium size, and small), however, combine the programs of both groups; hence, the combined function of wage and salary administration. It is claimed that the preparation of one plan, even with variations, is simpler and easier to explain to workers and supervisors. It is also believed that by combining the two programs, higher administrative expenses can more easily be avoided than when two separate programs exist.

Fundamental assumptions of wage and salary administration

Every field of endeavor is said to rest upon certain assumptions or foundations. These assumptions are general beliefs or propositions that appear reasonable and valid although, like many other assumptions in life, they have not been scientifically tested. On the basis of known research studies and current knowledge that is available, there is more evidence to support these assumptions than there is to doubt their validity. However, more research studies are needed to prove beyond a doubt that the following basic assumptions are the basis upon which the field of wage and salary administration rests.

1. An industrial enterprise must be reasonably competitive to survive. Therefore, efficiency in a firm is not only desirable but also a necessity.
2. Compensation should be primarily based on up-to-date values that employees and jobs have to the employee and to the employer. These *values can be measured in a consistent and systematic manner* by reasonable and fully qualified people. However, the criteria for measurement may be different for the various groups of employees and jobs evaluated, i.e., Administrative, Clerical, Crafts, Executives, Professional, Sales, and Supervisory.
3. Labor is a factor of production; therefore, its compensation must depend upon production. This means that wages or salaries have to be

earned through productivity. Higher wages and benefits cannot be given as "gifts" from management, except at the expense of others, such as the customer or the employer. If management is to be fair to all those concerned with the future progressive prosperity of the enterprise, higher wages and benefits can be granted only when "earned" through increased productivity.

4. Employee motivation is tied to the ever-changing needs and wants of employees. Human nature is such that employees rarely fulfill all their needs and wants. Economists and psychologists have established that the satisfaction of one human want automatically creates another want.

5. Money is a prime motivator of employees up to the point where employees can reach the standard of living they have set for themselves and their families.

6. Supplementary compensations (fringes) become more important as motivators after employees' wages or salaries provide them with the standard of living they have set for themselves. Supplementary compensations generally involve job security in healthful environments and provision for sufficient income after the employees' productive years cease.

7. More workers would rather be employed on a steady job, even though it may pay a lower wage, than on a job with less security.

8. Most employees have a sense of fair play and will be reasonable when dealing with a reasonable and responsible management. They will share with the employer the rewards of increased production which they help create. However, they will have a tendency to hold back their job efforts under such conditions as when: the outlook for a secure job is limited; basic practices have not been thoroughly tested; employees lack respect for their management; pay appears inequitable; compensation policies are not clearly understood; management fails to keep its word; and when decisions involving jobs and employees appear to be arbitrary and inconsistent.

9. Employees will not accept wage rates or salaries based on mere estimates or improperly evaluated comparisons. Whatever rates they accept will be only after the workers have been given adequate time and opportunity to be convinced that their work was accurately and correctly measured.

10. The function of wage and salary administration is inherently a responsibility to settle compensation problems (by cure or prevention) on the basis of what is right and fair for the common good of the employees, the employer, and the public at large.

The future of wage and salary administration

The last 25 years witnessed an unusually steady growth in the function of wage and salary administration. It has now become a recognized management position upon which business and industry depend for stable employer-employee relations. Continued growth and importance of the future role of compensation in an enterprise appear apparent. The factors that give us clues on the future of wage and salary administration are: technology, unions, and current trends in the United States.

Changing Technology

It is common knowledge today that 90 percent of all the engineers and scientists who have ever lived are alive today. This means that in the next 40 years we are likely to see dynamic changes in technology equal to those of the past 400 years. Ells has indicated that automation is eliminating almost 40,000 jobs a week and that from 1959 to 1964 new jobs were created at the rate of about 57,000 each week.[6] Others have estimated that as many as 70 percent of present-day jobs in manufacturing will disappear within the next ten years.[7] Half of the graduating college seniors today are accepting jobs that did not exist at the time they were born.

A recent edition of the *Dictionary of Occupational Titles* contains 6,000 job titles that were not listed in previous editions.[8] The day is coming when there will no longer be jobs that offer a lifetime career. It is expected that employees will change careers at least two or three times in a lifetime because today's skills will not hold tomorrow's jobs.

As factories become more automated, individual financial wage incentives become obsolete because most employees no longer can work independently but only as part of a team. This means that group or plant-wide incentives must be developed if employees are to become more fully motivated.

The statements above represent some of the mounting evidence to show that the future director of compensation is going to have his hands full in keeping abreast of job changes, writing new job descriptions, evaluating jobs, pricing jobs, and installing new incentive and pay plans.

Union Power

Unions continue to be strong and to exert steady pressure on managements to improve wage and salary conditions. In order to be even stronger, unions are attempting to organize and unionize the white-collar workers. Unions are developing progressive patterns of leadership and organization. They employ methods of systematic management and scientific research similar to those of large industrial enterprises, relying more and more on a highly educated, specialized staff of college- and university-trained personnel. Already unions are in a position to multiply their services not only by employing professionals but also

---

[6]Ralph W. Ells, *Is Automation Causing Unemployment?* (Chicago: National Research Bureau, Inc., 1964), p. 4.

[7]Roger M. Blough, "The Art of Being Secure" (From a speech to the Advisory Council of Pace College, New York, January 21, 1964).

[8]James I. Black, "Cybernetics and the DOT," *Employment Service Review* (August/September, 1967), p. 26.

by offering attractive salaries to develop leaders with almost limitless opportunities for financial advancement.[9] Consequently, under dynamic leadership union growth may be inevitable, which presents top management with the challenge to further develop effective wage and salary programs.

Current Trends

There are several trends in the United States that should keep wage and salary administration in the limelight for a long time and may even increase its importance in the future.

Since 1946 there have been annual across-the-board wage raises that the unions and workers have been able to gain from managements. There appears to be no end in sight. It seems that each year the only question is how much will the raises be.

Since the end of World War II, the American economy has generated about four new white-collar jobs for each blue-collar or farm job eliminated by changing technology.[10] Since 1956 the white-collar workers have outnumbered the blue-collar workers. Currently, there are over 33 million white-collar workers who represent approximately 49 percent of the labor force, while blue-collar workers total only about 36 percent.[11] The Bureau of Labor Statistics has forecast that by 1975, there will be about 12 million more white-collar jobs than there were in 1964. This would be about three times the anticipated increase of blue-collar jobs during the same period.[12] This trend is resulting in the white-collar world being diversified into a new, complex system of job classifications that may change even more rapidly in the future. As the white-collar workers grow in number, the various segments (clerical, professional, technical, administrative, sales, etc.) are growing stronger and exerting more pressures on managements to inform them more fully on the many phases of compensation and to justify the procedures used.

A recent development is the growing trend of governmental employees (federal, state, and local) to seek to bargain collectively with their respective employers in the same manner as in private industry. This movement will greatly expand compensation activities in the government.

As the level of education in America is continually rising, the American worker is more capable of participating in the activities that spell success to the company. He is more interested in greater participation in the business and in group and plant incentives such as profit sharing. At the same time, it is only

---

[9]Gus Tyler, *A New Philosophy for Labor* (New York: The Fund for the Republic, Inc., 1959).

[10]Thomas R. Brooks, "New Fit to the White Collar," *Dun's Review and Modern Industry* (September, 1963).

[11]*Statistical Abstract of the United States* (1968), p. 226.

[12]Howard V. Stambler, "89 Million Jobs by 1975?" *Occupational Outlook Quarterly* (May, 1967), p. 2.

natural for him to expect to learn more about the company's compensation methods and policies as they affect him. Even those firms employing twenty-five employees or less will need to do more in the compensation area as they are pressured by their employees.

It would appear that the majority of the 4.8 million firms in the United States need to improve their compensation matters. Too many companies are using job evaluation plans and other procedures that are 10 or 20 years old and badly in need of updating. Even the smallest firms will be doing more in the area of wage and salary administration as they become aware of its advantages, or are forced to do so because they are plagued with wage grievances. More managements in the future will have to obtain wage and salary experts, as the unions have done, if they are to meet labor's challenge in this field. It would appear that every company employing 500 or more employees has need for a full-time supervisor of compensation.

In summary, the apparent forces of changing technology, the strength of unions, and the various trends in our society point to an important role for wage and salary administration in every enterprise in the future.

REVIEW QUESTIONS

1. What three major economic parties or groups have an interest in a firmly established wage and salary program? Why?
2. Give a comprehensive definition of wage and salary administration.
3. What are the common misconceptions in connection with wage and salary administration?
4. What factors are involved in the adequate and equitable compensation of employees?
5. Explain the relationship between the general goals of: wage and salary administration, management, and employees.
6. Briefly explain each of the major goals of compensation.
7. What are the specific phases of wage and salary administration?
8. Should wage and salary administration be concerned with satisfying the public as well as capital and labor? Why?
9. How great a proportion of the national income do wage and salary earners receive?
10. How much concern does the typical employee have for wages?
11. Differentiate between a wage and a salary.
12. Select several of the fundamental assumptions of wage and salary administration and indicate from your experience whether you would agree or disagree with the assumptions.
13. Can you think of any circumstances that might indicate what the wage and salary function will be like in the years to come?

RESEARCH OR SEMINAR QUESTIONS

1. Of the nine major wage and salary activities (see Figure 1.3), which do you think is the most important? least important? Why?
2. Of the four major goals of wage and salary administration (see Figure 1.2), which do you think is the most important? least important? Why?
3. Since World War II, has wage and salary administration been accomplishing its goals or not? Explain your answer.
4. Is there a need for wage and salary administration in every company? What considerations should enter into the formulation, modification, and administration of every wage and salary program?

PRACTICAL EXPERIENCE ASSIGNMENTS

1. Contact and interview a wage and salary administrator (or the person performing this function) to discover what his typical routine is each day. Prepare to give a five-minute report to the class covering the tasks that the wage and salary man performs and the approximate amount of time (in minutes, hours, or percent of the day) he spends on each task each day. In your report, it will also be interesting to include a few comments about what the administrator considers to be his most difficult task.
2. During your summer vacation you worked at the Torrence Manufacturing Company, which employs 300 production workers. You and two other new workers started at $2.40 per hour in the milling machine department. The foreman who hired you promised a raise of five cents after four weeks and another five-cent raise after eight weeks, provided you are diligent and learn how to operate the milling machine.

   During the first few weeks you found out: (a) some workers doing much more complicated work than you receive only $2.50 per hour; (b) the John Jones Company, manufacturing similar goods, is paying 20 to 40 cents more per hour for the same jobs; and (c) some of the old employees are complaining bitterly that their incentive rates have been cut twice because of their high earnings.

   Explain what you think is lacking at the Torrence Manufacturing Company, and the possible reasons therefor.

CASE PROBLEM

1—1. THE PROGRESSIVE MANUFACTURING COMPANY[13]

Functional Organization For Wage and Salary Administration

Mr. John D. Carpenter, an ingenious practical mechanic, invented a portable tool suitable for various operations in garages and small shops. He decided to capitalize on the invention by doing all the designing, experimenting, and producing of the tool in his own little job shop. Only a few samples were produced at a time. His eldest son, John D. Carpenter, Jr., was an active employee, taking care of purchasing, receiving, storing of materials and supplies, and

---

[13] This case is analogous to an actual case known to the authors. The name, however, is fictitious.

shipping. His wife did the bookkeeping, paid the bills, and attended to the banking, correspondence, and billing.

The venture was very successful. Mr. Carpenter, Sr., in addition to his son, employed one toolmaker, four all-around mechanics, and one laborer to help in producing parts and assembling the tool in small quantities. Toolmaker A, who had a knowledge of drafting, assisted in making sketches and drawings. He helped to originate several additional models that were perfected and marketed. The four mechanics used a few simple machine tools to fabricate all the necessary parts. In this little group, Mr. Carpenter, Sr., formed the nucleus of a "line organization." (See Figure 1.4.) Various jobs and operations (functions) were performed interchangeably by the senior Mr. Carpenter and his mechanics. The small group (organization) performed numerous functionalized duties which, in large-quantity production, are subdivided, specialized, and produced by skilled, semiskilled, and unskilled labor at appreciably less cost.

A growing demand for the portable tools prompted the senior Mr. Carpenter to expand his small organization. Anticipating the possibility of extending his line with various additional products, he began to reorganize the job shop by renting larger quarters and hiring additional mechanics to take care of the demand. He also realized that the expanded organization must be "functionalized" on the basis of grouping supervisors and workers in several sections, as shown in the line organization chart, Figure 1.5. Hence, toolmaker A was promoted to foreman; and mechanics B, C, D, and E became assistant foremen, each supervising 8 workers. Mr. Carpenter's son, John D., Jr., became office manager, and the second son, Frank F., took over John D., Jr.'s old job of purchasing and shipping. The organization totaled 39 employees, after 32 additional workers were hired.

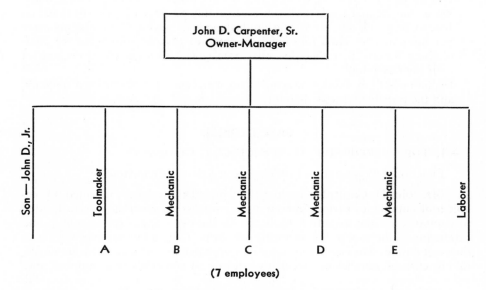

(7 employees)

FIGURE 1.4 Job Shop Line Organization

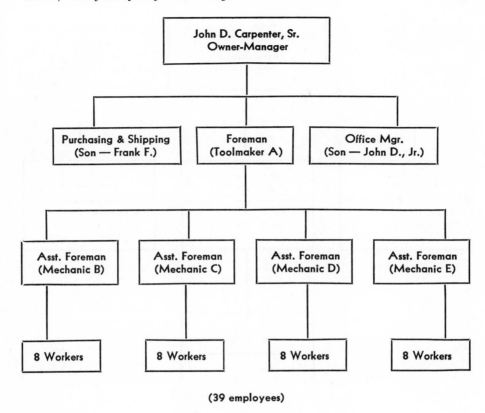

(39 employees)

FIGURE 1.5   MACHINE SHOP LINE ORGANIZATION

Mr. Carpenter's foresight, coupled with the assistance and encouragement of his sons, resulted in a rapidly growing enterprise. New duties and expanded activities required more personnel to handle the additional responsibilities and to emit authority. Toolmaker A advanced from foreman to superintendent; mechanic B from assistant foreman to assistant superintendent; and mechanics C, D, and E were promoted from assistant foremen to foremen. More specialized activities were introduced with the prospect of enlarging the organization still further.

Sales and profits increased rapidly, attracting banking interests that were eager to provide capital. Mr. Carpenter decided to form The Progressive Manufacturing Company. Manufacturing quarters were expanded and new specialized equipment gradually added. At the same time, the increased personnel organization commenced to branch out into functionalized (specialized) fields, forming a line and functional organization as shown in Figure 1.6.

The Progressive Manufacturing Company thus grew from its original small shop of 7 employees to a factory employing 300 workers, manufacturing multifarious products. Mr. John D. Carpenter, Sr., the president and founder,

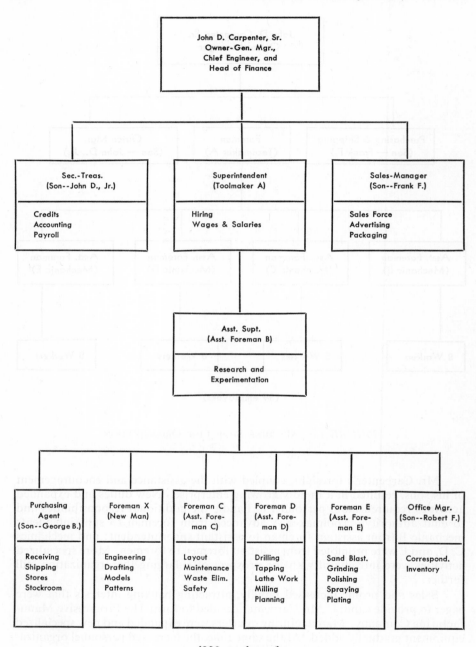

(300 employees)

FIGURE 1.6 Line and Functional Organization of The Progressive Manufacturing Company

is the principal stockholder. Each of his four sons occupies an official position. Once again John D., Jr., took on a new position, namely, secretary-treasurer; and George B. took on the position of purchasing agent. The president establishes policies and makes all final decisions pertaining to the business in general. The superintendent, foremen, and other department heads operate the factory with very little deviation from the original methods of operation and procedures. The only exception is that most of the old employees, those who have been with the company for a long time, are not producing at the normal capacity expected from skilled mechanics. They are retained as a gesture of goodwill, and in reciprocation for their proven loyalty.

Wages, in general, have been raised appreciably, but production is lagging. New employees are started at minimum wages only, to make up for the inflated production cost, but they have no opportunity for increasing their earnings through extra efforts because motivation of employees through incentives (piece rates or bonuses) has never been introduced. Assistant foremen in some departments are constantly vigilant. In some cases dictatorial pressure is resorted to in order to raise production, but to no avail. Many employees are dissatisfied and labor turnover is high. Sales and profits are dropping because the equivalent competitors' goods, which are priced lower, are in great demand.

Faced with continued losses, Mr. Carpenter's two eldest sons realize the necessity for another reorganization "to introduce new blood" as well as modern methods of factory management. They are convinced that the product designs and purely technical matters are well taken care of, but that compensation and human relations have been neglected. They also insist that executives and department heads be educated to comprehend the new trends in industrial relations. The consensus of the sons is that the superintendent, assistant superintendent, and foremen use obsolete and inefficient "rule of thumb" management, which should be superseded by effective systematic management.

Problems:

You, as a wage and salary administrator, have been engaged to appraise the situation, with specific concentration on compensation matters, and to recommend the reorganization and addition of managerial positions.

Prepare an outline suggesting what steps should be taken in order to improve conditions. Which new functions should be added? What policies should the new executives and staff men pursue to maintain industrial peace? How can the principles expressed by the slogan "Our business must satisfy the three parties — employer, employee, and consumer alike" be carried out practically for the benefit of all concerned? Your report should be accompanied by an organization chart showing your proposed new functions.

chapter **2**

HISTORICAL BACKGROUND
OF WAGE AND SALARY ADMINISTRATION

Anyone dealing with wages and salaries realizes that unions play a prominent role on the stage of the American economy. The fact that not only craftsmen and unskilled workers but also professional employees, such as hospital technicians and nurses, members of the engineering profession, specialists in the sciences, office clerks, and public school teachers, are affiliated with unions is sufficient evidence that unions dominate many of the decisions in the field of compensation. In view of this fact, an historic sketch of the growth and impact of unionism will be of interest to the wage and salary administrator. Therefore, in this chapter some historical events, such as those listed in Figure 2.1, are presented as a background for our study. We shall very briefly trace the early employer-employee relationship, the evolution of compensation in general, and the causes and effects leading up to the present wage and salary administration. Some of the events may help the wage and salary administrator gain a proper perspective of the need for a sound wage and salary program.

Early stages of compensation in Europe

History points to a direct connection between the early labor philosophies and employer-employee relations in Europe and the early capital-labor relations in the United States regarding their effect upon wages. It is neither within the

1630	Plymouth Colony and Massachusetts Bay Colony passed maximum pay laws (repealed 1635).
1786	Earliest authenticated strike — Philadelphia printers gained a minimum weekly wage of $6.
1840	President Van Buren established a 10-hour day for federal employees on public works without reduction in pay.
1847	New Hampshire passed first state law fixing 10 hours as a legal workday.
1868	Congress passed first federal 8-hour-day law (applied only to government laborers, workmen, and mechanics).
1870	The first written contract between coal miners and operators was signed on July 29. It provided for a sliding scale of pay based on the price of coal.
1875	First private pension plans in industry established at American Express Company.
1880's	Frederick W. Taylor started first individual wage incentive system in industry.
1881	First job evaluation studies made by Frederick W. Taylor at Midvale Steel Company.
1886	Birth of American Federation of Labor union.
1886	Westinghouse Electric Corporation first to grant paid vacations.
1887	Procter & Gamble started profit-sharing plan (oldest plan in existence).
1902	Hospitalization and medical programs were undertaken by Mutual Benefit Societies.
1906	General Electric inaugurated their suggestion plan.
1908	First workmen's compensation law for federal government employees was enacted.
1909	Commonwealth Edison Company of Chicago introduced a job classification plan.
1911	Wisconsin enacted first state workmen's compensation law (to be held constitutional).
1912	Massachusetts adopted first minimum wage act for women and minors.
1915	Alaska adopted first constitutional old-age pension law.
1918	Colorado Fuel & Iron Company, Pueblo, Colorado, was first company to change from 12-hour to 8-hour day without loss of pay.
1919	Michigan and Montana passed equal pay laws for men and women.
1920	Civil Service Retirement Act for federal employees enacted.
1925	Merrill R. Lott introduced first point method of job evaluation.
1926	Eugene J. Benge introduced first factor comparison method of job evaluation.
1931	Davis-Bacon Act provided for payment of prevailing wage-rates to laborers and mechanics on federal construction projects.
1932	Wisconsin passed first state unemployment insurance law.
1935	National Labor Relations Act (Wagner Act) established the first national labor policy of protecting the right of workers to organize and to elect their representatives for collective bargaining.
1935	Social Security Act (old-age, survivors, and disability insurance) passed.
1936	Walsh-Healey Public Contracts Act established labor standards (wages and hours) on government contracts of $10,000 or more.
1938	Fair Labor Standards Act established 40-hour week, minimum hourly wage, and overtime pay for employees in interstate commerce.
1942	Economic Stabilization Act froze all wages as of September 15, 1942, to mark the beginning of the modern era of wage and salary administration.

FIGURE 2.1 SIGNIFICANT DATES AND EVENTS IN THE HISTORY OF COMPENSATION IN THE UNITED STATES

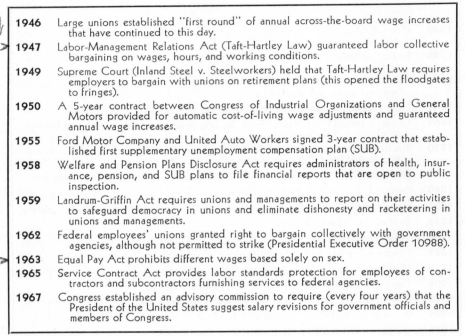

1946	Large unions established "first round" of annual across-the-board wage increases that have continued to this day.
1947	Labor-Management Relations Act (Taft-Hartley Law) guaranteed labor collective bargaining on wages, hours, and working conditions.
1949	Supreme Court (Inland Steel v. Steelworkers) held that Taft-Hartley Law requires employers to bargain with unions on retirement plans (this opened the floodgates to fringes).
1950	A 5-year contract between Congress of Industrial Organizations and General Motors provided for automatic cost-of-living wage adjustments and guaranteed annual wage increases.
1955	Ford Motor Company and United Auto Workers signed 3-year contract that established first supplementary unemployment compensation plan (SUB).
1958	Welfare and Pension Plans Disclosure Act requires administrators of health, insurance, pension, and SUB plans to file financial reports that are open to public inspection.
1959	Landrum-Griffin Act requires unions and managements to report on their activities to safeguard democracy in unions and eliminate dishonesty and racketeering in unions and managements.
1962	Federal employees' unions granted right to bargain collectively with government agencies, although not permitted to strike (Presidential Executive Order 10988).
1963	Equal Pay Act prohibits different wages based solely on sex.
1965	Service Contract Act provides labor standards protection for employees of contractors and subcontractors furnishing services to federal agencies.
1967	Congress established an advisory commission to require (every four years) that the President of the United States suggest salary revisions for government officials and members of Congress.

FIGURE 2.1   SIGNIFICANT DATES AND EVENTS IN THE HISTORY OF COMPENSATION IN THE UNITED STATES (*concluded*)

scope of this book nor its purpose to delve into the structure, internal government, and political aspirations of unions.[1] We shall, therefore, lightly pass over the beginnings of labor conditions in Europe and highlight the more outstanding advances made by American unions in their drive for higher wages and shorter work-days until they gained the present benefits of federal and state legislation.

Serfdom

The first revolutionary change in the economic status of labor in Europe occurred when slavery gave way to serfdom and the manorial system. The laborer and his family were provided with just enough food, shelter, and clothing to subsist. Although this compensation was meager, nevertheless, it was based on custom. The serf bound to the soil necessarily must have subsistence.

The Household Period

Then came the *household period*, when members of the household produced the family's needs in the home. All activities were performed according to rules

---

[1]For complete discussions of the structure, policies, and internal government of trade unions, see: John R. Commons *et al*, *History of Labour in the United States* (2 Vols.; New York: The Macmillan Company, 1918), and Florence Peterson, *American Labor Unions* (2d ed.; New York: Harper and Brothers, 1951).

established by the head of the family or a leader in the community. The group spirit of working together had its inception during this period.

The Handicraft-Guild Period

Socioeconomic progress was very slow during the household period. But, with the advent of trading, towns began to form, thus creating greater demands for goods. *Merchant guilds* sprang up to regulate trade on a monopolistic basis. Profits from these monopolies spurred producers of goods to organize *craft guilds*. Each guild decided who should produce certain goods, how many men might be employed, how each trade was to be taught, and the prices to be charged. The skilled worker emerged during this period.

The early stages of industrial development were fraught with the workers' apprehensive fears of losing their means of subsistence. Inventions did not raise the standard of living for the general public, but benefited only a fortunate few. Written contracts for the sale of inventions, and descriptions for patent applications specifically emphasized the advantage of employing children instead of skilled workers. Early European writers advised the inventors to own property and to employ workers at wages only sufficient to keep them from starvation. From such conditions evolved the so-called subsistence theory of wages, which certain groups accepted without question; but the skilled workers resented the meager compensation.

Specialized Tradesmen

Handicraft production developed specialized trades such as woodworking, metalworking, stonecutting, clothmaking, and leatherworking. As the handicraft industry progressed, labor began to divide into distinct classes. General leatherworkers became shoemakers and harnessmakers; woodworkers became cabinet makers producing furniture; and carpenters began producing wagons and building cottages. The master craftsmen and their helpers produced goods according to the master's own ideas. In Europe, each master craftsman was permitted to hire only a prescribed number of journeymen and apprentices.

Compensation for journeymen consisted of a small amount of money each week or month, plus food and shelter. To become the apprentice of a well-known master was the greatest compensation and incentive for a young man because, as a result, he gained prestige in the community. The next incentive for the apprentice upon completion of his term was the coveted privilege of traveling or journeying from one town to another[2] to work for prominent masters. Permission to work under contract for master craftsmen was an honor. The contractual relationship between employer and employee, in its crudest form, began

---

[2]Hence, the name "journeyman" — a craftsman of the Middle Ages — one who might travel 20 miles a day to seek employment.

at this stage of industrial development. Aspiring for leadership in the art, the master and the helper worked side by side to create a finished product. The interests they shared induced harmony and understanding between master and servant. The "employer-employee" relationship had not yet emerged.

The Cottage-Trade System

The beginning of craftsmanship specialization and apprenticeship led to the cottage-trade system. In some European countries, an entrepreneur supplied raw materials and tools to the workers who, in their own homes (which were called cottages — thus, the derivation of the term cottage-trade system), processed the raw materials into salable products. The worker's pay for his production was usually a specified amount per piece. Thus, the piece-rate method of wage payment originated with the cottage-trade system.

The cottage industry continues today unabated in some rural districts of Germany and Switzerland. Glassware, Christmas tree ornaments, small assembly units, and parts for instruments are typical cottage products.

Compensation during the colonial period in the United States (1607–1776)

The history of compensation during the colonization of the United States seems to have been generally overlooked by most writers of American history. However, the following write-up is an attempt to pull together what information is available on compensation practices during the time when the United States was primarily an agricultural nation.

Higher Wages

From the founding of Jamestown in 1607 to today, wages in the United States have been typically higher than in other parts of the world. Since most early settlers came from Europe, that continent is usually used in making compensation comparisons. Letters and reports from agents of the British companies engaged in colonial settlements and from early colonial governors expressed consternation amounting to distress over the "exorbitant demands" of craftsmen and laborers.[3] Actually, wages were not really extravagant, but they were higher than in Europe because labor was scarce in the United States and therefore could demand a higher wage. Labor remained scarce because men continued to move westward in settling the United States.

In the New England colonies, attempts were made to control higher wages by means of the governmental system. The Plymouth Colony and the Massa-

---

[3]U.S. Department of Labor, Bureau of Labor Statistics, *History of Wages in the United States from Colonial Times to 1928*, Bulletin No. 499 (Washington: U.S. Government Printing Office, 1929), p. 7.

chusetts Bay Colony passed similar laws in 1630 fixing a *maximum* rate of pay.[4] In the Massachusetts Bay Colony, carpenters and bricklayers were not allowed to accept over 48.6 cents a day for pay. If their employer furnished them food and drink, the workmen could not accept over 32 cents a day for pay. In 1633, an act was passed that fixed the following rates for a day's work: "master" workmen (building trades), 28 cents; master tailors, 24.3 cents; and "inferior" tailors, 16 cents.[5] The rates of pay were determined by the town constable and "two indifferent freemen." No information is available as to the criteria used for determining these rates of pay. To complicate the matter of computing wages was the problem of how much to charge for room and board. It was customary to provide board to workers at the place they worked. Board in Virginia in 1650 was worth $24.30 a year, while in Boston it was $50 a year. It was not until 1750 that board in Virginia cost $50 a year.[6] Employers who paid more than the established maximum rates of pay could be fined for violating the law. In 1635, the wage-fixing statute was repealed. The colonial authorities appointed a commission of 29 men to decide how to handle the wage question.[7] The Commission recommended that each town control its own wage rate.

Wage Differentials — Skilled v. Unskilled

Another distinction between Europe and the United States in compensation matters during the early part of the colonial period was the small wage differential between the skilled and the unskilled. In Europe, the pay differential was more pronounced than in the United States. There were even two instances on record in the United States in which it was specifically stated that *all work should be paid at the same rate*.[8] The men who worked upon the construction of the meeting house in Delham, Massachusetts (in 1637) and the mechanics and laborers who reconstructed a fort on Point Comfort in Virginia were all to receive the same wages.[9] The small pay differential between the skilled and the unskilled continued until almost 1800 when trade organizations which were coming into being emphasized the differences between the various crafts.

Pay Media

It is interesting to note that during the colonization of the United States, money was not the principal medium in which the workers were paid. In Virginia, wages were paid in pounds of tobacco because tobacco was the standard of value in which all supplies were purchased. Twenty pounds of tobacco a day (worth 30¢) was the going rate paid construction workers. In the New

---

[4]*Ibid.*, p. 9.
[5]*Ibid.*
[6]*Ibid.*, p. 23.
[7]*Ibid.*, p. 10.
[8]*Ibid.*, p. 12.
[9]*Ibid.*

England colonies, the medium of pay was beaver skins and "country pay" (which meant agricultural products such as corn).   In 1633, a tailor was paid one-half pound of beaver skins (worth about 8¢) for mending some blankets.   The standard medium in which workmen were paid was "corn" (a generic term that included several species of grain).   There was also the practice of forcing the laborers to take wine in pay for wages.   Legislation finally curbed this; however, workers then began to press their employers for an allowance of wine every day, over and above their wages (as present-day workers press for coffee breaks).   Legislation also curbed this practice.

There appear to be two main reasons why money was not used as the principal medium in which workers were paid.   First, money was scarce, while other media were not.   Second, what money was available consisted of a variety of currencies such as Spanish, English, and Dutch, and it was difficult to determine the equivalent value of each.   Since there were many inconveniences in paying people with tobacco, beaver skins, or grain, it was clear by 1776 that workers would soon have to be paid with money.

Compensation during the industrialization of the United States (1776–1942)

The era from the American Revolution to World War II (1776–1942) may be thought of as the period of time when the United States converted from an agricultural to an industrial nation.   It is marked by the Industrial Revolution, the growth and strength of labor unions, and the beginning of the field of management.   How these events relate to compensation follows.

The Industrial Revolution

The eighteenth and nineteenth centuries are regarded as years of transition from the cottage-trade system to the industrial era.   With the transition came new conceptions of ownership, productivity, and economy, which upset the early master-journeyman relationship.   England and the United States suffered a critical industrial revolution. Workers began demanding increased compensation as they struggled for higher standards of living.   In his *Wealth of Nations* (first published in 1776) Adam Smith wrote, "Every individual is continually exerting himself to find out the most advantageous employment for whatever capital he can command."   Regarding the use of machinery, Smith wrote:

> The great increase in the quantity of work . . . is owing to three different circumstances; first, to the increase of dexterity in every particular workman; secondly, to the saving of time, . . . and lastly, to the invention of a great number of machines which facilitate and abridge labour, and enable one man to do the work of many.[10]

---

[10]Adam Smith, *The Wealth of Nations* (Vol. I; London: G. Bell and Sons, Ltd., 1921), p. 9.

The Factory System. The invention of machinery, notably in the textile industry, at the end of the eighteenth century, lent impetus to the growth of the *factory system.* The increased consumption of cotton for manufacturing astonished even the most ardent objectors to machinery. From 1781 to 1785, about 10 million pounds of raw cotton were purchased by England for the manufacture of textiles, and by 1800, importation rose to 55 million pounds. The growth of the textile industry stimulated further thinking along technical lines, which in turn produced mechanical developments that gradually replaced the handicraft system.

Increased demands forced the handicraft artisan to use machinery in manufacturing goods to satisfy the desire for "luxuries." Most of the luxury items rapidly became daily necessities, thus raising the standard of living. In 1885, factory workers endeavored to own 25 items, 17 of which were considered essential. Fifty years later (1935) out of 500 items available, only 84 were considered essential.

The Production System. During the nineteenth century, the ingenuity of many brilliant Americans revolutionized production methods as well as means of transportation, introducing the *production system*, which, in turn, changed the methods of compensation. Free trade and abundant natural resources helped tremendously to establish various industries. Individual workers became indifferent to the final outcome of investments made by the "Captains of Industry." The breach between the owners and the workers widened, causing industrial strife.

The Impact of the Labor Movement in the United States

Management of an enterprise has always been affected by labor's demands for higher wages or for a share of the employer's profits. At no time in American history, however, has wage and salary administration felt the impact of union labor as during the last three decades.

The kindred spirit between artisans and all types of skilled, semiskilled, and unskilled labor was developed into a bond of common interest by strong unions which suddenly emerged as a powerful influence on the American scene. The stabilization of labor unions in the United States resulted in expanded collective bargaining and wage and salary demands. To understand the rapid growth and power of unionism, the wage and salary administrator should have at least a general knowledge of the labor movement in the United States.

Unions Organize for Protection. Labor organizations in the United States were founded long before factories overshadowed small shops. Workers had resolved to protect themselves against low wages and long workdays. Between 1790 and 1799, shoemakers, printers, carpenters, and other craftsmen organized "societies" in eastern cities and conducted strikes for higher wages and closed shops. The earliest authenticated strike of workers in the United States in a single trade occurred in Philadelphia in 1786 when the printers gained a minimum wage of $6 a week.[11] The shoemakers of Philadelphia entered into collective bargaining in 1799, and were emulated by the New York printers in 1809.

The labor philosophies that were developed and promulgated by the organized societies in the eastern cities had a strong influence on other labor groups, which led to the formation of the Mechanics' Union of Trade Associations in 1827. Subsequently, numerous societies organized into a United National Trade Union "to promote the moral, physical, and intellectual conditions of the working class." Various craft unions centralized in different cities and organized strikes to demand a ten-hour workday, but without success. Strike failures transformed pure trade-unionism into political action, which collapsed during the financial panic of 1837. A long period of unemployment ensued with over a decade of inaction on the part of union groups.

The general expansion of industry, coupled with the soaring prices that followed the discovery of gold in California in the 1850's, revived trade-unionism. Workers resumed their demands for increased wages and a shorter workday. Skilled workers claimed a "victory" in 1860 when they obtained a raise of 50 cents, thus increasing their earnings from $1.50 to $2.00 per day.

American Federation of Labor. In December of 1886, the officers from 25 unions assembled in Columbus, Ohio, to organize all trades and to form the American Federation of Labor (AFL). Although the AFL believed in the capitalistic system and principles of competitive enterprise, they adopted the policy of collective bargaining to deal with employers on wage matters.

Before the turn of the century and even during the first decade of the twentieth century, hundreds of items were manufactured under strenuous circumstances in homes and shops, nicknamed "sweatshops." The shops were overcrowded, inadequately lighted, unventilated, and lacked proper sanitary facilities. Men and women worked 10 to 12 hours per day, six to seven days a week. In 1910, about a half million children under 16 were employed in textile and silk mills, coal mines, glass factories, and other industries. Approximately 150,000 were between 12 and 13 years of age. The AFL labored incessantly for legislative measures to eliminate unsatisfactory working conditions, to abolish child labor, and to introduce workmen's compensation and the Fair Labor Standards Act. It is interesting to note that in 1912, Massachusetts passed the first minimum wage law in the United States.[12] In 1913, eight other states (California, Colorado, Minnesota, Nebraska, Oregon, Utah, Washington, and Wisconsin) followed the pattern set by Massachusetts.

---

[11]U.S. Department of Labor, Bureau of Labor Statistics, *Important Events in American Labor History 1778–1963* (Washington: U.S. Government Printing Office, 1964), p. 1.

[12]For further information see U.S. Department of Labor, *State Minimum-Wage Laws*, Leaflet No. 4 (Rev. ed.; Washington: U.S. Government Printing Office, 1963).

Congress of Industrial Organizations.   During the 1935 AFL convention, 32 of the participating unions were expelled from the AFL because they wanted to organize all the workers in the mass-production industries with no restriction as to trade or craft.   The expelled unions formed a "Committee for Industrial Organizations" and in 1938 met in a constitutional convention and formed the Congress of Industrial Organizations (CIO) on a permanent basis.

The CIO membership grew and new union locals developed rapidly to represent the activities of crafts, trades, and industrial nonskilled workers, in direct competition with AFL unions.   Jurisdictional disputes broke out, with violence between the two factions.   Prolonged bitter strikes with costly losses were forced upon employers — innocent bystanders — who were caught in the turmoil.   Eventually, both unions adopted similar written agreements regarding wages, incentives, fringe benefits, and working conditions.   Skilled mechanics resented the relatively small differential between their wages and that of the unskilled, such as the sweeper.   This accounted for the decline in the overall membership of the CIO in the 1940's.

AFL-CIO Merger.   The earlier AFL and CIO union disputes provided opportunity for communistic elements to bore from within the labor movement. These and other disruptive conditions drew the AFL and CIO closer together. They felt that the cohesive action of unified union locals would purge their ranks of the radical elements.   In December, 1955, the two national labor unions merged under the name of AFL-CIO.   It became apparent that the united labor groups had formed a coalition that was destined to become a powerful force in the socioeconomic and political life of our nation.   As a result of the unification, communist-controlled union locals were expelled and the Ethical Practices Committee was formed to investigate the corrupt activities and practices in the administration of national and local unions.

Employers Opposed to Union Organization.   Even in the early days of employer-employee relations, workers' trade associations were considered a threat to employers.   Companies and individual owners of small enterprises appealed to the courts to dissolve workers' associations on various charges.   In 1806, unions were prosecuted in the city of Philadelphia for "conspiracies in restraint of trade."   Their dissolution was ultimately effected under the old English common-law precept of "an association of workmen to raise wages is conspiracy against the public."

During the first decade of the twentieth century, employer associations lobbied for legislation to restrain trade-union activities and succeeded in obtaining federal court injunctions.   The old Amalgamated Iron and Steel Workers' Union was abolished in 1901 when steel corporations adopted antiunion policies and operated their mills with nonunion labor.   As late as 1919, the state of Kansas passed an act declaring strikes illegal and committing all disputes to an industrial court for decision. The Supreme Court, however, subsequently ruled that the act was unconstitutional.

The Effects of Growing Industrialization

In the glory of extraordinary successes gained through personal initiative and ingenuity, the early American industrialists often disregarded the welfare of their employees. It was felt that increases in the standard of living, and wages and compensation in general, were of secondary importance; compensation was looked upon as a necessary evil. E. D. Jones gives his impression as follows:

> The Captains of Industry seized leadership by right of ability, but, technically speaking, they secured it as the privilege arising from the ownership of great fortunes. . . . By virtue of having lived in a highly individualistic and self-confident society, they worked out rules of action, each man for himself. . . . Their organizations were mere extensions of themselves, and ruled as their households might be. Enterprises so conceived were incapable of serving as a rallying-point for the loyalty of the various classes of persons who might become connected with them.[13]

Although rugged individualism reigned supreme in industrial ownership, society accepted it as a natural phenomenon, while anticipating a better future. The possibility of acquiring luxuries and participating in the romance of discovery and invention were incentives of uncommon magnitude. Nevertheless, men and women began making concerted efforts to share in the fruits of discoveries and inventions by reason of their labors. These efforts gradually evolved a new concept of the relation between workers and the employer. During the early industrial period of our history, the doctrine of master and servant relationship still prevailed. The bargaining power of the servant was one of inequality. This condition became manifestly intolerable with the development of large-scale industry and particularly with the advent of the institution known as the corporation. In the first decade of this century a new concept came into being, namely that of "employer and employee," which implied a relationship of theoretical equality in bargaining power. The legal recognition of this concept is epitomized by the enactment of workmen's compensation laws, first in England in 1906 and in this country in 1911 in Wisconsin, followed subsequently by all the other states. This theoretical concept of equality of bargaining power furnishes the rationale for workers and organizations, and the pressure by employees for higher wages.

Specialization of Labor. The factory enterprise with its specialization and division of labor is now the primary factor in mass production. For instance, during the master-helper relationship, the cabinetmaker completed a whole set

---

[13]E. D. Jones, *The Business Administrator* (New York: The Engineering Company, 1914), p. 8.

of furniture including chairs, tables, cabinets, beds, dressers, and bookcases. Now the furniture industry is specialized not only in manufacturing one type of furniture such as bedroom, dining, and living room suites, but is also further subdivided into the specialized manufacture of a single item. One manufacturer produces chairs only; another manufactures tables; and a third specializes in bookcases or office desks only.

Industries took advantage of their large-volume production which made it practical to break down products into component parts, and the processes into individual operations and suboperations. Employers thus had to find new solutions to the additional problems of wage payment, new policies, and new methods of compensation.

It is obvious that the efficiency of a worker performing only a few operations will be increased so that the whole product can be completed within a remarkably shorter time and at a lower cost. Thus, it is possible to pay unskilled workers considerably more per hour than the early skilled worker earned. All workers can share and enjoy the benefits of mass production by acquiring an abundance of goods at minimum costs, thereby raising their standard of living.

Open- and Closed-Shop Disputes. At the end of World War I, it was difficult for commerce and industry to resume a peacetime status because of the friction between employers and trade unions. In October, 1919, President Wilson called a conference of employer, union, and public representatives "to bring capital and labor into close cooperation." The conference deadlocked because the trade unions demanded collective bargaining, while employers held firm against dealing with "outside groups," arguing that the arbitrary use of collective bargaining is "a menace to free society." Labor representatives maintained that "wage earners as free people have a right to organize and bargain collectively." Public representatives argued for the inclusion of company employee representatives as collective bargaining agents. The conference broke up without an agreement. Employers all over the country refused to accept closed-shop agreements, and continued practicing the "American Plan," with freedom of adherence to open-shop principles.

Union membership dwindled, but shop unions gained members through the influence of company work councils and employee representation plans. Most industrial corporations were successful with shop unions because of the company welfare plans and employer-employee cooperation programs.

The Employer's Changing Attitude. The tenacity of labor unions to improve working conditions and to gain recognition for the worker's human dignity provoked several liberal employers to influence employers in general to change their policies. They began to realize that their employees instinctively desired to improve their socioeconomic and family life.

Frederick W. Taylor's principles of scientific management, which emphasized high wages for employees and low labor costs for employers, and insisted that management practice human relations, changed the attitudes of some early leading industrialists.   Henry Ford I, who adopted the fundamental principles of scientific management in manufacturing and marketing, paid astonishingly high wages and his profit earnings kept increasing.   He envisioned an employer-employee relationship that would eliminate unions and change management policies, as stressed in the statement:

> There is a change coming. When the union of "union leaders" disappears, with it will go the union of blind bosses. . . . bosses who have never done a decent thing for their employees until they were compelled. If the blind boss were a disease, the selfish union leader was the antidote. When the union leader became the disease, the blind boss became the antidote. Both are misfits, both are out of place in well-organized society.[14]

Another incident will serve to exemplify how some early employers gave their recognition to fundamental managerial principles. For some time, unions agitated for a reduction of work-hours per day, contending that twelve-hours' production could be accomplished in eight hours and, in addition to the increased productivity, there would be a reduction in absenteeism, sickness, work injuries, and defective products. An eight-hour day seemed feasible when offset by worker reciprocity. On that basis, steel workers steadfastly demanded a shorter workday with hourly wage-base rates equivalent to the twelve-hour take-home pay.

Management in some steel mills believed that the twelve-hour day could not be curtailed without suffering losses. However, one liberal industrialist, Mr. J. F. Welborn, president of the Colorado Fuel and Iron Company, Pueblo, Colorado, proved that the twelve-hour shift was an unnecessary waste of energy. As early as November, 1918, the company changed from a twelve- to an eight-hour shift with resounding success. The workers' hourly wages were increased without company losses. In every department of the steel manufacturing operations, from the blast furnace to the wire mill, production per man-hour rose to larger percentages than under the twelve-hour shift, and the labor cost per ton was reduced. It was obvious that the change from a twelve- to an eight-hour day was both practical and successful with the result that on October 25, 1923 (15 years before the 40-hour week became law) the twelve-hour day was abolished in the steel industry.[15]

New Management Concepts. The enlightened views of the proponents of scientific management contributed to a clearer understanding of managerial

---

[14]Henry Ford, *My Life and Work* (New York: Doubleday, Page and Company, 1922), pp. 256–57.

[15]Information received from the American Iron and Steel Institute, July 8, 1959.

principles. Employers obtained cost reductions that enabled them to increase compensation periodically in accordance with higher costs of living. Liberal labor policies and new wage determination standards evolved rapidly.

New industrial and human relations principles had remained dormant during 1921–1922 because of the post-World War I depression. By 1923, however, the so-called Second Industrial Revolution overshadowed prior industrial changes. Employers and labor joined forces to increase productivity and to raise the standard of living through higher money wages and larger real earnings, thereby creating the so-called "purchasing power theory."[16] A new "living wage" concept, based on increased production and stabilized employment, was launched. It was agreed that if high wages and increased real income were to be sustained, the old principles of wage and salary determination would have to be replaced by new techniques of job and employee evaluations, work simplification, and new compensation methods. The productivity theory of wage determination was generally accepted.

Unions also changed their attitude toward scientific management. The AFL was the first labor union to realize the importance of increased productivity.[17] At its 1930 annual convention, the AFL adopted a declaration that partly reads: "We hold that the best interests of wage earners, as well as the whole society group, are served by increasing production in quality as well as quantity by high wage standards which assure sustained purchasing power to workers." Organized labor and adherents to scientific management principles worked hand in hand. Thus, the enlightened era of scientific management became firmly entrenched for the benefit of employer, employee, and the public.

The New Status of Unionism. Although the strength of unions had generally fluctuated a great deal during the growth of industry, the passage of the National Labor Relations Act (Wagner Act) of 1935 gave new status and strength to unions. The act guaranteed employees "the right to self-organization, to form, join, or assist labor organizations to bargain collectively through representatives of their own choosing." Hence, most company-dominated unions and employee representation plans were virtually terminated. The Act made collective bargaining an instrument of American national policy, thus paving the way for labor to organize and to bargain collectively without interference from employers. It boosted the growth of labor unions, thereby influencing wage and salary structures. When the United States Supreme Court legalized the Act (April 12, 1937), major industries such as the United States Steel Corporation, General Motors, and the Ford Motor Company eventually entered into collective bargaining agreements with the unions.

---

[16]Wage theories are discussed in Chapter 5.
[17]See William Green, "Organized Labor's Modern Wage Policy," *Research Series No. 1 of American Federation of Labor* (Washington, D. C., 1927).

Wage and salary administration since World War II (1942–present)

The period of time since World War II has had the greatest impact on the field of wage and salary administration. During this time, activities and events have moved rapidly and have stimulated interest and motivation in developing compensation procedures and practices from a rule of thumb concept to a more systematic and sound practice of management. This period is also marked by greater governmental intervention in more of the phases of compensation.

Compensation Known as Wage and Salary Administration

If there is any one period of time in which it can be said that wage and salary administration came into its own, it would appear to be during World War II. Although the basic groundwork for many phases of compensation had been laid in earlier periods of time (incentives in 1880's; merit rating during World War I and the early 1920's; job evaluation in the 1920's and '30's), it took some catalyst to crystallize the various phases of compensation into a meaningful and coordinated system. The catalyst was the United States Government Economic Stabilization Act of 1942, which froze all wages (World War II wage and salary controls were not terminated until 1946). This freeze was brought about because of a shortage of manpower that was created by the needs of the Army, Navy, and Marine Corps. During the war, the armed forces expanded to 15 million men mainly by taking employees from the labor force. The resulting scarcity of skilled workers caused employers to offer high wages and fringes to the employees who were still available. Many of those who were available began jumping from one job to another to get even higher wages with each move. This job jumping caused much industrial inefficiency and made it difficult to maintain essential war production schedules of airplanes, guns, ammunition, and the like. Since the government could not tolerate such chaotic conditions at home, the wage freeze was established.

Acceleration of Fringes

The wage freeze made it very difficult to grant a wage increase or to hire new workers without concrete justification for the action. Some companies felt that they were unfairly handicapped because the wage freeze came about without prior notice and prevented a justifiable wage increase previously promised to their employees. Some companies resorted to the granting of a fringe benefit or two in lieu of an increase in wages, since it was fairly easy to do this and still appease the employees. This practice opened the door to many fringes, the handling of which has accelerated into one of the present major challenges for the wage and salary administrator.

Formalizing of Wage and Salary Procedures

Another result of the wage freeze was that every company was forced to determine a way of evaluating jobs, pricing jobs, and granting pay raises based on valid criteria. Although many companies had some type of informal or formal procedure for these purposes, it was now becoming necessary to justify the procedures to the union and the government. Within a short time each company was busy reexamining, formalizing, and attempting to perfect its procedures, which were coming to be known as wage and salary administration. Previous to World War II, the various phases of compensation may have been handled by different departments such as the personnel department, the industrial engineering department, or the finance department; now an attempt was being made to coordinate and centralize the compensation activities in one department.

As time went on, the strength of the unions continued to gain, and in 1946 the unions were able to win the first of a series of annual across-the-board pay raises which have continued to the present time. These annual raises, like the wage freeze, forced managements to become more efficient in order to help pay for the raises granted. It also forced managements to make periodic wage surveys and more careful job evaluations as an objective basis for their decisions which the unions might question. The dynamic technological improvements developed during the war caused many changes in old jobs and created many new ones, all of which had to be dealt with to the satisfaction of the employer, the union, and the public.

During the early years following the war, there were a great many strikes — many of which were over wages. It has been said that since World War II, strikes have cost as much as $1 billion a year in lost wages alone.[18] These strikes increased the need for managements to know all the facts and facets of compensation and to have wage and salary data available for their collective bargaining with the unions. In large companies, these activities soon took the full time of one or more employees, and the person engaged in these activities was commonly referred to as the wage administrator or by some similar title. Some companies today, as in the past, have both a wage administrator and a salary administrator. At present, the procedures and techniques of wage administration are more advanced than those of salary administration, since wage administration primarily deals with employees who are unionized. It has been the constant pressure by unions that has forced managements to pay more attention to wage administration. However, there appears to be increasing pressure by the various groups paid on a salary basis (clerical, professional, technical, administrative, etc.) to force managements to improve the practice of salary administration. It would appear that at present the field of compensation is emerging from the

---

[18]Kenneth G. Slocum, "Strike Without Strife," *The Catholic Digest*, Vol. 28, No. 11 (September, 1964), p. 72.

technician stage to a total systems approach in which all facets of compensation must be tied together and related to all other business functions. The future challenge is to do this, while at the same time spending whatever money is available as wisely as possible.

Legislation governing compensation and collective bargaining

Persons interested in wage and salary administration are urged to become acquainted with the more important federal and state laws governing compensation and collective bargaining. The following descriptions of the laws are intended to give general perspective on how the laws affect employees and their compensation. Since statutes are subject to changes and amendments, inquiries for precise information on the application of the law in specific situations should be made to the local authorities in your vicinity. It should be realized that some states have supplementary laws that are more stringent than those described below. Some of the statutes are described in greater detail elsewhere in the book whenever required for proper understanding of the topic under consideration.

Workmen's Compensation Laws

Workmen's compensation laws (or industrial accident insurance statutes) constitute the first form of social insurance to develop widely in the United States. They provide some income protection for workers who are injured on the job and for their families in the event of fatal injuries. All states, since 1948, have had workmen's compensation programs. The Federal Employee's Compensation Act of 1908 covers workers who are employed by the United States government or whose employment is outside the jurisdiction of the United States. Together, these laws cover about four out of every five American wage and salary workers.

The main purpose of workmen's compensation laws is to eliminate the former uncertainties about receiving compensation damages when employees are injured on the job. Prior to the compensation act, the employer could defeat a damage claim under employers' liability laws or at common law. For instance, the employer could defeat a recovery claim if it was proven that the employee's injury was due to the ordinary risks of his work, if the injury was caused by the negligence of a fellow worker, or if the employee by his own negligence contributed to the injury. This system resulted in costly and sometimes lengthy court actions along with the uncertainty of whether damages could be collected.

A typical workmen's compensation law provides compensation for three kinds of disability — temporary total disability, permanent partial disability, and permanent total disability. The first involves disability that is temporary and leaves no permanent physical impairment; the second type is injury that may restrict the earning power of a worker; and the third is a disability that permanently terminates an employee's useful working life.

The large majority of industrial accidents, approximately 90 percent, involve temporary total disability. About 90 percent of these cases recover within a month and 75 percent in three weeks. The typical workmen's compensation law requires a one-week waiting period and allows no retroactive benefits for that week until the disability lasts beyond 28 days.

Workmen's compensation laws are intended to assure prompt payment of benefits to employees injured in the course of their employment, regardless of fault, with a minimum of legal formality. While the laws vary from state to state both as to coverage and benefits, they were originally intended to provide prompt medical care and weekly cash benefits for disabled workers at two thirds of their average wages, subject to dollar maximums. However, more than half of the states today have maximum benefits that are less than 50 percent of the state's average weekly wage. This means that the percent of benefits has deteriorated over the years since the 1910–16 era when most of the laws were passed.

A workmen's compensation law places a value on various parts of the human body. There are payments scheduled for injuries such as the loss of a finger, an arm, or an eye. The total amount payable is calculated by multiplying the maximum number of weeks allowed for the particular injury by the worker's weekly benefit. For example, a worker in Georgia who loses an arm is eligible for a maximum of $7,400 (200 weeks $\times$ $37). In the event of a fatal injury, the funeral expenses are paid and the survivors receive cash benefits.

The cost of the workmen's compensation programs is borne by employers as a part of the expense of production. The costs are about $1.04 for each $100 of payroll. In workmen's compensation, employers insure their risk either with a private stock or mutual insurance carrier, with a state fund (competitive or exclusive), or they self-insure. Workmen's compensation is the only social insurance that relies primarily on the private insurance mechanism for financing.

Classification Act of 1923

The *Classification Act of 1923* provided "the first systematic attempt by the federal government to achieve a uniform alignment of jobs and salaries among its various departments and agencies."[19] This, coupled with the *Brookhart Act of 1930*, gave coverage to the field service and central office employees of the federal government. The changing structure of the executive branch of the government has caused many changes in the Classification Act of 1923.

Since 1941 the pay schedules have climbed steadily upward through amendments, revisions, and repeals of original legislation. Of the several amendments,

---

[19]U. S. Department of Labor, *Wage Chronology — Federal Classification Act Employees, 1924–1964*, Bureau of Labor Statistics Bulletin No. 1442 (Washington: U.S. Government Printing Office, April, 1965), p. 1.

revisions, and appeals, the *Ramspeck Act of 1940* provided departmental employees with a system of appeals to the efficiency ratings assigned them. The *Mead-Ramspeck Act of 1941* (Public Law 200 of the 77th Congress) extended the efficiency ratings to the greater part of governmental employees beyond the departmental level. The *Classification Act of 1949* was a major revision of the 1923 Act and, as a result, the position classification of over 900,000 federal Civil Service employees was brought closer to the needs of the government. The *Performance Rating Act* of 1950 provided that upon the request of any officer or employee of a department, that department shall provide one important review of the performance rating of the employee or officer. In 1962 *Executive Order 10988* extended the right of collective bargaining to federal employees. The federal *Salary Reform Act of 1962* was a major revision of the pay plan part of the 1949 Act; the classification plan of the 1949 Act was not affected. The 1962 Reform Act is said to have accomplished the following: (1) established the "principle of comparability" between federal wages and those in the private sector of the economy for similar levels of work; (2) linked the other statutory salary systems (Postal Field Service, Foreign Service, and the Veterans Administration Department of Medicine and Surgery) with the Classification Act at certain key points, thus covering over 1.7 million federal employees; and (3) provided flexibilities in the use of within-grade rates. The *Salary Reform Act of 1964* "reaffirmed the 1962 principle of comparability and it continued the procedure of linking together the major statutory systems."[20] With the passage of this Act, the government was furnished "with a modern, effective compensation system that recognized the realities of the labor market in which it competes, while at the same time being just to both employee and taxpayer."[21]

Except to obtain a summary of the changes, there is no available substitute for the legal documents and the opinions of the government agencies charged with interpreting these documents.[22] A summary of the government's job classification procedure is given in Chapter 7.

Railroad Labor Act of 1926

This Act (which was amended in 1934, 1940, and 1952) provides for mediation, voluntary arbitration of wage disputes, and compulsory investigation by the National Railroad Adjustment Board before a strike can be called. The National Mediation Board deals with major disputes in cases of new contracts. If the Mediation Board cannot settle a dispute, or it is not resolved through arbitration, the matter is referred to the President of the United States, who

---

[20]Letter from Harold H. Leich, Chief, Program Planning Division, United States Civil Service Commission, Bureau of Programs and Standards, to Senator William Proxmire and forwarded to authors on October 8, 1964.

[21]*Ibid.*

[22]U. S. Department of Labor, *Wage Chronology — Federal Classification Act Employees, 1924–1964, op. cit.*

appoints a fact-finding committee. No strike is called for a period of 30 days, this time being used for deliberation by the fact-finding committee.

Davis-Bacon Act of 1931

The Davis-Bacon Act, also known as the Prevailing Wage Law of 1931 (amended in 1935, 1940, and 1964), specifies payment of certain prevailing wages, as determined by the Secretary of Labor, on federal construction projects. The projects may include altering or repairing public buildings under contract with the federal government or the District of Columbia, amounting to $2,000 or more. The requirements apply to all statutes that authorize the use of federal funds to aid nonfederal construction, such as state hospitals, airports, municipal buildings, and other housing projects.

A 1964 revision of the Davis-Bacon Act instructed the Secretary of Labor to include in prevailing wage determination the pattern of employer costs for fringe benefits including the following: medical or hospital care; pensions; life, disability, sickness, and accident insurance; vacation and holiday pay; unemployment benefits; and apprenticeships or similar training programs. Other benefits may be included if they are the pattern in the area.

Norris-La Guardia Anti-Injunction Act of 1932

This Act defines and limits the powers of federal courts that issue injunctions in labor disputes. The Act explicitly explains when and under what circumstances injunctions may be issued. It makes the so-called "yellow-dog contracts," in which a worker agrees not to join a union, unenforceable in federal courts.

National Labor Relations Act of 1935

This Act, also known as the Wagner Act, guarantees workers the right to organize and to choose their own representatives for collective bargaining with employers. The Act prohibits an employer from interfering with the formation or administration of any labor organization. It also provides rules and procedures for carrying out collective bargaining under the control of the National Labor Relations Board. The Board is empowered to hold elections in order to decide which union is to represent the workers in bargaining with the employer. As could be expected, the National Labor Relations Board met with opposition from employers who felt that the Wagner Act was one-sided. That is, employers maintained that the Act supported labor entirely, since employers and their representatives could not exercise their constitutional rights to freedom of speech among their own employees.

During World War II, employers and unions cooperated with governmental agencies in carrying out the war program in accordance with the National Labor Relations Act. After the war, however, there was strong public agitation to amend or to change the Act because it prohibited employers from performing certain labor practices. In addition, there was no provision against unfair union practices. Furthermore, the Act required a union to bargain for all employees, including nonunion workers. As a result, the National Labor Relations Act was amended by the Taft-Hartley Law of 1947, which officially became the Labor-Management Relations Act of 1947.

Social Security Act of 1935

The old-age, survivors, and disability insurance (OASDI) program in the United States, more popularly known as the Social Security Act, is probably the most important law for protecting the worker who becomes unemployed or disabled, or who retires or dies and leaves dependents. At present, about nine tenths of all gainfully employed persons are covered by the Act. The various amendments to the original act have mainly extended the number of persons covered and have increased the dollar amounts of the various benefits. The 1965 amendments provided a hospital insurance benefit program for persons age 65 and over with a supplementary health benefits program and an expanded program of medical assistance.

The Social Security Act of 1935 created a system of unemployment insurance to assist an unemployed worker during a period of time when he might be out of work. The aim of the program was to provide the jobless worker with at least 50 percent of his average weekly earnings during the period he qualified for unemployment compensation. In the early years of the program, the maximum weekly benefit in most states was $15. The average weekly wage at the time was $23; thus, the maximum benefit equaled 65 percent of the average wage.[23] Today, the typical maximum weekly benefit is $50; the average wage is nearly $120. Thus, the benefit represents only about 42 percent of the average wage.[24] Some companies have felt that unemployment compensation benefits are not enough for the unemployed man and his family to weather the layoff and therefore have instituted Supplemental Unemployment Benefit Plans (SUB).

All states have laws that levy a payroll tax on employers, according to an experience rating formula, to provide money for the unemployment benefits under the Social Security Act. The purpose of the experience rating formula is to vary a firm's unemployment tax directly according to its unemployment record (or experience). Thus, a firm having a lower record of unemployment pays a smaller amount of money into the fund.

The monthly old-age or disability insurance benefits are calculated according to a formula based on the worker's average wages. Workers and employers share the insurance costs equally, based on a certain percentage stipulated by law.

---

[23]James O'Brien, "The Shocking Erosion of the Jobless Pay System," *AFL-CIO American Federationist* (January, 1969), p. 18.
[24]*Ibid.*

Walsh-Healey Public Contracts Act of 1936

This Act (amended in 1940, 1942, and 1952) establishes minimum wages and maximum hours for work done on *government contracts* amounting to $10,000 or more. The Act provides that the Secretary of Labor must decide the minimum wages that contractors are to pay. The Act also contains regulations for the payment of one and one-half times the employee's wage-base rate for the hours worked in excess of eight hours in one day or 40 hours in one week. This Act further specifies that the goods must be produced under adequate safety and sanitation standards.

Fair Labor Standards Act of 1938

Commonly referred to as the Federal Wage and Hour Law, the Fair Labor Standards Act (FLSA) was enacted by Congress in 1938. It is a very significant federal law since it affects over a million establishments with 42.8 million workers. The Act covers those employees who are engaged in the production of goods for interstate and foreign commerce, including those whose work is closely related to or directly essential to such production. It also includes employees of farms, and certain retail and service establishments whose sales volume exceeds a prescribed amount, on the supposition that large financial operations must of necessity "affect commerce." The FLSA attempts to eliminate labor conditions detrimental to the health, efficiency, and well-being of the workers and to eliminate unfair competition based on these conditions. To accomplish these goals, the Act establishes minimum wages and overtime pay; it puts certain restrictions on the employment of children; and it prohibits wage differentials based on sex. The Act establishes a number of rules exempting certain classes of employees from the minimum wage-and-hour provisions, and releasing employers from payment of time-and-one-half for overtime on specific jobs. Some of the main provisions of the Act and its amendments follow.

Equal Pay Act of 1963. The Equal Pay Act of 1963 is considered an amendment to the FLSA. Under this act, the employer must not discriminate on the basis of sex by paying lower wage-rates to one sex than to those of the opposite sex for *equal* work on jobs requiring *equal skill, effort,* and *responsibility* which are *performed under similar working conditions.* An employer may pay a higher rate of pay to one sex than to the other where he can establish that the differential is based on a seniority system, a merit system, a system measuring earnings by quantity or quality of production, or on any factor other than sex. An employer must not reduce the wages of any employee to eliminate a prohibited wage differential based on sex. Although the law was designed primarily to protect women from discriminatory pay practices, it affords the same protection to men.

Minimum Wages. When the FLSA was passed in 1938, it provided a 25-cent-an-hour minimum wage. Subsequent amendments have increased the minimum wage and the types of businesses and employees that are covered by the Act. Under the 1966 amendments more than nine million additional workers were brought under the coverage of the Act. Coverage was extended for the first time to farm hands and service employees such as laundry workers, hospital orderlies, waitresses, bellhops, and school janitors. The 1966 amendments also established a series of steps in which the minimum wage was gradually raised to $1.60. Unless specifically exempt, all employees previously covered by the FLSA were paid at least $1.60 per hour effective February 1, 1968. All nonfarm workers newly covered by the act must be paid at least $1.60 per hour as of February 1, 1971. All farm workers previously covered by the act and its amendments were paid at least $1.30 per hour as of February 1, 1969. This is true whether the employees are paid by the hour, by salary, by piece-work, or by any other method. However, under certain conditions, the employer may pay special minimum rates to learners, apprentices, messengers, handicapped workers, and full-time students if a special certificate is obtained from the Wage and Hour and Public Contracts Division of the United States Department of Labor.

Overtime Pay. The FLSA requires all employers to pay to all persons covered by the Act at least one and one-half times the regular rate of pay for all hours worked over 40 hours each week. The regular rate of pay is not always the same as the hourly rate of pay. If an employee receives any supplementary earnings (such as bonuses, incentives, commissions), his regular rate of pay is found by totaling all his earnings and dividing by the number of hours worked.

The law does *not* require extra pay for Saturday, Sunday, or holiday work. It does not require vacation, holiday, or severance pay, or a discharge notice. Nor does it set any limit on the number of hours of work for persons 16 years of age or over.

Child Employment Restrictions. The FLSA forbids the employment of any child under 14 years of age. Children 14 or 15 years old may be employed outside school hours in a limited number of jobs such as office and sales jobs for a limited number of hours under regulated conditions. The employer must keep proof of a child's age on file to avoid violation of the law. Children 16 or 17 years old may be employed in any occupation other than hazardous occupations, such as jobs at the sawmill and gravel pit, driving or helping on a motor vehicle, operating elevators or other hoisting apparatus, or operating power-driven bakery machines or other power-driven machines declared hazardous by the Secretary of Labor. Other restrictions (hours, time, etc.) are governed by state statutes. Children 18 years and over may work in any occupation, including those declared hazardous.

Specifically exempt from the child-labor provisions of the law are:

1. Children engaged in the delivery of newspapers to the consumer.
2. Children employed in agriculture outside school hours for the school district where they are living while employed.
3. Children employed as actors or performers in motion picture, theatrical, radio, or television productions.
4. Children employed by their parents in jobs other than manufacturing, mining, or hazardous occupations.
5. Homeworkers engaged in making wreaths composed principally of natural holly, pine, cedar, or other evergreens (including the harvesting of the evergreens).

Employees Covered by FLSA. Which employees are covered under the minimum wage law provisions may cause some confusion. Prior to the 1961 amendment, coverage under the FLSA was determined by the nature of the work in which the individual employee was engaged. The question was: Does his job involve interstate or foreign commerce, or the production of goods for interstate or foreign commerce? Although the 1961 amendment did not change this yard-stick, it did set up an additional test — the "enterprise" concept.

The "enterprise" concept shifts the emphasis — as far as retail, wholesale, and service businesses are concerned — from the *individual employee* to the *firm* itself. If the firm qualifies as an enterprise, *all* its employees are now covered by the Act. Whether a firm is a covered enterprise depends on its annual gross volume of sales (at least $1 million) and the amount of goods purchased for resale (at least $250,000–$350,000) that have moved across state lines.

Generally, employees working in the following occupations, industries, or establishments are typical of those covered by the FLSA:

accounting firms	manufacturing
advertising agencies	mines
bakeries	oil fields
banks	processing
clothing firms	quarries
communications	radio
construction	sawmills
department stores (large)	seamen
distributing	telegraph
fuel	television
gas stations	transportation
insurance	utilities
lumbering	wholesaling
machinery	

Employees Exempt under FLSA. Employees working in the following occupations, industries, or establishments, are typical of those that *are exempt* from the minimum wage and overtime provisions of the FLSA:

administrators
agriculture
airlines*
amusement parks (seasonal)
announcers*
beverage service (local)
city government
county government
colleges
cotton gins
delivery drivers* (local)
domestics
dry cleaning
executives
farm workers
fish products*
fishermen
gas stations*
federal government
forestry (small)
fruit and vegetable transportation
hotels (small)

hospitals
livestock auctions
laundries (home)
motels (small)
news editors*
newspapers (small)
nursing homes
pipelines*
professional
railroads*
recreational establishments
restaurants
retail establishments (small)
salesmen (outside)
schools
service establishments (small)
state government
taxicabs
theaters
tobacco processing
transit companies (local)
trucking*

*Exempt from only the *overtime* requirements of the FLSA.

Wage and Salary Stabilization Act of 1942

Legislated during World War II, this Act gave the President of the United States authorization to control prices, wages, and salaries at levels existing on September 15, 1942. It made provisions for adjustments to correct inequities in wages, salaries, and prices affecting the cost of living.

The Act prevented employers of more than eight employees from making any changes in the wage and salary levels that were in effect on October 1, 1942. In cases of promotion, however, the employer could increase wages and salaries on the basis of rate levels that existed before the stabilization act became effective. Similarly, employers were permitted to raise wages and salaries for jobs that were evaluated in relation to other jobs at price rates existing prior to October, 1942.

The Act led to numerous directives issued from the office of the President. They included the placement of upper limits on wages and salaries that were controlled by an established National War Labor Board (NWLB). This Board, represented by employers, employees, and the general public, was charged with stabilizing wages and salaries and resolving disputes that could not be solved by unions and employers. The War Labor Board decisions insisted on job evaluation to determine what was alleged to be wage inequities. From this time on, job evaluation became an accepted factor in wage determination. In 1946 all World War II wage and salary controls were terminated.

Little Steel Formula of 1942

One of the first policies of the NWLB was the establishment of the Little Steel Formula, which permitted a general wage increase of 15 percent above the prevailing rates on January 1, 1941. The formula was first applied to workers in steel companies, based on a 15 percent increase in the cost of living from January 1, 1941, to May 1, 1942. It is significant to note that this policy was used in stabilizing wages throughout World War II and continued to be a factor in wage and salary determination thereafter.

The NWLB was also responsible for wage increases based on intraplant inequities, which led to a greater use of job evaluation, wage and salary surveys, and wage differentials as discussed in Chapters 6 through 13.

Labor-Management Relations Act (Taft-Hartley Law) of 1947

This Act is considered to be the most far-reaching labor legislation in the United States. It is administered by the National Labor Relations Board, which is composed of five members and a General Counsel. In addition, there is a Federal Mediation and Conciliation Service that acts as an independent agency of the federal government, divorced from the Department of Labor.

The Act revised and amended the Wagner Act of 1935 by guaranteeing workers the right to organize and to bargain collectively with their employers, or *to refrain from all such activities*. The Act permits employers "free speech" as long as there is no threat of reprisal, and places certain limitations on the activities of labor organizations as well as employers. Both employers and employees are protected against unfair labor practices that could be committed by unions, such as: compelling an employer to pay an employee for unperformed services, coercing employees to join a union, participating in jurisdictional strikes, and extracting excessive initiation fees from new union members. The unfair labor practices forbidden an employer are: restraining employees from joining a union, declining to bargain collectively with employee representatives, and influencing labor unions.

A union is certified as the collective bargaining agent after the majority of workers have declared their preference for it. Strike limitations include a 60-day "cooling-off" period during which neither a strike nor a lockout may occur. If an agreement is reached, neither the union nor the employer may change it before a 60-day notice has expired.

The Act abolishes new *closed-shop* agreements under which management must hire only union designated workers. *Union-shop* agreements are permitted only by the authorization of a majority of employees. Under these agreements, management may hire any worker, but must discharge said worker either if he does not join the union after his probationary period, or if he has lost his "good standing" after joining. However, union-shop agreements are not valid in states where such agreements are forbidden by state law.

The Taft-Hartley Law does not apply to employees in an enterprise where a labor dispute does not affect interstate commerce. Furthermore, the Act prohibits strikes that are intended to stop an employer from doing business with another employer involved in a strike (secondary boycott). It also *does not* apply to supervisors "having authority, in the interest of the employer, to hire, transfer, suspend, recall, promote, discharge, reward, or discipline other employees."

Welfare and Pension Plans Disclosure Act of 1958

This Act requires administrators of all health, insurance, pension, and supplementary unemployment compensation plans covering more than 25 workers to file with the Secretary of Labor descriptions and annual financial reports to be available for public inspection. The Act was amended in 1962 to require that descriptions and financial reports be filed only for plans covering 100 or more participants.

Landrum-Griffin Act of 1959

The Landrum-Griffin Act, officially known as the Labor-Management Reporting and Disclosure Act of 1959, was generally designed to promote democracy in union affairs, eliminate improper activities (racketeering and dishonesty) by labor and management, and force unions and managements to make reports on a number of their activities. Thus, the law features both regulation and protection of managements and unions.

Specifically, the Act provides certain protection for the rights of labor organization members; provides for the filing of reports describing the organization, financial dealings, business practices of labor organizations, their officers and employees, certain employers, labor relations consultants, and unions in trusteeship; safeguards union election procedures; sets standards for the handling of union funds; amends the Taft-Hartley Law to eliminate the "no-man's land" in NLRB cases; closes previously existing loopholes in the protection against secondary boycotts; and limits organizational and jurisdictional picketing. The statute is administered by the Department of Labor. The National Labor Relations Board administers portions of the statute amending the Taft-Hartley Act.

Service Contract Act of 1965

This Act provides labor standards protection for employees of contractors and subcontractors furnishing services to federal agencies. It requires that provisions regarding wages and working conditions be included in the contracts and bid specifications.

REVIEW QUESTIONS

1. Briefly trace the history of the methods of compensation to the present day.
2. (a) What were some of the effects of the Industrial Revolution on labor and management? (b) In what way did the introduction of the Factory System influence the standard of living?
3. Briefly trace the development of union organizations.
4. (a) What caused the formation of the CIO? (b) What were the main differences of organization between the AFL and the CIO?
5. Why were employers successful in opposing unions at the beginning of the nineteenth century?
6. Explain why the early manufacturers were known as the "Captains of Industry."
7. What was the result of specialization and its impact on American labor?
8. How does specialization affect the compensation of American labor?
9. Should the Fair Labor Standards Act apply to all employees in the labor force? Why?
10. (a) In what way did the "new-era capitalists" differ from the old "Captains of Industry?" (b) What main factors influenced the introduction of the eight-hour day in the steel mills?
11. (a) Briefly describe why and how the "new era of management" was introduced. (b) What effect did it have on wages and salaries? (c) What are the new management concepts?
12. Name some of the federal laws that influence the wages and the salaries which employers pay.
13. Which law or laws affect collective bargaining to the advantage of unions?
14. (a) To what extent does the Taft-Hartley Law favor employers? (b) In what way does the law differ from the Wagner Act? (c) What are the provisions made under the Taft-Hartley Law to avoid strikes?
15. What are the unfair labor practices forbidden unions and employers as provided by the Taft-Hartley Law?
16. Wage and salary administration has come into its own since World War II. Why?

RESEARCH OR SEMINAR QUESTIONS

1. What effects has the growth of labor unions had on management's employee policies?
2. List the arguments for and against the closed shop and explain why you think it should or should not be legalized.
3. What new developments in wage and salary administration can be expected in the near future?
4. Are the laws that the federal government has passed in the labor relations area making it more difficult for wage and salary administration to exist? Why?

PRACTICAL EXPERIENCE ASSIGNMENTS

1. At your local or campus library see how far back in history you can find any mention of the subject of wage and salary administration. Be prepared to report to the class the pertinent details you find.
2. Write a 200-word composition on the evolution of compensation in business and industry.
3. Write to (or talk with) your congressman, senator, or public official regarding his views on legislation dealing with wages. Find out whether he thinks that the present laws (federal, state, or local) are adequate or whether new ones are needed and why. Do you agree with him? Why?
4. Visit some union official or a member of management who takes part in the collective bargaining process between a union and a management. Find out the part that wages play in the collective bargaining process. What is the aim, theory, or principle under which this person's organization operates when bargaining for wages?

CASE PROBLEMS

2—1. UNIONIZATION OF TEACHERS

Minimum Wage Law for Teachers

It has been claimed for many years that teachers are underpaid. Teachers' salaries have been compared with those of truck drivers, garbage men, janitors, and other jobs that call for a limited amount of education. In some cases the teachers' salaries have been no higher than these jobs. At present there is a minimum wage law for most employees who are engaged in interstate commerce jobs.

In a fairly large midwestern city, one of the local unions has decided to try to organize the teachers and to have a minimum wage law passed that would reward teachers in proportion to their earned college degrees.

Problem:

Analyze the pros and cons of this proposition and be prepared to indicate whether you would be for or against such a law and why.

2—2. STABILIZATION OF EMPLOYER-EMPLOYEE RELATIONS

The Taft-Hartley Law

A considerable amount of material has been written pro and con about the "expansion of union powers and governmental control." Attempts are made to condemn or to justify the Taft-Hartley Law.

1. Do past experiences point toward increased management-labor cooperation?
2. Will current unionism survive?

3. Will new legislation be enacted to diminish union power?

4. In the long run, how can employer-employee relations be stabilized?

It is claimed that neither the 1935 nor the 1947 Congress anticipated all the implications of making wage and salary determination dependent upon compulsory collective bargaining and arbitration. Hopes are raised that the shortcomings in the rules governing labor-management relations will be corrected. Employers are opposed to picketing as an instrument of union coercion, especially the frequent locked-arm mass picketing. Furthermore, it is alleged that the Taft-Hartley Law permits organized labor to shut down entire industries, creating trade practices equivalent to the restraint of trade, which are not in the public's best interest. Employers feel that the antitrust law applied equally to the combined union organizations.

Labor unions launched a drive to repeal the Taft-Hartley Law (termed "slave-labor law") as soon as it was published. They strongly object to the provision permitting employers free speech on the grounds that workers are still being coerced.

Social-minded citizens argue that workers, as free American citizens, should not be forced to pay union taxes in order to work. This argument is supported by the fact that a number of states have right-to-work laws that prohibit union membership as a requisite for obtaining and holding a job. Against this argument, union supporters assert that "every employee should contribute his share because the union is his legal representative in collective bargaining." Therefore, unions aim to repeal the section of the Taft-Hartley Law that permits states to adopt right-to-work laws. On the other hand, employers urge a federal right-to-work law "to curb costly strikes and wage inflation which are a drain on the American economy."

Some personnel managers in industry contend that progressive unionism has become an integral part of the American capitalistic system. This is verified by the hundreds of management-labor agreements that function to the satisfaction of employers, employees, and the public, without work stoppages. It is also argued that the American labor movement is a great economic asset because the periodic demands of union leaders keep management on the alert constantly to improve productivity which, in turn, increases consumption and raises the standard of living.

Problem:

What is your reaction to the various claims set forth in the above paragraphs? As a wage and salary administrator, your function is to serve three parties — employer, employees, and the general public as buyers and consumers. Which side do you represent? State enough reasons to clearly justify your position.

chapter **3**

THE ROLE OF THE WAGE
AND SALARY ADMINISTRATOR
IN AN ENTERPRISE

The primary purpose of this chapter is to give a comprehensive picture of the job and the administrator who is in charge of compensation in an enterprise. To do this the discussion will focus upon the job of the wage and salary administrator, his qualifications, criteria for job success, and some guidelines for successful performance.

The job of the wage and salary administrator

The position of the compensation administrator has not yet been formalized into a standard pattern for every company. Probably no two wage and salary administrators are performing identical work. However, there are some common denominators that characterize the work of each. In order to understand better the job of the person in charge of remuneration, the discussion will cover the development of the job, its goals, titles, functions, responsibilities, and variations.

Origin and Organizational Development of Wage and Salary Administration

Wage and salary administration had its inception with the introduction of scientific management. Its functions were intermingled with the activities of the early practitioners who laid the foundation for systematic business organization at the beginning of the twentieth century.

When Frederick W. Taylor, his associates, and followers brought scientific management before the public, its identification with the term "efficiency" became widespread.[1] As a result, pseudo engineers and quack practitioners operated under the guise of "efficiency experts." The new science of management was discredited by ultraconservatives who envisioned a new industrial revolution that would deprive craftsmen of the use of their skills.[2] To avoid being referred to as a Taylor Systematizer or the derogatory "efficiency expert," a group of engineer-practitioners turned to the profession of industrial engineering and ventured into the field of wage and salary administration.

Wage and Salary Administration in the Field of Industrial Engineering. By the end of 1920, Taylor's principles of scientific management and human relations had been accepted and developed by his followers. They began laying the foundation for the modern wage and salary administration program to supplement time studies and piece-rate setting. Lichtner started discussing job analysis and the need for experienced analysts "who plan their work so as to enlist the help of the organization and win the confidence of management, supervisors, and workers."[3] He was followed by Lott, who — with a technical background — became personnel superintendent in a manufacturing concern. Lott wrote the first book on job evaluation "to be practical and useful" based on a progressive wage program.[4] He stressed the foundation of an equitable wage structure with emphasis on incentives to obtain "equal pay for equal service rendered."

The function of wage and salary administration has become a permanent part of the industrial engineering field because of its activities in setting work standards for job performance, and time standards for piece rates and other wage incentive plans. To accomplish the latter, the industrial engineer makes a job analysis of each step in the manufacturing process, along with very closely detailed specifications. All the elements involved in performing an operation are described sequentially. In addition, a job classification card is prepared describing the job, how the work is performed, and the type of operator and labor grade needed for the job.[5] Thus, in many companies it was natural for the industrial engineering department to absorb the function of wage and salary administration

---

[1]Harrington Emerson, *Efficiency as a Basis for Operation and Wages* (New York: The Engineering Magazine Co., 1911) and *The Twelve Principles of Efficiency*, published in 1919 by the same company.

[2]See *Procedures of American Federation of Labor* (November 10–22, 1913), p. 299.

[3]William O. Lichtner, *Time Study and Job Analysis* (New York: The Ronald Press Company, 1921), chaps. V and IX.

[4]Merrill R. Lott, *Wage Scales and Job Evaluation* (New York: The Ronald Press Company, 1926).

[5]Ralph M. Barnes, *Motion and Time Study* (4th ed.; New York: John Wiley & Sons, Inc., 1958), pp. 573–74.

activities. This condition still exists in many medium-size and large enterprises, such as the Western Electric Company where there is no wage and salary administration department; and the Armstrong Cork Company where members of the industrial engineering department's staff perform operation studies, job analysis, and job evaluation, and establish incentive wages.

Status of Wage and Salary Administration in Industrial Engineering. To find to what extent the industrial engineers are involved in about 30 wage and salary administration activities, Professor Ralph M. Barnes at the University of Iowa made a survey in 1948. He polled 80 companies and found that in 49 percent of the firms, the industrial engineering department head reports to top management, and in 51 percent, to factory or works managers. Of the 80 companies polled, 77 installed wage incentive systems, 71 developed complete wage payment plans, and 68 of the latter used job evaluation methods.[6]

In a similar survey in 1950, Professor Barnes polled 67 industrial companies to ascertain the industrial engineering practices in the Los Angeles area. The survey revealed that in 45 companies the engineers developed wage payment plans and wage incentives, 39 of which also installed job evaluation methods.[7]

A survey by the American Society of Mechanical Engineers (ASME) in 1952 showed that in 132 responding companies, industrial engineers performed wage and salary administration functions as follows: 79 installed wage incentives; 69 carried out complete job evaluation; 44 had charge of wage and salary administration; and 21 carried out employee rating.[8]

In 1943 the Work Standardization Committee in the Management Division of the American Society of Mechanical Engineers was engaged in defining the limits in the field of industrial engineering. The committee designed a chart similar to the one shown in Figure 3.1, which has been abridged to show only those activities that are of specific interest to the wage and salary administrator.

Figure 3.1 indicates how the industrial engineer carries out the function of wage and salary administration after methods and operations have been standardized. The activity of work measurement parallels the activities of wage and salary administration until wage payment procedures begin. The chart traces the relationship of motion and time study to wage and salary administration.

Wage and Salary Administration As a Function of Industrial Relations. Personnel management was founded during the 1920's and rapidly won recognition as a function in organizations. Like industrial engineers, personnel managers took on a number of functions related to the selection, employment, testing, and grading of personnel, as well as making job analyses for placement and wage

---

[6]Ralph M. Barnes, *Industrial Engineering Survey*, Industrial Engineering Report No. 10 (Iowa City: University of Iowa, 1949).

[7]Ralph M. Barnes and J. Bryan Sullivan, *Production Management Survey* (Los Angeles: University of California, 1950).

[8]H. B. Maynard (Editor in Chief), *Industrial Engineering Handbook* (New York: McGraw-Hill Book Company, Inc., 1956), Sec. 1, p. 21.

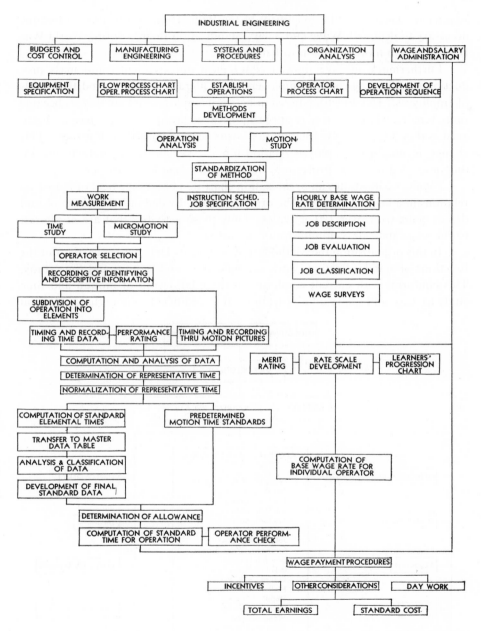

American Society of Mechanical Engineers

FIGURE 3.1   RELATIONSHIP OF MOTION AND TIME STUDY TO WAGE AND SALARY
ADMINISTRATION IN THE FIELD OF INDUSTRIAL ENGINEERING

payments. Then, with the enactment of the Wage-Hour Act in 1938, it became necessary to deal with Wage and Salary Stabilization Boards during World War II, and to give more attention to bargaining.

Furthermore, as inventions, technological improvements, and mass production increased, corporate employers hired literally hundreds and thousands of employees. The direct relationship between employer and employees became more remote, while the close relationship between groups of employees strengthened as they began to solve their mutual socioeconomic problems together. This change in employer-employee relationship — especially in manufacturing industries — led to a new profession, the *Industrial Relations Director.*

Figure 3.2 illustrates an organization chart that covers the field of industrial relations in a large company. The organization is divided into ten divisions and departments with over 120 activities. Only those activities that are of interest to the wage and salary administrator are listed.

In this organization the Methods and Standards Department carries out the functions of standardization, work simplification, and motion and time study. This conforms with current emphasis on the relationship of motion and time study to wage and salary administration. It is significant to note that writers on

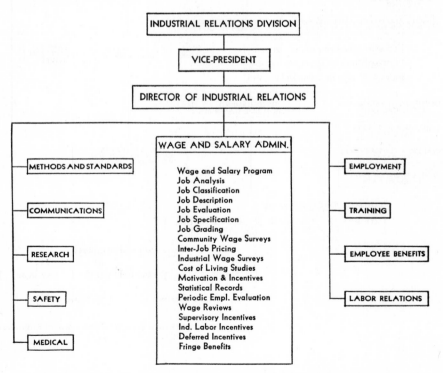

FIGURE 3.2   Relationship of Wage and Salary Administration
to the Field of Industrial Relations

personnel management and industrial relations emphasize the need for and use of time study.[9]   Professor Yoder urges that "The industrial relations worker should have a basic elementary understanding of time study, especially as it relates to wage and salary administration and compensation methods."[10] Similarly, industrial psychologists are giving special consideration to work methods, work simplification, job standardization, and motion and time study. Professor Gray's book *Psychology in Industry* devotes an entire chapter to the subject.[11]

Another interesting organizational setup shows the relationship of wage and salary administration to the field of industrial relations at Texas Instruments Incorporated, Dallas, Texas.   The organization chart in Figure 3.3 shows the

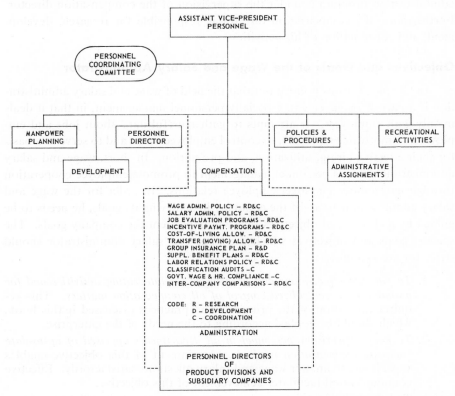

Texas Instruments Incorporated

FIGURE 3.3   Central Personnel Organization of Texas Instruments Incorporated and Its Functional Relationship to Wage and Salary Administration

[9]Dale Yoder *et al*, *Handbook of Personnel Management and Labor Relations* (New York: McGraw-Hill Book Company, Inc., 1958), pp. 5.32 through 5.40 and 16.50 to 16.53.
[10]*Ibid.*, p. 16.50.
[11]J. Stanley Gray, *Psychology in Industry* (New York: McGraw-Hill Book Company, Inc., 1952), pp. 119 to 140.

eight divisions of the industrial relations organization.[12]   Only those responsibilities of the compensation division that are of special interest to wage and
salary administrators are illustrated.   Note that the compensation director and
the personnel director are at the same level, both reporting to the Assistant Vice
President in charge of Personnel.   Also, Figure 3.3 indicates that the responsibilities of the compensation director include the development of wage administration policies as well as salary administration policies; incentive payment
programs; various supplemental wage and fringe benefit plans; labor relations
policy; governmental law compliances; and other responsibilities in addition
to the usual job evaluation programs, as well as activities generally considered as
wage and salary administration.   In other words, the entire wage and salary
administration program is under the supervision of the compensation director.
Furthermore, the compensation director is responsible for research, development, and coordination of his activities.

Objectives and Goals of the Wage and Salary Administrator

In Chapter 1 it was pointed out that the field of wage and salary administration is a part of management, especially personnel management, in that it deals
mainly with employees.   It attempts to gather useful data about jobs and employees, to motivate employees, to control employee costs, and to serve as a basis
for their effective hiring, utilization, and promotion.   In short, wage and salary
administration assists personnel management to promote employee cooperation
through harmonious employer-employee relations.   In order for the wage and
salary administrator to assist the company in achieving its goals, he needs to be
guided by a clear set of objectives that will implement the company goals.   The
specific goals and objectives which the wage and salary administrator should
strive for are as follows:

1. *To put into effect plans and procedures for integrating activities and for
   maintaining a centralized control of all compensation matters.*   This requires utilization of the principles and practices discussed in this book,
   which should be applied according to the needs of the enterprise.
2. *To keep supervisory personnel in all departments apprised of up-to-date
   company compensation methods.*   Attainment of this objective enables
   supervisors to answer wage and salary questions satisfactorily.   Effective
   communication facilitates achievement of this objective.
3. *To help the personnel department attract and maintain an efficient and con-
   tented work force by paying adequate wages and salaries.*   An adequate
   compensation program can be maintained by a continual surveillance of
   the cost of living as well as the demand for labor and competitive goods.
   Also, keeping pace with competitors' wage payments avoids abnormal
   labor turnover.

[12]We are indebted to Mr. R. G. Bartling, Compensation Director of Texas Instruments
Incorporated, for the chart and complete information regarding his division.

➤ 4. *To establish ways and means for minimizing pay inequities in order to eliminate dissatisfaction and grievances among employees.* Pay inequities are avoided by the introduction of job evaluation and job classification, which establish a job rate hierarchy based on job differentials and job pricing according to graded job difficulties. Employee morale is heightened, labor turnover is avoided, and pay-rate schedules are established according to the worth of each job.

5. *To pay equivalent pay rates for the same or similar jobs in the community or industry.* The going rates are generally ascertained by making periodic surveys in the community. Company rates are then adjusted and each employee is paid for his job according to the average rate in the community. To retain efficient employees, qualified workers are remunerated at a higher wage-base rate. Thereby, an organization of productive manpower is maintained for successful competition with other employers.

6. *To arrange periodic employee rating in order to compensate workers according to their worth as compared with other employees doing the same job.* Standards are established to measure an employee's ability apart from his job function. An appraisal of his past performance determines the amount of quantitative and qualitative output that may be above the expected rate of output. Similarly, an analysis of the worker's past behavior ascertains his regular attendance, punctuality, and other factors that contribute to his value as an efficient and loyal employee. Accordingly, his status with regard to an increase in wages and promotion is established.

7. *To control direct and indirect labor costs through established standards of performance and adherence to standard unit costs.* This objective can be realized by studying job operations in their sequence, by simplifying work methods, by eliminating unnecessary motions, and by standardizing the working conditions around the work area. Material handling standards and effective equipment maintenance are additional factors of control. Thus, standard costs can be maintained and excessive labor costs can be avoided.

8. *To balance production costs with remuneration on a basis of incentive wages for above average production.* Performance standards and time rates are set — on the basis of motion and time studies — to establish an average work pace. An incentive plan enables the worker to increase his earnings a certain percentage in proportion to his increased efforts.

9. *To strike a proper balance between direct wage and salary remunerations and supplemental compensation such as profit sharing, group insurance, pensions (deferred incentives), and various fringe benefits.* During the last 20 years supplemental compensations have become a part of the wage and salary program either as a result of union demand or as a matter of attracting employees in a competitive market. In either case, diligence and judgment must be exercised to keep immediate rewards and deferred payments in proper balance so as to gain profits.

10. *To maintain good human relations according to management creeds through effective communication on all employee compensation matters.* To uphold employee morale, human relations have become an important

part of management inasmuch as labor costs and other expenditures related to compensation are affected. To keep faith with the employees and to avoid misunderstandings, management must express its beliefs through the media of communications.

To meet these goals, the person in charge of compensation is usually given a title and assigned various functions and responsibilities, as discussed below.

Titles, Functions, and Responsibilities of the Wage and Salary Administrator

A research study made by the American Management Association (AMA) reveals that there is no consistency in describing the functions and titles of certain managerial positions.[13] The same is true of positions in wage and salary administration. It appears that the titles and descriptions of middle management positions are still in a formative stage, although the titles and job descriptions at the first-line supervisory level and those of production workers have received much attention and are now fairly well established.

In wage and salary administration, numerous titles are being used interchangeably for the same functions and responsibilities. Similarly, different functions and duties are sometimes carried out by administrators with the same title. This is due to the fact that the function of wage and salary administration has been erroneously interpreted to mean job analysis, and, by some, to mean job evaluation. To others, it means employee rating, and to still others, motion and time study, performance rating, or other subfunctions of compensation. Wage and salary administration should be regarded, however, as the all-inclusive function that comprises the activities cited in Figure 1.3, page 11.

Title Descriptions. Generally, those whose main function and responsibility is to coordinate and to control the company wage and salary program and to maintain the compensation structure are known under several titles as indicated:

TITLE	COMPANY
Director of Compensation and Benefits	Vick Chemical Company, New York, New York
Wage and Salary Administrator	Dresser Industries, Incorporated, Dallas, Texas
Coordinator Wage & Salary Administration	Henry J. Kaiser Company, Oakland, California
Manager Salary Administration	General Foods Corporation, White Plains, New York
Supervisor Wage Administration	Verton Aircraft Corporation, Morton, Pennsylvania

---

[13]C. L. Bennet, *Defining the Manager's Job* (New York: American Management Association, Inc., 1958).

Functions and Responsibilities. Wage and salary administration functions and responsibilities entail activities that are determined by the size of the organization, the kind of products and/or services, and the number of jobs involved. Naturally, the activities and responsibilities will vary from company to company. Nevertheless, the following activities and responsibilities are widely accepted as applicable to a majority of wage and salary programs:

1. Formulating wage and salary plans based on principles and policies acceptable to employer and employees.
2. Establishing criteria for wage and salary determination that may be considered "fair" for the purpose of collective bargaining.
3. Setting up and administering wage and salary evaluation systems, which involves analyzing and rating jobs to establish job differentials and job standards.
4. Recording and maintaining job and position descriptions, job specifications, and classification for comparative wage determination.
5. Analyzing each job and developing techniques in order to set differential and equitable wage-base rates within the organization as compared with wage rates in the entire industry.
6. Assigning newly created jobs to established labor classifications or developing new evaluations and classifications.
7. Making wage surveys to ascertain average going rates in the community or in the industry for comparison to keep wages and salaries in line with those of competitors.
8. Analyzing government wage regulations, company wage policies, and agreements with unions to maintain up-to-date wage rates.
9. Making policy recommendations regarding wages and salaries.
10. Making periodic checkups, rating and appraising employees to: change existing rates; grant wage increases if warranted; recommend promotions, special training, and transfers to further a worker's security.
11. Establishing fringe benefits and other supplementary compensations.
12. Recommending and administering plans for wage incentive systems.
13. Supervising job analysts, statisticians, wage or salary analysts, and other staff members, as well as the office clerks and stenographers in the department.
14. Supervising and maintaining records pertaining to all compensation.

Complementary Work. In many companies, the wage and salary administrator's function includes the following complementary activities:

1. Advising other managers concerning negotiations relevant to rates of pay, and governmental laws and regulations affecting wages.
2. Consulting with supervisors regarding company policies on wages and salaries.
3. Meeting with supervisors, individual employees — if requested by line supervisors of operating departments — and grievance committees to adjust differences arising out of wage and salary provisions.

4. Preparing reports to federal and state agencies and periodic reports to top management.
5. Writing reports periodically for executives and supervisors and examining reports received from related departments for corrections and changes.
6. Suggesting action to be taken in dealing with certain employees.
7. Establishing and maintaining procedures for receiving and submitting periodic information from and to other organizational departments that must be kept informed regarding changes, new rates, and other statistical data relating to their activities.

Figure 3.4 is a job description of the position held by one wage and salary administrator. It should help to portray the overall picture of this position. It may be interesting to note the approximate percentage of time this administrator spends on each duty and the degree of difficulty associated with each duty.

Place and Variations in the Functions of the Wage and Salary Administrator in an Enterprise

The place of the wage and salary administrator in the organizational setup of an enterprise is somewhat controversial due to varying opinions that are influenced by an admixture of historical and professional backgrounds. Thus, we find wage and salary administration placed under the treasurer, the personnel department, the industrial engineering department, the industrial relations division, the comptroller, and the standards department.

The reasons for the different locations of wage and salary administration are traceable to the rapid developments in modern industry and to some employers who rely upon expediency — rather than upon established objectives, formalized principles and policies — in setting up the organization. Also, the rapid growth of industrial engineering and personnel management, which has caused misconceptions regarding wage and salary administration requirements, accounts for some of the varying opinions about the place of wage and salary administration in an enterprise. To some employers, the simple man-specifications used by the personnel man in hiring have been enough to differentiate job values. Others have considered the piece-rate setting, with or without rate standards, sufficient for wage rates; and for still others, labor cost keeping in relation to production has been the essential part of wage control. Some still believe that the individual in charge of wage administration should report to the same administrative level as the one in charge of hiring. Others rightfully stress that the wage administrator should report to the same administrative level as the director of personnel.[14] No matter to whom the head of compensation reports, it is very important that he be

---

[14]Dale Yoder and Herbert G. Heneman, *Labor Economics and Industrial Relations* (Cincinnati: South-Western Publishing Company, 1959), p. 650. Also, Herbert S. Fuhrman, "Do We Forget the Principles of Wage Administration?" *Personnel*, Vol. XXII (March 1946), p. 284.

JOB DESCRIPTION

IDENTIFICATION DATA

A. Job Title Wage & Salary Administrator   **H. Job Analyst** James Moriarity

B. Alternate Titles Manager of Compensation   **I. Date** 2/13/--

C. Range of Pay $10,000–$20,000/yr.   **J. Verified by**

D. Promoted from Personnel Assistant or Job Analyst   **K. (His) Title**

E. May Lead to Director of Industrial Relations   **L. Sheet No.** 1 of 2 **Sheets**

F. Company L & Z, Inc.

G. Dept. Industrial Relations

WORK PERFORMED

A. Summary Statement:

Promotes compensation that is equitable and satisfactory to the employees and the employer by administering and recommending necessary changes in a wage and salary program in order to maintain the company in a competitive position in the industry and yet provide compensation that will attract, hold, and motivate the necessary labor force. May also be required to develop and install a wage and salary program.

B. Major Duties

	No. Hrs. or % of Time	Degree of Difficulty
1. Maintains the job evaluation program by issuing new job classifications, revising existing classifications, or deleting unnecessary ones through the application of the job evaluation plan so that company compensation will remain equitable.	25	C
2. Assists the company in maintaining the desired wage and salary relationships and levels by conducting wage surveys within the company and in the community, charting or graphing data for comparison, and making recommendations to the company.	5	C
3. Assists supervision by counseling them in evaluating employee performance so that employee progress can be determined and rewarded.	25	SC
4. Maintains and administers the wage and salary program by determining and keeping the necessary records to assure accurate, fair, and consistent treatment of employees.	25	R
5. Analyzes changes in government wage regulations, company policies, and labor union agreements for effects on the wage and salary program to keep up-to-date in the field.	5	SC

FIGURE 3.4   JOB DESCRIPTION OF ONE WAGE AND SALARY ADMINISTRATOR
(continued on next page)

B. Major Duties (continued)	No. Hrs. or % of Time	Degree of Difficulty
6. May develop and recommend a wage and salary program which would be equitable and satisfactory to employees by:		
a. Determining most suitable type of job evaluation plan — point method, factor comparison, job classification, ranking — and developing details of the plan.		
b. Analyzing and evaluating all jobs through job evaluation techniques to provide a basis for developing the wage and salary structure.		
c. Recommending type of wage structure — single rate, multiple-rate merit system, multiple-rate automatic progression system, etc. — and developing details of the structure.		
d. Determining the actual rates to be paid based upon prevailing rates in the community and company policies.		
e. Recommending the merit rating form, if one is to be used.	5	C
7. May assist Industrial Relations by performing a variety of tasks, such as representing the company at public functions, handling grievances, conducting research, and counseling employees, for the purpose of meeting the needs of the employees and the company.	10	C

C — Complex
R — Routine
SC — Semicomplex

WORKING CONDITIONS

Daily hours from 8 a.m. to 5 p.m., 5 days per week.

Weekly hours 40, overtime hours 1-2 a week.

Percent standing 25, walking 25, sitting 50.

Days of travel (out of town) 1 per month.

May be subject to calls for emergencies or special work such as: labor negotiations, grievances, community wage surveys, and professional conferences.

EQUIPMENT USED

Typewriter

Calculator

Duplicating machine

Electronic data processing machines

FIGURE 3.4 JOB DESCRIPTION OF ONE WAGE AND SALARY ADMINISTRATOR *(concluded)*

free from pressures (political, union, etc.) which would cause him to lose objectivity and fairness in carrying out his duties.

Place and Functions in Small Enterprises. The place, functions, and responsibilities of the wage and salary administrator are determined by the size of the company, the type of products, and the jobs involved. All employers need wage and salary administration in some form, but insufficient continuous activity does not warrant having one person devote all of his time exclusively to compensation matters.

In small manufacturing companies, the function of wage and salary administration, along with other functions, may be carried out by one individual under the supervision of the plant manager or superintendent. In other cases, the wage and salary specialist may be a member of the personnel department. Here, he generally devotes a part of his time to wage and salary administration, and the balance of his time is allotted to employee selection, placement, and employee services.[15] One study reported that 35 percent of the time was devoted to wage and salary administration.[16]

Place and Functions in Medium-Size and Large Enterprises. In most medium-size and large companies, the component functions of wage and salary administration are broad in scope, and implications are so far reaching that groups with industrial relations and/or industrial engineering backgrounds cooperate to carry out the component functions.

There are companies that distribute the various wage and salary administration functions among several people in different departments of the industrial relations division. These people devote only part of their time to the duties of wage and salary administration that are apportioned to them. Generally they are not supervised by a wage and salary administrator. Some companies that follow such a procedure are successful, while others experience difficulties because of insufficient control. Most companies find it more economical to centralize the specialized functions under one administrator, and at the same time effect better control.

Conditions warranting a wage and salary program have now reached a stage where this function should be placed as near the top level of the organization as feasible. Since the wage and salary program is constantly under the surveillance of employees and management, it is one of the most important segments of an enterprise. Wage and salary administration should be placed under the direction of a vice-president in charge of industrial relations; a vice-president in charge of personnel administration; or a director of wage and salary administration, who

---

[15]See *Jobs in Employee Relations*, Research Study No. 38 (New York: American Management Association, Inc., 1959).
[16]*Ibid.*, p. 28.

devotes specific attention to all the operative functional and staff personnel necessary for carrying out the whole program.

The individual responsible for the wage and salary administration program should be of sufficient stature to warrant top management's full support in carrying out his function. His level of authority should ward off any undue pressure to make decisions of expediency against his judgment of what is fair and just. He must be capable of rooting out any deficiencies in the personnel department that could weaken the wage and salary structure. Thus, the higher the jurisdictional level of the wage and salary administrator and the more freedom of action he possesses, the more assured is the success of the total compensation program. Therefore, it is logical for the wage and salary administrator to be responsible to the same administrative level as the personnel director.

Organization Structure of Wage and Salary Administration. Wage and salary administration may be considered functional only in the sense that specialized professional skill and knowledge are disseminated to all other organization units of the enterprise. In general, wage and salary administration is recognized as having a dual capacity, that of staff and managerial.

As a staff unit, wage and salary administration is charged with the responsibility of advising and aiding all foremen, supervisors, and executives to solve their compensation problems. Wage and salary administrators never interfere with the decisions of line management. However, in cases of grievances or employee misunderstandings pertaining to matters of compensation, they are always ready, if requested, to assist purely as staff.

Figure 3.5 shows a very good example of the staff relationship to the line executives at the Lockheed Aircraft Corporation. Note sketch 6, which explains the specific qualifications of the staff man who cooperates with other departments to create harmony either in the same or in different organizational levels. As foremen and supervisors become thoroughly acquainted with compensation problems and their solutions, they usually give the wage and salary administrator their most enthusiastic support.

Qualifications of the wage and salary administrator

The management of medium-size and large enterprises requires executives and departmental leaders with professional qualifications and special training in their respective fields of endeavor. Thus, the wage and salary administrator must be versed in the fundamentals of administration, management, and organization, as well as in the specialized field of employee relations. Whether the wage and salary administrator is in the position of director, administrator, or supervisor, his educational background and experience must be broad in scope.

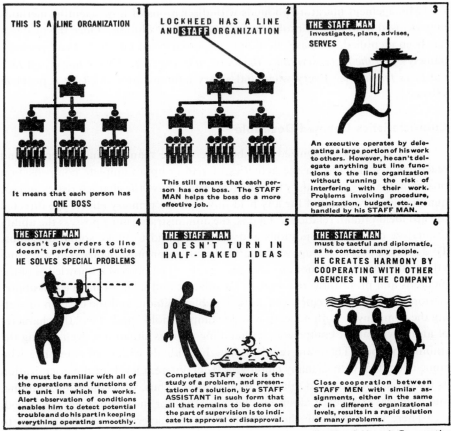

Lockheed Aircraft Corporation

FIGURE 3.5 THE STAFF POSITION. An explanation of the staff man's job and his relations to line executives at Lockheed Aircraft Corporation.

Systematic or Scientific Problem Solver

For a proper perspective of managerial requirements to establish wage and salary controls, a grounding in the fundamentals of scientific management is essential. In the past, it was generally erroneously thought that such fundamentals involved only motion and time study or financial incentives. However, scientific management involves a careful analysis to establish definite procedures for processing raw materials; production control; setting exact standards of performance; determining equitable wages and salaries; and establishing a methodology of motivation as well as various types of supplemental compensations. Success is contingent upon a systematic approach and control to determine whether all functionalized activities are performed in accordance with predetermined standards.

Management literature abounds with discussions of how scientific methods may be used to approach problems for a successful solution. Once the problem has been identified, the basic steps may be summarized into five "fact" phrases, namely: *find the facts; scrutinize the facts; filter the facts; fix the facts;* and *face the facts fearlessly.* Every wage and salary administrator must be a problem solver.

Characteristics Deemed Desirable

It is generally recognized that because of the many human interests and reactions associated with the activities of setting up a complete compensation program, the wage and salary administrator must have the characteristics and/or qualities usually required for any field in which the primary efforts are directed toward ideal human relations. That is, the administrator must possess the ability to analyze diversified conditions and situations, and to make sound decisions. To do this, a potential wage and salary administrator must realize that wage and salary administration is not an exact science; he must possess a knowledge of the methods and procedures required and available; and he must have a full appreciation of the value of employee morale, public opinion, and the costs in operating the company. Both education and training "mold" and "flex" the character of an individual for competency in handling various situations, even during the training period. There are relatively few individuals within an enterprise who come in contact with as many employees from different levels of the organization as the person in wage and salary administration. Thus, with education, training, and practical experience, desirable characteristics for the position are developed.

There is no question, however, that the characteristics which are akin to common sense are the most desirable ones for the wage and salary administrator to possess — the courage to live up to one's convictions; tolerance; patience and self-control; tactfulness; respect for another's viewpoint; recognition of other people's desires and aspirations; cooperation and reciprocity; a sense of fair play; willingness "to give and take" when dealing with individuals or groups (unions); and a pleasing personality, which embodies courtesy and neatness. In short, the wage and salary administrator must be fair, firm, and friendly.

Education and Experience Requirements

A college education, preferably graduate work with a major field in personnel administration, is usually a prerequisite for the position of wage and salary administrator. Emphasis should be placed on having satisfactorily completed courses in the specialized fields of business administration — business statistics, industrial management, industrial engineering (specifically motion and time study), manufacturing and production control, industrial relations, economics, sociology, industrial psychology, and above all, wage and salary administration.

In addition, several years' (four to ten) experience in phases of industrial relations, familiarity with wage and hour laws, and some knowledge of labor organizations are desirable. Experience as a staff specialist in wage and salary administration will also provide a valuable background. These requirements are needed to give the administrator an understanding of people and groups of people in order to know what makes people tick and to understand what their basic needs, wants, desires, and motivations are. Finally, proper education and experience will provide the administrator with the ability not only to understand employees but also to communicate with them by talking their language. Figure 3.6 contains a summary of the more important qualifications deemed desirable for the person serving as the wage and salary administrator.

Criteria of job success

Thus far, this chapter has treated primarily the job of the wage and salary administrator and the qualifications deemed desirable for him to possess. The role of the wage and salary administrator would be incomplete if no mention were made of the evaluation of the administrator. Although the evaluation of the success or failure of the wage and salary administrator is an individual matter and varies from company to company, the following suggestions indicate how an evaluation may be accomplished.

General Job Performance Standards

Every evaluation, in order to have a sound basis, must start with the objectives that are to be reached by the person holding the job. In Chapter 1, the general goals of wage and salary administration were identified as assisting the company in motivating employees to optimum job performance; controlling employee costs; providing a basis for effective hiring, utilization, and promotion of employees; and promoting employee cooperation through harmonious employer-employee relations. Although it may be difficult to identify specifically the role that the wage and salary administrator plays in achieving these goals, it can be ascertained whether or not the trends and conditions within the company point toward achieving these goals. If employees are not motivated, or costs are getting out of line, or employer-employee relations are deteriorating, questions should be raised as to what extent compensation matters have contributed to produce these undesirable conditions. Usually some approximate evaluations can be made from a study of these conditions.

Specific Job Performance Standards

A much more valid appraisal can be made by analyzing the specific duties and goals of the wage and salary administrator as outlined in Figure 3.4. These

MAN SPECIFICATION

(Desirable Qualifications for the Wage and Salary Administrator)

1. Appearance and Manner

> Neat in appearance
> Friendly, courteous, and personable
> Calm, rather than an excitable, nervous or argumentative manner

2. Education

> A college education or its equivalent. Some courses in the following are highly desirable: business statistics, personnel administration, wage and salary administration, motion and time study, psychology, sociology, industrial engineering, law, industrial management, and economics.

3. Work Experience

> Several years' (4–10) experience as an assistant to a personnel director or administrator. Some previous job experience with whatever groups of jobs are under the jurisdiction of the wage and salary administrator (clerical, crafts, supervisory, sales, executive, administrative, professional, etc.) is desirable.

4. Physical Fitness

> General good health
> No serious ailments that would incapacitate the person for more than a part of a day at a time

> Physical disabilities or limitations may not be a handicap provided they do not affect his attendance, and mobility or his ability to work with employees.

5. Attitude

> Concerned about human dignity, fair play, and the common good

6. Social

> An extrovert rather than an introvert
> Can work well on committees

7. Special Qualifications

> Security clearance required for some special organizations
> Citizenship required for some special organizations

FIGURE 3.6   MAN SPECIFICATION FOR THE JOB OF THE WAGE AND SALARY
ADMINISTRATOR

duties suggest the following questions that would be useful in evaluating the job performance of the compensation director:

> Are company compensation policies generally accepted by employees as being fair, consistent, and valid?
>
> Are job descriptions, job specifications, and job evaluations kept up-to-date?
>
> Are wage rates equitable and commensurate with job values?
>
> Are supervisors getting the assistance they need on compensation matters?
>
> Are compensation records adequate, accurate, and up-to-date?
>
> Are compensation activities attracting, holding, motivating, and rewarding employees?
>
> Are compensation costs in line with productivity?
>
> Are there any over-paid jobs in the company?
>
> Are wage grievances kept to a minimum?

For each answer to the questions above, the company must have some idea of what constitutes acceptable performance, outstanding performance, and job failure. For example, the question "Are wage grievances kept to a minimum?" means that the company must know or be able to determine what number or percent of grievances is considered as satisfactory or unacceptable. One company may decide that an average of one grievance per employee per year is a high rate and unacceptable, while another company may feel that this is reasonable and satisfactory. Still another company that has been continually plagued with grievances may feel that this is a very low rate and thus would be an outstanding record for them. In other words, each company has its own history and peculiar set of circumstances that need to be taken into account in establishing the specific performance for each rating of the criteria used for evaluation.

Guidelines for the wage and salary administrator

To assist the administrator in carrying out his role, several guidelines are suggested for integrating the wage and salary function with such factors as the organization, the management, other administrative units, the employees, the geographical locality, and the consuming public. The various guidelines that the wage and salary administrator should consider for each factor are discussed in the paragraphs that follow. These factors and guidelines are also graphically illustrated in Figure 3.7.[17]

---

[17]Adapted, with slight modification, from Herbert S. Fuhrman, "Some Basic Principles of Wage and Salary Administration" in *A. M. A. Handbook* (New York: American Management Association, Inc., 1950), p. 16. Reproduced with permission.

Design Compensation Program to Meet the Objectives of the Organization

The objectives of an organization usually indicate the kind of products to be manufactured or the type of services to be rendered. Accordingly, the compensation program must be designed to meet those objectives. Different products and the size of an organization will dictate the purpose, objectives, and policies of the wage and salary administration. Often, too, organization structures vary with the distribution and redistribution of functions. Hence, the program must be flexible so that it can be adjusted according to the organizational changes.

Adhere to Sound Management Principles

According to management principles, the wage and salary administrator must at all times act in the interests of both management and employees. Sound managerial policies require that the employees be compensated in proportion to controlled labor costs and standardized production; that is, the starting wage rates should not be overpaid and fringe benefits should not be overemphasized. Management should be solicitous about each worker's performance, his output, or his rendering of satisfactory services for fair and equitable compensation. As a matter of sound business policies, management must at all times give due consideration to satisfying the employer (stockholders) by paying dividends and at the same time providing a surplus for equipment replacement and needed expansion.

Thus, the wage and salary administrator must adhere to management principles and policies so that the program will be acceptable to management as well as to the employees, and make every effort to convince both parties of the program's feasibility.

Coordinate Compensation with Other Administrative Units

Top management is vitally interested in integrating the wage and salary administration unit with other units for effective production and control, since the compensation program influences the effectiveness and cooperative functioning of the entire organization. The unanimous acceptance of the compensation program by other units and the interchange of data and sound suggestions help to achieve top management's goals. Therefore, the compensation program must be directed toward simplifying and expediting rather than obstructing other administrative functions.

Win Employee Approval

Employees' attitudes are affected mostly through their take-home pay, since the livelihood of their families depends upon the method of compensation and the amount of pay received. It is a well-established fact that satisfactory com-

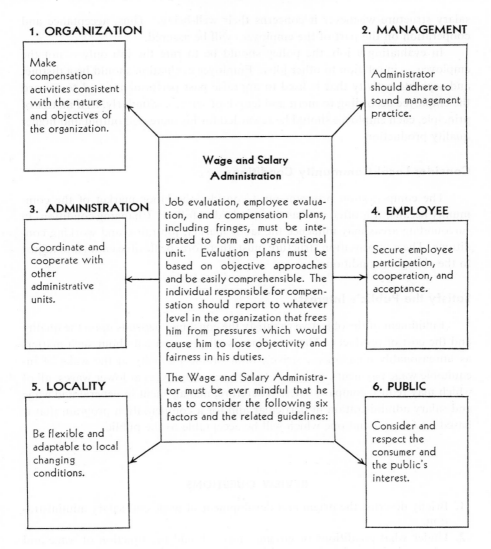

1. ORGANIZATION

Make compensation activities consistent with the nature and objectives of the organization.

2. MANAGEMENT

Administrator should adhere to sound management practice.

3. ADMINISTRATION

Coordinate and cooperate with other administrative units.

4. EMPLOYEE

Secure employee participation, cooperation, and acceptance.

Wage and Salary Administration

Job evaluation, employee evalua-tion, and compensation plans, including fringes, must be inte-grated to form an organizational unit. Evaluation plans must be based on objective approaches and be easily comprehensible. The individual responsible for compen-sation should report to whatever level in the organization that frees him from pressures which would cause him to lose objectivity and fairness in his duties.

The Wage and Salary Administra-tor must be ever mindful that he has to consider the following six factors and the related guidelines:

5. LOCALITY

Be flexible and adaptable to local changing conditions.

6. PUBLIC

Consider and respect the consumer and the public's interest.

FIGURE 3.7 FACTORS AND GUIDELINES FOR A COMPENSATION ADMINISTRATOR

pensation is reflected in an employee's morale, his job satisfaction, and his per-formance. In this respect, the underlying principle of the compensation program is to carry on activities that will ensure a fair day's pay for a fair day's work.

Employees are apt to feel that they are underpaid. Therefore, it is necessary to explain thoroughly the compensation program so that they can understand and accept it. Furthermore, as a matter of principle, employee representation should be included to help carry out the various phases of the entire wage and salary structure whenever it concerns their well-being. Thus, acceptance and cooperation on the part of the employees will be assured.

In evaluating a job, the policy should be to rate the job only — not the employee — in relation to other jobs. Employee evaluation should be a distinct and separate activity that is used to appraise past performance and to reward the employee according to merit and length of service. Similarly, as a matter of principle, each employee should be rewarded for his increased output and higher quality production.

Consider Local Community Conditions

The compensation program must consider the labor market of the community because it is often used as the standard to follow. Changing conditions in surrounding areas may influence the labor market, job rates, and working conditions. The compensation structure must, therefore, be flexible enough to adjust to the changing conditions.

Satisfy the Public's Interest

Fulfillment of the objective to satisfy the consumer depends upon the quality and the cost of products. The consumer is often concerned about such matters as unreasonably high prices, strikes, unfavorable publicity in the wake of inequitable wage payments, or layoffs to hire new employees at lower wages, all of which may reduce company sales. Therefore, management in general and wage and salary administration in particular aim for a compensation program that is based on fairness and one which will be acceptable to the public.

REVIEW QUESTIONS

1. Briefly describe the origin and development of wage and salary administration.
2. Under what conditions or circumstances should the function of wage and salary administration be placed in the Industrial Engineering Department? the Industrial Relations Department (or Personnel)?
3. (a) Which one of the objectives of the wage and salary administrator (pages 60 and 61) do you consider the most difficult to carry out? Why? (b) What recommendations do you have that would assist a company in satisfactorily carrying out this objective?
4. (a) Of all the various position titles that are being used to identify the wage and salary administrator, which one do you think is most appropriate? Why? (b) Can you coin a more fitting title?
5. What factors would you consider if you were assigned the task of formulating the functions and responsibilities of a wage and salary administrator?

6. When a company is not large enough to support a full-time wage and salary administrator, who should be assigned the collateral duties of wage and salary administration? Why?

7. What minimum qualifications do you think the wage and salary administrator must possess to perform satisfactorily? Arrange the qualifications in the order of their importance.

8. What specialized courses in business administration are necessary for the personal development of a wage and salary administrator?

9. What is the most basic and general performance standard not only for the wage and salary administrator but also for most jobs?

10. Answer each of the questions on page 73 using your own job experience to obtain the answers, or ask someone to help you by answering the questions as they apply to his company or a company he knows.

11. How do you think a wage and salary administrator should go about coordinating his function with other administrative units? What guidelines can he use?

12. What are the various facets of the role of the wage and salary administrator that are necessary to make the compensation function a success?

RESEARCH OR SEMINAR QUESTIONS

1. Is the wage and salary department more important to the worker or to management? Discuss.

2. To whom should the wage and salary administrator report? Discuss.

3. Of the ten objectives of wage and salary administration listed on pages 60 and 61, which is the most important? the least important? Explain.

4. What changes would you make in the job description of the wage and salary administrator given on pages 65 and 66? Explain each change and give the reason that you think it should be made.

PRACTICAL EXPERIENCE ASSIGNMENTS

1. Visit some company to find out which department handles the wage and salary function. Obtain enough information (and any available sample literature) to give a five-minute talk to the class on the role that wage and salary administration plays in this organization.

2. Draw up an abbreviated organization chart of a company to show the place of wage and salary in the organization. List the advantages and disadvantages of this arrangement. Where else might the wage and salary function be placed? Why?

3. Secure two different organizational charts. Compare them on the basis of the part that wage and salary administration plays. In terms of the role that wage and salary administration should play, which organization has placed wage and salary administration in the more ideal arrangement? Why?

4. Interview the head of compensation in two different companies and find out what was the most difficult decision each person was forced to make while on this job.

CASE PROBLEM

3—1. SOUTH MENTOR ZIPPER MANUFACTURING COMPANY

Wage and Salary Administration Policies

The South Mentor Zipper Manufacturing Company employs about 2,000 hourly-rate employees. In the last few months, management has seen signs of increased dissatisfaction among the employees over the wage policy.

Up until a few years ago, the wage administrative duties were not demanding and the plant superintendent controlled the program. The present program was put into effect in 1939. Since then, the company has grown from 200 employees to its present size.

Assume that you have just been appointed the first full-time wage and salary administrator. You have been asked to immediately survey the problem and to recommend a new or revised wage policy. Management requests a policy that will be fair and just, and one which will be acceptable to the union, management, and the public.

Problems:

Briefly describe what you assume is your role as a wage and salary administrator in a company of this size. Draw up what you consider to be some acceptable operating wage principles or policies that you will recommend to the company for adoption. Explain why each principle or policy should be adopted.

chapter 4

BASIC CONSIDERATIONS FOR SUCCESSFUL WAGE AND SALARY ADMINISTRATION

This chapter brings together the main concepts and interrelationships that a company management must understand if it hopes to administer a successful wage and salary program. If these conceptual foundations are ignored, the compensation program is built on a weak foundation and sooner or later the structure is bound to give way and result in failure. The basic areas that management needs to consider, each of which is discussed in this chapter, are Management; Philosophy; Productivity, Human Relations, and Motivation; Compensation Policies; Communication; Compensation Structures; and Responsibilities.

A management philosophy or creed

The top executives of a company frequently issue a formal set of statements or a general communication concerning the company's aims, policies, responsibilities, and obligations. These statements are generally referred to as a management philosophy. They may also be known as the company credo or management creed. These creeds contain the beliefs of management. They are expressions of the essential goals that guide the whole enterprise in fair conduct and fair dealing with workers, the owners (stockholders), raw material and equipment suppliers, employees, customers, and the general public. They reveal the basic attitudes of management. The creeds usually define the purpose of the company and its character. They create a company image and a particular "climate" within the business. They provide an overall guide to those in decision-making positions so they can act independently but within the framework of the firm's basic goals and principles. In short, the company creed lays down the very broadest policy from which all day-to-day operating policies, guides, and practices should flow.

Potential Benefits of a Well-Conceived Management Philosophy

When a company has established a well thought-out creed and has clearly communicated it to all employees, there are several advantages to be gained. First, employees can be expected to accomplish more easily a goal that has been clearly identified than one which has never been spelled out. Second, there is less employee confusion, dissatisfaction, and turnover when employees are working as a team toward a set of common goals. Third, employees are more easily motivated to produce their best when they are aware of the rewards to be gained and the importance that management places on employees in the organization.

Codes and Creeds Related to Wage and Salary Administration

Many companies regard their basic objectives, principles, and policies as a code of ethics, which becomes a "creed" for the entire company personnel to follow.[1] Some of the basic principles and policies of a few leading companies, presented in the form of codes or creeds, are given below to convey their importance in relation to wage and salary administration.

The value and significance of a creed to the Delaware and Hudson Railroad Company is substantiated by its vice-president, J. P. Hiltz, Jr., in the following perspicuous statement:

> *Our creed was prepared in writing to provide a starting point for the introduction of scientific management by informing our employees what top management expected the company to do and the way it was to do it. With this as a basis, it was felt that our employees would be better able to recognize their functions in carrying out the creed and would be better able to prepare job descriptions, performance standards, appraisals, etc.* I can't stress too strongly that I feel the creed is the beginning of scientific management. It is a starting point to which subsequent procedures and methods can be continually referred in order to check consistency.

The Bell & Howell Company, which enjoys an enviable reputation in its relations with employees, customers, and the general public, also recognizes the value of a creed. Long before Mr. Charles H. Percy became president of

---

[1]See Stewart Thomson, "A Survey of Company Creeds; Formulation, Uses, and Results," *Management Creeds and Philosophies*, Research Study No. 32 (New York: American Management Association, Inc., 1958).

the company, he accidentally discovered that workers had exaggerated misconceptions about the company affairs, especially regarding the margin of profits. Some employees erroneously calculated that the company earned an 85 percent profit which, in reality, amounted to only 8 percent.

In relating the incident, Mr. Percy stated: "I decided then that if I ever had the chance I would talk frankly and openly about financial matters within the organization." Shortly after becoming president, he lost no time in communicating with the employees not only on matters directly concerning them but also on all company matters, including finances. Hence, the company maintains a regular flow of information through formal and informal methods of communication.[2] Figure 4.1 shows an extract from their creed, which should interest the wage and salary administrator. This creed is worthy of consideration from the standpoint of human relations, as a pronouncement of objectives and policies, and is an excellent means of communication. It is of great importance as a basic consideration for wage and salary administration.

Another instance of transmitting sincere motives to employees as a creed is the expression of Procter & Gamble Company's beliefs, which have been taken from their employee handbook and reproduced in Figure 4.2. Each new employee receives the handbook as a goodwill gesture aimed toward making him "feel at home." In addition to information about the company, management, and matters of interest to the new employee, the company — eager to imbue every employee with its spirit and philosophy — introduces the booklet by listing "*certain fundamental beliefs*," which are expressions of a creed.

The Eastman Kodak Company, which is world renowned for its position in the photographic field, is equally progressive in human and industrial relations. The objectives, principles, and policies instituted by its founder, George Eastman, continue to guide the whole organization. Under his leadership, the company established various plans designed to provide a large measure of individual security. These and other plans that have been established after his time are described in *A Handbook for Kodak Men and Women*, which begins with "A Code of Industrial Relations," explaining the policies and principles that govern relationships within the company. The code includes 23 statements regarding various personnel subjects. These are thoroughly explained in the handbook and supplemented in more detail in other company booklets.

In short, a management philosophy or creed identifies what employees can expect from a company. When these expectations are acceptable to the employees, the creed becomes the vehicle for attaining mutual respect between the company and its employees. This trust and respect for fair play by management is basic to good wage and salary administration, because it is one of the signs of good human relations needed to motivate employees to be more productive.

---

[2]We are indebted to Mr. William Hodge, Director of Industrial Relations, Bell & Howell Company, for information pertaining to the means of communication referred to in this chapter.

A CREED FOR MANAGEMENT

There are over 64 million gainfully employed people in the United States. One-half of these work directly for American corporations, and the other half are vitally affected by business directly or indirectly. Our entire economy, therefore, is dependent upon the type of business management we have. Business management is therefore in many respects a public trust charged with the responsibility of keeping America economically sound. We at Bell & Howell can best do this by keeping our own company's program on a firm foundation and by having a growing group of management leaders to direct the activities of the company.

. . . Our basic objective is the development of individuals. In our own present program we are doing everything conceivable to encourage, guide, assist, and provide an opportunity to everyone to improve their abilities and skills, thus becoming more valuable to the company and enabling the company to improve the rewards paid to the individual for such additional efforts.

. . . But a company must also have a creed to which its management is dedicated. I hope that we can all agree to the following:

We believe that our company must develop and produce outstanding products that will perform a great service or fill a need for our customers.

. . . We believe that management must serve employees, stockholders, and customers, but that we cannot serve the interests of any one group at the undue expense of the other two. A proper and fair balance must be preserved.

We believe that our business must provide stability of employment and job security for all those who depend on our company for their livelihood.

We believe that we are failing in our responsibility if our wages are not sufficiently high to not only meet the necessities of life but provide some of the luxuries as well. Wherever possible, we also believe that bonus earnings should be paid for performance and output "beyond the call of duty."

. . . We believe in the necessity for constantly increasing productivity and output. Higher wages and greater benefits can never be "given" by management. Management can only see that they are paid out when "earned."

. . . We believe that every person in the company has a right to be treated with the respect and courtesy that is due a human being. It is for this reason that we have individual merit ratings, individual pay increases, job evaluation, and incentive pay; and it is why we keep every individual fully informed — through The Finder, through our Annual Report, through Family Night, through individual letters — about the present program of the company and also about our future objectives.

. . . We hope that every principle we believe in is right and is actually being practiced throughout the company as it affects every individual.

FIGURE 4.1   A CREED FOR MANAGEMENT. Principles and policies communicated to employees by Charles H. Percy, former president and chairman of the board of directors of the Bell & Howell Company.

WE BELIEVE . . .

The Procter & Gamble Company has been a successful business for over a century. Its success is based in large measure on the carrying out of certain fundamental beliefs which have developed as a result of experience gained over the years. The thinking and actions of the men who manage the business have been guided by these beliefs. Many of these beliefs have to do with the relations between the management and other employees. These are the beliefs most important to the employees of the Company — beliefs which every Procter & Gamble employee should know. They are the foundation on which the relations between the Company and all of its employees are built and will continue to be built.

① A fair day's wage for a fair day's work

The Company pays wages which match the wages paid by leading companies in the community for similar types of work. The Company expects from each employee an hour of work for each hour of pay.

② Extra pay for extra production

On jobs where output can be measured, and where the employee is willing, extra work produced brings extra pay. For every hour of work produced above standard the employee gets an extra hour of pay.

③ Steady work

High hourly rates mean little unless there is the opportunity to work steadily throughout the year. Because of the Guarantee of Regular Employment, Procter & Gamble employees know reasonably well what their income will be and can plan accordingly.

④ Clean, safe, and healthful working conditions

Cleanliness is our Company's business. Every effort is extended to carry the principle into the factories, the lunchrooms, the locker-rooms, the shower-rooms so that Procter & Gamble employees may have a clean, safe, and healthful place in which to work.

⑤ Adequate protection in time of real need

The Company's medical and health facilities, our Disability Benefit Plan, Hospital and Surgical Benefit Plans, and our Group Life Insurance Plan, are directed toward helping the employee when real trouble threatens. Through high wages and steady work, the Company offers the Procter & Gamble employee the American privilege of standing on his own feet, but if he faces trouble through illness he will have help at hand.

⑥ Opportunity for thrift and economic security

By sharing the profits through the Profit Sharing Plans, the Company adds to high, steady wages the extra dollars which give the Procter & Gamble employee the chance to save for his own home, the education of his children, and toward the days when he no longer can or no longer desires to work. These Plans, together with the Stock Purchase Plan and the Pension Plan offer him the opportunity for continued savings and the independence every American wants.

⑦ Opportunity to advance on merit

Procter & Gamble has been built from the bottom up. The way ahead is always open for the employee who has the ability.

⑧ The right to be heard and the right to express wants and desires

Through the medium of collective bargaining, employees have the opportunity to present and discuss with management their own ideas concerning wages, hours of work and other working conditions. Procter & Gamble employees have dealt with the Company through representatives of their own choosing for more than thirty years.

To say it briefly, since its founding the Company has always believed in dealing fairly with all the people in the business and has believed that the interests of the Company and its employees are inseparable.

FIGURE 4.2 A COMPANY'S BELIEFS. Principles and policies communicated to every employee in Procter & Gamble Company's Employee Handbook. Reproduced with permission.

Importance of productivity, human relations, and motivation

Psychologists and various authorities on industrial relations emphasize the value of good human relations as a means of motivating employees toward full cooperation and higher production. Such motivation is usually supported by attractive wage incentives. Therefore, it seems pertinent to point out the relationship that productivity, human relations, and motivation have toward the success of a compensation program.

Productivity and Its Relationship to Compensation

The subject of productivity, as related to compensation, has received considerable attention in the past two decades. Union demands for extra compensation, based on increased productivity, known as the *improvement factor,* have made productivity an important factor in collective bargaining. There is much discussion regarding the various facets of productivity and their relationship as a basis for pay. We shall now attempt to acquaint the reader with the subject matter and in the next chapter we discuss productivity as a basis of pay.

Meaning of Productivity. As civilization and the economic structure progressed, man learned to obtain or to produce the necessities of life by his own endeavor and ingenuity. For that reason it is erroneously assumed that productivity or *output* is the result of human labor only, thus entitling the worker to all the gains of increased productivity. Capital, efficient management, methods, materials, and machines are equally essential, however, and in some cases even more important in industry than human labor, especially in modern manufacturing. Nevertheless, human labor must be relied upon to utilize the methods and machine power in handling the material efficiently; that is, human energy and effort exerted over a certain period supply the necessary physical *input* in processing the products from raw materials.

Hence, in attempting to evaluate increased productivity, that is, creating a larger quantity of parts or finished products by an operator, the input must be considered. Human labor input — as differentiated from capital and materials input — is measured in terms of the number of man-hours required to produce the output of component parts and finished products or services.

The input-output action, that is, the input requirement relative to the level of output (quantity), is termed productivity. For our study, *productivity* means the measurement of the quantity and quality produced in terms of the man-hours expended in production.

Productive Labor. Human work, whether purely physical labor, mental effort, or directing others, is apparent in every undertaking. Ordinarily, the term "worker" or "producer" refers to a manual laborer rather than to a salaried or white-collar employee. In our study, however, anybody employed to perform labor in producing goods or rendering services is regarded as a *producer*. Hence, the term productive labor applies to the functions of purchasing, marketing, selling, office work, editing, manufacturing, transportation, or any other activity for which compensation is rendered. *Productive labor*, then, includes all human effort, whether mental or physical.

Importance of Productivity. Productivity is important because it has a bearing on our standard of living, the wages that employees can earn, and the profits that a company can earn.

Figure 4.3 indicates that population growth requires increased productivity. If the population in the United States is expected to increase 15 percent from 1960 to 1970, productivity in the United States has to increase 15 percent *just to maintain our present standard of living*. If our present productivity had to be shared with 15 percent more people, our present standard of living would be diluted and thus would decline. Most employees would like to see their present standard of living improve. To raise the standard of living, productivity must be greater than the growth in population.

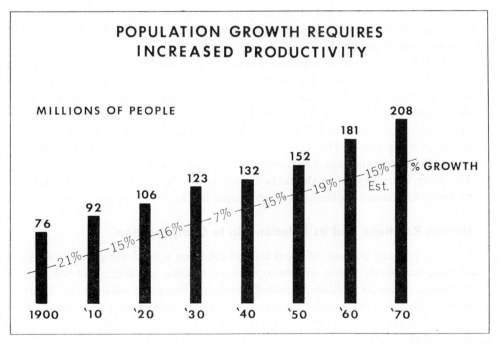

U. S. Department of Labor, 196

FIGURE 4.3 Productivity Needs to be Increased at the Same Rate as the Population to Maintain Our Current Standard of Living

Since labor is a factor of production, and it is only through production that wages are possible, it is necessary that productivity be increased to make it possible to pay greater wages. If wages are increased without being earned through increased productivity, some segment of the business (customers or stockholders) will have to pay this bill. Someone may be willing to do this for a short period of time, but over the long run no customer or stockholder is going to feel fairly treated if he has to pay for wage increases not earned through increased productivity or services.

A company should not expect to increase its profits without increasing productivity, since it is only through productivity that profits are possible. Employees and labor unions, along with customers, will not allow a company to increase its profits at their expense.

Improving Productivity. Improved products and services, as well as reduced man-hours per unit of production, stem from the proper utilization of machine power, work simplification, and improved methods of job performance, all of which have made unusual forward strides since the introduction of scientific management. Under systematic management the most complicated operation can be divided into small elements to develop the best method of job performance. This development led to specialization, which revolutionized productivity, increased money wages (nominal wages), and stimulated a wide distribution and consumption of goods.

In the early stages of industrial progress, the tendency was to make humans work like machines. Now, for the maximum production of goods to satisfy the needs of mankind and to raise the standard of living, the trend is toward the development of machines that work like humans. Nevertheless, the machine operators' cooperation is still needed, especially because of the short workday and high wage rates. This cooperative spirit can be secured by an organized motivation program that will satisfy the psychological needs of employees. Therefore, every supervisor should be trained to use the best techniques available to deal with human problems through proper human relations procedures.

Human Relations and Its Relationship to Compensation

The primary purpose of good human relations is to develop cooperative, efficient teamwork within an atmosphere of genuine satisfaction in job performance. Human relations, especially human relations in industry, is closely related either to work conditions, in general, or to some specific personal adjustment problems that concern individual workers or groups of employees. Ever since the Hawthorne studies[3] pointed out human and social relationships at the

---

[3]Conducted at the Western Electric Company, Chicago, Illinois. See F. J. Roethlisberger and William J. Dickson, *Management and the Worker* (Cambridge, Massachusetts: Harvard University Press, 1940).

workplace, employers and industrial relations directors have been conscious of the social and human aspects of a work situation, and are aware of their significance in maintaining employee cooperation and industrial peace. For instance, as a matter of proper human relations, more and more employers are now encouraging their employees to participate in certain phases of management. This is accomplished through suggestion systems, company committees, and such techniques as morale surveys, multiple management, and consultative management. These participating activities give employees an opportunity to make known their attitudes and interests, as well as to express their desires and needs in order to derive ultimate satisfaction from their work. Similarly, supervisors are trained to exercise human relations by improving job performance through work simplification, application of predetermined work control, and employee motivation.

Meaning of Human Relations. Human relations in industry is an all-inclusive term denoting goodwill, fair treatment, and a sympathetic understanding of human nature. Human relations is variously defined, interpreted, and applied in accordance with the activities and needs within an organization. In this book we are concerned with those phases of human relations that apply to employees doing productive labor. In other words, management should express a continual interest in the social and human aspects of a worker's environment, his attitudes, and desires. For our purpose, *human relations* is defined as: "The medium for effecting the maximum satisfaction of the economic, social, and psychological wants of all people having relations with an organization which has the objective of increasing productivity."[4] Therefore, the objective of human relations is to build the highest employee morale, or *esprit de corps*, among all employees. With the attainment of this objective, "Workers will usually produce at a higher rate of output and hence have higher earnings."[5] These are indeed the most realistic definitions and objectives of human relations in industry.

Spirit of Human Relations. Human relations presupposes adherence to the golden rule. Management and the supervisory force must recognize human dignity regardless of race, color, creed, or level of activity in the organizational setup. Human relations can be most effective if each employee — a human being and our greatest resource — is placed in a suitable environment. An understanding of the variables involved in the way that human beings work is also necessary. The employee is to be treated as an individual with a kindred spirit toward the organization, as a member of a team aiming for job security as well as a full share of earnings commensurate with individual contribution. Based on a give-and-take principle, the employer expects an employee to exert his best efforts and the employee expects an adequate and equitable compensation.

---

[4]John F. Mee (ed.), *Personnel Handbook* (New York: The Ronald Press Company, 1951), p. 893.
[5]*Ibid.*

Employee Representation. The instinctive desire for a gregarious social relationship common to all human beings may be nurtured through employer-employee activities such as harmoniously competitive production groups, company employee associations, or union organization. A balancing of human relations between management and workers is the mainspring to a better understanding of each other's problems. This can be accomplished whether a company has a union or not.

An excellent example of employee representation in a nonunion company is the Woodward Governor Company located in Rockford, Illinois. Since 1946, this company has operated under a term they call "Corporate Partnership." The partnership is between the stockholders and the workers. In addition to performing their assigned duties, worker partners are obligated to protect and promote the welfare of the company internally and to collaborate with the stockholder partners in the protection and promotion of the company's welfare externally. Thus, there are a number of committees (Legislative, Education, Recreation, Tax, Candidates and Elections, Contributions, Open Door, and Health and Safety) constituted within the company that are staffed with workers who have been elected to these memberships. Although the work of these committees has no direct relationship to the routine operation of the plant, through these committees the workers have greater participation and voice in the internal welfare of the company. Occasionally when management has to make a decision involving unusual circumstances, the workers may participate in full-scale discussion in an open assembly (and balloting if necessary) to determine what is best for the welfare of the company as a whole.

Mr. Irl C. Martin, chairman of the board and former president of Woodward Governor Company, reveals how he feels about committees having employee representation when he said:

> As head of the company, I am afforded an opportunity to discuss their decisions with them before posting. Whether I agree or not, I vote the way the committee recommends. After all, in a democracy votes are what decide issues and one vote is of no greater value than another. However, anything that affects this company affects each member proportionately, and I know that no one is going to damage himself intentionally by thoughtless or careless voting. Therefore, if, as head of this company, I can't sell them into my way of thinking, it is just as well that I accept their judgment — they may be right. Among sincere people a source of judgment generally is appreciated if its quality stands the test of time. To date, I am very proud of the judgment and civic integrity displayed by this committee.[6]

Unions have an excellent opportunity to cooperate effectively in many functions of the enterprise. Some employers recognize the benefits of union participation as evidenced by the following affirmation:

---

[6]From a talk, "A Business Philosophy," by Irl C. Martin.

Many of our best supervisors are doing a better job working with Union representatives in conducting the affairs of their departments than they did some years ago . . . . They no longer have the liberty to make all of the decisions . . . . nevertheless they are also making decisions which are less hasty and generally sounder than ever before.[7]

Joint (Bilateral) Actions. Union-management cooperation, known as joint or bilateral action, means that both act together. Mutual cooperation is the logical way to effect a better understanding. A good example of this is the 1960 Human Relations Research Committee (now commonly referred to as the Human Relations Committee) formed by the United Steel Workers of America (CIO) and 11 steel companies with whom they bargain collectively. The idea of the Human Relations Committee was born out of the turmoil and the tarnished relationships between the steelworkers and their companies in the 1959–1960 steel dispute. The aim of the committee is to improve relationships and promote peace in the steel industry.

The record so far has been very good. Several negotiations have been completed without a strike. A whole new and constructive relationship between labor and management in the steel industry has been formed, one that will enable both the industry and the employees to prosper while contributing more and more to the growing economy of our nation and the needs of its people.

Worker's Loyalty and Cooperation. A frequently asked question is whether the worker can serve two masters. Authorities aver that "dual worker loyalty" is possible. An exhaustive study of one of the largest packing houses convinced Professor Theodore V. Purcell, S. J.,[8] that the worker sees no essential conflict between the loyalties of the two overlapping organizations. He found that 79 percent of the workers felt a clear allegiance to their union as an institution; but 92 percent also felt allegiance to the company.

There is ample proof that, if workers are treated with proper regard for human dignity, they will loyally cooperate with an employer. The second largest shoemaking firm in the United States, the Endicott-Johnson Corporation in Johnson City, New York, is an example of worker loyalty. Not too long ago the corporation was in trouble because it was losing money and its sales and earnings were falling off. A New York City holding company was attempting to gain control of the company by stock purchase. Within a few weeks, 8,600 of the 9,000 workers participating in the company's pension plan signed petitions saying they would loan 20 percent of their retirement fund ($10 million) to the company

---

[7]E. H. Johnson (Director of Employee Relations, United Air Lines), "The Union Is Here to Stay," *Proceedings, National Management Engineering Clinic* (Chicago: Industrial Management Society, 1950), p. 17.

[8]Theodore V. Purcell, S. J., *The Worker Speaks His Mind On Company and Union* (Cambridge: Harvard University Press, 1953).

to use for whatever purpose it wished.[9] Another example of worker cooperation is the Minneapolis-Honeywell Regulator Company, where employees — with the mutual understanding and full cooperation of union leaders — cooperate whole-heartedly in a joint waste- and cost-reduction program to reduce losses in time, materials, and equipment. Other examples are the excellent cooperative setup of joint union-management action at the Nunn-Bush Shoe Company, Milwaukee, Wisconsin; and the union-management cooperation that saved the business of the Merrimack Manufacturing Company in Lowell, Massachusetts; as well as the Lapointe Tool Company in Hudson, Massachusetts; and the Adamson Company, manufacturers of steel tanks in East Palestine, Ohio, who were on the verge of bankruptcy.

Human Wants and Needs. A discussion on human relations would be incomplete without some mention of human wants and needs. Professor Davis offers the following specific viewpoint: "Human Relations as an area of management practice is an integration of people into a work situation in a way that motivates them to work together productively, cooperatively, and with economic, psychological, and social satisfaction."[10] Thus, this definition underlines the fact that *motivation* of people on the basis of their *wants*, as depicted in Figure 4.4, is an important part of human relations. According to Professor Davis, economic, social, and psychological wants are the boundaries of employee human relations which are satisfied within the limits permitted by the situation and the company's objectives and policies.[11]

The wants vary from one worker to another. Economic wants differ from the standpoint of items that are desired for daily needs and those of general satisfaction. They are obtained through work performance, compensation, and motivation (incentives). Social wants are satisfied through group relationships such as companionship, family life, belongingness, and social acceptance in the community. The psychological or personal wants seek to satisfy innate desires for recognition of human dignity and of individual initiative even when the worker must adhere to required standards. To satisfy these human wants is partially the concern of wage and salary administration.

Principles of Human Relations. The essential principles of satisfactory socioeconomic human relations in an enterprise that concern wage and salary administration are:

1. Placing employees in jobs they can perform most efficiently.
2. Providing for additional training to give each worker an opportunity for further development and promotion.

---

[9]"Communities Repay a Benevolent Firm," *The Milwaukee Journal*, (January 22,1961), p. 1, col. 7.
[10]Keith Davis, *Human Relations in Business* (New York: McGraw-Hill Book Company, Inc., 1957), p. 4.
[11]*Ibid.*, pp. 8–9. Figure 4.4 reproduced with permission.

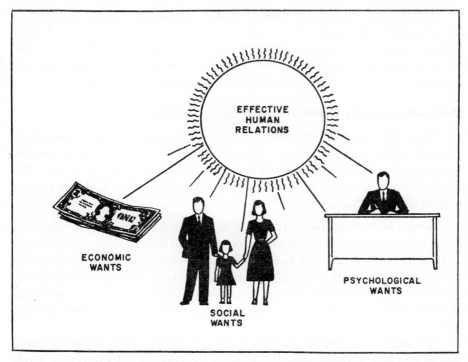

FIGURE 4.4 EFFECTIVE HUMAN RELATIONS. A means of satisfying the economic, social, and psychological wants of employees working together productively.

3. Furnishing the best tools, equipment, and facilities in a safe, sanitary environment.

4. Arranging for research to improve performance methods for higher production and better work with less human effort.

5. Developing effective organizational units, including indirect labor, coordinated to achieve a balanced production through cooperative efforts.

6. Encouraging employees to voice their opinions regarding personal well-being.

7. Formulating employer-employee committees to participate in solving problems directly related to the workers.

8. Setting up rules and standards as guides without demanding more than normal expectancy.

9. Compensating each employee equitably according to experience, skill, and individual ability.

10. Establishing financial incentives to imbue workers with the spirit and pride of accomplishment.

11. Promoting ways and means to provide steady employment and future economic security.

The first six principles of human relations are included in the activities of the personnel department. Inasmuch as they affect the worker and his job, however, wage and salary administration is also indirectly involved. The last five principles directly concern wage and salary administration since they are regarded as the needs that motivate a worker's behavior or action.

Motivation and Its Relationship to Compensation

Motivation has an important relationship to compensation because it is generally believed that when employees are more fully motivated, they can produce greater goods and services and thus merit increased wages or salaries. We shall attempt to give only a general overview of motivation here and treat it more fully in Chapter 18.

Nature of Motivation. *Motivation* is usually construed as an impelling force, or a powerful drive, from within the individual that stimulates innate wants and desires for intangible and tangible needs. The *intangible* needs may be recognition, praise, sympathy, and a desirable social status within the community. The *tangible* needs may be personal possessions such as a house, a car, adequate clothing, and other utilitarian goods or luxuries that can be obtained through incentive wages.[12]

The needs of a tangible nature are usually acquired after external stimulation to act; that is, the individual is inspired to action in order to obtain goods of an economic nature. In industry, management provides an incentive that motivates an employee to perform a certain quantity or quality of work for a specific reward, which is commonly termed a wage incentive. Thus, in connection with motivation, incentive is regarded as an external stimulus.

From the industrial relations standpoint, motivation and encouragement through incentives evolve into actual and definite means of satisfaction. They are actual and definite in that the incentives are tied in with job performance, which is rewarded by adequate and equitable wages that are enhanced through piece work, premiums, and bonuses.

Motivating Factors. Human relations must be integrated, or at least interrelated, with motivating factors. There are many positive and negative incentives that motivate employees. The wage and salary administrator has only a token interest, however, in the negative angle of motivation, such as reprimanding to secure obedience; monetary fines for defective work or tardy attendance; demotion for improper behavior; or discharge for not completing a standard amount of work in proper time. The positive factors that predominently motivate an industrial worker are:

---

[12]The subject of psychological and economic effects of wage incentives is discussed in Chapter 18.

1. Laudatory recognition of a job well done.
2. Opportunity for advancement within the sphere of one's own job.
3. Gratification from participating in solving management problems, or belonging to a group that represents the workers in all employer-employee relations matters.
4. Assurance that his work is properly organized under effective leadership.
5. Adequate and equitable compensation based on merit, skill, experience, and the going rate in the community.
6. Rewards for extra efforts in raising production.
7. Participation in company profits.
8. Security during retirement, and achieving company objectives aimed toward future security.

Laudatory Recognition. Recognition of a job well done generates contentment in job satisfaction. Being praised imparts a sense of importance within a worker's environment and inspires further endeavor to do his best. Commendation by supervisors, executives, and managers exerts a strong influence upon a worker, but when accompanied with periodic increases in wage-base rates or some other tangible reward, it is undeniably more satisfying.

Opportunity for Advancement. A worker generally yearns for an opportunity for advancement. The supervisor can help him satisfy this want by suggesting a procedure of substituting better methods to improve his job, and thereby encourage the worker to do more and better work. Another way to enhance his opportunity for advancement is through special training. When a worker continually performs high-quality work and exceeds the expected quota, he has demonstrated that he should be given consideration for promotion to the next better job.

Participation in Solving Management Problems. Employees will generally increase their output when given the opportunity to participate — either individually or in groups — in making decisions on matters concerning their welfare. According to Saltonstall, this is one of the basic satisfactions that employees want from their jobs.[13] The worker, as an individual, feels that he is doing his part and that his ideas are worth passing on to the employer as well as to his own work group. He wants to earn the respect of everyone within the work group by contributing his share "to help the gang"; and, as an employee, he would like to be assured that the employer appreciates his performance by being granted a voice in company affairs.

Organized Work Under Effective Leadership. Employees are inspired to do their full share if the daily routine is properly organized and supervised by men

---

[13]Robert Saltonstall, "What Employees Want from Their Work," *Harvard Business Review*, Vol. XXXI, No. 6 (November–December, 1953), p. 74.

or women whom they respect. Managerial leadership is evinced by workers who conscientiously or automatically follow well-defined organizational principles and standards that are effectively administered. Efficient organization pulsates with loyalty and cooperation in direct proportion to the spirit of unity and enthusiasm inculcated by management. Men generally look to their leaders for proper guidance and timely action.

Adequate and Equitable Compensation. In connection with the basic satisfaction of receiving fair wages, a worker, as an individual, expects his pay to be adequate and equitable in compensation for the hazardous conditions, job importance, skill and amount of effort expended; and, if more is produced, he should accordingly be paid more without cutting the standards.

Another motivating factor for a worker is satisfaction that his wages are at least equal to the wage-base rate in the community for the same type of work, and that he will receive additional compensation for increased production.

Rewards for Extra Efforts. While it is definitely established that certain nonfinancial motivating forces incite a worker to raise production, the factors of adequate wages and equitable remuneration are still considered as the most powerful incentives. An examination of contractual labor-management agreements will prove that compensation factors predominate. Therefore, it is reasonable to assume that when a worker consistently produces more than the normal (average) requirements, he expects additional remuneration in proportion to his results.

This motivating factor should be regarded by wage and salary administration as one of the most powerful. As further emphasized in Chapter 18, the value of wage incentives is uppermost in a worker's mind in order that he can satisfy his socioeconomic and psychological wants.

Profit Sharing. The factor of motivation through profit sharing as deferred compensation encourages a worker to maintain his interest in increased and better quality production. In addition, the worker's loyalty and favorable attitude toward the company remain steadfast. This favorable attitude also influences the community where the worker lives inasmuch as the company indirectly supports the community. If profit sharing is deferred until retirement, it provides the additional satisfaction of security, and encourages a worker to increase his earnings by contributing to the company's profits through efficient job performance.

Security to Satisfy Family Needs and Retirement. Employees are generally concerned about job security to take care of immediate family needs. Attitude surveys invariably reveal, however, that middle-aged and older workers are considerably anxious about their family needs in case of sickness or death, and old age. Thus, the motivation factor in this respect is highly influential in that it allays the worker's anxiety and concern for his family by providing hospitalization and group life insurance. Pensions and retirement plans are additional job security provisions. These positive incentives encourage a worker's utmost efforts to achieve the company's goal of earning profits and continuing in business as an important part of the economy.

Development of wage and salary policies

If men are to work harmoniously and effectively in a joint effort toward a definite goal, they must in some way be guided toward that goal. Policies serve as these guideposts. *Policies* are statements of intent by management that commit them to a course of action in achieving a goal. For example, if a company's policy is to pay employees according to merit, it means that the firm has committed itself to relate pay to employee results or merit. It means that the firm wishes to pay only for results. The various members of management then have to determine for each department the various forms of results to which pay will be tied. Compensation policies have to be developed if wage and salary administration is to succeed.

Importance of Policies

Wage and salary policies are important from the management point of view because they are the working guidelines that translate management philosophy into action toward company goals. If management expects its employees to be positively influenced to assist in achieving the company goals, it is necessary to have clearly defined policies that reflect respect for human dignity.

From the employee point of view, compensation policies reveal to the employee the basis of management decisions. Through management policies and decisions the employee learns whether management practices what it preaches, or whether the policies are misleading and really "window dressings." Good policies help to assure employees that their management is competent, knows where it is going, and is ethical in its dealings with both its workers and the public.

Policy Areas

Management needs to develop compensation policies according to the needs of the company and its employees. This means that all companies do not need the identical number or kinds of policies. Each firm must decide for itself which policies are needed to adequately guide the members of management and at the same time satisfy the needs of the employees. Many companies believe that formal compensation policies are desirable in the following areas:

Employee evaluation (merit rating)
Fringe benefits or services (pensions, vacations, holidays, leaves, insurance)

Incentive wages or salaries (bonuses, profit sharing, stock options, etc.)
Informing union of activities
Job analysis
Job descriptions
Job evaluation and classification
Job pricing
Job promotions, transfers
Method improvements
Motion and time studies
Overall level of company wages in the industry, community, or country
Posting of job openings
Premium pay (shifts, overtime, etc.)
Retroactive pay
Suggestion systems
Type of wage structure(s)
Use of training rates
Wage grievances
Wage or salary pay increases (or decreases)
Wage surveys

Many of the compensation policies in the areas above are written into the union-management contract and thus become a standard part of the union-management collective bargaining agreement.

The Employers Mutuals of Wausau, Wisconsin, has indicated that the objectives of its salary policies are, "To create opportunities for men and women to achieve a satisfactory career in the insurance business, and to reward them according to their contribution to the enterprise."[14]   In order to meet these objectives, this firm has adopted these specific salary policies:

1. Establishing and maintaining equitable salary relationships among all positions in the company.
2. Maintaining salary levels consistent with those in companies using similar skills and abilities.
3. Establishing policies and procedures to insure equitable administration of salaries in all departments and branches.
4. Maintaining a proper balance between the total salary expense and the company's financial goals.

Requirements of a Sound Policy

In drawing up compensation policies, there are many individual considerations such as coordination with other company policies, the historical background and traditions of the industry, and the needs and desires of the employees, that need to be kept in mind. However, the real measure of a sound policy is whether it can meet the tests of validity, flexibility, and clarity.

---

[14]Employers Mutuals of Wausau, Wisconsin, *Salary Program* (October 21, 1964), p. 1.

Policy Validity. A sound policy must accomplish what it is supposed to do and do that consistently. Unless present policy is accomplishing its goal, it should be modified to correct the condition or it should be scrapped. Employees will not tolerate a policy that is either unreliable or inconsistent.

Policy Flexibility. Policies need to be flexible in order to be current with the times. Our dynamic economy and its sociopolitical expansion call for an alert wage and salary administration to maintain flexible policies that may require periodic changes, especially regarding wage-base rates, job evaluation, employee classification, hiring rates, and trainee rates. Furthermore, as a matter of policy relative to changed time-base rates, it may be necessary to change piece-rate incentives, bonus percentages, employee ratings, and the overall motivation policies to maintain satisfactory human relations. Too many policies today need updating because they have not kept up with the times. Policies can be kept more current and flexible if a schedule is established for their periodic review.

Policy Clarity. There appears to be a strong relationship between the understanding of a policy and its clarity. Employees who cannot understand a policy rarely will accept it. Clarity of language assists understanding. Policies should be written in simple layman's language. Policies are not the place to show off one's vocabulary or attempt to impress employees with the author's education. Unless a policy is clearly written and promptly communicated to the employees, it cannot be effective.

Communication in wage and salary administration

Communication is a process of transmitting information through various channels in an organization, forming a chain of clear understanding from top-level management to workers at the bottom level and vice versa, thus integrating the members of the entire organization into a unified team of action. Its purpose is fulfilled when confidence and mutual understanding are developed between the employer, management, and employees.

Need of Communication

Communication should be an integral part of the wage and salary program if it is to be maintained effectively. Communication regarding compensation is of specific concern to all employees, overshadowing all other matters pertaining to their work situation. Whether an entirely new wage and salary program is to be introduced, old compensation methods revised, or new additions or significant changes made regarding employee security, the information should be "communicated" to the workers with clarity of purpose since it will have to be acceptable to them and their union representatives. Sibson believes that it is extremely important to communicate information to employees which substantiates that the company is living up to its basic written policies, because such information demonstrates to employees that company pay policies are living instruments which guide day-to-day actions, rather than merely window dressing.[15]   Unless employees know about the compensation program, how it is administered, and where to get questions answered, they are not likely to have much confidence in the program. To assume that the employees will somehow absorb the facts about the system without a well-planned communication program is to miss a very real opportunity for bettering the employee relations within the company.[16]

Executives are sometimes shocked to learn that their employees know so little about their companies. In a voluntary employee quiz given by a large electrical firm, the results showed that only a small percentage of employees knew the important facts about company matters.[17]   Only one employee in five knew or could guess the amount of the company's sales. Only 34 percent of the employees knew the amount of the sales dollar that went to employees for pay and benefits. Only one in five knew what the company's profits were. Only 4 percent of the employees knew to what extent pay and benefits had increased in the past five years. It would appear that little advantage is gained from paying an employee well unless he knows he is paid well. According to Newcomb and Sammons, many companies have found that lack of effective employee communications about their wage structure has cost them dearly.[18]

In every enterprise administrators and managerial executives must use some means of communicating with employees to impart a common understanding of the company's responsibilities to the owners, employees, and the community. In small organizations the relationship between executives and the comparatively few employees is close; hence, intercommunication is simple. Complaints and misunderstandings can be settled promptly on the spot.

In medium-size and large companies, however, the gap between top management and workers at the lowest organization level is relatively wide. Injustices and misunderstandings may cause grievances that disrupt the organization and business routine. Therefore, a well-organized communications system to prevent misconceptions, to ease tensions, and to keep employees working together as a cooperative team is a necessity.

---

[15]Robert E. Sibson, "Your Pay Program Must Be Sold," *Personnel Journal* (June, 1958).

[16]Theodore E. Weissinger, Manager, Salary Classification Division, Employee Relations Department, of the E. I. duPont de Nemours Company in Wilmington, Delaware, speaking before an American Management Conference, from *Notes and Quotes*, No. 314 (July, 1965), p. 3.

[17]"How Little We Know About Ourselves," *Employee Relations News (G.E.)*, No. 63–7 (February 25, 1963), p. 2.

[18]Robert Newcomb and Marg Sammons, *Employee Communications in Action* (New York: Harper and Brothers, 1961), chap. 7.

Communication Media

There is a great variety of media available to transmit intracompany compensation information. The more common media include written communications, printed booklets, pamphlets, bulletin boards, individual contacts, and group meetings.

Written communication in the form of instructions, memorandums, letters, records, and reports is generally more important than verbal communication since, if clearly presented, it can be retained for future reference. Although a personal follow-up may be necessary, the written communication is invaluable when it involves objectives, policies, and rules regarding wages, wage payments, financial incentives, and fringe benefits.

There is a variety of printed booklets used to acquaint employees with different phases of an enterprise. Such booklets range in size from small pamphlets to elaborate manuals that contain information about the company, its history, organization, policies, rules, safety measures, personnel practices, and products. Where compensation methods are well established, the booklet includes information about job structures, work measurement, hourly wage determination, incentive pay, overtime pay, special bonuses, profit-sharing plans, pension plans, group life insurance, stock purchase plans, and hospitalization and medical plans.

Some companies issue booklets that cover specialized information regarding compensation subjects. Booklets about profit-sharing plans, disability benefit plans, and pension plans are usually purely descriptive. Other booklets may include artwork and line drawings to supplement the explanations. The use of such techniques gives the worker a clearer understanding of what is involved and why certain procedures must be carried out according to predetermined rules or standards.

The Armstrong Cork Company issues a booklet entitled "Your Hourly Rate," which is illustrated with numerous cartoons. It tells how an employee's hourly rate is determined and explains step by step why various jobs receive different rates of pay as determined by job evaluation. The upper part of Figure 4.5 shows the first page of the booklet, which contains an illustration of how the factory payroll can be fairly distributed. The illustration in the lower part of Figure 4.5 appears toward the end of the booklet and depicts how the job requirements are balanced. The booklet ends with the statement and illustration shown in Figure 4.6.

For a number of years, the Owens-Illinois Corporation has conducted a salary education plan that continues to be an important phase of their wage and salary program. Each employee receives a booklet explaining how salaries are determined; how supplemental bonuses and fringe benefits are calculated; and

Armstrong Cork Company

FIGURE 4.5   BALANCING WORK WITH PAY. Portions of the first and last pages of the booklet, "Your Hourly Rate," explaining job evaluation and its factors.

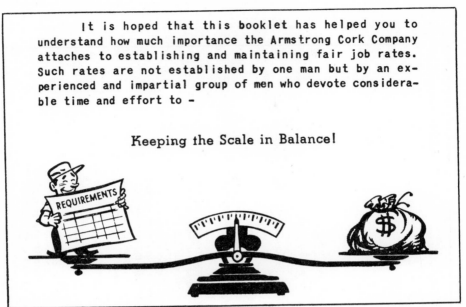

It is hoped that this booklet has helped you to understand how much importance the Armstrong Cork Company attaches to establishing and maintaining fair job rates. Such rates are not established by one man but by an experienced and impartial group of men who devote considerable time and effort to –

Keeping the Scale in Balance!

REQUIREMENTS

Armstrong Cork Company

FIGURE 4.6 KEEPING THE SCALE IN BALANCE

under what conditions they are paid. An "auxiliary" means of communication is a one-page form, "Your Salary Benefits," which is issued to each employee annually. It explains his individual benefits as of January 1 of that year. Figure 4.7 shows where entries are made on the form to supply explicit information regarding the individual's standing.[19]

Other excellent examples of good communications on compensation matters include the following firms and their publications: Eastman Kodak Company, "How You Are Paid"; McDonnell, "Retirement Income Plan"; and Owens-Illinois, "Money Plus — Your Salary Benefits."

Bulletin boards are usually placed in prominent locations within access of all manufacturing departments and offices. They are the most popular means of transmitting written communications. If the posters are kept up-to-date with well-arranged illustrations and catchwords, they arouse curiosity. The general consensus is that posted information regarding compensation matters, especially wage and salary changes, attracts the widest attention.

Written information, whether communicated by letter, announcements posted on bulletin boards, or by printed booklets, undoubtedly leads to an understanding of the compensation program. Invariably, however, some workers

---

[19]Reprinted with the permission of Walter F. Hosack of the Wage and Salary Administration Department, Owens-Illinois Corporation.

Your Salary Benefits—1968

This is a confidential summary of your Owens-Illinois salary benefits. Please note that these benefits were calculated as of **JANUARY 1** of this year and may not be strictly correct today if changes have occurred this year. If you have questions about them, please discuss them with your supervisor.

TO:

SERVICE

Your service with Owens-Illinois dates back to:

MO. _____ DAY _____ YR _____

SALARY

Your supervisor will answer any questions you may have about your salary and tell you your rate group number and the salary range for your group.

$ _____ PER WEEK

SICKNESS BENEFITS

If you should be unable to come to work because of an illness or injury, that began this year, you will continue to receive your salary for:

1/4 MONTHS _____

In addition, your O-I group insurance will pay you the following weekly disability benefit for nonoccupational disabilities for a period of up to 26 weeks after your Salary Sickness Benefits listed above have expired: (People in California ordinarily will receive this benefit only for periods of disability when they are not eligible for State Unemployment Compensation Disability benefits or Salary Sickness Benefits.)

$ _____ PER MONTH

If you are disabled and eligible for the Company Plan of Long-Term Disability insurance, you will receive these payments beginning when your Salary Sickness Benefits end. They will be coordinated with other benefits you may receive and can continue to age 65 if the disability lasts that long. Your maximum benefit amount is:

Your group insurance Comprehensive coverage also provides hospital, surgical and other medical expense benefits for you and your eligible dependents if you have included them in your policy. These benefits help you pay the cost of disabilities, when your covered medical expenses are over $25 in any calendar year. Under this plan you could receive payments of up to $25,000; $12,500 of which can be received in one calendar year. After retirement you and your spouse each receive $2,500 of Comprehensive Medical coverage at Company expense.

If you should be injured on the job, you would be entitled to workmen's compensation benefits, the cost of which is paid by O-I.

VACATIONS

Your Owens-Illinois service entitles you to the following vacation:

If this is your first vacation, you become eligible June 1 or after 12 months service, whichever comes first.

WEEKS _____ DAYS _____

SEVERANCE PAY

At your age and length of service, as of January 1 of this year, if you should lose your job permanently, through no fault of your own, your salary will be continued for the following number of 1/4 months: (Severance pay is not ordinarily given to people who resign and is never given to people who retire.)

1/4 MONTHS _____

EDUCATION PLAN If approved in advance, and completed successfully, night school courses will be reimbursed for 100% of tuition and correspondence courses for 75% of cost.

DEATH BENEFITS If you should die while an O-I salaried employee: Your dependents would receive a payment from Owens-Illinois equal to your salary for a period of the following number of ¼ months: (The length of time depends on the person's age and length of service at time of death.)

In addition, your beneficiary under the group insurance program would receive the following amount: If your death were accidental, this insurance amount would be doubled. Upon retirement, one-fourth of your active life insurance is continued at Company cost.

TRAVEL ACCIDENT INSURANCE In addition to the above death benefits, if you should die or become permanently and totally disabled as the result of an accident while traveling on Company business, your beneficiary or you would receive $100,000. Loss of a hand, foot, or eye, as a result of such an accident would pay you $50,000.

RETIREMENT BENEFITS The figures in Boxes 4 through 7 are estimates only. If you have questions not answered by this report, write the Retirement Department.

¼ MONTHS
$ DOLLARS

SALARY RETIREMENT PLAN			SOC. SEC	TOTAL INCOME
$			$	$
1. Total contributions made by you during the year 1967.	2. Your total contributions through December 31, 1967.	3. Your own contributions plus interest as of December 31, 1967.	5. Estimated monthly income at age 65, assuming future participation based on your and the Company's contributions to the Salary Plan as of Dec. 31, 1967. (See Note 1 below.)	6. Estimated monthly primary Social Security amount from age 65. (See note 2 below.)	7. Total estimated monthly retirement income after age 65.
These three columns will be blank if you joined the Plan May 1, 1967 or later and earn under $550 per month or have refused the Plan.		4. Monthly retirement income payable from age 65, which has already been provided by your and the Company's contributions to the Salary Plan as of Dec. 31, 1967. (See Note 1 below.)			

IMPORTANT REMEMBER TO NOTIFY YOUR PERSONNEL DEPARTMENT IF YOU WANT TO CHANGE YOUR BENEFICIARY UNDER THE SALARY RETIREMENT PLAN.

NOTE 1: This Figure includes your accrued benefits under both the former Contributory and Service Retirement Plans prior to Nov. 1, 1967 and will be used in calculating benefits if before age 65 you terminate, die or retire.

NOTE 2: The amount shown in Box 6 assumes that you have earned maximum coverage under Social Security since 1955, and have earnings of at least $7,800 a year starting Jan. 1, 1968 and each year thereafter until you reach age 65. If you earn less than the Social Security covered wage, you <u>may</u> receive less than the Social Security benefit shown.

Owens-Illinois Corporation

FIGURE 4.7 Effective Means of Communication. Policy of telling salaried employees about some of their fringe benefits.

will have certain doubts or questions since it is almost impossible to use a vocabulary and approach that will be correctly and unquestionably interpreted by different people in various groups. Therefore, a follow-up by verbal person-to-person communication will clarify some points about which a worker may be doubtful, inasmuch as "five minutes' conversation is more effective for the exchange of ideas or information than six weeks of correspondence."[20]

Another medium for presenting a wage and salary program to a large number of employees at one time is to hold open question-and-answer meetings. Many companies make it a rule to establish some occasion two to four times a year for employees to meet and to discuss company matters, primarily with reference to compensation. Most employees derive a certain amount of satisfaction from these meetings which concern their welfare. Employer-employee meetings also tend to inspire a feeling of belongingness. Low morale and grievances with respect to wages or salaries may thus be avoided.

Language of Communication

Communication is one of the most effective means in human relations of conveying management's philosophy and ideas. It sometimes is so complex, however, that it causes differences between the sender and the receiver. The communicator translates his thoughts or desires into words that the recipient often interprets according to his own ideas and attitudes. For that reason the communication process must be thoroughly planned, prepared, and couched in simple, easily understood terminology.

Leaders in management claim — from practical experience — that the basic language of managers too often is concentrated upon production efficiency. They forget that it should be translated into the vocabulary of a first-line worker who wants to know how it can benefit him. Otherwise there are "plenty of words but no communication."[21]

Reception of Communication by Employees

In most cases employees are receptive to simple-worded company communications regarding a sound wage and salary program, when convincingly presented. Adherence to principles of fairness in paying wages and salaries according to job values, experience, efforts, and expended energy develops trust and confidence in the program which is accepted voluntarily, without undue pressure from the management. One authority on communication underlines this contention as follows:

---

[20]Burleigh B. Gardner and David G. Moore, *Human Relations in Industry* (Homewood, Illinois: Richard D. Irwin, Inc., 1950), p. 44.
[21]William Oncken, Jr., *Communication and Human Relations*, Circular No. 23 (Pasadena: Industrial Relations Section, California Institute of Technology, October, 1958), pp. 2 and 6.

Only with trust can there be any real communication, and until that trust is achieved the techniques and gadgetry of communication are so much waste effort. Study after study has pointed to the same moral: before employees will accept management "facts," they must first have over-all confidence in the motives and sincerity of management.[22]

Separate compensation structures for employee groups

It is practically an impossible task to develop a single compensation structure that is applicable and satisfactory to all the different types of jobs and employees found in a company of 500 employees or more. In companies employing fewer than 100 employees, it may be possible to have a single formal compensation structure that will work satisfactorily for the majority of employees; but if the firm has a combination of 25 or more clerical and manual jobs, a single wage structure may be vulnerable in many areas because clerical and manual jobs have too many different aspects to be appraised satisfactorily with the same yardstick.

A firm should attempt to classify its jobs into broad categories (job families) that can be evaluated by a common set of appraisal factors. The most common practice is to have separate compensation structures for clerical employees (a salary structure) and for manual or shop employees (a wage structure). Many of the larger companies establish individual compensation structures for the following employee groups: sales; executives; supervisors; clerical; shop; and administrative, professional, and technical.

No matter how many compensation structures a company has, there should be some type of relationship or coordination between these structures so that together they represent an overall compensation system that does not appear to be a hodgepodge of structures. Each structure may have its own factors and yardsticks applicable to the employees and their jobs, but some plan for equating the separate structures into their comparative values to the company should exist. This subject is further discussed in Chapter 13.

Responsibility for wage and salary administration

Top management must play an important role in the success of a compensation program. The top executives are instrumental in formulating the philosophy of the company as well as in establishing the broad compensation policies from which all other compensation activities are drawn. Top management must also satisfy itself that various standards, controls, and administrative procedures have been established which are most likely to achieve the objectives of the compensation program. Finally, it is only top management that should decide how much

---

[22]William H. Whyte, Jr., *Is Anybody Listening?* (New York: Simon and Schuster, 1952), p. 23.

information is to be communicated to its employees.[23]   Thus, top management must believe in and support the various activities that encompass wage and salary administration. It may demonstrate this through its actions and deeds.

One of the most important evidences of top management's support of wage and salary administration is the appointment of a competent person to head such matters. In a company of 500 or more employees, this is a full-time job. In smaller companies it may only be a part of a person's job, but it is a definite part; and some qualified person within the organization must be given the responsibility to plan, organize, and coordinate all compensation matters.

Besides top management's support of compensation matters, all middle-level executives and first-line supervisors must be thoroughly convinced of the soundness of the wage and salary program and be fully informed so as to answer questions intelligently. Written messages, booklets, and other communications usually contain annotations such as, "Your supervisor can answer questions concerning the plan" or "Your supervisor will be glad to explain how it works." While many first-line supervisors are efficient in directing work, they may be ineffective communicators on wage and salary administration matters. Therefore, assistance from the wage and salary administration staff and other management executives should always be available to them.

In summary, compensation matters are a part of the job of every member of management. Top management must lead the way to a sound program of wage and salary administration by establishing the organizational framework and the endorsement that are needed to give employees confidence in the fairness, sincereness, and soundness of the program.

Checklist for successful wage and salary administration

The following list of considerations will aid in the establishment of a successful program of wage and salary administration. The suggestions are not intended to be all-inclusive nor to apply to all situations in a like manner. Their degree of applicability will vary from firm to firm but, in the main, they should serve as useful guidelines.

1. Select a competent person to take charge of all compensation matters. Top management must approve of this employee and provide him with the necessary authority and facilities for performing his job. (Chapter 3)
2. Establish the aims and objectives that the compensation program is to accomplish. (Chapters 1 and 2)
3. Develop and communicate compensation policies that will accomplish the aims and objectives previously decided upon. (Chapter 4)

---

[23]Edward N. Hay and Associates, "Salary Administration: The Role of Top Management," *Men and Management*, No. 148 (1964).

4. Analyze all company jobs to provide the factual basis for management decisions and for preparing job descriptions, job specifications, job performance standards, etc. (Chapters 11 and 12)

5. Establish plan(s) for setting up appropriate compensation structure(s) for all jobs in the company. This involves evaluating, classifying, and pricing all jobs in the firm. (Chapters 5–10, 13, 14, 24, 25)

6. Determine performance standards and the appropriate methods of compensation for all jobs. Supplementary compensations (fringes) are included in this category. (Chapters 15, 22, 23)

7. Establish plan(s) for motivating, evaluating, and rewarding all employees in the company. (Chapters 16–21)

8. Develop a set of periodical follow-up procedures for evaluating, controlling, maintaining, and updating the compensation program after it has been established. (Chapter 26)

REVIEW QUESTIONS

1. What does a management philosophy or creed have to do with wage and salary administration?

2. (a) Do you believe that every company should make available to its employees a creed of its philosophy? Why or why not? (b) If you think a company should make a creed available, how should it be done?

3. What does productivity mean to you?

4. What relationship does productivity have to wages?

5. Explain the importance of productivity to the standard of living, employee wages, and company profits.

6. (a) What is meant by human relations? (b) What is its objective? (c) How can good human relations be achieved?

7. (a) What is your reaction to employee representation? (b) What effect has it on wage and salary administration?

8. Why are the predominant motivating factors of industrial workers important to compensation?

9. Is it really necessary for a company to develop compensation policies in the areas of employee evaluation, fringe benefits, incentives, etc.?

10. Are there any tests that can be applied to a compensation policy to determine its soundness?

11. What relationship does communication have to good wage and salary administration?

12. What suggestions do you have to improve the overall picture of compensation communications?

13. Discuss the use of bulletin boards v. the person-to-person method of communicating compensation matters.

14. Comment on the statement "Only with trust can there be any real communication, and until that trust is achieved, the techniques and gadgetry of communication are so much waste effort."

15. Discuss what is behind the statement "Before employees will accept management 'facts,' they must first have overall confidence in the motives and sincerity of management."

16. Who should bear the responsibility of compensation matters?

RESEARCH OR SEMINAR QUESTIONS

1. Should union representatives be asked to participate and cooperate with management in the determination of the specific personnel plans to be adopted? Why or why not?

2. "Formal wage and salary administration is not necessary because the unions set the wages that a company must pay." Discuss this statement, explaining why you agree or disagree with it.

3. Do all the motivating factors listed on page 93 affect all workers in the same manner? Which factors are important for the young married woman? the 50-year old woman? the 26-year old male factory worker? the 31-year old middle executive?

4. In order for a wage or a salary to benefit the company as much as possible, what needs must it satisfy for the employee?

PRACTICAL EXPERIENCE ASSIGNMENTS

1. Contact a wage and salary administrator and ask him for a copy of whatever literature his company gives to the employees to present the firm's philosophy on compensation. Analyze this literature to determine the strong and weak points as presented in the material. Prepare a report outlining the strong and weak points discovered and your recommendations on how to bolster up the weaknesses.

2. Draw up what you consider to be an ideal creed on wage and salary matters.

3. Interview a friend, classmate, or worker to find out specifically what he wants or expects from a job. In what way can the wage and salary department assist in motivating him?

4. Prepare a list of rules or guides that management should follow in communicating wage and salary information to its employees.

5. Interview a wage and salary administrator to determine what he considers to be the more important considerations for successful wage and salary administration.

6. Talk to some workers of a company that has a published management creed or philosophy to find out whether or not they believe the company is "window dressing" or that it really means what it has said in the creed. What evidence did the workers give you to back up their feelings?

7. Interview three employees to find out why they do or do not read company booklets on wage and salary matters. What recommendations do you have to make the booklets more effective?

CASE PROBLEM

4-1. BERNARD CARLSON WOOD PRODUCTS COMPANY

Communication Problems in Human Relations

Mr. Bernard Carlson, a cabinetmaker of the old school whose versatility with a few tools enabled him to produce almost any wood item or piece of furniture, looked forward to owning a woodworking shop. After being employed on various jobs, including the production of wood blocks for engravers, Mr. Carlson succeeded in augmenting his own savings with a loan in 1938, making it possible for him to form the Bernard Carlson Wood Products Company in a small Michigan town, to manufacture wood blocks for engravers.

In the earlier years, book and magazine illustrations were reproduced solely from hand-engraved boxwood blocks. Boxwood logs were imported from Turkey and Venezuela, thus necessitating a sizable expenditure. To economize, the company also processed boxwood to prescribed dimensions for the manufacture of triangular and flat precision scales used by draftsmen, in addition to other items.

The company had enough advance orders to start out with twelve skilled workers. Business growth was so rapid that a large number of additional shop workers and office personnel had to be employed. Attracting highly efficient employees was no problem because Mr. Carlson, president and manager, enjoyed the reputation of being a good man for whom to work. Occasionally he worked alongside his men, addressing them by their first names, and the workers called him "BC." Because of the esprit de corps in the organization, labor turnover was practically nil.

Three months after World War II began, the production of boxwood products, along with many other items, almost ceased because of the changeover to war production. Due to the influx of government orders, Mr. Carlson's efforts were heavily concentrated upon complying with government contracts, thus lessening his personal contact with the employees. Furthermore, the business grew so rapidly that he decided to obtain additional capital, and thereby attract two stockholders who would participate in conducting the business.

Gunnard Mathiessen and George Steymack invested in 46 percent of the company stock with the understanding that Mathiessen would become factory superintendent and Steymack the chief furniture designer. During the ensuing years of war effort, the company expanded from 80 employees to 360 factory and office workers. Wages were continually raised to keep pace with the increased cost of living and labor demands. A sharp change in work conditions, however, developed a markedly large labor turnover. Production lagged and the company's reputation for prompt delivery of high-quality products suffered.

When some of the best workers began to leave, Mr. Carlson made a personal investigation among the oldest and most loyal employees. He learned that the factory superintendent constantly rebuked foremen and workers for low production and his attitude toward the workers was one of haughty aloofness. Upon being approached for a raise, Mr. Mathiessen invariably rejected the plea by remarking that a raise was not warranted because productivity was too low and the company was losing money.

Mr. Carlson was so disturbed over the turn of events that he discussed the matter during an executive meeting. Mathiessen declared that in similar situations elsewhere he solved the problem by laying off the troublemakers. He stated that a personal discussion of the situation with each foreman individually would gradually improve conditions. However, this kind of communication proved ineffective. Employees were prone to believe the rumor that the company was earning unusually large profits despite "the crabby old slave driver's" protestations to the contrary.

By the end of World War II, in September, 1945, the printing industry had developed photographic and metal-etching processes for illustrations in black and in color. Hence, the need for engraver's art on wood blocks almost ceased, and the Carlson Company was forced into a new line of products. Mr. Steymack began to design and manufacture children's furniture, kitchen cabinets, and office desks to keep the company in continual operation.

During the transition from war production to the new furniture lines, the shop workers began doubting the steadiness of employment at the Carlson Company. Their doubts rose when employees were gradually laid off, and over 40 employees left voluntarily within a three-month period. The employees began conjecturing that since boxwood products were no longer being manufactured and the war orders were cancelled, additional layoffs were imminent. The large labor turnover gave other workers in the community the impression that the company no longer enjoyed its former reputation.

Meanwhile, Mr. Steymack's unusual designs and first-class workmanship attracted the furniture market and the company received numerous big orders that they were unable to fill due to the labor difficulties. Mr. Mathiessen discussed the situation frankly with each foreman, imparting the information that Mr. Steymack was in the process of setting up incentive plans to compensate workers in accordance with increased output. Each new employee was to be informed by the foreman that the workers would share in the profits by receiving a monetary bonus at the end of the year. When this good news was carried to the other workers over the "grapevine," however, it met with disbelief, and the situation was not remedied. Attracting and retaining skilled woodworkers continued to be a serious problem.

Problems:

1. Comment upon Mr. Mathiessen's policy of industrial and human relations. Explain what actions the Bernard Carlson Wood Products Company should take to ensure a steady cooperative organization. What changes, if any, do you recommend?

2. How should the company proceed to convince the employees of steady lucrative employment? Are there any communication problems involved? If so, state your recommended methods of communication.

chapter 5

DETERMINING WAGES AND SALARIES

For centuries, economists, sociologists, and others interested in the earnings of labor have pondered over problems of wages and criteria of compensation. No definite solution has been found, however, that could be accepted and uniformly applied to formulate wage payments. Consequently, the search continues for basic principles that will serve as a foundation for wage and salary determination and that can be applied directly without exploring the vast field of economics. Granted, multitudinous "laws" and wage theories have been advanced, but none of the early wage theories are acceptable in view of our dynamic economy with its technological and scientific developments. For, as Walton Hamilton and Stacy May significantly state:

> Surely men enough have given themselves to fashioning "laws" of wages. If every tome meant increased understanding, we must long since have learned more than there is to know about the earnings of "labor"; ... explanations have come and gone to no good purpose; for more often than not the new has been no nearer than the old to a truth which is on speaking terms with reality.[1]

The utmost can be accomplished by solving individual problems on the basis of some realistic wage pattern proven to be acceptable and satisfactory. Therefore, standards that aid in deciding what is right and what is wrong, what is

---

[1]Walton Hamilton and Stacy May, *Control of Wages* (New York: MacMillan Co., 1923), p. v.

fair and what is unfair, in the determination of wages are a welcome solution to the problem.

The purpose of this chapter is to discuss the theory, practice, and problems of determining a wage or salary in an enterprise, To do this, the subject matter is broken down into the following major topics: the tests that a wage determinant (or pay formula) should be able to meet, a review of historical wage theories, an analysis of modern wage theories, and the yardsticks that are commonly used in determining compensation.

Tests of wage determinants

If a sound formula for determining wages is ever to be found, it should meet certain standards to be considered valid and acceptable. The more important tests that a practical and sound wage theory (or its determinants) would have to meet are:

1. Is it acceptable to the employer, the employees, and the public (consumers)?
2. Is it based on facts and systematic procedures?
3. Is it flexible enough to accommodate changing technology?
4. Does it promote cooperation and prosperity?

A discussion and explanation of each of these criteria follow.

Is the Wage Theory Acceptable to the Employer, the Employees, and the Public?

At the heart of industrial relation problems today (of which compensation is a very large part) is the question of how to share the good fortunes (technology, progress, prosperity, etc.) of a business. Labor appears to be continually looking for higher wages and a larger share of the prosperity pie. The owners (investors) are likewise concerned about greater returns on their investments, while the customers (public) complain about higher costs and less value for their money. This means that some equitable share for each of these three major groups needs to be determined for each company. The share for each group does not need to be the same for every company or industry, but should be governed by the local conditions.

Traditionally, owners, by right of the company property they owned (tools, machines, equipment, and facilities) believed that they were entitled to all the profits of their company because of the money they had invested at a risk. This concept has been regularly attacked within the last 50 years by various groups of people (labor, clergy, etc.) to the extent that it has lost many of its followers. As the general public has become better educated, there has developed the belief that employees also risk their careers and opportunities in employment with a company; and therefore they, too, are entitled to share in the general prosperity of the company. Rightly or wrongly, many people believe this; and because they are reluctant to work for a firm that believes that all profits should go to the owners, the old property-right concept of exclusive rights to profits by the owners has been forced into a reexamination. The social scientists believe that employees can be more easily motivated when they can share in the prosperity of the firm; thus, there has developed a trend in a number of companies to allow the employees to share in the progress and profits of the concern. Managements are learning that this sharing of company prosperity is bringing together in closer alignment the goals of both management and employees, and thus these two groups are willing to work more cooperatively to achieve a common end.

For any wage theory to be practical, it must reasonably satisfy the three groups of people that are essential to the success of any enterprise — the employer, the employees, and the consuming public. Each of these three groups plays a vital role in a firm's existence. Without the customer there would be no need for a company or its employees. Without management to coordinate the company's activities and to secure investors to loan money to the company for tools, machines, and facilities, the firm could not produce its product or render its service. Without employees the product or services could not be rendered. Although it is impossible to satisfy every person in these three groups, it is believed that most people are reasonable and can be satisfied with a wage structure that considers their various needs and expectations. In order to identify what a wage formula would have to contain to be acceptable to these three groups, an analysis of their expectations follows.

Employer's Expectations. The employer is generally considered to be the management group or team of each company. These persons are charged with the responsibility of seeing that the firm is productive (efficient), healthy, and sound, and continues in business because it is making a profit or rendering a worthwhile service. The management is expected to coordinate the interests of its employees, the owners, and the consuming public.

Management is generally considered to represent the owners (stockholders) of the firm because it is the owners who have hired management to manage the business. Management, therefore, is expected to see that the owners, who have risked their money to purchase the needed machines, tools, supplies, and facilities with which to conduct the business, receive a fair return (interest) on their financial investment.

Investors expect a greater return on their money from a company than they do from a bank because bank deposits (up to $15,000) are guaranteed against losses while loans to a company are not. Thus, a risk is involved because the firm may fail and the owners may lose their money. This means that to satisfy the investors, a wage formula must provide for an adequate return on the dollars invested by the stockholders or owners. The wages or salaries paid to the employees must not be so unreasonably high that the investors' returns are less than they would receive if they had loaned their money to a bank or some other safe financial institution. Investors' expectations, on the other hand, cannot be such that they will receive all the so-called profits made by the company. The employees are also risking their careers and talents and are therefore entitled to an equitable share of the good fortunes of the company.

There is no hard-and-fast rule or standard as to what a fair return is on money invested at a risk by the stockholders. The rate of return varies according to the individual complex of factors found in each particular company. However, a fair return may be approximated by finding out the average return paid by other companies of a similar nature.

If the management (employer) is to practice good management, its chief concern is to control costs by keeping all costs, particularly wages and salaries, commensurate with results. No economic system or firm can pay wages that are not earned. This means that wages and salaries are a cost of production and that increases in compensation have to be justified through increased productivity. It means that men and machines must continually produce so that unit costs are competitive with competing firms. Unless an employee does a fair day's work each day, his company cannot be competitive nor offer much security to its employees. If employees are to do a fair day's work each day, there has to be some method of measuring work to determine what a fair day's work is. Thus, there is a need for measuring work and setting standards by which to evaluate the productivity and results of employees.

Good management also realizes that wages and salaries need to be adequate to meet employer competition in the area. Employee compensation needs to be high enough to attract and recruit competent employees, to hire them, to motivate them to produce, and to reward them adequately for their results. Thus, good management requires that compensation rewards be based mainly on merit rather than on seniority. Finally, the employer is interested in keeping compensation disputes and grievances to a minimum.

Employees' Expectations. Wages, to the employee, are the price he charges for his skill, ability, physical strength, and time. Most employees expect that any compensation formula will provide them with enough money to support their families and to be able to maintain a decent standard of living. Their pay should give them reasonable financial security during their working career as well as later in retirement. Most workers would like some guarantee that they will earn a minimum amount each week and that they will be protected against wage-rate changes and reductions in earnings. Walter Reuther, the president of the auto workers' union, believes employees should have a guaranteed annual wage or salary just as management does because the worker also has expenses every week. Furthermore, employees believe they should receive their fair share of the company's prosperity and progress because they helped make this possible. They also find it difficult to understand why everyone should not be included in any bonus plan the company may have.

Employees are concerned that their pay be fair in comparison to other employees. They feel they should make good money when they work hard and have the opportunity to earn extra money when they work harder. They want a fair day's pay for a fair day's work. This means that there must be some satisfactory way to determine a fair day's pay for a fair day's work. Whichever method is used for this measurement, it should be based on accurate data rather than on arbitrary guesswork.

Since the Taft-Hartley Law has made it clear that wages, hours, and working conditions are topics that may be bargained for, employees feel that they should have some voice in the determination of their wages or at least have an avenue of appeal in the event that they are dissatisfied with their wages.

Employees today are suspicious of any pay plan that they do not understand. Past experiences with complicated pay plans have sometimes appeared to be management's schemes that were not fair to the worker. Employees, therefore, are not likely to accept a complicated plan that they cannot understand nor one which has not been fully explained to them.

In short, the employee expects a fair wage which, to him, means enough money to live according to the average standard of living similar to those who perform the same or similar type of work.

Public's Expectations. Public expectations of a compensation formula represent those of the community, society, and the consumer. The community and society expect that the employer will pay at least a living wage. This is important to the community because without a living wage, workers may have to be placed on welfare and have to be partially supported by the community. Such an employer would not be considered a good citizen in his community. Society, through the state and federal governments, has continually exerted pressure on the employer to pay a living wage by passing minimum wage laws.

While society is concerned about wages being too low, it is also concerned that the employer keep his costs and selling prices within the framework of value received. Customers are the sole reason for an organization to offer a product or a service. Without the customer, there can be no jobs. Customers expect that the product or service they purchase from the employer will be worth its purchase price. Since direct and indirect compensation costs can be as much as 75 percent of the selling price, the customer is concerned that these costs are not only merited but also fair and just. The "do-it-yourself" movement of people in painting, building, decorating, and other household jobs such as cutting children's hair is ample evidence that some craftsmen have priced themselves out of the market. Occasionally, the public goes on a "buyer's strike" and refuses to buy a product or service because it believes it would not receive adequate value for the cost of the product or service.

In summary, probably the most important test that any wage determinant, theory, or pay formula has to meet is its acceptability to the three groups of people who can make or break the company. Hence, their expectations can be tied to the various economic, legal, ethical, psychological, social, historical, and political aspects of the problem.

Is the Wage Theory Based on Facts?

Whatever wage formula is used to determine a wage or a salary, the compensation should be established and administered on the basis of facts and systematic procedures. Employees will not accept results based on guesses or arbitrary decisions. Such decisions, if used, eventually produce inconsistent results and cause employees to distrust management, even when management is sincere in its attempts to determine a fair wage or salary. Whenever the facts are lacking, they must be found. If the situation is so new that facts are unobtainable, this should be made clear to all concerned, and a committee of well-respected, competent persons should be appointed to arrive at a sound and acceptable decision. This will prevent employees from being underpaid or overpaid; thus, compensation inequities and complaints should be few in number.

Is the Wage Theory Flexible?

Any wage theory that is to stand the test of time must be flexible enough to accommodate the changes that continually occur in a dynamic society. In an earlier chapter, it was pointed out that increasing productivity is a necessity as long as our population continues to increase or as long as employees wish to increase their standard of living. To produce more with the same amount of human effort through technological improvement is a sound economic and social objective that discards the false philosophy of make-work and featherbedding and the erroneous idea that machines take the bread out of the workmen's mouths. To increase productivity, new and better tools, machines, and methods must be discovered. If a compensation formula prohibits or restricts technological improvements, little progress can be made. Therefore, a wage-payment plan must be flexible enough to work under changing conditions.

Does the Wage Theory Promote Cooperation and Prosperity?

A successful wage determinant should result in the employer and the employees working peacefully to promote the prosperity of the employees, the company, and the public. Any factor that in determining wages causes strife and industrial warfare weakens the firm and the security that goes with the company.

Summary

In summary, any pay plan or formula for determining wages and salaries should attempt to do the following:

1. Establish logical and justifiable relationships between the different amounts of compensation paid. This provides validity to the formula.
2. Provide a prudent man with enough compensation for him to establish and maintain the standard of living that is comparable to his job and standing in the community. This will attract him to the job.
3. Reward the employee commensurate with his contribution to the success of the company. This will keep him from quitting the job.
4. Be equitable to capital (the return to stockholders on their investment), to labor (a fair day's pay for a fair day's work), and to the public (getting the best product at the lowest cost). This is proof the formula is fair.

Having identified the criteria or tests that a sound wage determinant, formula, or theory has to meet, we can proceed to examine some of the earlier wage theories to learn what their strengths and weaknesses were and then proceed to an analysis of present-day theories and the various yardsticks that are now being used to determine wages and salaries.

Wage theories

A brief review of various traditional and contemporary wage theories will convince the student of wage and salary administration that *there is no single wage theory or formula that could be accepted by both labor and management as a common ground for settling disputes.* From time to time, both sides have made claims, often borrowing from economists whose theories were contradictory and, furthermore, usually were not compatible with twentieth century industrial progress. No classical wage theories have ever been put into actual practice to solve what has been termed the "eternal wage problem." The question arises, "To what degree does business behavior follow the theories postulated by economists in order to make decisions and determine wages?" One economist's answer is, "To a very limited extent."[2] Ask a manager of any large or small enterprise which theory he has accepted as a guide for wage determination. Invariably the answer will be, "We do not follow any of the theories found in economics textbooks. We use good, practical common sense to tie up wages with the many factors involved in offering the best product at lowest cost." The factors are these: simplest design of product, progressive means to obtain highest production, effective means of distribution, enough profits to offer the best compensation methods at the collective bargaining table and, at the same time, to be able to pay dividends.

---

[2]See Albert Lauterbach, *Man, Motives, and Money; Psychological Frontiers of Economics* (Ithaca: Cornell University Press, 1954).

The early theories were founded by political economists who used them as a working hypothesis in wage controversies favoring either labor or capital. The theories thus vary according to the social and economic outlook of the times in which they were written. Most of these theories are not valid today. It appears that of all the early economists, only Adam Smith emerged from an impressionistic hypothesis to some realistic facts. In analyzing production and productivity, he stressed specialization of labor, predicting the benefits of mass production and the currently recognized bargaining and productivity theories of wages. As early as 1776, he accurately predicted that demands for higher wages would increase with the growth of national wealth. In his wage doctrine, he agreed with the productivity theory, placing himself strongly in favor of the worker's aspirations by claiming:

> . . . The comfortable hope of bettering his condition, and of ending his days perhaps in ease and plenty, animates him to exert that strength to the utmost. Where wages are high, accordingly, we shall always find the workman more active, diligent, and expeditious, than where they are low.[3]

To provide the reader with a better understanding of the problem of determining wages and salaries, we shall describe the more popular wage theories that have thus far been advanced.[4] It is hoped that by a discussion of such theories, some "food for thought" will generate some new ideas that could crystallize into a future wage theory that would be acceptable to the employer, the employees, and the public.

The Just Price Wage

The *just price wage* (also referred to as the *just wage*) can be defined as that wage which will permit a person to live in a manner comparable to his job or station in life. Thus, the more prominent a position a man holds, the higher would be his just wage.

This theory was one of the earliest of the wage theories known to have a continuing influence on society.[5] Although the idea of the just wage is believed to have been stated by Plato (427–347 B.C.) and Aristotle (384–322 B.C.), it was reestablished by St. Thomas Aquinas (1225–1274 A.D.) and became the guiding philosophy of his era[6] and a few hundred years thereafter. The just price wage theory came about and gained wide acceptance in the Middle Ages because an increasing proportion of workers (artisans and craftsmen) had achieved the right

---

[3]Adam Smith, *An Inquiry into the Nature and Causes of Wealth of Nations* (Edinburgh, Scotland: Adam and Charles Black, 1863), p. 37.

[4]For a more complete and comprehensive discussion of wage theories, see H. G. Heneman, Jr., and Dale Yoder, *Labor Economics* (Cincinnati: South-Western Publishing Co., 1965), chaps. 20–22.

[5]*Ibid.*, p. 571.

[6]James M. Greene, "An Analysis of Scientific Management Wage Theories," *Advanced Management* (November, 1959), p. 17.

to sell their services for wages (for most workers were serfs or slaves supported by their masters). As greater numbers of workers offered their skills for sale to potential employers, the need arose to determine the price of labor.

The just price of an article was the price that was adequate, but no more than adequate, to cover the cost of production and based on the accustomed standards of living of the producers concerned.[7] A just price must be adequate to assure the continued availability of goods. A just wage must assure the continued availability of the services of independent craftsmen. Hence, wages should be set at a level that would permit craftsmen to live and to support their families on a scale that would maintain these supplies.[8] It was not assumed that the just price and the just wage could be determined with any great degree of accuracy, but they did serve as a guide in the conduct of exchange as well as in relationships among men. Based on the idea of a common Father and the brotherhood of men, the just wage theory assumed that men should behave as brothers and that no one should take advantage of another.

The strengths of the just wage theory appear to be twofold: (1) it assured the continued availability of the services of independent craftsmen, and (2) the employee was to be considered as a human being and paid as such, rather than treated as a commodity. Thus, human dignity, one of the more important factors in determining wages, was identified. This has been the major influence of the just wage theory on modern-day wage theory.

The weaknesses of the just price theory appear to be several: (1) an employee was unable to earn more wages than his present station in life called for; therefore, he could not raise himself to a higher station in life, (2) the theory conflicted with the realities of an economic enterprise in which wages are a cost of production and have to be earned through adequate productivity; otherwise, the just wage could put the employer out of business, (3) the theory failed to identify more than one factor (the ethical question) that is involved in wage determination, and (4) common acceptable standards as to what is just are still not clear nor agreed upon.

Modern theologians have indicated that a just wage must meet two requirements or tests of justice, namely, commutative justice and social justice. Commutative justice deals with the relations between individuals, while social justice deals with the relations between the individual and society. Let us briefly examine each of these tests of justice.

Commutative justice requires the exchange of value for value between the employer and the employee. For this reason it is sometimes called exchange justice. Since labor is considered one of the factors of production, its contribution or service toward that production has an economic value or price. The just

---

[7]*Ibid.*, p. 18.
[8]Heneman and Yoder, *op. cit.*, p. 572.

price is the market price determined under conditions of free and fair competition, apart from any influence of fraud, collusion, or monopolistic control of supply. Usually the price varies somewhat due to geographical factors, supply and demand, the efficiency among firms, etc. These various prices or values are often referred to as the going values or rates. An employee receiving a going wage (his wage is not lower than the lowest wage nor higher than the highest wage paid for his type of service) is receiving commutative justice. (Going wages may be determined by means of wage surveys, which are treated in Chapter 13.)

Social justice (or distributive justice) requires that society distribute to the worker a living wage in return for his contribution (or productive efforts or services) to society. A living wage is one that will enable a normal family of four (husband, wife, and two children) to meet the minimum living standards of health and decency. This amount has been estimated to be at least $100 per week in the United States. It would no doubt vary from country to country according to their economic productivity and conditions. (The cost of living and various standards and levels of living are treated in greater detail in the latter part of this chapter.) In general, commutative justice and social justice are met when the wage the employee is receiving falls within the going rates for his type of job, and this wage is adequate for him to support his family according to the minimum demands of health and decency.

Classical Wage Theories

From the height of the popularity of the just price wage theory to 1870, economists became much concerned about wages as they recognized payments for the services of labor as a major cost of production. They therefore began to theorize about what forces determine the prices paid for labor. Two wage theories that appeared, and have been considered classical theories ever since, are the subsistence wage theory and the wage fund theory.

The Subsistence Wage Theory. This theory, credited to David Ricardo (in 1817), related wages to population, labor supply, and subsistence. According to the theory, wages in the long run should naturally be set at the subsistence level (the wage that was only enough to provide food, clothing, and shelter) because this was the cost of producing and maintaining the labor force. The theory implied that if there is a temporary scarcity of labor, the wages will advance beyond that of strict necessity (subsistence) and in turn will cause more workers to marry and produce families; thus, the population will increase. The increase in population will then cause an oversupply of labor, which in turn lowers wages to a subsistence level.

The subsistence wage theory has generally been proven invalid, especially in those industrial countries where wages have continually been above the subsistence level. In the United States, where the average worker has for several decades been paid more than the subsistence level, there appears to be no lowering of wages to the subsistence level as a result of any population increases. Furthermore, this theory would never be acceptable to labor in the United States because its workers expect more than a subsistence wage and therefore would probably refuse to work for mere subsistence. On the other hand, the subsistence wage theory presently appears to apply to a limited extent in some of the nonindustrialized countries of the world.

Wage Fund Theory. The wage fund theory, advanced by John Stuart Mill in about 1837, held that employers had a given amount of money available for wages and each employee's share was determined by dividing the number of workers into the amount in the fund. Thus, wages would rise or fall with fluctuations in either the population growth or the size of the wage fund or both.

The wage fund theory would be unacceptable to labor today for several reasons. First, the wages were the same for all workers regardless of a worker's efficiency, seniority, or job difficulty. Second, if more workers were hired, each worker's proportionate wage share was decreased. Third, if a worker were to get an increase in wages, the number of workers had to be decreased. Thus, if one worker were to get ahead, another worker had to take a loss or the gain had to be at his expense. Economists William Thornton and Francis Wacker were very critical of this theory, and in 1869 Mill himself rescinded the wage fund doctrine, which led to the decline of the theory's influence.[9]

Although the wage fund theory failed to make clear what determined the amount of the fund, there are several wage incentive plans today (Scanlon, Rucker, Kaiser) that utilize the concept that a fixed percentage of money is to be given to labor. It would appear, as a result of this theory, that people were beginning to realize that sooner or later some method of determining an equitable way of splitting the economic pie would be needed.

In summary, the classical wage theories attempted to explain wage determination over the long term (subsistence wage theory) and over the short term (wage fund theory). In both theories, the worker had practically no opportunity to raise himself above his station in life. The theories may be looked upon today as having served as a catalyst to make people aware of the need for a sound wage theory and to stimulate thinking so that newer theories could be advanced.

Productivity Theories

Productivity theories concentrate on the relationship between wages, productivity, and employment. The theories usually emphasize the relationship between the wages and the productivity. They attempt to determine the productivity of labor and base the payment of wages according to this value. The

---

[9]Charles Brennan, *Wage Administration* (Homewood, Ill.: Richard D. Irwin, Inc., 1959), chap. 2, p. 15.

first ideas on the productivity theory were pioneered in about 1826 by Johann Heinrich Von Thünen, a German economist, but they did not receive much attention because the subsistence and wage fund theories were the vogue. However, by 1898 these classical theories had faded and two economists, John Bates Clark (an American) and Philip Henry Wickstead (an Englishman), are now considered chiefly responsible for advancing the marginal productivity theory.[10]

Marginal Productivity Theory. According to this theory, the wage that is paid to an employee should be equal to the extra value of productivity that he adds to total production (the other factors of productivity are assumed to remain constant). The value of the worker's production is determined by the return the employer can get for the worker's productivity. If all factors of production are kept constant, only a certain amount of production can be obtained. For every new employee hired, production will increase up to a point of diminishing returns when productivity per worker begins to decline. The employer can still continue to hire more workers as long as the wages he pays the worker are less than the income he gets from the sale of the increased production. However, as the employer continues to hire more workers, a point is eventually reached where the last worker hired just produces enough production to pay his wages. This last worker is called the marginal worker, and the increased production attributed to him is called the marginal productivity of labor; hence, the name, the marginal productivity theory of wages. The wage of the worker is equal in value to the production attributed to him, and his wage determines the wages of all workers since they are all doing similar work and are assumed to be of equal efficiency.

The concept of basing wages on productivity, as has been pointed out, is one of the early twentieth century theories. Most of its development took place within the first third of this century. However, its theory has continued to expand and be modified, and to this day is considered to be an important concept in determining wages.[11] Prominent contemporary economists, including Senator Paul H. Douglas and the late Professor Sumner H. Slichter, are on record as being strong advocates of the productivity theory of wages. Slichter has said, "It is high time that all groups in the community realize that real wages are tied to productivity and that collective bargaining cannot raise real wages faster than output per man-hour."[12] Senator Douglas, as a former professor, measured in some detail the increase in real wages as related to the increase in productivity. He pointed out that when productivity per worker was static, real wages were relatively constant.[13]

---

[10]*Ibid.*, p. 15.

[11]Heneman and Yoder, *op. cit.*, p. 587.

[12]Sumner H. Slichter, "Comments on the Steel Report," *Review of Economics and Statistics* (November, 1949), p. 288.

[13]See Paul H. Douglas, "The Modern Technique of Mass Production and Its Relation to Wages," *Proceedings of the Academy of Political Science* (July, 1927), pp. 17–42; Paul H. Douglas, *Real Wages in The United States* (New York: Houghton-Mifflin Company, 1930).

The United Auto Workers (UAW-CIO), International Ladies Garment Workers' Union (ILGWU), AFL, Machinists' Union, and other AFL unions recognized this principle as part of their wage determination formulas. They are cognizant of the fact that a wage formula can be economically sound only if directly related to productivity which has been increased through technological changes or the direct efforts of the workers.

Although the productivity theory of wages is still considered by many to be proper and just because workers are compensated on the basis of their productivity, there are a few difficulties connected with the theory.

First, it is many times impossible to know, much less to measure accurately, the amount of productivity that labor has solely contributed. If a firm has increased its productivity a certain percentage each year, what part of this can be attributed to labor? Everyone knows that there are other factors besides labor which affect productivity. Suppose all the productivity increases have been due to technology (or new machines) in which labor now actually does less work and finds the work easier? To add to the complexity of the problem, can labor's productivity be accurately measured while the other factors of production are in a constant state of change?

Second, it is important to realize that factors other than labor effort influence marginal productivity of labor. What relative weight or importance should be attached to the other factors? And how do you measure them? What is a fair and just reward that should be given to each of these factors?

Third, we have inadequate information on many of the forces behind the scenes that affect the factors of production. For example, do we know enough about the supply of labor, the demand for labor, the mobility of labor, the wants of buyers (and markets), and the needs of employers?

Lastly, the marginal productivity theory is a wage theory for the economy as a whole, but for the individual firm it is more a theory of employment. This is true because for the economy as a whole, the quantity of labor is relatively fixed and wages are the primary variable. For the individual firm the wage rate which may be paid is set within fairly narrow limits by competition for labor in the market, and employment is the primary variable.[14]

Even though the marginal productivity theory has its limitations, it has proved useful, especially in agriculture and in manufacturing. The average employee today is beginning to realize that higher wages can be earned only through higher productivity. The theory has also provided insight into some of the other variables (employment) that are part of wage determination. Such an understanding has led to modifications of wage determination and wage payment plans. A description of one of these modifications follows.

---

[14]Allan M. Cartter, *Theory of Wages and Employment* (Homewood, Ill.: Richard D. Irwin, Inc., 1959), p. 45.

Productive Efficiency Theory. The productive efficiency theory of wages is a refinement of the marginal productivity theory in that each worker is given a chance to increase (or decrease) his wages according to his productive efficiency as well as his productivity. This theory assumes that whenever a worker is given the opportunity to increase production through performance standards, his earnings will increase accordingly. On the other hand, his earnings will remain at an average or below the average level if his efficiency is below the performance standard adopted. Implied in the assumption that a worker will strive to increase his wage, if given the opportunity, is that he will be provided with the means to increase his production — standardized equipment, materials, methods, tools, working environment, etc.

Many contemporary economists and management authorities believe that, because of its realistic application, the productivity theory is the most constructive of the recent wage theories. Nevertheless, other factors, some of which have been mentioned in relation to marginal productivity, must be considered fundamental and cannot be overlooked when wage levels and salaries are determined. They are as follows:

1. Wage rates and salaries differ in geographical areas according to the standard of living and the cost of living.
2. Wages and salaries differ in the same locality or between localities according to grades of occupations.
3. Wages and salaries differ between localities according to variations in the skills and aptitudes of workers performing similar jobs.
4. Wages and salaries differ in the same locality or in different localities according to the supply and demand of workers in the respective professions, occupations, or trades, as well as according to their bargaining power.
5. Wages and salaries differ according to the creativeness and progressiveness of management, engineering, and marketing forces.

Tables 5.1, 5.2, and 5.3 contain facts and statistical figures to substantiate these fundamentals.

In summary, the productive theories of wages attempted mainly to relate wages and salaries according to production results. They are more analytical and less descriptive or empirical than the earlier wage theories. They sought to provide insight into functional relationships or general tendencies rather than to provide specific prescriptions that an employer could use in day-to-day wage and salary administration.[15] In spite of their difficulty in accurately measuring and equating wages to production, their fundamental concept has many advocates as evidenced by the large numbers of wage-payment plans that utilize this concept (profit sharing, progress sharing, bonuses, and other individual and group incentive plans).

---

[15]Heneman and Yoder, *op. cit.*, p. 607.

TABLE 5.1

DIFFERENCES IN AVERAGE HOURLY WAGE SCALES AND RANGES FOR SEVERAL UNION BUILDING TRADES (IN 100 CITIES)

TRADE	AVERAGE HOURLY WAGE	WAGE RANGE
Bricklayers................................	$5.86	$4.30–$6.60
Carpenters................................	5.55	3.70– 6.48
Electricians...............................	5.83	4.15– 7.10
Painters..................................	5.18	3.25– 5.98
Plasterers................................	5.49	3.63– 6.49
Plumbers.................................	5.92	4.45– 7.30
Building laborers..........................	4.06	2.07– 5.37
All trades................................	5.32	......

Source: United States Department of Labor: 10-414 Bureau of Labor Statistics (202) 961-3000 (May 6, 1969).

TABLE 5.2

SALARY DISTRIBUTION (AND DIFFERENTIALS) FOR FULL-TIME EMPLOYED SCIENTISTS BY FIELD, 1968

SCIENTIFIC AND TECHNICAL FIELD	LOWER DECILE	LOWER QUARTILE	MEDIAN	UPPER QUARTILE	UPPER DECILE
All fields............	$ 8,500	$10,400	$13,200	$17,000	$21,500
Chemistry..............	$ 8,500	$10,500	$13,500	$17,000	$21,000
Earth & marine sciences..	9,000	10,500	12,900	16,000	20,000
Atmospheric & space sciences..............	9,600	11,400	13,400	15,800	19,600
Physics.................	9,000	11,000	14,000	18,000	22,500
Mathematics.............	8,000	10,000	13,000	17,500	22,300
Computer sciences.......	10,300	12,000	14,100	17,000	20,300
Agricultural sciences.....	7,600	9,000	11,000	13,500	16,900
Biological sciences.......	7,500	10,000	13,000	17,600	23,000
Psychology.............	9,400	11,000	13,200	16,200	20,200
Statistics...............	10,200	12,000	14,900	18,200	22,000
Economics..............	9,800	11,700	15,000	19,000	24,000
Sociology...............	8,000	9,500	12,000	15,500	19,500
Political science.........	8,400	9,600	12,000	16,000	21,000
Anthropology...........	9,500	10,500	12,700	16,900	20,400
Linguistics..............	8,000	9,500	11,500	15,000	19,000

Source: National Register of Scientific and Technical Personnel, 1968.

TABLE 5.3

GEOGRAPHICAL AREA BASIC WAGE SCALE DIFFERENTIALS FOR UNION BUILDING TRADE WORKERS*

TRADE	ATLANTA, GA.	BUFFALO, N.Y.	CHICAGO, ILL.	CINCINNATI, OHIO	DALLAS, TEXAS	DENVER, COLORADO	DETROIT, MICH.	LITTLE ROCK, ARK.	LOS ANGELES, CALIF.	MILWAUKEE, WISC.	NEW YORK, N.Y.	ST. LOUIS, MO.	SEATTLE, WASH.	TAMPA, FLA.	WASHINGTON, D.C.
Bricklayers	$5.15	6.30	5.91	5.70	5.00	6.15	4.85	5.10	5.89	6.45	5.75	5.67	4.70	5.70	
Carpenters	$4.80	5.75	5.90	5.13	5.07	5.96	4.45	5.33	5.41	6.40	5.83	5.30	4.20	4.90	
Electricians	$5.70	6.70	6.20	5.23	5.67	6.25	5.25	6.10	5.87	5.67	5.65	5.85	4.80	5.90	
Painters	$5.30	5.65	5.23	4.78	4.88	5.45	3.85	5.60	5.16	5.20	5.36	5.21	3.75	4.97	
Plasterers	$4.92	5.58	5.13	4.77	5.10	6.07	4.44	5.40	5.02	6.10	5.75	4.88	4.48	5.07	
Plumbers	$5.45	5.85	6.06	5.37	5.26	5.96	4.79	5.79	5.77	5.85	6.26	5.90	4.90	5.81	
Building laborers	$3.05	4.45	4.80	2.88	3.55	4.65	2.85	3.97	4.68	5.20	4.53	4.60	2.70	3.33	

*These scales represent the minimum wage rates (excluding holiday and vacation payments regularly made or credited to the worker each pay period) agreed upon through collective bargaining between employers and trade unions. Rates rounded to closest penny.

Source: United States Department of Labor: 10-414 Bureau of Labor Statistics (20) 961-3000 (May 6, 1969).

Bargaining Theory of Wages

Although some ideas on this theory may be found in Adam Smith's 1776 writing,[16] it was not until about 1898 that John Davidson[17] proposed the theory that wages may be determined by a bargaining process between the workers and the employer. This concept was slow to take hold because it was introduced in an era in which the employer had very strong bargaining power. By 1929 the situation was slowly beginning to change. It was not until the 1930's, however, that the bargaining concept received a real impetus when the Wagner Act, which gave workers the right to organize and bargain collectively, was passed. Thus, the workers (and unions) were given a real opportunity to add strength to their bargain power and to cause the bargaining theory to become a reality and to this day remain as one of the leading methods for determining wages.

The bargaining theory of wages is based upon the assumption that there is no single wage rate for a particular kind of work. Instead, there is a range of possible wage rates. The upper limit of the range is determined by the highest wage the employer is willing to pay, and the lower limit is determined by the lowest wage for which the employee is willing to work. The employer and the workers bargain to determine the actual wage within the range that will be paid for the work. Thus, wages are determined by the relative economic bargaining strength of the employer and the employees.

The bargaining theory of wages may be regarded as a modification or an adaptation of the marginal productivity theory because it includes the union and can still function in the productivity theory framework. In advancing the bargaining wage theory, an effort is made to explain what happens in the labor market. According to this theory, employers are buyers of labor, which is considered a commodity. Workers are the sellers. For bargaining purposes, labor may be considered a commodity; but, in reality, labor is not a commodity that the purchaser (employer) can put into reserve. Labor cannot be separated from the worker for speculative investment. Nevertheless, buyers and sellers do bargain to determine what wage the worker is to receive. The final wage that is agreed upon will depend on the strengths of the buyer and seller. If the seller is strong, the wage will be high. If the buyer is strong, the wage will be low. If both parties are equal in strength, the wage will be very close to what the market determines the wage to be.

Union Impact on Wage Determination. It has been said that employees, bargaining individually, do not necessarily have the strength nor the ability to effect maximum wages and benefits from employers. This can be seen in the past when the old-time captains of industry kept their workers at a subsistence wage

---

[16]Smith, *loc. cit.*
[17]John Davidson, *The Bargaining Theory of Wages* (New York: G. P. Putnam's Sons, 1898).

level. Thus, the feeling arose that the workers could increase their chances of selling their services for a higher price if they could have a bargaining agent that represented all the workers. The recognition of the union as a legal institution and its great growth in the decades of the 1930's to the 1950's provided the employees with the bargaining agent necessary to engage in collective bargaining. That short period of "labor power" caused the bargaining theory of wages to attract more attention than at any other prior time. The assumptions and assertions that this theory is workable are justified if we consider the effective results attained during this short period.

After the drive to organize unskilled labor was launched in 1937, union membership increased to over 15 million within ten years. The rapid growth and strength of unions augmented their collective bargaining power, which gained notoriety as a wage-determination medium. Union leaders are firmly convinced that their influence improved living conditions and the general economic welfare through increased wage levels. They further claim that labor unions overbalanced the employees' traditional adherence to low wage levels. There are other claims, refuted by dependable United States Department of Labor Statistics, that through their bargaining power, unions have succeeded in obtaining nationwide uniformity in wages. As an examination of Table 5.3 shows, there is no nationwide wage uniformity for union building trade workers.

At this point it is not intended to give the impression that all employers persisted in low wage levels until unions forced the issue. Henry Ford, Sr., with his realistically practical doctrine of increased productivity and consumption, paved the way to higher wages without union demands. Similarly, a great many employers in medium-size and large industrial establishments may be credited with the aim to pay the highest wage within the respective industry without pressure from employees or unions.[18] For decades, manufacturing industries that never dealt with unions have raised wages periodically in spite of minor and major depressions.

It must be conceded, however, that labor union activities definitely influence the increasing of wage levels in well-organized union groups. To what extent wage levels should and can be raised solely through labor union bargaining is debatable, however, for once adequate and equitable wages are fairly established in an area or industry, they should not be increased merely by demand or pressure. Wage increases must be justified by gains in efficiency, productivity, and larger distribution of goods without additional expense. If unions disregard these fundamental considerations, inflation sets in and the economic structure of the nation is weakened. Usually, if there is a general increase in wages, prices rise and the increase in the amount of real wages is not in proportion to the increased amount of money wages. This is generally the aftermath even though the em-

---

[18]See James F. Lincoln, *Lincoln's Incentive System* (New York: McGraw-Hill Book Company, Inc., 1946).

ployer has done his utmost to attain maximum productivity through technological changes and additional specialized equipment. Concurrently, union bargaining power will have reached its limit unless the output per man-hour is somehow increased.

GM-UAW Bargaining Wage Formula. An excellent example of a bargaining wage formula is the General Motors (GM) two-year agreement of 1948 and the subsequent five-year agreement of 1950. After signing agreements with UAW-CIO (over 300,000 employees) and the IUEW-CIO in May, 1950, GM concluded negotiations with twenty international unions in over 100 different labor agreements covering 225 bargaining units.[19]

The GM original agreements with UAW in 1948 and 1950 provide annual improvement-factor wage increases under which employees participate in technological advancements and cost-of-living adjustments. The latter are hinged on the price index issued periodically by the United States Bureau of Labor Statistics (BLS). The GM agreement is based on a one-cent change in hourly wage rates for each 0.5 point change in the index. The cost-of-living agreement is termed an "escalator clause," which simply means that as the BLS index goes up, wages are increased; and as the BLS index goes down, wages are decreased. Significantly, the large union membership received the escalator clause more favorably than the leaders anticipated. The cost-of-living allowance was reduced by GM on three occasions, following decreases in the BLS index, with no noticeable dissatisfaction among the GM workers. This condition is a truly favorable reflection on GM leadership, their objectives, and wage policies, as well as the cooperation of progressive union leaders.

By the end of 1950, a great many unions, representing over 2 million members, adopted the GM-UAW wage agreement formula. It seems that this bargaining theory of wages has a sound basis since, according to one union leader, wages must be determined in terms of the economic realities. The ability to meet a particular wage necessarily depends on its relative efficiency and profit-producing possibilities.

Before leaving the bargaining theory of wages, a word should be said about some of its weaknesses. Pure bargaining power as a determinant of wages has the inherent weakness of viewing wages independently of other price relationships in the economy. The fact that the bargaining is over a wage within a range of possible wages emphasizes that factors other than economic are operating. Depending upon who has the most strength, extremely high or extremely low wages can result. It should be remembered that "strength" or "might" is not synonymous with what is "right." Extremely high wages are not equitable to the public nor to the owners. Extremely low wages are not equitable to the employee. It would appear that the determination of wages with all its determinants and

---

[19]See American Management Association *Personnel Series,* No. 136 (October, 1950).

problems is becoming so complex that collective bargaining may be inadequate to do the job in the future. For the past 20 years there have been continual rounds of wage increases won by unions. Some people believe this has been a cause of inflation since the wage increases have not always been earned through higher productivity. Others believe that unions and managements have worked in collusion to pass along unearned costs to the customer. In collective bargaining the public is not represented. This means that a corrupt or irresponsible union or management could take advantage of the public. Furthermore, there have been many wage strikes in the past 20 years, some of which have tended to disregard the public's interest by crippling the country's communications, defense industries, railroads, and other essential services. In 1963, the late President John F. Kennedy interceded to keep the steel companies from passing along wage increases for the public to pay. Finally, the questions should be asked, "Has the collective bargaining theory met the test of time?" "Will there be any real bargaining if either the employer or the employees succeed in achieving all or most of the collective bargaining power?"

Other Theories

There are many other theories about wages that have been advanced from time to time. Some of these theories have occasionally been used as a basis for arguments by unions and managements in their wage negotiations. The more prominent of the older and newer theories are the consumption theory of wages, the law of supply and demand, and the behavioral science theories of wage. Each of these will be briefly discussed.

Consumption Theory of Wages. This theory, also known as the *purchasing power theory*, had its inception in 1915 when Henry Ford, Sr., made the astounding announcement that he would pay a minimum wage of $5 a day, or about 100 percent higher than the prevailing wages. This action was considered a radical change in employer-employee relations. Many employers and economists deemed it the road to economic disaster, while others heralded it as a new wage theory. Mr. Ford's philosophy was that high money wages encourage greater consumption, increase the demand for more products, and thereby lower commodity prices. In 1920–1921 (war recession years), Ford increased the minimum wage to $6 per day and, during the depression of 1930, when most employers insisted on cutting wages to make profits, the Ford Motor Company raised the minimum wages for 100,000 employees to $8 per day. This step was heralded as an introduction of the equity principle (a fair day's wage) because Ford distributed his profits as a current wage rather than defer them for payment as a "profit share."

Mr. Ford's consumption theory won approval among industrialists and economists. Labor unions quickly adopted it as their own philosophy. It was accepted on the very simple supposition that high wages will encourage greater consumption, causing a larger distribution of consumer and durable goods, thereby creating more work for labor, increasing profits for employers, and lowering commodity prices.

The general well-being or prosperity in any country is measured by the consumption of all goods produced by agriculture, mining, and industrial development. But, as concluded from the bargaining theory and the productive efficiency theory, larger consumption can be induced by either one, two, or all three of the following means: (1) increasing individual productivity, (2) improving production methods, or (3) introducing specialized machinery. Here, Mr. Ford's philosophy takes on realism:

> It is not good management to take profits out of the workers or the buyers; make management produce the profits. Don't cheapen the product; don't cheapen the wage; don't overcharge the public. Put brains into the method, and more brains, and still more brains — do things better than ever before; and by this means *all parties to business are served and benefited.*[20]

Law of Supply and Demand. An investigation of the labor market will reveal that jobs requiring common labor command considerably lower wages than jobs requiring skill, because the supply of common labor is always proportionately greater than the supply of skilled labor. From this simple comparison, the reader can readily conclude that wages are governed by the law of supply and demand. If jobs are few and the supply of workers is plentiful, wages will fall. Conversely, if jobs are plentiful and there is a shortage of workers, wages will rise. In other words, there is no static equilibrium.

Although unskilled labor is now more steadily employed than fifty or sixty years ago, nevertheless, our industrial economy is not entirely adjusted to the point of regulating wages. This condition is not only prevalent among common laborers and shop workers but also among the so-called white-collar workers. Regional or geographical conditions, differentials in skills, as well as conflicting employer-employee relations, are deciding factors.

Behavioral Science Theories of Wages. Within the last few years there have been attempts by Jaques,[21] Belcher,[22] and others to integrate the findings of the behavioral scientists (psychologists, sociologists, anthropologists) into the past and present economic wage theories. These newer theories deal with wage levels of the firm, internal wage structures, individual wage determination, and wages as motivation.

---

[20]Henry Ford, *My Life and Work* (New York: Doubleday, Page and Company, 1924), p. 155.

[21]Elliott Jaques, *Equitable Payment* (New York: John Wiley and Sons, Inc., 1961).

[22]David W. Belcher, "Toward a Behavioral Science Theory of Wages," *Journal of the Academy of Management* (August, 1962), pp. 102–116.

Jaques relates pay to such factors as: the "time-span of discretion" in the job (length of time before an employee's superior needs to check the employee's work), the relationship between employee performance and his expected performance (as determined by an employee's expected growth curve which each employee is supposed to have, according to his age), and to the employee's special efforts (as motivated through a monetary reward). In short, Jaques' ideas are based upon the principles of the psychological growth of people and upon the social norms.

Belcher[23] has offered the following behavioral science implications that have a bearing on wage determination:

1. A behavioral science theory of wage level of the firm would include the following elements:
   a. the inducements-contributions utility balance
   b. the labor market as a social institution
   c. unions and employers as holders of power and influence
   d. nonfinancial rewards as substitutes for financial rewards

2. A behavioral science theory of internal wage structure would consist of the following elements:
   a. the force of social norms and tradition
   b. accommodation of sociologically diverse labor markets
   c. employers as wage-setting institutions
   d. the force of group power on the internal wage structure

3. A behavioral science theory of wages as motivation would deal with the following:
   a. basic motivations common to all individuals derived from basic individual needs and the common culture
   b. motives derived from reference groups and varying among the groups
   c. complexity of motivation in operation, i.e., multifactor, nonlinearity in effect, the possibility that some factors are positive motivators and others are negative motivators
   d. perceived alternatives and their consequences
   e. motivation as a function of organization design
   f. nonmotivated work

In concluding this section on wage theories, it should be kept in mind that all theories are speculative. They are the beliefs, ideas, or explanations of various individuals on what appears to be happening. They have not been proven through the test of time; otherwise, they would be considered laws. More research is needed to test these theories in order to improve them or to find the actual laws that are really in operation. Before such laws are discovered, the researchers need to find out much more about the forces behind each of the factors involved in wage determination.

---

[23]Adapted from David W. Belcher, "Toward a Behavioral Science Theory of Wages," *Journal of the Academy of Management* (August, 1962). Reprinted by permission.

Yardsticks commonly used in determining wages and salaries

The more common yardsticks that are used by the employer and the employee in determining wages and salaries are discussed in this section. Depending upon the circumstances, these yardsticks sometimes become the basis for both the unions and managements in arguing their cases in wage negotiations.

Ability to Pay

During the last few decades the ability-to-pay criterion has been a factor in the determination of wages. Management used it when certain wage demands were deemed to be excessive. Labor unions used it in times of prosperity, under the assumption that workers are entitled to their share of the excessive profits made by employers. Some economists used it as an "ethical proposition" to test the fairness of prevailing wages. From a purely business standpoint, employers oppose the ability-to-pay policy as a criterion for wage determination. Indeed, there are many different angles and problems to be considered before adopting this wage determinant.

General Principles. A proposal advanced in favor of the ability-to-pay criterion carries with it the assumption that our economy operates under perfectly standardized competitive conditions and that it has reached an equilibrium. Since our economy is rather complex and not balanced, the ability to pay cannot be accepted as a realistic solution to the problem of wage determination.

Management's Concept. Management is always on guard against paying more than necessary to attract the type of labor needed. Any increase in pay is usually offset or regulated by increased production without increasing the labor cost per unit, thus meeting the ability to pay. This is accomplished by applying standardization and work simplification principles, which are discussed in Chapter 15. Indirectly, then, the ability-to-pay principle always prevails even though it is not used as a wage criterion.

Attempts have been made to use the ability-to-pay principle in relation to the determination of selling prices.[24] This condition brings supply and demand as well as competition into the picture. The ability to pay higher wages is feasible if the additional cost can be transferred to the selling price without total sales being affected by competition. In the American free enterprise system, however, competition is keen and the profit-making factor predominates.

Labor Unions' Concepts. Labor unions continually demand that higher wages be paid out of profitable earnings. This raises the delicate question of how to divide earnings if no formal profit sharing plan has been agreed upon.

---

[24]See the discussion of the sliding scale as a method of wage payment, Chapter 17.

Hence, the criterion becomes one of profit sharing rather than ability to pay. On the other hand, if a union insists that wage payments be increased out of current earnings, the problem becomes one of determining the company earnings over short periods.

When a union presses for participation in the profits, such action may be very detrimental to both sides, unless both agree on some system of monthly production comparisons.[25]   The union would have access to company books, insist on a monthly profit and loss statement, and, in general, participate in running the business.   Insistence upon regulating the company's financial statements without capital investment could force the company out of business. Reports submitted to unions might reach competitors who would take full advantage of the information to increase production perhaps by means of different facilities, reduced costs, and lower selling prices.

We strongly recommend employer-employee cooperation and joint action in matters of work simplification, wage determination, job and employee evaluation, and stabilization of financial incentives. We do not believe, however, that management would agree to the aforementioned union concepts and principles, since such principles reflect socialistic or communistic philosophies.

The shoe industry in Brockton, Massachusetts, and its surrounding area, is a good example of a competitive enterprise in which unions caused extensive losses to employers, the closing of factories, and unemployment. Union leaders subsequently realized that competition limits the demand for wage increases and they explained their changed position with such statements as, "We realize that to drive our wage scale above what competition will stand is disastrous to all concerned."[26]

There have been instances where unions insisted on wage raises merely by estimating the ability to pay of companies. The position of companies would become so critical that they either had to go out of business or move to another city or state. Considering the catastrophic experiences of some shoe, hat, and metal-working industries, it appears that unions would usually make wage concessions, even to the extent of accepting radically reduced wages. In the Brockton shoe industry, for example, unions agreed to concessions such as the following: "We are in favor of offering to any and all manufacturers in the District a price low enough for them to bring back the business that has been lost to this District."[27]

A similar occurrence took place in Vassar, Michigan, where the AFL-UAW local union offered the management of the Eaton Manufacturing Company's foundry a reduction of 62 cents per hour (from $2.68 to $2.06) in order to prevent

---

[25]See the Scanlon Plan in Chapter 20, page 577, and the section on profit sharing, Chapter 20, page 569.
     [26]George P. Schultz, *Pressures on Wage Decisions* (New York: John Wiley & Sons, Inc. 1951), p. 132.
     [27]*Ibid.*

its closing. The management claimed that a "militant and noncompromising union" caused the foundry to lose its competitive position. The foundry, with a payroll of two million dollars, was the town's principal industry. The company stated that it would take 18 months to two years to regain the position it held in the competitive field before the closing announcement.[28] In view of union concessions, it is interesting to note that a union staff member admitted ". . . 'ability to pay' may be the single most important element in the union's formulation of wage policy."[29]

A Fair Day's Pay for a Fair Day's Work

For over fifty years, the AFL and other national labor unions used the slogan "A fair day's pay for a fair day's work." Later, management transposed the slogan to "A fair day's work for a fair day's pay." Each party made this its battle cry without giving a concrete definition of what is "fair" in relation to a day's pay or a day's work.

Similarly, whenever management and representatives of labor get together around the bargaining table, the discussions often turn into heated arguments over "fair wages," "just wages," and "satisfactory wages." No other terms have caused more differences of opinion than these three terms, especially when applied without distinctive interpretation. Seldom do those who argue for fair, just, and satisfactory wages actually give a clear definition. Yet, this is imperative if collective bargaining and wage and salary determination are to be firmly established. Fair, just, and satisfactory wages can be considered only in the light of what is deemed a fair day's pay, which, in turn, is related to a fair day's work.

A Fair Day's Pay. The concept of *fair* with regard to wages varies from one organization to another. Even two people within the same organization may not have the same interpretation of the term; it may mean *just, average,* or *equitable.* These terms, like the term fair, have no quantitative meanings. The synonym "just" would be reasonable if there is an understanding of what is right and what is wrong in conformance with a set standard. "Average" may be acceptable if there is a norm to go by in order to distinguish between high and low, thereby arriving at an average.

Invariably, fair and just wages are also related to equitable wages, which the worker has a right to as full compensation for his production. To what extent his wages may be regarded as equitable depends upon an evaluation of how much time he spent and how much skill, effort, ingenuity, and responsibility the worker exercised on his job. Thus, we may assume that *fair and just wages become satisfactory wages when the worker is convinced that his job has been properly*

---

[28]*Chicago Tribune* (June 17, 1955).
[29]Jack Barbash, *The Practice of Unionism* (New York: Harper and Brothers, 1956), p. 128.

classified, evaluated, and rated to a grade entitling him to a price for his labor that is equitable in accordance with the bargaining process. For wages to be accepted as fair, the worker must also be convinced that his wage-base rate, as well as his potential incentive wages, is at least the same as elsewhere in the community. Furthermore, an equitable wage, as referred to above, is the compensation based on a wage structure that reflects the requirements of a job in relation to other jobs (discussed in Chapters 6 through 13), and the worker's qualifications to perform the job.

A Fair Day's Work. The understanding of a fair day's work depends on using a definite norm as a standard. The norm can be attained if the work is analyzed and if work methods are determined. Then, by using measuring techniques and performance ratings (discussed and illustrated in Chapter 15), an average can be obtained that is the quantity of work to be produced per day by a qualified worker with average skill and effort. Hence, the standard of a day's work becomes a constant that may be considered fair, regardless of a day's pay. The fair day's pay (wage-base rate) is agreed upon by collective bargaining, or by the "going rate" in the community, which may fluctuate due to unforeseen conditions. But, once a work standard is accepted by mutual consent of labor and management, it should not be subjected to bargaining. It becomes a norm for a specific job like the established standard weight of a pound or the number of inches in a foot, which are not subject to bargaining. It is worth remembering at this point that a fair day's work is generally not attainable under time-wage payments, since in most cases no performance standards exist.

Standards of Living and Levels of Living

Standards of living and levels of living are common terms in a workingman's life. They influence the determination of wages and salaries mainly through collective bargaining. "Millions of workers' wages are adjusted periodically under their union contracts for changes in the 'cost of living,' which are almost invariably measured by the Bureau of Labor Standards consumer price index."[30] Even though there is a growing familiarity with and greater usage and publicity of these "living" terms, the relationship of "living" to wages is far from clear. In order to clarify the situation, we shall discuss what constitutes a standard of living and what income is associated with various levels of living. This should give the reader a better idea of how much compensation one needs for his labor or services in order to live according to a desired standard or level of living.

Standard of Living Defined. Of the many available definitions of the standard of living, Webster's dictionary gives one of the most useful for the compensation field. *Standard of living* is defined as "a minimum of necessities,

---

[30]George Leland Bach, *Economics: An Introduction to Analysis and Policy* (4th ed.; Englewood Cliffs, N.J.: Prentice-Hall, Inc., 1963), p. 76.

comforts, or luxuries that is essential to maintain a person or group in customary or proper status or circumstances."[31] "The standard of one's living is judged today in large measure by the number and kinds of durable goods and costly articles in his possession, as well as by his consumption of items yielding cultural and aesthetic satisfaction."[32] Figure 5.1 depicts the common categories and ingredients of which the standard of living is composed. The different standards of living that a person may attain are associated with the varying amounts and the quality of those items that go to make up his standard of living. We shall now describe several levels of living and the compensation that is associated with each one.

COMPONENTS OF A STANDARD OF LIVING	
Common CATEGORIES......	and some of their INGREDIENTS
G O O D S Food.................	Meats, fruits, vegetables, beverages, etc.
Clothing..............	Hats, coats, suits, shoes, etc.
Transportation..........	Plane, bus, car and its upkeep
S E R V I C E S Housing..............	Buy or rent house, furniture, appliances and utilities
Medical Care...........	Doctor and dentist, drugs, and insurance
Recreation.............	Sports, movies, reading materials, radio-TV, etc.

FIGURE 5.1   Common Categories and Ingredients of a Standard of Living

Levels of Living.   The nonmanagerial working class of people have been divided into four levels of living: (1) poverty level, (2) subsistence level, (3) health and decency level, and (4) comfort level. The main features of each of these levels are described below. Note that each of the levels of living has the three basic elements of food, clothing, and shelter, but varying amounts of the individual ingredients.

Poverty Level. The *poverty level* is the lowest level of living and is considered to be below the minimum standards of decency. It implies insufficient income for the basic necessities of life. On this living level, a family is not on a self-

---

[31]*Webster's Seventh New Collegiate Dictionary* (Springfield, Mass.: G. & C. Merriam Company, 1963).

[32]Theodore N. Beckman, *Credit and Collections: Management and Theory* (7th ed.; New York: McGraw-Hill Book Company, 1962), p. 130.

supporting basis, but exists because of inroads or serious encroachments that it makes upon its own health or upon its supply of material possessions. The family at this level of living resides in substandard housing with a diet usually below that considered essential for an adult male doing moderately heavy labor. Resources for recreation or unexpected expenses are nonexistent.

The United States Department of Labor has indicated what incomes are associated with the poverty level for a single person and for a family of almost any size whether on a farm or in the city.[33] (See Table 5.4). It should be made clear that *income is not identical to a wage or a salary received from the employer.* Income refers to the total amount of money received and thus includes wages and salaries as well as other sources of remuneration. A wage or a salary is not equivalent to take-home pay as there can be deductions for taxes, union dues, etc. On the other hand, *most wages and salaries that are stated do not include fringe benefits* which, on an average, amount to an additional 25 percent of total compensation. Not all employees would spend this fringe money for the same items. This means then that allowances need to be made in equating the income associated with the poverty level and a wage or salary.

TABLE 5.4

FAMILY INCOME ASSOCIATED WITH THE POVERTY LEVEL OF LIVING

| NUMBER OF PERSONS IN FAMILY | INCOME OF THESE AMOUNTS OR LESS IS CONSIDERED AS POVERTY* | | | | | | | |
| | NONFARM INCOME | | | | FARM INCOME | | | |
	YEARLY	MONTHLY	WEEKLY	HOURLY	YEARLY	MONTHLY	WEEKLY	HOURLY
1	$1,800	$150	$ 34.60	$ .86	$1,500	$125.00	$ 28.80	$ .72
2	2,400	200	46.15	1.15	2,000	166.67	38.46	.96
3	3,000	250	57.69	1.44	2,500	208.33	48.08	1.20
4	3,600	300	69.23	1.73	3,000	250.00	57.69	1.44
5	4,200	350	80.77	2.02	3,500	291.67	67.31	1.68
6	4,800	400	92.30	2.30	4,000	333.33	76.92	1.92
7	5,400	450	103.84	2.59	4,500	375.00	86.53	2.16
8	6,000	500	115.38	2.88	5,000	416.67	96.15	2.40
9	6,600	550	126.92	3.17	5,500	458.33	105.77	2.64
10	7,200	600	138.46	3.46	6,000	500.00	115.38	2.88
11	7,800	650	150.00	3.75	6,500	541.67	125.00	3.13
12 or more	8,400	700	161.53	4.04	7,000	583.33	134.62	3.37

*Amounts of income are based on a 40-hour week for a 52-week year (fringe benefits excluded).

Source: United States Department of Labor, 1969, as reported in *AFL-CIO News*, Vol. XIV, No. 49 (December 6, 1969), p. 7.

---

[33]*AFL-CIO News*, Vol. XIV, No. 49 (December 6, 1969), p. 7.

Subsistence Level. The *subsistence level* is slightly above the poverty level but is still considered an inadequate level of living by present "market basket" standards. Families living at this standard receive enough income for physical sustenance but not enough to meet the major emergencies of illness, accidents, and old age, or to enjoy social pleasures that cost money. Generally, subsistence level families will insist upon availing themselves of certain pleasures; consequently, they tend to be somewhat undernourished and appreciably overcrowded.

The American Institute of Public Opinion, better known as the Gallup Poll, gives an indication of the income associated with this level of living. The Gallup Poll asked this question: "What is the smallest amount of money a family of four (husband, wife, and two children) needs each week to get along in this community?" The results showed that the median average amount that the non-farm public thinks is the minimum that a family of four needs each week to get along is $120 (or $6,240 a year).[34] Another question in the poll revealed that the average nonfarm family spends about $33 a week for food.[35] We estimate that the annual income of $4,000–$6,500 is most closely associated with the subsistence level of living.

Health and Decency Level. The *health and decency level* of living is slightly above the subsistence level and is therefore sometimes referred to as the "subsistence plus" level. This level of living requires sufficient income to enable a family to house itself decently in four or five rooms, to purchase an adequate quantity of food containing sufficient calories to meet the family needs, and to buy reasonably priced but neat clothing. In addition, there should be a small balance of money for recreation and sundries. It is believed that the average urban family living at the health and decency level spends approximately 25 percent of their income for food, 10 percent for clothing, 30 percent for shelter, 15 percent for transportation, 7 percent for medical care, and 5 percent for recreation.[36] We estimate that the annual income of $6,500–$8,600 is most closely associated with the health and decency level of living.

Comfort Level. The *comfort level* of living is often thought of as the representative (median) American standard of living wherein a family is able to maintain a level of living, according to the prevailing standards of what is needed for health, efficiency, the nurture of children, and for participation in social and community activities. This level of living is much more liberal in its provisions for clothing, housing, insurance against industrial risks, amusement, and recreation than the health and decency level.

---

[34]George Gallup, American Institute of Public Opinion syndicated column in the *Milwaukee Journal* (January 25, 1970), p. 3, Accent Section.
[35]*Ibid.*
[36]Katherine R. Murphy, "Contrasts in Spending by Urban Families: Trends Since 1950 and Variations in 1960–61," *Monthly Labor Review*, Vol. 87, No. 12 (December, 1964), p. 1410.

An indication of the income associated with the comfort level of living can be gained by examining the median incomes of *families* in the United States. According to the Bureau of Census, Department of Commerce, the median income for all nonfarm families in 1962 was approximately $6,000; in 1965 it was $6,900; and in 1968 it was about $8,600.[37] The annual income that we most closely associate with the comfort level of living is whatever the annual median *family* income is of the typical American workman. See Table 5.5 for the annual median family incomes and what these are equivalent to on a monthly, weekly, and hourly basis. The table has been extended so that as annual median incomes rise in the years ahead, their equivalents in monthly, weekly, and hourly rates can be easily ascertained.

In 1970, the Bureau of Labor Statistics released a family budget study containing three standards of living for an urban family of four for the spring of

TABLE 5.5

**ANNUAL MEDIAN FAMILY INCOMES CONVERTED INTO
MONTHLY, WEEKLY, AND HOURLY AMOUNTS**

YEAR	MEDIAN FAMILY INCOME			
	ANNUAL	MONTHLY	WEEKLY	HOURLY
1962	$6,000	$500	$115	$2.88
1965	6,900	575	133	3.32
1968	8,600	717	165	4.13
↑	8,800	733	169	4.23
	9,000	750	173	4.33
	9,200	767	177	4.42
F	9,400	783	181	4.52
U	9,600	800	185	4.61
T	9,800	817	189	4.72
U	10,000	833	192	4.81
R	10,200	850	196	4.90
E	10,400	867	200	5.00
	10,600	883	204	5.10
Y	10,800	900	208	5.19
E	11,000	917	212	5.29
A	11,200	933	215	5.38
R	11,400	950	219	5.48
S	11,600	967	223	5.58
	11,800	983	227	5.67
↓	12,000	1,000	231	5.77

Source: United States Department of Labor and the Bureau of Census, as reported in *AFL-CIO News*, Vol. XIV, No. 34 (August 23, 1969), p. 8.

[37]The Bureau of Census, as reported in *AFL-CIO News*, Vol. XIV, No. 34 (August 23, 1969), p. 8.

1969. To maintain a moderate living standard at that time, a family required an annual income of $10,077.[38] Today, this figure would be even more. The Bureau also reported a "lower" annual budget of $6,567 that would maintain an "austere" standard for a family of four. In addition, the study reported a "higher" annual budget of $14,589 for a fuller, more expansive life.

All three budgets assume that maintenance of health and social well-being, the nurture of children, and participation in community activities are desirable and necessary goals. The consumption expenditures for food, housing, transportation, clothing, medical care, gifts, education, and recreation account for 82 percent of the low budget, 79 percent of the moderate budget, and 76 percent of the higher budget.

It would appear that the Bureau's "lower" budget and our health and decency level of living are similar. However, the moderate budget is higher than the comfort level, while the Bureau's higher budget appears to be on the edge of a "luxury" level.

Standards of Living Limitations. On an overall basis, the standard of living, at best, is useful only as a broad guideline for determining the wages or salaries that are in keeping with various levels of human dignity. The limitations of using the standard of living as a basis for determining wages and salaries are many. Precise and concrete standards have not, as yet, been agreed upon. It is difficult to establish valid standards because of the many dynamic variables, such as individual differences in values, requirements, tastes, and managing money, that are involved. Different geographical locations, fringe benefits, buying habits, and size of family are also influential. Another limitation of the standard of living is that the income associated with it is not synonymous with a wage or a salary. Adequate allowances need to be made for fringes and payroll deductions before income and standard of living can be equated. The Consumers' Price Index appears to be a useful device for indicating whether the costs for a standard of living are rising or falling.

The Value of the Job and the Employee

More than any other consideration, today's determination of an employee's total wage or salary appears to be based on the value of the job and the value of the employee to the company. Most companies, whether they realize it or not, use some form of job evaluation to determine the relative value or importance of the job to the company. The companies likewise use some form of merit rating or employee evaluation to determine the relative value of the individual to the firm. Thus, the combined values of the job and the employee form the basis for his total compensation.

---

[38]"Urban Family Income Needs Rise Above $10,000 Level," *AFL-CIO News*, Vol. XV, No. 3 (January 17, 1970), p. 1.

In using these two factors to determine a wage or a salary, the relationship between the job and the individual should be clarified. It is already known that jobs ordinarily do not increase at a uniform rate of complexity. This is one reason why it is said that executive positions are worth a great deal more than the lower level jobs. It should be likewise recognized, however, that the part an individual plays in the success of a job varies greatly. For example, at the one extreme (the unskilled or "muscle" jobs) the duties are very routine, relatively simple, and such that any person not physically handicapped can perform the job. There is very little difference between the performance of one worker or another doing similar jobs. This is another way of saying that the nature of the job does not allow the individual to exert much individuality. Because of this condition, some people would say that the job "makes the employee."

If one looks at the other extreme of jobs or positions (executive, professional, or "brain" jobs), the duties are generally diversified, complex, and can be performed by only a small number of persons. Of those who can perform the duties of the position, the results are usually different due to the individual differences of persons. Positions of this nature depend on the individual abilities of the person holding the job or position. This means, then, that at the higher job levels the individual really "makes the job or position," since it is what the person puts into the job that governs its success or failure. This concept is graphically illustrated for general comparison in Figure 5.2. From the diagram in Figure 5.2, it should be observed that as an employee advances in rank in a company due to his ability, a greater percentage of his pay should be based more on the part he plays as an individual and less on the job or position he holds. If this concept is kept in mind, it should be easier to understand and to determine the relationship between the job and the individual in determining the pay of an employee.

In appraising the relative values of the job and the employee to determine compensation, it should be apparent that many of the factors previously discussed such as productivity, labor supply and demand, bargaining power, motivation, ability to pay, the standard of living, and efficiency are a part of this concept. It is, therefore, a very useful method of determining pay as long as the employees and the employer can agree on the criteria used in the evaluations and if it also serves the public interest.

Summary and conclusion

In this chapter an attempt was made to identify the various wage theories and yardsticks that have been advanced for the determination of wages and salaries. An attempt was also made to cite the tests that any wage determinant would have to meet. At present, there is no specific theory or special single formula that can be used in wage determination. Traditional and contemporary theories should be examined in view of origin and today's economic conditions.

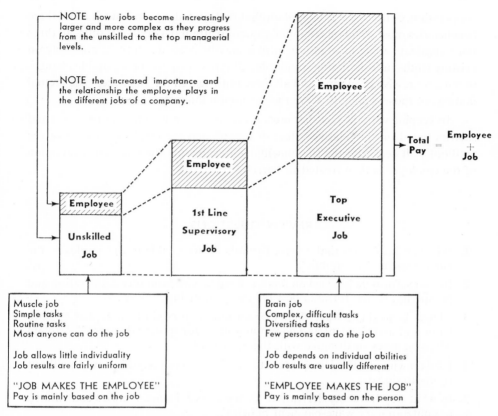

FIGURE 5.2 The Theoretical Relationship Between the Job and the Employee

It is apparent, however, that some wage theories resolve themselves into a few logical and practical principles that affect wage determination. So long as we do not approve of socialism or communism, the governing factors in wage determination seem to be collective bargaining, production costs, and productivity. Capitalistic enterprise with its profit system must rely on productivity, marketing, and distribution for profits to pay wages, salaries, and dividends.

Any policy to establish proper compensation will constantly be affected by variables involving the employer, employee, and consumer. All are interested in the ultimate results, however, even though the interest of each is divergent or directed into different channels. The employee's main interest rests in the equity of his wage differential, the security of his job, and increased real wages. The employer is willing to raise wages and salaries to the highest level if he can obtain a fair profit to pay dividends as the deserved interest on invested capital. The public desires to purchase commodities at the lowest prices. Thus, all three — employer, employee, and the public — have a common goal. All will benefit by cooperation, collective action, and mutual understanding. Inasmuch as all three beneficiaries must stand on common ground to attain the desired results, all three must eliminate waste in whatever form it may be present; all three must rely on existing truths in formulating standards; all three must accept inevitable changes in our progressive economy; and all three must search for and accept the factual findings of those willing to serve their common interests.

In keeping with the fact that most firms are presently determining wages and salaries based on the relative values of the job and the employee, Part 3 of the textbook will deal with the fundamentals of evaluating the job. The evaluation of the employee is then treated in Part 4.

REVIEW QUESTIONS

1. Why is it important that a wage formula be acceptable to the employer, the employees, and the public?

2. If a wage formula is based on facts, is flexible, and promotes cooperation and prosperity, is that formula best for every company? Why?

3. "There is no single wage theory or formula that could be accepted by both labor and management as a common ground for settling disputes." Explain why you agree or disagree with this statement.

4. Explain why you think employers today do or do not pay a just wage without trying to do so.

5. In what way have any derivations of the classical wage theories contributed to contemporary wage-payment policies?

6. Which wage theory do you feel comes closest to being the most fair and just to the greatest number of workers? Why?

7. Differentiate between the marginal productivity theory and the productive efficiency theory.

8. What role did the unions play in making the bargaining theory of wages feasible?

9. (a) Name the best-known contemporary wage theories. (b) Which is most applicable to present-day conditions?

10. (a) How are wages affected by an escalator clause? (b) Where and when did the escalator clause originate?

11. Is the productivity theory of wages acceptable? Explain in detail, including the factors which must be considered when the theory is applied.

12. In what way is the consumption theory of wages identified with other wage theories? Explain.

13. Discuss the merits and demerits of the law of supply and demand theory of wages and the proposed behavioral science theory of wages.

14. Is it fair for labor unions to demand pay raises based on the company's ability to pay? Cite a case to support your answer.
15. What is the relationship between a fair day's pay for a fair day's work and work standards?
16. What relationship should the American standard of living have in determining the worker's wage?
17. Describe the standards of living applicable to the working class according to the four standards or levels established by the United States Department of Labor.
18. Why is it important that the value of the job and of the employee be considered when compensating an employee?

RESEARCH OR SEMINAR QUESTIONS

1. What action by the government can affect the wage and salary programs of established companies?
2. Do the economic "laws" that were explained in this chapter in any way still operate today? Explain.
3. Do you agree with the statement, "A man's pay is determined by the job and the operation of the man within the job"? Explain.
4. What are the advantages and disadvantages of tying wages to the cost-of-living index?
5. Where should the line be drawn between what you pay for the job and what you pay for the man?

PRACTICAL EXPERIENCE ASSIGNMENTS

1. Cite a job you have worked on and indicate, in the order of importance, the two most important factors you think should be used to determine the worth of that job. Tell why you chose these factors. Ask a relative what he considers to be the two most important factors that should be used to determine the worth of his job. What reasons does he give to justify the factors he chose?
2. Make up a list of all the factors and conditions that affect the determination of an individual's wage. Which is most important? Why?
3. Figure 5.2 on page 143 graphically portrays the relationship between the job and the individual. See what information you can get (at the library, from a company, or from friends, etc.) to supply monetary values or percentages to the figure.
4. Discuss Figure 5.2 on page 143 with a wage and salary administrator to get his ideas on how this concept can be better portrayed.

CASE PROBLEM

5 — 1. The Quick Loan Finance Company

Determination of Wages and Salaries

The Quick Loan Finance Company is about to be established. It will be a one-office company that makes loans to customers in amounts up to $1,000. Customers may borrow money to consolidate their debts, and to buy automobiles, appliances, etc. The employees of the company will consist of the office manager, assistant manager, receptionist-clerk, and two field representatives (bill collectors).

The owner of the proposed company is a close friend of yours. He has come to you for advice regarding a basis for determining the wages and salaries of the employees of his loan company. He is aware of the existing traditional theories of wage payments, but prefers not to use any of them.

Problems:

You are to propose a new wage theory that you feel is an improvement over those existing today. Point out how your theory differs and is an improvement over the present systems.

chapter **6**

FUNDAMENTAL CONSIDERATIONS IN EVALUATING JOBS AND POSITIONS

This chapter is the first of several dealing with the various phases of job evaluation. The purpose of this chapter is to introduce the topic of job evaluation. To do this, the discussion will center around the nature of job evaluation, its uses and benefits, the theory of job evaluation, its evolution and acceptance, and some of its organizational considerations.

The nature of job evaluation

The United States Employment Service defines *job evaluation* as the process of determining the relative values of individual jobs in an organization so as to establish a wage classification system for that organization.[1] The job evaluation process involves an orderly, systematic method and procedure of ranking, grading, and weighting of jobs to determine the value of a specific job in relation to other jobs. It takes into account all requirements and surrounding conditions of the job. Through a system of *rating*, taking into consideration a number of graded "factors" according to responsibilities and difficulties involved, a measurement is established that serves to appraise jobs as accurately as possible for

---

[1] Ester Becher, *Dictionary of Personnel and Industrial Relations* (New York: Philosophical Library, Inc., 1958), p. 160.

the purpose of determining wage differentials and equitable wage-base rates. Job evaluation thus provides a means to guide the employer and employees in the bargaining process and facilitates wage adjustments.

Job evaluation serves as a measuring stick to compare and to measure the value of jobs on the basis of some common denominator, usually expressed in units, such as *points*. Research and factual experience have proven that through methodic and systematic job evaluation, it is possible to obtain acceptable results in establishing job differentials.

Equivalent Terms

Because the process of job evaluation usually involves such activities as occupational analysis, job analysis, and occupational rating, these terms are sometimes erroneously considered as equivalent to job evaluation. The term job evaluation is now generally accepted and known to include occupational classification, job analysis, job description, job specification, and job rating (occupational rating), all of which will be fully discussed later.

Job Evaluation Is Not Pricing Jobs

In a very broad and general interpretation of the term job evaluation, it is possible to say that the pricing of jobs is a part of job evaluation. However, we believe that there are several good reasons why it would be a mistake to consider the pricing of a job as part of job evaluation.

First, the technique of job evaluation is to be used to measure jobs and develop valid standards for measuring other jobs. It is necessary that such a standard be a fixed one (like a three-foot yardstick) rather than a fluctuating one. The pricing of a job would fluctuate from time to time like the price of a pound of butter. Furthermore, pricing is a negotiable item that the union and management can bargain over each year in their collective bargaining. The evaluation of jobs can be performed by management or jointly by the union and management; but once it has been performed, it is *not* negotiable nor should it be negotiable or subject to change any more than the length of a yardstick can be changed from year to year. How can any measuring stick or standard be so called if it is subject to fluctuations?

Second, job evaluation for many years has been most closely related to the rating of jobs in terms of points, units, or classes without regard to money values. The single exception is that of the factor-comparison method of job evaluation which originally priced a job at the same time it was evaluated. Today, most companies do not attempt to price jobs simultaneously with their ratings of the jobs. It would cause considerable confusion for many years to come to include job pricing as part of job evaluation. The authors know of no job evaluation manuals that evaluate the job in terms of money. Thus, to say that job evaluation includes the pricing of jobs would be inconsistent with many years of established practice. It would require that the title of job evaluation manuals be renamed to make their titles correct, or that the manuals be somehow revamped in order that the evaluations be in terms of job prices or pay.

Finally, job evaluation should not include pricing the job because if a union should be dissatisfied with the pricing of the job, the whole technique of job evaluation could be rejected despite its many good features. The one feature of having a fair and valid method of measuring job values serves as a valuable tool for solving disputes and grievances about jobs. What is there to substitute for this measuring stick that would be considered consistent, fair, valid, and acceptable if the whole technique of job evaluation were to fall in disfavor?

In short, job evaluation should identify the relative degree of importance of each job in the company. This relationship between jobs, when known, assists in the establishment of a price for each job. The pricing of a job rarely has a fixed and direct relationship to the job evaluation. Pricing a job involves more considerations than the job evaluation itself. The pricing of jobs should be a separate procedure based on supply and demand — the natural and competitive forces in the labor market — and the company's labor policy. Job evaluation should precede job pricing by establishing the job value in definite units, such as points, that never change as long as the job is not changed. To consider job pricing as part of job evaluation would *force* joint union-management evaluation of jobs. This would not be considered good management for at least two reasons: (1) some unions are not competent to establish valid job standards, and (2) some unions are so powerful that they could force mismanagement of the business by establishing standards that are not in the best interests of the company or its employees.

Uses and benefits of job evaluation

The essential aim or purpose of job evaluation is to determine objectively the value of each job or position in the company. To be valid, these values must be fair and acceptable to both the management and the employees. When this has been accomplished, the job evaluation may benefit all concerned because it can be used as a sound basis for each of the following.

To Assist in the Pricing of Jobs

Job values of one firm can be compared with job values and wages of other firms in wage surveys of the community and industry. Thus, it will help to identify the level of wages of the firm in the area and influence the company's wage policy. This information will also be useful in determining equal pay for equal work.

To Discover and Eliminate Employee Wage Inequities

This must be done if a sound and balanced wage structure is to be possible within a department or the plant. Identifying and correcting wage-base rates which are out of line will help to convince employees that there is no favoritism. It will also eliminate some grievances and prevent potential employer-employee strife. In short, job evaluation can serve as a method of settling wage inequities that arise as well as identifying them and preventing them.

To Provide a System for Evaluating Newly Created Jobs

All job evaluation methods need to provide a uniform and consistent system for evaluating new jobs that are created as technology advances. Thus, the job evaluation provides yardsticks that are flexible enough to accommodate continuing industrial job changes.

To Provide a Foundation for Employee Evaluations

Job evaluation data (through job descriptions and job specifications) provide the basis for setting job performance standards and incentives that are required in evaluating employees and granting merit pay increases.

To Assist in Other Company Personnel Functions

Job evaluation data also provide the basis for assisting the company in personnel work such as determining the qualifications of employees in their proper selection, hiring, training, transferring, promoting, and counseling.

To Assist Company in Nonpersonnel Functions

Job evaluation data provide the basis for assisting nonpersonnel management functions such as measuring work, simplifying work, estimating costs, developing safety measures, and standardizing terminology.

In conclusion, a valid job evaluation program has many uses and benefits, all of which contribute to improved industrial relations and greater company effectiveness. There is a real need in every company to have some form of job evaluation that includes all the jobs from the top to the bottom of the organization. It is just as important to evaluate managerial positions as it is nonmanagerial jobs. Any organization that expects to distribute its payroll dollars fairly has to be able to sort out its jobs in order of importance (or value) because this is one of the more influential yardsticks used to justify job compensation.

The theory of job evaluation

Having identified job evaluation as a necessary management tool that attempts to assure that each job is paid a fair rate according to its value in relationship to all other jobs in the company, we can proceed to an examination of the tool to learn the theory and beliefs commonly involved in its process.

The process of determining the relative (not absolute) values of individual jobs in an enterprise is subjective and results in a qualitative measure. That is, the process is one involving a qualitative judgment. This means that the process is not a scientific one and can be expected to be only reasonably accurate. Job evaluations are no more exact than the estimates and judgments upon which the job evaluations are based. For the job evaluation judgments to be reasonably valid and acceptable to both the employee and the employer, they must come from persons who are not only objective and respected for their fairness but also technically competent, knowledgeable, and reasonable (unselfish). Such persons need to be interested in the common good of the employees, employer, and the community.

In theory, job evaluations are believed to be more accurate when the job is broken down into various parts that can be evaluated separately and objectively. In this way, the overall final job value is more likely to represent a more valid value than if each job were evaluated only on an overall basis. An overall evaluation is thought to be less accurate because evaluators often become biased when they are influenced by the performance of the employee holding the job. Then, too, overall evaluations are more likely to be general or arbitrary since they rarely give consistent weighting and similar consideration to the more important factors that make the job worth its cost. The various parts into which the job is broken down are the job factors that are believed to be important and for which compensation should be paid. They are the reasons a higher wage rate is paid for some jobs than for others.

Most theorists believe that all jobs have some common denominators (yardsticks or factors) running through them which can be identified and used to evaluate the jobs. Job evaluation authorities generally agree that the following common denominators are required in different degrees in all jobs: skill, effort, responsibility, and job conditions. Once it is agreed that there are common denominators and they have been identified, it is then a matter of attaching weights or values to them and attempting to make the subjective evaluations (or judgments) as objective as possible. This means that the more objective the judgments can be made, the easier the job evaluation results are likely to be found consistent and fair and accepted as valid.

In practice, it does not matter much which method of job evaluation is chosen as a basis for evaluation as long as it is considered fair and valid by the employees whose jobs are to be appraised. A method of job evaluation is more likely to be acceptable when the evaluation factors that it uses are considered important, measurable, and related to the jobs.

One indication of the quality of evaluations is how well they stand the test of time. If there are continual arguments about the values of a number of jobs or some specific job, it may be a sign of clerical error or invalid job evaluations. However, once valid job evaluations have been made and accepted, they should *not* be subjected to the collective bargaining process. Valid job evaluations should be considered permanent standards just like the pound, the mile, and the yardstick. These standards should not be subject to change just because of the relative strengths of the union or of management. Strength and bargaining power are not synonymous with what is right or fair. This does not mean that the *wage* at which the job is priced cannot be changed through collective bargaining. It means that the basic value (in units or points) should not be changed unless the job changes. The *pricing* of the job may change just like the price of a pound of butter changes. However, the pound as a standard unit never changes.

An indication of the permanence and stability of a job evaluation method is its ability to handle job changes. A satisfactory method must not be so rigid that it cannot accommodate new jobs that are created. The method must be flexible enough to integrate new jobs smoothly and at the same time be able to eliminate the obsolete jobs. There must be procedures for keeping abreast of job changes and reevaluating present jobs that change substantially. If our society is to continue to gain a higher standard of living, improved technology and industrial change will need to continue. This means continual job changes. An adequate job evaluation method will not break down as a result of such changes.

There are those people who do not believe in either the theory of or the tool of job evaluation for one reason or another, which will be brought out at the appropriate time in this textbook. If new and better tools and theories for managing an enterprise are to be developed, they must come from people who not only are dissatisfied with what we now have but who also have the interest and ability to make constructive criticisms. It is easy to criticize job evaluation, but what is there to replace it that would be considered more fair, valid, and acceptable to the employee, the employer, and the public?

The evolution of job evaluation

With the introduction of the factory system and its specialization, jobs were evaluated as a whole without considering their detailed aspects, that is, without examining the component parts of the jobs. Thus, job evaluation had its unwitting inception during the handicraft-guild period when each job was given a certain money value, or was evaluated in terms of payments in commodities instead of money.[2]

Early Need for Job Evaluation

The problem of wage and salary payments on an equitable basis was felt by the United States government before the industrial revolution was intensified.

[2]See Chapter 2.

As early as 1838, government clerks submitted a petition to Congress calling attention to the evils of wage inequalities, requesting that a law be passed "apportioning and fixing salaries to duties so that all clerks performing like duties should receive like salaries."[3] In 1893, President Cleveland directed that ratings in governmental agencies should apply in promotions *from one grade to another*. In its report of 1902, the United States Civil Service Commission summarized and recommended necessary changes for a reclassification of the services *on the basis of duties performed*. These early stages indicated the need for job evaluation in establishing equitable wages and salaries.

The first actual job evaluation studies were made by Frederick W. Taylor at the Midvale Steel Company in 1881. Taylor's job evaluation concerned itself with the proper description of jobs and division of jobs into operations and suboperations (elements), mainly for the purpose of establishing time-base rates, which in turn were converted into wage rates. While it is true that those job time studies have little resemblance to present methods of job evaluation and rating, nevertheless, they may be considered the beginning of job evaluation methods.

To solve some of its wage and salary problems, the Commonwealth Edison Company of Chicago introduced job classification plans as early as 1909. Similar plans were introduced by consultant industrial engineers for employees of the city of Chicago in 1912.

A Realistic Approach to Job Evaluation

During the 1918-1928 decade, job evaluation gained impetus from the introduction of job analysis and job specifications in the field of personnel management. In 1925, Merrill R. Lott described his method of job evaluation and wage scales in the magazines, *Manufacturing Industries* and *Management Administration*. Shortly thereafter, Lott paved the way to an equitable wage program by introducing the first point method of job evaluation as a "Scientific Plan."[4]

With the growth of unionism in the 1930's and its effect upon bargaining power, as well as the enlightened point of view of some industrialists to compensate labor according to job differentials, pressure was exerted to introduce job values that could show the equitable relationship to other jobs for the purpose of fair wage-base rate setting.

Union pressure was most conspicuously effective when the CIO organized all factory workers, both skilled and unskilled. Unskilled workers, the so-called lower class, were generally employed at low wages. Demands for wage increases

---

[3]Philip W. Jones, *Practical Job Evaluation* (New York: John Wiley & Sons, 1948), p. 122.
[4]Merrill R. Lott, *Wage Scales and Job Evaluation* (New York: The Ronald Press Company, 1926), p. 20.

by these lower paid workers brought about the perplexing problem of wage adjustments. It was easy for the unions to discover wage-rate inequities, thereby proving to their union members that employers took advantage of unorganized workers. Wages in general were adjusted upward without recognizing the fallacy of disregarding the differentials in wage rates. Then both management and the CIO leaders had to find ways and means to justify wage increases on a differential basis that only job evaluation could provide.

From 1937 to 1939, two outstanding associations representing American industry, the National Electrical Manufacturers' Association (NEMA) and the National Metal Trades Association (NMTA), introduced job evaluation plans for rating hourly paid jobs in factories. They used the point-rating method, which was developed by L. B. Michael and L. V. Fisher at the Western Electric Company, and later widely publicized and installed by A. L. Kress. It was heralded as the most useful tool in setting up equitable and sound wage structures.[5] The respective plans were not only successfully used by NEMA and NMTA member companies, but have since been adopted, with modifications, and widely used by hundreds of plants in various industries.

Reasons for Accepting Job Evaluation

It may be said that World War II was the largest contributing factor to hasten the acceptance of job evaluation as an important technique in the stabilization of wage and salary programs. In the first place, a large number of new jobs, occupations, and positions were rapidly created without having been properly classified, bringing up the question, "How much is the new job worth?" In many cases there was no guide for evaluating the job. The second cause was the loss of skilled manpower to the armed forces. The skilled workmen had to be replaced with semiskilled or unskilled labor at the wage-base rates of those who left. The third cause was the overbidding of high rates by companies that had expanded through increased war orders. These three conditions forced commerce and industry to adopt job evaluation plans.

The situation was intensified when the Economic Stabilization Act went into effect in October, 1942, freezing all wages prevailing on September 15, 1942. Employers who paid low wages before that date were prohibited from offering increases, thus losing workers who could obtain the same jobs elsewhere at higher wages. Neither could such employers hire new employees at the higher prevailing rates without adopting a job evaluation plan, thereby proving to the National War Labor Board that their jobs corresponded with those in the same industry where job evaluation and higher wage-base rates existed before September 15, 1942.

---

[5]A. L. Kress, "How to Rate Jobs and Men," *Factory Management and Maintenance*, Vol. IIIC, No. 10 (October, 1939).

Labor leaders were equally handicapped. Unions could obtain wage increases for their members only by complying with the Wage and Salary Stabilization Law. Hence, unions had to reconcile themselves with management procedures as far as the installation and administration of job evaluation programs were concerned. The resultant effect can now be witnessed by the many collective bargaining contracts that contain clauses pertaining to job evaluation techniques.

Status of Job Evaluation

A few statistics will indicate the status of job evaluation and its widespread use. According to Professors William R. Spriegel and E. Lanham, who completed surveys of job evaluation practices and procedures in various non-industrial and industrial organizations, seventy banks reported formal plans, of which eight had installed their job evaluation plans in the ten-year period of the 1930's. From surveys of job evaluation in department stores, aircraft industries, and automobile and automotive parts industries, it appears that job evaluation programs gained momentum during the 1940's.[6]

A survey by the Bureau of National Affairs in 1954 showed that two thirds of the larger companies (1,000 employees or more) and three fourths of the small companies use job evaluation.[7] In 1957 D. H. Rosensteel polled 110 companies throughout the country on supervisory compensation. He found that 77 percent of the companies use job evaluation plans to establish salaries.[8] A survey completed in 1957 by the Bureau of Business Research, University of Texas,[9] covering 852 firms, shows that the proportion of firms making job analyses increased from 66 percent in 1947 to 82 percent in 1957. Similarly, the use of job evaluation increased from 55 percent in 1947 to 72 percent in 1957. It is also interesting to note from Figure 6.1 that the use of job analysis increased almost 100 percent between 1930 (when the first survey was made) and 1940.

In 1960 in a study of 320 companies, Patton[10] found that 65 percent of all hourly employees were covered by job evaluation plans. Less than one percent of the companies said job evaluation was unsatisfactory. In contrast, a 1947 study at Princeton University reported that 20 to 30 percent of the companies indicated that job evaluation was unsatisfactory. Not all sections of the United

---

[6]For a study of statistics and procedures, see Wm. R. Spriegel and E. Lanham, *Personnel Studies*, Nos. 1 through 6 (Austin, Texas: The University of Texas, Bureau of Business Research).

[7]"Wage and Salary Administration," *BNA Personnel Policies Forum Survey No. 28* (November, 1954), p. 2.

[8]D. H. Rosensteel, "Supervisory Compensation — An Interim Report," *Personnel*, Vol. XXXIII, No. 4 (January, 1957), pp. 354–61.

[9]William R. Spriegel, John Robert Beishline, and Alfred G. Dale, *Personnel Practices in Industry* (Austin, Texas: The University of Texas, Bureau of Business Research, 1958).

[10]John Patton, "What 320 Companies Say about Job Evaluation," *Factory* (October 1960), p. 108.

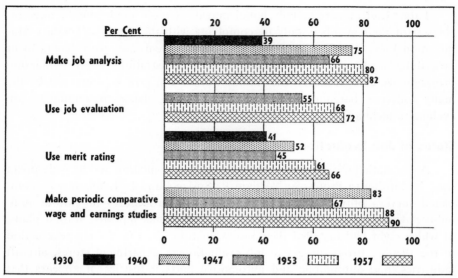

Bureau of Business Research, University of Texas

FIGURE 6.1   PERCENT INCREASE IN THE USE OF JOB ANALYSIS, JOB EVALUATION, MERIT RATING, AND WAGE STUDIES — 1930 TO 1957

States have accepted equally the tool of job evaluation. Patton concluded that there is more resistance to job evaluation in the East (three times as much) than in the central or western states.[11] In a 1961 study of 219 West Virginia firms, only 46 percent of the companies used some form of job evaluation.[12] In a 1968 National Job Analysis Methods Survey of some 899 firms, about 76 percent reported that they have job analysis programs and that approximately 89 to 93 percent of these firms are using job analysis for setting wage and salary levels (job evaluation).[13] A major problem of job evaluation today is how to keep job information current.

Acceptance of job evaluation by employees (and their unions) appears to have a close relationship to the employee's understanding of the method, his confidence and respect for those who establish and administer the plan, and his belief that the evaluations are reasonably accurate, consistent, and fair to all concerned. Unless a firm makes a special effort to meet these requirements, an otherwise valid and technically sound job evaluation plan may be rejected or prove to be unworkable.

[11]*Ibid.*

[12]Thomas S. Isaack, "Personnel Practices of West Virginia Firms," *West Virginia University Bulletin,* Series 63, No. 12-1 (June, 1963), p. 22.

[13]Summary of "National Job Analysis Methods Survey" by Bureau of Business Research, California State College, Long Beach, and Los Angeles Foundation, California State College, 1968, pp. 1 and 4.

Job, position, and occupation defined

Although the term job in job evaluation is well established and its meaning generally understood by those who deal with the subject, a definition and clarification seems necessary inasmuch as the terms "job," "position," and "occupation" are sometimes used interchangeably.

Job and Position

Any group of tasks, physical or mental work, service, or duties regularly assigned to and performed by any one person may be termed a *job*. When we refer to a job, we consider work performed by an employee, and its relationship to work performed by other employees. In the popular sense, however, any assignment or task performed by manual laborers, such as factory workers, is regarded as a job. On the other hand, work of a mental and clerical character, such as that performed by professional and office workers, or the duties of one in official rank who supervises and directs by authority, is termed a *position*. Viewed in connection with *job evaluation*, both categories serve the same purpose since they involve work to be evaluated. Job evaluation, therefore, applies to jobs performed for hourly wages and for positions commanding salaries, since job is a colloquial term applying to any position.

Occupation

The term *occupation* generally refers to a trade or profession in which one is regularly engaged. Also, it is often applied to a group of similar or closely related jobs with common characteristics. The same job groups may be found in different companies. For example, three toolmakers belonging to one occupational group may be engaged in three different jobs. One may specialize in punch and die work, the second might work in jigs and fixtures only, while the third could specialize in cutting tools.

Organizational considerations for job evaluation

Experience has shown that the installation and the maintenance of job evaluation in large companies require numerous professional specialists who are part of the organization. Therefore, a detailed plan of the organizational setup and the activities must be worked out in advance for a sequential distribution of the work load so as to obtain the best results from the program. The one best qualified to supervise certain important activities during the installation process must be selected with utmost care. Furthermore, it should be remembered that after installation of the job evaluation program, the same personnel will have to be retained in order to maintain the various activities and possibly be in daily contact with first-line supervisors and workers.

Too often managers are confronted with difficulties because they rush into some ready-made plan without proper investigation and without regard for the differences in their own organizational setup. Often, too, the workers are not informed of the job evaluation, which results in grievances and union arguments that lead to eventual rejection and discontinuance of the whole program. Thus, much of the success of the job evaluation program depends directly upon how diligently the methods, techniques, and personnel are selected to install and to carry out the program.

Who Is Responsible for the Program?

The job evaluation function and related activities are performed either under the supervision of the industrial engineering department or under the direction of the industrial relations division, as discussed in Chapter 3. The number of personnel will, of course, depend upon the size of the company, the variety of products, and the kind of items produced or services rendered.

In small companies (less than 200 employees) the person who performs the functions of wage and salary administration will also carry out the installation of job evaluation. Or, in very small companies, the personnel manager and one of his assistants may perform the function of job evaluation in addition to other correlated duties.

Whoever is in charge of this very important function should have full authority and the active support of top management. Top management should clearly understand and fully realize that after job performance measurement and methods standardization, job evaluation is next in importance in wage and salary administration.

In large and medium-size companies, the director of industrial relations usually is most concerned with the job evaluation program since he is in charge of all the activities related to manpower administration. A specialist generally carries out this function. Being between top management and the various functions of personnel management, the industrial relations director can appreciate the needs of job evaluation and, at the same time, is in the best position to convince top management of its benefits, such as providing equitable wages, effecting better production, and improving industrial relations. Top management must have faith in job evaluation as the best measuring tool to establish standards for job differentials and, at the same time, to aid in creating equitable wage differentials.

Number of Job Evaluation Plans to Use

Another consideration in organizing for job evaluation is the number of job evaluation plans that the company may wish to use. Questions arise as to what jobs should be evaluated and whether one or more plans should be used to appraise these jobs. It should not be assumed that all companies always evaluate all jobs and in doing so use only one plan.

In theory, all jobs should be evaluated and this could be done by using only one plan of job evaluation. In practice, however, all jobs may not be formally evaluated for one reason or another, and in medium- and large-size companies it is rare to find that one plan is used to evaluate all jobs. What are the reasons behind these practices?

First, let us stress that all jobs in every firm should be evaluated, whether formally or informally (unwritten), as a basis for fair distribution of the payroll dollars. In firms having fewer than 25 jobs, an employer may feel that it may not be necessary to have a *formal* job evaluation program *if* it is obvious to the employees what the order of importance is of the various jobs. If the employees are satisfied that the pay is equitable for the various jobs, there may be no need to spend the time and money for a formalized program as long as these conditions exist. However, sooner or later, conditions may change. The company may expand and the increased total number of jobs may be impossible to keep track of on an informal basis. Or, new employees may join the company and may question the traditional values that have been assumed to exist between the jobs. If an informal plan remains in effect, it may become difficult to convince the new employees that the plan is fair because the evaluations may appear to them to be based on the whims of the employer or on faulty yardsticks. If this should happen, a formal job evaluation plan is needed if the employer is concerned about being respected by his employees for his fairness.

Second, assuming the employer has recognized the need for a formal plan of job evaluation, he has to decide whether he will use one or more plans. A single plan may work satisfactorily for almost any number of jobs that are homogeneous — that is, if they are of a similar type or nature such as clerical, factory, managerial, and sales. If jobs are of a heterogeneous nature, they can still be evaluated under one plan *if* there are not too many of them (over 25) and *if* it is easy to measure their relative values. The acid test of whether to evaluate diversified jobs under one plan is dependent upon whether the employees will accept the plan. If it is doubtful that they will accept such a plan, it is better to revert to more than one plan.

Most medium- and large-size enterprises have more than one plan of job evaluation. The more common plans that have been devised are for the following groups of jobs: shop (manual), office (clerical), and supervisory (lower levels), sales, and executives. Companies are said to use more than one plan of job evaluation in order to satisfy the complaints of different groups of employees who are unhappy when their jobs are all evaluated under one company plan. These employees say their jobs are "different" and should be evaluated by a special set of factors more appropriate to their jobs. Sometimes, for administrative ease, a firm will have one plan covering all salary employees and another plan covering the wage employees. Or, the sheer bigness (size) of some companies may make it more desirable and effective to divide and administer the job evaluations into more than one plan. Furthermore, some jobs are "exempt" from certain provisions of the Fair Labor Standards Act, while other jobs are not. Then, too, some jobs are more difficult to compare than others. Finally, the prevailing compensation being paid for the various groups of jobs may not change proportionately nor simultaneously, thus making it advantageous to have more than a single plan of job evaluation for an enterprise.

Importance of the Job Evaluation Committee

Perhaps no other activity in wage and salary administration can be as greatly benefitted by an advisory committee with union participation as job evaluation. The value of committees and union participation in job evaluation is fully discussed in Chapter 8, but here we should like to emphasize two reasons for their importance. In the first place, job evaluation, as one of the most important activities in wage and salary administration, literally affects every employee in the company organization. Since no managerial executive is completely familiar with all jobs, a properly selected committee will naturally contribute a great deal of information that could easily be overlooked by one individual. Secondly, the committee, which includes union representatives, can be very influential in having the job evaluation plan accepted. In other words, since the workers are represented by one of their own group, they feel that the adopted plan will be carried out to everyone's satisfaction.

Installation and Operating Costs

When the installation of a job evaluation plan is suggested to top management, the question of cost usually is raised. This is natural since the outlay of money for the salaries, wages, etc., for the additional activity must be considered as an added overhead cost. Such costs can be fairly approximated. If it is a question of whether higher productivity and profit earnings will immediately offset the expenditure, however, the answer cannot be entirely anticipated since job evaluation does not solve all the deficiencies and problems of wage and salary administration. Job evaluation includes the cost of installation plus the cost of operation and maintenance. But, its many benefits continue long after installation. The installation cost depends upon the number of jobs in the plant. In other words, the time it takes to describe the jobs, write the specifications, and price the jobs determines the time required to complete the installation and its cost.

The operation and maintenance cost is governed by the number of jobs as well as by the number of employees in the organization. It also depends upon the number of existent inequities. The more numerous the inequities, the longer it takes an analyst to rectify the situation. Besides the cost for the analyst's time, there is also the possibility of having to adjust wages upward in order to meet the wages for equivalent jobs in the community. Hence, the payroll is increased without the immediate benefit of increased production.

On the other hand, a maladjusted wage structure may disclose numerous overpaid jobs. After discovering the unwarranted overpayments, management will pay newly hired employees the lower wages prevalent in the community, resulting in certain savings. Above-level rates being received by some employees at the time adjustments are made should not be reduced, however. Many companies have learned that reducing the wages to the properly evaluated level lowered the morale not only of those employees whose wages were affected but also of sympathetic coworkers who felt that the reductions were unjustified. Thus, labor turnover, loss of goodwill, and decreased production exceeded any gain from the wages that were reduced to the properly evaluated level. Wherever employees receive wage rates for certain jobs that are higher than the evaluated rate, usually the rates can be adjusted by training for higher paid jobs, granting the authority to instruct by reason of seniority rights, or by assignment to become a group leader.

The Employers' Association of Milwaukee, having a membership of over 400 firms comprised of diverse manufacturing and service firms, utilities, financial firms, and hospitals, has found that installation costs for a job evaluation program are contingent on the number of classifications involved, the knowledge and experience of the job evaluators, and the nature of the plan used. Employing well-trained analysts with an engineering background and six to eight years' experience plus eight to twelve months' training with job evaluation systems and wage administration procedures, the Association has found that a job evaluation study for factory, office, and technical classifications rarely exceeds an average of two hours' analyst's time to evaluate each job, write and/or dictate descriptions, and summarize and prepare a wage analysis of the total study. The clerical work involved to complete the study is not included.

The cost of job evaluation may vary considerably from one plant to another, this being contingent on the number of company personnel involved in consultation and evaluation. In the smaller companies these may be limited to the Association's analyst and one full-time company managerial employee who confer with and evaluate jobs with foremen or supervisors. The larger companies usually increase the size of the staff to be oriented by the Association's analyst in order to expedite the program. Firms that do not have a service facility or staff experience and knowledge of job evaluation procedures usually engage a management consulting firm to obtain the services of a specialist to guide and expedite the program. Members in a national trade association long associated with this service may obtain the services of an experienced analyst for around $125 each day plus expenses. Engaging a reputable management consulting firm that performs job evaluation services usually involves higher fees plus expenses. The Employers' Association of Milwaukee has a nominal fee for member firms of approximately one third of the consulting firm's fees, for job evaluation and wage administration services only; other services are included in the membership fees of the Association.

To estimate the cost of a job evaluation installation with any degree of accuracy would be very difficult. The experience of the Employers' Association of Milwaukee of two hours for each classification may or may not be applicable in all cases. Job evaluation is not a mechanical process but involves judgments and decisions on the part of the analyst and the company personnel assigned as well as the foremen and supervisors who participate in the evaluation procedures. Professional management consulting firms prefer to contract on a time basis or a fixed amount for each classification evaluated depending on the nature of the industry, size of the firm, etc. These costs are directly out of pocket and do not include the salaries and other costs for company personnel who participate.

Maintenance of the job evaluation plan is dependent, to a great extent, upon the changes that the jobs undergo because of advances in engineering and methods. Although a basic job evaluation plan may change relatively little in ten years, some of the jobs are bound to change because of new tooling, technology, product changes, market changes, and union attitudes. When it is determined that a job must be reevaluated, the time and cost of this are estimated to be about one half of the original evaluation time and cost.

Evaluation of administrative, managerial, professional, and supervisory positions requires considerably more time than factory and office jobs as these positions are more complex and extensive in scope and require the consideration of organization structure, operating policies, and personalized tendencies. An estimate, based on experience, indicates that in large part the analyst's time, if comprehensive description matter must be developed, would probably be double the time required for the more standard factory and office classifications.[14]

One company has indicated that the cost for each first-line supervisory job evaluated was $65. The evaluation costs included those of the job analyst, the job incumbent, the incumbent's supervisor, the evaluation committee (four persons), and the stenographer. From the observation of those well-managed companies having sound job evaluation plans, it seems evident that the installation and the operation of these plans have proved successful and profitable from the standpoint of improved employee relations, the installation and administration costs notwithstanding.

---

[14]Information received from Mr. E. E. Ross, Director of the Wage and Salary Division of the Milwaukee Employers' Association, 1966.

The personnel director of a large hospital in the Midwest reported that it cost about $50,000 for the initial installation of a point plan of job evaluation in their hospital and that the maintenance of the plan costs about $2,500 a year. The hospital administrators feel that this was a good investment because it enabled them to pay higher wages through increased efficiency due to better methods and training, with a resulting 10 percent gradual reduction in the hospital staff.

The Need for Effective Communication

Since the installation of a job evaluation plan is usually the initial step in formulating a sound wage and salary program, it is generally conceded that education and convincing communication are most important at this stage of the program. It stands to reason that if the first attempt to introduce changes and improvements is fully explained to everyone concerned, the ensuing benefits derived from the initial installation are convincing proof of the philosophy and integrity of those responsible for the installation. All other phases in completing the wage and salary program can then proceed without difficulty.

We should like to repeat that a well-organized communication system prevents misconceptions, eases tension, avoids unnecessary grievances, and keeps employees working together as a cooperative team. Thus, as soon as top management issues the go-ahead for the installation of a job evaluation program, all supervisors, employees, and members of the personnel department should be thoroughly informed regarding the purpose of job evaluation, the method to be used, and the process by which it will be carried out. Plans should also be made to "educate" middle management and especially first-line supervisors. In other words, a great deal of instruction is required to get across the reasons why job evaluation is being undertaken, how it is processed, and finally how the results were accomplished.

Figure 6.2 shows the manner in which the employees of the Stewart-Warner Corporation were informed how job evaluation was used as an aid in setting new rates. Although a similar communication was issued before, the information was reprinted to inform the newer employees regarding the job evaluation methods used in the enterprise.

With Figure 6.2, we introduced the reader to the point method of job evaluation, which is very widespread in commerce and industry. We shall discuss the preliminary details of this method in the next chapter when we compare it with other methods. Then, all details necessary to carry out the installation of the point method plan are explained in subsequent chapters through Chapter 13.

Here's How Job Evaluation Was Used
As an Aid to Set New Rates

The new wage schedule which went into effect last week as a result of the wage agreement signed yesterday, is based upon a systematic job evaluation survey which required the work of five highly trained men working for more than a year to properly study and rate the 750 different jobs performed by S-W employees.

This program directly affects every S-W employee. In order that all may better understand what job evaluation means and how it operates, the following article which was prepared by R. J. Muldoon, chief of the job evaluation section of the Personnel Department, and which appeared originally in the March 20th issue of your plant paper, is being reprinted:

There is no mystery or secrecy about job evaluation. It is simply a systematic method of comparing the requirements of one job with those of another.

Job evaluation is nothing more or less than an additional way of making certain that our wage policy is applied fairly over the entire organization.

It does NOT set rates.

It DOES make sure that a value is set upon each job in fair proportion to the value of every other job in the plant.

It does NOT measure YOUR abilities.

It DOES measure what the JOB requires of you.

Naturally, you want to know how a value was set on your particular job, and this article will attempt to answer that question.

In determining the worth of your job, certain factors which are common to all jobs are considered. These are Skill, Effort, Responsibility and Job Conditions. These major factors are so large that it is impossible to accurately review them as a whole. The most logical procedure then, is to analyze each of the elements which go to make up the major factors.

These elements are as follows:

SKILL

1. Education: This element appraises the schooling or technical training which is ordinarily required to learn a job.
2. Experience: This element appraises the length of time usually required by an individual with the specified education or trade training to learn to perform the work satisfactorily.
3. Initiative and Ingenuity: These elements deal with the independent action, exercise of judgment, making of decisions or the amount of planning which the job requires.

EFFORT:

4. Physical Demand: This element appraises the amount of physical effort required.
5. Mental and Visual Demand: Alertness required, concentration and coordination of manual dexterity with mental attention are considered in rating this element.

RESPONSIBILITY:

6. For Equipment: This element appraises the responsibility for preventing damage to the equipment or process used in the performance of the job.
7. For Material: This element appraises the responsibility for preventing waste or loss of raw material or partially finished products through carelessness.
8. For Safety of Others: This element appraises the care which must be exercised to prevent injury to others.
9. For Work of Others: This element appraises the responsibility which goes with the job for instructing or directing the work of others.

FIGURE 6.2   ANNOUNCING A POINT METHOD PLAN OF JOB EVALUATION
AT THE STEWART-WARNER CORPORATION

JOB CONDITIONS:
10. Working Conditions: This element appraises the surroundings or physical conditions under which the job must be done and the extent to which those conditions make the job agreeable.
11. Hazards: This element appraises the accident hazards connected with or surrounding the job.

Each of the above elements is broken down into five different degrees, and each degree assigned a specific number of points. For example, under the education factor the toolmaker's job would require a four-year apprenticeship and receive 56 points, while the simpler or laboring job would only require the ability to read and write and receive 14 points.

In rating the various jobs, every effort is made to insure the greatest possible degree of accuracy and impartiality. Briefly, the procedure is as follows: Two men from the job evaluation group tour a department accompanied by the department head or foreman and observe the various types of work being done, the equipment used, the effort required and the working conditions. Additional information, such as education and experience required for the job and responsibility for equipment and materials is obtained from the department head.

The jobs are then written up by one of the men, checked by the other, reviewed by the Job Evaluation group as a whole, and rechecked by the head of the group. If there is any question as to the correctness of the rating of any particular job, other members of the rating group observe the job and the correct rating is determined.

After a point rating was established for each job according to the above procedure, all the jobs in the plant were then divided evenly into groups or labor grades, according to their point value. Minimum and maximum rates based on the prevailing rates for the various types of work in the Chicago area as found by the War Labor Board were then set up and progressive rates worked out for each labor grade in proportion to its point value, allowing for progression within the labor grade.

From this outline it will be apparent that the job evaluation plan gives each worker the satisfaction of knowing that his job is in the same classification and carries the same rate of pay as other comparable jobs elsewhere in the plant, and that the rates of pay provided in all classifications are comparable to or above the rates being paid for similar work in other plants.

Reprinted by permission of Mr. R. J. Muldoon, Personnel Director

FIGURE 6.2 ANNOUNCING A POINT METHOD PLAN OF JOB EVALUATION
AT THE STEWART-WARNER CORPORATION (*concluded*)

REVIEW QUESTIONS

1. (a) What is job evaluation? (b) What does it involve?

2. Should job evaluation include job pricing? Explain.

3. List and explain the benefits that can be derived from a well-planned job evaluation program.

4. In what way is job evaluation a subjective process?

5. How can the process of job evaluation be made more valid?

6. (a) What are the common denominators that are required in varying amounts in all jobs? (b) Why can these be considered "common denominators"?

7. What is necessary to make job evaluation more likely to be accepted by the employees?

8. Once the point value of a job has been set, what circumstances would justify a change of the rating?

9. Once job evaluation ratings have been agreed upon by management and employees, should they be subject to collective bargaining?

10. (a) Who made the first job evaluation studies? (b) When were they made? (c) What did they consist of?

11. What hastened the acceptance of job evaluation? Why?

12. Explain the difference between the terms job, position, and occupation.

13. Who should be responsible for the job evaluation function?

14. (a) Should all jobs be evaluated? (b) When should the evaluation be informal and when should it be formal?

15. If a formal plan of evaluation is to be used, how many plans should be used?

16. What are two reasons why union participation in setting up job evaluation is so important?

RESEARCH OR SEMINAR QUESTIONS

1. If a company is working smoothly without a job evaluation program, should one be established? Explain your answer.

2. What are some of the ways that management can gain labor's support for a job evaluation program? Explain the possible drawbacks of each method.

3. What are the major reasons for the failure of job evaluation programs in industry? How can each of these be overcome?

4. What facts about job evaluation, if any, should management tell their employees? What facts should they omit? Why?

PRACTICAL EXPERIENCE ASSIGNMENTS

1. Interview an officer of some union and report to the class the union's attitude or position on the technique of job evaluation.

2. Contact some local business concern that employs a job evaluation plan. Learn what you can about the plan and why the firm chose this method. Be prepared to present your findings to the class for comment and discussion.

3. Obtain a job evaluation plan that dramatically shows the difference between job evaluation points and dollars for the job. List the reasons why this separation is important.

4. List the advantages of a formal job evaluation plan over an informal plan. List the cases when an informal type plan can be useful.

5. Contact a company that utilizes a committee type of job evaluation and find out who (job titles) is on the committee and why they selected the committee form over the one-man type.

CASE PROBLEM

6—1. THE PROGRESSIVE MANUFACTURING COMPANY

Investigation of Job Evaluation

Your inquisitive observation of conditions at The Progressive Manufacturing Company (Case 1 — 1) revealed that all wages and salary matters were handled by the secretary-treasurer, Mr. John D. Carpenter, Jr. After conferring with him, he admitted that he did not pay much attention to wage and salary administration from the standpoint of job differentials, wage differentials, or employee relations. Furthermore, there was no established policy. He depended upon the decisions of the old superintendent and foremen who always set wage rates arbitrarily.

You convinced Mr. John D. Carpenter, Jr., that the industrial relations in The Progressive Manufacturing Company need to be brought up-to-date, as explained in your recent report. Since employer-employee relations are on a decline, Mr. John D., Jr., feels that the wage and salary program should be set up first. You have agreed that the initial step should be the installation of a job evaluation plan, which should be fully discussed at the next meeting of the president's advisory committee.

You are asked to prepare a complete report so as to convince the entire committee of the advantages in installing a job evaluation plan. You should anticipate a lengthy, quizzical discussion of all the details.

Problems:

Prepare a paper for distribution to the committee members prior to the meeting.

1. Briefly explain why the relationship between the job and the individual must be considered.

2. What should be the relationship between the employer's wages and the employees' pay rates?

3. Explain the meaning of job evaluation and inform the committee regarding the advisability of its early acceptance. At the same time, briefly explain the purpose of job evaluation.

4. What organizational matters should be taken up at this meeting?

chapter 7

BASIC METHODS USED
TO EVALUATE JOBS

Job evaluations cannot be any more accurate than the job information and facts that are used as a basis for the evaluations. In an actual installation of a job evaluation program, the fact-finding process (called job analysis) would precede the rating of the jobs. However, in *learning* the essentials of job evaluation, we believe that the learner must first become acquainted with the various methods of job evaluation in order to know what to look for when he learns how to analyze jobs. Thus, the essential methods and procedures of job evaluation are treated (Chapters 6 through 10) before the analysis and preparation of job descriptions and job specifications (Chapters 11 and 12).

Various formal and informal job evaluation processes are known and described under "classes," "forms," "groups," "methods," "plans," "systems," and "types," depending upon the attitude and experience of the users. The term *method* seems to be generally accepted and widely used to describe and differentiate between the established basic plans. The purpose of this chapter is to discuss the four basic methods of job evaluation that are being utilized in the United States. Through such a discussion the reader should become aware of the theory of each method and the procedures, strengths, limitations, and conditions under which it functions best. However, space does not permit a description of the various job evaluation methods that are intermarriages or offshoots of the four basic methods.

Basic methods of job evaluation

Job evaluation methods have been divided into different classes, of which the following are commonly known as basic:

1. Ranking method.
2. Job classification method.
3. Factor comparison method.
4. Point method.

The Occupational Analysis Branch of the United States Department of Labor divides the four basic methods into two groups of *nonquantitative measures* and *quantitative evaluation measures,*[1] as illustrated in Figure 7.1. In this chapter we shall briefly describe the four basic methods in the nonquantitative and quantitative measures, as classified by the Department of Labor.

Nonquantitative evaluation measures

Under this classified group, the ranking and job classification methods are discussed. They are relatively very simple, briefly describing the job, including the duties, responsibilities, difficulties, and qualifications. No endeavor is made to apply compensable factors in order to obtain quantitative measures of job value. The ranking and classification methods are, therefore, regarded as nonquantitative measures.

The Ranking Method

Ranking, the simplest method, also known as the "rank-order," "order-of-merit," and "order-of-importance" system, is the oldest method used to determine the economic value of a job. It was quite popular in the first few decades of the twentieth century. As newer methods were developed, it has been overshadowed by the other three basic methods. Today, this method is mainly used in very small firms. Its usefulness may depend upon how the ranking is carried out and by the number and nature of the jobs to be evaluated.

The Theory of Ranking. As the name implies, all the jobs in the company are ranked (compared or evaluated) on the basis of their *overall* importance to the enterprise. Generally, little or no attempt is made to break the job down into specific, weighted rating factors. However, the evaluator may have general factors in mind such as the difficulty of the job or the responsibilities involved in the job. The evaluation process may resemble what takes place when a woman goes to the hat shop to buy a hat. She tries on many hats and in her own mind rates or ranks the hats in the order of their desirability or importance to her. If her husband were to ask her for the reason for her number one choice she may,

---

[1]U.S. Department of Labor, U.S. Employment Service, *Industrial Job Evaluation Systems* (October, 1947), p. 64.

NONQUANTITATIVE MEASURES		QUANTITATIVE EVALUATION MEASURES	
Ranking Method	**Job Classification Method**	**Factor Comparison Method**	**Point Method**
The job analysis. A narrative description of the job with the duties, responsibilities, degree of difficulty, and required qualifications clearly brought out.		**The job analysis.** A narrative statement of duties and qualifications. In addition, the job is broken down into the important compensable factors, such as required experience and training, mental effort, and physical effort. The amount to which each factor is present in the job is indicated by a short narrative statement.	
Method of Relating Jobs Jobs are ranked in their order of relative difficulty or value to the company, and grade levels are sometimes defined after the jobs have been ranked.	**Method of Relating Jobs** Jobs are allocated to grade levels which are defined arbitrarily prior to evaluating jobs.	**Method of Relating Jobs** Jobs are related by factorial comparison. The factors used are assumed to be fundamental to all jobs and of universal application. The point values are set after analysis of jobs from existing rates of key jobs, and the degrees of each factor are expressed by sample jobs.	**Method of Relating Jobs** Jobs are related by factorial analysis. A restricted number of fairly specific factors is selected for application to a limited number of types of work. The point values are predetermined before analysis of jobs and are decided arbitrarily, and the degree of each factor is expressed by a definition.

Taken from Industrial Job Evaluation Systems, United States Department of Labor

FIGURE 7.1 COMPARISON OF THE FOUR BASIC METHODS OF JOB EVALUATION

or may not, be able to give an answer that would satisfy anyone but herself. The ranking method of job evaluation sometimes falls in this category. If the ranking method is to prove useful and be accepted by the firm's employees, there must be some meeting of the minds on the overall job evaluations. If this becomes a problem, it may be resolved by coming to an agreement on the general considerations (or the basis) on which the evaluations should depend.

Mechanics of Ranking. Ranking should not be attempted until up-to-date job descriptions are available to the evaluator. Ranking is commonly carried out by the chief executive or by a committee under the supervision of an executive in collaboration with supervisors and department heads. Ranking may be arranged by title only, or by combining title, job content, and compensation rates. The title of each job is placed on a card which may also include the job content to facilitate judgment as to which job is more or less important in relation to other jobs. Where many jobs are to be ranked, it is advisable for each member of the committee to rank the jobs of his own department or section. Then, by comparing the rankings of all departments a decision can be reached as to how the departmental rankings can be integrated into an overall company ranking. Where disagreements of rankings may occur, they may be resolved through discussion or by pooling the judgments so as to come up with average rankings. The collective judgment of the committee will also aid in tabulating the final results, including the setting of compensation rates.

The number of ranks varies with the number of jobs (or positions) and the type of organizational activity. Figure 7.2 shows a convenient form that may be used to rank jobs by a paired-comparison method of ranking. Table 7.1 shows examples of jobs, arranged in rank order and price, and grouped into three activity fields.

Advantages and Disadvantages. The advocates of the ranking method of job evaluation point out, first, that it can be successfully used in small shops or in offices where comparatively few jobs have to be evaluated. Second, it is simple, easily understood, and better than no method of job evaluation at all. Finally, the method is relatively inexpensive and easy to install because it involves little paperwork.

The critics of the ranking method point out, first, that the rankings may cause considerable grievances and loss of time in explaining them because they are often incorrectly based on the employee performing the job rather than on the job itself, or because the evaluations are very subjective and have no definite or consistent standards to justify the rankings. A second disadvantage is that the method may become difficult to use for a large number of jobs because the evaluation process becomes cumbersome and there may be no one person who knows all the jobs and is thus qualified to evaluate them. Third, ranking does not measure nor indicate the distance between the jobs ranked. Some employees are

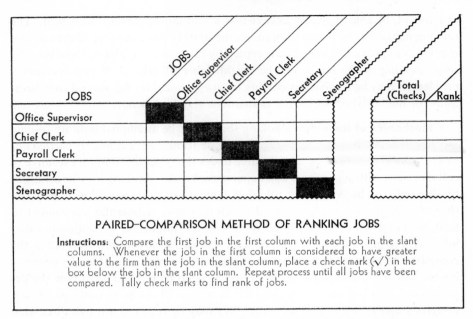

PAIRED–COMPARISON METHOD OF RANKING JOBS

Instructions: Compare the first job in the first column with each job in the slant
columns. Whenever the job in the first column is considered to have greater
value to the firm than the job in the slant column, place a check mark (√) in the
box below the job in the slant column. Repeat process until all jobs have been
compared. Tally check marks to find rank of jobs.

FIGURE 7.2   Form Used to Rank Jobs by Paired-Comparison Method

interested in knowing how close to or far apart they are from the jobs above and
below them in rank.

In conclusion, the ranking method of job evaluation can be highly satisfactory when there are only a small number of jobs to rank (less than 25) and
when the employees trust and respect the employer's integrity in ranking the jobs.

The Job Classification Method

The second of the basic methods of job evaluation to be developed was the
job classification method, which is also known as the *grading method*. This method
appeared in the early 1920's. It is said that the pioneer work in developing this
method was done by the Bureau of Personnel Research at the Carnegie Institute
of Technology in 1922.[2]

Shortly thereafter, the federal government's position classification method
originated with the Classification Act of 1923.[3] This act was amended many
times and was finally replaced by the Classification Act of 1949. This act with its
many amendments remains as the principal legal authority for classifying positions within the federal government.[4] At present, the United States government

[2]E. Lanham, *Administration of Wages and Salaries* (New York: Harper and Row Publishers, 1963), p. 165.

[3]U.S. Civil Service Commission, *Classification Principles and Policies*, Personnel Management Series No. 16 (June, 1963).

[4]*Ibid.*, p. 13.

TABLE 7.1

EXAMPLES OF JOBS IN THREE DIFFERENT ACTIVITY FIELDS

Arranged In Rank Order

RANK ORDER	JOB GROUPS AND COMPENSATION RATES					
	PROFESSIONAL JOB TITLE	SALARY RANGE (PER MONTH)	OFFICE AND CLERICAL JOB TITLE	SALARY RANGE (PER MONTH)	SHOP AND MFG. JOB TITLE	WAGE RANGE (PER HOUR)
1.	Chief Engineer	$1,707	Manager-Office Services	$625	Tool and Die Maker	$4.20
2.	Personnel Director	1,376	Tabulating Machine Operator	496	Machinist (general)	3.55
3.	Chief Accountant	1,329	Accounting Clerk	461	Turret Lathe Operator	3.20
4.	Office Manager	1,079	Stenographer	403	Screw Machine Operator	3.00
5.	Accountant	964	Switchboard Operator	395	Multiple Drill Press Set-up and Operator	2.90
6.	Auditor	857	Key-punch Operator	376	Engine Lathe Operator	2.80
7.	Job Analyst	847	Bookkeeping Machine Operator	372	Maintenance Electrician	2.70
8.	Engineering Technicians	713	File Clerks	368	Welder	2.60
9.	Senior Draftsman	585	Messenger	281	Packers (shipping)	2.50
10.	Tracers	361			Laborers (material handling)	2.40
11.					Brazier	2.30
12.					Janitor	2.20

Note: Titles, salaries, and rate ranges are illustrative and for comparison purposes only.

is the largest single utilizer of the classification method of job evaluation. Some 2,400,000 employees are believed to have their jobs evaluated by this method.[5] The method has been used mostly for the evaluation of office and clerical jobs.

The Theory of the Job Classification Method. The underlying idea behind the job classification method is the belief that any number of jobs can be sorted out and classified into a number of predetermined classes, grades, or groups, on the basis of some common denominators that run through the jobs.

[5]From a letter written by Harold H. Leich, Chief of Program Planning Division, U.S. Civil Service Commission, Bureau of Programs and Standards, October 9, 1964.

The common denominators often used are the levels of responsibilities, abilities or skills, knowledge, and duties. The job classes or grades are arranged (ranked) in an overall order of importance according to the common denominators.

The classification idea is often utilized in analogous ways. In a supermarket, one section of the store is reserved for meats; another section houses the canned goods; still another, the vegetables, the fruits, baked goods, etc. In short, the merchandise has been classified or grouped according to some common denominators or characteristics. Another example is the post office department that classifies letters and mail by geographical location or zone. Thus, the classification method of job evaluation assumes that predetermined classes or groups can be established that will indicate a relative value or class for every job in the enterprise.

Examples of the Classification Method. One company classified all jobs into groups as follows: Policy-making, Administrative, Executive, Professional, Semiexecutive, Skilled, and Semiskilled. The Philadelphia Electric Company divides its classification scheme into eight groups or classes according to: (1) General Management, (2) Departmental and Associate Management, (3) Major Supervision or Highly Technical Service, (4) Highly Skilled Service or Minor Supervision, (5) Skilled Service, (6) Semiskilled Service, (7) Slightly Skilled Service, and (8) Primary Service. Table 7.2 shows how these eight groups fit into the two major divisions of Top Management and Operating Practice.

The federal government has one job classification method that covers mostly all of its jobs and positions (professional, scientific, clerical, administrative). This method is known as the General Schedule and has 18 job classes (GS-1 through GS-18). These job classes differ in the level of job difficulty (duties), responsibilities, and qualification requirements of the work performed. See Figure 7.3 for examples of how the job classes are described. Figure 7.4 shows the key phrases that differentiate one governmental job class from another. It can easily be seen from Figure 7.4 that the lower the job class number, the less difficult the job becomes. The higher the job class number, the greater are the responsibilities and qualifications necessary to fill that job.

From an analysis of the various job classification methods being used, grade descriptions contain many of the following areas as the basis for the different job class levels:

1. Difficulty of work (simple, routine, varied, complex)
2. Volume of work (small, average, great)
3. Responsibility (little to great in dollars, people, etc.)
4. Supervision given or received (none, limited, general, close)
5. Experience required (none, to 10 years or more)
6. Special knowledge necessary (none, some, normal, highly technical)
7. Judgment involved (none, limited, shared, independent)

TABLE 7.2

TABLE OF CLASSIFICATION

Service Grades		Accounting	Clerical Service	Engineering	Designing	General Administration	Construction	Monthly Basis
I. MANAGEMENT:	A					President		7800–8500
1. General Management	B					Sr. Vice-President		6000–7000
	C					Vice-President		4000–5000
	D					General Manager		3500–4500
	E					Asst. Genl. Manager		2500–3000
2. Departmental and Associate Management	A	Controller						2000–3500
	B							1800–2350
	C							1600–2150
	D							1450–1950
	E	General Auditor		Chief Engineer				1300–1750
	F							1150–1570
	G			Mech. Engineer				1000–1400
	H							900–1350
	I	Auditor		Asst. Mech. Engineer				800–1100
	J	Office Manager						700–1000
II. OPERATING PRACTICE:	A	Senior Accountant		Senior Engineer	Chief Designer Squad		Asst. Supt.	675–800
3. Supv. or Highly Technical Service	B		Genl. Off. Supvsr.		Chief Senior		Supvsr. Asst.	660–750
	C	Accountant	Supvsr. Storekpr.	Engineer	Designer Supvr.		Supvsr.	640–700
	D		Chief Clerk		Lay-out		Senior Foreman	620–675
4. Highly Skilled or Minor Supervision	A	Junior Accountant	Asst. Chief Clerk	Junior Engineer	Designer		Foreman	600–625
	B		Senior Clerk A		Senior Fieldman		Gang Leader	580–600
	C	Book-keeper	Senior Clerk B	Engineer Asst.	Asst. Designer		Machinist 1st Class	525–575
	D		Bill Computer		Fieldman		Machinist 2nd Class	460–550
5. Skilled Service	A	Asst. Bookkpr.	Clerk A		Junior Designer		Bench Worker	420–500
	B		Balance Clerk		Senior Draftsman		Press Operator	400–475
6. Semiskilled Service	A		Clerk B		Draftsman		Machinist Helper	380–450
	B		Posting Clerk		Junior Draftsman		Special Laborer	370–425
7. Slightly Skilled Service	A		Asst. Clerk		Tracer		Laborer	350–400
	B		Junior Typist		Junior Tracer			340–360
8. Primary Service			Junior Clerk				Shop Boy	200–250

Note: Titles, placements, and rate ranges are illustrative only.

Source: J. O. Hopwood, *Salaries, Wages and Labor Relations* (New York: The Ronald Press Company, 1945). (Rate ranges have been updated.)

Grade-General Schedule 1 includes all classes of positions the duties of which are to be performed, under immediate supervision, with little or no latitude for the exercise of independent judgment, (1) the simplest routine work in office, business, or fiscal operations, or (2) elementary work of a subordinate technical character in a professional, scientific, or technical field.

Grade-General Schedule 5 includes all classes of positions the duties of which are (1) to perform, under general supervision, difficult and responsible work in office, business, or fiscal administration, or comparable subordinate technical work in a professional, scientific, or technical field, requiring in either case (A) considerable training and supervisory or other experience, (B) broad working knowledge of a special subject matter or of office, laboratory, engineering, scientific, or other procedure and practice, and (C) the exercise of independent judgment in a limited field; (2) to perform, under immediate supervision, and with little opportunity for the exercise of independent judgment, simple and elementary work requiring professional, scientific, or technical training equivalent to that represented by graduation from a college or university of recognized standing but requiring little or no experience; or (3) to perform other work of equal importance, difficulty, and responsibility, and requiring comparable qualifications.

Grade-General Schedule 9 includes all classes of positions the duties of which are (1) to perform, under general supervision, very difficult and responsible work along special technical, supervisory, or administrative experience which has (A) demonstrated capacity for sound independent work, (B) thorough and fundamental knowledge of a special and complex subject matter, or of the profession, art, or science involved, and (C) considerable latitude for the exercise of independent judgment; (2) with considerable latitude for the exercise of independent judgment, to perform moderately difficult and responsible work, requiring (A) professional, scientific or technical training equivalent to that represented by graduation from a college or university of recognized standing, and (B) considerable additional professional, scientific, or technical training or experience which has demonstrated capacity for sound independent work; or (3) to perform other work of equal importance, difficulty, and responsibility, and requiring comparable qualifications.

Grade-General Schedule 13 includes all classes of positions the duties of which are (1) to perform, under administrative direction, with wide latitude for the exercise of independent judgment work of unusual difficulty and responsibility along special technical, supervisory, or administrative lines, requiring extended specialized, supervisory, or administrative training and experience which has demonstrated leadership and marked attainments; (2) to serve as assistant head of a major organization involving work of comparable level within a bureau; (3) to perform, under administrative direction, with wide latitude for the exercise of independent judgment, work of unusual difficulty and responsibility requiring extended professional, scientific, or technical training and experience which has demonstrated leadership and marked attainments in professional, scientific, or technical research, practice, or administration; or (4) to perform other work of equal importance, difficulty, and responsibility, and requiring comparable qualifications.

FIGURE 7.3 Examples of General Schedule Descriptions for the Federal Government Job Classification Method

Grade-General Schedule 18 includes all classes of positions the duties of which are (1) to serve as the head of a bureau where the position, considering the kind and extent of the authorities and responsibilities vested in it, and the scope, complexity, and degree of difficulty of the activities carried on, is exceptional and outstanding among the whole group of positions of heads of bureaus; (2) to plan and direct or to plan and execute frontier or unprecedented professional, scientific, technical, administrative, fiscal, or other specified programs of outstanding difficulty, responsibility, and national significance, requiring extended training and experience which has demonstrated outstanding leadership and attainments in professional, scientific, or technical research, practice, or administration, or in administrative, fiscal or other specialized activities; or (3) to perform consulting or other professional, scientific, technical, administrative, fiscal or other specialized work of equal importance, difficulty, and responsibility, and requiring comparable qualifications.

FIGURE 7.3   EXAMPLES OF GENERAL SCHEDULE DESCRIPTIONS FOR THE FEDERAL GOVERNMENT JOB CLASSIFICATION METHOD (*concluded*)

Job Classification Guidelines. While the job classification method is comparatively simple in application, the following basic guidelines should be adhered to if good results are to be achieved: (1) identifying the job classes or grades that will cover all the jobs to be evaluated, (2) describing the job classes and their characteristics, (3) classifying (slotting) each job into one of the predetermined classes, (4) assigning money values to the job classes and their jobs, and (5) installing a periodic checkup.

Advantages and Disadvantages. The advocates of the job classification method of job evaluation point out, first, that it is relatively easy to use and understand because most employees already have an idea of how job classes can be logically established. Second, the results are fairly satisfactory, especially for small firms, because a great deal of time and technical help are not needed.

The critics of the job classification method point out as a first disadvantage that the overall classifying of each job is a very subjective process and may cause grievances and distrust among the employees. This can happen for a number of reasons: (1) The blanket classifying of a job has few concrete and consistent factors to justify the rating. (2) Some jobs may appear to fall into more than one classification. (3) Job classifications may be unduly influenced by their existing wages or salaries or by the employees who hold these jobs. Another disadvantage is that the method can become cumbersome as a firm expands because job class descriptions may no longer be adequate and newer ones become more difficult to write due to the complexity created by the added jobs.

In conclusion, the job classification method of job evaluation can be highly satisfactory when there is either a small number of jobs to classify or the jobs to be classified lend themselves to natural or logical groupings.

General Schedule Job Classification No.	JOB FACTORS AND THEIR VARYING REQUIREMENTS		
	DIFFICULTY	**RESPONSIBILITY**	**QUALIFICATIONS**
1.	simplest routine work		
2.	routine work		some training or experience
3.	somewhat difficult	somewhat responsible	working knowledge
4.	moderately difficult work	moderately responsible work	moderate training, good working knowledge
5.	difficult work	responsible work	considerable training, broad working knowledge, college graduate
6.	difficult work	responsible work	broad working knowledge, special and complex subject
7.	considerable difficulty	considerable responsibility	comprehensive and thorough working knowledge
8.	very difficult	very responsible	comprehensive and thorough working knowledge
9.	very difficult	very responsible	administrative experience, sound capacity for independent work
10.	highly difficult	highly responsible	somewhat extended administrative experience
11.	marked difficulty	marked responsibility	marked capacity for independent work
12.	very high order of difficulty	very high order of responsibility	leadership and attainments of a high order
13.	work of unusual difficulty	work of unusual responsibility	leadership and marked attainments
14.	exceptional difficulty	exceptional responsibility	leadership and unusual attainments
15.	outstanding difficulty	outstanding responsibility	leadership and exceptional attainments
16.	unusual difficulty and national significance	unusual responsibility and national significance	leadership and exceptional attainments involving national significance
17.	exceptional difficulty	exceptional responsibility	exceptional leadership and attainments
18.	outstanding difficulty	outstanding responsibility	outstanding leadership

FIGURE 7.4   KEY PHRASES FROM UNITED STATES GOVERNMENT JOB CLASSIFICATION METHOD THAT DIFFERENTIATE ONE JOB CLASS FROM ANOTHER

Quantitative evaluation measures

Under this classified group, the factor comparison and point methods are discussed. The job evaluations are somewhat complex, requiring statements of duties and qualifications as well as breaking down jobs into a number of compensable factors. Each factor is described and evaluated either in a quantity of money (dollars and cents), or in a number of points. Thus, through these methods quantitative job values are obtained.

The Factor Comparison Method

The *factor comparison method* of job evaluation was originated and installed at the Philadelphia Rapid Transit Company by Eugene J. Benge in 1926. This method is also known as "the key job system," "the job comparison system," and "the job-to-money method." It has some characteristics of the ranking and the job classification methods but differs considerably in structure and application. The factor comparison method is more widely used than the ranking and the job classification methods. Its popularity is surpassed only by the point method of job evaluation.

The Theory of Factor Comparison. Benge and his followers believed that the following five evaluation factors can be found to exist in all jobs: skill, responsibility, physical effort, mental effort, and working conditions. All jobs should be compared on these critical factors. The basic idea of factor comparison is that all jobs should be compared and evaluated independently on each of the evaluation factors. Thus, all jobs are compared independently five different times, once for each factor. On the factor of skill, jobs are compared and ranked in the order they require skill — from the most to the least. All jobs are likewise compared and ranked according to the responsibility, physical effort, mental effort, and working conditions of the job. The five separate rankings are then assigned monetary values. When these five values are added together, they result in each job having an overall monetary value or a base-rate price on it. When the factor comparison method was first devised, it was not only a method of evaluating jobs but also one of pricing the jobs at the same time. Modern theorists do not advocate retaining the feature of pricing a job simultaneously with its evaluation because our economy is too dynamic and constantly fluctuating, causing continual turmoil. It is believed better to evaluate jobs in terms of points or units which can be considered permanent standards that are only subject to change when the job changes. The pricing of the job is, then, a separate activity and can fluctuate to meet any changing conditions without destroying the job evaluations. In a stable economy, the evaluation and pricing of a job simultaneously could be considered an advantage and retained as such.

The heart of the factor comparison method of job evaluation is the use of "key jobs." Benge and his followers believed that the whole process of evaluating company jobs could be made easier and more valid by first selecting and evaluating a number of "key jobs." *Key jobs* are those well-known jobs (such as the tool and die maker, machinist, and patternmaker) which, over a period of time, have unofficially become standards for comparison because they have not changed much. When a number of key jobs can be agreed upon as presently being correctly priced (base rate), these key jobs can be first processed through the factor comparison procedure and then used as bench marks (guideposts) for evaluating the remaining jobs in the company.

Although Benge used five factors to evaluate jobs, he believed that as many as seven factors could be used satisfactorily. However, most present-day factor comparison plans have retained the original five factors. When more factors are added, the evaluation process requires more time and paperwork and has a tendency to become unduly complex and cumbersome.

Steps of Evaluation by Factor Comparison. The procedure for evaluating jobs by the factor comparison method involves the following six steps:

1. *Selection of Key Jobs.* Select 10 to 20 key jobs that represent a cross section of all jobs to be evaluated. These key jobs should range from the lowest to the highest paid jobs, as agreed upon by a committee representing workers and management. All committee members should be in accord on the terminology used in descriptions, definitions, and compensation rates.

2. *Analysis of Jobs and Comparison of Factors.* Descriptions of the key jobs are analyzed by each member of the committee. If job descriptions are not clear, the respective jobs may have to be observed firsthand and the operator interviewed for description. Once the analysis of jobs is completed, members of the committee critically study definitions of the five basic factors. See Figure 7.5 for the definitions used by the originators of the factor comparison method. An agreement on factor definitions and job requirements is imperative before ranking is started.

3. *Ranking the Selected Key Jobs According to Factors.* Key jobs are ranked according to factors, one factor at a time, in the order of their relative importance. The ranking should first be arranged numerically, as illustrated in Table 7.3. Note that in the factor column "Mental Requirements," the highest rank (1) is given to the job of patternmaker, while the lowest rank (10) is assigned to the rammer. In the factor column "Skill Requirements," the highest rank is assigned to the patternmaker (rank 1), but rank 9 is assigned to the rammer. On the other hand, in the factor column "Physical Requirements," the highest rank (1) is selected for the rammer, seventh place (rank 7) for the patternmaker, and the lowest rank (10) is assigned to the job of substation operator.

4. *Application of Money Values to Factors.* After the committee establishes the average wage-base rates or salaries for all ranked key jobs, the money value for each key job is divided among the five factors according to the importance of the respective factor to the key job. Let us take three key jobs as examples. Assume that the patternmaker receives $4.20 an

MENTAL REQUIREMENTS

"include all those elementary factors having to do with basic intelligence required and the necessary training of that intelligence, usually acquired by processes of formal education."

SKILL REQUIREMENTS

"include all those elementary factors involving development of abilities by application to and practice in actual working, or practical, situations."

PHYSICAL REQUIREMENTS

"Ratings are based on such physical factors required as strength, height, weight, health, physique, and the degree to which their use is required on the job."

RESPONSIBILITY

"Comparison of responsibility among positions being evaluated is based on the comparative moral 'accountability' placed on the incumbent of the position by his employer. Consideration should be given to the probability of error or improvement and the possible consequences of such error or improvement. This involves comparison of such phases of the responsibility element as the number of checks or inspections given to the work, the type and grade of supervision received, the scope of the decision limits permitted the incumbent of the position, the relative values of the raw and finished products, and all other factors having to do with the effect of the job on profit or loss."

WORKING CONDITIONS

"Under the factor 'Working Conditions' should be included all those considerations having to do with disagreeable or hazardous features of the job."

Source: Eugene J. Benge, Samuel L. H. Burk, and Edward N. Hay, *Manual of Job Evaluation* (New York: Harper and Brothers, 1941), pp. 100–102.

FIGURE 7.5 Definitions of the Five Factors Used by Benge in the Factor Comparison Method of Job Evaluation

hour; the rammer, $2.80 an hour; and the substation operator, $3.00 an hour. The money values are then distributed for each factor of the three jobs as shown in Table 7.4.

5. *Comparison of Ranked Key Jobs With Monetary Scales.* When members of the committee agree to distribute the adopted wage-base rates according to the ranked and evaluated factors, the pooled rankings are set up in a reference master table as illustrated in Table 7.5. Key job titles are arranged vertically in the extreme left-hand column sequentially from the highest to the lowest paid key job. In the next column are entered the hourly wage-base rates agreed upon by the committee. The monetary scales, representing the factor ranks for each key job as well as the rank

TABLE 7.3

SAMPLE RANKING OF KEY JOBS

Factor Comparison Method

RANK	MENTAL REQUIREMENTS	SKILL REQUIREMENTS	PHYSICAL REQUIREMENTS	RESPONSIBILITY	WORKING CONDITIONS
1	Patternmaker	Patternmaker	Rammer	Substation Operator	Rammer
2	Substation Operator	Machinist	Poleman	Patternmaker	Poleman
3	Machinist	Substation Operator	Laborer	Machinist	Laborer
4	Pipe Fitter	Pipe Fitter	Pipe Fitter	Pipe Fitter	Pipe Fitter
5	Painter	Painter	Machinist	Drill-press Operator	Painter
6	Drill-press Operator	Drill-press Operator	Painter	Painter	Drill-press Operator
7	Carpenter's Helper	Carpenter's Helper	Patternmaker	Carpenter's Helper	Machinist
8	Poleman	Poleman	Carpenter's Helper	Poleman	Carpenter's Helper
9	Laborer	Rammer	Drill-press Operator	Rammer	Patternmaker
10	Rammer	Laborer	Substation Operator	Laborer	Substation Operator

Source: Adopted from U.S. Department of Labor, U.S. Employment Service, *Industrial Job Evaluation Systems* (October, 1947).

numbers, are registered under the five major (critical) factors. The total distributed money values for each factor, added horizontally, equal the established hourly wage-base rate.

Since this master table serves to compare all other jobs with the key jobs for setting wage-base rates, it is imperative for each committee member to critically reexamine the ranking of amounts assigned to all jobs under each factor. Any discrepancies or misconceptions in the minds of the raters should be corrected before the chief analyst releases the comparison master table for use in evaluating other jobs.

6. *Evaluation of All Other Jobs.* Having established a measuring stick for ranking jobs and evaluating factors in money values, the committee is ready to complete the evaluation of all jobs that can be compared with the key jobs. The procedure is the same as used for establishing the key jobs, except that the rankings and money evaluations can now be accomplished by using the master Table 7.5 for comparison.

It is advisable to consider one job at a time in its relative position to the key jobs and their evaluated basic factors. Each factor of the job in

TABLE 7.4

MONEY VALUES APPORTIONED TO FIVE FACTORS FOR THREE KEY JOBS

Factor Comparison Method

FACTORS	KEY JOBS AND GRADED MONEY RATES		
	PATTERN- MAKER MONEY RATE	RAMMER MONEY RATE	SUBSTATION OPERATOR MONEY RATE
Mental Requirements............	$1.23	$0.17	$0.90
Skill Requirements..............	1.52	0.25	1.05
Physical Requirements...........	0.47	1.26	0.12
Responsibility..................	0.72	0.28	0.81
Working Conditions.............	0.26	0.84	0.12
Total Wage-Base Rate	$4.20	$2.80	$3.00

Note: Titles and rate ranges are illustrative and for comparison purposes only.

TABLE 7.5

FACTOR COMPARISON METHOD

Rankings and Money Values

KEY JOB TITLE	HOURLY WAGE- BASE RATE	FACTOR RANKINGS AND RATES									
		MENTAL REQUIREMENTS		SKILL REQUIREMENTS		PHYSICAL REQUIREMENTS		RESPONSI- BILITY		WORKING CONDITIONS	
		RANK	RATE	RANK	RATE	RANK	RATE	RANK	RATE	RANK	RATE
Patternmaker.......	$4.20	1	$1.23	1	$1.52	7	$0.47	2	$0.72	9	$0.26
Machinist..........	3.55	3	0.75	2	1.13	5	0.64	3	0.67	7	0.36
Pipe Fitter.........	3.48	4	0.59	4	1.04	4	0.70	4	0.59	4	0.56
Poleman...........	3.46	8	0.38	8	0.59	2	1.24	8	0.45	2	0.80
Painter............	3.30	5	0.56	5	1.02	6	0.63	6	0.56	5	0.53
Substation Operator.	3.00	2	0.90	3	1.05	10	0.12	1	0.81	10	0.12
Drill-Press Operator.	2.90	6	0.52	6	0.93	9	0.38	5	0.58	6	0.49
Rammer...........	2.80	10	0.17	9	0.25	1	1.26	9	0.28	1	0.84
Carpenter's Helper..	2.60	7	0.47	7	0.86	8	0.44	7	0.52	8	0.31
Laborer............	2.50	9	0.32	10	0.18	3	1.05	10	0.25	3	0.70

Note: Titles and rate ranges are illustrative and for comparison purposes only.

question is studied to establish money values according to the five basic factor ranks. The total of the five factor money values becomes the new wage-base rate for the job.[6]

---

[6]For a more complete discussion of the factor comparison method, see Eugene J. Benge, Samuel L. H. Burk, and Edward N. Hay, *Manual of Job Evaluation* (New York: Harper & Brothers, 1941).

Advantages and Disadvantages. The advocates of the factor comparison method of job evaluation point out, first, that the method provides each company with its own tailor-made job evaluation plan to meet specifically its own needs. Second, once the evaluation scales are set up, it is relatively easy for most anyone to evaluate other jobs, without using highly trained specialists. Finally, the job-to-job comparisons on each factor are said to produce a valid evaluation because they assure that jobs are compared on a comparable yardstick.

The critics of the factor comparison method point out, first, that obtaining adequate key jobs can prove to be a problem. This is especially true when the union and the management are not on good terms. In some cases there may not be a large enough number of or a range of jobs that are either available or can be agreed upon. In other cases, gradual changes in key jobs (duties, going rates, working conditions, etc.) sometimes take place without being noticed, thus causing the rating scales to become inaccurate. In short, without adequate and dependable key jobs, the factor comparison method cannot be used and still be valid. Another criticism is that the method is difficult to set up and to explain the rationale behind the original rating scales. Finally, considerable time and clerical work are required.

In conclusion, it can be said that the factor comparison method can be satisfactorily used for most any kind of job and size of company. However, it is more successfully used in a company when the union-management relations are harmonious and when there is no difficulty in agreeing upon an adequate number and range of key jobs to be used as the basis of the evaluation.

The Point Method

Merrill R. Lott is credited with having introduced the first point method of job evaluation when, in 1925, he described this method in the two magazines, *Manufacturing Industries* and *Management Administration*. The point plan idea was quick to catch on and today it is by far the most widely used of all the job evaluation methods.

The Theory of the Point Method. The basic idea of the point method of job evaluation is the belief that a number of evaluation factors can be found that run through the various jobs to be evaluated. After these evaluation factors have been identified and agreed upon, each is assigned an overall value (a number of points) and is then subdivided into a number of gradations (degrees) so that it becomes a measuring stick. Each job is then measured in terms of the various measuring sticks (factors), and the sum of the measurements gives an overall value of the job in terms of points. Thus, jobs can be quantitatively evaluated on the basis of whatever factors are considered important. The factors, in turn, can each be assigned whatever weight or value is considered commensurate with its individual importance.

The theory of the point method is similar to that of the factor comparison method in that both methods start out with the belief that a job should be broken down and evaluated on the basis of several evaluation factors that run through the jobs to be evaluated. However, the factor comparison method has tended to use the five factor requirements (mental, skill, physical, responsibility, and working conditions) as universal and critical factors on an overall and comparative basis. The point method theory, although in basic agreement with the idea that skill requirements, effort, responsibility, and working conditions are the common denominators of most jobs, stresses that these broad categories should be further broken down into more specific factors. Then, the factors should be further subdivided into degrees that can be specifically used as separate quantitative yardsticks rather than merely as comparative ranking tools. The point method almost always uses different weights for its factors than does the factor comparison method. Furthermore, the point theory disregards community rates (or going rates) in evaluating jobs, while the factor comparison theory utilizes basic wage rates as the basis for evaluating its key jobs.

A Sample Breakdown of the Point Method Factors. Table 7.6 shows a typical example of how the basic factors of skill, effort, responsibility, and job conditions have been broken down into 11 subfactors and six degrees and the number of points that has been allotted to each. These 11 subfactors are used in many point methods and are commonly referred to as factors. Each subfactor is divided into a number of *degrees* to serve as a scale for measuring the distinct levels of each factor. The degrees, in turn, are evaluated separately by a number of *points*. The mathematical sum of all evaluated subfactors in units of points represents the total point score of the job.

Note that 50 percent of the total points in the whole plan have been assigned to the basic factor of skill. The basic factor of skill has been subdivided into three subfactors that go to make up one's total skill. It is generally assumed that almost every job requires some education on the part of the worker who performs it. The question is how much education is needed? Numerous unskilled jobs do not require more than the ability to read and sign one's name. Such jobs are 1st degree, evaluated at 12 points, as indicated in Table 7.6. Certain assembly jobs call for some figuring, requiring a grammar school education or its equivalent. These are 2d degree, deserving 24 points. Jobs such as toolmaking and patternmaking require a high school education, and come under the 3d degree with 36 points. Other jobs requiring college training may come under the 5th or 6th degree, evaluated at 60 and 72 points. Thus, gradations expressed in degrees are necessary to establish the various qualifications needed to measure the distinct levels for each job. For a complete analysis of the remaining factors, degrees, and assigned points, see the point job evaluation manual in Chapter 10, pages 248 to 258.

TABLE 7.6

POINTS ASSIGNED TO FACTORS AND DEGREES

| FACTORS AND SUBFACTORS | % | DEGREES AND POINTS | | | | | | WEIGHT IN PER-CENT |
		1st Deg.	2d Deg.	3d Deg.	4th Deg.	5th Deg.	6th Deg.	
SKILL	50							
1. Education & Job Knowledge.....		12	24	36	48	60	72	12
2. Experience & Training..........		24	48	72	96	120	144	24
3. Initiative & Ingenuity...........		14	28	42	56	70	84	14
EFFORT	15							
4. Physical Demand...............		10	20	30	40	50	60	10
5. Mental and/or Visual Demand...		5	10	15	20	25	30	5
RESPONSIBILITY	20							
6. Equipment or Tools.............		6	12	18	24	30	36	6
7. Material or Product.............		7	14	21	28	35	42	7
8. Safety of Others...............		3	6	9	12	15	18	3
9. Work of Others.................		4	8	12	16	20	24	4
JOB CONDITIONS	15							
10. Working Conditions............		10	20	30	40	50	60	10
11. Unavoidable Hazards..........		5	10	15	20	25	30	5
TOTAL	100%	100	200	300	400	500	600	100%

Differences Between the Two Point Methods. There are two point methods: (1) the *straight point* method, and (2) the *weighted point* method. These two methods differ in the allotment of points to factors and to degrees.

In the straight point method, all basic factors as well as subfactors are considered of equal importance. Each factor receives the same number of degrees, and the same number of points is allotted to each factor for the same degree. (See Table 9.7, page 238.)

In the weighted point method, now almost exclusively used, each basic factor differs from another in importance. Similarly, the number of points assigned each basic factor as well as subfactors differs according to the relative importance of factors. (See Table 7.6 for differences in point allotments.)

Acceptance of the Point Method. After Merrill R. Lott paved the way for the point method of job evaluation, a variety of weighted point methods emerged which proves its value. Each method has its variation in the number of factors, definition of factors, division into degrees, description of degrees, and the method of weighting and scoring, as can be noted from Table 7.7. This variation has been found necessary because the structure of most job evaluation plans is built to suit the particular requirements of an enterprise, depending upon the processes, products, and parts manufactured or services rendered. The factors and degrees may differ, but the techniques used in developing the plan are the same. For instance in dividing the basic factor Responsibility, all six plans shown in Table 7.7 assign a number of points for Equipment or Processes, Material or Product, and Safety of Others. In three companies, however, conditions are such that they have to consider additional subfactors. We find that some work under

TABLE 7.7

COMPARISON OF SIX WEIGHTED POINT METHODS FOR PRODUCTION JOBS

FACTORS AND SUBFACTORS	% NEMA-NMTA*	AN ELECTRIC COMPANY	REVERE COPPER & BRASS, INC.	U.S. STEEL CORP.	NATIONAL FOOTWARE ASSOC.	JOHNSON WAX CO.
SKILL						
Education...........	14	8	...	2.4	8.4	...
Experience...........	22	...	...	...	12.8	39
Initiative.............	14	...	...	...	10.6	5
Training Time........	...	21	15.7	9.3	...	...
Mentality............	...	13	...	8.1	...	...
Manual Dexterity....	...	10	10.5	4.7	...	...
TOTAL	50%	52%	26.2%	24.5%	31.8%	44%
EFFORT						
Physical.............	10	10	10.5	5.8	8.5	14
Mental and/or Visual.	5	5	10.5	5.8	12.8	4
TOTAL	15%	15%	21.0%	11.6%	21.3%	18%
RESPONSIBILITY						
General.............	...	...	...	15.1	...	...
Equipment or Processes.........	5	5	5.3	9.3	12.8	10
Material or Product...	5	5	21.1	23.3	12.8	14
Safety of Others......	5	5	5.3	4.7	6.4	5
Work of Others......	5	3	...	...	...	...
TOTAL	20%	18%	31.7%	52.4%	32.0%	29%
JOB CONDITIONS						
Working Conditions..	10	10	10.5	6.8	8.5	4
Unavoidable Hazards.	5	5	...	4.7	6.4	5
Health Hazards......	...	...	5.3	...	...	...
Current Expense.....	...	...	5.3	...	...	...
TOTAL	15%	15%	21.1%	11.5%	14.9%	9%
Total of All Factors	100%	100%	100%	100%	100%	100%

*The percentage figures shown in the NEMA-NMTA plan also indicate the number of points allotted to the first degree of each individual factor.

both the NEMA-NMTA and the electric company plans requires that workers be responsible for the Work of Others. Hence, the subfactor Work of Others was added to Equipment or Processes, Material or Product, and Safety of Others. Similarly, note that some work at the United States Steel Corporation requires General Responsibility on the part of the worker. Therefore, they regarded this subfactor important enough to assign 15.1 percent of the points to it. Along the same lines, certain subfactors that are of importance in one enterprise would be unimportant in another. Thus, if the head job analyst, the committee, the union, and those who are to administer the plan feel that the objectives will be fully achieved, a different combination of subfactors may be accepted as long as the basic factors Skill, Effort, Responsibility, and Job Conditions are included.

The method that has gained the widest acceptance, and which will be used in our future discussions for setting up a job evaluation plan, is the one originally developed at the Western Electric Company by Mr. L. V. Fisher and later adopted by the National Electric Manufacturers' Association (NEMA) and the National Metal Trades Association (NMTA). The point method is by no means an "exact science," but it may be considered systematic enough to approach the scientific method. Thus, a large degree of objectivity in evaluation and rating is achieved. As we shall see later, application of the point method is adaptable to all employee group levels within commerce and industry. From the standpoint of its resultant benefits and value to an up-to-date wage and salary program, the point method can be installed with no apparent difficulty in any organization where a multitude of jobs exist.

The point methods are based on the concept that only those factors should be used which are common to all jobs. The factors serve as a yardstick to evaluate a job according to the differences in values attached to each factor.

Advantages and Disadvantages. The advocates of the point method of job evaluation point out that it has many advantages. First, the overall job ratings are more valid than other evaluation methods because there is usually greater general agreement and consistency in the ratings among the raters. With repeated use, the method appears to have even greater validity because accuracy and consistency of the ratings tend to increase with continued use. Second, by evaluating the job independently of money rates, the evaluators are not influenced by pressures from unions, workers, or management because pricing the basic wage rate for the job is a separate process. Third, the individual rating factors and their various degrees have helped to make the subjective evaluation process more objective. Fourth, the method has great flexibility because it allows a wide choice of factors, degrees, and points that can fit the peculiar circumstances of each organization. It does not matter whether the enterprise is large, small, complex, expanding, or the like; the method can be adapted to meet the firm's needs. Fifth, evaluating jobs in terms of points makes the placing of jobs into classes quite easy and logical; it assists in pricing jobs; and it can show the relative quantitative differences in jobs. Finally, most authorities believe there is less chance of making rating errors or manipulating the ratings (cheating) because the ratings and their basis can be easily understood by most employees.

The critics of the point method point out, first, that professional talent is required to tailor-make a plan for a company. It is not a task for the inexperienced. Second, a large amount of time is consumed installing the method. Third, a large amount of clerical detail is also required.

In conclusion, the advantages far outweigh the disadvantages of the method. The impressive list of advantages has gained great acceptance for the point method in all types and sizes of enterprises. Its popularity and usage have surpassed all other basic job evaluation methods put together. In short, it has been found to be the best all-around method of job evaluation in existence.

Criteria for selecting a method of job evaluation

It is not difficult to select the proper method of job evaluation if the objectives and purposes have been clearly defined and definitely decided. Before the program is started, however, all methods should be studied to ascertain which is best fitted for the types of jobs or positions involved. The introduction of a job evaluation method is generally regarded as one of the most outstanding changes or innovations in an organization. It is, therefore, inadvisable to accept any method merely because it is used in another company. Unless the method is tailored to suit the jobs of a particular company, it will fail, since misunderstanding, poor judgment, and incorrect values usually ensue. Any one method may give satisfactory results provided it is administered and supervised by competent personnel, and if it includes management's vigilance in order to avoid complications. Normally, complications and conflicting grievances will be avoided if the inherent differences in the evaluation methods are understood.

To assist a company in selecting a method or plan of job evaluation, the following criteria are offered as guidance.

Is the Method Valid?

This question deals with how technically sound the method is; that is, whether it will do what it is supposed to do and do that consistently. To be valid the method must systematically and correctly evaluate jobs and do this consistently so that inequities can be eliminated as well as be prevented. Employee grievances on this matter are an indication of validity. Although most methods can be valid under the proper set of circumstances, the validity of the ranking and the classification methods is generally limited to small companies. If either of these methods will do the job, there is little need to saddle a small company with a more elaborate, sophisticated, and expensive method than may be needed. On the other hand, if a small company has future expansion plans, it eventually may have to convert to one of the quantitative methods that can handle a large number of jobs. If this is the situation, the company may be wise to adopt the more flexible method in the beginning.

Is the Method Practical to Use?

This question deals with the feasibility of the method and its procedures and administration within the framework of the company circumstances. All too often a method is chosen on the basis of one person who is most familiar with a certain method instead of choosing the method that is best for the company circumstances. One important consideration to be weighed is the attitude of the union. A firm needs to know whether the union is receptive to a method of job evaluation and whether it believes that the job evaluations should be conducted jointly by the union and management or by management alone. Other considerations include the need to examine the available job evaluation methods to determine whether they can be administered without undue red tape and whether present company record-keeping machines lend themselves best to one of the methods. Will the procedures of this method cost more than they are worth? The answers to these questions will help to evaluate the merits of the various methods under consideration.

Are Qualified Personnel Available to Install and Maintain the Method?

This question brings out the need for staffing the job evaluation activities. Qualified people have to be available or the evaluations can be a waste of time and money. Not only must well-respected and competent employees be available but they must also be allowed adequate time to carry out the evaluations properly. When present employees are neither available nor competent, a firm has a choice of hiring a qualified person to assume the responsibilities, or engaging a team of professional consultants to install the method and teach present employees to maintain it.

Will the Method Be Acceptable to the Workers and Management?

Workers look for a method that is consistent and equitable. They are not likely to accept any method that they cannot understand because they cannot see the fairness of the method. Highly technical and complex methods tend to make employees suspicious of management's intentions, especially if union-management relations are not good. Management personnel, especially first-line supervisors, need to understand the method thoroughly to accept it. Unless they understand the method, they cannot be expected to explain it nor to support it because it becomes a source of embarrassment to them. Assuming a job evaluation method is valid and practical, acceptance of it by top management may be based on what costs the company can afford and the amount of time required to install the method.

After a method of job evaluation has been selected, various procedures are used in its installation and administration. These procedures are the subject of the next chapter.

REVIEW QUESTIONS

1. Should every job in an organization be appraised by some job evaluation method? Why?
2. What is the difference between the quantitative and nonquantitative measures of job evaluation?

3. What general advantage do the quantitative measures of job evaluation enjoy over the nonquantitative measures? vice versa?

4. Explain the implications of using the ranking method of job evaluation.

5. Can a committee be used to advantage in the ranking method or will its use tend to make the job more difficult?

6. (a) Enumerate and briefly explain each of the four basic methods of job evaluation. (b) Under what conditions would you recommend that each of these methods be used?

7. Identify and explain each of the guidelines that should be followed in evaluating jobs through the use of job classification.

8. (a) What is a key job? (b) How is it used in the factor comparison method of job evaluation?

9. Why is the point method more commonly used in industry than the factor comparison method?

10. Why is the selection of key jobs essential in the operation of the factor comparison method?

11. What are the steps of evaluation when using the factor comparison method?

12. Compare and contrast the point method of evaluation with the factor comparison method.

13. Draw up a chart that compares the advantages and limitations of each of the four major job evaluation methods.

14. What is the difference between the straight point method and the weighted point method?

15. Which of the four methods of evaluation has met with the best acceptance? Why?

16. List the criteria that you think should be met in selecting a job evaluation method.

17. Should a company devise its own method of job evaluation to fit its particular needs, or should the company adopt a standard type plan that has been proven satisfactory by other companies?

RESEARCH OR SEMINAR QUESTIONS

1. Compare and contrast the quantitative and nonquantitative job evaluation methods and indicate the circumstances under which each can operate.

2. Why is job evaluation subjective rather than objective no matter which method is used? How can it be made more objective?

3. Is there any way to set up a method that has the advantages of both the point method and the factor comparison method?

4. How should a company go about setting up a job evaluation program?

PRACTICAL EXPERIENCE ASSIGNMENTS

The first four assignments consist of evaluating a sample set of 12 production jobs. Assignments 5 through 8 are an alternate set of assignments consisting of evaluating a sample set of 12 office and clerical jobs. In each set of assignments the four basic methods of job evaluation are used. These assignments should give you a better understanding of the methods, their problems, advantages, and limitations. The set of jobs may be evaluated individually by each student, or by committees of students, or both. The first four assignments might also be split up or assigned according to the instructor's preference and the circumstances that prevail in the locality.

1. Using the set of 12 production job descriptions or job titles on pages 194 and 195, evaluate the jobs via the ranking method. Rank the jobs in the order of value to the company. Place the rank of the job on the description in the upper left-hand corner.

2. Using the set of 12 production job descriptions on pages 194 and 195, evaluate the jobs via the job classification method. Classify each job according to one of the following classifications:

   (a) General management.
   (b) Department and associate management.
   (c) Major supervision or highly technical service.
   (d) Highly skilled service or minor supervision.
   (e) Skilled service.
   (f) Semiskilled service.
   (g) Slightly skilled service.
   (h) Unskilled service.

   Place the letter of the classification of the job on the job description in the upper right-hand corner.

3. Using the set of 12 production job descriptions on pages 194 and 195, evaluate the jobs via the factor comparison method. Consider the following jobs as key jobs that are paid the hourly rates as indicated:

Key Job	*Rate/hr.*
Janitor — Power Sweeper	$3.35
Craneman — $7\frac{1}{2}$ Ton	3.78
Punch Press — Set Up	4.00
Machinist Q — Maintenance	5.00

   Place the amount that each job is worth on the job description in the lower left-hand corner.

4. Using the set of 12 production job descriptions on pages 194 and 195, evaluate the jobs via the point method. Use the point rating manual found in Chapter 10, page 248. Place the number of points that each job is worth on the job description in the lower right-hand corner.

5. Using the set of 12 office and clerical job descriptions or job titles on pages 196 and 197, evaluate the jobs via the ranking method. Rank the jobs in the order of value to the company. Place the rank of the job on the description in the upper left-hand corner.

6. Using the set of 12 office and clerical job descriptions on pages 196 and 197, evaluate the jobs via the United States government job classification method. Classify each job according to one of 18 General Schedule (GS) job classes. Place the letter of the classification of the job on the job description in the upper right-hand corner.

7. Using the set of 12 office and clerical job descriptions on pages 196 and 197, evaluate the jobs via the factor comparison method. Consider the following jobs as key jobs that are paid the weekly rates as indicated:

Key Job	*Rate/Week*
Key-Punch Operator and Verifier — 100	$126
Telephone Switchboard Operator — 220	130
Secretary — 160	178
Tabulating Machine Operator — 80	170

Place the amount that each job is worth on the job description in the lower left-hand corner.

8. Using the set of 12 office and clerical job descriptions on pages 196 and 197, evaluate the jobs via the point method. Use the point rating manual found in Chapter 10, page 259. Place the number of points each job is worth on the job description in the lower right-hand corner.

CASE PROBLEM

7—1. COUNTY OIL COMPANY

Selection of a Suitable Job Evaluation Method

A wealthy retired manufacturing executive has become bored with retirement and has decided to establish his own oil company in your county. He plans to build 25 identical gasoline service stations in various sections of the county. He plans to staff each station with the following employees: a station manager, an assistant manager, two gas pump attendants, a grease man, and a car washer.

Problem:

You have been asked to recommend a suitable job evaluation method for the company. Make your recommendation and describe fully the reasons for your choice. Feel free to supply whatever additional details or assumptions you need to come to a conclusion on the case.

JANITOR — POWER SWEEPER

Rank _____   Class _____

Operate riding and electric types of powered floor cleaners or polishers, 16" diameter or larger. Also, perform routine sweeping and cleaning duties of a manual nature in shop and office sections. Includes: remove collected refuse, service rest and wash rooms, mop and polish floors, dusting, etc.

#F-C Units _____   # Points _____

CRANEMAN — 7½ TON

Rank _____   Class _____

Load and unload all incoming gondola and flat railroad cars and trucks. Place material in incoming area for inspection. Lift, carry, and place inspected materials for stock and shop operation as directed. Responsible for inspecting crane frequently to insure safe operation. Report all signs of weakness or obvious defects to the Maintenance Department.

#F-C Units _____   # Points _____

DRILL PRESS — RADIAL

Rank _____   Class _____

Set up, adjust, and operate a radial drill press to drill, tap, bore, ream, and spot face a variety of standardized work. Setups involve some blocking, aligning, and securing of work pieces; jigs and fixtures used on greater part of work. Occasional simple layout required. Speeds and feeds, tooling, and operational sequences standardized.

#F-C Units _____   # Points _____

PUNCH PRESS — SET UP

Rank _____   Class _____

Set up and adjust a variety of primary and secondary operations on presses ranging from 10-ton to 600-ton capacity to produce parts in accordance with tolerances and requirements. Includes compound, progressive, and universal types of dies. Responsible for setting up, adjusting, and synchronizing with the press such auxiliary equipment as dial feeds, hitch feeds, roll feeds, straighteners, scrap cutters, conveyors, limit switches. Inspect first piece with instruments, such as, 1" micrometer, rule, fixed gauges, dial indicator. Refer parts requiring other measuring instruments and procedures to departmental Inspector.

#F-C Units _____   # Points _____

ELECTRICIAN — MAINTENANCE

Rank _____   Class _____

Plan, lay out, install, and maintain a wide variety of complex electrical equipment such as machine tool controls, electronic controls, elevator controls, power house and substation equipment. Aid supervision in establishing secondary power and lighting distribution centers. Balance loads. Install power and lighting equipment in accordance with the Electrical Code. Includes determining the size of conduit, size of wire, voltage drop, temperature rise, etc. Aid Engineering Department in determining accessibility for wiring on special controls. Direct work of lower class electricians when used as helpers.

#F-C Units _____   # Points _____

ASSEMBLER

Rank _____   Class _____

Perform a variety of repetitive bench assembly and miscellaneous related operations to assemble small- and medium-size units in accordance with prescribed methods. Assemblies generally involve a limited number of different parts, rather liberal tolerances, and some adjusting of movable parts. Must recognize ill-fitting and defective parts or malfunctions affecting quality or appearance. Examples of miscellaneous operations are hand stamping, riveting, drilling, staking, gauging, packaging.

#F-C Units _____   # Points _____

TOOL AND DIE MAKER

Rank _____ Class _____

Plan, lay out, and perform all bench and machine operations to construct, alter, and repair intricately designed and constructed tools, dies, fixtures. Perform difficult machining operations requiring complicated set-ups involving the improvising of tooling and machines. Perform critical bench and assembly operations to fit, align, calibrate, adjust, assemble, and finish work. Includes developing of details where complete design specifications are not provided.

#F-C Units _____ # Points _____

MACHINE OPERATOR

Rank _____ Class _____

Perform repetitive operations on small and medium-size punch presses and spot welders, involving handling of a variety of small, light-weight parts. Tools range from simple holding fixtures to intricate, progressive punch press dies. Operation does not include setup. Inspect finished parts by comparing with sample piece, using fixed gauges or templates.

#F-C Units _____ # Points _____

LATHE — ENGINE

Rank _____ Class _____

Plan, lay out, set up, and perform a variety of operations such as turning, boring, reaming, facing, threading on fairly complicated parts having close tolerance and finish requirements. Speeds, feeds, tooling generally prescribed or selected within limited range; however, must be altered by operator to meet varying conditions and materials. Work from fairly complicated drawings and specifications; use a variety of precision-measuring instruments.

#F-C Units _____ # Points _____

MACHINIST Q — MAINTENANCE

Rank _____ Class _____

Diagnose troubles on a wide variety of precision tools such as automatic and hand screw machines, boring mills, boring bars. Plan, lay out, and perform machining operations to make replacement parts when necessary. Operate all types of machine tools such as boring mills, boring bars, planers, shapers, lathes, milling machines, profilers, drill presses. Tear down machine, usually with aid of helper, replace broken or worn parts, scrape ways, etc.; reassemble with particular care paid to aligning and fitting parts. Adapt standard machines to special purposes — make any parts necessary.

#F-C Units _____ # Points _____

TOOLKEEPER

Rank _____ Class _____

Maintain records and inventories, and issue tools, equipment, supplies, etc. Plan storage of tools and fixtures in crib. Responsible for determining and maintaining the proper levels of inventory. Responsible for controlling issuance of supplies and equipment. Required to handle and move dies with hand truck to make up the loads for various destinations.

#F-C Units _____ # Points _____

JANITOR SWEEPER

Rank _____ Class _____

Perform routine sweeping and cleaning duties of a manual nature in shop and office sections. Includes: remove collected refuse, service rest and wash rooms, mop and polish floors, dusting, etc.

#F-C Units _____ # Points _____

10. ACCOUNTING CLERK (BOOKKEEPER)

Rank _____   Class _____

Keeps a complete and systematic set of accounting records with or without the use of accounting machines . . . and/or is a member of an accounting department whose training permits handling of such assignments as: determining proper accounting entries; preparing accounting reports; analyzing accounting records to determine causes of results shown. May direct the work of junior clerks or bookkeepers. (However, exclude supervisors and persons at policy-making levels.)

#F-C Units _____   # Points _____

40. GENERAL CLERK

Rank _____   Class _____

Performs fairly complex and responsible clerical duties in accordance with standard practice. Work usually requires independent analysis, exercise of judgment, and a general knowledge of department or company policies or procedures related to work performed. Work not usually subject to detailed verification. (Exclude supervisors and those assuming responsibility at policy-making levels.)

#F-C Units _____   # Points _____

70. PAYROLL CLERK

Rank _____   Class _____

Maintains payroll records. Calculates earnings based on time cards or similar records. Posts calculated data to payroll sheets. May make out checks and assist paymaster or other officer in making up and distributing pay envelopes. May compile periodic payroll reports or earnings records.

#F-C Units _____   # Points _____

80. TABULATING MACHINE OPERATOR

Rank _____   Class _____

Operates all types of tabulating machines, including tabulators, reproducers, interpreters, collators, sorters, and multipliers in producing a variety of tabulations from punched cards. Sets up machines and wires plug boards according to established practice or from diagrams. May make minor adjustments to equipment. (Exclude supervisors or operators in charge of machine room or other operators, and those capable of planning complex wiring diagrams to meet special problems.)

#F-C Units _____   # Points _____

100. KEY-PUNCH OPERATOR and VERIFIER

Rank _____   Class _____

Operates numerical or alphabetical key-punch machine and/or verifier to record/verify a variety of data by means of perforations in tabulating cards. Requires thorough knowledge of source materials, card forms, complex setups; gives close attention to selection of information, sequence of recording and use of proper columns. Usually required to machine verify the work of other key-punch operators and must be an experienced operator.

#F-C Units _____   # Points _____

220. TELEPHONE SWITCHBOARD OPERATOR

Rank _____   Class _____

Operates at a multiposition switchboard (usually full-time) handling all types of telephone calls with courtesy, tact, and speed. May operate various types of in-plant communications systems; should have good knowledge of firm's personnel. May keep records on calls and do other minor clerical duties if clearly subordinate to operator assignment.

#F-C Units _____   # Points _____

120. CALCULATING MACHINE OPERATOR

Rank _____ Class

Operates calculating machine (Comptometer or other type) a major part of time to perform varied or complex computations and including the basic computations of adding, subtracting, multiplying, and dividing. Frequently required to exercise judgment in selection and application of data; knowledge of background subject matter usually necessary. Generally checks and verifies computations. (Exclude employees whose jobs require only incidental use of calculating machine or who use it only for adding and subtracting.)

#F-C Units _____ # Points

140. DUPLICATING MACHINE OPERATOR

Rank _____ Class

Operates stencil, fluid (spirit), or simple offset-type office duplicator. Responsible for mechanical operation and makes necessary minor adjustments and repairs to produce good quality reproduction.

#F-C Units _____ # Points

150. FILE CLERK

Rank _____ Class

Arranges, sorts, and files routine material (correspondence, cards, invoices, or other records) that has already been classified or indexed. May classify and index simple material. Removes material from file on request and may keep record of disposition. No previous clerical or filing training required.

#F-C Units _____ # Points

160. SECRETARY

Rank _____ Class

Performs with skill and efficiency the complete secretarial job for a high-level executive or a person responsible for a major functional or geographic operation. Does work of a confidential nature and is able to relieve principal of designated administrative details as well as acting for him in matters not requiring his presence. Requires initiative; judgment; knowledge of company practices, policy, and organization. May direct the work of a small number of clerical or stenographic employees.

#F-C Units _____ # Points

180. STENOGRAPHER

Rank _____ Class

Records and transcribes dictation of more than average difficulty, rapidly and accurately, by use of shorthand and/or transcribing machine. May perform related clerical duties. Must have general knowledge of the firm's organization, products, terminology and procedures, and must use judgment in carrying out assignments with minimum supervision. May plan the setup for and type complicated tables, unusual reports, or similar material. Should also be able to do volume typing with speed and accuracy.

#F-C Units _____ # Points

200. TYPIST

Rank _____ Class

Types rapidly and accurately on different machines varied material of a nature requiring a general knowledge of the organization, terminology, and procedures. Plans the setup and arrangement for typing complicated tables, reports, and other material from rough drafts. Must use judgment and skill in carrying out assignments with a minimum of supervision. May do related clerical work as a minor portion of overall assignments.

#F-C Units _____ # Points

chapter 8

PROCEDURES USED
TO EVALUATE JOBS

The success of a job evaluation method depends upon the ways and means that are planned and executed in accordance with predetermined broad objectives and policies. The plan should be convincingly fair in order to withstand objections when changes or new procedures are introduced due to unprofitable business conditions. Otherwise, the plan will be questioned by the rank-and-file workers, regarded unfavorably by supervisors, and resisted by union leaders.

For a job evaluation method to succeed, any possible difficulties should be anticipated and precautions should be taken to minimize them, thereby avoiding misunderstandings and unfavorable criticism by union members and the supervisory force. Ready acceptance of the method assures smooth workability and successful administration of the program, especially if the employees and supervisors are convinced that decisions are not biased nor is favoritism practiced.

Installing a job evaluation and rating plan

The process of developing a job evaluation and rating program consists of a number of well-defined steps that shall be discussed in detail. It involves setting up an organizational procedure that takes into consideration the main features of job classification, job analysis, job description, job rating, job grading, and job pricing. When setting up a job evaluation plan, it is advisable to take a long-range point of view since many personnel activities may be directly or indirectly affected by job evaluation. For instance, in addition to their main purpose of stabilizing the wage and salary structure, job analysis and job descriptions may also be utilized as aids in employment procedures, training, work method improvements, employee evaluation, and other organizational activities.

Steps and Techniques in Installing the Plan

The following outline and description of the steps necessary to take in installing a job evaluation and rating plan have been drawn from the authors' experiences in installing point plans, without resorting to any specific pattern. The sequence of these steps and techniques may vary in some companies, and fewer steps may be required when using some of the other job evaluation methods discussed in Chapter 7. To make the presentation of techniques and the explanation of installations as realistic as possible, we shall utilize data being used successfully by both small and large companies as factual examples.

Under normal conditions it is advisable to proceed in accordance with the steps enumerated below:

1. Convince top management of the resultant benefits when starting a job evaluation program in accordance with predetermined objectives.
2. Appoint a chief analyst or job evaluation engineer to supervise the program from its inception to its final installation and administration.
3. Authorize the chief analyst, or job evaluation engineer, to develop the program and to prepare details of procedure for the guidance of a committee. At the same time, top management should decide which jobs should first be evaluated and rated — shop jobs, office jobs, or professional jobs.
4. Inform supervisors and employees of the intention to install a job evaluation plan, and explain the objectives involved.
5. Select a committee to cooperate in the evaluation and installation of the plan. Give special attention to union attitudes and the selection of union members to represent the workers. The chief analyst should explain the objectives, procedure, and method to be used.
6. Decide on standard terminology and design of forms, including those needed to collect preliminary data. This step is especially important if a new tailor-made plan is to be inaugurated.
7. Prepare an occupational classification.
8. Decide on the number of basic job factors and subfactors (characteristics or attributes), including their descriptions and definitions. Establish weightings (in percent) according to the importance of the basic factors. At the same time, decide on the number of degrees for each factor, and the specific number of points to be allotted for each degree.
9. Prepare a manual to assist in the use of standard factors, definitions, evaluations, and ratings. For this purpose, select a number of key jobs. Evaluate and assign a total number of points for each key job in accordance with the established procedure. Then evaluate all other jobs.

10. Decide on the procedures that will be used to collect data. Analyze jobs and prepare job descriptions for specifications and ratings.
11. Set up 10 to 15 job grades (job classes) for job ranking purposes to establish a relationship between point ratings and wage-base rates. Assign money values to job grades (pricing the job) in accordance with union agreements or a wage survey.
12. Construct a scatter chart with a wage curve. The curve is known as a "trend line," "line of average relationship," "mean curve," and "line of correlation." Establish range limits, and correlate job grades with the existing wage-base rates. (The charting of wage and salary rates is discussed in Chapter 13.)
13. Establish new wage-base rates or adjust existent wage-base rates to fall in line with the established midpoint for each job grade on the mean curve or trend line.
14. Follow up and periodically check results after installation of the plan. Provide a procedure for corrections and readjustments to meet economic changes, and to keep the job evaluation program up-to-date at all times.

Gaining the Interest and Support of Top Management

A job evaluation program is seldom successful if there is insufficient interest by top management. Top management must be thoroughly convinced that the installation and upkeep of a job evaluation and rating plan will eliminate friction and unfavorable wage-rate adjustments. Creation of a factual program with established standards to pay wage-base rates on an equitable basis is of deep concern to both management and the workers. The many successful job evaluation programs that have been installed in large, medium-size, and small companies prove the need for such a plan for industrial peace and profitable employer-employee relations. These are facts that must be recognized by top management.

Furthermore, top management should pave the way by issuing a statement of policy to employees long before any activity for setting up the plan begins. The statement of policy should cover the most important phases of the program, thus avoiding future embarrassing misunderstandings. The program should be clearly presented to supervisors and employees alike, including a brief outline of the scope and procedure in conformity with some of the steps outlined above. Some companies deem it sufficient to make their announcements in the manner illustrated in Figures 8.1 and 8.2.

Appointing a Chief Job Analyst to Serve As Coordinator

If top management is convinced of the necessity of setting up a job evaluation program, a chief analyst should be appointed to concentrate on processing the program, to coordinate all activities, and to represent management whenever important decisions have to be made. Any executive or staff employee who is conversant with all phases and techniques of job evaluation and who has the

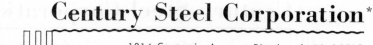

Century Steel Corporation*

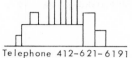

1214 Carnegie Avenue, Pittsburgh, PA 15219

Telephone 412-621-6191

April 15, 19--

To All Employees of the Manufacturing Division:

Subject: Job Evaluation and Rating Plan

At a meeting held on April 13, 19-- by management representatives of the Century Steel Corporation and representatives
of the employee organizations, it was mutually agreed to undertake a study of all jobs and positions for the purpose of
establishing fair and equitable wage-base rates and salaries.

To accomplish this task, a Joint Job Evaluation Committee
was formed which will function under the direction of Mr.
John F. Melvin, the Job Evaluation Engineer.

We wish to assure all employees that the committee will be
unbiased in evaluating the JOBS, without reference to the
workers performing the jobs.

UNDER NO CONDITION WILL THERE BE
ANY WAGE-BASE RATE REDUCTIONS

It is the objective and aim of the company to have all jobs
evaluated to determine a fair value of a particular job in
relation to all other jobs. Certain jobs are out of line,
needing adjustment upward. Consequently, there is a possibility that a number of employees will benefit by increases
on that basis.

All employees will be informed of the procedure and progress
made by the joint committee.

CENTURY STEEL CORPORATION

Robert S. Tumser
Works Manager

dm

*Fictitious company name and location.

FIGURE 8.1 LETTER TO EMPLOYEES ANNOUNCING THE JOB EVALUATION
PROGRAM

analytical ability to make a thorough study of wages and salary administration
may be selected as the chief analyst or the "job evaluation engineer." Successful
installations have been made by company employees who hold staff positions
such as chief engineer, industrial engineer, chief statistician, head of methods
department, personnel manager, time study engineer, and chief of wages and
incentives division.

Century Steel Corporation*

1214 Carnegie Avenue, Pittsburgh, PA 15219

Telephone 412-621-6191

May 1, 19--

To All Employees of the Manufacturing Division:

It has come to our attention that some workers doubt that job evaluation and job rating can accomplish fair results.

To substantiate the mutual value of job evaluation for the employer
and employee alike, we quote the following excerpt from a bulletin
prepared by the Technical Division, United States Conciliation Service, Department of Labor, November, 1944, which is self-explanatory:

> "Job evaluation is one of the most highly developed of
> the various techniques used to measure the relative worth
> of jobs and is being increasingly looked upon as the best
> solution to the problem of wage determination. It pro-
> vides labor and management with a yardstick to measure
> all jobs within a company; assures that all jobs receive
> the same consideration; is the means of determining the
> worth of a new or revised job; establishes a logical rela-
> tionship between jobs in the separate divisions or depart-
> ments of a plant; and eliminates as far as possible the
> sources of irritation caused by inequalities and incon-
> sistencies.... Job evaluation is essentially the study of
> the content of each job, without regard to personalities,
> to establish objectively the relative worth of one job to
> another within a given plant."

The task of achieving our objective may look difficult. However,
with your wholehearted cooperation and help we shall accomplish our
purpose to the satisfaction of all concerned. Some employees may
have to fill out questionnaires, others will be interviewed by a
member of the committee. Please do your utmost to respond with
accurate information.

Mark W. Gerhardt	Robert S. Tumser
Edward A. Adams	Works Manager
Ralph M. Holmes	
Gregory J. Caldwell	John F. Melvin
Union Representatives	Job Evaluation Engineer

dm

*Fictitious company name and location.

FIGURE 8.2 Follow-up Letter Assuring Benefits from Job
Evaluation

When a staff member is selected for the important position of chief job
analyst, it should be ascertained that he is just and fair in all matters of human
and industrial relations. In the absence of such staff or professional employees,
a consultant management engineer should start the program and carry it through
to its complete installation. During that period, someone should be appointed
as chief analyst to assist the consultant in coordinating the important details and
to eventually take over the activity as a special function.

As stated elsewhere, ready-made plans *with modifications* can be installed with good results by any member of the organization as long as he is thoroughly conversant with the job requirements, adopting only those features of the plan that fit the company conditions. On the other hand, if it is essential to design a tailor-made plan, it may be advantageous to obtain the services of a consultant who specializes in job evaluation, and thereby benefit by his experience. This is especially desirable in those situations where union members are distrustful of the employer. The consultant, being an "outsider," may be of inestimable value in conciliating the employees and in gaining their confidence. Thus, matters will be simplified for the job analyst acting in his capacity as the coordinator of all activities in the interests of employer and employee alike.

Preparing the Evaluation and Rating Program

As soon as the job analyst has been authorized to proceed with the program, his first responsibility is to prepare a detailed outline of procedure to guide those who will participate in the evaluation and rating. This is especially important if the work is to be carried out by a joint job evaluation committee comprising union members and management representatives. The outline should point out which employee group level will be affected first; the evaluation method to be used; the manner in which the evaluation and rating, as such, will be carried out; how decisions will be made regarding the selection of factors, their descriptions and definitions; how facts and information, in general, will be collected; and how job pricing will be accomplished.

When top management and the chief analyst agree on the details of procedure, the next step is to inform all supervisors, unions, and employees of the intention to install a job evaluation plan. The information may be submitted by notices posted on bulletin boards, or by letters sent to each employee, after the company has favorably discussed the preliminaries with representatives of either the union or employees. The same representatives should be willing to become members of a committee that will eventually function in setting up and installing the plan. This is, perhaps, the most important step. It leads toward an understanding that the employees will have a voice in most of the decisions on job evaluation, and that the employees' interests will be guarded by their representatives on the committee. The first notice or letter should also indicate that further bulletins explaining the main points of the procedure and the workings of job evaluation will be either posted on bulletin boards or mailed to each employee.

One Man's Plan Not Desirable

Some failures in the introduction of a job evaluation plan are directly traceable to a "one man's plan." Such plans invariably comprise poorly chosen factors, degrees, and their definitions, which affect the establishment of base rates. This is understandable because one individual cannot be expected to have a thorough acquaintance with all the jobs and their necessary requirements. Granted that a study of job conditions and job environments can be made by a properly qualified analyst, nevertheless, certain important details may be overlooked. This would not happen, however, if supervisors, operators, and union stewards participated as committee members in all the activities of job evaluation. In order to ascertain the varying degrees of difficulties and objectionable or unimportant features of some jobs, specific information about the job performance and a detailed knowledge of multitudinous operations are required, which only the supervisors and operators are able to disclose.

Since job evaluation is used as an aid in setting wage rates which, in turn, are subject to collective bargaining, it stands to reason that a lack of union participation will invariably result in opposition to the whole idea of one man's decisions. It is common knowledge that some unions harbor a traditional distrust of management's unilateral methods of decision making concerning the setting of wage rates. Therefore, the union should not only be informed of what is transpiring, but should also become an active participant in carrying out the program. Thus, any disagreements which may stem from possible claims that one man's decisions in establishing details are biased may be avoided.

In many cases where only one individual carries out the installation of a job evaluation plan, rumors, misunderstandings, and unfavorable reactions cause distrust, even when employees are informed of the "new wage system" prior to the installation. Experience has proven that employees assume that the "newfangled ideas" will affect their wages, or that some incentive plan will be combined with the new wage system to reduce their earnings. Human reaction among the rank and file is such that the fear of one who suspects a reduction will influence all others even though their fears are unfounded and they will not be affected by any reductions whatsoever. An assurance that present wage-base rates will not be reduced,[1] as incorporated in the letter to employees in Figure 8.1, will do much to clear the air, but will not be effective unless employee representation is included to carry out the program.

Selecting a Job Evaluation Committee

To avoid adverse reactions and to assure success, a committee should be selected to act in an advisory capacity as well as to actually participate in completing the various tasks involved in evaluation and rating. Members of the committee should be selected to represent management, immediate supervisors, the union, and the workers whose jobs are to be evaluated. To inspire further confidence and trust, employee representatives should be elected by the workers

---

[1]In Chapter 13 the problem of how to avoid rate reductions without causing wage inequities or losses to the employer will be discussed.

themselves. Thus, when some misconception has to be corrected, or when management appeals to the employees for cooperation through written communication, inclusion of the names of their chosen representatives, as shown in Figure 8.2, will be more influential and will lend an atmosphere of confidence.

As soon as the committee is organized, the chief job analyst should prepare the necessary preliminary forms and manuals, and arrange a training program to familiarize the committee members with the principles, objectives, and techniques of job evaluation. Such training and orientation may take many hours or even weeks, but it should be regarded as time worth spending. If all committee members clearly understand what is involved, the collection of factual information, job analysis, evaluation, and rating will proceed considerably smoother than if the members "have to find their way." Disagreements may be caused by personal prejudices, lack of job knowledge, or misunderstanding of the factors and degrees involved. One of the advantages of the committee arrangement is that by exchanging ideas, clarification and conciliation will be facilitated and differences of opinion may be compromised. Hence, evaluation will be completed without undue friction and misunderstandings. The smooth workings of the committee and its progress should be reported to the employees periodically in a brief explanation.

Union reaction to job evaluation

It is sometimes assumed that most unions oppose job evaluation just as they opposed time and motion study and financial incentive plans in earlier years. Opposition to job evaluation did prevail in some dispersed locals where the "old guard" of the AFL horizontal craft unions was in power. This cannot be said, however, of the majority of today's enlightened AFL and CIO leaders. Wherever CIO unions had refused job evaluation, it was not because of their disagreement with the principle, but rather because they were not given the opportunity to voice their opinion and to participate in the program. Let us examine the record.

During 1946–1947, the American Management Association's Research Department examined 100 contracts covering office employees in a representative cross section of business and industry. They found that approximately 50 percent of the contracts included clauses on existing job evaluation programs, and that about 8 percent contained clauses on a proposed job evaluation plan to be installed within a certain period. A survey made by Smyth and Murphy discovered that out of 36 companies having job evaluation plans, 47 percent of the programs were union-management installations.[2] A survey completed by author Langsner in 1953 indicated that, of 172 agreements contracted with labor unions, 33 percent contained bargaining clauses pertaining to job evaluation. In a study

---

[2]R. C. Smyth and M. J. Murphy, "How Industry Is Using Time Study and Incentives," *Factory Management and Maintenance*, No. 1 (January, 1945).

of 320 companies by Patton in 1960, 83 percent of the companies indicated that the job evaluation program was recognized in the union contract.[3]

Joint Union-Management Job Evaluation

Let us reemphasize one of the fundamental principles stressed in the introductory chapters that a successful enterprise, regardless of size, serves three groups proportionately alike — the employer, the employee, and the buying public. Properly applied, this principle is the essence of a sound union-management relationship. In the employer-employee relationship, one should not take advantage of the other. For, just as unions may overestimate their importance, thereby endangering the interests of their own organization, management, representing the employer, may underestimate the value of employees, thus jeopardizing the welfare of the employer, the employees, and the public.

The old idea of management's insistence on the prerogative to unilaterally install job evaluation appears to be giving way to the acceptance of union-management decisions. In the study by Patton, 18 percent of the companies said that their unions participated with management in their job evaluation programs.[4] In 34 percent of the companies, the union even helped management select the plan of job evaluation to be used.[5] In 25 percent of the companies, the managements made concessions to the union on job evaluation matters. However, some managements still refuse participation by unions because they believe this to be solely a management prerogative or because they feel that the union is irresponsible. It would appear that managements have much more to gain than to lose by inviting *qualified* and *responsible* unions to join them in their job evaluation programs. When such a union participates in job evaluation, it is believed that employees are more likely to understand and accept the results of the evaluations because the union had a hand in making them. This places some obligation on the union to defend such decisions. Joint participation has also been known to build trust and confidence between the employees and the employer as well as to eliminate a number of grievances. Furthermore, union participation tends to help satisfy the needs of some employees to contribute. The critics of joint union-management participation in job evaluation point out that this arrangement has some disadvantages. Management no longer has the complete say-so on decisions and may find that the process of job evaluation takes more time. On the other hand, if management has to spend much time justifying its unilateral decisions, the joint decision may actually consume more time in the short run but less time in the long run. Unions are sometimes accused of working too closely with management and they may be called upon to defend job evalua-

---

[3]John Patton, "What 320 Companies Say About Job Evaluation," *Factory* (October, 1960), p. 108.
[4]*Ibid.*
[5]*Ibid.*

tions. We believe unions have to assume such responsibilities whenever they wish to participate in managerial decisions.

The answer as to whether management should handle job evaluation alone or jointly with the union should be made on the basis of which method will accomplish the evaluations with greater objectivity, fairness, understanding, and acceptance. When a union accepts management's invitation to participate jointly in job evaluation, the union-management committee is the vehicle used to perform the necessary work.

The Union-Management Committee

The joint union-management committee of a fairly large manufacturing company is normally composed of two groups: (a) the *permanent committee* (known also as the steering committee), and (b) the *advisory committee.*

The permanent committee may consist of:

1. The chief job analyst, acting as chairman and coordinator.
2. A representative from the personnel department.
3. A representative from the time study or methods department.
4. The factory manager, or superintendent.
5. The general foreman or a foreman's representative.
6. A representative from the local union, or the chief steward.
7. An employee from the office (preferably a union member if union organized).
8. A union member from the manufacturing departments.
9. A union member from the assembling departments.
10. A union member from the maintenance department.
11. A union member representing shipping, receiving, and housekeeping departments.

The advisory committee functions only whenever either an occupational job group or all jobs of a department are being described and evaluated. In such cases the department manager or foreman, the department steward, or any other union member acting as representative of the department automatically become members of the advisory committee. After the jobs of a department have been described and evaluated, the advisory committee of that department ceases to function. If the jobs of another department are to be described and evaluated, a new advisory committee is selected from that department.

The union-management committee of a smaller company can function just as effectively with a smaller representation from management and workers, as long as management and union members are equally represented. As stated before, employee representatives should be selected by the employees themselves.

Why Unions May Object to Job Evaluation

Unions are sometimes indifferent and other times even adamant about job evaluation. Patton found that there is three times as much resistance to job evaluation in the East as in the central or western states.[6] The lack of union interest and cooperation in job evaluation matters may be due to any number of reasons. However, the main reasons unions may object to job evaluation appear to be as follows: (1) management shortcomings, (2) differences in union or management views on job evaluation, and (3) a lack of job evaluation knowledge by unions.

Management Shortcomings in the Use of Job Evaluation. At its inception, job evaluation underwent some trials and errors that created false impressions and misconceptions. In some instances, wage-base rates may have been cut after a program went into effect, thus causing justifiable resentment and opposition. Today many managements are failing to see to it that employees understand job evaluation. One study showed that more than half of the employees have a poor understanding of job evaluation.[7] The same study pointed out that only 20 percent of the companies use a committee to evaluate jobs and that 56 percent of the companies have only one person assigned to handle the entire program. It is difficult to understand how any one person can be so knowledgeable that he can make the hundreds of judgments involved in evaluating jobs without being accused of being arbitrary. It is well to remember that to be a success, a job evaluation program must earn the general respect of the company employees. There are very few individuals capable of doing this job single-handed. Managements have also been criticized for providing inadequate training for their job analysts. Employees have been quick to complain about job evaluation programs that are erroneously claimed to be scientific and about those that are unduly complicated and technical. Finally, some managements draw criticism for poorly administering an otherwise valid job evaluation program.

Conflicting Views of Unions and Managements. Generally, managements rely heavily upon job content as the basis for job evaluations. Some unions have objected to this because they believe that there are other considerations that should be used to evaluate the worth of a job. For example, should a dead-end job (one having no promotional outlook) be worth more than one which is a stepping stone to a better job? Should supply and demand be considered? Should the prestige or security of the job be considered? These are questions that may be difficult to answer. In the evaluation of jobs, the evaluator must keep in mind that only job factors are to be evaluated and not the people who fill the jobs. When one speaks of such considerations as supply and demand, prestige, security, promotion, and the like, these are primarily factors that apply to persons filling the job and therefore are not generally either suitable nor practical to use as job evaluation factors. They may be used in pricing jobs after the job

---

[6]*Ibid.*
[7]*Ibid.*

evaluations have been made but are not commonly accepted as job evaluation yardsticks. On the other hand, any job evaluation method that utilizes factors to evaluate jobs (such as the point method and the factor comparison method) can incorporate any factor that is believed to have a true basis for evaluating the job.

Two union leaders, Solomon Barkin, representative of the Textile Workers' Union of America, and William Gomberg, former representative of the International Ladies' Garment Workers' Union (ILGWU), AFL, have written articles containing conflicting views about job evaluation. Barkin, although recognizing that job evaluation has brought some beneficial results, believes it is a management tool favoring management and that it does not favor collective bargaining.[8] Gomberg's position is as follows:

> It seems that the problem which job evaluation presents to collective bargaining is not so much how to fight it as a management tool, but rather how to reshape it into a more useful collective bargaining instrument. . . . If the tail of job evaluation succeeds in wagging the dog of collective bargaining, it is largely because the dog does not know how to use its tail. Cutting it off by rejecting job evaluation is much like cutting off one's nose to spite one's face. . . . Mr. Barkin seems most anxious to preserve complete freedom to dicker and bargain without any fundamental guiding principles except the loose term, collective bargaining.[9]

Uninformed Unions. Some unions reject job evaluation because they are uninformed or have been misinformed about the true nature of job evaluation. Being misinformed may be due to early abuses of job evaluation by managements. In other instances, it may have been that unions were remiss in learning about the true nature of job evaluation. Somehow, some unions even today still fail to see the distinction between the evaluation of jobs and the pricing of jobs. They fail to understand that once jobs have been fairly evaluated in relationship to each other, these values must remain as stable standards without fluctuation as long as the job does not change. The pricing of a job can be accomplished only *after* the job has been evaluated. Job evaluation and job pricing are not synonymous, for pricing a job is a bargainable topic and the price can vary with the times. Job evaluation should be performed in a manner acceptable to the union, but once the evaluations have been made, they are not subject to change by bargaining. They should be changed only if a clerical error or a change in the job is made. To do otherwise is to establish a "rubber yardstick" that could be used to manipulate jobs in favor of either the management or the union. No union or management should advocate this.

---

[8]Solomon Barkin, "Wage Determination; Trick or Technique," *Labor and Nation*, I (June–July, 1946).
[9]William Gomberg, "A Collective Bargaining Approach to Job Evaluation," *Labor and Nation*, II (November–December, 1946). Quoted with Dr. Gomberg's permission.

Fields in which job evaluation is being applied

At the close of World War II, the vast majority of all job evaluation plans were primarily designed for shop and factory workers because there was great pressure on managements by unions. Today, the older factory plans are being polished and refined while managements are being faced with increasing pressure to evaluate all technical, clerical, professional, administrative, executive, and supervisory jobs, because sound management also requires a defensible evaluation of these positions.

Job and Position Groups

Job evaluation and rating plans are now sucessfully installed in the following six job and position groups:

Group Plan 1. For jobs performed by shop and factory workers, utility, general service, and hospital employees who receive compensation on an hourly wage-base rate.

Group Plan 2. For jobs of office and clerical employees in factories, banks, utility companies, department stores, and hospitals who receive salaries, as well as for nonexempt employees being paid hourly wage-base rates.

Group Plan 3. For jobs and positions of supervisors, such as foremen, office managers, store managers, nurse supervisors, hospital housekeepers, and chief accountants.

Group Plan 4. For jobs of salesmen, demonstrators, distributors, sales engineers, and other functions performed in the sales and marketing fields.

Group Plan 5. For jobs of specialists, professional and technical positions, such as engineers, draftsmen, designers, hospital specialists, inspectors, and X-ray technicians.

Group Plan 6. For positions of managerial and leading executives, department heads, operating division heads, chiefs of technical and experimental divisions, superintendents, works managers, and managers in charge of production, sales, and other functions.

Whether each of the six groups is to be considered individually or in some combination depends upon the products manufactured or the services rendered. The fundamental principles of evaluation are the same for all groups. However, the techniques may differ in many respects, especially in the number of factors, their definitions, degrees, and the assigned number of points.

As stated in Chapter 7, there is no specific need for a fully developed point method if the salaried clerical positions, supervisory jobs, professional, and technical positions are few. In such cases, a small number of factors may be established and the ranking method may be applied. The pricing of jobs can be accomplished by comparison and by general inquiry in the community relative to salaries paid for the same or similar positions.

If the point method is selected for a large or medium-size company, the best procedure is to design a tailor-made plan for each group since the jobs, processes, techniques, and equipment vary with each company. Point method plans designed by trade and professional associations, such as the National Electrical Manufacturers' Association (NEMA), the Life Office Management Association (LOMA), and the National Footwear Manufacturing Association, Inc. (NFMA), have proven so effective, however, that the same plan has been adopted with slight modifications for all their members.

Illustrative Cases of Job Evaluation Plans

The National Electrical Manufacturers' Association (NEMA) was the first to adopt a uniform point method plan for hourly rated shop jobs of its member companies (1937). About 12 years later, it adopted the same kind of "yardstick" to evaluate *technical, accounting, clerical, supervisory*, and *general salaried jobs*. NEMA introduced its salaried job plan with the following statement:

> Notwithstanding the wide use of job rating for evaluating factory jobs, little has been done in establishing sound salary structures, based on job rating, to assure the elimination of inequities among the clerical, supervisory, and technical groups. The extension of job rating into this area is one of the most constructive steps a company concerned with sound employee relations can take.[10]

Table 8.1 lists twenty key jobs that NEMA uses for example purposes, utilizing the same six factors for all key jobs.[11]

TABLE 8.1

KEY JOBS USED BY NEMA AS EXAMPLES FOR JOB DESCRIPTIONS AND RATING SHEETS FOR SALARIED JOBS

Dictating Machine Operator	Secretary— Class B
Expediter	Stenographer
Foreman — Conveyor Assembly	Supervisor — Cost Section
Foreman — Tool Room	Supervisor — Safety and Health
Interviewer — Employment	Tabulating Machine Operator
Key Punch Operator — Class A	Telephone Operator
Mail Clerk	Telephone Operator-Receptionist
Messenger	Time Study Man — Class A
Nurse — Industrial	Tool Designer — Class B
Sales Engineer	Typist

Source: National Electrical Manufacturers' Association.

---

[10]*Manual of Procedure for Use of NEMA Salaried Job Rating Plans* (New York: National Electrical Manufacturers' Association, 1949), p. iii.

[11]*Ibid.*, p. 13.

S. C. Johnson & Son, Inc., manufacturers of wax products and chemical specialties, employing approximately 2,000 workers, developed six distinct job evaluation plans classified as: (1) factory plan, (2) office plan, (3) specialized and technical plan, (4) sales plan, (5) supervisory plan, and (6) executive plan. The point method is used in all six plans. These plans were installed in 1946, and some revisions were made in 1953, 1961, and 1965.[12]

The Revere Copper and Brass Corporation established four distinct group plans that are used in all seven of its divisions which are located in different cities of the United States. The plans are for: (1) hourly rated occupations in the production departments, (2) clerical positions, (3) supervisory positions, and (4) functional and technical positions.

The Bell & Howell Company, manufacturer of precision photo and movie equipment, employing about 9,400 workers, uses three distinct plans. Two of these plans are designed and administered in conformity with NMTA plans. One serves for all hourly rated shop workers, and the other for salaried and hourly rated office workers, including professional and technical employees and supervisors. A third plan of the company's own design is used for executive and administrative positions.

The Life Office Management Association (LOMA) made an exhaustive study of the various plans that existed prior to 1939, before it recommended its own point plan for insurance company offices. In 1948 some minor changes were made, but the original plan remained in effect. During the past two decades, however, progress in the field of job evaluation has outdated LOMA's original point plan. Thus, LOMA has worked out the LOMA Key Job Comparison System especially for evaluating clerical jobs in life insurance companies. This plan covers five job families of clerical workers that are further broken down into 23 key jobs as shown in Table 8.2.

Occupational and job classifications

Occupational classification is the grouping of jobs into general classes relating to the same occupation or profession which usually requires similar skills, techniques, and qualifications for specific jobs.

Job classification is an identification of specific jobs within an occupational group. Jobs are separated and individually defined according to job content following adopted criteria such as duties, work environments, processes, training, experience, responsibility, and physical exertion. Through job classification, broad occupational families can be separated into subgroups or job families that have the same factors as common denominators. The group may be distinguished by appropriate headings, job or position titles, codes, and distinctly classified descriptions.

---

[12]Information and data received from D. L. McClelland, Chemical Engineer, S. C. Johnson & Son, Inc., 1966.

TABLE 8.2
JOB FAMILIES AND KEY JOBS USED BY LOMA FOR EVALUATING CLERICAL JOBS IN LIFE INSURANCE COMPANIES

PROCESSING	ACCOUNTING	SECRETARIAL	OPERATION	SUPERVISOR
File Clerk	Junior Accounting Clerk	Clerk-Typist	Key-Punch Operator	Unit Leader
Senior File Clerk	Accounting Reviewer	Contract Typist	Senior Key-Punch Operator	Unit Supervisor
MIB Coder	General Ledger Clerk	Transcriber	Tabulating Machine Operator	Assistant Section Supervisor
Examiner	Accounting Approver	Senior Transcriber	Senior Tabulating Machine Operator	
	Accountant	Stenographic Secretary Secretary Executive Secretary		

Job Definitions

The *Dictionary of Occupational Titles*[13] contains definitions of 21,741 jobs that are known by 35,550 titles. For best results, the occupations have been initially classified into nine major groups, then arranged into occupational divisions and job subdivisions. The classification structure provides a code range of one to six digits to cover the scope of the groups and divisions. The first digit indicates the major occupational categories; the second digit indicates major occupational divisions within the groups; and the third digit indicates specific occupations within the divisions. The fourth digit indicates a job's relationship to data or "information, knowledge, and concepts, related to data, people, or things, obtained by observation, investigation, interpretation, visualization, or mental creation." The fifth digit indicates the job's relationship to people. The sixth digit indicates the job's relationship to things or those inanimate objects such as substances, materials, machines, tools, equipment, and products that are distinguished from human beings. In reading the fourth, fifth and sixth digit, it is important to remember that the *more* complex the relationship, the *lower* the assigned number. A 0 or 1 indicates a highly complex relationship, whereas an 8 indicates a relatively insignificant relationship. Figure 8.3

---

[13]U.S. Department of Labor, *Dictionary of Occupational Titles*; Vol. I, *Definitions of Titles*; Vol. II, *Occupational Classifications* (3d ed.; Washington: U.S. Government Printing Office, 1965).

shows a sample job broken down by its Occupational Categories, Occupational Divisions, and Divisional Groups, and codification as to relationships between the job and data, people, and things.

Occupational classification aids job description and rating if there are a number of different jobs in the same category. It also helps to classify the jobs into levels or grades from highest to lowest or lowest to highest for the purpose of determining the value in number of points and monetary worth, as explained in Chapter 13.

Need for Standard Classification

The unusually rapid development of specialization, the increased number of new products and new jobs, as well as the introduction of new professions and inventions, have caused our terminology to become complex. Job titles and job descriptions differ within the offices and plants of one company and, more so, in the same industry. Similarly, the same terms used for different jobs cause confusion regarding actual values and differential compensation. We therefore stress the importance of standard classification and job description, as further evidenced by the following example of occupational classification.

In earlier years, a pair of shoes was completely finished by one or two shoe-makers. With advanced mechanization and specialization, however, shoe-making has been divided into 40 to 80 different jobs and 100 to 250 operations, depending upon whether slippers, shoes, or boots are being manufactured. Thus, in the present shoe manufacturing industry, shoemakers in the old sense have been replaced by workers on jobs under different categories. Some of these jobs are arranged in five classes as listed below. They show the need for occupational classification and proper titles in order to describe job contents.

Job Classification A
CUTTER
1. Sock Lining Cutter
2. Trimmings Cutter
3. Outside Cutter

Job Classification B
HEEL WORKER
1. Heel-Lift Cementer
2. Heel Sander
3. Heel Slugger
4. Heel Breaster

Job Classification C
LASTER
1. Side Laster
2. Bed Laster

Job Classification D
SANDER
1. Rubber Lift Sander
2. Heel Sander

Job Classification E
TRIMMER
1. Heel Seat Trimmer
2. Insole Trimmer
3. Heel Trimmer
4. Edge Trimmer

SAMPLE JOB: Machine Repairman, Maintenance
NUMBER: 626.281

Coding: 6 2 6 . 2 8 1

MAJOR OCCUPATIONAL CATEGORIES (9)	OCCUPATIONAL DIVISIONS (84)	DIVISIONAL GROUPS (603)	RELATIONSHIP OF JOB TO DATA	RELATIONSHIP OF JOB TO PEOPLE	RELATIONSHIP OF JOB TO THINGS
0, 1 Professional Managerial and Technical	0 Metal Machining Occupations	0 Motorized Vehicle and Engineering Equipment Mechanics & Repairmen	0 Synthesizing	0 Mentoring	0 Setting up
2 Clerical and Sales Occupations	1 Metal Working Occupations	1 Aircraft Mechanics and Repairmen	1 Coordinating	1 Negotiating	1 **Precision Working**
3 Service Occupations	2, 3 Mechanics and Machinery Repairman	2 Rail Equipment and Repairmen	2 **Analyzing**	2 Instructing	2 Operating-Controlling
4 Farming, Fishing, Forestry, and Related Occupations	4 Paperworking Occupations	3 Marine Mechanics and Repairmen	3 Compiling	3 Supervising	3 Driving-Operating
5 Processing Occupations	5 Printing Occupations	4 Farm Mechanics and Repairmen	4 Computing	4 Diverting	4 Manipulating
6 **Machine Trades Occupations**	6 Woodworking Occupations	5 Engine, Power Transmission, and Related Mechanics	5 Copying	5 Persuading	5 Tending
7 Bench Work Occupations	7 Machining Stone, Clay, Glass, and Related Materials	6 **Metal Working Machinery Mechanics**	6 Comparing	6 Speaking-Signaling	6 Feeding-Offbearing
8 Structural Work Occupations	8 Textile Occupations	7 Printing and Publishing Mechanics and Repairmen	7, 8 No Significant Relationship	7 Serving	7 Handling
9 Miscellaneous Occupations	9 Machine Trades Occupations	8 Textile Machinery and Equipment		8 **No Significant Relationship**	8 No Significant Relationship
		9 Special Industry			

FIGURE 8.3 Explanation of *Dictionary of Occupational Titles* Coding, Using Sample Job

Each classification indicates the lowest and the highest grade in sequence of job numbers. Under "Trimmer," heel seat trimming and insole trimming are two jobs receiving the lowest number of points (lower job grade), while edge trimming receives a higher number of points since it is the highest graded job in the "trimming family." However, after all occupations are classified by job grades (explained in Chapter 13), the Sock Lining Cutter and the Heel Breaster may receive the same number of points and thus be entitled to the same wage-base rate. Similarly, the Heel Seat Trimmer, Insole Trimmer, and Heel Sander are placed in the same job grade, each receiving the same number of points and the same wage-base rate.

It is interesting to note that the *Dictionary of Occupational Titles* lists 109 different job titles for heel making, of which only 41 are coded and defined. Thus, 68 heel jobs are different in name only. For instance, the job of a "Heel Buffer" is the same as brusher, buffing machine operator, cuffer, polisher, rasper-machine operator, remover, roughener, ruffer, sander, sander polisher, and scourer.[14]

The shoe manufacturing industry serves as an example for hundreds of other industries in which jobs and positions have changed rapidly and have increased in large numbers. Old and small, as well as large, industries are still handicapped by confusion on account of adherence to improperly used terminology. One medium-size company used the terms "lap sealing" (by machine), "brazing," "soldering," and "lap welding" interchangeably for "making a weld." The same wage-base rate was paid for all jobs which, of course, is out of line since each job requires a different skill and training. Only through job analysis, proper description, evaluation, and rating were the inequities disclosed.

We have noted specialized jobs, which in the shoe industry are grouped under occupational headings. In the same manner, there is a need to classify the occupations of office work, and factory work such as toolmaking, grinding, lathe work, boring, millwork, drilling, screw machine work, welding, and others. Finishing and assembling jobs in metalworking industries are different from those in the woodworking industry. Various clerical and office jobs in banks differ from those in department stores. In each of these activities, occupational and job classifications are necessary for each identification, division, or combination of specific jobs. Obsolete titles and descriptions are thereby eliminated, while up-to-date procedures are discovered that require new titles and job definitions. Hospitals, with their complex and various occupations, are efficiently managed if a distinct occupational and professional classification exists. While some administrators deem it a physical impossibility to introduce job evaluation in a hospital, others have succeeded outstandingly in installing and operating job evaluation plans through occupational classification and accurate descriptions of jobs and positions.

[14]*Ibid.*, Vol. I, pp. 81, 357–358.

REVIEW QUESTIONS

1. (a) Should the management of a firm try to install a job evaluation plan using entirely its own employees? Why? (b) Under what conditions should the firm seek outside help?

2. What systematic steps should management take if it hopes to develop and to install a sound system of job evaluation?

3. (a) Should the plan for job evaluation be discussed with representatives of unions? (b) Should a union representative assist in evaluating the jobs? Why?

4. (a) What is the effect of union participation in a job evaluation study? (b) What responsibilities must be accepted by the union?

5. (a) What should the chief job analyst's job duties consist of? (b) What qualifications should he have?

6. In what manner should a job evaluation program be announced to the employees so that it is clearly and objectively understood?

7. What methods might be used by management to explain a job evaluation plan to workers in a plant?

8. (a) In establishing a job evaluation program, how many committees is it advisable to establish? (b) What type or types of committees are recommended?

9. (a) How many members should there be on a job evaluation committee? (b) Should the committee be composed of an equal number of representatives from management and labor or more of one than the other? Why?

10. (a) What is a job family? (b) Of what use is it? (c) What function does the key job have?

11. Why is a "one man's plan" of job evaluation considered to be undesirable?

12. What are some categories or groups of jobs to which job evaluation plans have been successfully applied?

13. Is there a need for job evaluation of executive positions? Explain.

14. Should job evaluation be used to determine the salary range for all clerical, sales, and semitechnical office positions? Why?

15. Of what use can the *Dictionary of Occupational Titles* be to the wage and salary administrator?

16. (a) How often should a company's job evaluation system be checked for accuracy? (b) What means should be used to check the accuracy?

RESEARCH OR SEMINAR QUESTIONS

1. What are the advantages and disadvantages to both managements and unions of having a union participate in job evaluation?

2. How substantial a change must come about before a job should be reevaluated? Should reevaluation be made at a regular time interval such as once a year?

3. What is the primary function of the wage and salary administrator as a member of the evaluation committee?

4. What qualifications should the job evaluation raters possess? Why?

PRACTICAL EXPERIENCE ASSIGNMENTS

1. Divide the class into groups of four or five students and develop the approach that should be used to install a job evaluation program in your school. Present each approach to the entire class for their comments.

2. Select one of your largest local department stores and nominate the persons (job titles) that you would recommend to serve on the permanent job evaluation committee. Explain the reasoning behind your recommendations.

3. Outline a practical procedure for your school's administration to inform the deans, department chairmen, and functional department heads of the intention and plan to install a point plan of job evaluation.

4. Draw up a list of reasons why it is important to keep the workers well informed about the intention to install or alter a job evaluation program.

CASE PROBLEM

8—1. PERRY BUILDING SUPPLY COMPANY

Procedure to Evaluate Jobs

The Perry Building Supply Company is a medium-size building materials distributor that is situated in a city in western New York. The company buys building materials such as face brick, cement, reinforcing steel, aluminum windows, doors, and tile from the manufacturers and sells them to lumber dealers and contractors throughout the state.

The company employs 80 men in its two warehouse yards. These employees include truck drivers, jeep drivers, laborers, machine operators (for cutting and fabricating steel reinforcing rods), and two derrick operators in the steel yards. All the warehouse-yard employees belong to a union. They are all paid by hourly wages which are determined through union-management collective bargaining.

The Perry Company office staff consists of 15 women, an office manager, and his assistant. The office staff are all nonunion and are paid monthly salaries.

The assistant office manager is a recent college graduate. Part of his job is to handle personnel functions. He has recently received a complaint from the receptionist who is dissatisfied with her salary. She heard that a filing clerk was earning more than she and thinks that this is unfair since she has more seniority than the clerk. A similar dissatisfaction is also present in the warehouse yards. The two derrick operators are being paid less than the truck drivers and they think that this is unfair since their job requires more skill and responsibility than that of the drivers.

The assistant office manager feels that a job evaluation system should be set up for the office and the yard in order to alleviate this situation. He spoke to the office manager about this and the office manager agreed, but he stated that he did not think that the company president would concur. The office manager also believes that the job evaluation system should be limited to the office employees since the yard workers are unionized.

The president of the Perry Company is third in the line of family presidents this company has had. His grandfather founded the business and his policies have been carried on ever since.

Problem:

The office manager has suggested to his assistant that he write a report to the president on the situation. Assuming that you are the assistant office manager, write a report in which you make recommendations as to a course of action that should be taken.

chapter 9

SETTING UP A POINT PLAN
OF JOB EVALUATION

After having classified the occupations and jobs, the chief analyst and his committee are ready to proceed with the technique of job evaluation, using the point method. Although the procedural steps for establishing a job evaluation program were pointed out in the preceding chapter, it is deemed necessary to outline the specific procedure for setting up a point method. The details will be discussed sequentially as enumerated below. Only the first three steps are described in this chapter, however; the remaining four steps will be discussed in Chapters 10 through 13.

1. *Prepare a list of factors, and define and tentatively weight each factor.* The selection of factors depends largely upon the types of jobs or positions to be evaluated. Since only those factors are used which are common to all jobs, it is evident that the factors for executive or professional positions will differ from those for manual labor or office jobs. Factor definitions should vary accordingly.

2. *Determine the number of degrees for each factor that serves as a measuring stick.* It is imperative to measure factor values for each job in order to evaluate and to rate objectively. For that purpose, each factor is divided into degrees from the lowest to the highest rating. The number of degrees for each factor varies with the plan and the accuracy of measurement desired. To prevent indiscriminate rating and misunderstanding, the analyst must clearly define each degree.

3. *Assign a number of points to each degree for final factor weighting.* The number of points depends upon the importance of the factor to the job,

and the number of degrees involved. Some methods include a larger number of points than others, and the number of degrees and scoring percentages vary accordingly (See Table 9.1 on page 232). As explained in detail later, the points are extended either in arithmetic or geometric progression.

4. *Select a number of key jobs.* Key jobs serve to establish a guide for comparison of classified jobs. The key jobs are also included in the *Job Evaluation Manual* to guide analysts, evaluators, and raters.

5. *Study and analyze jobs, gather information, and prepare preliminary job descriptions.*

6. *Prepare final job descriptions, specifications, and rating sheets.*

7. *Rank the jobs according to differences in the number of points scored to establish job grades, which in turn are to be translated into wage-base rates and job pricing.*

Selecting, defining, and weighting factors

The term *factor* has various meanings. One of Webster's definitions is: "Factor is one of the elements, circumstances, or influences that contribute to produce a result." This definition is applicable to our discussions. Such terms as Attributes, Characteristics, Elements, Factors, and Traits are used interchangeably by industrial engineers, psychologists, and authors of management literature. All of these terms have the same meaning when applied to job evaluation and rating. Since the term "factor" is primarily used, however, we shall use that term in our discussions of job evaluation as well as employee evaluation.

Factors serve as a yardstick in measuring jobs. The selection of basic factors (and any subfactors) may be regarded as the heart of the point method of job evaluation. It is essential that the factors selected fit the company needs and be applicable to the jobs to be evaluated. To obtain satisfactory and lasting results, we recommend that a committee be assigned the task of selecting a number of factors that will evaluate the jobs validly and be mutually acceptable to both management and the union. The committee should adopt some criteria for selecting suitable factors.

Criteria for Selecting Suitable Factors

The selection of suitable factors can begin as soon as the decision has been made as to the number of jobs (or job groups) to be evaluated. Small firms may prefer to evaluate all of their jobs under one set of factors while large firms may decide to have a separate set of factors for each of the various categories of work (clerical, factory, sales, supervisory, executive, etc.).

The first requirement for the selection of suitable factors is that the factors be common denominators that can be found in varying amounts in the jobs to be evaluated. Unless each factor runs through each job and is variable from one job to another, there will be difficulty in comparing the relative worth of the jobs in attempting to reach an agreement on final evaluation.

The second requirement for the selection of suitable factors is that each factor should be considered important, measurable, and acceptable. The answers to the following questions will help determine whether the factor meets all these tests:

1. Is the factor important? An important factor contributes to the success of the job. It helps determine the worth of the job. It is a factor for which management is willing to pay. Employees recognize such a factor as necessary for the success of a job. An important factor lends validity to the job evaluation.

2. Is the factor measurable? For a factor to be measurable, it must be possible to determine or observe the amount or frequency of its use in different jobs. If reasonable measuring or rating of the factor is debatable, the factor should be discarded.

3. Will the factors be acceptable to the personnel involved? To be acceptable, the factor needs to be understandable and considered fair and practical. Acceptability of a factor by the vast majority of employees concerned is more easily met when a respected committee is chosen to select the factors (rather than a single individual appointed by management).

The third and final requirement for the selection of suitable factors is that collectively they will adequately cover the jobs without overlapping each other. Too few factors may result in an inadequate coverage of the jobs and cause employees to doubt the validity of the job evaluations. Too many factors may result in undue complexity and needless clerical red tape in administration for management. Sometimes too many factors cause overlapping of factors; thus, some part of the job is counted twice in the evaluation.

When the selection of factors begins, the following three problems are usually encountered: (1) which factors should be selected for a certain group or specific job groups, (2) whether the same factors can be utilized in different industries, and (3) the number of factors to be adopted. Since there are no definite rules to follow in solving these problems, the nearest approach is to investigate existing practices and to benefit from factual examples in commerce and industry.

Factors for Specific Job Groups. The problem of selecting factors should be considered only after top management has decided which job group is to be evaluated first. As mentioned previously, there are six possible group divisions in the field of application. The job evaluation factors will differ according to the job contents and the governing conditions within a specific job group. It will be noted in subsequent examples and in the job evaluation manuals in Chapter 10 that the same factors are used for similar groups or for different groups. In some cases the same factors are accepted, but they are either modified or differently defined. In other words, the same factor receives a different meaning when interpreted and described for another job group. They may also be given a different weight because their importance is different.

Same Factors in Different Industries. The possibility of using the same factors as measuring sticks under different conditions in various industries has been found to be practical. This is verified by the fact that the shoe industry has adopted the same factors as those used in the metal industry.

In the early stages of job evaluation, it seemed necessary that the "type" and number of factors had to differ extensively in manual and in professional jobs, such as baking, steelmaking, the manufacture of wood furniture, scientific instruments, shoes, chinaware, electrical goods, machine tools, and clothing, as well as in the services of utility companies and hospitals, to mention only a few. As the method of job evaluation developed, however, the number of factors decreased considerably, and application of the same factors became almost universal for jobs in different industries.

The Number of Factors to Use. The problem usually confronting the job evaluation analyst is how many factors to adopt. There is no single solution to this problem unless one is completely familiar with the group levels, occupations, and the jobs involved. For example, the activities and specific jobs of hourly paid workers in a manufacturing plant require a different number of factors than the jobs in insurance company offices.

It is the general consensus that evaluation will be inadequate if only three or four factors are employed. On the other hand, the use of 20 to 40 factors, as suggested by some authors, becomes complicated and causes overlapping and burdensome refinements. The most successful plans use between 6 to 16 factors. Even psychologists, who in the early stages of job evaluation generally favored a large number of factors, now seem to prefer a smaller number. One prominent psychologist states:

> The findings of the psychological laboratory support the judgment of the practical job analyst who insists upon reducing the number of factors to be appraised to a minimum consistent with the adequate differentiation of jobs.[1]

Since job contents and job conditions differ in industries and in group levels, the number of factors will vary and specific factors will differ accordingly. To acquaint the reader with some typical factors used in various industries and business enterprises, several examples with specific references to evaluation plans for workers in shops and salaried positions are given on the following pages.

---

[1]Morris S. Viteles, "A Psychologist Looks at Job Evaluation," *Personnel*, Vol. XVII, No. 3 (New York: American Management Association).

Factors Used in Plans for Hourly Rated Jobs

The most widely used job evaluation plans for shop jobs in the metal and electrical industries in the United States are those of the National Metal Trades Association (NMTA) and the National Electrical Manufacturers' Association (NEMA). These plans are considered similar because they are based on the basic factors of Skill, Effort, Responsibility, and Job Conditions. The basic factors are further divided into the following 11 subfactors:

SKILL

1. Education
2. Experience
3. Initiative and Ingenuity

RESPONSIBILITY

6. Responsibility for Equipment or Process
7. Responsibility for Material or Product
8. Responsibility for Safety of Others
9. Responsibility for Work of Others

EFFORT

4. Physical Demand
5. Mental or Visual Demand

JOB CONDITIONS

10. Working Conditions
11. Unavoidable Hazards

The basic NEMA and NMTA plans, with slight adaptations, have been successfully used in many industries. The tanning, wood, paper, and chemical industries are some typical examples. Since 1938, over 250 plans of the NEMA and NMTA type have been installed in the metropolitan Milwaukee, Wisconsin, area alone.

The National Footwear Manufacturers' Association, Inc., adopted the same basic factors and subfactors as those used by NEMA and NMTA, with the exception of the factor Responsibility for Work of Others, which is used for supervisory jobs. Shoe manufacturing operations are entirely different from those in metal manufacturing industries; nevertheless, shoe manufacturers deemed it advisable to adopt the same type and number of factors. Of course, job descriptions, grade definitions, and ratings are entirely different.

The United States Steel Corporation uses the same point plan for its hourly rated production, maintenance, and nonconfidential clerical jobs in the processing shops. The joint union-management committee designed the plan with exceptionally good results by using the following twelve factors. These factors have been adopted by all steel companies and their subsidiaries.

1. Preemployment Training
2. Employment Training and Experience
3. Mental Skill
4. Manual Skill
5. Responsibility for Materials
6. Responsibility for Tools and Equipment
7. Responsibility for Operations
8. Responsibility for Safety of Others
9. Mental Effort
10. Physical Effort
11. Surroundings
12. Hazards

The Sperry Gyroscope Company formed a joint union-management committee to establish its job evaluation plan. The committee adopted seven basic factors for all hourly paid jobs. Four of these factors are broken down into subfactors according to the following arrangement:

I. EDUCATION
  A. Schooling or Its Equivalent
  B. Experience and Training Required

II. SKILL
  A. Manual Skill Required
  B. Mental Skill Required

III. RESPONSIBILITY
  A. For Safety of Others
  B. For Spoilage of Productive Parts and Productive Material
  C. For Damage to Machines and Equipment

IV. ACCURACY

V. PHYSICAL EFFORT

VI. MENTAL EFFORT

VII. WORKING CONDITIONS
  A. Hazards to Self
  B. Surroundings
  C. Connected Expense

At Sperry, Education, Skill, Responsibility, Accuracy, Physical Effort, and Mental Effort are considered *primary factors*. Working Conditions are considered *secondary factors* "because they are not an inherent part of the job. They must be taken into account only after the primary requirements have been studied." Latrell reports that Sperry has used their factors for the past 23 years.[2]

The John Jones Company,[3] manufacturer of asbestos products, uses the following five basic factors and 16 subfactors for its shop workers:

MENTAL REQUIREMENTS
  1. Education
  2. Judgment
  3. Initiative
  4. Application

SKILL
  5. Equipment Use
  6. Material Use
  7. Dexterity

RESPONSIBILITY
  8. Supervision
  9. Safety of Others
  10. Cost of Error

WORKING CONDITIONS
  11. Accident Hazard
  12. Surroundings
  13. Clothing Spoilage

PHYSICAL REQUIREMENTS
  14. Strength
      (average weight lifted per hour)
  15. Application
  16. Fatigue

The Industrial Management Society (I.M.S.) designed a plan that was first published in 1937, and currently is in use.[4] It comprises 11 basic factors (termed attributes) and 23 subfactors arranged in the following order:

[2]Letter to authors in 1966 from T. F. Latrell, Salary and Wage Manager, Sperry Gyroscope Company, Great Neck, New York.
[3]Fictitious name. Manufacturer's name withheld by request.
[4]Letter to authors in 1966 from Robert J. Mayer, Executive Manager of Industrial Management Society, Chicago, Illinois.

BASIC FACTORS	SUBFACTORS
1. Physical Effort..........................	Endurance
	Exertion Strength
	(Measured in Pounds)
2. Hazards..............................	Accident
	Health
3. Job Conditions.........................	Discomfort
	Strain
	Clothing Spoilage
4. Supervision...........................	Supervision Received
	Responsibility for Work
	of Others
5. Responsibility for Safety of Others.........	
6. Responsibility for Equipment and Material..	Tools and Machines
	Losses on Performed Work
7. Knowledge............................	Knowledge of Equipment
	Knowledge of Methods
	Knowledge of Materials
8. Schooling.............................	Education
	Mental Training
9. Judgment and Initiative..................	Making Decisions
	Carrying Out Decisions
10. Mental Capability.......................	Ingenuity
	Initiative
	Versatility
11. Physical Skill..........................	Dexterity
	Precision

The Armstrong Cork Company manufactures a large variety of linoleum, tile, accessories, and floor coverings in several plants. In each plant the Industrial Engineering Department maintains a system of job classification to evaluate hourly rated jobs in accordance with the following basic factors and subfactors:

BASIC FACTORS	SUBFACTORS
1. Time Required.....................	Practical Experience
	Technical Knowledge
2. Effort[5].............................	Physical Exertion
	Visual or Mental Concentration
3. Manipulative Skill..................	Dexterity
	Precision
4. Judgment..........................	Decisions
	Job Knowledge Requirements
5. Responsibility......................	Reliance
	Job Complexity
6. Leadership.........................	Type of Job Performed by Group
	Number of People in Group
7. Working Conditions..................	Personal Discomfort
	Job Conditions
8. Accident Hazards....................	Severity or Type
	Probability

---

[5]John V. Valenteen, Manager of Central Industrial Engineering, Training and Research, Armstrong Cork Company of Lancaster, Pa., reported to authors in 1966, that the factor "Physical Effort" was changed to "Effort."

The Employer's Association of Milwaukee developed a plan[6] containing the following factors that are being used to evaluate both hourly and salaried jobs by the majority of private hospitals in the metropolitan Milwaukee area:

1. Education
2. Experience
3. Complexity of Duties
4. Responsibility for Preventing Errors and Losses
5. Responsibility for Contacts with Others
6. Responsibility for Confidential Data
7. Physical Demand
8. Working Conditions
9. Hazards

(*For Supervisory Occupations Only*)

10. Character of Supervision
11. Number of Employees Supervised

Factors Used in Plans for Salary Rated Jobs

As stated before, the National Electrical Manufacturers' Association (NEMA) pioneered in the introduction of a uniform point method for salaried jobs long after the shop plan with eleven factors was successfully used by its members. NEMA uses only six factors for nonsupervisory salaried jobs "in order to keep the plan as simple as possible," while NMTA increased the number to nine, as listed below. Both added two factors for supervisory jobs.

NEMA	*NMTA*
Education	Education
Experience	Experience
Complexity of Duties	Complexity of Duties
Monetary Responsibility	Supervision Received
Responsibility for Contacts with Others	Errors
Working Conditions	Contact with Others
	Confidential Data
For Supervisors:	Mental or Visual Demand
Type of Supervision	Working Conditions
Extent of Supervision	
	For Supervisors:
	Character of Supervision
	Scope of Supervision

The Life Office Management Association (LOMA) with 24 years of experience evaluating clerical jobs in the life insurance business is presently using the following six factors:[7]

1. Education
2. Job Knowledge
3. Contacts
4. Responsibility
5. Supervision
6. Working Conditions

---

[6]Permission granted by C. A. Anderson, Manager of Employer's Association of Milwaukee, in 1966 to quote factors used in this plan.

[7]Information received on January 14, 1966, from Donald Krueger, Personnel Department, Northwestern Mutual Life Insurance Company, Milwaukee, Wisconsin.

The Continental Illinois National Bank and Trust Company of Chicago uses the following six factors:[8]

1. Preparation and Training
2. Organization of Details
3. Supervision over Others
4. Resourcefulness
5. Tact and Agreeableness
6. Responsibility

Alden's, Inc., a mail-order house in Chicago, adopted the four basic factors of NMTA, but introduced some slight changes in the subfactors to suit its own job conditions. The four basic factors and their 25 subfactors are listed below:[9]

I. RESPONSIBILITY
1. Money and Property
2. Equipment
3. Materials
4. Service and Goodwill
5. Safety of Others
6. Supervision

II. JOB CONDITIONS
7. Discomfort
8. Accident Hazard
9. Health Hazard
10. Clothing Spoilage
11. Adoption Period

III. EDUCATION AND SKILL
12. Education
13. Technical Education
14. Additional Qualifications
15. Experience
16. Dexterity
17. Precision
18. Versatility
19. Initiative and Ingenuity

IV. MENTAL AND PHYSICAL EFFORT
20. Perseverance
21. Concentration
22. Judgment
23. Acuteness of Senses
24. Strength
25. Endurance

The joint union-management committee of the United States Steel Corporation found the following seven factors were sufficient for the salaried clerical and technical jobs:

1. Preemployment Training
2. Employment Training and Experience
3. Mental Skill
4. Responsibility for Performance
5. Responsibility for Contacts
6. Working Conditions
7. Responsibility for Direction

Note that the same joint union-management committee provides twelve factors for hourly paid jobs in the shops as explained on page 224, while for salaried jobs only seven factors are used, three being the same as those used for shop workers.

The Employer's Association of Milwaukee developed a plan for nonexempt Clerical and Technical Occupations (Designers, Drafting, Technicians) that has been used to evaluate jobs in well over 200 companies (industry, banks, insur-

---

[8]Letter to authors in December of 1965 from C. D. Foster, Assistant Cashier, Personnel Division, Continental Illinois National Bank and Trust Company of Chicago, Illinois.
[9]Information received from Harry Ruter, Manager of Industrial Relations, Aldens, Inc., Chicago, Illinois.

ance, and service firms). The eight factors that are being used in their latest plan are as follows:[10]

SKILL	RESPONSIBILITY
1. Education	4. Responsibility for Trust
2. Experience	5. Responsibility for Accuracy
3. Complexity of Work	6. Responsibility for Contracts
	7. Responsibility for Work of Others

EFFORT

8. Mental and/or Physical Requirements

A review of the examples will indicate that four or five basic factors and six to sixteen subfactors are sufficient for a plan, depending on the group level. Four or five basic factors are not sufficient in themselves, however, to discern the difference between one job and another. After adopting the basic factors, it should be comparatively easy to decide on subfactors to suit the variation of jobs within activities of specific groups in the enterprise. Some companies may use the same factors for two or three different groups but change the definitions and weighting to suit the differences. It will be found, however, that invariably a choice of factors *for each group level* is preferred since it will reduce cost and confusion, and be more acceptable to supervisors and workers alike.

Defining the Job Evaluation Factors

After the selection of factors has been completed, it is then necessary to define the factors, to weight them tentatively, to divide them into degrees, to define each degree, and to apply final factor weighting by establishing a definite number of points for each degree. This procedure is necessary so that when jobs are evaluated, the factor and degree values are the same for all concerned.

Avoid Ambiguity. Factors should be defined in simple everyday language so that each committee member and worker will understand the definitions. Avoid too brief a definition since it will invariably be misunderstood and cause different interpretations for the same job. The best results are obtained if each committee member defines one factor at a time. A discussion of definitions will bring out some errors or misconceptions that should be corrected immediately. Then when grievances arise, arguments with union representatives can be avoided.

If the definitions are adopted from a ready-made plan, the analyst and the committee must ascertain that the terminology adequately fits their own conditions. If the definitions are clear and ambiguity is avoided, the division into degrees and the weighting of factors will not only be simplified but the measurements will also be fair and accurate.

---

[10]Permission granted by C. W. Anderson, Manager of Employer's Association of Milwaukee, in 1966 to quote factors used in this plan.

Examples of Factor Definitions in Two Different Plans. Examples of how the factors Experience and Physical Demand are defined in each of two plans used successfully by the Sperry Gyroscope Company and the Armstrong Cork Company may well serve the purpose of explaining the required differences in the terminology.

Experience. Sperry Gyroscope Company combines Experience with Training under the basic factor Education. Definition: *"Experience* is the minimum period of time the average person requires to obtain competency in a specific job, trade, or occupation,"

Armstrong Cork Company uses the factor Experience as a subdivision of Time Required. Definition: *"Practical Experience* refers to the prerequisite job experience and the time necessary to become familiar with the work location, personnel, job requirements, records, reports, operating policies, and safety requirements, and to operate with no more than a normal amount of supervision on the job."

In each manual of the two companies, further clarification is provided by a discussion that follows the definitions.

Physical Demand. Sperry uses Physical Effort as a basic factor without any subdivision. Definition: *"Physical Effort* evaluations are based upon the demand for expenditure of energy, or physical exertion required of employees for certain occupations, and the frequency with which such physical exertion occurs."

Armstrong employs Effort as a basic factor with the subdivisions of (1) Physical Exertion and (2) Visual and Mental Concentration. Definitions: *Effort* may be defined as the expenditure of physical effort inherent in a job as regards fatigue in order to perform a satisfactory job at a normal rate of operation. A normal rate of operation may be considered as that rate expected to perform a day work task. It is not necessarily the use or display of physical strength but rather the fatigue resulting. Inducement to work at a greater activity than a normal rate, with the resulting greater fatigue, is rewarded by earnings on production incentive." Effort includes *Physical Exertion.* "This refers to the muscular fatigue to the employee resulting from the physical demands of the job. In determining the physical exertion of a job, consideration will be given to the application of effort in handling and/or lifting materials or objects; the application of force in pushing and pulling materials or objects; and the bodily motions and positions required during the above applications. The consideration of these factors will indicate the relative physical exertion and the resulting muscular fatigue induced."

From the foregoing examples, it may be seen that the terminology of definitions will differ considerably as long as the job contents in one company differ from those in another. The definitions of the Sperry Gyroscope Company may appear too brief, but experience has proven that literally hundreds of plans in metal industries have successfully used similar brief definitions. The definitions of the Armstrong Cork Company may appear too lengthy, but apparently its shop conditions and raters require a more fully explained interpretation in order to avoid ambiguity. Of course, the mere definition of factors in any plan by itself will not be sufficient unless the factors are divided into clearly defined degrees for the sake of clarity.

Weighting of Factors

To date, there has been no standard procedure developed nor a generally accepted formula to follow in the weighting of factors. The weighting of factors remains an individual judgment that each company can and should make according to its own circumstances. The weighting of factors should be decided upon by a job evaluation committee according to the relative value that is attached to each of the factors within each job evaluation plan.

After the various factors to be used have been decided upon, they should be ranked in their order of importance (according to their overall effect on the success of all the jobs being evaluated). The committee may ask itself, "What is the most important factor that contributes (or is needed) for success in all jobs included in the job evaluation plan?" In a precision-tool industry or factory plan, the factor is likely to be Experience. In an executive plan, the most important factor may be Accountability (or Responsibility). In an office, or clerical, plan it may be Job Knowledge. The most important factor is the one that is most appropriate according to each company's individual needs and particular circumstances.

After the various job evaluation factors have been ranked in their order of importance, the factors should be assigned a percent value. The percentage of all factors should total 100 percent. In other words, the committee needs to distribute 100 percentage points among the various factors according to their relative degrees of importance to the overall success of all the jobs in the company's evaluation plan.

Table 9.1 shows a comparison of the relative weights that several companies have assigned to the various factors they use for evaluating production jobs. Note that the basic factor of Skill has been assigned anywhere from 24.5 percent to 52 percent. Note also that the basic skill factor has been broken down into subfactors and assigned different percentages according to the different values placed on these by the respective companies. Much study should be made of the various successful plans in use in order to gain insights on why these plans are successful. This is especially important when a national union has various locals in different companies. The union employees of one firm are more than likely to compare various job evaluation plans to determine whether the differences in plans are justifiable.

TABLE 9.1

COMPARISON OF SIX WEIGHTED POINT METHODS FOR PRODUCTION JOBS

FACTORS AND SUBFACTORS	% NEMA- NMTA*	AN ELECTRIC COMPANY	REVERE COPPER & BRASS, INC.	U.S. STEEL CORP.	NATIONAL FOOTWARE ASSOC.	JOHNSON WAX CO.
SKILL						
Education........	14	8	...	2.4	8.4	...
Experience........	22	...	...	...	12.8	39
Initiative.........	14	...	...	...	10.6	5
Training Time....	...	21	15.7	9.3	...	...
Mentality.........	...	13	...	8.1	...	...
Manual Dexterity..	...	10	10.5	4.7	...	...
TOTAL........	50%	52%	26.2%	24.5%	31.8%	44%
EFFORT						
Physical..........	10	10	10.5	5.8	8.5	14
Mental and/or Visual..........	5	5	10.5	5.8	12.8	4
TOTAL........	15%	15%	21.0%	11.6%	21.3%	18%
RESPONSIBILITY						
General..........	...	...	...	15.1	...	...
Equipment or Processes.......	5	5	5.3	9.3	12.8	10
Material or Product........	5	5	21.1	23.3	12.8	14
Safety of Others...	5	5	5.3	4.7	6.4	5
Work of Others ...	5	3	...	...	...	...
TOTAL........	20%	18%	31.7%	52.4%	32.0%	29%
JOB CONDITIONS						
Working Conditions.....	10	10	10.5	6.8	8.5	4
Unavoidable Hazards........	5	5	...	4.7	6.4	5
Health Hazards...	...	...	5.3	...	...	...
Current Expense...	...	...	5.3	...	...	...
TOTAL........	15%	15%	21.1%	11.5%	14.9%	9%
Total of All Factors..	100%	100%	100%	100%	100%	100%

*The percentage figures shown in the NEMA-NMTA plan also indicate the number of points allotted to the first degree of each individual factor.

Following the allocation of percentages to the various factors, the next step in weighting factors is to assign a total number of points to each one according to the percentages previously agreed upon. Determining whether to assign a large or small number of points to the various factors, according to the predetermined factor percentages, may be governed by the administrative aspects of the plan as well as by the method of subdividing the factors into degrees. Generally, the initial weighting given to the various factors (in both percents and points) is a tentative decision because the number of points decided upon is also affected by the number of degrees into which the factor is subdivided and by the method of allocating these points within each degree. All of these considerations need to be coordinated to be able to satisfactorily administer the plan. A discussion of these considerations is presented next.

Determining the number of degrees

The point method of job evaluation is based on predetermined weights for each factor; therefore, each of the adopted factors must be divided into a system of degrees and weighted to furnish a point scale that is properly divided for measurement of the same factor for different jobs. The value of the same factor may be very low for one job and very high for another, as expressed in lowest and highest number of points.

Due to the variations in jobs or positions, various plans differ in the number of degrees, definitions, and allotted number of points. An investigation of numerous plans discloses that divisions in degrees vary from 3 to 12. The total number of points for *all factors* varies from 0 to 150 for the lowest degree, and from 500 to 2,000 for the highest degree. The variations are justified since they represent a large variety of jobs requiring less or more factors and a smaller or larger number of degrees to clarify definitions. The number of degrees into which a factor is subdivided may be based on such considerations as administrative ease and precedent, or according to some logical unit of measurement appropriate to the nature of each particular factor to be used. In any event, the decision on the number of degrees needs to be justified on some sound basis. The next few pages disclose pertinent information and common practice in determining the number of degrees to use.

How Many Degrees?

Opinions differ regarding the number of degrees required for an effective plan. There is as much disadvantage in using too few degrees as in using too many. The job analyst and his committee must consider primarily to what extent the degrees should differ in accordance with a clear description of the degrees. A small number of degrees will limit the range of differences required for certain jobs. On the other hand, if the number of degrees is too large, the description of each degree will not only be time consuming but will also be so minute that it will cause misunderstanding and lose its effectiveness.

Number of Degrees for Hourly Plans. A special study of various job evaluation methods by the authors disclosed that most shop plans for hourly paid jobs use four to six degrees for each factor. In such plans, the tendency is to use a uniform number of degrees for all factors. The original plans designed by NEMA and NMTA — introduced in the majority of manufacturing plants —

use five degrees that are uniformly divided for all factors. The plan shown in Table 9.2 provides a uniform division into six degrees for each factor according to the needs of industries where a more refined distinction between degrees is required. (See Figure 10.2, page 248, for definitions of degrees.)

TABLE 9.2

FACTORS, DEGREES, AND WEIGHTED POINT VALUES FOR HOURLY EMPLOYEES

Factors and Subfactors	%	Degrees and Points						Weight in Per- cent
		1st Deg.	2d Deg.	3d Deg.	4th Deg.	5th Deg.	6th Deg.	
SKILL	50							
1. Education & Job Knowledge......		12	24	36	48	60	72	12
2. Experience & Training...........		24	48	72	96	120	144	24
3. Initiative & Ingenuity...........		14	28	42	56	70	84	14
EFFORT	15							
4. Physical Demand...............		10	20	30	40	50	60	10
5. Mental and/or Visual Demand....		5	10	15	20	25	30	5
RESPONSIBILITY	20							
6. Equipment or Tools.............		6	12	18	24	30	36	6
7. Material or Product.............		7	14	21	28	35	42	7
8. Safety of Others...............		3	6	9	12	15	18	3
9. Work of Others.................		4	8	12	16	20	24	4
JOB CONDITIONS	15							
10. Working Conditions.............		10	20	30	40	50	60	10
11. Unavoidable Hazards...........		5	10	15	20	25	30	5
TOTAL	100%	100	200	300	400	500	600	100%

Number of Degrees for Salaried Plans. When establishing the number of degrees for salaried jobs, it will be found that some factors may require division into a greater number of degrees than others.

The NEMA salary rating plan illustrated in Table 9.3 shows a variation in the number of degrees from five for most of the factors to six for Education and eight for Experience.

An examination of the Revere clerical and supervision position scales, illustrated in Figure 10.3, page 259, and Figure 10.4, page 264, shows a variation of four to six degrees for clerical positions and three to five degrees for operating supervision positions.

Examples of Degrees and Values for Two Factors

For comparison purposes we shall consider the factors Experience and Physical Demand, their divisions in degrees, and their assigned number of points, in two different plans, those of NMTA and Sperry Gyroscope Company.

Experience. The factor Experience is divided by NMTA into five degrees with an allotted number of points for each degree as listed in Table 9.4.

TABLE 9.3

**FACTORS, DEGREES, AND WEIGHTED POINT VALUES
FOR SALARIED EMPLOYEES**

FACTORS	DEGREES AND POINTS							
	1st	2d	3d	4th	5th	6th	7th	8th
1. Education...............	20	40	60	80	100	120		
2. Experience................	25	50	75	100	125	150	175	200
3. Complexity of Duties.........	20	40	60	80	100			
4. Monetary Responsibility......	5	10	20	40	80			
5. Contacts...................	5	10	20	40	80			
6. Working Conditions..........	5	10	15	20	25			
Add for Supervisory Jobs Only								
7. Type of Supervision..........	5	10	20	40	80			
8. Extent of Supervision........	5	10	20	40	80			

Source: National Electrical Manufacturers' Association.

TABLE 9.4

**DEGREES AND NUMBER OF POINTS ASSIGNED TO EACH DEGREE
FOR FACTOR *EXPERIENCE***

DEGREES	TIME REQUIRED	No. OF POINTS
1st Degree	Up to three months	22
2d Degree	Over three months up to one year	44
3d Degree	Over one year up to three years	66
4th Degree	Over three years up to five years	88
5th Degree	Over five years	110

Source: National Metal Trades Association.

Experience and Training is the factor used by Sperry Gyroscope Company. The factor is divided into 32 degrees, each degree evaluated into the number of months as the minimum time required to become proficient on the job. Each degree is designated by a letter code from A to Z and from AA to AF, in the manner shown in Table 9.5. The lowest number of points is 12 for one month or less, with an arbitrary increase of the number of points (no specific increment) for each degree until the 32d degree, AF, is reached with an assigned number of 125 points for ten years (120 months) as the highest. Due to space limitations, Table 9.5 contains only a partial list of the coded degrees, their time in months, and the assigned number of points.

In the two plans reviewed above, note that the time element is an important measuring unit for the factor Experience. Division into degrees and their definitions assist the rater in evaluating the factor for the respective job in units of months or years. However, the rater is confronted with a different situation when evaluating the factor Physical Demand.

TABLE 9.5

**DEGREES AND POINTS ASSIGNED TO EACH DEGREE
FOR FACTOR** *EXPERIENCE AND TRAINING*

DEGREE CODE	STEP DEFINITION	TIME IN MONTHS	No. OF POINTS
A to C	Requires a short period of training work, not exceeding a total of three months.	1 or less 3	12 25
D to L	Requires experience gained through job training or on related work in addition to job training, the total being over three months but not exceeding one year.	4 12	30 50
M to Y	Requires previous experience on related work in addition to job training, the total being over one year but not exceeding three years.	13 36	51 79
Z to AA	Requires a broad background of necessary practical knowledge obtained from previous experience and association with related work in addition to job training, the total being over three years but not exceeding five years.	48 60	88 96
AB to AF	Requires expert knowledge in a skilled occupation obtained from practical experience gained over a period exceeding five years.	72 120	103 125

Source: Sperry Gyroscope Company, Inc.

Physical Demand. Physical Demand, Effort, Physical Effort, and Physical Requirements are used interchangeably and all have the same meaning. The analyst should consider measurements of *strength and physical effort, fatigue, endurance,* or *application.* Either one or all of these measurements must be defined to avoid ambiguity or controversy.

Strength and Physical Effort can be expressed in total pounds lifted, carried, pushed, pulled, or moved per hour or per day.

Fatigue is the resultant effect of physical and mental demands, disagreeable temperatures, fumes, noise, monotony, insufficient illumination, glare, and constant exposure to hazards.

Endurance measures the frequency with which lifting, carrying, pulling, pushing, or moving occurs.

Application is similar to endurance since it measures the continuity of physical effort required for the job expressed in a percentage of the total time required to exert physical effort.

Thus, such terms as "little," "light weight," "short," "long," and "frequent" in any definition should be explicitly explained in units of measurement, unless illustrations of some key jobs are used to explain such terms and to clarify degree definitions in order to avoid ambiguity (See Figure 10.1, page 244).

The joint job evaluation committee of Sperry Gyroscope Company apparently realized the pitfalls of inconsistency in using ambiguous terms such as those indicated above. For that reason, the company expressed the definitions of degrees for the factor Physical Effort in concise measuring units, as illustrated in Table 9.6.

Assigning points to each degree

As previously explained, the installation of a job evaluation plan by the point method makes it possible to evaluate jobs more objectively than by other methods. It is therefore apparent that a rating scale should be established for each compensable factor in order to express its value in a number of points. It was also emphasized that to further facilitate objectivity and insure validity, factors are divided into a number of degrees, each degree receiving a point score to differentiate it from other degrees. Two point methods have been in use, namely, the straight point method and the weighted point method.

TABLE 9.6

DEGREES, WEIGHTS, PERCENTAGE OF FREQUENCY, AND POINTS ASSIGNED TO FACTOR *PHYSICAL EFFORT*

		FREQUENCY OF EFFORT			
WEIGHT LIFTED OR EQUIVALENT EXERTION IN PUSHING OR PULLING		LOW 10% or less time	MODERATE 11%– 25% of time	HIGH 25%– 50% of time	SUSTAINED Over 50% of time
CODE	DEFINITION OF DEGREES	G	H	J	K
A	Less than 1 pound..............	0	5	10	15
B	1 to 5 pounds. Include use of light hand tools in this degree....	7	12	17	22
C	5 to 25 pounds. Include work such as using hand lift trucks....	14	19	24	29
D	25 to 50 pounds..............	21	26	31	36
E	50 to 100 pounds..............	28	33	38	43
F	Over 100 pounds..............	35	40	45	50

WORKING POSITION OF OPERATOR

CODE	DEFINITIONS	POINTS
M	Operator sits, or sit-stands intermittently	0
N	Operator stands or walks continuously	10
O	Stands, walks, and works in awkward positions	20

(Add points from both charts for total)

Source: Sperry Gyroscope Company, Inc.

Straight Point Method

The allotment of points to factors and degrees is very simple when using the straight point method, as shown in Table 9.7. Note that each of the five factors has an equal number of points. Being equally weighted, the factors have no relative difference in values. The difference in the number of points for each degree is exactly the same for all factors — ten points. The straight point method is now used very little because uniformity in the number of points for each factor rarely indicates the relative importance of each factor as compared with the other factors.

TABLE 9.7
ALLOTMENT OF POINTS — STRAIGHT POINT METHOD

FACTORS	DEGREES					
	1	2	3	4	5	6
	POINTS					
1. Education and Job Knowledge......	20	30	40	50	60	70
2. Experience and Training...........	20	30	40	50	60	70
3. Initiative and Ingenuity...........	20	30	40	50	60	70
4. Physical Demand.................	20	30	40	50	60	70
5. Mental or Visual Demand.........	20	30	40	50	60	70

Weighted Point Method

The weighted point method is widely used because, as explained before, in the majority of jobs and positions, certain factors are of much more value than others. Having established the relative importance of each basic factor, sub-factor, and the division into degrees, the analyst finds it comparatively simple to apportion the proper number of points to each degree.

The number of points for each factor in the weighted point method is usually based on a definite percentage assigned to each basic factor and a related weight percent to each subfactor. The commonly used factors, as enumerated in Table 9.2, are those established by the National Metal Trades Association, the National Electrical Manufacturers' Association, and the National Footwear Manufacturers' Association, Inc., and used by their member companies. The number of degrees and relative weights in points will differ according to the types of jobs and the kinds of industries. However, the weighted point plan presented in Table 9.2 serves for evaluating hourly rated jobs in the average metal plants as well as in wood furniture plants. Other industries may use the same factors and number of degrees, but the definitions as described in the manual in Figure 10.2, page 248, and the allotted number of points may differ. It should be remembered that the total number of points is not significant *as long as they are distributed in a predetermined relative proportion among all sub-factors and their degrees.*

Assigning Points to Degrees

Whether a firm wishes to utilize the straight point or the weighted point method for differentiating between factors and degrees, there is still need for some systematic way of allocating points to the different degrees of each factor. There are two systems or progressions being used to assign points to degrees, the arithmetic progression and the geometric progression. In the arithmetic progression, points are allocated to each degree according to a constant *number* of points (10, 20, 30, 40, 50) because the differences between one degree and another are thought to be related in a constant, *fixed* increment. In the geometric progression, points are allocated to each degree according to a constant *percent* of points (10, 20, 40, 80, 160) because the differences between one degree and another are believed to be related according to a constant, *increasing* increment. A further word about each follows.

Arithmetic Progression. Critics of the point method question the validity of assigning a constant number of points as a difference between degrees. They assert that the variation in the increase of value from one degree to another is not always in accordance with the uniform increment. Therefore, it is believed the difference in points should not be constant. They claim that either an arbitrary progression selected by trials or a geometric progression is preferable to the arithmetic progression in order to conform with the increased values between the higher degrees. Although no convincing mathematical proof is advanced to substantiate the accuracy of constant differences between degrees, nevertheless, the constant variation in points is generally accepted by workers, who rely on the decision of committee members. It becomes a "matter of course" to them that if the committee decided on a relative worth of 10 percent for the subfactor Physical Demand, and the allotted minimum number of points for the first degree is based on one point for each percent, then the subfactor Physical Demand receives 10 points, and each additional degree is worth 10 points more on the basis of an arithmetic progression. The authors have found that this reasoning is acceptable to workers when explained by the rater or committee members.

Geometric Progression. Analysts who prefer the geometric progression scale believe that the difference between the last two degrees should be greater than that between the first two degrees. They assume that each degree increases a certain percentage in value; therefore, the number of points should increase accordingly. If the geometric progression scale were to be utilized in Table 9.2, the point values 12, 24, 48, 96, 192, and 384 (or such values as 3, 6, 12, 24, 48, and 96) would be assigned the six degrees for the subfactor Education and Job

Knowledge. Similarly, point values for Unavoidable Hazards would be 5, 10, 20, 40, 80, and 160; or such values as 1.25, 2.5, 5, 10, 20, and 40. The geometric progression may appear more accurate when pricing jobs. As stated before, however, experience has proved that arithmetic progression is easier than geometric progression for workers to understand and is preferred by shop stewards and union leaders.

In summary, the selection, definition, and weighting of factors and degrees are determined by the various circumstances found in each firm. The committee charged with this responsibility should study the various successful plans in existence that most closely parallel their circumstance and make appropriate modifications. There is no sound and lasting substitute for the results that can be obtained when a conscientious committee thoroughly discusses these facets and makes sound decisions that are easily defensible.

REVIEW QUESTIONS

1. List and describe the procedural steps necessary for establishing a point program of job evaluation.
2. What are the three requirements for the selection of suitable factors for a point program of job evaluation?
3. What is the point plan of job evaluation built around?
4. Should different factors be used if different job groups are going to be analyzed? Why?
5. (a) How many factors should a job evaluation plan utilize? (b) What determines the exact number?
6. What type or level of language should be used when defining the terms in the job evaluation manual? Why?
7. What determines the number of degrees into which each factor should be subdivided?
8. (a) What are the advantages and disadvantages of assigning points to each degree by the straight point method? (b) by the weighted point method?

RESEARCH OR SEMINAR QUESTIONS

1. Explain the stand you take as to whether each of the following should be considered in determining the worth of a job:
   (a) Promotional possibilities — whether the job is a dead-end one or not.
   (b) Supply and demand of workers — the availability of people in filling the job.
   (c) Number of hours worked per week.
2. What is the "perfect" number of factors to be used for a point plan of evaluation of clerical jobs? Why?

3. What advantages does the point plan of job evaluation have over the other plans that have been explained in this book?

4. In determining the factors that each point plan uses, what criteria should be evaluated?

PRACTICAL EXPERIENCE ASSIGNMENTS

1. Form committees of four or five students and draw up a set of factors, degrees, and points that would make a sound point plan for the evaluation of teaching jobs in a college or university.

2. Draw up a list of reasons why a point plan of job evaluation that works well for one company may not be suitable for another company even if the two companies are in the same industry.

3. Select, as a class, a company in your area that utilizes a point plan of job evaluation. Divide the class into groups of 4 or 5 and investigate the plan, looking for its strong points and possible weaknesses, and recommend how the weaknesses may be corrected or reduced.

CASE PROBLEM

9—1. THE QUICK-DRY PAINT COMPANY

Installing Job Evaluation

Mr. Brush is the president of the Quick-Dry Paint Company, a family owned and operated concern. This firm manufactures paints and mirrors and distributes paints, mirrors, glass, wallpaper, and a small line of sundry items in the hardware line to various hardware dealers and decorators. The company also contracts for window glass and thermopane installations. It maintains retail outlets in several states.

The company employs 150 people in its office, plants, and retail outlets. There are approximately 40 different jobs, which include secretaries, typists, bookkeepers, billers, sales clerks, salesmen, stock clerks, glaziers, dock workers, packers, foremen, truck drivers, maintenance men, and general factory and warehouse help. About one fifth of the nonsales and office workers belong to the Teamsters, Paint & Varnish Workers, or Glaziers unions.

Due to grievances about wage inequities that have been brought up recently, the company officials have decided that, in order to remedy the situation, they must install a job evaluation system.

Problem:

You, as the Personnel Manager, are given the task of setting up a usable evaluation system to eliminate the existing and any possible future wage inequities. Outline the procedure that should be followed to set up a point plan of job evaluation.

chapter 10

JOB EVALUATION MANUALS

Of the seven procedural steps required to set up a job evaluation point plan, we have so far discussed three steps: (1) selecting, defining, and weighting factors; (2) determining the number of degrees for each factor; and (3) assigning a number of points to each degree. In this chapter we shall discuss step number 4, which pertains to the contents and usage of job evaluation manuals. Illustration of three complete sample manuals which are actually used in industry will enable the reader to obtain a full insight into the development of a manual, the definition of various factors and degrees, the allotment of point values to each degree, and the selection of key jobs.

An examination of the most outstanding job evaluation plans discloses the use of separate job evaluation manuals for each employee group level. The manual serves as a reference to determine the relative value of jobs, and sets the pattern to guide analysts, committee members, supervisors, and union leaders.

Contents of job evaluation manuals

A job evaluation manual should contain the most important information needed by the evaluator for direction and comparison when analyzing and evaluating jobs. The manual is the authoritative source of information for those who assist in setting up the job evaluation plan, as well as for new committee members and for grievance committees after the plan has been installed. Therefore, for effective guidance, the manual should present vivid examples with concise and complete explanations for all items agreed upon by the committee.

There is no definite standard or established uniformity as to the size and contents of job evaluation manuals. Companies and chief job analysts each have their own conceptions of what form the manual should take. The format may differ from the printed pocket size, 4 x 6½", flexibly bound 116 pages issued by United States Steel Corporation, to the 8½ x 11", solidly bound handbooks issued by Industrial Fasteners Institute (Cleveland, Ohio), or to the printed "Joint Job Evaluation Manual," 8½ x 11", issued by the Sperry Gyroscope Company of Brooklyn, New York.

Although detailed instructions will vary from company to company, a complete and useful job evaluation manual should contain the following information:

1. Introduction, including appreciative acknowledgment of assistance from committee members and union representatives.
2. Objective and scope of job evaluation program.
3. Use of manual.
4. Principles and definitions of commonly used terms.
5. Procedure for collecting information.
6. Number of factors, degrees and points. (A setup similar to Table 9.2, page 234, and Table 9.3, page 235, will suffice.)
7. Definition of each factor and degree.
8. Example of job descriptions.
9. Sample rating form.
10. Brief explanation of job pricing.
11. Table of point range and pay grades (similar to Table 13.1, page 316).

Manual Illustrations

To facilitate matters and to assist in objective judging, writers of some manuals include illustrative aids consisting of drawings, diagrams, and photographs that depict actual operations of the evaluated key jobs or similar jobs in the same plant. Figure 10.1 shows a very impressive set of two photographs and a drawing to illustrate three degrees (step definitions) of the factor Education. Similar illustrations are utilized by the Sperry Gyroscope Company in its joint job evaluation manual for degrees of other factors. Photographic illustrations can be economically obtained by using 35 mm. cameras with film rolls for 20 to 36 pictures. The 35 mm. size films may be used for direct reproduction or for enlargements up to 3¼ x 4¼" without losing accuracy and sharpness.

A well-prepared manual written in plain language will be a source of authority to curb arguments and grievances. Such a manual must contain instructions that are supported by illustrations or examples for guidance, definitions of factors, and acceptable weighting of degrees.

SCHOOLING OR ITS EQUIVALENT   13
★ ★

CHARACTERISTIC: EDUCATION — A. SCHOOLING OR ITS EQUIVALENT			
CODE	STEP DEFINITION	POINTS	EXAMPLE

A. Job requires only the understanding of simple verbal instructions.
    0 to 12

B. Work may require reading and understanding written instructions. May use simple arithmetic such as counting.
    13 to 25

C. May use piece part drawings showing detailed items with a limited number of dimensions. May use precision measuring instruments such as micrometer. May make calculations involving decimals, fractions or percentages.
    26 to 37

Sperry Gyroscope Company

FIGURE 10.1   ILLUSTRATIVE DEGREE DEFINITIONS

Measuring Scales

In the preceding chapters we discussed the selection of factors, their division into degrees, and the adequate weighting of degrees and factors. Tables 9.2, page 234, and 9.3, page 235, show at a glance the number of factors, degrees, and points desirable for shop and salaried workers. Using the tables as a guide, the analyst can readily set up *measuring scales* in which he defines all factors, establishes degrees, and assigns the weighting in points. The scales then serve as a basis for developing the manual which, in turn, assists the analyst in gathering factual data, making job analyses, selecting key jobs, and rating jobs.

Ready-Made Measuring Scales. As stated before, a number of point plans that have been prepared by trade associations and institutes are now widely used by their members and, with modifications, by other industries. If a ready-made plan is adopted, however, we again emphasize the advisability of defining the factors and degrees to suit local conditions. Any one of a number of plans and their scales may serve as a sample guide. Although the three manuals presented in this chapter have proven very successful, they should be considered as guiding examples only.

Sample Scales. The scales illustrated in Figure 10.2 conform with the factors, degrees, and weighted points shown in Table 9.2, page 234. The definitions of factors and degrees are in accord with the job contents in metal and woodworking industries where the scales are used most effectively.

Figures 10.3 and 10.4 illustrate the point scales for clerical jobs and supervisory positions used for over 23 years by Revere Copper and Brass, Inc. Revere utilizes different plans for each of four groups — shopworkers, clerical positions, supervisory positions, and functional and technical positions. The same four plans are used by six different Revere factory divisions in the United States. The jobs are classified by occupation, and each individual classification is analyzed.

The first factor termed "Elemental Factor Value" used in all Revere plans carries a philosophy and an approach that is characteristic of Revere. The plan is entirely different from all other existing plans, since the measurement of all jobs within a certain group starts with a common evaluation of the factor "Elemental Factor Value." The allotted points for this common factor are: 40 points for all jobs in the shops; 45 points for all clerical positions (see Factor No. 1, Figure 10.3); 30 to 45 points for six different supervisory positions (see Factor No. 1, Figure 10.4); and 35 to 55 points for functional and technical positions. The definition of the first factor in all four groups is the same, namely, "As a basis for employment, the company demands certain characteristics which are considered essential for all positions — or jobs — such as willingness to work, a certain ambition, neatness, personality, honesty, dependability, certain physical specifications, etc. . . ." (Compare Factor No. 1, Figures 10.3 and

10.4.) The unusual success of the Revere plans is best expressed by one of the executives in the foreword of the manual, which is reproduced in Figure 10.3.

The student of wage and salary administration and the job evaluation practitioner should keep the aforementioned manuals in mind when comparing job descriptions and specifications for evaluation and rating purposes, which are discussed in Chapter 12.

Key Jobs

Key jobs, also known as *benchmark jobs* and *pilot jobs*, are commonly known to have the same characteristics in different organizations within one industry or locality. Key jobs are regarded as standards. They should be selected and carefully studied by the committee as representative patterns for comparison and guidance to define degrees and to rate objectively. For those who may question the validity of evaluation and rating, key jobs help to understand better how the rater arrived at certain degrees and point allotments. Furthermore, key jobs are of immense value in ascertaining that the manual is a sound and reliable source to guide the committee members in their evaluation and rating.

Representative key jobs are selected from the lowest to the highest paid jobs. Through the pooled judgment of the committee it can readily be decided which are the lowest, medium, or highest paid jobs. All key jobs should be listed in ranking order to determine the difference in relative values, thereby facilitating proper selection.

It is recommended that each committee member evaluate and rate all key jobs. This procedure will familiarize all members with the routine and, above all, give each member an opportunity to compare his evaluation and rating with those of other members. Each factor of the selected key jobs should be evaluated by all committee members at one time. The grading of each factor should be compared and discussed, disagreements settled, and a uniform evaluation and rating arrived at. If all key jobs are evaluated by each member, one factor at a time, and completed according to the manual, it is assumed that the manual will be sound for evaluating all other jobs. On the other hand, if there are too many disagreements as to the grading and the allotted number of points, the definition and weighting of some degrees may have to be revised and acceptable standards established.

Considerations in the use of job evaluation manuals

For those who are anxious to get as much out of the job evaluation manuals as they can and thereby obtain ratings that will gain respect for being fair, objective, and valid, the following suggestions are offered.

1. Job evaluation ratings have the best chances of being accepted and considered valid when they are made by a joint union and management committee composed of reasonable, fair-minded, and knowledgeable persons who are respected for these qualifications. Ordinarily the larger the number of qualified employees doing the rating, the more reliable and relevant the ratings are likely to be; thus, the committee concept aids validity.

2. All persons asked to evaluate jobs should be given adequate instructions and practice in performing job evaluations before they are allowed to make official job evaluations.

3. Ratings cannot be any more valid than the accuracy of the data contained in the job specifications.

4. When evaluating a number of jobs, it is considered a better practice to evaluate all of these jobs on only one factor at a time, rather than evaluate one job at a time using all the factors. The only time it would appear desirable to evaluate a job completely on all its factors is when a new job needs to be slotted into the existing job classification plan. Even then this job would be compared on each factor with several jobs already previously evaluated and firmly established in the job classification plan.

   When a rather large number of jobs (50 or more) are to be evaluated, the total evaluation time can be shortened somewhat if the more well-known jobs (key jobs) are first evaluated and then used as guides or bench marks for evaluating the remaining jobs. This procedure should also assist in achieving greater validity and acceptance of the evaluations.

5. Objective ratings require that only the job requirements be kept in mind while performing the evaluations. If raters are evaluating the job based on the employee who is performing the job, the ratings are bound to be biased in some manner. In other words, raters must think of what the job requires of anyone rather than what qualifications the present employee has or how well he is performing the job.

6. Ratings should not be considered final nor official until each member of the job evaluation committee has evaluated the jobs independently and then has met with the other members of the committee to reconcile any variations in rating results. The procedure for reconciling any differences should be agreed upon before the ratings are made. Most evaluation results differ because of some misunderstanding of the terms used or the "apparent facts" about the job. Usually these differences are easily cleared up when a closer check of the job is made. Occasionally differences of opinion may persist. Such varying viewpoints may be resolved by the pooling of all the committee ratings or by arbitration.

7. Employees and raters cannot expect the job evaluation ratings to be absolutely perfect because they are based on judgment. Therefore, the ratings should not be advertised as being absolutely perfect but, rather, as the result of the best considered human judgment of fair-minded and knowledgeable employees.

1. EDUCATION AND/OR JOB KNOWLEDGE

The factor measures the extent of education or knowledge required by the worker to perform the job successfully. The education or knowledge may be the result of native intelligence, formal schooling, self-study, or company-sponsored educational courses.

Degree	Job Requirements	Point Value	Key or Benchmark Jobs
1st	Understands verbal instructions to perform simple repetitive jobs. Ability to read simple written instructions and write plain production figures.	12	Hand Drill Press Operator Laborer — Common Loader — Shipping Machine (Plain) Operator Punch Press Oper. — Blanking Wood Sander — Hand
2d	Required to operate simple machines. Read plainly written specifications, packing and shipping instructions. Should be able to add, subtract, multiply, and divide plain figures. Required education — grammar school or its equivalent.	24	Assembler (Plain subassemblies) Drill Press Oper. — Sensitive Grinder & Polisher Pipe-Fitter — Helper Punch Press Oper. — General
3d	Sets up and operates simple machines. Has to read simple drawings and understand simple mathematical formulas. Uses micrometers, precise calipers, and judges close dimensions. Two years' high school or its equivalent.	36	Assembler — (Complicated subassemblies) Automatic Screw Mach. Oper. Drill Press Set-up Oper. Machinist's or Millwright's Helper Tool Maker — (Small Tools)
4th	Produces jigs and fixtures. Assembles precision apparatus. Reads and interprets drawings and blueprints of accurate work in process. Uses a variety of gages. Requires a technical education equivalent to four years' technical high school.	48	Instrument Maker (Surveying) Machinist — First Class Milling or Automatic Machine Set-up Man Millwright Tool Maker — Jigs and Fixtures Tool and Die Maker
5th	Assembles, repairs, or inspects high-grade machinery using a variety of precision gages. May supervise a small group of workers (section leader). Requires education equivalent to two years' college.	60	Electrician Layout Man Metallurgical Inspection Microscope Adjuster Tool & Die Making Section Head
6th	Directs the operation of complex production units requiring mechanical and electrical engineering principles. Prepares and integrates schematics for laying out work and equipment. Requires four years' technical education or engineering training.	72	Automation Adjuster Calibrater and Tester Chief Electrician

FIGURE 10.2 Scales for Shop Workers. Factor and Degree Definitions, Point Allotments, and Key or Benchmark Jobs.

2. EXPERIENCE AND TRAINING

The factor measures the time required by the worker to learn how to do the job, or the experience necessary to perform the job competently. Produced work should be of a quantity and quality to justify continuous employment. Avoid confusing experience with formal schooling.

DEGREE	JOB REQUIREMENTS	POINT VALUE	KEY OR BENCHMARK JOBS
1st	Requires a comparatively short period of training or experience — up to three months.	24	Drill Press Operator Laborer Punch Press Operator Shipping Clerk Stocker
2d	Requires training on the job or related work — over three months but not exceeding one year.	48	Assembler (Intricate subassemblies) Pipefitter — Helper Turret Lathe Operator Welder, Arc
3d	Requires specific job experience. Learning time over one year but not exceeding three years.	72	Automatic Screw Machine Oper. Machine Assembler Millwright — Helper Punch Press Die Setter Radial Drill Press Operator
4th	Requires broad practical knowledge. Three to five years' experience.	96	Grinder, Ext. and Int. precision Lathe Operator — Engine Machinist — General Milling Mach. Operator and Set-up man Millwright
5th	Requires five to six years' training. Highly skilled in his occupation.	120	Automatic Screw Machine Set-up Operator Boring Mill Set-up Operator Molder Tool and Die Maker
6th	Requires six or more years' training and experience. An expert in constructing tools, apparatus, or complicated instruments. Capable of instructing others to become competent workers.	144	Assembler — (Surveying Instruments) Constructor — Apparatus

FIGURE 10.2 SCALES FOR SHOP WORKERS (*continued*)

3. INITIATIVE AND INGENUITY

The factor measures the nature and extent of initiative, ingenuity, and self-reliant judgment required to perform the job. The factor is also a measure of capacity to make decisions and the ability to develop a method of procedure.

DEGREE	JOB REQUIREMENTS	POINT VALUE	KEY OR BENCHMARK JOBS
1st	Performs job according to verbal or simple written instructions. Simplest type of job, requiring no decisions.	14	Hand Drill Press Operator Laborer — Common Loader — Shipping Machine (Plain) Operator Punch Press Operator
2d	Makes occasional minor routine decisions covered by simple and fully described instructions. Very little judgment required.	28	Assembler (Small Subassembly) Drill Press Operator — Sensitive Grinder & Polisher Pipefitter — Helper Punch Press Operator — General
3d	Shows ability to make frequent routine decisions of immediate importance. May have to make occasional routine decisions even if complete descriptions are available.	42	Assembler (Complicated Subassembly) Automatic Screw Mach. Operator Millwright's Helper Tool Maker — Small Tools
4th	Makes independent decisions using initiative and judgment regarding procedure, policy, and operation methods when definitely prescribed decisions are not available.	56	Assembler (Machine) Electrician Machinist — First Class Millwright Tool and Die Maker
5th	Encounters jobs of a semicomplex nature. Must make his own decisions to complete the job.	70	Calibrating and Testing Instrument Maker (Surveying) Layout Man Metallurgical Inspection
6th	Needs a high degree of originality to think through an extremely difficult and complex job. Develops new methods and makes independent decisions to obtain highest results.	84	Chief Electrician Millwright — Leader Tool & Die Making Section Head

FIGURE 10.2 SCALES FOR SHOP WORKERS (*continued*)

4. PHYSICAL DEMAND

The factor measures and compares application, endurance, fatigue, and strength under normal or abnormal conditions. Relates to expenditure of physical exertion inherent in a job to be performed at a normal pace. Consideration must be given to muscular exertion required for material handling, use of tools, and operation of machines. Also, consider weights when the job requires pushing, pulling, or lifting; frequency of weight handling, speed and time required to complete a job is equally important. Observe bodily motions and positions (sitting, bending, standing, kneeling) required in a day's work.

DEGREE	JOB REQUIREMENTS	POINT VALUE	KEY OR BENCHMARK JOBS
1st	Very light physical exertion sustained. Minimum of effort required for observation (sitting). Light assembly work and lifts weights of 1 to 10 lbs. 25% of total time.	10	Assembling, light Counting (by Scale Weighing) Crane Operator Inspection (visual) Light Material Handling
2d	Light physical exertion using hand tools. Works regularly with materials weighing 10 to 20 lbs. 25 to 50% of working time. Operates gasoline truck, tractor, or machines where machine time exceeds handling time.	20	Lathe Operator (Engine) Machinist (General) Stock Handler Tool Maker Truck Operator (Gasoline)
3d	Moderate physical exertion. Lifts, pushes, or pulls 20 to 30 lbs. 50% of the time. Job may require coordination of eyes, hands, and feet.	30	Assembler (Floor) Die Maker Laborer Millwright Sprayer and Painter
4th	Partially heavy physical exertion. Works in awkward positions, climbs ladders or stairs, pushes, pulls, or lifts 30 to 40 pounds over 50% of the time.	40	Carpenter Laborer Material Handling — Heavy Painter Trucker (Hand)
5th	Heavy continuous exertion in abnormally hot or cold temperatures. Uses heavy hand tools such as picks, hammers, bars, or heavy pneumatic tools. Lifts 40 to 50 lbs. over 50% of the time.	50	Blacksmith Chipper Coal Shoveler Grinder of heavy castings
6th	Exceptionally heavy work with continuous exertion in abnormal temperatures. Pushes, pulls, or lifts 50 lbs. or over in awkward positions over 50% of the time.	60	Foundry Worker Laborer (Loading cars) Painter (Handling Ladders) Trucker

FIGURE 10.2 SCALES FOR SHOP WORKERS (*continued*)

5. MENTAL AND/OR VISUAL DEMAND

The factor measures the degree of nervous fatigue resulting from performing the job. Consider mental or visual concentration and attention required to perform a fair day's work. Also, consider the complexity of the job, evaluating the time necessary to visualize the job.

DEGREE	JOB REQUIREMENTS	POINT VALUE	KEY OR BENCHMARK JOBS
1st	No mental effort required. Simplicity of the job or automation does not call for adjustments. May require visual attention at infrequent intervals.	5	Hand Trucker Machine Loader Stocker
2d	Job consists of rough work requiring limited mental and visual attention. No testing or checking required. Repetitive or automatic operations may require frequent visual attention.	10	Laborer Machine Operator (Automatic) Machinist's Helper Millwright's Helper Sweeper
3d	Job consists of repetitive work requiring mental and/or visual attention. Machine operations need adjustments from time to time. Inspection of work with close tolerances. Machine set-ups or operation of trucks or tractors in close areas.	15	Assembler (Subassemblies) Drill Press Operator Hand Screw Machine Operator Trucker (Power)
4th	Calls for close work with continuous mental and visual concentration. Necessitates coordination of mind and eye for inspection of close tolerances or keeping machines precisely adjusted.	20	Assembler (Accurate work) Cam Cutter Lathe Operator (Engine) Millwright Milling Machine Operator
5th	Necessitates very close work requiring highest mental and visual concentration. Work may require magnifying apparatus for close inspection.	25	Assembler (Precision Instr.) Grinding (Precision) Inspection (Microscopic) Layout Man Set-up Man
6th	Requires extremely accurate and diversified work with constant concentration of mental and visual effort. Work is of a precise nature calling for extreme exactness in planning and organization.	30	Adjuster of Automatic Equipment (Automation) Watchmaking

FIGURE 10.2   SCALES FOR SHOP WORKERS   (*continued*)

6. RESPONSIBILITY FOR EQUIPMENT OR TOOLS

The factor measures the degree of responsibility placed on the worker to prevent loss of, or damage to equipment and/or tools. The degree is measured according to probable cost of repair or replacement of equipment such as machines, dies, fixtures, jigs, dial gages, Johansson blocks, micrometers, precision calipers, optical gages, cutting tools, electric hand drills, or pneumatic tools.

DEGREE	JOB REQUIREMENTS	POINT VALUE	KEY OR BENCHMARK JOBS
1st	Uses simple hand tools with remote probability of damaging equipment. Probable loss not over $10.	6	Assembler (Plain Subassembly) Laborer (Common) Sweeper
2d	Uses tools and equipment which are not easily damaged. Probable loss $10 to $50.	12	Assembler (Subassemblies) Janitor Packer Stocker Trucker (Hand)
3d	Uses tools and equipment requiring some attention to prevent damage. Probable loss $50 to $500.	18	Automatic Machine Operator Blacksmith Chipper Drill Press Operator Trucker (Power)
4th	Uses tools and equipment requiring moderate attention to prevent damages on dies, power-driven equipment, motor-driven trucks, etc. Probable loss $500 to $1,000.	24	Lathe Operator Lens Grinder Punch Press Operator Truck Driver Welder
5th	Considerable attention required to prevent loss of tools or damage to complex machines. May involve some production losses. Probable loss $1,000 to $2,000.	30	Assembler (Using Optical Instr.) Craneman Molder (Precision) Punch Press Set-up Man Tool and Die Maker
6th	High degree of attention and continued care required to prevent damage to precision machinery and equipment where entire responsibility is placed on the operator. Probable loss $2,000 and over.	36	Automation Machine Adjuster Complicated Line Set-up Man Dividing Machine Operator — (Surveying Instruments)

FIGURE 10.2 SCALES FOR SHOP WORKERS (*continued*)

7. RESPONSIBILITY FOR MATERIAL OR PRODUCT

The factor measures the degree of responsibility placed on the worker to prevent spoilage of material, damage, or waste of products. The activity may consist of manufacturing, transporting, stocking, loading, unloading, or inspecting materials, parts, or assembled products. When evaluating this factor, consider monetary losses involved in the cost of materials and labor necessary for replacements.

DEGREE	JOB REQUIREMENTS	POINT VALUE	KEY OR BENCHMARK JOBS
1st	Job is very simple. Damage to materials or products unlikely to occur. Probable loss $25 or less.	7	Assembler (simple) Counter and Packer Grinder (rough) Janitor Laborer (common)
2d	Job requires ordinary care to prevent material spoilage or damage to product. Losses occur occasionally. Probable loss due to scrapping of material or damage to product is between $26–$100.	14	Drill Press Operator Punch Press Operator Screw Machine Operator Sprayer Trucker
3d	Job is of a repetitive nature requiring fairly close attention to prevent spoilage of material or damage to product. Probable losses $100–$200.	21	Arc Welder Band Saw Operator Boilermaker Crane Operator Milling Machine Operator
4th	Job requires close attention to produce parts or assemblies. Constant checking is of importance even though job is mechanically controlled. Probable losses $200–$500.	28	Automatic Screw Machine Set-up Man Grinder (Ext. and Int.) Lathe Operator Millwright 2d class Tool and Die Maker
5th	Job requires very close attention due to complex set-up. Material spoilage and damage to products difficult to prevent. Probable losses $500–$1,000.	35	Lens and Prism Polisher Millwright 1st class Tool Heat Treater Tractor Operator Wire Drawer
6th	Exceptionally close attention required to prevent spoilage and damages to expensive material and precise set-up. Work involves exceedingly close tolerances. Subject to damage due to transportation or handling. Probable loss is over $1,000.	42	Airplane Pilot Diamond Cutter Power Plant Engineer Precision Jig Borer Roll Maker — Precision

FIGURE 10.2 SCALES FOR SHOP WORKERS (*continued*)

8. RESPONSIBILITY FOR SAFETY OF OTHERS

The factor measures the degree of responsibility placed on the worker to maintain proper precautions for the safety of others. Consider negligence of the person performing the job as cause for probable injuries to a number of persons at any one time. Accidents to the worker himself are to be evaluated under the factor "Unavoidable Hazards." It should be remembered that the employer is responsible for all accidents which may occur on his premises.

DEGREE	JOB REQUIREMENTS	POINT VALUE	KEY OR BENCHMARK JOBS
1st	Job requires little care to prevent injury to others. Work is performed in areas where others are not exposed to accidents.	3	Assembler (Light, Bench) Counter (Scale) Hand Stamper Inspector (Visual) Packer
2d	Job is performed in area where only one other person is exposed. Probable injuries are very limited (1st-degree burns, cuts, abrasions, bruises, etc.).	6	Drill Press Operator Electrician's Helper Inspector (Roaming) Laborer (Common) Millwright's Helper
3d	Ordinary care is required in accordance with prescribed safety precautions. Work is performed in areas where others are occasionally exposed to 2d-degree burns, cuts, abrasions, bruises, etc.	9	Chipper Grinder (Surface) Molder (Foundry) Punch Press Operator Stock Handler (Using Ladder)
4th	Considerable care and attention required to prevent lost-time injuries to others. Failure to comply with safety precautions would probably result in 3d-degree burns, crushed bones, eye injury, loss of finger, etc.	12	Agitator (Steel Mill) Carpenter Electrician (Maintenance) Molder (High Speed) Oil House Stockkeeper Sprayer
5th	Job requires a high degree of constant attention to prevent incapacitating injuries to others (loss of arm, leg, eye).	15	Craneman Elevator Operator Millwright Motor Truck Operator (Congested Area) Wood Shaper
6th	Extreme care and highest degree of judgment necessary to avoid accidents to others (permanent total disability).	18	Airplane Tester Blower (Steel Mill)

FIGURE 10.2 SCALES FOR SHOP WORKERS *(continued)*

9. RESPONSIBILITY FOR WORK OF OTHERS

The factor measures the responsibility placed on a worker to set up equipment for, and instruct or direct other workers. It does not involve the disciplinary or supervisory capacity of a foreman or departmental manager. It only concerns the worker who has a helper, or the "Section Leader" who has several workers with him doing the same or closely related work. Consider the size of the group, required teamwork, degree of controls exercised, effect of leadership, and percentage of time spent with his group.

Degree	Job Requirements	Point Value	Key or Benchmark Jobs
1st	Job requires little or no responsibility for work of others.	4	Janitor Laborer (Common) Lathe Operator Oiler Punch Press Operator
2d	Job requires responsibility for directing or instructing one or two helpers or assistants.	8	Carpenter Electrician Machinist Millwright Molder
3d	Job requires a crew of three to six workers. Leader is responsible for set-up and continuity of production.	12	Automatic Screw Machine Crater Drill Press Set-Up Man Inspector Punch Press Set-up Man
4th	Job requires responsibility to operate a medium-sized production unit including 6 to 9 workers. Leader spends 50% to 60% of his time instructing and directing his helpers.	16	Carpenter Group Leader Electrician Group Leader Plater Polisher and Buffer Tool and Die Maker

5th	Job consists of operating a major production unit requiring set-up work and responsibility for instructing and directing 9 to 15 workers.	20	Working Group Leader of:
			  Automatic Screw Machines
			  Drill Presses
			  Forge Hammers
			  Tapping Machines
			  Turret Lathes

6th	Section Head is responsible for instructing, directing, and supervising over 15 workers.	24	Section Head of:
			  Optical Grinders
			  Tool and Die Makers
			  Truckers
			  Welders

FIGURE 10.2 SCALES FOR SHOP WORKERS *(continued)*

10. WORKING CONDITIONS

The factor measures the environment and general conditions under which work is performed. Consider disagreeable features such as cold, dampness, darkness, dirt, dust, fumes, grease, glare, heat, noise, oil, use of coolants, vibration, wearing respirator, and other disagreeable conditions surrounding the job to which the worker is exposed. Evaluate these elements and to what extent they may affect the worker, as well as additional expenses.

DEGREE	JOB REQUIREMENTS	POINT VALUE	KEY OR BENCHMARK JOBS
1st	Agreeable working conditions. Job has no effect on personal comfort.	10	Assembler (Various jobs) Coil Winder Elevator Operator Packer Stockroom Attendant
2d	Average working conditions. Disagreeable features have a slight effect on worker's well-being.	20	Lathe Operator Milling Machine Operator Pipe Fitter Tapper Tool Maker
3d	Working conditions include minor disagreeable features. Worker can become accustomed to surrounding conditions within a week or two. Is exposed to abnormal conditions 20% of working time.	30	Electrician (Maintenance) Machinist (Maintenance) Painter (Maintenance) Punch Press Operator Welder
4th	Unpleasant working conditions. Worker is continually exposed to dirt, grease, noise, and oil. Temperatures do not exceed seasonal standard by more than 5 to 10 degrees.	40	Automatic Screw Machine Operator Heat Treater Nail Machine Operator Sander Sprayer
5th	Disagreeable working conditions due to constant noise or fumes. Worker is exposed to temperatures exceeding seasonal standard 12 to 15 degrees 50% of the time.	50	Acid Dipper Forge Hammer Operator Grinder Polisher and Buffer Riveter
6th	Continuous disagreeable working conditions due to disturbing influences of excessive cold, dirt, fumes, heat, or noise. Worker may be exposed to these elements over 50% of the time.	60	Craneman Furnace Tender Ink Mixer (Carbon) Sign Painter

FIGURE 10.2 SCALES FOR SHOP WORKERS *(continued)*

11. UNAVOIDABLE HAZARDS

The factor measures the degree of risk assumed by the worker being exposed to accident and health hazards. Accidents may occur even though all safety precautions, procedures, and devices have been installed. Consider the severity of an unhealthy condition as well as the frequency and extent of injuries that will probably occur through accidents. It is assumed, of course, that the worker is observing all safety regulations.

Degree	Job Requirements	Point Value	Key or Benchmark Jobs
1st	Very little accident or health hazard present.	5	Assembler (Bench) Janitor Packer of light material Sweeper Watchman
2d	The worker may incur minor cuts, abrasions, bruises, or slight burns. Health is not affected and there is no loss of working time.	10	Inspector (Roaming) Crane Operator Laborer (Common) Tool Crib Attendant Trucker (Hand)
3d	The work is of a nature that an accident may cause bruises, cuts, eye injury, or muscle strain, effecting three to four days of lost working time.	15	Arc Welder Bricklayer Crater Drill Press Operator Punch Press Operator
4th	The work involves exposure to occupational diseases. Or, job may cause serious burns, eye injuries, finger-tip cuts, hernia, respiratory irritations, and other injuries, effecting loss of one to two weeks' earnings.	20	Band-Saw Operator Chipper Punch Press Setter Sander Truck Driver
5th	The work involves exposure to health or accident hazards which may cause the loss of several fingers, an arm, a leg, or partial eyesight. The worker may lose three to six weeks' earning power.	25	Buffer and Polisher Grinder (High Speed) Heat Treater Power Shear Operator Shaper (Wood)
6th	The occupation exposes the worker to occupational diseases or accidents leading to incapacitation or disfigurement causing loss of six weeks' to one year's income, or total disability.	30	Agitator Operator (Steel Mill) Dye Mixer Electrician Lineman (High Tension) Sand Blaster

FIGURE 10.2 Scales for Shop Workers *(concluded)*

REVERE CLERICAL POSITION EVALUATION PLAN

Definitions of various factors used and explanation of the various degrees comprising each factor

---

Used on all clerical positions

FOREWORD

The use of Job Evaluation as a means of establishing proper proportional spreads between dissimilar jobs has spread rapidly during the last several years.

However, there are still a great many people who look upon Job Evaluation as a devisement of complicated formulas and expressions which can be intelligently understood or applied only by those people with advanced education and training along similar lines of endeavour.

Revere, in devising its own plans, has laid particular stress on the need for simplicity, so that its plans can be easily understood and so that the rating procedure can be reduced to a plain common-sense level rather than to a highly intellectual one.

We believe this attempt has been successful.

John H. Eikenberg*
Vice-President — Industrial Relations
Revere Copper and Brass Incorporated

*Now, Chairman of the Board.

FACTOR No. 1 — ELEMENTAL FACTOR VALUE

Point Value

As a basis for employment, the company demands certain characteristics which are considered essential for all positions, such as willingness to work, a certain ambition, neatness, personality, honesty, dependability, certain physical specifications, etc., and, therefore, when considering wage differentials between jobs, we do not attempt to rate these common factors but instead base all rating differentials on the prime position factors above these common ones.

Lack of these characteristics are obvious and will destroy all chances of promotion.

To grant a value for these characteristics and to value them similarly for all jobs, we are inserting a constant factor which we will call "Elemental" and assign it 45 points.   45

Revere Copper and Brass Incorporated

FIGURE 10.3 Evaluation Manual and Scales for Clerical Positions

FACTOR No. 2 — EDUCATIONAL REQUIREMENTS

This factor is rated according to the minimum education necessary to allow an understanding of the position. It should be remembered here that it is the desire to concentrate on the requirements of the position and not the value of the education acquired by the man employed in the position.

Degree   Point Value
1. Grammar School or equivalent............................   0
2. Up to 2 years High School or equivalent....................   2–4
3. Up to 4 years High School or equivalent....................   6–8
4. Up to 2 years Special Training above a High School Education
   or its equivalent......................................   10–12
5. Up to 4 years Special Training above a High School Education
   or its equivalent......................................   14–16

FACTOR No. 3 — PRACTICAL EXPERIENCE REQUIRED

The degree of this factor is determined by the amount of experience judged necessary to fulfill minimum position requirements.

Degree   Point Value
1. Where no experience is necessary.........................   0
2. Where some experience is preferable, but can be accumulated
   during 3 to 4 months' employment with the company.........   1–3
3. Where sufficient experience would necessitate approximately one
   year of employment with the company in related positions......   4–6
4. Where the necessary experience would require approximately
   three years' employment with the company in related positions..   7–9
5. Where considerable experience is necessary in related positions so
   as to acquire a thorough overall knowledge; this experience to
   absorb approximately five years..........................   10–12
6. Where extensive experience is imperative in order to fulfill the
   position requirements. This would be considered as requiring over
   five years' company experience in related positions............   13–15

FACTOR No. 4 — ANALYTICAL REQUIREMENT AND COMPLEXITY OF WORK

This factor recognizes the difficulties and complications of the assigned task and measures the extent to which the work involved requires analytical ability, exercise of judgment, initiative and ingenuity.

Degree   Point Value
1. Where the assigned task is of a simple nature and obvious conditions can be readily recognized...........................   0
2. Where the assigned tasks consist of routine or standard matter,
   but demand recognition of a deviation from the accepted routine   1–3
3. Where the assigned tasks necessitate a weighing of facts and the
   exercise of a limited amount of judgment in decisions. It also
   involves performance of several different kinds of clerical or
   manual operations.......................................   4–6

FIGURE 10.3 Evaluation Manual and Scales for Clerical Positions
(continued)

Degree	Point Value
4. Where the assigned tasks make it necessary to devise data, requiring certain initiative and ingenuity, solve special problems, and make reliable decisions.....................................	7–9
5. Where it is necessary to ascertain certain facts, weigh them and present important or costly decisions to management without the benefit of guidance..	10–12
6. Where unusual and important facts must be weighed and analyzed, calling for an extreme exercise of good judgment and where independent action is essential and will have a bearing on quality or cost..	13–15

FACTOR No. 5 — ACCURACY

This factor considers the importance of the work as regards its opportunity for errors and the relative magnitude of the consequences. It also recognizes the availability of supervision to detect errors promptly and the amount of dependence placed on the accuracy with which the task is performed.

Degree	Point Value
1. Where possibility of error is negligible. All jobs require a certain degree of accuracy..	1–2
2. Where preliminary routine work is assigned and where errors are possible, but easily detected and corrected....................	3–4
3. Where the cost of correction will be considerable due to the difficult nature of the work and the degree of dependence placed on the performances..	5–6
4. Where work is of a very complicated nature and where cost of correction will be great in either time or money..............	7–8

FACTOR No. 6 — MEMORY

This factor values the necessity for retaining a variety of facts which may be associated with others, and will have a bearing on the efficient performance of the position.

Degree	Point Value
1. Where this element is relatively unimportant.................	0
2. Where it is desirable to retain simple facts about current orders and standard practices...................................	1–2
3. Where a retention of a variety of facts adds greatly to the efficiency of the task..	3–4
4. When the retention of a variety of repetitive facts or figures is necessary for constant use and where the memorized facts are difficult to retain because they are not associated with others............	5–6
5. Where the efficiency of the task depends largely upon the retention of non-repetitive complicated facts, which would be extremely costly if time were taken to consult written data..............	7–8

FIGURE 10.3 EVALUATION MANUAL AND SCALES FOR CLERICAL POSITIONS
(continued)

FACTOR No. 7 — MANUAL DEXTERITY

This factor is intended to attribute a value to those tasks which require a degree of dexterity, but which involve only a few of the other factors because of the nature of the work.

Degree	Point Value
1. Ordinary Clerical Work....................................	0
2. Adding Machine and Calculator Operators...................	1–2
3. Typists, Tabulator Key Punchers, Filing, Telephone Operators, Waitresses..	3
4. Dictaphone Operators, Stenographers, Elliott Fischer Operators, Comptometer Operators....................................	4
5. Bookkeeping Machine Operators...........................	5

FACTOR No. 8 — SUPERVISIONAL REQUIREMENTS

This factor values the degree of supervision exercised over the work of others, and takes into consideration the nature of the work as well as the number of employees.

Degree	Point Value
1. Where no supervision is exercised.........................	0
2. Where a group of employees must be supervised, but where the nature of the work calls for little directing, instructing, training, or planning..	1–3
3. Where a small group of not more than five in number must be supervised, but where it is frequently necessary to train and instruct, direct and plan the work involved....................	4–6
4. Where a group of more than five is involved, and where the nature of the work calls for frequent instructions, training, planning, and directing..	7–9
5. Where a small group is involved, but where the nature of the work involves the direction of highly skilled, specialized tasks or work of a complicated nature....................................	10–12
6. Where a large group is involved and where the nature of the work requires a co-ordination of varied phases of highly skilled technical or complicated work....................................	13–15

FACTOR No. 9 — CONDITIONS OF WORK

This factor takes into consideration the physical effort expended and the place of work.

Degree	Point Value
1. Sound-proof office or where only slight noises are apparent......	0
2. Noisy office or room.......................................	1
3. Where much walking or standing is necessary to the efficient performance...	2–3
4. Where the position consists almost entirely of standing or walking and where work must be done under extremely noisy conditions.	4–5

FIGURE 10.3 Evaluation Manual and Scales for Clerical Positions
(*continued*)

FACTOR No. 10 — CONTINUITY OF WORK

This factor refers to the degree of continuous performance without benefit of interruptions or breathing spells due to necessary conversations with others, etc.

Degree	Point Value
1. Where ample time for stoppage of work is possible due to any causes	0
2. Where work is varied and necessitates some stops for discussion or advice	1
3. Where the work is routine and planned for long periods with little opportunity for interruption	2–3
4. Where it is imperative to stay at the task constantly with rare opportunities afforded for breathing spells	4–5

FACTOR No. 11 — PHYSICAL STRAIN ON SENSES

This factor recognizes the nervous or eye-strain connected with certain tasks or positions.

Degree	Point Value
1. Where there are few involuntary interruptions or very little close figure work which demands concentrated vision	0
2. Where part of the work involves eye-strain	1
3. Where the major portion of the work involves constant eye-strain or close figure work	2–3
4. Where numerous involuntary interruptions are part of the day's work, requiring much concentration and nervous strain to again pick up the trend of thought or stoppage point	4–5

FACTOR No. 12 — RELATIONS OR CONTACTS

This factor measures the extent and relative difficulty and importance of the work handled with and through other departments or other companies in connection with the effect these contacts may have on plant or public relations.

Degree	Point Value
1. Where this factor is negligible	0
2. Usual contacts with other departments within the company on matters involving flow of work which has been standardized to a large extent and requires no decisions	1–2
3. Contacts with other departments within the company on matters involving decisions or disposal of certain activities which may lead into many discussions as to the best disposal or decision	3–4
4. Contacts within the company or with the public or both which involve the making of substantial adjustments which involve money or company policy	5–6
5. Contacts within the company or with the public or both which involve important agreements or disposal of serious matters which could greatly affect future relations	7–8

FIGURE 10.3 EVALUATION MANUAL AND SCALES FOR CLERICAL POSITIONS
(*concluded*)

REVERE OPERATING SUPERVISION
POSITION EVALUATION

Definitions of various factors used and explanation of the various degrees comprising each factor

---

Used only for supervisory positions

FACTOR No. 1 — ELEMENTAL FACTOR VALUE

As a basis for employment, the company demands certain characteristics which are considered essential for all positions, such as willingness to work, a certain ambition, neatness, personality, honesty, dependability, certain physical specifications, etc., and, therefore, when considering wage differentials between jobs, we do not attempt to rate these common factors, but base all rating differentials on the prime position factors above those common ones.

Lack of these characteristics are obvious and one lacking them would not be considered for a supervisory position.

To grant a value for these characteristics and to vary it according to the importance of these elements to the company, we are apportioning a set value as follows:

	Point Value
Superintendent or Assistant Superintendent	45
General Foreman	42
Assistant General Foreman	39
Foreman	36
Assistant Foreman	33
Group Leader or Section Operator	30

FACTOR No. 2 — TECHNICAL KNOWLEDGE REQUIRED

This factor recognizes the degree of intellectual knowledge necessary to a comprehensive understanding of the work elements involved. It is formal or literal education as opposed to real or practical knowledge.

Degree	Point Value
1. *Elementary* — Where little technical knowledge is required to conduct operations and where mental application is predominantly ordinary routine	1–6

Revere Copper and Brass Incorporated

FIGURE *10.4* EVALUATION MANUAL AND SCALES FOR SUPERVISORY POSITIONS

Degree **Point Value**

2. *Advanced* — Where a special knowledge of tools, equipment, and processes, and their effect one upon the other, which may be gained through experience, but which represents routine training rather than mental application.................................... 7–12

3. *Trained* — Where a thorough training is required in the operation of and application of definite technical rules or laws gained through study of cause and effect, or prescribed by higher supervision, technical staff or written advice. Representing mental application above routine instructions................................. 13–18

4. *Skilled* — Where one must possess a technical knowledge beyond routine stage having the equivalent of a technical course of study in the subject, where intellectual application exceeds practical or routine and where original thought is frequently demanded..... 19–24

5. *Expert* — Where one must possess technical knowledge of the subject matter, equivalent to a full university course in the subject, and who, through practice or further study, has developed technical knowledge to predominantly intellectual application. Capable of creative, analytical or original thought.................... 25–30

FACTOR No. 3 — PRACTICAL KNOWLEDGE REQUIRED

This factor assigns a value to the training derived from practical routine which may be gained only from actual contact and experience. It portrays the necessary accumulation of knowledge of the methods and tricks of the trade, non-technical in nature, which cannot be reduced to formulae or written instruction, but which govern quality and/or quantity of production.

Degree **Point Value**

1. *Elementary* — Simple repetitive operations, few in number, easily assimilated, well covered by instructions or precedent.......... 1–6

2. *Ordinary* — Involving knowledge that may be gained in a year of practice, yet cannot be transferred by verbal nor written instructions.. 7–12

3. *Trained* — Processes demanding knowledge that may be fully assimilated only after 2 or 3 years of practice................... 13–18

4. *Skilled* — 4 to 5 years of practical experience necessary to a full comprehension of a trade. To have practiced a standard and gained comprehension above the trained men................. 19–24

5. *Expert* — Requiring a high degree of ability to absorb intangible factors which control processes where variables are unlimited and requirements stringent. Marked skill to the point or degree of adaptability of a doctor or specialist......................... 25–30

FIGURE 10.4 EVALUATION MANUAL AND SCALES FOR SUPERVISORY POSITIONS (*continued*)

FACTOR No. 4 — EXERCISE OF JUDGMENT

This factor measures the degree of concentration necessary in the exercise of judgment as called for in the use of Factors 2 and 3.

Degree   Point Value

1. *Little* — Little demand for exercise of judgment. Experience governs variables.. 1–6

2. *Normal* — Some demand for judgment, but where process operations are covered by instruction or automatic through habit. Where advice is available from supervisory staff members or instructions, or where there are standard and relatively few operations... 7–12

3. *Exacting* — Where the demand for good judgment is imperative and independent judgment is necessary, but where ample time is available for reference and consideration. Demand for decisions are not too frequent.................................. 13–18

4. *Concentrated* — Where the demand necessitates quick decisions, using definite instructions or routine as a basis of such decision, but analyzed independent of aid. Demands are frequent....... 19–24

5. *Intense* — Where high mental ability to correlate cause and effect, to improvise remedy, to meet unexpected and serious development with good snap judgment, is demanded. Where demands are very frequent and must be made without the benefit of a higher source of information.................................. 25–30

FACTOR No. 5 — DEMAND FOR LEADERSHIP

This measures the ability to absorb and carry out company policies, rules and regulations, to understand worker psychology and to maintain satisfactory relations within the scope of his jurisdiction.

Degree   Point Value

1. *Little* — Where policy is predetermined and there is little demand for personal leadership, such as group leaders................ 1–5

2. *Average* — Where policies must be applied but are handed down by higher supervision in the mill or department. Where complete responsibility is not assumed but considerable tact is required in policy application....................................... 6–10

3. *Great* — Where full responsibility is vested for the policies and the relationship between management, supervision, and workers, of a mill or department... 11–15

4. *Extreme* — Where policy is determined and responsibility is vested for more than one mill or department.. 16–20

FIGURE 10.4 Evaluation Manual and Scales for Supervisory Positions (*continued*)

FACTOR No. 6—PLANNING

This factor measures the quantity of planning necessary as well as the difficulties involved coordinating types of processing.

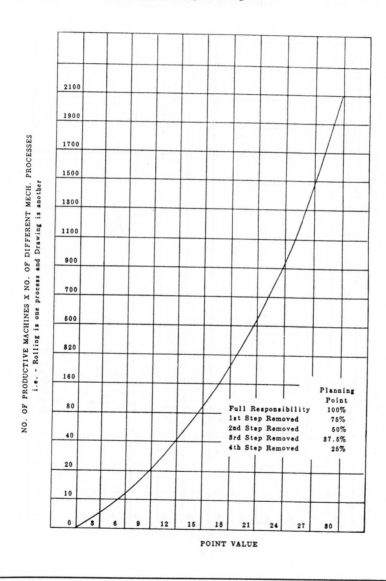

FIGURE 10.4   EVALUATION MANUAL AND SCALES FOR SUPERVISORY
POSITIONS (*continued*)

FACTOR No. 7 — No. OF MILL EMPLOYEES

This factor measures the value to be assigned for numbers, whose quality and/or quantity of production and employee relationship and conduct are affected directly by the functional activities of the subject supervisor.

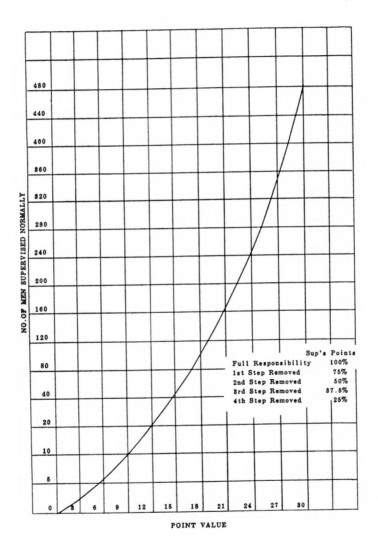

FIGURE 10.4   Evaluation Manual and Scales for Supervisory Positions (*continued*)

FACTOR No. 8 — CONDITIONS OF WORK

This recognizes the influence the process has on health and body.

Degree	Point Value
1. Ordinary processes requiring no unusual exposures which are foreign to the average fabricating mill......	1–6
2. Where exposure to elements of heat, fumes, dust, extensive noise, etc., is necessary......	7–12
3. Where high health or accident hazards are present......	13–18

FACTOR No. 9 — LIABILITY OF DAMAGE TO PRODUCT

This factor recognizes the importance of the work as regards the relative magnitude of the consequence of spoiled work.

Degree	Point Value
1. *Little* — Where only breakdown operations are involved and where there is small possibility of great or costly spoilage before discovery	1–6
2. *Average* — Where rundown operations are involved or where simple finishing operations offer little chance of error because of the check provided......	7–12
3. *Great* — Finish rolling or fairly complicated fabricating operations or any other process where a large cost has been built up with possibility of spoilage through lack of knowledge. Casting, because of the large possibilities of quantity spoilage, would be included in this class......	13–18

FIGURE 10.4 EVALUATION MANUAL AND SCALES FOR SUPERVISORY POSITIONS (*concluded*)

REVIEW QUESTIONS

1. What is the primary purpose of a job evaluation manual?
2. What information should be contained in a job evaluation manual?
3. How can job evaluation manuals be made more valid?
4. How can the evaluation of a large number of jobs be made more accurate? less time consuming?
5. "Employees and raters can expect job evaluation to be perfect." Explain why you agree or disagree with this statement.
6. (a) How can the quality of job evaluation ratings be improved? (b) Are the qualities of the raters important? Why?
7. When might the "pooled judgments" of raters become "pooled ignorance"?
8. Are the instructions that accompany the job evaluation manual important? Why?
9. (a) What is the importance of the use of key jobs in job evaluation? (b) How should the key jobs be used?
10. How can job evaluation ratings be made more objective?

RESEARCH OR SEMINAR QUESTIONS

1. Why must "responsibility" be given such a heavy weight when the worth of jobs is being evaluated?
2. Who should determine which jobs are key jobs, and how should the key jobs be determined?

PRACTICAL EXPERIENCE ASSIGNMENTS

1. Using the *Revere Clerical Position Job Evaluation Manual* found on pages 259 to 263, evaluate the following clerical jobs in your school as you understand them: typist, secretary, receptionist, and clerk.
2. Make up a list of topics that every rater should be instructed on before he is allowed to officially rate jobs according to the point plan.
3. Draw up a list of the strengths and possible weaknesses of the *Revere Clerical Position Job Evaluation Manual* found on pages 259 to 263. Make recommendations for correcting or reducing the weaknesses.

CASE PROBLEM

10—1. IRONSIDES FOUNDRY, INC.

Reevaluating Job Ratings

Ironsides Foundry, which concentrates in specialized castings, has had a poor profit picture for the last two years. Sales have dropped from $60,000 per month to $50,000. The average unit casting cost has risen from 25¢ to 30¢ per pound of castings produced. Profits have dropped from 8% to 1% of sales.

The company has a union shop and employs 200 workers, of whom 80 are molders. Hourly wages are slightly higher than the going rates in the community. The company uses the metal trades point system of job evaluation. Workers are, in general, satisfied, but management feels it has to do something to improve the cost and profit situation.

Mr. Steel, the president, has been thinking about handling the situation by completely modernizing the foundry. At present, the foundry is a rather dirty and hazardous place to work. Mr. Steel feels that modernizing the plant can accomplish these things:

1. Improve efficiency of operations and quality of product.
2. Improve employee morale through safer and more pleasant working conditions: improved lighting, ventilation, dust collection, safety devices, etc.
3. Reduce the job point ratings on many jobs. This would come about as a result of removing many of the undesirable and hazardous working conditions for which the company has had to pay heavily.

Problem:

The president has given you (the Personnel Director in charge of wages) his thinking on the problem and wants your recommendation on items 2 and 3. What will it be? Be prepared to justify your solution.

chapter **11**

METHODS AND TECHNIQUES
OF ANALYZING JOBS

If the fundamentals of the first four steps in setting up a job evaluation plan, discussed in Chapters 9 and 10, are understood and if the job evaluation committee is organized under the leadership of the chief job analyst, the actual process of carrying out step five can proceed. Step five involves studying and analyzing jobs, gathering information, and getting ready for the preparation of job descriptions and specifications.

Meaning and purpose of job analysis

Job analysis is basically the researching of a job to obtain the necessary information to serve some purpose. Job analysis may be thought of as a fact-finding process about a job or jobs. It is the very foundation upon which decisions in wage and salary administration (and the entire business) are based. Unless reliable and accurate information about a job can be obtained, there can be no facts; nor can valid and acceptable decisions about jobs be made.

Job analysis is multifariously interpreted in various situations for different purposes. Its usage, application, and definition have undergone diverse changes and adaptations. Therefore, it is necessary to consider the meaning and purpose of job analysis in relation to the activities and contemplated usage.

Job analysis is frequently interpreted to mean any one of its three subdivisions: "job description," "job grading," and "job classification." This is confusing since each of these three terms represents a related part of job analysis. Normally, job analysis precedes the preparation of job descriptions, job grading, and job classification. At times, the term job analysis is used to designate a written record, and at other times it means the investigation of functions and activities, or the description of positions that involve duties, qualifications, and attributes. It is also occasionally used to establish specifications that characterize different trades. Since we shall use the term job analysis in connection with subjects related to wage and salary administration, it seems advisable to discuss briefly the distinctions in its application.

Basic Divisions of Job Analysis

Job analysis is identified with many different uses which are an outgrowth of the arts and sciences developed in commerce and industry. In most manufacturing companies, there are at least two types of job analysis: one made by the industrial engineering division for the *study of processes, simplified methods, work measurement, and incentive rate setting;* and the other for use in personnel administration *specifically for job evaluation, employee evaluation, and the selection and proper placement of employees.*

For our purpose, however, the uses of job analysis may be classified into five basic divisions, each requiring different techniques of applications to serve as a foundation for:

1. Job evaluation and rating to ascertain job requirements, working conditions, health and safety requirements, and standardization of job terminology.
2. Evaluation and rating of employees to ascertain their qualifications and to facilitate promotion, upgrading, counseling, and transferring from one job to another.
3. Preparing specifications for recruitment, selection, placement, training, and guidance of employees.
4. Standardizing jobs to establish performance standards and detailed operation elements of doing work in order to set time rates for wage incentive plans.
5. Studying and analyzing work processes and procedures to find better methods of doing work in connection with work simplification.

Job Analysis for Job Evaluation

Job analysis for job evaluation and rating purposes concerns itself mainly with wage and salary administration to establish differential job structures and to remove inconsistencies in differentials of wage structures. It is accomplished through the standardization of job terminology, description, classification, and job grading. It also provides factual data concerning health and accident hazards as well as pertinent information for collective bargaining.

For the purpose of job evaluation, *job analysis* may be defined as the process of gathering information and determining the component elements of a job by observation and study. It involves analyzing and recording identifying information about the job and its duties; its requirements in terms of skill, effort, and responsibility; the equipment used on the job; and the working conditions under which the job is performed. The information and data obtained are recorded in job descriptions and job specifications.

Job Analysis for Evaluating Employees

During World War I and shortly thereafter, job analysis was adopted by psychologists for the classification of personnel and the evaluation of employees. Since then, the predominant aim of such analysis has been to determine and to correlate traits, abilities, aptitudes, and interests of employees with job success and failure. Such studies aid merit rating by facilitating promotions, transfer, counseling, and increases in wage and salary rates, thereby strengthening the wage and salary structure through periodic wage and salary adjustments. This type of job analysis is discussed in Chapters 14 and 15.

Job Analysis for Recruitment and Placement of Employees

The position of employment manager came into being because of the growing number of employees in manufacturing industries, and the introduction of new jobs and processes. The employment managers developed more up-to-date employment procedures that utilized job analysis in its new aspect of employee procurement.

Since the formation of the National Personnel Association, job analysis has become increasingly more important as a tool of the personnel management profession. Job analysis is applied specifically as an aid to recruiting, testing, placement, training, vocational counseling, promotion (upgrading) of employees, and safety administration. All these functions are correlated with general compensation wage scales, financial incentives, fringe benefits, and working hours to insure satisfactory and gainful employment. Job analysis for recruitment and placement of employees is essentially concerned with the discovery of employee qualifications that appear to be responsible for the employees' success or failure on the various jobs in a firm.

Job Analysis for Establishing Performance Standards

Job analysis, as originated by Frederick W. Taylor in 1881, led to the breakdown of each job into its constituent parts known as *operations* and *elements*. It was applied to time studies mainly to establish performance standards and to set piece rates. Thereafter, job analysis brought to light all the unnecessary activities and motions that cause loss of time, energy, and wages. Wastes that ordinarily escaped notice were readily detected. The functions of job analysis and time study were so closely related — because every aspect of a job must be studied in both activities — that some authors were inclined to utilize what seemed to them the more inclusive term of job analysis as a substitute for the term time study.[1]

Job Analysis for Work Simplification

At its inception, job analysis was adopted by Taylor's followers for the sole purpose of finding how long it took to do a job. But, as time progressed, job analysis aided in developing better methods for setting time-base rates as a basis for financial incentive plans. Job analysis serves to improve production methods, as a phase of work simplification, by correlating processes, operations, motion economy, job standardization, and time rating.

From the foregoing discussions of the basic divisions of job analysis, it is evident that the scope of job analysis varies according to the intended purposes of job study. Since each job study requires a technique and application different from others, obviously a clear distinction is necessary.

The job analyst

The person who performs a job analysis is commonly referred to as a *job analyst*. Sometimes the person is called a salary analyst if he is mainly analyzing salary positions. In either case, the analyst performs essentially the same work of collecting, analyzing, and developing occupational data relative to jobs, job qualifications, and work characteristics as a basis for compensating employees in a fair, equitable, and uniform manner. He also writes job descriptions and specifications and prepares narrative and statistical reports, reflecting such data as physical demands, working conditions, skills, knowledges, abilities, training, education, and related factors required to perform jobs. He may also conduct related occupational research, utilizing publications, professional and trade associations, and other media to verify or standardize data.

The *Dictionary of Occupational Titles* lists four levels or grades of job analysts. Each of the levels differs in the degree or class of work performed. The first grade is a training status in which the person is under instruction and learning to become an analyst. The second grade refers to an analyst who works mainly on routine and the more simple job assignments. The grade three analyst performs a greater variety of wage and salary assignments. The grade four analyst performs the more difficult assignments and may even develop, install, and administer a program. In short, an analyst may perform a range of work that at the lower levels assists the wage and salary administrator and at the higher

---

[1]See E. H. Anderson and G. T. Schwenning, *The Science of Production Organization* (New York: John Wiley & Sons, Inc., 1938), p. 46.

levels closely parallels the work of the wage and salary administrator. It would appear that a firm employing 2,000 or more employees would have need for the full-time services of an analyst.

The desirable qualifications that a competent job analyst should possess are many. Among the more important are the following. First, he needs to be knowledgeable in the practices of the business or industry in which he is to analyze jobs. Second, he should be personable and have the ability to secure the cooperation of the different types of employees that an analyst has to interview. Third, he should have an analytical ability to see the relationships between the duties and the jobs involved and objectively and honestly collect and report data on them. Fourth, he needs to be able to communicate clearly and succinctly at various educational levels. This means speaking and writing so that he is easily understood by any employee who can read and write.

In a study on what some 320 companies say about job analysts, only 38 percent of the companies prefer to select men from within their companies to become analysts. [2] Seventy-three percent of the companies expect an analyst to have at least two years of college background. Sixty-five percent of the companies train the analyst by assigning him to work with experienced men. Thirty-eight percent of the companies that are giving the analyst less than six months' training consider this satisfactory, while 12 percent of the companies find this length of training period unsatisfactory.

Job analysis procedures

The completeness and accuracy of the information obtained about jobs may be dependent upon how the jobs are analyzed. Job descriptions and job specifications cannot be any more accurate or valid than the quality of the job analysis. Unless the job analysis is done properly, it may have to be redone. This should be avoided since any analysis is a time-consuming activity and a relatively expensive one. In order to secure detailed, valid, and authoritative job information, the following job analysis procedures are suggested.

Preparing for the Analysis

There are several advantages to be gained by the proper preparation for a program of job analysis. Valuable time will be saved by eliminating the necessity of asking embarrassing questions on elementary points. Thus, the analyst will be able to interview and observe more quickly and intelligently. Proper preparation will also pave the way for more effective and acceptable analyses.

For the analyst to prepare effectively for job analysis, he must first know for what purposes the job analysis data will be used. If the data are to be used for

---

[2] J. A. Patton, "What 320 Companies Say about Job Evaluation," *Factory*, Vol. 118 (October, 1960), pp. 108–111.

employment, compensation, training, and safety work, the analysis must be more comprehensive than if the data are to be used for only one of these purposes. When the data are to be used for wage and salary purposes, the analyst should also know what method of job evaluation will be employed because the preparation of the job questionnaire should be tailored according to the factors or the information needed in the job evaluation process. See Figure 11.1 for a sample job analysis questionnaire used in the analysis of factory jobs by means of a point plan of job evaluation.

A job analyst needs to make a good impression as soon as he begins his analysis. Therefore, to gain the respect and cooperation of the various employees he will encounter, the analyst should secure some background information about the firm and its different departments. Sometimes a plant tour will give an overall picture of plant operations, processes, and work flow. An organizational chart may identify departmental relationships, titles of jobs to be analyzed, and company personnel. Discussions with officials and key employees will reveal where the greatest needs are for analyses and where good cooperation can be expected in order to get off to a good start. The *Dictionary of Occupational Titles* and the current *Occupational Outlook Handbook* are two valuable reference books that can help the analyst become acquainted with the necessary job and occupational information. Reviewing whatever local or national job descriptions are available may also provide background information.

Management should pave the way for the analyst by publicizing the purpose and expectations of the analyses. Arrangements must be made to introduce the analyst to the various personnel throughout the plant who will be involved. By means of these preparations, management shows its backing of the activity and the degree of importance attached to it and establishes a climate for the necessary cooperation between the analyst and the personnel with whom he will work.

With the help of the wage and salary administrator, the analyst should determine where to begin the analysis so that the program gets off to a good start and is productive as soon as possible. Consideration should be given to the following questions in making the decision of where the most promising place is to begin the company analysis program. In what departments is there a pressing need for the analysis? Which departments recognize this need? In which departments are the personnel enthusiastic about an analysis? Usually it is best to select a department greatly in need of the analysis, where the need is recognized, where cooperation may be easily obtained, and where the analyst has some background so that he and the program can get off to a good start and gain the respect of the employees.

One item that is often overlooked in preparing for job analysis is the amount of time that may be needed to perform the analysis. Although it is very difficult to estimate accurately the exact amount of time that different job analysts may require, the following guidelines are offered for consideration. In a national job

JOB ANALYSIS QUESTIONNAIRE

I. IDENTIFYING INFORMATION

A. Job title_____
B. Alternate titles_____
C. Time on this job:_____yrs.____mo.
D. Rate of pay_____
E. Promoted from_____
F. May lead to_____
G. Company_____
H. Dept. or location_____

I. Job analyst_____
J. Date_____
K. Verified by_____
L. His title_____
M. His time with co.____yrs.____mo.
N. Sheet no. _____of_____sheets

> **PLEASE READ THE ENTIRE FORM**
> **BEFORE MAKING ANY ENTRIES.**

II. JOB SUMMARY — What is the overall purpose of your job? How is it done? and Why?_____

III. DESCRIPTION OF WORK PERFORMED

A. Major Duties — Enumerate the job tasks that you perform regularly (tell <u>What</u> is done, <u>How</u>, and <u>Why</u>). Indicate the approximate number of hours or percent of time you spend on each duty per week. Indicate whether the duty is Routine (R), Complex (C), or Semicomplex (SC).

	No. Hrs. or % Time	R, C, SC
1.		
2.		
3.		
Etc.		

B. Other Duties — List any other tasks you perform irregularly or occasionally. How often?

   1.
   2.
   Etc.

IV. EQUIPMENT, TOOLS, AND MATERIALS USED ON THE JOB

List any machines, tools, and materials that you have to use on your job which require training or instruction to use them properly._____

V. JOB REQUIREMENTS (Minimum)
A. Education and/or Job Knowledge

   1. What is the lowest grade of grammar, high school, or college education that should be required of a person starting in your position?_____

   2. If any special courses are needed, name them._____

FIGURE 11.1 A Sample Job Analysis Questionnaire for a Point
Plan of Job Evaluation

B. Experience and Training

  1. What is the lowest amount of past experience which would enable a new employee to learn and perform the duties of your job satisfactorily?_____

    (Name the kind of experience, where, and how it could be obtained, and the time required to acquire it).

  2. Given the above education and experience (in A & B), what would any new employee (new to your position) have to learn that would not have been learned in past training and experience?_____

  3. What is the shortest period after starting the work that he could learn what those new factors are and how to handle them?_____

  4. After learning these new factors (in B2) how long would it take the new employee in your position to obtain sufficient practice in doing the new work to reach the point at which he would be just "barely satisfactory"?_____

C. Initiative and Ingenuity
Indicate the nature and extent of routine, initiative, originality, self-reliance, or judgment which are required by the job duties._____

D. Physical Demand
Specify any particular physical qualifications or requirements that are needed for your job (height, weight, strength, eyesight, health, appearance, etc.)_____

E. Mental and/or Visual Demand
Describe any degree of mental or visual concentration or attention that is required as part of your job (minimum, close work, nervous fatigue, constant attention, etc.)

F. Responsibility for Equipment or Tools
What is your responsibility ($) to protect or to prevent loss of, or damage to, equipment, tools, dies, machines, etc.?_____

G. Responsibility for Materials or Products
What is your responsibility ($) to protect or to prevent spoilage of material or waste of products? (in handling, storage, producing, inspection, selling, etc.)_____

H. Responsibility for Safety of Others
What is the nature and extent of your responsibility to maintain proper precautions for the safety of others?_____

I. Responsibility for Work of Others
What is your responsibility to instruct and direct (or supervise) the work of others? (List the job titles, number of people on each job, and what the general purpose of their work is.)_____

FIGURE 11.1 A SAMPLE JOB ANALYSIS QUESTIONNAIRE FOR A POINT
PLAN OF JOB EVALUATION (*continued*)

J. Working Conditions

1. Indicate the conditions present in the location and nature of your work (Mention any unfavorable, undesirable, or disagreeable features as: cold, dampness, glare, dirt, fumes, grease, noise, etc.)_____

_____

_____

2. Daily hours: from_____to_____Days per week_____

3. Weekly hours_____overtime hours_____(day, week, month)

4. % standing_____walking_____sitting_____lifting_____
   climbing_____bending_____kneeling_____other_____

5. Days of traveling (out of town)_____(per week, month, year)

6. Must person join the union after probationary period?_____

7. What emergencies or special work are you subject to call?_____

K. Unavoidable Hazards — What dangers, risks, or accident hazards are present in your work?_____

L. Please list any other requirements not covered above (personal or special) which are important. (age, male or female, attitude, security clearance, license, citizenship, foreign language, bonded, etc.)_____

VI. PERFORMANCE STANDARDS AND JOB SUCCESS

A. List the factors that should be considered in evaluating the degree of success or failure of employee performance on this job. (quality, quantity, etc.)_____

_____

B. Specify after each factor the efficiency or job performance standards that would indicate each of the following employee ratings: Failure, Satisfactory, Outstanding.

FIGURE 11.1 A SAMPLE JOB ANALYSIS QUESTIONNAIRE FOR A POINT PLAN OF JOB EVALUATION (*concluded*)

analysis methods survey,[3] respondents were asked to estimate the average time needed to complete one job analysis (this estimate included the gathering of data and the writing of a job description). For hourly rated employees, about one half of the respondents averaged four hours or less to complete the analysis of one job, while one fourth spent five to eight hours. For salaried workers, one third averaged four hours or less, and another third averaged five to eight hours. In short, it would appear that for most jobs, close to four hours should be allotted for each analysis, while the more difficult jobs may require twice as much time.

[3]Summary of "National Job Analysis Methods Survey" by Bureau of Business Research, California State College, Long Beach, and Los Angeles Foundation, California State College, 1968, p. 2.

Conducting the Analysis

After proper preparation has been made for the analysis of jobs, the job analyst is ready to begin gathering the necessary job information. The more uses to which the information is to be put, the more information that should be collected. If in doubt, it is always better to collect too much information and later discard some of it than to have to make a second trip to get additional information because not enough was collected.

Information to be Collected. In general, the information that needs to be collected for every job analysis can be grouped into the following six areas: (1) Identifying Job Information, (2) Job Summary, (3) Description of the Work Performed, (4) Equipment, Tools, and Materials Used on the Job, (5) Job Requirements, and (6) Performance Standards for Job Success.

Identifying Job Information. This section of the job analysis (see the job analysis questionnaire in Figure 11.1) pulls together in one place pertinent information about the job's correct title, location in the plant, pay, etc. Such information identifies key facts about the job in the overall company job hierarchy.

Job Summary. This is a simple statement of the overall purpose of the job, how it is done, and why. A job summary assists employees and management in quickly locating a specific job about which they need further information.

Description of the Work Performed. This section is intended to identify the specific kinds of major and minor duties that are part of the job itself. It may also indicate the approximate percentage of time spent on each duty and whether the duty is considered to be a routine one, complex, or somewhere in-between. This information is vital to the company when recruiting, hiring, training, and compensating its employees.

Equipment, Tools, and Materials Used on the Job. This section identifies the various machines, tools, and materials that are used in connection with the job. This information is needed when hiring and training a person, when determining the degree of skill needed to perform the job, and when evaluating the job.

Job Requirements. This section spells out the minimum demands that are called for by the job. These demands are properly referred to as job specifications. This information is an absolute necessity for evaluating the worth of a job during job evaluation. The information that is sought should be tailored around the factors that are to be used in the plan of job evaluation. This means that the information sought for all company jobs will only be the same if only one plan of job evaluation is to be used. If a different plan of job evaluation (one having different factors) is used for clerical jobs, factory jobs, executive jobs, etc., a different set of job requirements and information will be sought for each plan to be used. Job requirements information is also useful for recruiting and selecting employees when it is translated into qualifications that a prospective employee needs to have to perform the job. Job requirements (job specifications) are thus used for wage and salary purposes in evaluating jobs, while employee qualifications (or man specifications) are chiefly used in employing persons.

Performance Standards for Job Success. No job analysis would be complete without finding out what job standards are used to evaluate the performance of an employee performing the job. There must be some basis for determining whether an employee is a success or a failure on the job. The performance standards indicate at least what performance is considered as failure, satisfactory, and outstanding. This information is needed for determining employee promotions and pay raises and in evaluating hiring procedures.

Methods of Gathering Information and Data. The gathering of factual job information (job review) serves the purpose of making a correct job analysis, preparing permanent job descriptions and, thereafter, objectively evaluating and rating jobs. Obviously the analyst must thoroughly understand the job and the factual data submitted to him.

There are five methods of securing job information:

1. Observing jobs and interviewing employees.
2. Sending separate questionnaires to workers and supervisors.
3. Obtaining job descriptions from the time study department.
4. Planning a conference with the supervisor and a select group of workers.
5. Using a combination of the enumerated methods.

Observing Jobs and Interviewing Employees. Experience has proven that the job analyst's personal interview with an employee benefits everyone concerned, even though it is somewhat more expensive than the questionnaire method. The interview may take place in the analyst's office or in a general conference room. However, not being within the environs of the job, the analyst is at a disadvantage, especially if unfavorable conditions exist. It is more advantageous to observe the job in process, to interview the worker, and to interview immediately the supervisor for additional information and verification.

Prior to the interview, the departmental supervisor should be contacted regarding the job to be observed and the worker to be interviewed. The supervisor then introduces the analyst and puts the employee at ease. Thus, hesitancy and confusion are reduced. If the employee is in a cooperative mood, his answers will probably be accurate and complete. When the analyst is convinced that the job duties and all requirements are correctly interpreted by the employee, all information should be recorded on a job analysis questionnaire form similar to Figure 11.1. After reading the recorded information to the employee and obtaining his confirmation of its correctness, the supervisor should be consulted for final verification.

If an employee is on a piece rate or bonus job, the analyst should make sure that the worker is paid his full wage-base rate for the time spent on the interview. The analyst creates goodwill by expressing his appreciation and assuring the worker that he will be informed if any changes are required. This is especially important if the worker assisted in filling out the job information sheet.

Sending Questionnaires to Workers and Supervisors. Companies differ in their approach when developing the contents of questionnaires. Some companies use the same questionnaire for workers and supervisors, while other firms use a simple questionnaire for workers and a more elaborate one for supervisors. The simple form may contain questions referring to the title of the job, duties performed, type of equipment used, skill required, supervision rendered or received, and working conditions. This information is not only useful to the analyst but also educational for the employee. Figure 11.1 lists some of the pertinent questions that may be asked shop workers. This form may also be used as a sample questionnaire for salaried employees.

When designing questionnaire forms, simplicity and completeness should be the pattern. Some personnel-minded analysts are apt to combine information needed for selection and employment with information required for job evaluation. As a result, the form becomes "top heavy," complex, and often confusing. A combination of unnecessary and complex information should be avoided.

To assure proper usage of the questionnaire, the analyst should decide in advance whether the "checklist type" or "prose type" form, or a combination of both, will be used for collecting and recording data. Since there are no set rules by which to determine the preferred type, the decision will be contingent upon the nature of the jobs and the observer collecting the data. The *checklist* type of questionnaire has the advantage of being definite; it saves time in making entries. Most of the information can be given by the employees by simply checking a number or a descriptive phrase that most closely describes their job situations. The analyst should not, however, design the forms so briefly that the collection of important factual information and data is overlooked. The *prose type* form of questionnaire is used when the company finds it necessary to have each employee write a description of his own job. This should be a preliminary description since the final description will be completed by the analyst. Explanations to guide the employee in filling out the form are enhanced by indicating the purpose of the job description. Furthermore, it is advisable to include a cautionary note, such as: "Note, the job is being analyzed, not the employee or the employee's ability to prepare the job description." When the analyst confers with supervisors or workers, he should investigate all the job details involved. Information not included on the form can then be added. However, there is the danger of "overanalyzing" through too many lengthy discussions with those being interviewed.

Although the questionnaire should contain all pertinent questions along with brief instructions on how to answer each question, it is advisable to accompany the questionnaire with a letter explaining how the employee is to proceed. The letter should also include some encouragement for the employees so that they will give the questionnaire their prompt and wholehearted attention. One type of accompanying letter is illustrated in Figure 11.2.

Century Steel Corporation*

1214 Carnegie Avenue, Pittsburgh, PA 15219

Telephone 412-621-6191

May 30, 19--

To All Employees of the Manufacturing Division:

The enclosed questionnaire has been prepared by the Job Evaluation Committee to gather information regarding your jobs. To obtain an accurate and fair job evaluation, we need the assistance of employees who actually perform the work on every job. Only then can we complete the best job descriptions.

Please study the questionnaire before answering any of the questions. If you understand all questions, fully answer each question as accurately as possible to assist your committee member, who may also be one of the job analysts. Make your answers clear so that they will be easily understood by anyone who has to make an analysis of your job. Most questions can readily be answered by making a check mark √ .

If you do not understand some questions, ask your supervisor, the committee member of your department, or the steward to assist you.

We greatly appreciate your help and sincerely hope that you will give this questionnaire your immediate attention, returning it to the committee on or before the due date indicated in the questionnaire.

Mark W. Gerhardt	John F. Melvin
Edward A. Adams	William Lawrence
Ralph M. Holmes	David Meyer
Gregory J. Caldwell	Paul K. Dick
Richard T. Kerr	Edward A. Parker

dm

*Fictitious company name and location.

FIGURE 11.2 LETTER ACCOMPANYING A QUESTIONNAIRE

Questionnaires for clerical workers and supervisors have been used with good results. Similarly, results are equally good when workers in shops are assisted by their supervisors or section heads in answering questionnaires. A steward's assistance should be given special consideration since he has considerable influence with coworkers and the union. The worker should be cautioned, however, to answer questions according to his own interpretation without any undue influence.

If a questionnaire is sent to the worker through the supervisor's office, a double function is accomplished by instructing the supervisor to assist the worker when necessary and, at the same time, to add his own information or corrections. If changes are required, the employee should be immediately informed. After comparing the answers on the employees' questionnaires against those received from supervisors, the analyst may notice differences in job titles and inconsistencies in descriptions that must be rectified before the forms are presented to the committee for discussion. From the authors' own experiences, it may be definitely stated that the employee questionnaire in itself cannot be depended upon for job descriptions. Corrections and clarifications are usually required.

The approach and the methods to be used in collecting information for job analysis are controversial among authorities. Some prefer to obtain job information by interviewing employees and supervisors, while others favor questionnaires that are sent to employees and supervisors. No specific rule can be established. As a matter of fact, both methods are acceptable as long as accuracy of information and time consumption are considered. Either one, or both methods combined, may be used contingent upon which is most effective at the lowest cost. Questionnaires speed the process of gathering information on a large number of jobs. Precautions should be taken, however, to see that workers interpret the questions correctly and supply the information in proper form.

After studying the advantages or disadvantages of both methods, the chief analyst and his committee make the decisions. They know which method will work best at the lowest cost, since they are in immediate touch with the situation. Whichever method is adopted, it is imperative to contact employees for their views and reactions. Besides offering firsthand information, this practice has a psychological effect on employees. It gives them assurance that they are assisting in evaluating their own jobs.

Obtaining Job Descriptions from the Time Study Department. Job descriptions for motion and time studies are written for the sole purpose of dividing the job into its operations and suboperations (elements), with a view toward establishing time standards and the "one best way" of performing a job. The best method of performing the job, however, is of no specific concern to the job analyst for job evaluation purposes. Time study engineers use the four factors, Skill, Effort, Conditions, and Consistency, for "leveling" purposes to ascertain a normal or average pace in performing the job. However, these factors are not included in the job descriptions, but they are necessary for performance standards. Nevertheless, the job evaluation analyst might receive assistance when evaluating factors and degrees by conferring with the industrial engineer or the time study man.

Planning a Conference with Supervisors and Workers. Whether the interview, the questionnaire, or both methods, are used to collect information, the analyst is dependent upon the supervisor, who is completely familiar with the job, to participate in answering questions and clarifying job requirements. To cut expenses, the analyst may find that the supervisor's information by itself is sufficient. Such job evaluation, however, may be regarded as one-sided. It is therefore recommended that the worker be called to the supervisor's desk where the analyst can make immediate entries while both the worker and supervisor give their reactions. Otherwise, the supervisor may either overestimate or underestimate the importance of jobs.

Using a Combination of Methods. A very complete job analysis can be undertaken by combining the methods described. A brief questionnaire is sent to the employees, who are instructed to examine the questions thoroughly, to answer them fully, and to send the questionnaire to the supervisor within a designated period. At the same time, a more elaborate questionnaire is sent to the supervisors with a request that it be returned to the analyst at approximately the same time that the employees send theirs to the supervisor. The supervisor reviews the employees' answers, enters his own information, makes corrections if needed, and returns the questionnaires to the analyst. If necessary, the analyst then interviews some workers to verify the answers. Thereafter, a conference is held with the supervisor and a group of employee representatives to further clarify the job contents for final adoption. The information is critically reviewed, analyzed, and edited by the chief analyst and the whole job evaluation committee, who finally decide on job descriptions, specifications, and evaluation according to the job manual.

Some Guidelines in Conducting an Analysis. Conducting an analysis, like interviewing, is more an art than a science. There are no foolproof or guaranteed formulas. A person becomes a skilled analyst by much practice and experience. A person who hopes to conduct satisfactory analyses should keep the following guidelines uppermost in his mind when he attempts to analyze a job:

1. The proper official should be contacted for permission to make the study. He can select a suitable departmental supervisor or foreman for the analyst to work with and to give the analysis the backing and any added assistance it needs. The departmental supervisor or foreman can be

consulted regarding the best time, place, and location to make the analysis. He will likewise introduce the analyst to the worker and pave the way for establishing rapport and getting the necessary cooperation and results. He can also check any job data and technical terminology that may be confusing to the analyst.

2. Each job should be analyzed in a consistent manner. The worker should be encouraged to think and talk according to a logical sequence of the duties performed. Generally, jobs are observed through a complete work cycle (from the time a unit of work or task has begun until it has been completed). For those jobs having unusually long cycles or no cycles at all, it may be more advantageous to observe the most important or difficult or most time-consuming tasks first in order to report on a descending order of the tasks being performed and to be able to write up the jobs in a consistent and comparable manner.

3. The facts about the job should be secured and reported as they actually exist (not as they once were or as they may exist in the future). It is not in the realm of the analyst to discuss, determine, comment, or report on the efficiency (quality or quantity) aspects of the job being analyzed. Facts are to be sought, not opinions nor preferences. It is not appropriate for an analyst to take issue with the worker's statements nor to show any partiality to any existing job grievances or job classifications. The attitude of an analyst is crucial in obtaining the cooperation of the employee, who must be treated with courtesy and respect and as an equal.

4. A minimum of notes should be taken while observing the job, as it tends to make workers nervous and less cooperative. Notes can and should be expanded as soon after the analysis as possible. In interviewing the worker, the analyst's questions should be tailored to the level of the employee being interviewed. The questions should seek to find out what duties the worker performs, why they are done, and how they are performed (methods, tools, and equipment used). The questions should obtain information about the job requirements (skill, effort, responsibility, and working conditions) as well as the performance standards set for the job. A job analyst should have a job analysis questionnaire (similar to Figure 11.1) and use it as a guide for analyzing each job. There is no substitute for a comprehensive questionnaire and knowing how to use it effectively. It is important to stress also that to date there has been no single all-around universal job analysis questionnaire devised that will serve satisfactorily for analyzing all the jobs that are evaluated by different plans of job evaluation. The questions in the job requirements section of a job analysis questionnaire (see Figure 11.1, Section V) will need to be adapted to the specific plan of job evaluation to be used.

5. The job analysis should be completed on a friendly note. Sometimes the information obtained from the worker is reviewed in summary fashion to check the worker's agreement. An expression of thanks to the employee for the time and cooperation he has extended to the analyst is always in good taste.

Putting the Analysis to Use

What happens to the facts and the data after they are collected in the job analysis? When the job analysis has been made for only wage and salary purposes, the data are used in the preparation of job descriptions and job specifications. If the analysis is to be used for employing persons, man specifications are developed. The data may also be used to identify the topics and subject matter for training employees and for accident prevention. Job analysis data are also valuable for counseling employees and making appropriate recommendations for transferring and promoting employees.

Before an attempt is made to put any of the data to the above uses, several preliminary checks should be made. First, the data should be double checked for legibility, correctness, and completeness. It is a simple task to do this immediately after the analysis has been completed, as the analyst has not had much time to forget the details nor have his contacts become too cold to get quickly any information he missed. Second, should there be any inconsistencies or controversies regarding the job titles, job codes, duties, and the like, the immediate superior of the worker should be contacted as he should be able to clarify or verify the situation. Third, there should be an attempt to establish some system or code for filing the analyses so that they are easily accessible by those who have need for such job data.

When these preliminary checks have been made to ascertain that the job analysis data collected are complete, accurate, and dependable, the data are ready to use. For compensation purposes, this primarily involves drawing upon these data for preparing job descriptions and job specifications which are used for evaluating jobs. The subject of the next chapter is the editing and utilization of the job analysis data to prepare job descriptions and specifications in a style suitable for wage and salary administration.

REVIEW QUESTIONS

1. Briefly describe the main functions or objectives of a job analyst.
2. (a) What are the principal methods that a job analyst has at his disposal to make a job analysis? (b) What are the chief advantages and limitations of each method? (c) Under what conditions or circumstances would you recommend use of each of the methods?
3. How much information should be collected in the job analysis interview?
4. What is the purpose of the job summary?
5. List the guidelines for conducting a job analysis and explain why each is important.
6. How does a job analyst go about securing the cooperation of employees and supervisors?
7. (a) List the desirable qualifications of the job analyst. (b) Why is each of these important?

8. What, if any, preparation should be made before each job analysis interview? Why?

9. (a) What are the major elements in the job analysis questionnaire? (b) Why is each important?

10. What areas should be covered in a job analysis interview? Why?

11. Under what circumstances is the questionnaire method of job analysis advisable? Why?

12. (a) What does the term *job analysis* mean to you? (b) For what various management functions can it be used to good advantage?

13. Explain the significance of job analysis in relation to job description and job specifications.

14. What can management do in order to insure favorable employee reaction to job analysis?

15. Should jobs be described as they actually are or as they should be? Why?

16. If a job questionnaire contains directions for completing the form, is it necessary to write a letter to the employees explaining the reasons for the analysis as well as giving them instructions? Why?

RESEARCH OR SEMINAR QUESTIONS

1. What are the advantages and disadvantages of having the supervisor perform his own job analysis in compliance with procedures established by the wage and salary administrator?

2. If, when using the interview form of job analysis, you find that the employee does not remember many of the things that he does, what can you do to complete the analysis?

3. How can you be sure you have all the pertinent information about a job before writing a job description?

4. What are some possible methods that may be used to "break down" the employee's job in such a way as to facilitate the writing of the job description?

5. (a) Draw up a list of the minimum qualifications that a person should possess if he hopes to qualify for the position of job analyst in a company large enough to support one full-time job analyst.
   (b) Recommended a method for developing or obtaining each of these minimum qualifications.

PRACTICAL EXPERIENCE ASSIGNMENTS

1. Make an analysis of a friend's job by interviewing him to collect information and data. Retain the data for use in Practical Experience Assignment 1, page 312, in which you will be asked to prepare a job description and a job specification for the point plan of job evaluation.

2. Have one of your classmates fill out a job questionnaire on a job he has held. The questionnaire on pages 277 to 279 may be used, or another type of questionnaire may be supplied by your instructor. Check carefully to see

that the information is accurate and complete enough for use in preparing a job description and job specification for the point plan of job evaluation.

3. Observe some employee while he is working on his job. Record the information that you think is necessary so that you could later prepare a job description and job specification for the point plan of job evaluation.

4. The job analyst does not know all the jobs in a given company. Make a list of steps or safeguards that he should take to make sure that the facts he gathers are correct, accurate, and unbiased.

CASE PROBLEM

11—1. WILSON SAW COMPANY

Reanalyzing Jobs

The Wilson Saw Company, manufacturers of power-chain saws, employs 2,100 men. Although a job evaluation point plan has been functioning for a year, there is some discontent among the workers arising from so-called wage inequities. The point plan (similar to that of NMTA) was installed a year ago to remedy wage inequities that were a constant source of employee dissatisfaction.

A job analysis was performed for each job, and descriptions and specifications were prepared on the basis of the data in the analyses. In preparing each analysis, the analyst interviewed a typical worker for each job, chosen by the foreman in whose department he performed the work. The analysis was verified by interviewing the worker's immediate supervisor. Later the job descriptions and specifications for each job were verified by the appropriate supervisor.

Three or four of the supervisors have been with the company for many years and have received their promotions for performing outstanding work as machinists. The remaining supervisors have been promoted directly from machine operator positions or have been recruited from outside the company.

Although the work performed in several of the departments tends to fall into similar labor grades (most semiskilled machining operations), the wages in those departments tend to be dissimilar. The wages in the departments headed by the former machinists tend to be higher than those in the other departments.

Problems:

1. What are some possible explanations for the differences in wages?

2. Should the company require another analysis of the jobs? If not, why not? If yes, should the analysis be undertaken for all jobs, those paying the lowest wages, or those paying the highest wages? Why?

3. What can the analyst do to increase the accuracy of his analyses?

chapter 12

PREPARING JOB DESCRIPTIONS
AND SPECIFICATIONS

In this chapter we shall deal with the preparation of job descriptions and job specifications for rating — the sixth step in the procedure of setting up a point plan in a company.

Job descriptions and job specifications differentiated

From the standpoint of job evaluation, *job descriptions* are combinations of simply written short statements that describe the contents and essential requirements of jobs or positions. *Job specifications*, on the other hand, are explanations of the specific job requirements within a uniform framework of job factors so that the job may be more easily rated during the job evaluation process. To comprehend the significant implications of the two terms in job evaluation, it seems advisable not only to explain their meanings and applications but also to introduce sample descriptions and specifications for both clarification and comparison purposes.

Illustrative Job Descriptions and Specifications

A comparison of the illustrative job descriptions, Figures 12.3, 12.4, and 12.5, used by various enterprises reveals differences in approach. In each case, the compiled informational data are of assistance in preparing specification rating sheets, such as those shown in Figures 12.7, 12.8, and 12.9.

While it is true that each style of job description and specification for rating will have to conform with a tailor-made job evaluation program, there is no reason why accepted patterns should not be adopted. Therefore, as samples for comparison purposes, we are introducing a number of practical illustrative forms that are used in commerce and industry. A close study of the samples will disclose the differences, thus making it possible for the reader to adopt those features that are most suitable for his requirements.

Importance of Job Descriptions and Job Specifications

The job analyst's proficiency and effort in collecting information and compiling pertinent facts are reflected in the job descriptions and specifications. The correct processing of these records is of paramount importance since they specify the fundamental data for evaluation and rating of job or position factors. The job must be clearly described, leaving no doubt as to its proper definition, so that each member of the job evaluation committee, as well as members of grievance committees, will have the same idea of what the job represents. Then, too, every employee should know what his job is if he is expected to do it well. The importance of job descriptions and specifications can also be seen in their usefulness to replace guesswork with dependable information about a job. Finally, it should be remembered, at this point, that the eventual pricing of jobs, as well as administrative functions, depends basically on job descriptions and specifications.

Job descriptions

Every employee has a right to know what his job is. Yet, there are literally thousands of people working today in jobs that are only vaguely defined. Many jobs do not even have a job description. The next few pages will discuss the various facets of job descriptions in order to clarify their meaning, usefulness, and preparation.

Nature and Purpose of Job Descriptions

A *job description* consists of a body of informational data compiled from job analysis, presented in organized statements that identify and describe the contents of a specific job or position. It details the tasks involved for a proper conception and a complete understanding of the job. Relevant facts affecting the job, including a description of the characteristics required for the whole job, such as type of equipment used, physical and mental skill required, responsibility involved, working conditions, and possible hazards encountered, are clearly recorded to present a detailed overall picture of job conditions and requirements.

Job descriptions are a basic source of job facts and serve as useful guidelines for personnel management. Since they serve so many purposes, they are essential to good management. Well-managed companies use job descriptions in many ways. They are used as a rational basis for wage and salary administration in that they assist in preparing job specifications as well as in comparing and evaluating jobs and employees. Descriptions are used for the employment function as an aid in identifying employee qualifications that are necessary in recruiting, selecting, hiring, promoting, transferring, and counseling employees. Job descriptions are used by managers in designing and improving company organizational efficiency. The descriptions can reveal the duty assignments and clarify job relationships and responsibilities of personnel. They often prevent overlapping of duties and poor work flow. Finally, job descriptions are used in training employees. They are especially helpful in inducting a new employee, thereby giving him an overall view of his job as well as an idea of the importance of the various job duties and responsibilities.

Although job descriptions are many times used as a guide in instructing employees on the job, the job description should not be considered as an instruction sheet on how to do the job. A true instruction sheet covers a great many more details than a job description. A good job description is general enough to describe the typical and more important tasks or duties that an employee is expected to perform. It cannot and should not be expected to cover every possible task. Employees should be informed that no job description can be expected to contain all the duties required of a job, since no writer of job descriptions could possibly foresee the future and see how the job will change and thus include all the future duties that may become part of the job. This means that an employee can be asked to do any task comparable to the accepted duties identified in the job description. It means also that an employee should not be able to use the argument "I don't have to do that task because it is not in my job description." On the other hand, if employees are regularly asked to perform new tasks or duties of a much more difficult level than the ones indicated in the job description, an employee's complaint has validity. In this case, the original job has changed, and therefore the job description should be rewritten and the job reclassified. In summary, it may be said that good job descriptions replace guesswork with facts that serve as a sound basis for a multitude of company decisions which have to be made.

Contents of Job Descriptions

The first official job descriptions published by the United States Department of Labor varied in their contents according to occupations. For example, the description of an All-Around Tailor job contains six distinctive parts: (1) Job Title, (2) Job Summary, (3) Work Performed, (4) Relation to Other Jobs, (5) Specialized Qualifications, and (6) Special Information.[1] In publications describing machine-shop jobs, some job descriptions contain as many as ten

---

[1]U.S. Employment Service, *Job Descriptions for the Garment Manufacturing Industry* (Washington: U.S. Government Printing Office, 1939), pp. 147–148.

parts. For example, the job descriptions of a Milling Machine Operator or an All-Around Machinist contain, besides the above enumerated parts, additional information on (7) Machine Description, (8) Special Tools and Equipment, (9) Material Worked On, and (10) Working Conditions.[2] Note that these job descriptions were *primarily intended for the use of public employment offices and related vocational services.*

Job descriptions that are especially useful for wage and salary administration, as well as for a variety of uses, contain information grouped around four areas: (1) Job Identification, (2) Work Performed, (3) Working Conditions, and (4) Equipment Used. See Figure 12.1 for an illustration of the areas that pertain to the job of the wage and salary administrator. The Job Identification area in Figure 12.1 includes items A through L that identify the job title and alternate titles used as well as other pertinent information involving pay, department, date of description, analyst, etc. The Work Performed area includes a summary statement of the job and a listing of the most important duties of the job. The approximate percent of time spent on each duty and the degree of skill required are helpful in evaluating the job and in hiring and training employees. The Working Conditions area identifies the environment and circumstances under which the job is performed. This information is also useful in evaluating the job and in employing personnel for the job. The Equipment Used area identifies whatever tools, materials, and supplies are used in connection with the job. Only those tools and equipment that are complex enough to require instruction for their operation are listed. Such information is likewise essential to an evaluation of a job and to the employing of a person to perform the job.

Obviously there is no specific prescription on how much detailed information should be included in a job description. It is advisable to decide in advance on the style and number of desirable parts (or sections) to be used, which may conform with those previously indicated. Essential details can then be included to fit conditions.

Guidelines in Preparing Job Descriptions

Since job descriptions serve a variety of purposes, they are not likely to ever become completely standardized. However, there are some common guidelines in their preparation that should be considered no matter where the job descriptions are used nor what format a firm prefers.

Clarity and simplicity of expression are prerequisites of both job descriptions and job specifications. If job descriptions are to be read, understood, and accepted by all levels of employees, the descriptions must be written in a plain and simple layman's language. A job description is not expected to be a masterpiece of English literature, but one that uses a minimum number of well-chosen

---

[2] U.S. Employment Service, *Job Descriptions for Job Machine Shops* (Washington: U.S. Government Printing Office, 1938), pp. 55–57.

JOB DESCRIPTION

1. JOB IDENTIFICATION

A. Job Title Wage & Salary Administrator

B. Alternate Titles Manager of Compensation

C. Rate of Pay $15,000/yr.

D. Promoted from Personnel Assistant or Job Analyst

E. May Lead to Director of Industrial Relations

F. Company XYZ

G. Dept. Industrial Relations

H. Job Analyst Herbert Zollitsch

I. Date 7-22-

J. Verified by Adolph Langsner

K. (His) Title Factory Manager

L. Sheet No. 1 of 2 Sheets

2. WORK PERFORMED

A. Summary Statement:

(WHAT)　　　　　　　　　　　　　　　(HOW)

Promotes more efficient employee performance by planning, organizing, and controlling all matters of compensation so that they will be equitable and satisfactory to the employees and the employer.

(WHY)

B. Major Duties

	Percent of Time	Degree of Skill
1. Recommends company compensation policies by developing and proposing wage and salary criteria and plans that will be acceptable to the employees and employer.	5	C
2. Analyzes jobs by interviews and other techniques to secure job facts necessary for evaluating and classifying jobs, setting standards, etc.	20	SC
3. Evaluates and classifies jobs through job evaluation techniques so as to provide a basis for company wage and salary structures.	10	C
4. Assists the company in pricing jobs by conducting wage surveys and collecting wage data so that wage rates will be equitable and commensurate with the values of the jobs.	5	C
5. Sets up wage and salary structures by plotting the company jobs on a graph to serve as a basis for determining company policies, eliminating wage inequities, etc.	5	R
6. Assists supervisors in evaluating employee performance by working with supervisors to determine job performance standards and evaluation forms so that employee progress can be determined and rewarded.	10	SC

FIGURE 12.1　A JOB DESCRIPTION FOR A MANAGERIAL JOB

B. **Major Duties (continued)**

	Percent of Time	Degree of Skill
7. Assists supervisors in securing greater efficiency and productivity by providing various wage incentive plans and fringes so that employees will be motivated to working more efficiently.	10	C
8. Administers and maintains company wage and salary programs by keeping records and performing the necessary housekeeping chores to keep the programs sound and equitable.	25	R
9. May assist the Director of Industrial Relations by performing a variety of tasks (such as: representing the company at public functions, handling grievances, conducting research, preparing job descriptions and specifications, counseling employees, and advising management) for the purpose of meeting the needs of the employees and the company.	10	SC

3. **WORKING CONDITIONS**

Daily hours from 8 a.m. to 5 p.m., 5 days per week.
Weekly hours 40, overtime hours 1-2 a week.
% standing 25, walking 25, sitting 50.
Days of travel (out of town) 1 per month.
May be subject to calls for emergencies or special work such as:
   labor negotiations, grievances, community wage surveys,
   and professional conferences.

4. **EQUIPMENT USED**

Typewriter	Duplicating machine
Calculator	Electronic data processing machines

FIGURE 12.1 A JOB DESCRIPTION FOR A MANAGERIAL JOB (*concluded*)

words to say something concisely. Unimportant and short words such as "a," "and," and "of," are generally omitted; thus, a telegraphic style of writing is employed. At the same time, words should not be used that are open to varying interpretations by employees because the wrong impression may be given. If true impressions are to be made, the words used must be clear enough to convey the right idea. If words having a double meaning must be used, they should be adequately explained. If the analyst is in doubt about the clarity and understanding of any words, he should test the words on a few employees who are known to be objective in their answers. Some simple words that can be used to advantage in preparing job descriptions and specifications are listed in Figure 12.2. The terminology used in job descriptions for identifying the job and describing the work performed, the equipment used, and the conditions of work should be as standardized as possible or at least have general acceptance because the descriptions are used for such a multitude of purposes.

HELPFUL TERMINOLOGY FOR ANALYZING JOBS AND PREPARING JOB DESCRIPTIONS AND SPECIFICATIONS

ACTION WORDS: (Verbs)

accounts for	details	lifts	repairs
acts	determines	maintains	requests
adjusts	directs	makes	reworks
analyzes	discovers	manipulates	reviews
answers	drafts	marks	schedules
applies	drives	mixes	secures
approves	estimates	observes	selects
arranges	examines	obtains	sells
assigns	figures	operates	sets
assists	files	orders	shoots
cares for	finds	organizes	sits
carries	follows	performs	sketches
checks	formulates	places	stamps
cleans up	gauges	plans	stands
climbs	handles	prepares	stores
compares	inspects	processes	supervises
composes	installs	proposes	systematizes
computes	instructs	pulls	takes
conducts	interprets	pushes	teaches
constructs	investigates	reads	totals
controls	issues	receives	types
coordinates	itemizes	recognizes	uses
decides	judges	records	walks
designates	keeps	refers	works
designs	lays out	removes	writes

THINGS ACTED UPON: (Nouns)

assemblies	fittings	methods	service manuals
blueprints	formulas	models	sketches
books	gauges	orders	specifications
castings	graphs	parts	standards
cars	handbooks	patterns	supplies
charts	instruction manuals	problems	subassemblies
correspondence	instruments	processes	tables
decisions	letters	products	technical literature
diagrams	machines	records	telephones
drawings	manuals	reference books	templates
equipment	materials	reports	tools
errors	memos	requisitions	trucks
			working drawings

QUALIFYING WORDS: (Adjectives)

accurate	dirty	hot	strong
adequate	dry	humid	sufficient
average	dusty	inside	suitable
cold	effective	kind	superior
complex	efficient	noisy	uncomfortable
correct	excessive	normal	weak
cramped	extreme	outside	wet
difficult	high	proper	

FIGURE 12.2   Some Simple Words That Can Be Easily Understood

A job title is an important facet of job description terminology that needs to receive special attention in adopting standard terminology. In the graphic arts industry, it has been said that the only job that has a title understood in the United States for men working on web offset presses is the "first pressman."[3] Every job from there downward is cluttered with a completely confusing assortment of titles. For example, the third man on a large multi-unit web offset press is called a "feeder," but he is also known by such other titles as "roll tender," "first feeder," "first assistant," "brakeman," "first operator," "second assistant to the pressman," "first perfecting operator," "first multicolor feeder," "first helper," "compensator," and "tension man."

General confusion in job titles is also indicated by the recent trends by various groups of employees to have their traditional job titles changed to ones with more prestige. A few examples should illustrate the point. Garbage collectors would like to be called sanitation engineers or refuse disposal officers; undertakers prefer the title of funeral directors; milkmen would like to be called dairy salesmen; and janitors prefer the title custodian or building superintendent. In Great Britain, even the tramps like to be known as wayfarers.

Job titles, to be useful inside and outside the company, should be consistent and meaningful and represent the main function of the job. The title used should be the one that is generally accepted by most employees as indicative of the true nature of the job. It is a mistake for firms to give everyone a misleading or a highly glamorous title that does not fit the job. If this is done, it can cause problems with those employees who legitimately have earned such titles and who naturally resent anyone being given a title who has not earned it. Furthermore, it is questionable whether ambitious, hard-working people will have any desire or motivation to achieve higher positions if the job titles have become meaningless through careless use.

Job titles and codes must be current and correct. These can be checked against those found in the *Dictionary of Occupational Titles*, which covers some 230 different industries and contains almost 22,000 jobs known by 36,000 titles. The *Occupational Outlook Handbook* is another valuable source of information on jobs.

Style and format are pretty much determined by the use of the job description and the personal preference of the firm. However, practically all job descriptions contain a Job Summary section and a place for listing the major duties. In both of these areas the statements should utilize a standard style. They should begin with an action word (a verb). They should at least tell WHAT is to be done, HOW it is to be done, and WHY it is to be done. The WHAT identifies the goal of the duty and indicates the end results that are to be accomplished. The WHAT signifies what the employee is paid to do. The HOW identifies the

---

[3]Lithographers and Photoengravers International Union, *Impact of Web Offset*, 1964 brochure, p. 21.

method or means that is being used to accomplish the WHAT (or the goal of the duty). The WHY explains the purpose or reason for performing the duty (WHAT). It is the justification for having the duty performed. If a firm is to be efficient and maintain that efficiency, the WHAT, HOW, and WHY of job duties need to be clearly spelled out and continually evaluated and reevaluated. Otherwise, the firm may be living in the past because it is supporting jobs and duties that no longer are very efficient nor economically justifiable. (See Figure 12.1, which illustrates the WHAT, HOW, and WHY principles.)

Sometimes the inexperienced writer of job descriptions confuses the HOW for the WHAT because he has difficulty identifying HOW the job or task is done. For example, a simple duty may be written up as "Types letters to save the time of department staff employees." This statement appears to indicate WHAT is done and WHY, but not HOW it is done. Possibly the HOW could be added by saying "Types letters manually to save the time of department staff employees." However, knowing that the letters are typed manually does not appear to add anything to the statement except another word. Yet, there appears no alternative to better describe the HOW. In this situation (and in many others) the words "types letters" can be considered *HOW* the employee is *turning out* letters for the department and not *WHAT* is being done. In short, when it seems difficult to determine HOW something is being done, the job description writer should ask himself whether he does not already have HOW something is being done (the statement he has been considering as the WHAT), and therefore the WHAT is all that really needs to be determined.

Many companies find it useful to list the job duties in some consistent manner in order that the job descriptions are more meaningful to all employees concerned. Such companies usually list the duties in a descending order from the most time-consuming duty to the least time-consuming duty. Some companies prefer to list the duties from the most important to the least important or from the most difficult to the least difficult. Others may list the duties in a chronological order or by the job cycle. Before preparing job descriptions, it is therefore suggested that consideration be given to whatever advantages and disadvantages there might be to the firm and its employees in adopting a standardized form in the listing of the duties on each job description.

Sometimes the preparation of job descriptions may cause special problems. A case in point is when the management of a firm is very concerned about employee reaction to job descriptions and wants to be sure that each job description is such that an employee can be asked to do any reasonable task not specifically mentioned in his job description but comparable to it. This may present a dilemma to the inexperienced writer of job descriptions. If there is fear that employees will complain about being asked to perform any reasonable and comparable task not specifically referred to in the job description, the following phrase may be listed after the last of the normal job duties in order that every specific job duty need not be listed:

> May be called upon to perform other duties comparable to the above as the above duties describe only the typical, primary features of the job (and should not be construed as describing all the duties which are part of the job).

Another case in point is when the company is afraid that their employees would complain about filling in on a lower classification job when the regular employee is ill or temporarily unavailable. Under these circumstances, the following phrase could be listed after the last of the normal duties in order to make it easier for management to assign lower job duties:

> May be called upon to perform any or all of the work assigned as regular duties for any jobs in subordinate classifications.

Of course it should be understood that an employee should be guaranteed his regular pay during the time he is temporarily filling in for a lower classification employee.

Variations in Job Descriptions

Because job descriptions are used for a number of different reasons, it is only natural that job descriptions vary some to accommodate these reasons and to allow for any individual preferences a firm may have. The job description in Figure 12.3, prepared for the hospital service, refers to some characteristics that specifically pertain to the person doing the job. The brief description in Figure 12.4 is prepared mainly to describe the job of a hand screw machine setter-operator, and emphasizes the requirements of the job itself. A comparison of these two job descriptions reveals the difference between job descriptions that may also be used for recruitment, and descriptions used for job evaluation. The job description in Figure 12.4 primarily brings out pertinent facts that aid in defining some factors (termed "attributes") necessary for rating the job.

The two job descriptions in Figures 12.3 and 12.4 have been compared specifically to show the vast differences between them due to the types of jobs as well as the purposes for which these jobs were described. The one is written for a service-rendering job and stresses the qualifications of the person performing certain duties. The other is written for a job performed in a metal manufacturing industry and stresses the job itself, which is evaluated in number of points according to the importance of factors (Numbers 1 to 11, in Figure 12.8).

To further distinguish the specific differences in job descriptions, study the job description in Figure 12.5, which is used in the metal industry to describe a melting job in a steel mill. Compare it with the job description in Figure 12.4, which is also designed for use in the metal industry, but for a job of an entirely

GUARDIAN HOSPITAL
JOB DESCRIPTION SHEET

JOB TITLE:_____Ambulance Driver_____ JOB SYMBOL:_____

OCCUPATIONAL
DICTIONARY TITLE:___Ambulance Driver (5-36.020)_____ CODE NO.____6-394___

DEPARTMENT:_____Admitting (On daily dispatch basis)_____

SUMMARY: Carries or assists patients into and out of vehicle, using a stretcher. Transports sick or injured by ambulance and renders first aid. Cleans ambulance and performs minor repairs on same.

DUTIES: Transports sick or injured persons by motor vehicle of up to 1 1/2 ton rated capacity.
Carries or assists patients into and out of vehicle, in a manner to minimize the aggravation of their condition, with or without use of a stretcher.
Improvises stretchers when necessary and may administer first aid. Drives ambulance rapidly during emergency, terrain permitting, and possibly through congested areas.
Keeps vehicle in a clean and orderly condition and makes minor repairs and adjustments. Checks oil pressure and level, gasoline, water in battery and radiator, and tire pressure to insure that these conditions are satisfactory for immediate and continued use of the vehicle.
Prepares reports indicating departures and arrivals on calls. Makes trips for the delivery of packages and mail.
Replaces dirty linen after each trip and dresses stretchers.

EDUCATION: High school education is preferred. Courses in first aid and automobile mechanics are desirable.

TRAINING &
EXPERIENCE: One year of experience driving an automobile. Should know how to make minor repairs to an automobile and be familiar with traffic regulations and location of city streets. Worker receives on-the-job training in methods and procedures.

INITIATIVE
& INGENUITY: Tact and sympathy in dealing with a variety of types of patients. Considerable initiative and judgment involved in moving patients, administering first aid, and in driving vehicle rapidly through crowded streets. Works under general supervision performing tasks that are usually routine, but which may require occasional independent decisions.

PHYSICAL
DEMANDS: Lifts and carries patients. Eye, hand, and foot coordination; color vision; and depth perception to drive vehicle. Stoops, and pulls stretcher.

EQUIPMENT: Motor vehicle up to 1 1/2 ton rated capacity. May be required to operate vehicle up to 2 1/2 ton rated capacity.

WORKING
CONDITIONS: Spends most of working day in clean, heated, well lighted, and ventilated office. Drives ambulance in all types of weather. Is subject to traffic hazards, infections from diseased patients, and injury from violent patients.

PROMOTION TO: No formal line of promotion

SUPERVISED BY: SUPERINTENDENT OR HOSPITAL ADMINISTRATOR.

FIGURE 12.3 Job Description Sheet for Ambulance Driver

different nature. Note the varying approach, technique, and composition. The distinctive differences appear logical because the jobs fall into dissimilar categories performed in two industries, each being completely divergent in nature.

On the other hand, it is interesting to note at this point that the job description in Figure 12.5 has a setup, style, job title, and terminology which is exactly the same as that now adopted by all steel manufacturers in the United States.

```
┌─────────────────────────────────────────────────────────────────────┐
│ FORM 2                                                               │
│ I. M. S.        JOB DESCRIPTION SHEET                                │
│ ─────────────────────────────────────────────────────────────────── │
│ PLANT JOB                                                            │
│ TITLE      Hand Screw Machine, Setter-Operator    PLANT NO.          │
│ ─────────────────────────────────────────────────────────────────── │
│ OCCUPATIONAL                                                         │
│ DICTIONARY TITLE                                  CODE NO.           │
│ ─────────────────────────────────────────────────────────────────── │
│ DEPT.                                             DEPT. NO.          │
│ ─────────────────────────────────────────────────────────────────── │
│ DESCRIPTION OF JOB                          TOTAL POINTS:            │
│                                                                     │
│                                                                     │
│       Set up and operate Hand Screw Machine such as #2 Brown and    │
│       Sharpe, or other similar equipment machining up to 1" round   │
│       ferrous or nonferrous alloys.  Limits are close and difficult │
│       to maintain on several dimensions to approximately ±.001"     │
│       where required.  Includes planning setups on new parts from   │
│       manufacturing layouts, prints, and specifications.  Requires  │
│       sharpening of tools.  Involves setting of cross slide and com- │
│       plicated turret positions, feeds, speeds, etc.  Hand feed     │
│       on cross slide and turret with automatic stock feeding and    │
│       chucking.  Requires handling bar stock weighing up to 35#     │
│       and tote pans up to 50#.                                      │
│                                                                     │
│                                                                     │
│ ─────────────────────────────────────────────────────────────────── │
│ APPROVALS:                                                          │
│                                                                     │
│                                                                     │
└─────────────────────────────────────────────────────────────────────┘
```

Industrial Management Society

FIGURE 12.4 JOB DESCRIPTION SHEET FOR A HAND SCREW MACHINE
SETTER-OPERATOR

The job evaluation was undertaken and completed with the participation and full cooperation of the United Steel Workers of America. Uniformity in titles, descriptions, and terminology made it possible for the United Steelworkers' Union to bring about unified action in wage bargaining, and the establishment of equity in wage-base rates for the same jobs in the entire steel industry.

Job specifications

The term job specification, like the term job analysis, has received various definitions depending on the user's point of view and the field of application. The next few pages will discuss job specifications in order to clarify their meaning, usefulness, and preparation.

JOB DESCRIPTION_____ Republic Steel Corporation_____

Department _____ Open Hearth _____   Standard Code_____ 0121 AG 0190   C W S B _____

Sub Division_____ Charging & Melting _____   Standard Title_____ First Helper--Open Hearth _____

Plant _____ Canton _____   Plant Title _____ First Helper _____

Date_____ 5/25/-- _____   Plant Code_____ 164-21 _____

Primary Function To operate and produce steel in one basic open hearth furnace as directed by the senior or junior melter.

TOOLS AND EQUIPMENT: 112 ton stationary basic open hearth furnace, door controls, sledges, shovels, rabble rods, tapping bars, patching spoon, test spoon and mould, melter's glasses, oil and gas recording flow meters, steam pressure gauge, etc.

MATERIALS: Used--Hot metal, all grades of scrap, limestone, pig iron, broken moulds, iron ore; spar, dolomite, magnesite, ferro-alloys, aluminum, nickle, molybdenum oxide, spiegel; sinter, coal, fuel oil, coke gas, compressed air, steam, etc.
                   Produced--High-grade alloy steels.

SOURCE OF SUPERVISION: Senior or Junior Melter.

DIRECTION EXERCISED: 2nd and 3rd Helpers.

WORKING PROCEDURE:
Directs second helper and group of six third helpers (1/6 of time).
Controls fuel consumption of furnace.
Regulates fuel mixing device for proper combustion.
Reverses furnace at frequent intervals to obtain maximum efficiency from fuel and furnace and to prevent damage to furnace brick structure.
Checks the charging of scrap to prevent damage to furnace and steel.
Melts and prepares heat for final additions as directed by the melter.
Directs charging machine operator.
Cleans air and fuel ports using a bar through the port bulkhead and doors.
Rams taphole with tapping rod to release steel from hearth into ladle (assisted by 2nd helper and 3rd helpers).
Observes heat working in furnace to detect boil which would result in breakout through banks or bottom.
Assists in making all furnace additions as instructed by melter.
Inspects furnace bottoms for holes.
Rabbles or blows molten metal out of holes.
Shovels refractory materials into holes and shallow spots in furnace bottom and back.
Opens slag hole to flush slag at proper time.
Pours test samples of the heat using hand ladle.
Directs the setting of the hot metal spout in front of furnace after determining time for hot metal addition.
Shovels dolomite to rebank door after hot metal charge.

REVIEWED AND APPROVED BY:

_____ John Jones _____ 3/15/-- _____
UNION SIGNATURE AND TITLE   DATE

_____ Frank Smith _____ 3/15/-- _____
COMPANY SIGNATURE AND TITLE   DATE

UNION COPY ☐   COMPANY COPY ☒

The above statement reflects the general details considered necessary to describe the principal functions of the job identified, and shall not be construed as a detailed description of all of the work requirements that may be inherent in the job.

Republic Steel Corporation

FIGURE 12.5 JOB DESCRIPTION OF A STEEL MILL JOB

Nature and Purpose of Job Specifications

Strictly speaking, a *job specification* (or job rating sheet) consists of a body of informational data compiled from a job analysis and presented in organized statements that identify and describe the minimum job requirements in terms of its skill, effort, responsibility, and working conditions. In short, a job specification specifies what the job requires in skill, effort, responsibility, and conditions of work. The job specification is chiefly used as the basis for rating jobs in the job evaluation process. Because most job evaluation plans have more than the four basic factors of skill, effort, responsibility, and working conditions, most job specifications specify the job requirements in refinements of the four basic factors. For example, skill is often subdivided into the education, the experience, and the initiative and ingenuity required for the job. Effort is often subdivided into the physical and mental effort required of the job, etc. Thus, the data contained in the job specification, by specifying the minimum requirements of the job, actually serve as the justification or basis for the rating the job receives in the job evaluation process.

Job specifications are often confused with man (or employee) specifications, which are used for employment purposes. A *man specification* specifies the minimum qualifications that an employee must possess to be considered for hire. There is a distinction between job specifications (which are used for wage and salary purposes) and man specifications (which are used for employment purposes). However, the distinction is not always clear nor apparent, and thus much confusion is perpetuated. It should be remembered that the job specification deals with job requirements, and the man specification deals with employee qualifications. Figure 12.6 shows areas wherein the job specification and the man specification are the same and different.

The job specification is sometimes used in conjunction with employment because some of its specifications (especially education and experience) imply what qualifications a person needs to possess to be hired. However, it is unwise to rely on the job specification for identifying all the necessary qualifications of a person for hire because the job specification specifies only the job requirements and not employee qualifications. If the job specification is to be used to aid employment, the various job requirements have to be translated into meaningful worker qualifications before the job specification can be of much use. Many companies analyze the completed job specification to determine what physical, mental, emotional, and other qualifications a person needs to meet the job specification requirements. It is more preferable to list all the qualifications needed by the employee for the job and call this a "Man Specification," an "Employment Specification," or an "Employee Specification," as these terms more appropriately describe the nature of that specification. If this were done, there would be little confusion between the job specification and the man specification.

Contents of Job Specifications

The contents of job specifications are mainly determined by the method of job evaluation for which the specification serves. As most job evaluation plans are of the point variety, we shall use the point method to discuss the application of job specifications.

JOB SPECIFICATION v. MAN SPECIFICATION FOR AN AMBULANCE DRIVER JOB

FACTORS	JOB SPECIFICATION (Identifies job requirements and is used for wage and salary purposes)	MAN SPECIFICATION (Identifies employee qualifications and is used for employment purposes)
Education	Requires high school	Must be a high school graduate
Experience	Requires 1 yr. driving	Must have driven 1 yr.
Physical Demands	Requires lifting of 100 lbs.	Must be strong, weigh at least 150 lbs.
	Drives ambulance	Must have driver's license
Mental Demands	Requires keen vision Requires mental alertness	Must have 20/20 vision Must have quick reflexes
Responsibility for Equipment	Requires driver-maintenance on vehicle Requires first aid on vehicle	Must have some mechanical experience or training Must have passed a first aid course
Working Conditions	Exposed to all kinds of weather	Must be in good physical condition
Unavoidable Hazards	Exposed to a variety of diseases	Must be healthy to resist diseases

Requirements are: SIMILAR { Education, Experience }

DISSIMILAR { Physical Demands ... Unavoidable Hazards }

FIGURE 12.6   Areas Where the Job Specification and the Man Specification Are the Same and Different

    Job specifications, like job descriptions, have an identification section at the top of the form that covers the necessary pertinent data such as job title, department, date, and total point rating.

    The main body of a job specification consists of a series of vertical columns of the chief features that are part of the specification. The columns may contain the specific job evaluation factors; the job facts pertinent for each job evaluation factor; the degree the job facts represent on each factor; and the points each degree is worth, according to the evaluators. At the bottom of most job specifications is a place for tallying the job points, the date, a place for the signature of the job evaluation committee members and any persons designated to approve the rating, and a place for any remarks that anyone wishes to make. Figures 12.7, 12.8, and 12.9 are typical examples. Occasionally, job specifications include either the job summary or job duties from the job description, or both.

		JOB SPECIFICATION AND RATING SHEET	
DG = Degrees			
PTS = Points		Substantiating Data	Total Points: __332__
Job Title:	Ambulance Driver		Job Symbol:
Occupational Dictionary Title:	Ambulance Driver (5-36.020)		Code No 6-394
Department:	Admitting (on daily dispatch basis)		

FACTORS	DG/PTS.	BASIS OF RATING
Education	3 / 38	High school education is preferred. Courses in first aid and auto mechanics are desirable.
Experience	2 / 32	One year experience driving an automobile required. Worker receives on-the-job training in methods and procedures.
Initiative & Ingenuity	3 / 42	Requires tact and sympathy in dealing with a variety of types of patients. May be required to improvise splints and administer first aid with limited supplies. May be required to drive through heavy traffic in difficult weather and poor road conditions.
Physical Demand	3 / 26	Occasionally lifts and/or carries patients for short distances. Eye-hand-foot coordination necessary. Drives vehicle, stoops, pulls, and pushes stretcher.
Mental or Visual	3 / 36	Frequent mental and visual attention required. Individual must remain constantly on the alert while driving vehicle and attending to patients being transported.
Responsibility for Equipment	3 / 22	Completes driver-maintenance on vehicle. Responsible for first aid equipment in vehicle.
Judgment	3 / 30	Judgment required when negotiating traffic. Judgment required in administering first aid and transporting patients.
Safety of Others	3 / 26	Drives ambulance transporting seriously ill patients. Maintains ambulance in a manner that it is always ready to complete emergency calls. Assists in first aid.
Work of Others	2 / 22	In addition to ambulance driving, assists in comforting patients in admitting office, washing and maintenance of other vehicles, simple routine office jobs.
Working Conditions	4 / 28	Spends part of day in well-lighted, ventilated, office. Some time is spent in maintaining vehicle in garage area. Drives in all types of weather. Subject to traffic hazards, exposure to cold and hot weather.
Unavoidable Hazards	4 / 30	Drives through all kinds of traffic under all weather conditions at all hours of the day. Is exposed to a variety of miscellaneous diseases.

FIGURE 12.7 JOB SPECIFICATION AND RATING SHEET FOR AMBULANCE DRIVER (Related to Job Description Sheet, Figure 12.3.)

Guidelines in Preparing Job Specifications

There are two procedures that may be followed in preparing specification and rating sheets. One procedure requires an analyst to record the facts related to the job, leaving the assignment of degree numbers and point rating to the

	ATTRIBUTE		No. of	

FORM 3 I.M.S.

JOB RATING SHEET

PLANT JOB TITLE   Hand Screw Machine, Setter - Operator   PLANT NO. _____

OCCUPATIONAL DICTIONARY TITLE   CODE NO. _____

DEPT.   DEPT. NO. _____

NO.	TITLE	No. of Pnts.	BASIS OF RATING
1.	PHYSICAL EFFORT	6	Lifts bars, parts, tools, etc., up to 30# and tote pans up to 50#. Turret and cross-slide operated by hand.
2.	HAZARDS	4	Minor scratches and bruises, usually no serious accidents. Possibility of skin disturbances from oil.
3.	JOB CONDITIONS	6	Ordinary shop wear on clothing. Some discomfort from small chips flying into clothing and smoke from heavy cuts.
4.	SUPERVISION	2	Works under general instructions with detail instructions available if required.
5.	RESPONSIBILITY FOR THE SAFETY OF OTHERS	1	Very little possibility of injury to others except when stocking up machine or handling tote boxes.
6.	RESPONSIBILITY FOR EQUIP. AND MATERIAL	4	Possible to cause damage of $100 to equipment. Errors due to setup and running jobs would not ordinarily be more than $50 per week.
7.	KNOWLEDGE EQUIP. & TOOLS METHODS MATERIAL	8 8 4	Requires expert knowledge average to complex tools. Requires expert knowledge of average methods. Requires working knowledge of a wide variety of common metals.
8.	SCHOOLING	7	Requires an education sufficient to read blueprints, do calculations of feeds, speeds, R.P.M., etc., write simple reports and records.
9.	JUDGMENT AND INITIATIVE	10	Requires judgment of average nature based on precedent, and definite initiative in setting up.
10.	MENTAL CAPABILITIES	7	Requires some ingenuity in layout and setting up, also versatility since several different kinds of work are done.
11.	PHYSICAL SKILL	5	Not much dexterity required and only about average precision.
	TOTAL	72	

REMARKS:

Industrial Management Society

FIGURE 12.8   JOB RATING SHEET FOR HAND SCREW MACHINE, SETTER-OPERATOR (Based on Job Analysis Sheet, Figure 11.4, and Job Description Sheet, Figure 12.4.)

committee. The other procedure, a common practice, is to have the one who made the job analysis also prepare the specification, including evaluation and rating, since the *specification is a product of job analysis and job description.* This second procedure is preferable because the job study and factual description of

JOB CLASSIFICATION___Republic Steel Corporation--Canton

Plant Title _First Helper_____   Standard Title _First Helper--Open Hearth_

	Factor	Reason for Classification	Code	Classification
1.	Pre-Employment Training	This Job requires the mentality to learn to: Direct the operation of an open hearth furnace and determine the analysis of product.	C	1.0
2.	Employment Training and Experience.	This job requires experience on this and related work of from 37 to 48 months of continuous progress to assimilate knowledge of wide variation in grades of steel manufactured.	H	3.2
3.	Mental Skill	Plan the operation of the unit well ahead of performance so as to obtain proper physical and chemical conditions for additions, flushing and finishing the heat.	E	2.8
4.	Manual Skill	Must use heavy hand tools. Operate refractory gun.	B	.5
5.	Responsibility for Material	Close attention to maintain slag lines and hearth lining One heat could be lost through breakout. The cost would be the value of the product less scrap value plus labor cleanup. Estimated Cost 150 tons x ($25 - 15).) plus $2 cleanup/ton or $1,800.	D	5.3
6.	Responsibility for Tools and Equipment	A high degree of care and knowledge of combustion and chemical principles required to avoid damage to brick work and hearth of furnace.	E High	3.0
7.	Responsibility for Operations	Has joint responsibility with melter for maximum production and continuity of operation on a major operating unit.	F	4.0
8.	Responsibility for Safety of Others	Has control of a unit where a number of hazards exist such as splashes from hot metal or slag, explosions caused by moisture in additions.	D	1.2
9.	Mental Effort	Close mental or visual application required to direct charging, observe melt down, make additions, take and make tests, finish off heat, tap furnace, rabble heat.	D	1.5
10.	Physical Effort	Moderate physical exertion required operating valves and controls, shoveling refractories or additions, rabble heat, punch out tap holes, observe operations and direct crew.	C	.8
11.	Surroundings	Exposed to extreme heat while tapping, making additions and bottoms.	C	.8
12.	Hazard	Occasionally exposed to burns from splashes and spills of molten metal.	C	.8

REVIEWED AND APPROVED BY:	Job Class 25 Total 24.9
John Jones .... 3/15/-- UNION SIGNATURE AND TITLE .... DATE	Described By: C. N. Lamielle Date 5-25---
Frank Smith .... 3/15/-- COMPANY SIGNATURE AND TITLE .... DATE	Classified By: C. E. Klopfenstein
UNION COPY ☐ COMPANY COPY ☒	Approved By: H. J. Jones

Republic Steel Corporation

FIGURE 12.9 SUBSTANTIATING SPECIFICATION RATING SHEET OF JOB DESCRIPTION, FIGURE 12.5

the job places the analyst in a position to use objective judgment in rating the job fairly. Any changes or corrections may subsequently be made when the specification rating sheets are reviewed and finally passed upon by the job evaluation committee. If committee members differ in rating any one degree, a discussion will either bring about rerating or a compromise.

The definition of each factor, as illustrated in the job evaluation manual, must be followed closely to ascertain what the substantiating data for each sub-factor should be. The best procedure is to enumerate and to record each sub-factor for every hourly paid job in a sequence such as that outlined in the manual, Figure 10.2, pages 248 to 258, beginning with (1) Education and Knowledge, and ending with (11) Unavoidable Hazards. Similarly, the specification and rating sheet for supervisory jobs should start with (1) Elemental Factor Value, and end with (9) Liability of Damage to Product, according to the manual, Figure 10.4, pages 264 to 269, if that manual is used.

To evaluate each factor according to degrees described in the manual, the analyst should bear in mind that specific requirements in the specifications must be based on measuring units for the basic factor affecting the job. For instance, in Skill, the specification for the subfactor Education and Knowledge must take into consideration kind of schooling, extent or number of years of schooling, and specific need of certain technical knowledge. Specification for the factor Experience and Training should be expressed in terms of weeks, months, or years; and the specification for the factor Initiative and Ingenuity should be expressed in terms of abilities to follow and to work from detailed instructions, or to do certain planning and independent thinking if there are no standards to follow. Similarly, specifications for all other basic factors should follow the pattern in the manual to record measuring units for each subfactor.

Variations in Job Specifications and Their Ratings

From the illustrative examples, it will be noted that the technique, division into sections, definitions, methods of grading and rating vary from one enterprise to another. This is necessary from the standpoint of installing tailor-made job evaluation programs in diversified enterprises. That is, the job evaluation program must meet the specific needs of each individual enterprise. As stated at the beginning of this chapter, however, it should be realized that a pattern may often be followed when the program is used within the same industry.

Two examples will clarify the need of tailor-made job evaluation programs with their characteristic job specifications. The examples will also show the possibility of following a pattern that is used within the same industry. The job specification (job classification) of a First Helper — Open Hearth job, classified in the specification rating sheet, Figure 12.9, at the Republic Steel Corporation is entirely different from the setup of the Millwright job specification and rating, Figure 12.10, of the Stewart-Warner Corporation. Factor number 5, Responsibility for Material, specifies an estimated cost of about $1,800 as the measuring unit for code D which, in turn, calls for a numerical classification of 5.3. Similarly, factor number 6, Responsibility for Tools and Equipment, indicates under code E a probable damage of "High," with a numerical classification of 3.0. The manual which is used as a guide by the Republic Steel Corporation and the job specification shown in Figure 12.9 are also used in all other steel mills of the United States.

JOB RATING FORM

STEWART-WARNER CORPORATION

JOB CODE __0412__

JOB NAME _____ MILLWRIGHT A _____ MAINTENANCE DEPT. __65__

FACTORS	DEG/P	BASIS OF RATING
TOTAL POINTS	380	
EDUCATION	4/48	Use shop arithmetic and handbook formulas. Work from drawings, sketches, and layouts. Use a variety of tools and measuring instruments. Knowledge of elementary mechanics, power transmission, construction details, and assembly methods common to all machines. Equivalent to 4 yrs. high school and 3 yrs. trades training.
EXPERIENCE	4/96	3 to 4 years experience and training.
INITIATIVE AND INGENUITY	4/56	Install and move ordinary equipment and machine tools requiring accuracy and care in aligning. Prepare machine foundations. Install line shafts and power drives. Judgment required to dismantle, move, and install machines with minimum interference to production and perform a variety of construction and maintenance work.
PHYSICAL DEMAND	3/30	Continuous physical effort moving or handling equipment. Heavy items handled with assistance. Some time spent in difficult work positions. Lifts 20 to 25 lbs. fifty percent of working time.
MENTAL OR VISUAL DEMAND	4/20	Continuous mental or visual attention dismantling and moving machines, erecting line shafting, aligning and leveling equipment.
RESPONSIBILITY FOR EQUIPMENT OR PROCESS	4/24	Improper handling or use of hoisting equipment or power tools may result in damage seldom over $25.
RESPONSIBILITY FOR MATERIAL OR PRODUCT	4/28	Improper aligning, lack of care in moving or rigging machinery or equipment may result in losses seldom over $250.
RESPONSIBILITY FOR SAFETY OF OTHERS	5/15	Failure to safeguard work, carelessness in rigging or moving machinery or handling tools and material, especially on overhead work, may result in lost time accidents to others.
RESPONSIBILITY FOR WORK OF OTHERS	2/8	Responsible for directing and instructing one helper.
WORKING CONDITIONS	3/30	Work in all parts of the plant under varying working conditions of heat, cold, grease, and dirt. (20% to 30% of working time.)
UNAVOIDABLE HAZARDS	5/25	May crush hand or foot while moving equipment or handling material. May fall from ladder or scaffold.

RATED BY	E. G. Sanczuk	DATE 6/11/--	STEWARD CONTACT
COMPANY APPROVAL		UNION ACCEPTANCE	

WORK COPY

Stewart-Warner Corporation

FIGURE 12.10 JOB SPECIFICATION AND RATING FOR MILLWRIGHT

The specification and rating sheet of a Millwright's job, Figure 12.10, is prepared for an entirely different metal industry. The pattern follows the definitions of factors and rating according to the manual for shop workers, Figure 10.2, pages 248 to 258. The arrangement of factors, definitions, measuring units, and point allotments is specified and substantiated in the specification sheets of many

JOB EVALUATION

Job Name____ Inseamer. Dict. of Occup. Titles: Goodyear Welt Sewing Mach. Operator (4.61.221)

Code Number____ S-1792 ____ Date ____ Dec. 4, 19-- ____ Factory ____ Shoe ____ Dept.____ Bottoming

DUTIES:— Operates Goodyear Stitching Machine that sews a narrow leather strip (welt), automatically fed from roll on machine to lip of the insole of a shoe by guiding shoe, sole upwards, under needle of machine and stitching through welt, upper, and lining, and insole lip against which upper and lining have been lasted. A rounded needle pulls the thread through upper part of shoe and welt. Stitches measure 1/4 of an inch.

    Must be able to interpret specifications. Must possess knowledge to make machine adjustments and simple repairs.

    Requires 2 to 3 years training to be proficient. Works with light material in standing position, outstretched arms, pressing and releasing foot pedal.

    Damages to product or equipment may amount to $250. No responsibility for work or safety of others.

    Working conditions, noisy, dusty, and machine vibrations. Is in danger of losing a finger from automatic knife cutter and hurt eyes from flying broken needles or staples.

	RATING FACTORS	SPECIFICATIONS	POINTS
Mental Requirements	1. Education	Education or Training Required. 2 yrs. H.S. - 2 yrs. TR.	72
	2. Judgment	What decisions have to be made? Quality of work and tolerances	28
	3. Initiative	Is new course of action required? Occasionally	42
	4. Application	What % of total time is mental application required? Constant alertness	25
SKILL	5. Equipment Use	Equipment used Inseaming machine (Goodyear Stitching Machine)	10
	6. Material Use	Use of Material Leather welt	10
	7. Dexterity	Manual Dexterity Requires continuous effort	30
RESPONSIBILITY	8. Supervision	How many men are supervised by the operator on this job? None	
	9. Safety of Others	Does the performance of this job endanger the safety of others? No	
	State how	How many are endangered?	
	10. Cost of Error	How could the equipment or product be damaged? Holding the shoe at the wrong angle will damage insole and welt	15
	Is damage likely to occur? Yes	What is amount of probable resulting loss? $250	
WORKING CONDITIONS	11. Accident Hazard	Is there above normal possibility of injury? Yes State how Flying broken parts of needle, or knife that works automatically, and staples	15
	12. Surroundings	Are there disagreeable surroundings? Yes State how Vibration from machine, dust, wet welt, outstretched working position	30
	13. Clothing Spoilage	Will job result in excessive wear to clothing? No State how	
PHYSICAL REQUIREMENTS	14. Strength	What is unit weight lifted? 1 to 10 lbs.	10
	What is total average weight lifted per hour? 4 lbs.		
	15. Application	During what % of total time is physical effort being expended? 25% to 40%	10
	16. Fatigue	Give points to following factors:— Physical Demands 5 ; Mental Demands 5 Distracting Noise 10 ; Qual. of Illum. 5 ; Degree of Monotony 5	30
		TOTAL POINT RATING	327

How will the operator on this job be paid?   Incentive ____ P.R. ____ Hourly Rate?____ ;Other?____ Hourly rate guaranteed

Type of operator required.____ Male

Approved by _____ Ind. Engineer

FIGURE 12.11 JOB EVALUATION FOR INSEAMER
(Combination of Job Description, Specification, and Rating.)

plants in similar industries. In other words, manual Figure 10.2 can serve other enterprises producing similar goods, but does not fit the basic steel industries.

Still another example is the *combined job description and specification in one form*, illustrated in Figure 12.11. This example illustrates some good features in that it gives the analyst and rater a concise description of the job and defines the rating factors briefly and clearly. Note that this specification considers five basic factors, each of which is shown separately in one box with the respective subfactors. Also note the interrogatory method of specifying the requirements and possible conditions for each factor.

REVIEW QUESTIONS

1. (a) State in your own words the difference between a job description and a job specification. (b) What are the purposes of each?
2. What are some of the other uses of job descriptions in addition to that of job evaluation?
3. Why are job descriptions necessary to the successful operation of any job evaluation plan?
4. What subject matter should be included when writing a job description?
5. There are many examples of job titles that are "glamorized" or "dressed up" to add dignity and prestige to the job. Is this recommended as good practice? Why or why not?
6. (a) As part of the job description, of what value is an appropriate job title? (b) Should job titles be chosen by function, for administrative purposes, or for some other purpose?
7. If in preparing a job description and specification you find that the job is not performed in the correct manner, should you write the job up as it is performed or as it should be performed? Why?
8. Why is accuracy important in writing job descriptions?
9. What is the difference, if any, between a job specification and a man specification?
10. Is the job description a good tool to use as an instruction sheet to tell the employees how to perform the job duties? Explain your answer.
11. Prepare a set of guiding principles that a job analyst should keep in mind when preparing job descriptions.
12. Sometimes the inexperienced writer of job descriptions confuses the *How* and the *What* in his description. How can this difficulty be overcome?
13. The job specification can be used in hiring because it contains all of the job's requirements. Explain why you agree or disagree.
14. Why is the *What*, *How*, and *Why* format, employed in the job description, important?
15. Are job descriptions ever likely to become standardized? Why?
16. What can be done to avoid the difficulty of the employee refusing to perform a related task that is not contained in the job description?

RESEARCH OR SEMINAR QUESTIONS

1. What are the dangers of an incomplete job description in regard to employer-employee relations?
2. What differentiates the job description from the job specification?
3. Explain the difference between the job specification and the job standard of success.
4. Discuss the various ways of writing up job descriptions. What problems do you encounter? What can be done to help eliminate these problems?

PRACTICAL EXPERIENCE ASSIGNMENTS

1. In each of the Practical Experience Assignments 1, 2, and 3, pages 288 and 289, you were asked to collect information and data for a job. (a) Using these data, prepare a job description for one of the jobs. (b) Next, prepare a job specification for the same job.
2. Exchange the job description and job specification you prepared in Practical Experience Assignment 1 with another member of the class. Analyze your classmate's job description and job specification by citing the following:
   (a) Its strong points.
   (b) Its weaknesses.
   (c) How you would correct the weaknesses.
3. Prepare a job specification for the point method of job evaluation for the position that a wage and salary administrator would hold in a company that is large enough to support only one full-time man in the wage and salary area.
4. (a) Prepare a job description for the position of job analyst in a company large enough to support a full-time analyst. (b) Prepare a job specification for the same position.
5. (a) Prepare a job description for some full-time job that you have held in the past. (b) Prepare a job specification for the same position.

CASE PROBLEM

12—1. GREENBRIER METAL PRODUCTS, INC.

Accurate Job Titles

As head of the wage and salary department in Greenbrier Metal Products, Inc., a large manufacturing plant, you report directly to the vice-president in charge of manufacturing. Your department is currently involved in a reappraisal of the job titles of employees.

During your preliminary work on this subject, you are given a formal written grievance from the union steward. The grievance states that certain specific job titles are crude and undignified, and suggests that these job titles should be changed. A suggested list of job titles for the jobs in question is also presented along with the grievance. In your opinion, the job titles submitted by the union are vague and do not accurately describe the jobs. Upon examination, you find that the job titles that are in present use are descriptive of the work actually done and, furthermore, are similar to those used in like industries.

The vice-president in charge of manufacturing states that you have full authority to decide on this issue. However, he cautions you to be careful in your dealings with the union because at this time the company is producing at full capacity to fulfill certain important commitments, and cannot afford any reductions due to difficulty with the union.

Problems:

1. How would you answer the union's grievance?
2. How would you explain your position to the union and to your superior?
3. Should the company sacrifice clarity and uniformity in its job titles in order to build up the morale of certain workers?
4. Why should management risk trouble with the union to preserve a few job titles?
5. How would it be possible to arrive at some compromise that would be also acceptable to all parties?

chapter 13

PRICING THE JOBS
AND DETERMINING THE
PAY GRADES AND RANGES

After job evaluation and rating, including a clarification of the job titles, have been completed, a new or changed wage and salary structure can be introduced. The procedure of deciding which job title and job description fits an employee in order to place him in a definite job grade should be carried out on a factual basis. It is imperative that each employee receive an equitable wage-base rate that is commensurate with his evaluated job. It is also important to check to see that each employee's old job title coincides with the job title established in job evaluation.

To facilitate matters and to strengthen the wage and salary structure, all job evaluation committee members should participate in wage stabilization. In Chapter 8, the importance of employee participation in the job evaluation program was discussed. The importance of these principles is reemphasized here, because at no time is the pooled judgment of committee members more desirable than in determining equitable wage-base rates for evaluated jobs. The compromising "give and take" of committee members, especially of a joint labor-management committee, is significant in ranking jobs and in stabilizing wage standards according to pay grades.

314

Determining equitable wage-base rates and salaries

Under the weighted point method of job evaluation, the determination of equitable wages and salaries according to job differentials is the final step in the program. The process involves the following procedures, which are listed in the order of their discussion:

1. Determining pay grades based on a number of points according to a scoring scale.
2. Classifying occupations according to job titles and pay grades.
3. Coding jobs for identification.
4. Investigating current wages and salaries in the same industry and within the community.
5. Charting basic wage and salary rates.
6. Establishing the wage curve.
7. Converting pay grade points into money values.
8. Adjusting existing wage-base rates and salaries to conform with established pay grade values and current wages in accordance with the line of correlation.

Determining pay grades

Where a large number of jobs exist, it is impractical to establish individual wage-base rates for jobs with slight differences. Invariably, management encounters administrative difficulties in distributing very small increments in wage differentials. To overcome such difficulties and to avoid numerous complaints and grievances, a pay grade setup has been found to be most satisfactory.

A *pay grade* includes a combination of different jobs, with approximately the same number of point ratings, arranged in the sequence of their evaluated importance. Each pay grade is composed of a number of points grouped in ranges, arranged in an ascending step-like form according to pay grade numbers.

In the early development of job evaluation plans, there was a tendency to set up an extremely wide point range for each grade, with an equally extreme variation in the number of points, thus making it practically impossible to have jobs upgraded. Unions objected to this procedure and thereby forced some employers to the opposite extreme — assigning only a few points for each pay grade, with equally small wage-rate increments. Some unions rightfully claim that if the spread of points is narrow, the upgrading potential is more favorable. On the other hand, the large number of pay grades necessary for such fine divisions becomes complicated to administer and is equally undesirable to workers. Therefore, the tendency now is to divide evenly the adopted total number of points and to provide equal numbers such as 20, 30, or 40 points for each pay grade. Slight deviations, however, will not lessen the benefits of job evaluation.

As an example, Table 13.1 presents the pay grade numbers, score ranges, and wage-base rates from a job evaluation plan adopted by a union-management committee and subsequently used by several companies with successful results. Table 13.1 and the scatter chart in Figure 13.6 list 14 pay grades arranged in positions relative to a 500-point scale as provided in the plan. The first pay grade starts with a score range of 100 to 160 points, and the rest of the pay grades show increments that were arbitrarily established.

TABLE 13.1

PAY GRADE NUMBERS, SCORE RANGES, AND WAGE-BASE RATES

Data for Figure 13.6

PAY GRADE	SCORE RANGE IN POINTS	WAGE-BASE RATES MINIMUM	MAXIMUM
1	100–160	$2.70	$3.30
2	161–191	3.24	3.96
3	192–222	3.58	4.38
4	223–248	3.89	4.75
5	249–274	4.22	5.16
6	275–300	4.49	5.49
7	301–326	4.77	5.83
8	327–352	5.07	6.19
9	353–378	5.35	6.55
10	379–404	5.65	6.91
11	405–429	5.94	7.26
12	430–453	6.24	7.62
13	454–477	6.48	7.92
14	478–500	6.75	8.25

Note: Wage-base rate values are illustrative and for comparison purposes only. The values may be changed to suit conditions.

When the committee considered the number of jobs that had to be fitted into the grades, the management representatives suggested adopting 10 grades. However, the union representatives insisted upon a much larger number. After compromising, the committee agreed upon 14 grades and, as shown in Table 13.1, provided 60 points for the first pay grade with an increased 30 points each for pay grades 2 and 3, while pay grades 4 to 10 received increments of 25 points for each grade. Then, the number of points for the highest pay grades decreased slightly until pay grade 14 received 22 points.

The lowest pay grade received a wide score range of 60 points so that trainees starting at a wage rate below the minimum could be upgraded to the minimum and maximum wage-base rates within the first pay grade, as soon as they showed increased skill and improvement in their work. Similarly, the committee's purpose in introducing a relatively large number of grades with fewer points in each score range above the first pay grade was to permit a worker who had developed more skill and experience in one grade to advance to a higher pay grade as soon as possible.

Contrary to other plans that start with the highest cardinal number for the lowest pay grade, Table 13.1 indicates the lowest grade as Number 1 and the highest grade as Number 14. This arrangement makes it possible to add additional grade numbers if new jobs that exceed the highest point values are added. It is also more consistent and logical when the highest pay grade represents the highest pay.

Pay Grade Terms

Pay grades are also known as "labor grades" or "classes," "job grades" or "levels," and "salary grades" or "levels." The term pay grade is used throughout this book in preference to other terms because it appears to identify better the fact that all jobs are classified into pay categories rather than on some ambiguous basis. If a pay category is referred to in terms of either a labor grade or a job grade, confusion may result because each of these terms has various connotations. In some companies certain jobs have a traditional social prestige that is highly esteemed by employee groups. For example, an employee may be a first-class worker within his group; but, assume that after his job is evaluated, it is graded Number 5 in the point score range. Then, according to some job evaluation plans, he becomes a fifth "labor class" or "labor grade" worker within the group and it has a demoralizing effect upon him. The employee assumes that there is a change in his status within the group, and he resents it, with a deep grudge against job evaluation. He cannot readily comprehend why his work suddenly is "devaluated" to a fifth "labor class" or "labor grade," giving him the feeling of being demoted to a lower level. Psychologically, workers are not so antagonistic toward "pay grade" as toward "labor class" or "labor grade," which have a more personal connotation. They consider it "a matter of course" that it is the job which is graded in relation to other jobs, and not an employee as compared with other employees.

How Many Pay Grades?

There is no accepted definite answer to the question, "How many pay grades shall we establish?" The number of pay grades will vary according to the existing number of jobs and employee group levels. If all office, clerical, technical, and professional jobs are evaluated as one employee group, the range will have to be wider between the lowest evaluated office jobs and the highest professional jobs. Hence, the combination will require a larger number of pay grades than if only the office and clerical jobs are evaluated in one group, and technical and professional jobs in separate groups. In a large majority of enterprises, shop jobs, office jobs, and professional and supervisory jobs are evaluated separately, thus requiring varied numbers of pay grades. The trend is away from having one wage structure for the whole company that contains enough job pay grades to handle all the jobs. Firms and business practice have become too large and complex to cling to a single compensation structure. Single-structure wage systems suffer from inflexibility in that they do not meet changing jobs and conditions adequately. Too often job ratings are forced to fit the system. Thus, pay grades and wage structures are now molded around the job cluster, job family, or some similar groupings of employees. It is becoming more common to set up separate wage structures for the following groups of employees: shop, clerical, draftsmen and technicians, administrators, engineers and scientists, sales, supervision, and executives. However, in each wage structure the question of how many pay grades must be decided.

Authorities agree that an excessive number of grades is undesirable. While there was considerable variation in the number of labor grades employed for nonsupervisory shop jobs, both during the 1951–1956 and the 1961–1966 periods, the mode was 12 grades during the former period, and 10 during the latter.[1] One bilateral committee that participated in a joint job evaluation of a manufacturing company with 440 evaluated jobs, decided on 14 grades, as shown in Table 13.1. Another manufacturing company evaluated 260 jobs, and adopted 20 pay grades with a 10-point grouping. Difficulties were experienced, however, in the latter case because a comparatively small number of points per pay grade was assigned, thus necessitating a revision and modification of the job evaluation plan. The NMTA plan, which has been very successful, uses only 10 pay grades with 20 points for each grade.

Classifying occupations

In Chapter 8 we discussed job classification in relation to analysis, description, and specification based on the use of factors as common denominators. Now, we are concerned with the classification of jobs within specific occupations, arranged according to a simple numerical coding system and alphabetical sequence. The occupational classification aids in fitting job titles to the workers who are compensated according to newly established pay grades. It also is of considerable aid in comparing jobs when making wage and salary surveys.

After all jobs have been described in accordance with appropriate titles, and after specifications and rating have been completed according to factor degrees and allotted points, classification data can then be recorded in an orderly fashion. Forms such as Figure 13.1 are designed with columns in which code numbers, titles and departments, job classes, degree and number of points for each factor, pay grades, and total number of factor points may be recorded. Under the original NEMA and NMTA evaluation plans, similar forms are used

---

[1]Richard M. Story, "Trends in Wage Administration," *Business Studies* (Denton, Texas: North Texas State University, Fall, 1967), p. 114. Also, in the unpublished results of a 1964 questionnaire, over 20 of 38 companies were using from 10–16 pay grades.

DEPARTMENTAL SUMMARY SHEET—JOB RATING

CODE NO.	PRODUCTION DEPT.	JOB CLASS	SKILL EDUCATION DEG.	PTS.	EXPERIENCE DEG.	PTS.	INITIATIVE AND INGENUITY DEG.	PTS.	EFFORT PHYSICAL DEMAND DEG.	PTS.	MENTAL-VISUAL DEG.	PTS.	RESPONSIBILITY EQUIP. OR PROCESS DEG.	PTS.	MATERIAL OR PRODUCT DEG.	PTS.	SAFETY OF OTHERS DEG.	PTS.	WORK OF OTHERS DEG.	PTS.	JOB CONDITIONS WORKING CONDITIONS DEG.	PTS.	HAZARDS DEG.	PTS.	PAY GRADE	TOTAL POINTS
71	Punch Press Setup & Oper. (4)	C	2	24	3	72	2	28	3	30	3	15	5	30	2	14	3	9	3	12	3	30	4	20	6	284
72	Riveting Hammer & Swedging (22)	C	2	24	1	24	2	28	2	20	2	10	2	12	2	14	1	3	1	4	4	40	2	10	2	189
73	Router Machine Operator (4)	C	2	24	1	24	2	28	2	20	1	5	2	12	2	14	1	3	1	4	4	40	2	10	2	184
74	Screw Mach. Automatic Setup (40)	A	3	36	4	96	3	42	3	30	3	15	4	24	4	28	4	12	4	16	4	40	3	15	9	354
75	Screw Mach. Automatic Setup (40)	B	3	36	3	72	3	42	3	30	3	15	4	24	4	28	4	12	3	12	4	40	3	15	7	326
76	Screw Mach. Automatic Oper. (40)	C	3	36	2	50	2	30	3	20	2	12	2	13	4	28	1	3	1	4	4	38	2	10	4	244
99	Shaper Setup Operator (3)	2	2	24	3	72	2	28	1	10	2	10	2	12	2	14	5	15	2	8	3	30	2	10	4	233
100	Setup Trim & Ripsaw (1)	2	2	24	4	93	2	28	2	20	2	10	2	12	2	14	5	15	2	8	3	30	2	10	5	264
101	Trim & Ripsaw Operator (3)	2	2	24	2	48	2	28	2	20	2	10	2	12	2	14	4	12	3	12	3	30	2	10	3	220
102	Wood & Celluloid Worker (3)	2	2	24	3	72	2	28	1	10	2	10	2	12	2	14	2	6	1	4	3	30	4	20	4	230

FIGURE 13.1 OCCUPATIONAL CLASSIFICATION BY FACTORS, PAY GRADES, AND TOTAL POINTS.

Arranged in numerical coding and alphabetical sequence.

as summary rating sheets. Some companies also use such forms to classify jobs by pay grades in an ascending or descending order.

Besides placing each job in a specific pay grade to establish differences in wage-base rates, the classification facilitates arriving at decisions for rate changes and for equitable compensation when transferring employees from one job to another. Having the occupational classification before him, the foreman or supervisor can immediately distinguish the difference in job values; thus, he will be alert when an employee is requested to do jobs of higher or lower grades. If a worker is asked to perform two jobs of different point values, unions will invariably insist that he be paid at the wage-base rate of the higher pay grade regardless of the time he spent on lower paid jobs.

Once a pay grade is established, it becomes standard. The grade does not change unless the whole job or some of its elements are changed. On the other hand, the wage-base rate is flexible. It does change from time to time. The changes or adjustments are discussed on page 351 under the main heading, "Adjusting Existing Wage-Base Rates and Salaries."

Coding jobs for identification

The coding of positions and occupations is necessary for general references, cross comparisons, verification of new rates or changed jobs, corrections, changes in job descriptions, and for other similar purposes, such as placing new or changed jobs in the proper group structure.

By adopting a numbering system, such as shown in the occupational classification by pay grades, Figure 13.1, an occupational code can be of simple structure. Each job of a certain category is designated by a code number. Note that screw machine jobs are grouped under code numbers 74 to 76. Job code number 74 designates automatic screw machine setup job Class A, pay grade 9, and has an evaluated rate of 358 points, while job code number 75 designates Class B, and has an evaluated pay grade 7, with a rate of 326 points.

Some companies prefer to use a code system with two, three, or four digits so that they can tie in the job title with the department and pay grade. Hence, the code for the first automatic screw machine job referred to above would be designated as 4019. The first and second digits refer to Screw Machine Department No. 40, the third digit to Automatic Screw Machine Job Class A, and the fourth digit indicates pay grade 9.

Investigating current wages and salaries

The investigation of current wages and salaries, through wage surveys, provides a valuable source of information that is helpful in pricing jobs (starting pay) and in establishing wage and salary levels, following the job evaluation process. The next few pages will point out the role that wage and salary surveys can play in wage and salary administration.

A *wage survey* is a statistical picture of what the wages for a particular geographical area, occupation, industry, or city were at a given time or are at the present time. The purpose of a wage survey is to collect comparable wage data that will enable a particular firm to determine on what wage levels it wants to operate or has to operate and to assist in reducing, if not eliminating, inequities which may be in existence within that firm. A survey should relate to a defined universe, that is, to some totality of firms or establishments. Since it is rare that the entire universe can be studied, a survey is usually a sample that reflects the universe. The survey is aimed at collecting wage data that are reasonably comparable among the firms included in the survey and to those firms which intend to make use of the survey. Although wage rates throughout the country are not uniform or consistent, each industry does have a range of pay that can be associated with it. Also, facts about wages, related benefits, and salaries take on added importance as the daily language of industry is supplemented with such terms as "prevailing wage rates," "equal pay for equal work," "collective bargaining," "escalator clauses," and "fringe benefits," to mention just a few. It is for these reasons that every manager should know what is happening to wages in his field of interest in his community as well as throughout the country. It should be noted, however, that because of the many diverse areas of wages and the tight schedules that managers have, managers usually do not have the opportunity to devote special time and effort to wage situations beyond their immediate field of work. The wage and salary administrator can therefore perform a real service to the firm by informing all concerned of the uses, limitations, and know-how that are associated with wage surveys.

Uses of Wage Surveys

Properly conducted wage surveys prove to be valuable to the general public, management, labor, and the unions as a tool in determining equitable treatment of all parties concerned.

The general public can consult a wage survey in an attempt to determine the effects of wages upon the cost of the products or services that are purchased. Wage surveys also help the general public to see the positions of both labor and management in collective bargaining sessions when the union is threatening a strike because management does not want to meet the union's wage demands. The general public is, therefore, more informed about various wage situations and is better able to understand the union and management positions in collective bargaining and the pricing decisions of management.

From management's standpoint, wage and salary surveys are of vital importance in keeping the company's job rates up-to-date and in line with those of other companies for the same jobs. This facilitates the formulation of policies and the stabilization and maintenance of a sound wage and salary structure. Once a wage and salary structure is established, wage and salary surveys enable management to compare its wage structure to the community, its industry, and other geographical areas. Large companies with multiplant operations and many thousands of workers find wage surveys useful as a means of checking the validity and equitability of the internal wage structure. On a larger scale, wage surveys prove useful in the evaluation of the labor costs involved in establishing a new plant or in relocating a plant.

Reference to wage surveys will enable employees to gain an indication of what the average wage for various jobs is throughout their community and country, and will sometimes answer their questions concerning unfair treatment by management. Just the fact that wage surveys are available can increase employee confidence in the management of a company.

Unions, as representative of employee interests, and management have found it practical and satisfactory to determine their own wage-base rates after a wage survey has been conducted to obtain sample wage differentials of comparable jobs from similar industries within the community or surrounding areas. The use of a wage survey by unions and management places them in a better position to modify or revise the wage and salary structure in a competitive labor market. If wages and wage administration issues have to be arbitrated, up-to-date dependable data can be presented to arbitrators as evidence.

Advantages and Limitations of Wage Surveys

In order to appreciate and utilize wage surveys more fully, students of wage and salary administration should be aware of their limitations as well as their advantages.

Advantages. An important question to ask at this point is, "What advantage or advantages are there about wage surveys that make them useful?" The first advantage is one of regularity. Surveys conducted by the federal government are made regularly and can be considered up-to-date in spite of the necessary time lag that takes place between the collection and the publication of the data. Table 13.2 lists 86 occupational areas in the United States in which annual wage surveys are conducted by the Bureau of Labor Statistics. The table also indicates the month the data were collected and the month the survey is available for purchase from the United States Government Printing Office in Washington, D.C. Wage and salary surveys have a broad scope in relation to the number of locations from which the data are drawn. Wage and salary surveys, when used to establish a common ground for collective bargaining, are advantageous in that a greater degree of confidence between the workers, management, and the public can be produced. If the public knows what wages are being paid, a more

TABLE 13.2

**THE 86 OCCUPATIONAL AREAS (CITIES) WHICH ARE SURVEYED ANNUALLY
FOR EARNINGS AND RELATED BENEFITS BY THE BUREAU OF LABOR
STATISTICS**

OCCUPATIONAL AREAS (CITIES) SURVEYED	USUAL MONTH OF SURVEY	USUAL MONTH DATA ARE AVAILABLE
Akron, Ohio	June	July
Albany-Schenectady-Troy, N.Y.	March	April
Albuquerque, N. Mexico	April	June
Allentown-Bethlehem-Easton, Pa.-N.J.	Feb.	April
Atlanta, Georgia	May	July
Baltimore, Maryland	Nov.	Jan.
Beaumont-Port Arthur, Texas	May	June
Birmingham, Alabama	April	June
Boise, Idaho	July	Sept.
Boston, Mass.	Oct.	Dec.
Buffalo, N.Y.	Dec.	March
Burlington, Vt.	March	April
Canton, Ohio	April	June
Charleston, W. Va.	April	June
Charlotte, N.C.	April	June
Chattanooga, Tenn.-Ga.	Sept.	Oct.
Chicago, Illinois	April	July
Cincinnati, Ohio	March	April
Cleveland, Ohio	Sept.	Nov.
Columbus, Ohio	Oct.	Dec.
Dallas, Texas	Nov.	Jan.
Davenport-Rock Island-Moline, Iowa-Ill.	Oct.	Dec.
Dayton, Ohio	Jan.	March
Denver, Colorado	Dec.	Feb.
Des Moines, Iowa	Feb.	April
Detroit, Michigan	Jan.	April
Fort Worth, Texas	Nov.	Jan.
Green Bay, Wisconsin	Aug.	Oct.
Greenville, S.C.	May	June
Houston, Texas	June	Aug.
Indianapolis, Ind.	Dec.	Feb.
Jackson, Miss.	Feb.	April
Jacksonville, Florida	Jan.	March
Kansas City, Mo.-Kansas	Nov.	Jan.
Lawrence-Haverhill, Mass.-N.H.	June	July
Little Rock-North Little Rock, Ark.	Aug.	Oct.
Los Angeles-Long Beach, Calif.	March	June
Louisville, Ky.-Ind.	Feb.	April
Lubbock, Texas	June	July
Manchester, N.H.	Aug.	Oct.

(Table 13.2 is concluded on following page)

TABLE 13.2 (concluded)

Occupational Area (Cities) Surveyed	Usual Month of Survey	Usual Month Data Are Available
Memphis, Tenn.-Ark.	Jan.	March
Miami, Florida	Dec.	Feb.
Midland and Odessa, Texas	June	Aug.
Milwaukee, Wisconsin	April	June
Minneapolis-St. Paul, Minn.	Jan.	March
Muskegon-Muskegon Heights, Michigan	May	June
Newark and Jersey City, N.J.	Feb.	April
New Haven, Conn.	Jan.	March
New Orleans, La.	Feb.	May
New York, N.Y.	April	Aug.
Norfolk-Portsmouth-Newport News-Hampton, Va.	June	July
Oklahoma City, Okla.	Aug.	Oct.
Omaha, Nebraska-Iowa	Oct.	Dec.
Paterson-Clifton-Passaic, N.J.	May	July
Philadelphia, Pa.-N.J.	Nov.	Dec.
Phoenix, Arizona	March	May
Pittsburgh, Pa.	Jan.	March
Portland, Maine	Nov.	Jan.
Portland, Oregon-Washington	May	June
Providence-Pawtucket, R.I.-Mass.	May	June
Raleigh, N.C.	Sept.	Nov.
Richmond, Va.	Nov.	Jan.
Rockford, Illinois	May	June
St. Louis, Mo.-Illinois	Oct.	Jan.
Salt Lake City, Utah	Dec.	March
San Antonio, Texas	June	Aug.
San Bernardino-Riverside-Ontario, Calif.	Sept.	Jan.
San Diego, Calif.	Nov.	Jan.
San Francisco-Oakland, Calif.	Jan.	March
San Jose, Calif.	Sept.	Jan.
Savannah, Ga.	May	June
Scranton, Pa.	Aug.	Nov.
Seattle-Everett, Washington	Oct.	Nov.
Sioux Falls, S. Dakota	Oct.	Dec.
South Bend, Ind.	March	May
Spokane, Washington	June	July
Tampa-St. Petersburg, Fla.	Sept.	Oct.
Toledo, Ohio	Feb.	April
Trenton, N.J.	Dec.	March
Washington, D.C.-Maryland-Virginia	Oct.	Dec.
Waterbury, Conn.	March	April
Waterloo, Iowa	Nov.	Jan.
Wichita, Kansas	Oct.	Dec.
Worcester, Mass.	June	July
York, Pa.	Feb.	April
Youngstown-Warren, Ohio	Nov.	Jan.

factual conclusion can be reached concerning the merits or demerits of labor's demands and management's assertions. Labor will have more reason to feel that they are being treated fairly if they are able to compare their wages with those of their fellow workers in different parts of the country. This type of confidence is very helpful to the whole economy because management and labor should work together as a team rather than as opposing forces. Another advantage of wage surveys comes to light when management wishes to compare its wage structure with those prevailing in other sections of the country. This comparison enables management to check its wage structure in regard to being above or below the industry, and the national or regional average. It may also enable management to determine if it is treating workers equitably and whether wage grievances are justified.

Limitations. A wage survey, like any other business tool, is subject to limitations. Most wage surveys are based upon a sample of representative wages for selected jobs in a company, industry, or geographical area. Since a sample of select jobs does not include all the jobs in any firm, a great deal of skill and judgment has to be exercised in interpolating the sample data to the remaining company jobs for which the survey data are not available. This is no easy task unless the firm has carefully determined the relative relationships among job values through the technique of job evaluation. Because the wage survey is based on a sample, it might also be of limited usefulness if the sample is not truly representative, or is too small to be of much value. Also, when reading the results of a wage survey, the user must be certain as to which statistical measure (median, mode, mean or average) is being used. The arithmetic mean reflects the average of all values, those that are extremely high as well as those that are extremely low. The median wage is midway between the lowest and the highest rates after they have been arranged in rank order; thus, the median wage is influenced by the number of wage rates in the survey. The modal wage is the one that occurs most often and is influenced by the type of sample used. Even if the sample is representative and the results are presented fairly, the survey may be of limited usefulness because the "universe" from which the sample is drawn may be faulty. For example, a manufacturing company that assembles small electric motors may request information from a manufacturing company that assembles chairs; thus, the universe of "assemblers" in the chair industry is faulty for surveying wages of "assemblers" for electric motors, unless the same or similar job evaluation plan is being used. A very important point to remember when using or conducting wage surveys is, "Statistics are valuable only to the extent that they are TRUE, ACCURATE, and COMPLETE."[2] In wages, as in many other fields, statistics generally serve to guide decision making rather than to determine

[2]H. M. Doty, "Survey Methods and Wage Comparisons," *Labor Law Journal* (April, 1964), pp. 222–23.

decisions automatically. The use of statistics almost always involves interpretation and judgment. No single wage survey will supply all the answers.

Wage and salary surveys are also subject to limitations arising from the comparability of the data. The surveys are of limited usefulness if the jobs for which the data are given are not comparable. Jobs with the same job titles may be radically different between companies; or when jobs are broken down into classes such as Machinist A, B, C, the criteria used to differentiate these may vary considerably between companies. Even if job titles and classifications are comparable, the wage survey may be of limited usefulness because of the amounts reported as wages. Wages given can be based on straight incentive (piece work), straight time, straight time plus overtime, measured day work, etc. Also to be considered are the factors which make up the wage figure. Does this figure include supplementary compensation (fringe benefits) or is it straight time? For purposes of comparison, the cost composed of straight time plus all fringes would be the best to use. This is the cost to the company of keeping the employee. The steel companies call this the "employment cost." However, as yet, wage survey methodology has not advanced to the point of standardization on this concept. It would appear that this must come in the future if wage surveys are to be more useful. At present most surveys report data on only the straight-time earned rates of the incumbents in the surveyed jobs.

Other limitations that cut into the effectiveness of wage surveys are: secrecy shrouds many companies when they present information about their wage structure; some companies tend to inflate the wages that they report; and because surveys are for a limited number of jobs, the dynamics of supply and demand for the jobs reported may not be taken into account. Finally, the time lag between the collection period and the time that wage surveys are available for use may limit their usefulness. This time lag can make wage surveys obsolete even before they are presented for use, especially if a period of nine months or a year elapses from collection period to presentation date.

Who Conducts Wage Surveys?

Some large companies conduct their own wage and salary surveys, while others prefer to obtain assistance from employer associations, banks, manufacturing associations, and the chambers of commerce who make quarterly surveys among their own members. For instance, the American Management Association, the Administrative Management Society (formerly the National Office Management Association), the Metal Trades Association, the National Furniture Manufacturer's Association, and several consulting firms conduct wage and salary surveys nationally and locally. These surveys have the advantage of gathering data based on jobs that have standardized titles and job contents similar to those published in the *Dictionary of Occupational Titles*.

The Federal Salary Reform Act of 1962 established the policy that federal salary rates shall be comparable with private salary rates for the same levels of work. Section 503 of the Act provides that the salary comparison shall be based on appropriate annual surveys conducted by the Bureau of Labor Statistics (BLS).[3] The published surveys of the federal government cover a whole range of occupations from tool and die maker to sweeper and from chief accounting clerk to office boy. From July, 1960, to June, 1961, BLS expanded its community wage survey program from 60 to 85 geographical areas. As of November, 1967, the survey includes 86 geographic areas, which constitute a sample of all Standard Metropolitan Statistical Areas. Bulletins are usually published for each labor market within three months of the survey. At the conclusion of each annual round of surveys, a summary bulletin, relating to the individual labor markets, is prepared. An annual bulletin containing national and regional projections of wage and salary levels and distributions, and of selected establishment practices (e.g., standard hours of work separately for plant and office employees) is also issued. Indexes of trends in occupational wages and salaries are also presented.

In addition to the "Occupational Wage Surveys," there are "Specific Industry Surveys," "Surveys of Collective Bargaining Agreements," and national surveys in such fields as "Professional, Administrative, Technical, and Clerical Work." Described below are some of the more important surveys that the government makes available to the public through federal depository libraries and for sale from the United States Printing Office in Washington, D.C.

Occupational Wage Surveys of specific metropolitan areas (see Table 13.2) are among the most important surveys that the government makes available. These surveys are conducted for 86 different labor markets as representative of at least 227 Standard Metropolitan areas and are primarily concerned with "occupational earnings and related wage benefits on an area wide basis."[4] The industry divisions included in these surveys are manufacturing, transportation, communications and other public uilities, wholesale and retail trade, finance, insurance, real estate and services; but the extractive industries, construction, and government operations are excluded. Occupations studied within these areas are professional and technical, maintenance and power plant, custodial and material movement, and office-clerical. The earnings given are for full-time workers and do not include premium pay for overtime, weekend, holiday and late shift work; but cost-of-living bonuses and incentive earnings are included. Also, at the end of each survey bulletin there are a number of occupational (job) descriptions that should prove to be useful in comparing the wages of different areas and occupations. Figure 13.2 shows examples of the type of occupational

---

[3]Testimony by Ewan Clague, Commissioner of Labor Statistics, U.S. Department of Labor, before the House of Representatives, Committee on Post Office and Civil Service, September 24, 1963, p. 1.

[4]U.S. Department of Labor, *National Survey of Professional, Administrative, Technical, and Clerical Pay,* Bulletin 1585 (Washington: U.S. Government Printing Office, 1968), p. 2.

ELECTRICIAN, MAINTENANCE

Performs a variety of electrical trade functions such as the installation, maintenance, or repair of equipment for the generating, distribution, or utilization of electric energy in an establishment. Work involves *most of the following:* Installing or repairing any of a variety of electrical equipment such as generators, transformers, switchboards, controllers, circuit breakers, motors, heating units, conduit systems, or other transmission equipment; working from blueprints, drawings, layout, or other specifications; locating and diagnosing trouble in the electrical system or equipment; working standard computations relating to load requirements of wiring or electrical equipment; and using a variety of electrician's handtools and measuring and testing instruments. In general, the work of the maintenance electrician requires rounded training and experience usually acquired through a formal apprenticeship or equivalent training and experience.

HELPER, MAINTENANCE TRADES

Assists one or more workers in the skilled maintenance trades, by performing specific or general duties of lesser skill, such as keeping a worker supplied with materials and tools; cleaning working area, machine, and equipment; assisting worker by holding materials or tools; and performing other unskilled tasks as directed by journeyman. The kind of work the helper is permitted to perform varies from trade to trade: In some trades the helper is confined to supplying, lifting, and holding materials and tools and cleaning working areas; and in others he is permitted to perform specialized machine operations, or parts of a trade that are also performed by workers on a full-time basis.

MACHINE-TOOL OPERATOR, TOOLROOM

Specializes in the operation of one or more types of machine tools, such as jig borers, cylindrical or surface grinders, engine lathes, or milling machines in the construction of machine-shop tools, gages, jigs, fixtures, or dies. Work involves *most of the following:* Planning and performing difficult machining operations; processing items requiring complicated setups or a high degree of accuracy; using a variety of precision measuring instruments; selecting feeds, speeds, tooling and operation sequence; and making necessary adjustments during operation to achieve requisite tolerances or dimensions. May be required to recognize when tools need dressing, to dress tools, and to select proper coolants and cutting and lubricating oils. For cross-industry wage study purposes, machine-tool operators, toolroom, in tool and die jobbing shops are excluded from this classification.

KEYPUNCH OPERATOR

Class A — Operates a numerical and/or alphabetical or combination keypunch machine to transcribe data from various source documents to keypunch tabulating cards. Performs same tasks as lower level keypunch operator but in addition, work requires application of coding skills and the making of some determinations, for example, locates on the source document the items to be punched; extracts information from several documents; and searches for and interprets information on the document to determine information to be punched. May train inexperienced operators.

FIGURE 13.2 Examples of the Type of Occupational (Job) Descriptions Found in United States Department of Labor Occupational Wage Survey Bulletins

KEYPUNCH OPERATOR (continued)

Class B — Under close supervision or following specific procedures or instructions, transcribes data from source documents to punched cards. Operates a numerical and/or alphabetical or combination keypunch machine to keypunch tabulating cards. May verify cards. Working from various standardized source documents, follows specified sequences which have been coded or prescribed in detail and require little or no selecting, coding, or interpreting data to be punched. Problems arising from erroneous items or codes, missing information, etc., are referred to supervisor.

SECRETARY

Performs secretarial and clerical duties for a superior in an administrative or executive position. Duties include making appointments for superior; receiving people coming into office; answering and making phone calls; handling personal and important or confidential mail, and writing routine correspondence on own initiative; and taking dictation (where transcribing machine is not used) either in shorthand or by Stenotype or similar machine, and transcribing dictation or the recorded information reproduced on a transcribing machine. May prepare special reports or memorandums for information of superior.

STENOGRAPHER, GENERAL

Primary duty is to take dictation from one or more persons either in shorthand or by Stenotype or similar machine, involving a normal routine vocabulary; and transcribe dictation. May also type from written copy. May maintain files, keep simple records, or perform other relatively routine clerical tasks. May operate from a stenographic pool. Does not include transcribing-machine work. (See transcribing-machine operator.)

FIGURE 13.2 Examples of the Type of Occupational (Job) Descriptions Found in United States Department of Labor Occupational Wage Survey Bulletins *(concluded)*

(job) descriptions found in the United States Department of Labor occupational wage survey bulletins.

Linked to the labor market survey program is the "Annual Nationwide Survey of Professional, Administrative, Technical, and Clerical Pay," which covers a wide range of white-collar occupations (jobs) in a broad spectrum of American industry. These surveys were designed specifically to meet the needs of the federal government for information on pay for work comparable to that through GS Grade 15 in the Federal Classified Service.[5] All industries that are major employers of the selected occupations are surveyed. The industry list includes manufacturing, transportation, communication, and other public utilities; wholesale and retail trade; finance, insurance, and real estate; and the small proportion of service industries devoted to engineering and architectural

[5]Clague, p. 2.

services and commercially operated research, development, and testing laboratories. The survey is limited to the nation's metropolitan areas and to establishments employing 250 or more workers since about 75 percent of all federal employees and more than 80 percent of Classification Act employees work in metropolitan areas. Small establishments have been excluded (since the 1960 survey) because they contribute very little to survey results, particularly for professional and administrative jobs.

There are 77 occupations (or job categories) for which salary data are selected from the following: accounting, legal, engineering and scientific, drafting, personnel management, clerical supervision, and clerical. Some specific typical jobs include personnel directors, job analysts, typists, keypunch operators, and file clerks. The 77 occupations studied, covering a wide range of pay levels, are numerically important in industry as well as in the federal service. Occupational definitions used in the collection of salary information reflect duties and responsibilities in industry but are translatable to specific pay grades (GS-1 through GS-15) applying to Classification Act employees. For each occupation a mean and a median salary are given on a monthly and an annual basis. A range of salaries is also given for the first and third quartiles. This information is shown in Table 13.3.

"Industry Wage Studies" are conducted for 70 (50 manufacturing and 20 nonmanufacturing) industries on a recurring 3- to 5-year cycle. Among the manufacturing industries are: Food and Kindred Products, Tobacco Manufacturers, Textile Mill Products, Lumber and Wood Products, Printing, Chemicals, and Transportation. The nonmanufacturing industries include: Mining, Wholesale and Retail Trade, Services, Building Trades, and Transportation. Included in the survey are averages and distributions of wage rates for representative jobs on a nationwide, regional, selected area, size of establishment, or some other basis depending upon the scope of the study and the industry. The Industry Wage Studies are differentiated from Occupational Wage Surveys in that the Industry Wage Studies treat specific industries on a nationwide basis, whereas the Occupational Wage Surveys treat a group of occupations in selected standard metropolitan areas.

Other studies published by the government treating the subject of wages and industrial relations are Union Wage Scales, Distribution of Employee Earnings, Employer Expenditures on Selected Supplementary Employee Remuneration Practices, Collective Bargaining Agreements, and Wage Chronologies. Figure 13.4 shows a list of government surveys and a brief description of each. The great degree of specialization that each of these studies involves is exemplified by the preface to the Wage Chronologies, which describes them as:

> A series of reports which trace the changes in wage scales and in related benefits, usually embodied in collective bargaining agreements made by specific employers or combinations of employers. The chronology series is

intended primarily as a tool for research, analysis, and wage administration. As such, the series deals only with selected features of the history of collective bargaining or wage determination. Reference to job security grievance procedure, methodology of price rate adjustment, and similar matters are omitted.

It is this degree of specialization that makes it desirable for the user of government information to become acquainted with at least two or three different types of information, such as Occupational Wage Surveys, Wage Chronologies, Industry Surveys, and Collective Bargaining Agreements. Figure 13.3 shows a list of regional offices from which information can be obtained.

U.S. Department of Labor, Bureau of Labor Statistics, Washington, D.C. 20212

Also, from the following Bureau of Labor Statistics Regional Offices:

- Federal Building, Government Center, Boston, Mass. 02203

- 341 Ninth Avenue, New York, N.Y. 10001

- 1371 Peachtree Street, N.E., Atlanta, Ga. 30309

- 219 South Dearborn Street, Chicago, Ill. 60604

- 450 Golden Gate Avenue, San Francisco, Calif. 94102

- Federal Office Building, 911 Walnut Street, Kansas City, Mo. 64106

- 411 North Akard Street, Dallas, Texas 75201

- Box 1784, William Penn Annex, Philadelphia, Pa. 19105

FIGURE 13.3 OFFICES WHERE UNITED STATES DEPARTMENT OF LABOR WAGE AND SALARY STUDIES AND SURVEYS MAY BE OBTAINED

General Criteria for Conducting a Wage Survey

Although it may be time-consuming and expensive for an individual company to conduct its own wage survey, there may be occasions when a wage survey is necessary and must be conducted. Given below are some general criteria to be considered when a company elects to conduct its own wage and salary survey. These points are not intended to show how a wage survey should be conducted but to show some of the more important factors essential to good wage and salary surveys.

Planning. As in any other business endeavor, planning is vitally essential to the success of wage and salary surveys. It is in this stage that the purpose of the wage survey must be established. Is the wage survey an attempt to find out starting wages, incentive pay, supplemental wages (fringes), or all of these data?

TABLE 13.3

TYPICAL INFORMATION AVAILABLE ON AN ANNUAL BASIS FROM THE DEPARTMENT OF LABOR ON PROFESSIONAL, ADMINISTRATIVE, TECHNICAL, AND CLERICAL PAY[1]

Occupation and Class (See Definitions in Appendix C)	Number of Employees[3]	Monthly Salaries[4]				Annual Salaries[4]				Percent Increase in Mean Salaries[2]
		Mean	Median	First Quartile	Third Quartile	Mean	Median	First Quartile	Third Quartile	
				Middle Range[5]				Middle Range[5]		
ACCOUNTANTS AND AUDITORS										
Accountants I	4,693	$621	$623	$575	$666	$7,451	$7,476	$6,900	$7,992	6.6
Accountants II	9,683	690	680	625	749	8,277	8,160	7,500	8,988	5.8
Accountants III	24,119	781	773	705	840	9,367	9,276	8,460	10,080	5.5
Accountants IV	16,669	939	925	850	1,008	11,273	11,100	10,200	12,096	5.8
Accountants V	6,557	1,128	1,108	1,008	1,243	13,531	13,296	12,096	14,916	5.8
Auditors I	724	637	625	575	700	7,645	7,500	6,900	8,400	6.3
Auditors II	1,795	726	719	650	800	8,707	8,628	7,800	9,600	4.2
Auditors III	3,773	831	820	740	908	9,977	9,840	8,800	10,896	5.6
Auditors IV	2,637	1,025	1,002	925	1,100	12,303	12,024	11,100	13,200	5.8
Chief accountants I	837	1,024	1,000	916	1,161	12,289	12,000	10,992	13,932	4.4
Chief accountants II	1,343	1,178	1,151	1,050	1,266	14,135	13,812	12,600	15,192	8.4
Chief accountants III	784	1,381	1,364	1,250	1,500	16,577	16,368	15,000	18,000	4.4
Chief accountants IV	301	1,587	1,583	1,442	1,699	19,046	18,996	17,304	20,388	0.8
ATTORNEYS										
Attorneys I	218	778	736	683	875	9,338	8,832	8,196	10,500	(6)
Attorneys II	959	858	806	760	912	10,293	9,672	9,120	10,944	7.0
Attorneys III	1,110	1,050	1,003	912	1,166	12,602	12,036	10,944	13,992	6.4
Attorneys IV	1,657	1,274	1,251	1,110	1,391	15,283	15,012	13,320	16,692	6.0
Attorneys V	1,428	1,495	1,447	1,300	1,666	17,936	17,364	15,600	19,992	4.2
Attorneys VI	691	1,846	1,833	1,625	2,083	22,152	21,996	19,500	24,996	3.4
Attorneys VII	408	2,403	2,373	2,081	2,765	28,841	28,476	24,972	33,180	5.7
OFFICE SERVICES										
Managers, office services I	282	765	766	683	810	9,183	9,192	8,196	9,720	7.3
Managers, office services II	721	912	916	833	990	10,948	10,992	9,996	11,880	5.3
Managers, office services III	381	1,142	1,117	1,000	1,292	13,707	13,404	12,000	15,504	5.3
Managers, office services IV	62	1,358	1,304	1,200	1,429	16,291	15,648	14,400	17,148	5.7
BUYERS										
Buyers I	2,395	612	608	541	670	7,344	7,296	6,492	8,040	4.5
Buyers II	9,132	722	715	641	783	8,660	8,580	7,692	9,396	5.5

Buyers III	12,878	855	845	759	939	10,260	10,140	9,108	11,268	4.5
Buyers IV	4,599	1,036	1,015	925	1,120	12,431	12,180	11,100	13,440	5.3
PERSONNEL MANAGEMENT[7]									
Job analysts II	384	735	733	650	819	8,820	8,796	7,800	9,828	8.1
Job analysts III	682	867	859	770	950	10,401	10,308	9,240	11,400	8.1
Job analysts IV	523	1,048	1,038	925	1,166	12,577	12,456	11,100	13,992	5.1
Directors of personnel I	1,153	919	900	825	990	11,029	10,800	9,900	11,880	6.0
Directors of personnel II	1,733	1,101	1,083	966	1,208	13,215	12,966	11,592	14,496	6.6
Directors of personnel III	1,132	1,334	1,316	1,133	1,499	16,005	15,792	13,596	17,988	4.5
Directors of personnel IV	391	1,643	1,521	1,374	1,875	19,715	18,252	16,488	22,500	2.8
CHEMISTS AND ENGINEERS									
Chemists I	1,768	672	660	615	734	8,061	7,920	7,380	8,808	6.2
Chemists II	4,419	744	740	687	800	8,931	8,880	8,244	9,600	5.3
Chemists III	9,292	849	833	775	912	10,187	9,996	9,300	10,944	4.8
Chemists IV	10,395	1,063	1,040	939	1,180	12,751	12,480	11,268	14,160	5.9
Chemists V	8,015	1,272	1,270	1,145	1,391	15,263	15,240	13,740	16,692	6.0
Chemists VI	4,340	1,444	1,431	1,300	1,581	17,324	17,172	15,600	18,396	4.5
Chemists VII	1,897	1,713	1,666	1,533	1,875	20,561	19,992	18,396	22,500	2.2
Chemists VIII	508	2,118	2,054	1,833	2,382	25,416	24,648	21,996	28,584	3.0
Engineers I	12,361	752	760	716	788	9,023	9,120	8,592	9,456	7.6
Engineers II	32,113	814	808	765	858	9,771	9,696	9,180	10,296	7.6
Engineers III	82,667	914	910	841	980	10,963	10,920	10,092	11,760	6.1
Engineers IV	109,538	1,091	1,083	990	1,185	13,095	12,996	11,880	14,220	5.4
Engineers V	71,257	1,269	1,251	1,130	1,380	15,223	15,012	13,560	16,560	4.8
Engineers VI	38,444	1,447	1,447	1,291	1,596	17,361	17,364	15,492	19,152	4.6
Engineers VII	12,789	1,685	1,670	1,505	1,834	20,216	20,040	18,060	22,008	4.6
Engineers VIII	2,971	1,940	1,859	1,708	2,120	23,280	22,740	20,496	25,440	4.7

[1]For scope of study, see table in Appendix A of the Bulletin.

[2]For limitations of percent increase in average salaries as a measure of change in salary scales, see p. 5 of the Bulletin.

[3]Occupational employment estimates relate to the total in all establishments within scope of the survey and not to the number actually surveyed. For further explanation, see p. 35 of the Bulletin.

[4]Salaries reported relate to the standard salaries that were paid for standard work schedules; i.e., the straight-time salary corresponding to the employee's normal work schedule excluding overtime hours. Nonproduction bonuses are excluded, but cost-of-living payments and incentive earnings are included.

[5]The middle range (interquartile) used here is the central part of the array excluding the upper and lower fourths of the employee distribution.

[6]Not reported in 1967.

[7]Insufficient data were obtained for level I to warrant presentation of average salaries.

Source: U.S. Department of Labor, Bulletin 1617 (January, 1969), p. 14.

SURVEY TITLE	DETAIL OF DATA AVAILABLE
Occupational wages — Metropolitan area studies	Averages and distributions of wage and salary rates for office clerical, skilled maintenance, custodial and material movement jobs — area-wide and by industry division. Work schedules and supplementary benefits and special analyses of wage structures and relationships.
Occupational wages — Industry studies	Averages and distributions of wage rates for representative jobs — nationwide, region, selected areas, size of establishment and other characteristics, depending upon industry and whether studied nationwide or in selected areas only. Work schedules and supplementary benefits and special analyses.
Occupational wages — Professional, administrative, technical, and clerical categories	Averages and distributions of salary rates for about 85 occupation work level categories of professional, administrative, technical, and clerical jobs.
Union wage scales	Averages and distributions of union scales of wages and hours by industry, trade, region, etc. Scales by trade in individual cities. Averages and increases in average wage scales by trade and for industry as a whole. Employer contributions to funds for health and welfare insurance, pensions, and vacations.
Current wage developments	For major situations, amount and nature of changes in wages and related benefits, identified by individual companies and unions, with number of workers affected, listed by industry group and location. Quarterly and annual statistical summaries of major wage developments and semiannual summaries of all wage changes in manufacturing.
Employee earnings distributions	Distributions and averages of earnings and hours of work, nationwide and by broad economic regions, metropolitan and non-metropolitan, and for selected individual industries and industry groups. (The 1966 studies cover retail trade and selected industries in nonmetropolitan areas in the South and North Central Regions and 9 small metropolitan areas in the South.)
Wage indexes	Indexes of wage and salary changes. National, and in some cases regional, indexes for such selected occupational groups as teachers, policemen and firemen, and Federal Classified Act employees. National and regional indexes (all industries combined, manufacturing) and selected city indexes for industrial nurses and office clerical, skilled maintenance, and unskilled plant workers; selected city indexes for production workers in machinery industry.

FIGURE 13.4   WAGE AND INDUSTRIAL RELATIONS SURVEYS THAT ARE AVAILABLE AT THE UNITED STATES GOVERNMENT PRINTING OFFICE IN WASHINGTON, D.C.

Source: "Major BLS Programs — A Summary of Their Characteristics" (1966 ed.), pp. 10–15.

SURVEY TITLE	DETAIL OF DATA AVAILABLE
Employer expenditures on selected supplementary employee remuneration practices (including the composition of payroll hours)	Percent of payroll and cents per hour employer expenditures for paid leave, premium pay, legally required payments, and private welfare plans. Ratio of paid leave hours to total hours paid for.
Analysis of health, insurance, pension, and other employee-benefit plans	Prevalence. Digests of plan provisions. Detailed analysis of selected provisions. Administrative and financial characteristics.
Public file of current collective bargaining agreements	File available for public use in Washington, D.C. Copies of specific agreements available at cost of copying.
Collective bargaining agreements analysis	Prevalence of contract provisions by major industry groups, subject matter, and other classifications. Contract clauses illustrating different approaches.
Work stoppages	Monthly: number of work stoppages, workers, and man-days idle. Annually: industry, areas, States, issues involved, duration, method of settlement. Special tabulations and analytical studies issued at irregular intervals.
Wage chronologies	Historical record showing amounts and characteristics of changes in wages and related benefits and plant practices.
Directory of national and international unions and union membership	Listing of national and international unions and State labor organizations, with names of key officials, number of members, and related information. Sections on union membership, structure, and functions; geographic and industrial distributions, trends, size of unions, women members, white-collar members, etc.
Union constitution provisions	Analysis showing prevalence, nature, and substantive characteristics of selected provisions.

FIGURE 13.4 WAGE AND INDUSTRIAL RELATIONS SURVEYS THAT ARE AVAILABLE AT THE UNITED STATES GOVERNMENT PRINTING OFFICE IN WASHINGTON, D. C.

(*concluded*)

Second, the number of companies to be included in the survey must be determined. For the first survey at least 10 or 12 firms are recommended for a reliable sample. Third, the type of firms to be contacted must be determined. It is recommended that companies of a comparable nature be contacted. For example, a manufacturing company wishing to conduct a wage survey for its office staff should contact other manufacturing companies rather than a bank or an insurance company. Fourth, wage and salary surveys cannot be collected overnight; thus, when planning a survey, enough time must be allotted for collection, analyzation, and presentation. Tolles and Raimon have estimated that "the modal time-lag between the distribution of employer association survey forms and the distribution of wage survey results is about six weeks."[6] This, however, should be recognized as an average figure and that it may take more or less time for each individual case. Fifth, the company must decide upon the method by which it is going to collect the data. Will a mailed questionnaire, a telephone interview, or a personal interview be used to collect the data? It is advisable to send a questionnaire first, then follow it up by telephoning or writing to inquire if and when the surveying company's representative may collect data. A visit to the respondent's personnel department or wage and salary administration offices by a representative who is capable of answering all questions satisfactorily should clear up any doubts or uncertainties. Also, in case of differences, the person-to-person contact may result in an agreement on standardized descriptions to conform with those of other institutions, thus establishing accurate information for future surveys. The following points, important in the planning phase, should be considered when using a questionnaire.

Generally, the questionnaire will vary according to industries and information desired. Figure 13.5 illustrates a typical wage survey questionnaire form. To establish fair, equitable, starting rates comparable to those of other employers, the chief job analyst and his committee should select a number of stable key jobs, preferably those used for evaluation and rating as described in the company's manual. If there are several key jobs for the same job title, they should be classified by letters A, B, C, D, etc. The lowest and highest key jobs will thus be included. It is imperative that the job titles be standard and in conformity with those prevailing in the respective field of activity, or community, as well as those in the *Dictionary of Occupational Titles*. A brief summary or condensation of a clear-cut job description should accompany each questionnaire, since the job titles alone may be misleading, especially when job content terminology differs. For instance, the job content described for "Head Clerk — Payroll" may differ entirely from the job content under the same title used by the company or institution from which the information is requested.

---

[6]N. Arnold Tolles and Robert L. Raimon, *Sources of Wage Information: Employer Associations*, Cornell Studies in Industrial and Labor Relations, Vol. III (1952), p. 330.

WAGE AND SALARY SURVEY DATA SHEET

Name of participating company_____Code_____

Address_____ Business_____

Survey No._____Data furnished by_____Title_____Date_____

	SHOP	OFFICE	SALARY	INCENTIVE
1. Number of employees in your company..	_____	_____	_____	_____
2. Minimum hiring rates................	_____	_____	_____	_____
3. Do you use training rates for new employees?...........................	_____	_____	_____	_____

4. Number of hours worked.

	Per week	_____	_____	_____	_____
	Per year	_____	_____	_____	_____

5. What method of progression do you use

Within the range	_____	_____	_____	_____
Automatic Increase	_____	_____	_____	_____
Merit Increase	_____	_____	_____	_____
Part Automatic — Part Merit	_____	_____	_____	_____

6. Are you granting rest periods

With pay	_____	_____	_____	_____
Without pay	_____	_____	_____	_____

7. Do employees working on holidays receive

Straight hourly rate	_____	_____	_____	_____
Time and one-half	_____	_____	_____	_____
Double time	_____	_____	_____	_____
Other compensation	_____	_____	_____	_____

8. What is the average percentage of base rate paid as supplemental wages?....... ____% ____% ____% _____%

9. In percent of base rates how much do you pay for a 40-hour work week?

Afternoon shift	___%	___%	___%	____%
Night shift	___%	___%	___%	____%
Saturday	___%	___%	___%	____%
Sunday	___%	___%	___%	____%
Holiday	___%	___%	___%	____%

10. Do you supply work clothes and laundry? _____ _____ _____ _____

11. Do you use a single rate (SR)   SR _____ _____ _____ _____
or a rate range (RR) for each job?   RR _____ _____ _____ _____

12. If you use an incentive plan, briefly explain the incentive method used_____

_____

_____

(Continued)

FIGURE 13.5   General Wage Survey Form

WAGE AND SALARY SURVEY DATA SHEET (continued)

	Shop	Office	Salary	Incentive

13. What are the average incentive earnings per hour as a percentage of base rate?... ____% ____% ____% ____%

14. Do you pay supplemental wages (Fringe Benefits)?
    Annual Bonus____ Attendance Bonus____ Christmas Bonus____ Profit Sharing____
    Stock Purchase Plan____ Seniority Bonus____ Vacation with Pay____ Paid Holiday____
    Other Payments _____

	Shop	Office	Salary	Incentive

15. Are you guaranteeing an annual wage?
    Yes ____ ____ ____ ____
    No ____ ____ ____ ____
    If "yes," please explain amount and number of weeks per year, etc._____

16. Which of the following holidays do you grant with pay?

	Jan. 1	Feb. 12	Feb. 22	May 30	July 4	Labor Day	Thanksgiving	Dec. 25
Shop								
Office								
Salary								
Incentive								

17. Are vacations granted with pay

	Shop	Office	Salary	Incentive
After 1 year employment	____wks.	____wks.	____wks.	____wks.
" 2 " "	____ "	____ "	____ "	____ "
" 3 " "	____ "	____ "	____ "	____ "
" 4 " "	____ "	____ "	____ "	____ "
" 5 " "	____ "	____ "	____ "	____ "

18. If you have employee benefit plans, excluding social security and workmen's compensation, who contributes —

	Company only	Employee only	Both Company	Employee
Accident Insurance			____%	____%
Life Insurance			____%	____%
Hospitalization Insurance			____%	____%
Pension			____%	____%
Savings			____%	____%
			____%	____%

19. If sick leave is granted with pay, how is it paid?

	Shop	Office	Salary	Incentive
Full Pay				
% of Base Rate	____%	____%	____%	____%

20. Attached are condensed descriptions of key jobs designated by our job numbers as indicated below. These jobs will also be used in repetitive surveys. Please fill in correct current data.

Job Code No.	Job Code No.	Job Code No.	Job Code No.
_____	_____	_____	_____
_____	_____	_____	_____
_____	_____	_____	_____

FIGURE 13.5   GENERAL WAGE SURVEY FORM (*concluded*)

The primary concern in job evaluation is to help determine wage-base rates of jobs that are executed under normal day-shift conditions. The survey questionnaire, however, may reach employers who pay beginners high wage-base rates to attract the best workers. On the other hand, some employers may pay low beginners' wage-base rates to induce the workers to depend on incentive rates for higher earnings. Similarly, workers on second and third shifts may receive 5–10 percent more pay per hour than day-shift workers. Therefore, data on different compensations are valuable not only to determine the types of compensation included in the wage and salary structure of other companies, but also to serve as a guide to secure accurate samples of base rates in order to assure a correct average of prevailing wages.

It should be remembered that some companies pay supplemental wages in the form of various "fringe benefits," also called "nonwage payments," and claim the advantage of paying lower average wage-base rates than their competitors. Therefore, inquiry should also be made regarding the status of supplemental compensations, such as pensions, paid vacations, financial incentives, group insurance, overtime premiums, merit payments, premium payments for shift differentials, and premium payments for Saturdays or holidays. Thus, the survey will make data available regarding supplemental wages in addition to ascertaining what the starting wage rate and the frequency of increases are. Furthermore, the survey will definitely assure all concerned that supplemental wages are to be considered a distinct addition to the wage and salary structure.

Another very important feature of such a survey is to determine to what extent incentive plans affect overall earnings. The chief analyst and his committee will be in a better position to make concrete decisions if all wage payment facts are available. This is especially important where bargaining is involved.

Analyzation and Summary. As soon as all questionnaires are received, they should be edited and coded. The codification of participating companies is necessary to keep the data confidential. Survey data are then analyzed and compiled by comparing company key jobs with those reported by the respondents to determine minimum, average, and maximum rates of pay for each key job. Opinions differ, however, whether the arithmetic mean, median, or modal method of computation should be used.

Arithmetic means are obtained by adding all rates received from the survey respondents for the same job and then dividing the total by the number of rates. *Median rates* appear in the middle of an uneven number of rate figures, that is, midway between the lowest and highest rates after they have been arranged in rank order. If the set of numbers is even, the median is commonly arrived at by adding the two middle figures and dividing by two. *Modal rates* are those that occur most frequently.

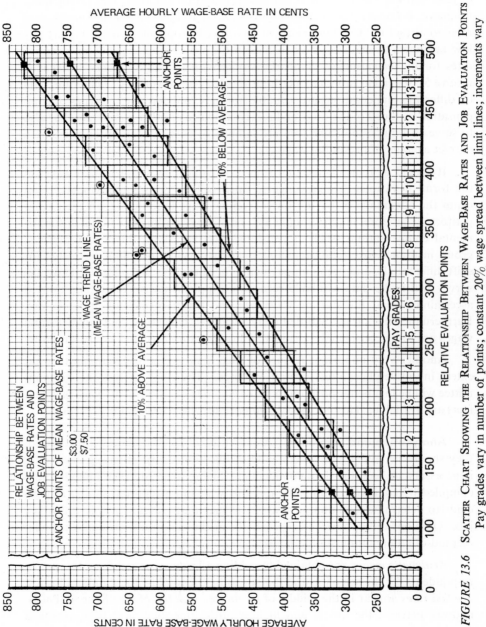

FIGURE 13.6   SCATTER CHART SHOWING THE RELATIONSHIP BETWEEN WAGE-BASE RATES AND JOB EVALUATION POINTS

Pay grades vary in number of points; constant 20% wage spread between limit lines; increments vary according to Table 13.1; trend line lies between anchor points.

Most job evaluation authorities agree that the fairest method to use in summarizing the data is to add all figures, and divide by the number of survey participants, thereby obtaining an arithmetic mean from the entire survey for component jobs of equal importance. It is also agreed, however, that a special study should be made of those returns from participating companies whose averages are considerably out of line. The extreme differences may disclose information that must be taken into consideration before an average trend line is arrived at. When extreme wage differences show up, it is often more satisfactory to select the median rate as more representative of the rate for each job.

Charting basic wage and salary rates

After the number of pay grades has been decided and an occupational classification similar to Figure 13.1 is completed, the next step is to prepare a graphic chart showing the plotted results of the wage and salary survey as well as the present status of the organization's wage and salary structure.

Charting the Data

To acquaint the reader with the important characteristics and techniques of converting job evaluation points into money values, a scatter chart has been introduced in Figure 13.6. Such a chart is commonly used in point rating methods to show the wage rates and wage distributions at a glance. The rates may either coincide with those of the community or be out of line, either above or below the survey average. By examining the chart, all concerned can visualize to what extent any discrepancies in the present wage rates have to be adjusted. In other words, the money value may be out of line in relation to the job within pay grades.

In charting the data, the jobs, as indicated by dots, are plotted in relation to the wage-base rate on the vertical scale (ordinate), and the pay grade point values, on the horizontal scale (abscissa). The next step is to decide which job represents the lowest average wage rate (within the lowest pay grade) and which job is regarded as the highest average wage rate within the newly adopted wage structure. Midpoints of the lowest and highest wage rates serve as *anchor points* to establish the trend line. The straight trend line drawn through the center of both anchor points is also known as the *line of correlation* (or the *line of regression*).

Line of Correlation

The line of correlation is considered the *basic wage curve,* since it is placed in a position that indicates the average relationship between points of established pay grades and money values regarded as wage-base rates. This curve is also known as the "conversion line," "wage trend line," "line of average relationship," "mean-wage-rate line," and "median line." The term trend line is used justifiably to indicate the correctness of a certain procedure in wage payments, whether arrived at in charting the curve by inspection or as a result of a union negotiated agreement. In other words, the trend line indicates the wage trend.

Establishing the wage curve

Normally, when the wage trend line is constructed on the scatter chart, the line appears curvilinear. However, since the majority of employees are not statistically trained, they tend to shy away from or to resist curved line charts that they do not understand. Therefore, it is customary practice to draw a straight line that represents the best fit for the data plotted, since the majority of employees can more easily understand such a trend line. There are two methods commonly used to determine the straight-line wage trend: by inspection or by using the least squares method for calculations.

The simplest technique for establishing a straight-line wage trend is to plot on the graph a midpoint (an anchor point representing the average rate) for the lowest pay grade (#1) and a midpoint for the highest pay grade and to draw a straight line connecting the two anchor points. The scatter chart, Figure 13.6, shows $3 at the midpoint of the lowest pay grade, also representing the lowest average wage-base rate, and $7.50 at the midpoint of the highest pay grade, representing the highest average wage-base rate. After the straight line has been drawn through the midpoints representing the lowest and highest anchor jobs, the correlation of average hourly base rates and pay grade points of all other jobs can easily be plotted.

The upper and lower limits of each pay grade may now easily be determined by drawing two more straight lines at a fixed percentage distance from the wage trend line. In Figure 13.6, two additional anchor points were established on a perpendicular 10 percent above and 10 percent below the midpoint (anchor point) for the lowest pay grade. Two more anchor points were plotted 10 percent above and 10 percent below the midpoint of the highest pay grade (No. 14). By drawing straight lines through the anchor points above and below the wage trend line, the minimum and maximum pay rates for each pay grade were established.

The anchor point method of establishing the wage curve as explained above is the accepted practice. It is now commonly adopted in various enterprises, especially where a joint labor-management committee exists. Some authorities claim, however, that the anchor point method does not produce a perfect wage curve. From the purely mathematical or statistical point of view, the claim may be justified, since calculations and plottings established by the method of least squares do reflect a somewhat truer wage curve.[7] On the other hand, however,

---

[7] For a study of the least squares method, see John Stockton, *Business and Economic Statistics*, (3d ed., Cincinnati: South-Western Publishing Co., 1966), pp. 354–361.

calculations by the least squares method are not understood by the workers, most supervisors, and some managers. Inquiries and tests have indicated that union representatives and workers generally prefer the inspected straight line curve, constructed by the anchor point method. The slight discrepancies are regarded as negligible in lieu of clarity and better understanding by the workers. The administrative executive or the engineer desiring to ascertain the degree of accuracy in an anchor point curve may, however, use the least squares method for checking and for verification purposes.

Converting pay grade points into money values

Money values have not been included in our discussions previously for the very reason that money values are constantly subject to changes and adjustments. After the pay grades and their point values are stabilized and the surveys completed, the conversion of points into money can commence. Many have regarded this procedure as the most crucial part of wage and salary determination. If jobs have been objectively evaluated and rated, however, conversion into dollars and cents is merely a matter of correlating the established point values to a money scale, as illustrated in Figure 13.6.

Correlating Points to Money Values

Before correlation is started, the job evaluation committee should decide what the pattern of wage-base rate comparison should be. Shall the pattern be based on the lowest and highest company wage rates? Shall the matter of establishing anchor points be subject to bargaining after an intercompany survey has been completed? Or, shall the pattern be based on results of an industrial and community survey? Also, shall there be single-rate steps for individual jobs, or shall there be wage-rate spreads within each pay grade? Shall the rate increments be constant or shall they vary according to pay grades and their point values? Whatever the pattern may be, it is necessary to establish a wage curve to be used as the line of correlation for the purpose of establishing wage-rate steps.

If, for example, the committee decides to use single rates, with specified increments, for each pay grade, a step structure as illustrated in Figure 13.7 results. In this example all jobs have been classified into 12 grades, each grade receiving 40 points. The wage-base rate for any one job within pay grade 1 is $3. An increment of 25 cents is provided for each of the other 11 pay grades. Superficially, this plan appears simple and plausible. The plan becomes complicated, however, because it does not include a definitely planned wage progression. There are no minimum and maximum wage rates with spreads in between to make progressions possible.

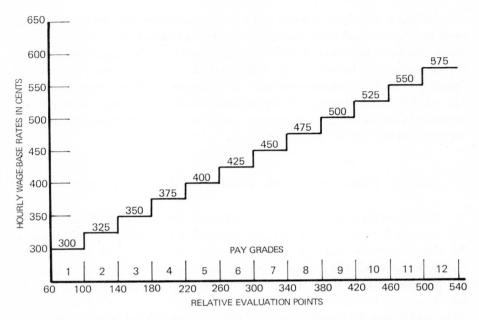

FIGURE 13.7   WAGE STRUCTURE CONTAINING SINGLE-RATE STEPS FOR INDIVIDUAL JOBS, A CONSTANT PAY GRADE INCREMENT OF 25¢, AND A PAY GRADE WIDTH OF 40 POINTS

Wage Progression

A sound wage and salary structure provides for a system of wage and salary increases over certain periods of time, without the necessity of entering into speculative bargaining with unions or capitulating to pressure from nonunion employees. Regardless of the wage progression system that is used, it should provide the employee with the opportunity to receive periodic pay raises so that the employee may advance from the minimum to the maximum rate paid in his pay grade. It should also permit promotion from one pay grade to another. This is known as *upgrade progression.*

Nowadays starting employees are interested in learning more than just the starting pay of a job. They want to know what pay raises can reasonably be expected as they demonstrate progress with the company. It is therefore important that a firm communicate the company's method of wage progressions through the pay grade range. Today's enlightened management realizes that every employee should know the salary range for his job and the system upon which pay raises are granted. This includes the basis upon which the increase is granted as well as the time interval of the raise and the amount of the raise. However, some companies are still operating under the mistaken idea that giving out such salary information is dangerous. Giving out wage information that each employee is entitled to know about his job can be used to create a favorable climate within the organization. A company's willingness to discuss appropriate aspects of compensation has an immeasurable salutary effect on employee relations. Secrecy and suspicions of favoritism that once existed are no longer the rule in well-managed companies. Today, fairness and honesty prevail. A good wage and salary administrator wants an employee to let him know whenever he feels that a wage inequity exists. When an organization creates such a climate, there is little opportunity for suspicion and distrust between labor and management to exist.

As shown in Figure 13.8, wage progressions may be classified into three basic types: (1) automatic, (2) merit, and (3) a combination of both automatic and merit.

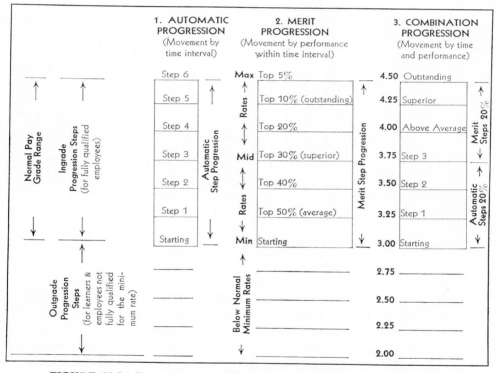

FIGURE 13.8   Basic Types of Wage Progression Connected with a Pay Grade (Hourly)

Automatic Progression. When a company grants one or more wage increases according to a specified period of time, it is considered an *automatic pay raise* or *automatic progression*. For example, if a person is employed on a job whose starting pay is $3 per hour, the company might automatically raise his pay 25 cents per hour for each additional six months of satisfactory employment (for a limited or unlimited number of years.) If this were the case, after six months of satisfactory service, the worker would be earning $3.25 per hour. After a year of satisfactory service, he would be earning $3.50 per hour, etc. In other words, as long as the employee is satisfactorily performing his job, he is automatically entitled to receive a set raise in pay in accordance with a previously determined period of time. Table 13.4 illustrates the automatic wage progression in use by the federal government.

TABLE 13.4

THE 10-STEP WAGE PROGRESSION USED BY THE FEDERAL GOVERNMENT

PER ANNUM RATES AND STEPS — JULY 12, 1969

	1	2	3	4	5	6	7	8	9	10
GS- 1	$3,889	$4,019	$4,149	$4,279	$4,408	$4,538	$4,668	$4,798	$4,928	$5,057
GS- 2	4,360	4,505	4,650	4,795	4,940	5,085	5,230	5,375	5,520	5,665
GS- 3	4,917	5,081	5,245	5,409	5,573	5,737	5,901	6,065	6,229	6,393
GS- 4	5,522	5,706	5,890	6,074	6,258	6,442	6,626	6,810	6,994	7,178
GS- 5	6,176	6,382	6,588	6,794	7,000	7,206	7,412	7,618	7,824	8,030
GS- 6	6,882	7,111	7,340	7,569	7,798	8,027	8,256	8,485	8,714	8,943
GS- 7	7,639	7,894	8,149	8,404	8,659	8,914	9,169	9,424	9,679	9,934
GS- 8	8,449	8,731	9,013	9,295	9,577	9,859	10,141	10,423	10,705	10,987
GS- 9	9,320	9,631	9,942	10,253	10,564	10,875	11,186	11,497	11,808	12,119
GS-10	10,252	10,594	10,936	11,278	11,620	11,962	12,304	12,646	12,988	13,330
GS-11	11,233	11,607	11,981	12,355	12,729	13,103	13,477	13,851	14,225	14,599
GS-12	13,389	13,825	14,281	14,727	15,173	15,619	16,065	16,511	16,957	17,403
GS-13	15,812	16,339	16,866	17,393	17,920	18,447	18,974	19,501	20,028	20,555
GS-14	18,531	19,149	19,767	20,385	21,003	21,621	22,239	22,857	23,475	24,093
GS-15	21,589	22,309	23,029	23,749	24,469	25,189	25,909	26,629	27,349	28,069
GS-16	25,044	25,879	26,714	27,549	28,384	29,219	30,054	30,889	31,724	......
GS-17	28,976	29,942	30,908	31,874	32,840	......	......	......	......	......
GS-18	33,495	......	......	......	......	......	......	......	......	......

Waiting Periods: One year to advance from Step 1 to 2; from 2 to 3; from 3 to 4.
Two years to advance from Step 4 to 5; from 5 to 6; from 6 to 7.
Three years to advance from Step 7 to 8; from 8 to 9; from 9 to 10.

When pay raises are granted automatically, beginning from the minimum starting wage for the pay grade, they may also be referred to as *ingrade progressions*. In enterprises where unskilled or inexperienced workers are hired as learners and go through a training period, the workers may progress from a very low hiring rate (learner's rate) to the starting or minimum rate received by a fully qualified employee. In this case, the automatic progression may be referred to as an *outgrade progression* since it is outside the regular established minimum and maximum rates paid to a fully qualified employee. Thus, an automatic progression of pay raises may apply in or outside the regular rate range. Unions tend to favor the automatic raise because it is an easy and simple way to decide who qualifies for a raise. They sometimes resist the merit progression system of pay raises because they may disagree with management's decision as to who deserves the raises.

Merit Progression. When a company grants wage increases on the basis of the individual's performance or merits, that is, his personal contributions or demonstrated abilities, the increase is considered a *merit raise* or *upgrade progression*. The next two chapters describe the theory and practice of evaluating the employee. The employee evaluation obtained would be used as the justification for granting or rejecting a merit pay raise. This type of wage raise is generally considered at specific predetermined time intervals, just like those used in the automatic progression. Management tends to favor this type of pay raise, in preference to the automatic pay raise, because it rewards employees more in relationship to their contributions or value to the company.

Combination of Automatic and Merit Progression. When, because of satisfactory service or due to union bargaining, a company grants some pay raises automatically for a period of time, and other pay raises due solely to individual merit, the increase is considered a *combination progression*. Many combination progression plans developed because neither management nor the union was completely sold on the use of the automatic or merit progression system alone. The combination wage progression is likely to provide for automatic pay raises from the minimum or starting pay for qualified workers, to the midpoint or half-way mark of the wage range. Merit raises then provide the basis for advancing in pay from the middle of the wage range to the maximum paid for the pay grade. In the combination progression, most employees eventually advance from the minimum wage to the middle of the pay range, while only the outstanding employees earn enough merit raises to reach the maximum wage in the rate range.

Pay-Grade Rate Ranges

Generally, most wage structures consist of pay grades having a wage spread (or steps) going from a minimum to a maximum rate of pay for each pay grade. The minimum or starting rates are usually governed by the competitive wage rates being paid in the community or industry for people who are barely qualified for the job. The rates in between the minimum and maximum rates serve to pay employees according to their various performances or efficiencies. (See number 3 wage progression in Figure 13.8). The maximum rates are set as a wage control to prevent pay costs from getting out of line. The theory of having a pay-grade wage spread is that it can serve as an incentive to motivate employees to perform at a greater efficiency than if there were no wage spread incentive. Then, too, a pay-grade wage spread allows for the reward and recognition of those employees who merit an increase in pay because of their performance, seniority, etc.

Some wage structures are characterized by a constant sum of money spread or increment (as shown in Figure 13.9), while the majority of wage structures usually provide a constant percentage spread of money (as shown in Figure 13.10). There is no general agreement among authorities as to what the ideal

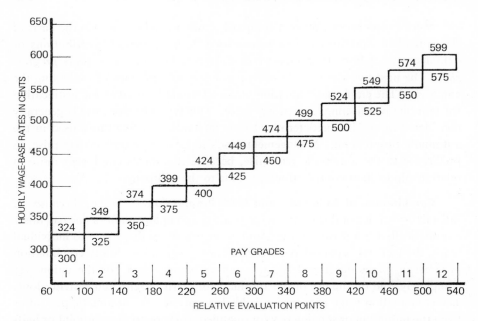

FIGURE 13.9   WAGE STRUCTURE CONTAINING A CONSTANT INDIVIDUAL PAY GRADE
SPREAD OF 24¢ AND A CONSTANT 25¢ INCREMENT FROM ONE PAY
GRADE MINIMUM TO THE NEXT

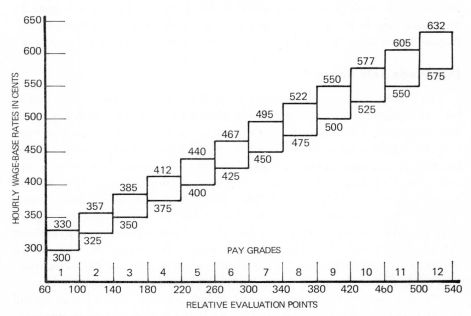

FIGURE 13.10   WAGE STRUCTURE CONTAINING A CONSTANT 10% INDIVIDUAL PAY
GRADE SPREAD AND A CONSTANT 25¢ INCREMENT FROM ONE
PAY GRADE MINIMUM TO THE NEXT

pay-grade rate spread should be. It appears to be an individual company matter that is dependent upon the employees' needs and desires and the firm's circumstances. Most authorities believe that to motivate employees, a pay grade spread should be at least 20 percent. That is, the minimum (or starting) rate is 10 percent below the average wage trend line and the maximum rate is 10 percent above this line (see Figure 13.6). Most companies are more likely to have a spread of somewhere between 30 and 40 percent. Pay grades for management personnel usually have greater spreads than those for unionized personnel. A few wage structures for executives have pay grade spreads as high as 100 percent.

Pay-grade rate ranges that have too much spread between the minimum and maximum pay may be identified by either or both of the following situations: the starting rates are too low to attract competent employees; or, the top rates are too high for the value of the work performed. Pay-grade rate ranges that have too little spread between the minimum and maximum pay may be identified by either or both of the following situations: starting rates are higher than necessary to attract competent employees; or, top rates are too low to keep competent employees. In short, a pay-grade rate range that is best is one in which the minimum rate can attract competent employees and the maximum rate will not only motivate the employees to be more efficient but will also serve to retain competent employees in the company. Much research needs to be conducted to establish more reliable guidelines.

Pay-Grade Rate Steps

The number of steps within each pay grade differs among various plans. Figure 13.11 is an example of one type of hourly occupational rate step used by a number of firms. The 12 pay grades provide 5 steps (A, B, C, D, and E) for raises within each grade. Each step is worth a 15-cent per hour raise ($6 per week or $312 per year).

Overlapping Pay Grades

Most wage structures, such as that in Figure 13.6, page 340, have pay grades that overlap each other because of two distinct advantages. First, the overlapping allows a greater pay grade spread that permits greater flexibility in fitting rates to jobs, granting pay raises, and in transferring and promoting employees from one pay grade to another. Second, the overlapping pay grade plan is less costly because cost curves rise sharply when there is no overlap. It is sometimes claimed that overlapping may cause employee resentment when a worker is promoted to the next higher pay grade since the top step of the lower grade is above the midpoint step on the next higher grade. This may seem unreasonable, but in practice little resentment is experienced because an employee in a lower

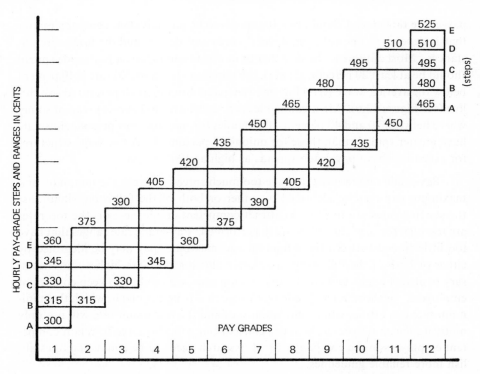

FIGURE 13.11   Sample Hourly Pay Grade Step-Wage Structure

pay grade who receives more pay than an employee in a higher pay grade has some compensating qualifications such as more seniority, experience, or skill or in some other way qualifies for this higher pay. Both labor unions and management prefer overlapping because a wide range of pay can be obtained horizontally and vertically within each pay grade, as illustrated in Figure 13.6. Overlapping permits flexibility by establishing a larger number of increases within the same grade over a longer period, an advantage which is more desirable than the limitations experienced with the structures illustrated in Figures 13.7 and 13.9.

    If employees have a complete understanding of the underlying principles involved and if the wage structure is simple without complicated formulas, there are no difficulties to overcome provided that the jobs are properly weighted and that an incentive system supported by employee evaluation exists. Variations in employee capabilities, intangible contributions, and length of service can then easily be taken care of. A chart with a trend line and a sufficient spread between the minimum level and the maximum level for each pay grade has proven satisfactory. The minimum and maximum line levels also make it clear to employees that they are within the pay range as compared with community rates.

Adjusting existing wage-base rates and salaries

After the occupational pay grades and scatter charts have been completed, discrepancies in pay will usually be found. Some workers may be receiving considerably more or less than the newly established averages specify. Since the main objective of installing a job evaluation program is to correct wage and salary inequities, all adjustments should go into effect as soon as practical after the evaluation is completed.

Rate Adjustment Problems

When forced to make rate adjustments, management is usually confronted with the following three problems:

1. What should the general company policy be if all employees are underpaid? Should underpaid employees be upgraded to the minimum or average rate levels?
2. What shall be done with respect to those employees whose wage-base rates are above the established average, but just below the maximum rates?
3. What should the general company policy be in regard to overpaid employees? Should they be dropped to the maximum, should they be trained for a job that will allow them to retain their present high rate, or should they stay in the same job at the same rate, or how should the problem be handled?

A clear-cut objective and a fair policy will eliminate unfavorable expediences, discourage favoritism, dictate adjustments based on fairness, and above all, create an equitable balance to correct unfair conditions. Solutions to the problems listed above may be found in accordance with the general discussion in the following paragraphs.

All rates of fully qualified workers that fall below the minimum line should be adjusted upward to a new rate within the pay grade in accordance with the company's wage progression policy. Each employee will have to be examined individually in light of the policy to see where he should fit into the range. However, a fully qualified employee should receive at least the minimum rate set up in the evaluation and then move through the range in accordance with the company's progression policy.

It may not be possible for a company to adjust the rates to their proper level all at once. Of the many reasons why the adjustments are made over a period of time, two are more common. First, old line management may not want to admit their error and therefore refuse to give large rate increases. Second, the company may be operating on very tight margins or fixed price contracts that may make it impossible to make the proper adjustments quickly without forcing a loss due to the increase in costs. The adjustment may require a series of steps that gradually brings the rate up to the proper level. When this is necessary, the employees should be told what the adjustment schedule is and why the company cannot make the entire adjustment at one time.

Avoid Wage Cutting

If plotted wage dots appear above the maximum line, they indicate overpayment and should be red circled for special attention and adjustment, as shown in Figure 13.6, page 340. This is a difficult problem to solve and to overcome where the number of overpaid employees is comparatively large.

In earlier years when job evaluation was first introduced, there was a persistent tendency to reduce the overpaid high rates either to the newly evaluated average or even to the minimum rates. Some employers discharged workers who were considered to be overpaid, without remedying conditions through adjustments. Such practices lowered the workers' morale and gave unions legitimate cause to refuse acceptance of job evaluation. On account of "rate cutting," they opposed job evaluation as "a tool of management to reduce a worker's legitimate earnings." If, after the new rate structure is in effect, it is discovered that a few employees are overpaid, the best policy is not to make any reductions. It is well to inform those employees, however, that they are overpaid, and at the same time appeal to their sense of fair play for full cooperation to produce the maximum according to their higher wage rates.

It cannot be overemphasized that whenever a worker is paid more than the newly established maximum, it is poor policy to cut wages after introducing job evaluation. An attempt should be made either to train and to upgrade the employee to another job that is commensurate with his current higher wage-base rate or he should be left on the job until a promotion occurs on the basis of employee evaluation and rating, which will be discussed in Chapters 14 to 16. The worker may have been with the company many years, thereby being entitled to a higher rate on the basis of seniority or because of distinguishing qualifications even though the job, as such, places him in a lower pay grade level. For example, assume that the employee has been with the company over 10 years. He should be capable of instructing new workers, or assuming the additional responsibility of inspection, thus entitling him to retain the higher rate. In an era or an economy of continuous annual wage raises, a simple solution to the overpaid employee would be to "freeze" his wages until the annual wage raises have caught up to his rate of pay.

Special Treatment of Abnormally High-Rate Recipients

If the high rates are the result of more production or better performance, that is, if one worker is producing more efficiently than another in quantity or quality per hour, then the higher rate should be regarded as an established award for efficiency, provided no incentive plan exists. On the other hand, if the differences are the outcome of rates haphazardly established by supervisors, the company should acknowledge its errors and continue paying the higher rates until conditions are rectified. Common sense reasons that if higher wages could be paid before, without losing profits, the company should be able to continue paying the higher rates until the employees are properly placed in other jobs. One employer upgraded some overpaid employees to positions that afforded opportunities for assisting in the work simplification program, thereby entitling them to higher rates. Agreements should be reached with unions and the fact publicized that due to seniority and other qualifications, the older employees will retain the higher rates as a gesture of goodwill and good faith until conditions are rectified, but that all new employees will receive the newly evaluated rates unless the cost of living and other conditions warrant increases.

Salary Adjustments

Although this chapter has stressed equitable wage standardization for hourly paid employees, it must be emphasized that the fundamental principles apply equally well to the standardization of salaries for supervisory, professional, technical, and managerial positions.

The evaluation of jobs and positions on supervisory, professional, and managerial levels involves detailed planning and full management cooperation. Without the inclusion of management, its criticism and acceptance of ultimate results, a detailed salary administration program would never be effective. The project must be planned to engage *all levels of management* in gathering job information and in the necessary evaluation judgments. Chapters 24 and 25 discuss this phase of wage and salary administration in more detail.

REVIEW QUESTIONS

1. (a) Why are pay grades used? (b) Would it be desirable to establish a different rate of pay for each job that has a different point value? Why?

2. Discuss the relative merits of ingrade progression in contrast to upgrade progression.

3. What are the advantages of having overlapping wage-rate ranges?

4. From an administrative point of view, how many pay grades are desirable within a wage structure?

5. From what sources might a company obtain information concerning the wages of the community, of its respective industry, and for a particular area of the country?

6. (a) Why is a community survey desirable in the establishment of pay scales?
(b) What difficulties may be encountered in securing and using such a survey?
(c) What are the common shortcomings of the use of local wage surveys?

7. (a) What are the various methods available to handle "red circle" (overpaid) jobs? (b) What are the advantages and disadvantages of each method? (c) Where should each method be used?

8. What difficulties are encountered in determining whether the wages in a particular plant are in line with community rates for comparable jobs?

9. Are wage increases by ingrade progression fair to the workers? Why?

10. How can small companies receive the advantages of wage surveys without incurring prohibitive costs?

11. Describe the different ways that a wage curve may be used by a company.

12. How are rating points converted into money rates?

13. (a) How is the correctness of a wage rate judged, once the point value of the job has been determined? (b) Is there any constant standard of "correctness?"

14. What consideration should be given to "dead end" jobs when the rate range is being determined?

15. How do you set the upper and the lower limits for a pay grade?

16. Is it ever advisable to cut wages after a wage survey reveals that your company is paying higher rates than any other company? Why?

17. What are the advantages of coding jobs for identification?

RESEARCH OR SEMINAR QUESTIONS

1. How can a public utility such as the telephone company conduct a wage survey when its skilled craftsmen such as a "central office repairman" have no direct counterpart in industry?

2. In using wage surveys, how can fair comparisons between rates be made when the measure of the efficiency, productivity, or contribution of the employees covered by the survey is unknown?

3. What should a multiplant company's policy be toward wage differences in different areas of the country? Should such a company have different rules in different plants? Why or why not?

4. Which one of the following rate increases would you recommend be used in your company? Give the reasons for your recommendation.
(a) Automatic progression.
(b) Merit progression.
(c) Combination of automatic and merit progression.

5. Identify the topics that should be covered in a wage survey questionnaire and explain why they are important.

PRACTICAL EXPERIENCE ASSIGNMENTS

1. Wage surveys are in themselves dangerous because of the number of things that they do not tell you but which still may be important. Draw up a list of the types of information frequently omitted from a wage survey which may greatly alter how it should be interpreted.

2. Obtain from a company of your choice their method of advancing an employee through a pay grade. Evaluate their method by citing the following:
   (a) Its strong points.
   (b) Its weak points.
   (c) How you would correct the weaknesses.

3. Draw up some guiding principles that a company might follow in handling wage inequities that are discovered during a job evaluation program.

CASE PROBLEM

13—1. THE PROGRESSIVE MANUFACTURING COMPANY

Adjusting a Wage Structure

After continued complaints from the union regarding wage-base rate inequities, James Carpenter, president of The Progressive Manufacturing Co., ordered a job evaluation program for the factory employees. He also authorized his company to be one of 15 participating members of a local wage survey. Results of the job evaluation and wage survey on key jobs are recorded in Table 13.5, page 357.

Problems:

1. Using the alphabetical job code letters in Table 13.5, prepare a scatter chart on graph paper by plotting the present weighted average rates of pay for each job (column 4). Label the horizontal axis on the graph "Job Points" and the vertical axis, "Wage-Base Rates." By observation or the least squares method, draw the company's present wage curve.

2. Using a different colored pencil and the same job code letters in Table 13.5, prepare a scatter chart on the same graph paper for the wage survey data (column 5). By observation or the least squares method, draw a wage curve for the wage survey data. Compare the company's and the community's wage curves and indicate what you have learned from them.

3. Set up an appropriate number of pay grades for the 26 jobs. Indicate the minimum and the maximum number of points assigned to each pay grade and the jobs that fall into each job grade. Record your results in columns 1, 2, 3, and 6 of Table 13.6, page 358. Explain your theory or reasoning in choosing the number of pay grades that you did.

4. Using the information in columns 4 and 5 of Table 13.5, determine whether you would recommend any changes in the weighted average pay for any of

the 26 jobs. Record in column 6 whatever new or old weighted average rates of pay you wish to recommend for each job and explain your adjustments. Using another colored pencil, plot these data (in column 6) on the same graph paper with the other curves obtained in Problems 1 and 2. By observation or the least squares method, draw the proposed new weighted average curve.

5. Compare the three wage curves that you plotted in Problems 1, 2, and 4 and make recommendations on the following:

(a) A proposed new midpoint for each pay grade. (Enter the data in column 7 of Table 13.5 and plot these on a new graph with the pay grades you chose in Problem 3. You may want to draw 3 lines on this graph to represent the 3 curves you previously plotted in order to see the various relations involved.)

(b) The minimum and maximum rates for each pay grade. Enter your recommendations in columns 4 and 5 of Table 13.6 and plot these data on a graph to determine whether your wage structure contains any wage inequities.

(c) Identify any red circle jobs and explain how you would handle them.

(d) How employees are to advance from the minimum to the maximum pay in the pay grade and any short- or long-range wage policies you believe are desirable.

6. Assume that, six months after your adjustments take effect, the company is being pressured by the union for a general pay raise.

(a) Figure out what the latest rates would be if there were an across-the-board blanket raise of 20 cents per hour and enter these rates in column 8 of Table 13.5 (added to rates in column 6).

(b) Figure out what the latest rates would be if there were an across-the-board blanket raise of 10 percent and enter these rates in column 9 of Table 13.5 (added to rates in column 6).

(c) Decide which pay raise you would recommend if the company were forced to grant a raise. Before making your decision, you may want to make comparisons by plotting 4 curves on another graph (community wage survey curve, the proposed weighted average rate curve, the proposed 20 cents across-the-board raise curve, and the 10 percent proposed raise curve.) Explain why you recommended the 20¢ raise or the 10 percent raise.

TABLE 13.5
WAGE STRUCTURE DATA

1	2	3	4	5	6	7	8	9
					PROB. 4	PROB. 5a	PROB. 6a	PROB. 6b
JOB CODE	JOB TITLE	POINT RATING	PRESENT WEIGHTED AVE. #RATE/HR.	WAGE SURVEY WEIGHTED AVE. #RATE/HR.	PROPOSED NEW WEIGHTED AVERAGE RATE	PROPOSED NEW MIDPOINT OF PAY GRADE	20¢ RAISE	10% RAISE
A	Watchman	161	$1.82	$2.28	2.15		2.55	2.57
B	*Punch Press Operator	170	2.18	2.50	2.25	2.35	2.45	2.47
C	*Opr. Small Drill Press	188	1.93	2.52	2.40		2.60	2.64
D	Helper (Machine shop)	210	2.08	2.70	2.70		2.90	2.97
E	Drill Grinder	220	2.38	2.75	2.78		2.98	3.06
F	Maintenance Helper	220	2.29	2.76	2.76	2.73	2.95	3.03
G	Grinder External	240	2.79	2.85	2.86	3.12	3.06	3.14
H	Milling Machine Opr.	260	3.05	2.95	3.10		3.20	3.41
I	Packer	260	2.63	2.90	3.05		3.25	3.36
J	Grinder (centerless)	275	2.84	3.00	3.25		3.45	3.58
K	*Opr. Big Drill Press	282	3.00	3.38	3.30		3.50	3.63
L	Assembler	282	2.74	3.18	3.18		3.38	3.50
M	Auto. Screw Mach. Opr.	288	2.91	3.20	3.22		3.42	3.52
N	Boring Mill Opr.	310	2.96	3.45	3.40		3.60	3.74
O	Maintenance Ma	320	3.16	3.50	3.45		3.65	3.80
P	Inspector	323	3.70	3.55	3.48		3.69	3.87
Q	*Welder	340	3.22	3.65	3.70		3.90	4.07
R	Painter & Sprayer	340	3.05	3.60	3.55		3.76	3.91
S	Toolmaker	355	3.22	3.65	3.75	3.55	3.95	4.13
T	Carpenter	380	4.14	3.83	3.90		4.10	4.25
U	Pattern Maker	386	3.93	3.83	3.92		4.14	4.36
V	*Drill Maker	390	4.02	4.09	4.05		4.25	4.45
W	Overhead Craneman	406	3.58	3.99	4.00	4.02	4.20	4.40
X	Screw Machine (set-up)	410	4.13	4.20	4.15	4.43	4.35	4.52
Y	Model Maker	440	4.35	4.50	4.45	4.43	4.55	4.90
Z	Electrician (main.)	490	4.55	4.83	4.76	4.74	4.90	5.17

*Employees on these jobs are in short supply; thus, competition is keen in filling them.

#The weighted average is developed by dividing the sum of all the hourly rates by the sum of the total number of persons holding the jobs.

TABLE 13.6

RECOMMENDED WAGE STRUCTURE FOR THE PROGRESSIVE MANUFACTURING CO.

1 PAY GRADE	← PROB. 3 →		← PROB. 5b →		← PROB. 3 →
	2 MINIMUM POINTS	3 MAXIMUM POINTS	4 MINIMUM RATE/HR.	5 MAXIMUM RATE/HR.	6 CODE OF JOBS IN PAY GRADE

chapter 14

BACKGROUND, THEORY, AND
METHODS OF
EMPLOYEE EVALUATION

In preceding chapters the evaluation of jobs performed by shop and office employees has been discussed. It was pointed out that job evaluation determines the value of specific jobs in relation to other jobs, but does not include the evaluation of employees. In this chapter the background, theory, and methods that form the basis for evaluating employees are discussed so that they can be appropriately compensated according to their merits.

Employee evaluation is the subjective process of appraising the relative value of an employee to the company in terms of his abilities, job performance, and potential (for a specific period of time). Usually the evaluation consists of a judgment made by one person of the way a subordinate employee has been fulfilling his obligations to the firm since his last evaluation. The subjectiveness of the appraisal process can be greatly reduced by using systematic and organized procedures to evaluate the employee in terms of concrete standards. Periodic appraisals of each employee are usually made throughout his career with the company. In a manner similar to job evaluation, a number of appraisal factors may be selected to assist the rater in being more objective and impartial in the evaluation process.

An analysis of employee evaluation programs shows that there is a variety of purposes for which employee evaluation is being used. Some of the most frequently used purposes of employee evaluation are to compensate employees, to aid in formulating employee development plans, to assist in personnel counseling, to aid in making transfers and promotions, and to enable the employee and the employer to know how well the employee is doing in his work.

The importance of formally evaluating employees periodically cannot be overlooked or overemphasized. Every employee of every firm is continually being informally evaluated whether one realizes it or not. There is no way to stop it, nor should there be, because in a competitive society a firm cannot hope to survive very long unless it regularly appraises its manpower resources and takes appropriate action according to sound management practices. Thus, employee evaluation is a necessity because it serves to inform both the employer and the employees of the strengths and weaknesses of the firm's personnel and makes it possible for management to develop plans and make decisions that attempt to utilize the company manpower to its greatest advantage.

Benefits of employee evaluation

In spite of the fact that the purposes of employee evaluation may differ greatly, depending upon the company organization, the nature and type of services, the objective, and the expected results, the following benefits can be generally derived from the information that is obtained from the employee evaluation when it has been properly established:

1. It furnishes reliable information for the proper *placement, counseling,* and *guidance* of employees. Thus, if the employee is improperly placed, corrections can more easily be made.
2. It gives confidence to the employee as well as to management in that all concerned are assured that *supervisors will try to be neither prejudiced nor biased* in dealings with their subordinates. The tendency toward being unduly influenced by outstanding characteristics (favorable or unfavorable) is also reduced.
3. It establishes a basis and common ground for the supervisor and the employee to *discuss the correction or removal of any shortcomings or weak points* that hamper the employee's progress.
4. It establishes dependable records that indicate the need or requirements for *training*.
5. It enhances *employee morale*, contributing directly and indirectly to self-improvement. The employee knows "where he stands" at all times.
6. It aids employees in demonstrating their strong points, desirable characteristics, and abilities, thus assuring them of not being overlooked for *advancement*.
7. It can provide wage increases as incentives for increased production and efficiency *if financial incentive plans do not exist*. As a matter of fact, it is

claimed that improvement in productivity is noticeable under an employee evaluation plan. Friendly rivalry and competition result from having been "evaluated and rated."

8. It serves as a basis for discovering abilities and latent capacities, thereby creating a determinant for *promotion.* This condition is especially advantageous when union seniority claims enter the picture.

9. It helps to identify workers who possess the necessary skills and capabilities for *transfer* to another job or department if a shortage of work or legitimate dissatisfaction occurs.

10. It helps to provide a *periodic wage or salary increase* if a job evaluation plan has been installed and if minimum and maximum rates for classified jobs are in effect. Assume that $3 is the established average hourly rate for a job and that the differential is 15 percent above and below the line of average relationship. Thus, there is a spread of 90 cents. If an employee starts at a minimum of $2.55 and his rating entitles him to receive increases of 15 cents every six months, he would receive six increases of 15 cents each over a period of 36 months. Similarly, any salary range can be adjusted depending upon the job classification and job values.

11. It helps to relieve employee tension and *encourages faith in management's fairness and justice in cases of work curtailment or layoffs.* Employees will react favorably if they are assured that aside from seniority (as favored by unions), ability and capacity, based on employee evaluation, are also determinant factors. In the event of discharge or layoffs, union representatives can be convinced of a worker's inefficiency or inability.

12. It helps to settle disputes in arbitration cases. Where unions have not participated in setting up the plan, arbitrators often request employee evaluation records for examination.

Terminology used to evaluate employees

The extremely rapid growth of employee evaluation plans in commerce, industry, and government agencies has placed the subject and its terminology in a heterogeneous condition. Frequently, an employer or a personnel manager is in somewhat of a quandary as to which method, plan, or system is most advantageous. This is understandable considering the comparatively large number of synonyms — titles and descriptive terms — used in personnel management and allied literature. Regretfully, the confusion is noticeable in the claims and counterclaims regarding certain plans, methods, factors, and other phases of employee evaluation used in commerce and industry.

The terms "employee evaluation," "employee appraisal," and "merit rating" are most commonly used. We have adopted the term employee evaluation in an attempt to clarify a much discussed subject and its terminology. As previously explained and as subsequent discussions will elucidate, we are seeking to establish the employee's value to the enterprise and his value as a member of a group, as differentiated from job evaluation. In employee evaluation we are also concerned with the *evaluation of the relative worth of one employee as compared with another.*

A search for proper terminology disclosed over 70 different titles and descriptive terms being used in the literature of personnel management, psychology, and industrial management. Included in the long list are such terms as appraisal and development rating, behavior rating, efficiency rating, employee job rating, measuring performance, measuring and rating employee performance, occupational rating, performance rating, and worker's appraisal. From this long listing, it would appear that if the terminology for evaluating employees had been designed to create confusion, it could not have been much more successful.

Need for Clarification and Consistency

The question may arise, "Why be so extremely concerned about terminology, description, and definitions?" The answer is obvious if proper consideration is given the fact that employee evaluation is a subject of utmost significance in dealing with employees, employees whose livelihood wholly or partly depends on how this phase of wage and salary administration is interpreted and determined. Workers are on the alert and are distrustful of the employer's "schemes" to regulate wages and incomes. Any technique to evaluate and measure traits and performance is always met with misgivings. This is attested by the many unsatisfactory results and failures in employee evaluation.

It is to be anticipated that new and important changes affecting human beings will not always be free from imperfections. It must be recognized, however, that employees expect their leaders — in this case management and personnel administrators — to achieve complete orientation through survey, inquiry, and research of that which existed in the past and which has been predominantly accepted as standard for practical application. Thus, when management presents a new program, it should be supported by indisputable facts. New ideas and new terminology should be made clear and understandable to employees.

In managing large groups of employees with various backgrounds, as well as in personnel relations consulting, experience has convinced the authors that the introduction of progressive managerial control, requiring new terminology coupled with standardized procedure, brings satisfactory results for all concerned if thoroughly explained and consistently applied. This is especially true when dealing with the AFL-CIO, or with other representative unions whose terminology in contractual agreements becomes a model for the local unions.[1]

It is not the purpose of this book to discuss all the undesirable terms. However, we shall cite some of the terms which may be regarded as ambiguous or even deceptive when used to mean employee evaluation.

---

[1]For a discussion of misunderstandings and wrong impressions due to improper terminology and differences in presenting data to employees, it is recommended that the reader review Chapter 8, pp. 207 to 209.

Employee Job Rating

This term gives the impression that both employees and jobs are evaluated or rated at the same time. Logically, this is impractical since it is contrary to the long-established principle — over 60 years — of functionalization and specialization. The use of the expression employee job rating causes confusion since:

> . . . much of the negative experience in rating practice is attributed to the lack of distinction on the part of foremen and management, between men and jobs. For this reason, many firms regard job evaluation as a prerequisite to effective employee rating.[2]

Measuring Performance, Performance Rating, and Measuring and Rating Employee Performance

These three differently described employee rating systems are commonly misconstrued. The expressions have long been regarded as terms that refer to the setting of *performance standards* or *time-rate standards of output* in time studies for productivity control. Performance rating for leveling the quantity of work to be performed by the average worker (normal output), as well as performance rating tables, has been used widely since 1925 by time study engineers.[3]

Employee evaluation, on the other hand, is the evaluation and recording of a worker's value on his job, as expressed by the judgment of his superior and other raters in terms of selected, well-defined factors that are graded in degrees. Factor grading in degrees is considered reliable enough to be accepted as *objective judgment* in establishing criteria for transfer, promotion, wage-base rate increases, wage incentives, and other benefits to the employee as well as to the employer. As explained later, measurements in quantitative and qualitative units are a part of employee rating only under specific conditions. In most enterprises the rater can obtain quantity and quality data from the production control departments.

Merit Rating

Although the expression merit rating is used considerably, its meaning is not always properly understood. "Merit" denotes a praiseworthy quality deserving a reward. This definition, however, could be misleading. When his status is being evaluated, a worker may get a false impression. The assumption is, "I am going to get a raise or be promoted because the 'old man merit rated' me." In reality, just the opposite may occur. He may be told that he must be on the job on time or he must improve his work, otherwise he will be demoted or transferred to a

---

[2]*Studies in Personnel Policies*, No. 8 (New York: National Industrial Conference Board, 1938).

[3]For a discussion of performance rating in time study, the reader is referred to Chapter 15.

lower paid job. Of course, "merit" in its true sense means a token of approval, excellence, or punishment, as well as reward. But, generally, the rank-and-file employee thinks of "merit" only in terms of excellence or reward.

The term merit rating is also used in connection with taxation for social security benefit payments. Employers are taxed a certain percentage of their payrolls for the unemployment insurance program. To encourage stabilized employment, however, some states provide an incentive for employers by reducing their tax rates or by allowing complete exemption from the payroll tax. The tax saving may then be credited against the employer's federal tax payment as if it were actually paid. The procedure of attaining the tax reduction is termed merit rating. [4]

Thus, it can be readily appreciated that the more concerned we are with the acceptance of clear and accurate terminology, the less irritation and confusion will be experienced in setting up an acceptable wage and salary structure for employees.

Evolution of employee evaluation

Employee evaluation is not new. It has existed informally for centuries. When wages and salaries had to be determined, employers always judged and evaluated employees on their personality and behavior as well as on their proficiency and skill. Many governmental agencies, including the Army and the Navy, used informal ratings during the nineteenth century.

First Formal Plan

The first formal employee "merit rating" plan in industry is credited to Robert Owen, a Scottish cotton-mill owner, who started a set of "character books" at the beginning of the nineteenth century. According to Professor Yoder's report, "Each employee had such a book in which his daily reports were recorded, and each was also provided with a character 'block,' each side of which was colored differently and represented an evaluation of the employee ranging from bad to excellent. The blocks were displayed on the worker's bench." [5]

First Department Store Plan

In 1915, Lord & Taylor's department store of New York introduced a "rating sheet for salespeople" that proved to be most successful in rating employees. The rating system included such factors as health, appearance,

---

[4]Herman Feldman, "Merit Rating in Job Insurance," *Personnel Journal* (September, 1935), pp. 86–93.
[5]Dale Yoder, *Personnel Management and Industrial Relations* (New York: Prentice-Hall, Inc., 1948), p. 327.

manner, initiative, industry, accuracy, loyalty, cooperation, responsibility, and knowledge.[6]

Influence of World War I

In 1917, Dr. Walter Dill Scott was chosen by the United States Army to select a group of psychologists and army officers to prepare a testing and rating system that would enable army officers to judge and rate draftees for proper placement, promotion, and better service. Thus, the army rating scale, also known as the man-to-man rating scale, came into being.

After World War I (1919), psychologists, as well as former enlisted men and army officers, used the army rating scale to introduce the testing and rating system into commerce and industry. This resulted in the employment of psychologists on a full-time and consulting basis by large and medium-size companies. The psychologists then introduced employment tests, rating systems, and, in general, made radical changes in the employment procedures and in personnel management.[7]

Acceptance of Employee Evaluation Plans

In 1923, the Classification Act set up basic rules for the rating and grading of government employees. Thereafter, employee evaluation was introduced at such a rapid pace that many employers depended solely on ordinary human judgment to rate others, and overlooked the shortcomings and difficulties involved. Of 195 companies with approximately 2,390,000 employees, surveyed by a group of personnel consultants in 1930, 41 percent used employee evaluation and rating. Members of the same group made a survey in 1953, covering 628 companies with 4,900,000 employees, which showed that 61 percent used employee evaluation.[8] A survey of 852 firms completed in 1958, indicated that 66 percent use formal employee evaluation.[9]

A survey by the National Industrial Conference Board in 1930 disclosed that 94 companies employing 618,127 persons had formal rating plans, some of which were started in 1923 or earlier.[10] In 1938, The American Iron and Steel Institute established "Merit Rating of Employees" plans for its members.[11] During the same year, the National Metal Trades Association vigorously introduced employee evaluation among its members.

---

[6]George D. Halsey, *Making and Using Industrial Service Rating* (New York: Harper & Brothers, 1944).

[7]For an interesting discussion of the beginnings in applied psychology, see Scott, Clothier, and Spriegel, *Personnel Management* (5th ed; New York: McGraw-Hill Book Company, 1954), Chapter 15.

[8]*Ibid.*, pp. 615 and 631.

[9]William R. Spriegel and others, *Personnel Practices in Industry* (Austin, Texas: Bureau of Business Research, The University of Texas, 1958).

[10]*Studies in Personnel Policies*, No. 8 (New York: National Industrial Conference Board, 1938).

[11]"Merit Rating of Employees," *Personnel*, Vol. XV, No. 1 (August, 1938).

In 1953, the management department at Northwestern University made a survey to establish the trend and correlation between motion and time study, job evaluation, employee evaluation, and financial incentives. Replies from 203 participating companies, ranging from 56 to 12,000 employees, revealed that 86 percent of the participants use formal employee evaluation.

In 1962 in a study of 185 companies conducted by the St. Louis Chapter of the Administrative Management Society (then, the National Office Management Association), 159 firms (85 percent) reported that they had employee evaluation programs. [12]

Spriegel, who has made periodic studies of employee evaluation since 1930, reports that formal methods of evaluating performance have grown fairly steadily. [13] His studies show that about two thirds of all companies polled have some kind of employee appraisal and that managers, too, are being appraised in 45 to 60 percent of the companies. In a 1968 study of some 681 firms that are using job analysis, 58.8 percent of the firms said they were using job analysis to appraise salaried personnel. [14]

Current Status of Employee Evaluation

Although the statistics would indicate that most large and medium-size companies now have employee evaluation programs, one study of 567 companies showed that 256 companies that once had such programs have since discontinued them. [15] In recent years there has been a growing concern about the effectiveness of evaluation programs. There has also been criticism that the programs require too much time and are too complicated. It would appear that at present we are going through a period of reappraising all the aspects of employee evaluation programs. In an attempt to assist those who are anxious to improve their programs or to establish new ones, we are devoting the remainder of this chapter and all of the next to the fundamentals of employee evaluation. We will begin by discussing the theory of employee evaluation so as to establish a framework of what the process is all about.

Theory of employee evaluation

Although there has been an abundance of material written about employee evaluation, there still appears to be a great deal of confusion regarding its theory

---

[12]St. Louis Chapter, National Office Management Association, "Survey of Hiring Practices, Indoctrination-Evaluation and Release," *NOMA Management Quarterlies*, Personnel, Unit 9 (July, 1962), p. 9.

[13]William R. Spriegel, "Company Practices in Appraisal of Managerial Performance," *Personnel* (May–June, 1962), pp. 78–82.

[14]"Summary of National Job Analysis Methods Survey," by Bureau of Business Research, California State College, Long Beach, and Los Angeles Foundation, California State College, p. 4.

[15]Spriegel, *loc. cit.*

and how an evaluation can be satisfactorily accomplished. Some of the confusion stems from a controversy over whether employees should be evaluated on the basis of the job contributions (results) they produce in the company or on the basis of the employees' characteristics. Historically, the early forms of employee evaluation concentrated heavily on personal traits. More recently, the trend is toward evaluations based on job performance or results. The reason there has been a shift to evaluation by results is that a company pays for results and its success depends upon results. Although an argument can be made that relationships can be found between results and such personal traits as initiative, dependability, and perseverance, it has never been proven that possession of these traits guarantees results. Certainly various personal traits do contribute to job success, but the same set of traits does not always produce the same results. Successful people rarely possess an identical set of personal traits, but they do always produce results, or they would not be considered successful. Thus, certain traits are not always responsible for the results that are obtained.

In order for a firm to determine what should be the proper basis of an employee evaluation, the firm must first decide on what uses it will make of the employee evaluation. In other words, the aims or objectives of the evaluation program determine the criteria to be used in the evaluation process. If the firm plans to use the results of employee evaluation for a variety of purposes such as pay raises, promotions, transfers, and training, the evaluation will need to uncover whatever employee data have a bearing on these purposes.

The Dual Purpose of an Employee Evaluation Program

It would appear that every firm should be interested in evaluating all employees in two major areas. The first is to evaluate each employee on his degree of job success (job performance), and the second is to identify those factors (conditions, circumstances, and personal qualifications) that can improve job performance. In other words, an employee evaluation program should serve a dual purpose. The evaluation of job performance identifies the contributions the employee is presently making toward the success of the company. Therefore, these contributions represent his present value to the company and should be used as the basis for granting wage increases or other awards commensurate with the contributions. The identification and the appraisal of the employee's qualifications serve to evaluate primarily the future value or worth of the employee to the firm. Every employee evaluation program should help the employee discover what he might do to develop himself in order to improve his present job performance (and thereby increase his pay) and also to qualify eventually for a better job. Today, with an ever-increasing population and the unions' demands for an annually increasing standard of living, it is necessary for firms to increase their productivity and efficiency each year. This places a responsibility on all employees to increase their job performance continually in order to earn and enjoy the higher standards of living they are demanding. It also makes it necessary for management to evaluate job performance to see how well the company is doing and who has earned pay raises and to evaluate those job factors and qualifications that are the means of continually improving job performances. Thus, an employee evaluation program really consists of two separate evaluations which may, or may not, be tied to each other. See Figure 14.1 for a graphic presentation of this concept.

Normally, the evaluation of the employee's job performance (his proficiency) consists in gathering data that represent a measure of the quality and quantity of the work performed or the goals or results that he has obtained. In the evaluation of the factors that affect job performance, notations need to be made on only pertinent conditions, circumstances, and employee qualifications. In the evaluation of employee qualifications, data are gathered that represent evidence of the employee's mental and physical abilities, his interests, and his personality. The mental abilities may be expressed in terms of his ability to learn, his knowledge, initiative, ingenuity, alertness, etc. The employee's physical abilities may be expressed in terms of his state of health and vigor, his strength, coordination, manual or finger dexterity, skill, etc. The employee's interests may be expressed in terms of his goals, ambitions, likes, and dislikes. Employee personality is often expressed in terms of character traits such as dependability, friendliness, judgment, cooperativeness, and attitude. An employee evaluation program which identifies the pertinent parts of the above information gives the company vital information that can be translated into the employee's present value to the firm and his potential worth to the firm. Every management should be interested in this information if it hopes to survive tomorrow's competition successfully. However, too many firms fail to realize that the dual purpose of an employee evaluation program calls for dual ratings rather than one overall employee evaluation rating which tends to cause confusion and is not an accurate appraisal of either an employee's present or anticipated worth.

A basic assumption that must be made in evaluating employees is that all individuals differ. Employees differ in their mental and physical abilities, interests, and personalities; and because of these differences, employee job performance differs. If employees did not differ or if the job performance differences were insignificant, it would be a waste of time appraising employees. The evaluation itself attempts to measure the differences to determine the relative value of the employee to the firm. Differences in employee job performance indicate differences in present values of the employees to the firm, while differences in qualifications indicate differences in potential or future values to the firm. It should be apparent that there should be a relationship between job results and rewards (pay raises) if the firm hopes to motivate and retain competent employees. On the other hand, every firm needs to develop, motivate, and utilize every employee to the utmost; therefore, some knowledge about each employee's

MAJOR AREAS OF AN EMPLOYEE EVALUATION PROGRAM

Evaluation Areas	Examples of Factors Used in the Evaluation Area	What Factors Are Used for:	Explanatory Remarks
(1) Employee Job Performance or Proficiency (Present worth to firm)	Quality and Quantity or Job Goals or Objectives to be obtained, Etc.	To determine basis for rewards (financial and non-financial)	Factors can be assigned weights in accordance with each firm's needs and desires. Overall proficiency rating determines present worth of employee to the firm and the amount of any pay raise or award that is to be granted.
(2) Circumstances, Conditions, and Employee Qualifications that affect employee's job performance (Future worth to firm)	Employee Qualifications: **Mental** { Ability to learn / Job knowledge / Initiative / Ingenuity / Alertness **Physical** { Vigor and Drive / Manual skill / State of health **Other** { Ambition / Dependability / Judgment / Attitude / Etc. and/or Conditions and Circumstances that handicap employee in the improvement of job perfomance	To determine the various causes of high and low performance so as to improve job performance and promotional possibilities of the employee	Factors are useful only insofar as they relate to improvement of an employee's job performance and promotability. Factors may, or may not, be rated so as to produce an overall estimate of promotability, transfer, discharge, etc.

FIGURE 14.1   THE DUAL PURPOSE OF AN EMPLOYEE EVALUATION PROGRAM

personal qualifications is necessary. In short, every firm should have two purposes and two ratings in evaluating employees. The problem the firm faces, then, is to decide what rewards should be given for each of these goals and to communicate this information to all concerned.

Pay Raises — The Primary Reward of Employee Evaluation

In any employee evaluation, pay raises should be the primary reward and should be in proportion or in relation to job performance. If very desirable personal qualifications accompany high job performance, the reward for personal qualifications can be promotion to a higher paying job. If the job performance is only average or below average, personal qualifications may indicate transfer of an employee to a more suitable job, or they may serve to pinpoint the nature and extent of the training the company should offer to the employee to help him become more productive. An evaluation of personal qualifications really serves only to help the employee obtain the opportunity to earn greater pay through self-improvement.

Pay raises should be granted chiefly on the basis of increased job productivity or efficiency. The following reasons are given to support this concept:

1. A company pays for job results because it is only through results that any wage is possible. Therefore, a firm must have job results to be successful.
2. Results can be quantified into more objective measures of job success than personal qualifications. Results are generally more tangible to observe and not only easier to establish but also easier to measure as they are less subjective.
3. Evaluating a person against an objective job standard of success is a much more acceptable method of appraising an employee than comparing him with another employee on character traits, which may cause undue rivalry and animosity. The evaluation can always be performed even if there is no other employee doing a job, whereas making comparisons between employees depends upon at least one other employee presently performing the job.
4. Job performance measured by results is a strong psychological motivator.
5. Evaluating employees by results produces more accurate criteria to use in validating company personnel selection procedures than criteria based upon character traits.

The process of evaluating an employee on the basis of results requires that some performance standard be developed which identifies the various degrees of job success. The development of such a yardstick is difficult, and many firms have failed to produce a satisfactory one. This may be the reason that a number of companies are not completely satisfied with their employee evaluation plans. Once a suitable standard is formalized, it is a simple matter to evaluate an employee by comparing his performance with the job performance yardstick.

In short, to evaluate properly an employee for a pay raise, the following steps must be carried out:

1. An identification of a number of levels (at least three) of job performance for each job in the firm.
2. The compilation of data on each employee for a period of time to determine what his job performance record has been.
3. A comparison of the employee's actual job performance record with the job performance standards (yardstick) to determine what rating the employee has earned.

An explanation follows on how each of these three evaluation steps may be executed.

Identification of Job Performance Standards

Every job in a company is assumed to be an asset to that company. That is, the job is supposed to be necessary because it makes a positive contribution toward the success of the company. If this assumption is true, there has to be some minimum level of job performance (in terms of time, service, quality, and quantity) established to indicate whether or not a job is "paying its way." Any job performance below this minimum level would constitute unsatisfactory performance because the job would be costing more than it contributes to the company's success.

The member of management who has direct supervision over the job is probably the most qualified person to determine which job results are an asset and which are not. The immediate supervisor should be able to identify for each job in his area at least three performance levels — unsatisfactory performance, satisfactory performance, and outstanding job performance. It is recommended that, whenever possible, job performance standards be set by mutual cooperation of the supervisor and his employees so that the standards will be readily acceptable to the latter group. There are several ways to establish performance levels for each job. What is unsatisfactory performance may be determined by a study of the performance records of those employees who have failed on the job. Why did the unsuccessful employees fail? What minimum performance is needed for the company to break even? to make money? In a similar manner, the determination of what is satisfactory and outstanding performance can be accomplished by studying the performance records of past and present successful employees. What do successful employees do that makes them a success?

From a study of the successful employees' records, the supervisor can (1) establish the necessary performance standards based on the average (or median) production made by a large number of workers, (2) determine what the ideal worker (a composite of the many workers) could produce, or (3) decide on the average performance expected by noting what the average worker produces.

From known industrial experience and an employee's record study, there should be little difficulty in establishing the various performance standards for the various degrees of job success; and whenever possible, these standards should be as concrete and as objective as possible. Figure 14.2 illustrates the types of data that can be used to accomplish this purpose.

Number of units produced per day (quantity of parts, assemblies, letters, etc.)

Number of transactions completed per day (sales, customers, telephone calls, etc.)

Worth of transactions completed per day ($)

Number of commendations received (during some period of time)

Earnings or commissions earned per month

Quantity and quality of suggestions made that were adopted each month

★ ★

% increase or decrease in profits (according to some period of time)

% increase or decrease in sales or market position (per unit of time)

% increase or decrease in unit costs

★ ★

Number of times raw or in-process inventories have turned over (per unit of time)

Number or % of parts rejected, spoiled, or scrapped (per unit of time or job)

Number or % of errors (clerical or otherwise) **made** (per unit of time or task)

Number of days or % of times absent from work (per month)

Number of chargeable accidents worker has had per unit of time (6 months)

Amount of money lost per month in accidents, scrap, etc.

Number of complaints received (during some unit of time)

FIGURE 14.2 Types of Data Useful As Criteria for Establishing Objective Job Performance Standards

In summary, an identification of the various degrees of job performance can be compiled by answering such questions as: What does an employee have to do to succeed on the job? or get fired? What is the company paying the employee to perform? What job performance (quality and quantity) should be considered as failure? satisfactory? outstanding?

Employees and supervisors who either lack the necessary experience to establish job performance standards or who do not have access to past performance records as a guide will need to estimate what performance can be reasonably expected. Such performance goals, of course, are considered temporary and must be adjusted as experience is gained. It is much better to make an educated guess and establish some temporary performance standards than to have no standard at all. There can be no employee evaluation without a job performance standard for comparison. Although temporary standards have the disadvantage of having to be altered, they are the means of eventually arriving at more accurate and practical standards.

There are some jobs in every organization for which the establishment of concrete performance standards may prove difficult. Jobs involving engineering, administration, and professional and technical work are typical examples that appear to defy the setting of performance standards. These are nonroutine jobs that are dynamic and constantly changing. Because of this, these jobs generally require short-range performance objectives or standards. A basis for evaluating the employees on these jobs may be made by having the employee and his superior establish some reasonable performance goals or objectives to be attained within a period of time (say 6, 9, or 12 months). If these goals are in keeping with the company objectives, the goals then become the job performance standards expected and are a means of evaluating the employee's success on the job for the period of time specified. This process of establishing job performance standards and evaluating employees on nonroutine jobs is often called *employee evaluation by objectives.*

If this first step of identifying various concrete job performance standards for each job is not carried out, the supervisor has only one alternative in evaluating employees — comparing their performances with each other. This method could give a performance ranking of the various employees, but the validity of the evaluation is questionable because there has been no performance standard established as to what is satisfactory or unsatisfactory. It may even be that the performances of all the employees are unsatisfactory. Or, they may all be above average. A firm might not realize soon enough that it is losing money on a job unless the minimum performance that is necessary for the job to be an asset to the company has been first determined as objectively as possible. It is very difficult to determine sound job performance standards when they are primarily based on people rather than on job requirements because emotions, personalities, friendships, social pressures, and other human factors are present that can distract and influence the correct setting of adequate performance standards.

Compilation of Employee Job Performance Data

Compiling employee performance data involves some systematic method for recording and keeping track of employee progress from one employee evaluation period to the next. Most companies have a permanent record folder for each employee that contains a formal rating form to record unusually good or poor performance. For identifying individual performance of factory workers, it may be only a question of looking over the various records such as worker production, scrap, earnings, and punctuality that are readily available in the plant. Some raters employ the technique of keeping an employee record of critical incidents (unusually good and poor performances) as a factual basis for evaluating their employees. Appropriate objective notations should be entered periodically by the employee's immediate supervisor on the employee evaluation form that eventually becomes part of the employee's permanent record folder. Record keeping is essential in order to determine the current and past performances that have been achieved and to aid in setting job standards. Records can then be used to identify what success rating each employee's performance warrants. True employee evaluations are based upon the whole record compiled since the last employee evaluation, not on just what the employee did last week or today.

Comparison of Employee Job Performance with Job Standards of Success

The last step in the employee evaluation process is to compare the worker's performance since his last evaluation with the established job performance standards to determine what rating the employee has earned. This step can be very simple or complex. It is a very simple operation to compare the output of a production worker with the output expected. For example, if a punch-press operator punches out 600 metal discs per hour, it is easy to see that, when compared with the following performance standards, the operator has earned the rating of "above average":

QUANTITY STANDARD	EVALUATION	
0–399 /hr.	Unsatisfactory Performance	
400–499 /hr.	Marginal	"
500–599 /hr.	Average	"
600–699 /hr.	Above Average	"
700 & up /hr.	Outstanding	"

Evaluating worker performance ceases to be a very simple step when there are several criteria that have to be considered to arrive at an overall evaluation. For example, a production worker's performance may be expected to include both quantity and quality so that the overall evaluation would be arrived at from the table at the top of the next page.

The overall evaluation above considers not only the number of pieces produced (quantity) but also the percent of pieces that are satisfactory (quality). The evaluator has to know whether the quantity and the quality are each worth 50 percent of the total evaluation or whatever weights have been assigned to them. When more than two criteria are used, the problem of total evaluation becomes more complicated because appropriate weights have to be assigned to

TABLE 14.1

JOB PERFORMANCE STANDARDS

Quantity Standard	Evaluation	Quality Standard	Evaluation
0–399 pcs./hr.	30%	12–15% rejects	10%
400–499 pcs./hr.	40%	9–12% "	15%
500–599 pcs./hr.	50%	6– 9% "	20%
600–699 pcs./hr.	60%	3– 6% "	25%
700 & up pcs./hr.	70%	0– 3% "	30%

Quantity Evaluation + Quality Evaluation = Employee Evaluation

Key to Employee Evaluation Rating:

85%–100% = Outstanding Performance
70%– 85% = Above Average   "
55%– 70% = Average   "
40%– 55% = Marginal   "
0%– 40% = Unsatisfactory   "

each criterion. Various examples of evaluation criteria and the weights that companies have assigned to them are illustrated in the next chapter. We turn now to the various methods and techniques that have been used successfully in the employee evaluation process.

Methods of employee evaluation

The various employee evaluation methods, also known as "types," "plans," and "systems," are more or less tied up with the kind of scales, processing procedures, or types of forms used. There are no accepted standards as to which method is the best for all purposes. Before a definite method or plan is adopted, the existing methods, if any, should be studied, and their advantages and disadvantages weighed to ascertain which method will best conform with the formulated objectives. Methods of employee evaluation may be thought of as different approaches to the measuring of the employee's worth. Each method should attempt to achieve maximum objectivity and minimum subjectivity so that the evaluation results can be considered valid and acceptable.

The extremely large variety of employee evaluation methods may be divided into five specific "basic" groups which will be discussed in the following order:

1. Simple ranking and order-of-merit methods.
2. Man-to-man comparison method.
3. Rating scale method.
4. Checklist method.
5. Employee evaluation by objectives.

Simple Ranking and Order-of-Merit Methods

Probably the least sophisticated of the various employee evaluation methods available to employers are the simple ranking and order-of-merit methods.

Simple Ranking Method. The *simple ranking* method, also known as the *grading* method, is an old one. Before systematic and methodical employee evaluation was developed, employers classified their employees by ranks. Thus, an employer or supervisor would designate John Jones as the best, George Miller as second best, Joe Crawford as third, and so on down the line until he had evaluated the entire employee group. They were rated on their overall usefulness and value to the organization. No attempt was made to describe and to evaluate their performances, traits, qualifications, or characteristics. The simple ranking method lends itself to use only in very small organizations (less than 25 employees) and then only when a suitable criterion is established as a basis for the rating. Without the use of an acceptable rating criterion, the employees and the rater are in a quandary as to how the ratings can be justified.

Order-of-Merit or Rank Order Method. With the advent of specialization and expansion in commerce and industry, ranking had to take on a more refined form. This led to the *order-of-merit* method, also known as the *rank order* method. The rater grades the employees as a group in rank order from highest to lowest on the merits of performance and other characteristics. The rater assigns the highest number to the best performer and the lowest number (1) to the poorest performer. The order-of-merit method is an improvement over the simple ranking method only when the order-of-merit method uses more than one criterion as a basis for the evaluation. For each criterion that is used as a basis for evaluating employees, a separate ranking is required. Thus, the order-of-merit method represents a pooling or an average of several rankings. Its success depends on how well the employees accept the criteria used for the rankings and how much respect the employees have for the rater's honesty.

Forced Distribution. To provide distinctions in the grouping of employees, the *forced distribution* method is utilized. An overall ranking of employees that meets a statistical standard is thus obtained. The forced distribution method is based on the principle that the abilities of a group follow a normal distribution, with very few at the bottom, very few at the top, and the majority falling in between. According to those who favor this method,[16] workers are rated on two factors, Job Performance and Promotability. All other factors recognized and proven to be useful in evaluating employees are either combined in these two

---

[16]Joseph M. Dooher and Vivienne Marquis, *Rating Employee and Supervisory Performance* (New York: American Management Association, 1950), p. 18.

factors or are eliminated. It is claimed that "job performance is the basic factor in determining an employee's value," and all other factors contribute to the employee's job performance.

Forced distribution differs from ordinary ranking and comparison methods in that a five-position percentage scale of 10-20-40-20-10 is provided for the job-performance factor, thus forcing the rater to evaluate the employees in five distinct groups. Accordingly, the rater allocates 10 percent of the group as highest, 20 percent next highest, 40 percent at the middle, 20 percent next to the lowest grade, and 10 percent as the lowest grade, as illustrated in Figure 14.3. After computing, on the basis of the percentages indicated above, the number of employees that will fall into each of the five subgroups, the employees are given rating numbers 1, 2, 3, 4, or 5, depending upon the position they hold within the subgroup. No descriptive phrases are provided for the scale numbers. On the back of each rating sheet, however, a list of factors is provided for the rater to indicate the reason for his overall job performance rating.

The advantage of this method is that it "forces" the supervisor to eliminate rating too many on the highest or middle scale. Obviously, the rater will not

---

EMPLOYEE RATING CHART

Dept. No. 25

Employee's Name Joe Jackson   Rated by F.Kuhn   Position Foreman   Date Rated 7/18/--

JOB PERFORMANCE: INSTRUMENT TESTING

( )   (X)   ( )   ( )   ( )
Highest 10%   Next high 20%   Middle 40%   Low 20%   Lowest 10%

POSSIBILITIES FOR PROMOTION

(X)   ( )   ( )
Promotable   Possible   Unlikely

FIGURE 14.3 FORCED DISTRIBUTION CHART FOR EMPLOYEE RATING

express himself in favor of the poorest workers as medium or fair, since he is "forced" to place them among the lowest 10 percent.

For the promotability rating as shown in Figure 14.3, a three-position scale indicates which employees are *promotable*, those *likely to be promoted*, and those who *should not be promoted*.

Man-to-Man Comparison Method

The *man-to-man comparison* method, also known as the *army rating scale*, has some characteristics of the rank order method, but differs distinctly from it in that the method provides a rating scale expressed in points. The man-to-man comparison method was developed during World War I for rating all commissioned officers periodically during their service and prior to separation from service. The original army rating method is based on five factors. Each factor is separately described on a master chart and rated in five grades: highest, high, middle, low, and lowest, with a number of points for each degree resulting in a possible maximum of 100 points and a minimum of 20 points. The five factors and range of grade points possible are:

1. Physical Qualities......................(highest 15 — lowest 3)
2. Intelligence..........................(highest 15 — lowest 3)
3. Leadership...........................(highest 15 — lowest 3)
4. Personal Qualities.....................(highest 15 — lowest 3)
5. General Value to the Service............(highest 40 — lowest 8)

A number of key men are chosen as "standard," their names placed on cards, and then rated by the rating officer using one factor at a time. The highest rated man is placed at the top and the one considered lowest at the bottom, as the two "anchor men." One each is then selected for the middle, and halfway on each side of the middle. All men to be rated are sorted in relation to the five "standard" key men in each of the five basic factors.

In industry, each rater develops his own master chart to serve as a standard for comparison. For example, assume the rater wishes to establish his standard for the factor Dependability. He will proceed to establish his chart as illustrated in Figure 14.4, selecting the most highly dependable man he knows, or has known before, for the highest grade. Similarly, he chooses the poorest or least reliable for the lowest grade, with three others in between. The rater then compares all his men to be rated with those on the chart. Suppose Hans Miller is to be rated. Then the rater questions himself whether Miller compares with George Jackson or with Arthur Roberts. He finally decides that Miller compares closest to John Shultz. Accordingly, Miller gets 16 points. In the same manner the rater compares all men with the anchor men on other factors and then totals the ranked points for each man.

Failure of the Man-to-Man Comparison Method. The man-to-man comparison method served its purpose better than any other ranking plan; nevertheless, it failed in industry because of its burdensome application. In the first place, the method depends upon the sole acquaintanceship of one rater with the five men used as the standard for comparison; thus his comparisons will never agree with those of another rater. Secondly, it is evident that a separate master chart is required for each factor to be rated, with a different grade for each of the five anchor men. Referring to Figure 14.4, Jackson is highest for Dependability but may be lowest for Quantity of Work.

EMPLOYEE EVALUATION AND RATING

MASTER CHART

RATER: John Jones   **COMPARISON FACTOR:** Dependability

Consider the manner in which the employee applies himself to his job. Does he carry out instructions? Is he reliable, accurate, and thorough?

Descriptive Rating	Anchor Men	Grade	No. of Points	Employees Rated
Justifies utmost confidence. Requires no supervision.	Geo. Jackson	Highest	20	
Applies himself well. Only occasional supervision required.	John Shultz	High	16	Hans Miller
Fairly reliable. Needs average supervision.	Frank Henry	Middle	12	Joe Fritz F. Nelson Arthur Cheske
Willing but needs frequent follow-up.	Ed Hughes	Low	8	
Unreliable. Needs constant supervision.	Arthur Roberts	Lowest	4	John Smith

FIGURE 14.4 MAN-TO-MAN COMPARISON MASTER CHART

Paired-Comparison Method. Another method that falls in the man-to-man comparison category is the *paired-comparison* method in which each employee is paired with every employee in the group employed on the job. It is left to the supervisor or rater to decide by comparison which of the two employees paired is more valuable. The rater then either underlines the name of the preferred employee, or crosses out the one that is not as desirable. The employee's score is established by counting the number of times his name is underlined. After all employees of a group have been compared, a list is prepared to show the rank of each employee in order of merit, according to the number of times his name was underlined. Figure 14.5 illustrates the method of pairing six employees. The ranking of the names involved is: (1) Sanczuk (highest); (2) Boldt; (3) Smith; (4) White; (5) Gunner; and (6) Gregg, who was not underlined, lowest.

EMPLOYEE COMPARISON RATING

RATER Carl Smith   TITLE Foreman   DEPT. NO. 627   DATE RATED 8/21/--

---

TO THE RATER: Judge your employees on the basis of their present jobs. Pair the comparison of each factor separately, regardless of comparison on the other factors (characteristics). Be sure to underline the name of the employee who, in your judgment, is the superior of the two. Your comparison should be based on the questions affecting the characteristic.

FACTOR TO BE RATED: Attitude

Questions:
Is the employee an exceptionally good team worker?
Is he going out of his way to cooperate with others?
Is he always receptive to changes and new ideas?

EMPLOYEES' NAMES: Adolph Boldt, Dave Gregg, John Gunner, Edward Sanczuk, George Smith, Arnold White

Boldt — Gregg	White — Boldt	Gregg — Smith
Gregg — Gunner	White — Gregg	Gunner — Boldt
Gunner — Sanczuk	White — Gunner	Gunner — Smith
Sanczuk — Smith	White — Sanczuk	Sanczuk — Boldt
Smith — White	Gregg — Sanczuk	Smith — Boldt

FIGURE 14.5 PAIRED-COMPARISON METHOD

The paired-comparison method is applicable only to very small groups (up to 10 or 12 employees). Considering the fact that in a group of 30 employees, over 430 comparisons have to be made, it is obvious that the job of rating large groups becomes burdensome and time-consuming.

Rating Scale Methods

A variety of *rating scale* methods is used advantageously to overcome the shortcomings of subjective ranking ratings. The design of rating scales serves the specific purpose of saving time, utilizing a technique that calls for "objective judgment." In general, the mechanics provide defined factors (traits, characteristics) at the left of the chart or rating form as illustrated in Figure 14.6. In

EMPLOYEE RATING CHART

Office.............................Date............ Total Points.................................

Name.. Rated by ....

Position.. Approved................................

1. QUANTITY OF WORK: Some employees are capable of unusually high, sustained output. They know their jobs thoroughly and consistently produce more than is expected of the average employee.
   Others produce what is expected of them and have a good general knowledge of their jobs. They may produce at a relatively steady pace or they may work rapidly at times with corresponding periods of below-average output.
   Still others produce very little more than is required as a minimum necessary to hold their jobs.
   Somewhere between the extremes will be found varying degrees of work output. Consider this employee carefully on the basis of what you have observed since the date you last rated him. Write in specific examples of behavior on which your judgment is based.

   | 1 Unusually High | 2 | 3 Average | 4 | 5 Minimum |

2. QUALITY OF WORK: Some employees consistently turn out work of high quality. They rarely make mistakes. When they finish an assignment it is complete, with no loose ends.
   Others usually turn out acceptable work with an average number of errors.
   Still others make frequent mistakes. Their work lacks neatness and is usually

   | 1 Consistently High | 2 | 3 Average | 4 | 5 Frequent Mistakes |

   He should be rated carefully on the basis of what you have observed since you have last rated him. Write in examples:

6. ABILITY TO DEVELOP: Some employees have great capacity for growth. They absorb and retain from their experience so that they become constantly more valuable to their employer. Their judgment matures and improves as they learn. Their associates and supervisors tend increasingly to depend on them.
   Other employees never seem to learn beyond the immediate demands of their job. They never contribute a new idea and never impress anyone with their capacity for additional responsibility. They never give anyone reason to think of them when promotions are being made.
   Somewhere between these extremes this employee should be rated. Think carefully of specific instances of his performance since the date you last rated him and rate accordingly. Write in examples:

   | 1 "Going Places" | 2 | 3 Average | 4 | 5 Will Never Be Promoted |

FIGURE 14.6 EMPLOYEE RATING CHART WITH FACTOR DEFINITIONS OPPOSITE A CONTINUOUS (GRAPHIC) RATING SCALE

order to evaluate an employee's qualifications and qualities for the purpose of measuring his relative value, the rater is required to check or underscore the rated value on a line with ascending or descending degrees, based on a total of 10, 20, 50, or 100 points.

Rating scales are divided into two systematic classes:

1. *Graphic scales*, also known as *continuous scales*.
2. *Step* or *multiple-step scales*, also known as *discontinuous scales*.

Graphic Rating Scales. The original graphic rating scales were arranged as plain lines without gradations, one end representing the maximum and the other end the minimum. The rater checked the end of the line that suited his opinion of the ratee. This procedure was indeed simple, but crude. The rater needed a more exacting means to provide a method that could be depended upon as a standard to guide him in making decisions. A variation of "continuous" scales was then developed, with the scale usually divided into five to ten degrees, each division indicating a value in points.

Continuous scales are known to be "alphabetical," "numerical," "percentile," and "adjectival" or "descriptive." Each scale measures a specific factor, such as Dependability in Figure 14.7. Usually, the horizontal scale is placed to the right of the defined factors as shown in Figure 14.6.

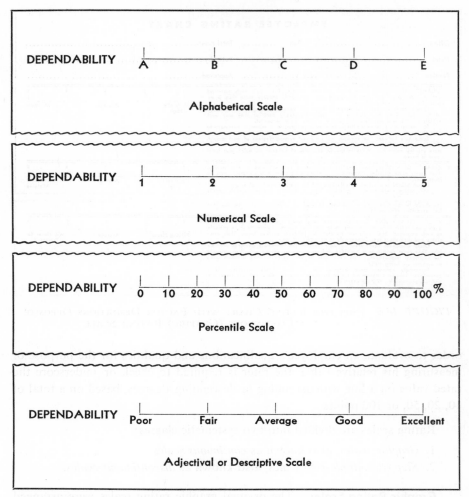

FIGURE 14.7   Continuous Scales, Also Known As "Graphic Scales"

Alphabetical and numerical scales are used where the rating scale is predetermined and the degrees are evaluated by letters or numbers. There are, however, numerous modifications.

Adjectival rating scales, such as "poor," "fair," "average," "good," and "excellent," refer to a grouping of adjectives in ascending order on a line usually divided into five parts. The rater checks the graded adjective that is applicable to the ratee. Descriptive grading or rating may also be a phrase or short sentence. The use of descriptive grading facilitates a common agreement among all raters and helps them to understand better the highest and lowest degrees. A foreman will not hesitate to rate his poorest employee because of the description. Neither will he rate his employees as "best" unless they are equal to the description. Any descriptive phrase in rating, as illustrated in Figure 14.8, is better than the mere adjectives "poor," "fair," "average," "good," and "excellent."

EMPLOYE RATING REPORT
(NON-SUPERVISORY)

NAME_____ NO._____ Department_____ TOTAL POINTS_____ Job_____

Time in this job_____ Total Service_____ Age_____

Date of previous review_____ Date of this review_____

QUANTITY OF WORK: Consider the volume of work produced under normal conditions. Disregard errors. Before checking, consult any production records maintained and compare his output with that of others in the same work.	Very slow worker	Volume below average	Is a normal or acceptable producer	Turns out more work than average	Exceptionally fast. Unusually big producer	
QUALITY OF WORK: Consider accuracy of work, regardless of volume. Before checking, consult any production records maintained and compare the percentage of his bad work with that of others on the same job.	Work almost worthless	Quality below average	Quality acceptable	Quality above average.	Exceptionally accurate.	
KNOWLEDGE OF WORK: Consider his understanding of all requirements of his job which may have been gained through experience or general and special training.	Inadequate knowledge	Some knowledge but requires considerable instruction	Needs but few instructions on usual work	Well informed. Knows all operations except those rarely encountered	Exceptional. Thorough knowledge of all phases of his job	
WORK HABITS: Consider work neatness, safety habits, care of equipment, etc.	Careless and sloppy	Just fair	Passable	Reasonably careful and neat	Habits are excellent	
PUNCTUALITY AND ATTENDANCE: Consider absences and tardiness in the light of their causes.	Record is very unsatisfactory	Record is bad	Record is acceptable	Record is good	Record is excellent	

FIGURE 14.8 EMPLOYEE RATING REPORT WITH DISCONTINUOUS SCALES
Eleven defined factors, 5 descriptive degrees without adjectival degree headings.

The division of a scale depends upon the refinement desired and the rater's ability to judge discriminately. For some raters, however, the fine discriminations proved to be a disadvantage and were impractical. The disadvantages were overcome by the development of the step or multiple-step scales (discontinuous scales).

Step or Multiple-Step Scales. Figures 14.8 and 14.9 illustrate *multiple-step* or *discontinuous* scales. Note that degree adjectives such as "poor," "below average," "average," "good," and "excellent" usually placed at the top have been purposely omitted by the company using form Figure 14.8. It was felt that the rater might be influenced by the degree headings, without reading the words or phrases after each factor for objective guidance.

A widely used and successful type of multiple-step scale is the one developed by the National Metal Trades Association (NMTA), partly shown in Figure 14.9. Four questions are set up as a yardstick against each of the six factors. Each question has two squares that the rater must consider before making his decision, thus assuring more accurate rating. Note part 7 of the instructions, in which the rater is cautioned: "If the specification adequately fits the employee, place an X in the left square. If he does not quite measure up to the specification but is definitely better than the specification for the next lower degree, place an X in the right square." Each square has its rating number, R-1, R-2, etc., which makes it possible to recognize eight different degrees in rating an employee on any one factor in terms of points. In reality, the NMTA method may be regarded as a combination of the graphic scale and the checklist method, since it involves

EMPLOYE RATING REPORT

NAME__________ NO.______ TOTAL POINTS______ GROUP______

DEPT.__________ OCCUPATION__________ CLASS______

RATED BY__________ DATE______ APPROVED BY__________ DATE______

INSTRUCTIONS—Read Carefully

Each employe's ability and fitness in his PRESENT occupation or for promotion may be appraised with a reasonable degree of accuracy and uniformity, through this rating report. The rating requires the appraisal of an employe in terms of his ACTUAL PERFORMANCE. It is essential, therefore, that snap judgment be replaced by careful analysis. Please follow these instructions carefully:

1. Use your own independent judgment.
2. Disregard your general impression of the employe and concentrate on one factor at a time.
3. Study carefully the definitions given for each factor and the specifications for each degree.
4. When rating an employe, call to mind instances that are typical of his work and way of acting. Do not be influenced by UNUSUAL CASES which are not typical.
5. Make your rating with the utmost care and thought; be sure that it represents a fair and square opinion. DO NOT ALLOW PERSONAL FEELINGS TO GOVERN YOUR RATING.
6. After you have rated the employe on all six factors, write under the heading "General Comments" on the back, any additional information about the employe which you feel has not been covered by the rating report, but which is essential to a fair appraisal.
7. Read all four specifications for Factor No. 1. After you have determined which specification most nearly fits the employe, place an X in the small square over it. If the specification adequately fits the employe, place an X in the left square. If he does not quite measure up to the specification but is definitely better than the specification for the next lower degree, place an X in the right square. Repeat for each factor.

FACTOR	R-1 / R-2	R-3 / R-4	R-5 / R-6	R-7 / R-8
What Has He Done?	☐ ☐	☐ ☐	☐ ☐	☐ ☐
1 QUALITY OF WORK THIS FACTOR APPRAISES THE EMPLOYE'S PERFORMANCE IN MEETING ESTABLISHED QUALITY STANDARDS.	DOES HE CONSISTENTLY DO AN EXCELLENT JOB? ARE REJECTS AND ERRORS VERY RARE?	DOES HE USUALLY DO A GOOD JOB? DOES HE SELDOM MAKE ERRORS?	IS HIS WORK USUALLY PASSABLE? MUST YOU SOMETIMES TELL HIM TO DO A BETTER JOB?	IS HE CARELESS? DOES HIS WORK ONLY GET BY? DOES HE OFTEN MAKE MISTAKES?
QUANTITY OF WORK	☐ ☐	☐ ☐	☐ ☐	☐ ☐
Can You Rely on Him?	☐ ☐	☐ ☐	☐ ☐	☐ ☐
5 DEPENDABILITY THIS FACTOR APPRAISES YOUR CONFIDENCE IN THE EMPLOYE TO CARRY OUT ALL INSTRUCTIONS CONSCIENTIOUSLY.	WHEN YOU GIVE HIM A JOB TO DO, HAVE YOU THE UTMOST CONFIDENCE THAT YOU WILL GET WHAT YOU WANT WHEN YOU WANT IT?	DOES HE FOLLOW INSTRUCTIONS AND DO WHAT YOU EXPECT HIM TO DO WITH LITTLE FOLLOW UP?	DOES HE GENERALLY FOLLOW INSTRUCTIONS BUT OCCASIONALLY NEED FOLLOWING UP?	DOES HE REQUIRE FREQUENT FOLLOW UP, EVEN ON ROUTINE DUTIES?
6 ATTITUDE THIS FACTOR APPRAISES THE EMPLOYE'S OPEN-MINDEDNESS, AND HIS WILLINGNESS TO COOPERATE IN CARRYING OUT SAFETY AND OTHER COMPANY POLICIES.	☐ ☐ IS HE AN EXCEPTIONALLY GOOD TEAM WORKER? DOES HE INVARIABLY GO OUT OF HIS WAY TO COOPERATE? IS HE ALWAYS READY TO TRY OUT NEW IDEAS?	☐ ☐ DOES HE MEET OTHERS HALF WAY AND GO OUT OF HIS WAY TO COOPERATE? IS HE USUALLY READY TO TRY OUT NEW IDEAS?	☐ ☐ DOES HE USUALLY COOPERATE, BUT WITH SOME RELUCTANCE TO ACCEPT SUGGESTIONS AND TRY OUT NEW IDEAS?	☐ ☐ DOES HE COOPERATE ONLY WHEN HE HAS TO? IS HE UNWILLING TO TRY OUT NEW IDEAS? DOES HE HAVE LITTLE INTEREST IN HIS JOB?

FIGURE 14.9 NMTA DISCONTINUOUS (MULTIPLE-STEP) SCALE
Combining graphic scale with checklist method.

some features of both. For any of the rating scale methods to be effective, both the employees and the rater must have a clear understanding of the performance standards that are represented by each rating step or division on the rating scale.

Checklist Method

The *checklist* method, also known as the *factor comparison rating plan*, is composed of numerous statements concerning a certain activity or performance, using phrases or questions that refer to a specific factor. The rater checks the statement in a space provided as shown in Figure 14.9, or answers by checking "yes" or "no" after the question describing the appropriate characteristic of the ratee, as illustrated in Figure 14.10. Some checklists, like those illustrated in Figure 14.11, require a check mark ($\sqrt{}$) for "adequate," a minus sign ($-$) for "weak," and a plus sign ($+$) for "outstanding." A numerical value, graded according to high or low performance, or according to the evaluation of a trait, is provided for each statement or question. The complete rating is determined from a total of all statement values.

The checklist method forces the rater to think critically about the employee's performance in terms of its important factors and to make a study of the employee's specific strengths and weaknesses. By answering the specific questions posed, the rater tends to think more systematically about his subordinate and to suppress some of the bias and subjectivity that are connected with the simple ranking and order-of-merit methods. The specific statements that the rater has

FACTOR	DESCRIPTIVE QUESTIONS	Check Answer	
		YES	NO
ATTITUDE			
	1. Is the employee an exceptionally good team worker?		
	2. Does he go out of his way to cooperate with others?		
	3. Is he receptive to changes and new ideas?		
	4. Does he have a constructive attitude toward his company?		
	5. Does he have a constructive attitude toward his associates?		
ADAPTABILITY			
	1. Does he learn new duties quickly?		
	2. Does he adjust himself to new conditions without difficulty?		
	3. Does he apply himself to new work without difficulty?		
	4. Is he willing to learn when a new situation arises?		

FIGURE 14.10 "Yes and No" Checklist

U. S. CIVIL SERVICE COMMISSION

REPORT OF
EFFICIENCY RATING

ADMINISTRATIVE–UNOFFICIAL   ( )
OFFICIAL:
REGULAR ( )   SPECIAL ( )
PROBATIONAL ( )

As of .... based on performance during period from .... to ....

....
(Name of employee)   (Title of position, service, and grade)

....
(Organization—Indicate bureau, division, section, unit, field station)

ON LINES BELOW MARK EMPLOYEE		CHECK ONE:

√ if adequate
– if weak
+ if outstanding
	1. Study the instructions in the Rating Official's Guide, C. S. C. Form No. 8828A.
	2. Underline the elements which are especially important in the position.
	3. Rate only on elements pertinent to the position.
	   a. Do not rate on elements in *italics* except for employees in administrative, supervisory, or planning positions.
	   b. Rate administrative, supervisory, and planning functions on elements in *italics.*
		Administrative, supervisory, or planning.......... ☐
		
		All others.......... ☐

_____ (1) Maintenance of equipment, tools, instruments.
_____ (2) Mechanical skill.
_____ (3) Skill in the application of techniques and procedures.
_____ (4) Presentability of work (appropriateness of arrangement and appearance of work).
_____ (5) Attention to broad phases of assignments.
_____ (6) Attention to pertinent detail.
_____ (7) Accuracy of operations.
_____ (8) Accuracy of final results.
_____ (9) Accuracy of judgments or decisions.
_____ (10) Effectiveness in presenting ideas or facts.
_____ (11) Industry.
_____ (12) Rate of progress on or completion of assignments.
_____ (13) Amount of acceptable work produced. (Is mark based on production records? _____)
                                (Yes or no)
_____ (14) Ability to organize his work.
_____ (15) Effectiveness in meeting and dealing with others.
_____ (16) Cooperativeness.
_____ (17) Initiative.
_____ (18) Resourcefulness.
_____ (19) Dependability.
_____ (20) Physical fitness for the work.

_____ (21) *Effectiveness in planning broad programs.*
_____ (22) *Effectiveness in adapting the work program to broader or related programs.*
_____ (23) *Effectiveness in devising procedures.*
_____ (24) *Effectiveness in laying out work and establishing standards of performance for subordinates.*
_____ (25) *Effectiveness in directing, reviewing, and checking the work of subordinates.*
_____ (26) *Effectiveness in instructing, training, and developing subordinates in the work.*
_____ (27) *Effectiveness in promoting high working morale.*
_____ (28) *Effectiveness in determining space, personnel, and equipment needs.*
_____ (29) *Effectiveness in setting and obtaining adherence to time limits and deadlines.*
_____ (30) *Ability to make decisions.*
_____ (31) *Effectiveness in delegating clearly defined authority to act.*

STATE ANY OTHER ELEMENTS CONSIDERED

_____ (A) ....
_____ (B) ....
_____ (C) ....

STANDARD Deviations must be explained on reverse side of this form	Adjective Rating		Adjective Rating
Plus marks on all underlined elements, and check marks or better on all other elements rated..............................	Excellent	Rating official..	....
Check marks or better on all elements rated, and plus marks on at least half of the underlined elements.................	Very Good		
Check marks or better on a majority of underlined elements, and all weak performance overcompensated by outstanding performance..............	Good	Reviewing official..	....
Check marks or better on a majority of underlined elements, and all weak performance not overcompensated by outstanding performance............	Fair		
Minus marks on at least half of the underlined elements............................	Unsatisfactory		

Rated by ....
           (Signature of rating official)   (Title)   (Date)

Reviewed by ....
           (Signature of reviewing official)   (Title)   (Date)

Rating approved by efficiency rating committee .... Report to employee ....
                                     (Date)   (Adjective rating)

FIGURE 14.11   RATING FORM USED BY THE UNITED STATES CIVIL SERVICE COMMISSION

to study have several advantages. They provide a concrete basis for discussion with the subordinate, give useful data to check the employee's progress, and provide specific information for management's review. The checklist method appears to be psychometrically sound as it follows a number of established principles of psychological test construction in terms of item analysis, score distribution, reliability, and validity.

Employee Evaluation by Objectives

One of the most recent methods to be devised for evaluating employees is the concept known as evaluation by objectives (or measurement by results). This method is based on the premise that the only real measure of how individuals perform is whether they achieve specific results. In this method, a number of short-range goals (targets or objectives) are established that appear to be within the capabilities of the employee to perform. The goals may be established by the employee, the supervisor, or both. The goals become the job performance standards upon which the employee is to be evaluated for the period of time for which the goals were established.

For example, an employee and his supervisor might each make up a list of, say, five to ten goals or specific objectives that each believes should be achieved by the employee within a definite period of time (usually 6, 9, or 12 months). The employee and his superior show each other their lists and, through discussion, decide on the more important goals that contribute to the overall department and company objectives. For best results, the goals need to be within the reach and control of the employee attempting them; otherwise it would be unfair to evaluate the employee on activities outside his accountability. An example of the goals or results that a sales representative and his superior might have agreed upon to be met within the next 12 months is shown in Figure 14.12.[17]

The goals in Figure 14.12 are expressed in relative objective terms that can be easily measured at most any period of time. Figure 14.13 shows the actual employee evaluation that was made at the end of the year.[18] Note the actual results that the sales representative achieved on each goal and the corresponding ratings he received. His overall rating of superior was based on an interpretation of the individual ratings. From the evaluation of the sales representative's job performance, an individual development program was proposed to assist him in his present job and to aid him in preparing for a future promotion. Figure 14.14 outlines the proposal that was drawn up.[19] Counseling the employee and assisting him to help himself are a vital part of any employee evaluation program if either the company or the employee is to get the most from the employee performance appraisal.

The method of evaluating employees by objectives is quite a departure from the majority of traditional methods of evaluation that have been in use. In the first place, each employee has his own individual set of job performance standards to be achieved, and he is generally well versed in how they will be measured. Second, the employee usually is the key person in the establishment of the goals or job performance standards to be met. Third, the evaluation is primarily job

---

[17]R. C. Johnson, "A Practical Approach to Management by Objectives," *Business Studies* (Denton, Texas: North Texas State University, Spring, 1965), p. 26.

[18]*Ibid.*, p. 27.

[19]*Ibid.*, p. 28.

PERFORMANCE PLANNING, APPRAISAL, AND DEVELOPMENT PROGRAM

Date   January 5, 19—

Name   Brown   James   E.   **Position Title**   Sales Representative
          (Last)   (First)   (Initial)

Location   Denver   **Department**   X Division   **Section**

Attach
Additional   PERFORMANCE PLANNING
Sheets as   GOAL SETTING — OBJECTIVES — END RESULTS EXPECTED
Required   For the forthcoming year 19--.

NOTE: Record below the individual's goals, budgets, and expected end results for the forthcoming year. The accountability as set forth in the individual's position description is also a basis of reference in formulating objectives, goals, and the end results expected.

1. Based upon sales potential, "A" product sales are to be increased 10% over last year's sales.

2. Develop five new accounts or reactivate five inactive accounts during the forthcoming year.

3. Sell an average of six new "B" products per month.

4. Through better planning of trips, reduce automobile expense by 8%.

5. An inventory turnover of 2.25 has been projected for parts for "A" and "B" products.

6. Sell an average of_____feet of "C" product per month.

7. Sell for the year a minimum of six complete turn-key installations of product "D."

Source: North Texas State University

FIGURE 14.12   JOB PERFORMANCE GOALS THAT A SALES REPRESENTATIVE
PLANNED TO MEET

oriented in that the employee is evaluated almost entirely on the results or goals he achieves rather than on his personal traits or qualifications.

Advantages of Employee Evaluation by Objectives. There are many advantages that this method of evaluating employees is believed to have. The more important of these are as follows:

1. Both the employee and his supervisor are in substantial agreement as to the specific evaluation criteria that are to be used for the evaluation. This common understanding of evaluation criteria is generally rare in other evaluation methods. Recent research studies conducted at the General Electric Company have found that job performance improves most when specific goals are established and when the employee participates in the goal-setting procedure.[20]

---

[20]Herbert H. Meyer and others, "Split Roles in Performance Appraisal," *Harvard Business Review*, Vol. 43, No. 1 (January/February, 1965), p. 124.

Attach Additional Sheets as Required	PERFORMANCE APPRAISAL For the current year 19--.					
List Below Current Goals — Objectives End Results Expected and/or Accountabilities Taken from Position Description	**Performance Measures (Descriptions Below)**					
Please Check in Appropriate Column Opposite Each Factor Rated		**1**	**2**	**3**	**4**	**5**
1. Based upon sales potential, "A" product sales are to be increased 10% over last year's sales. Results were a 15% increase.					X	
2. Develop five new accounts or reactivate five inactive accounts during the forthcoming year. Results were five new accounts.				X		
3. Sell an average of six new "B" products per month. Results were an average of eight.					X	
4. Through better planning of trips reduce automobile expense by 8%. Results were a reduction of 3%.			X			
5. An inventory turnover of 2.25 has been projected for parts for "A" and "B" products. Results were turnover of 2.0.			X			
6. Sell an average of_____feet of "C" product per month. Results were an average of_____feet per month.					X	
7. Sell for the year a minimum of six complete turn-key installations of Product "D." Results were six installations.				X		

Individual's Overall Performance Evaluation
(Circle appropriate word describing overall performance)

Unacceptable   Acceptable   Average | Superior | Outstanding

(Performance Measures)

1. Unsatisfactory — Significant improvement required
2. Generally satisfactory — Not fully up to standard. Development or other action needed
3. Fully satisfactory — Normal expectancy performance. Measures satisfactory to all standards
4. Above expectancy — Performance consistently exceeds standards. Contribution is above expectancy overall
5. Exceptional and Outstanding Performance — Performance is of unusually high quality. Contribution is unique and is easily and generally identified and accepted as such.

Source: North Texas State University

FIGURE 14.13 The Employee Evaluation That the Sales Representative Received

Attach Additional Sheets as Required	INDIVIDUAL DEVELOPMENT PROGRAM For the forthcoming year 19--.			
Description of Individual's Development Needs	**Plan for Training and Development of Individual Based on Prescribed Need (Methods and Sources)**	**Proposed Dates To:**		**Date Completed**
		Begin	**Complete**	
Development Plan of Action for Current Position				
1. Needs further development in salesmanship techniques.	1. Enroll in evening or correspondence course on "Principles of Industrial Salesmanship."	1-1	10-1	
2. Employee needs to expand knowledge of "turn-key" product sales.	2. Attend the next training session at the plant.	Next scheduled meeting preferably first half of year.		
3. Needs to expand knowledge of the revisions to "A" product including application and specification.	3. Recommend that the company develop a training course.	Begin as soon as possible	7-1	
4. Automobile operating expenses have been higher than company average.	4. (a) Review of pamphlets on practices relating to economical operations of an automobile.	1-1	3-1	
	(b) Discussion with superior relative to efficient operation of automobile.	1-1	12-31	
Development Plan of Action for Promotion Preparation				
1. In preparing for sales management, needs to learn principles of supervision.	1. Read three books on sales management and management from company library.	2-1	12-31	
2. Should develop knowledge of District Sales Manager's functions.	2. (a) Counseling sessions with District Sales Manager	1-1	12-31	
	(b) Provide vacation relief for District Sales Manager	6-1	6-22	

*Source: **North Texas State University***

FIGURE 14.14 A Proposal for the Development of the Sales Representative (Based on His Evaluation)

2. The subordinate, and most of the time the supervisor, knows at all times how well he is performing. This information can be a source of pleasure and satisfaction if the employee is performing well. On the other hand, if his progress has been less than expected, the employee may be motivated to some action to improve the performance. In most other plans of evaluation, the employee is not likely to really learn how well he is performing until the end of the rating period. In some cases, employees are not even informed then.

3. More teamwork and cooperation between the employee and his superior are generated than in other methods because the two employees concerned are mutually interested in obtaining the same job goals and they are ever aware of the progress that is being made. It is a known fact that employees will invariably work harder toward achieving goals that they themselves have set. The cordial relationship that exists between the employee and his supervisor paves the way for whatever informal discussions and corrective actions may be needed at any time to improve job performance. In other methods of employee evaluation, corrective action would normally not be taken until the end of the evaluation period. It is then sometimes too late to be effective.

4. The evaluation of employees by objectives is a much more flexible method of evaluation than other methods because individualized job performance standards can be adapted to practically any level of employee or to any type or job, no matter how dynamic either may be. This is an especially important advantage because there are many nonroutine jobs that are held by technicians, administrators, scientists, engineers, executives, and the like that almost defy setting performance standards that are acceptable to these employees. Furthermore, the periodic setting of job performance standards means that appropriate standards can usually be set to keep pace with changing technology and progress.

5. This method of evaluating employees for pay raises comes closest to a true merit rating system in which pay increases are earned through productive results.

Limitations of Employee Evaluation by Objectives. No method of evaluating employees has yet been found to be perfect. Some of the limitations and difficulties of evaluating employees by objectives are as follows:

1. It is difficult to know how much weight and monetary reward to place on each of the job performance objectives that has been established for evaluation. As yet, there has not been enough experience to provide adequate guidelines.

2. There are occasions when some difficulties may be experienced in either setting or agreeing upon practical and realistic job performance standards. There is room for honest disagreements between the employee and the supervisor; and there are cases where either one or the other, or both, is inadequate in performing this task. In other situations, individual standards may be difficult to set when output is extremely intangible or where the employee is part of a work team.

3. Evaluating employees by objectives has little chance of success in a firm whose management has failed to (or is unwilling to) define its goals clearly (and the results it expects) and then communicate these to the employees. It is difficult, if not impossible, for employees to establish goals that are in keeping with the firm's goals unless they are informed of the company's forecasts, plans, etc. Likewise, if the management of a firm is autocratic or unreceptive to employee participation and constructive criticism, the method of evaluating employees by objectives may be ineffective.

4. Optimizing individual employee job goals may be destructive of long-run company goals. Unless the various employee job goal objectives are subordinated and coordinated into a total management team effort, there is the danger that an individual or a department may attain the type of results that make it look good; but these results may have been obtained at the expense of other components within the company, and thus they may be detrimental to the long-run best interest of the firm. This difficulty in evaluating employees is also applicable to other methods of evaluating employees and is not peculiar only to the evaluation by results method.

REVIEW QUESTIONS

1. For many years employee evaluation has been considered to be a subjective process. How can this subjectiveness be reduced?

2. What are the main purposes of employee evaluation?

3. Briefly trace the history of employee evaluation.

4. What conditions probably brought about the introduction of formal employee evaluation plans?

5. What are the main benefits that can be obtained from a formal system of employee evaluation?

6. How prevalent has the practice of employee evaluation become in the past ten years?

7. What areas should be covered on the form used to evaluate employees?

8. What are the differences between the evaluation of an employee's job permance and an employee's qualifications?

9. What is the most important assumption that must be made when setting up a plan of employee evaluation? Why?

10. Assume that an employee evaluation has two parts: (1) one that measures production, and (2) one that measures personality. (a) What connection should pay have to each of the two parts? Why? (b) What are the reasons for the two parts?

11. (a) Why may ranking one employee's performance in relation to others give invalid results? (b) How can this be corrected?

12. (a) What methods are available to collect information to evaluate employees once job standards have been set? (b) When would these methods be used?

13. What are the steps involved in employee evaluation?

14. What are the main advantages and disadvantages of the various forms of employee evaluation?

15. Examine the rating scales presented in Figure 14.7, page 382. Can any of these scales be used alone or is some additional information necessary? Why?

16. Why do the authors consider the term "employee evaluation" to be better than "merit rating"?

RESEARCH OR SEMINAR QUESTIONS

1. If an employee complains of being given an unfair employee rating by his immediate supervisor, do you think that there should be some "appeal procedure"? Explain your answer.

2. Should a merit increase be granted to an employee if he has not earned it, even though you think that he will prove to be valuable in the future? Explain your answer.

3. In addition to the facts given in Question 2, you find out that if you do not give the employee a salary increase, he will leave. Will this additional fact change your answer? Explain your reasoning.

4. Because of a tight labor market, an employee is given a job for which he lacks some of the qualifications. Should his performance on those factors be included in the overall evaluation or should these factors be discounted until he has had a chance so gain the necessary qualifications?

PRACTICAL EXPERIENCE ASSIGNMENTS

1. An employee confronts you, the wage and salary administrator, and states that he should be evaluated by objectives rather than by a rating scale plan. The employee has no concrete evidence to support his feelings; he merely regards the present system as inequitable to his particular position. How would you handle such a situation?

2. Design a "Student Evaluation Form" that college teachers and counselors might use as a method of evaluating seniors who are soon to graduate. This form would be a confidential reference check report made available to the person who recruits college seniors for placement in his organization.

3. As a committee member you are requested to study and evaluate the present company employee evaluation plan. Outline a simplified procedure that you would suggest to be followed by such a committee. What criteria would be essential to such a study, taking into consideration any possible conflict of interests within the company, such as among the union, employees, and stockholders?

CASE PROBLEM

14—1. THE SOUNDPROOF INSULATOR COMPANY

Discussing Employee Evaluation with Employees

Warren Jones had just graduated from college and was hired by the local Soundproof Insulator Company. Warren was led to believe at the time of employment that he was shortly to become a supervisor in one of the service departments. Since he was fresh out of college, however, it was felt that he should take the company management training course first and then get at least six months of "seasoning." This he did, and after the six months of experience, Warren heard he had received an employee evaluation rating of "satisfactory." Since Warren had not been informed of the meaning of a satisfactory report, he felt he was performing quite well. In fact, he felt he was really doing so well that he could expect a promotion in the immediate future to the anticipated opening of service supervisor.

About one month after the employee evaluation report, Warren happened to be in another department working on an assignment when a supervisor's manual caught his eye. Since Warren knew he was hired as a potential supervisor and was being groomed for the position, he took the liberty of quickly thumbing through the manual. One of the topics that caught his attention was employee evaluation. To his utter amazement and shock, Warren learned that a person receiving an employee evaluation rating of satisfactory was considered a marginal employee and unless this employee showed definite improvement within a short time, he was to be dropped from the company.

Warren became worried. He didn't know what to think. He could hardly believe that he was a marginal worker since his supervisor had never shown nor mentioned any dissatisfaction with his work or progress. In fact, his supervisor hadn't even discussed the rating with him.

Problems:

1. Identify the wage and salary administration problems that appear to you.
2. If you were Warren, what would you do? Why?
3. What are the advantages and disadvantages of discussing employee evaluations with the employee?
4. Would it be good or poor management practice for Warren's supervisor to discuss Warren's evaluation with him? Why?
5. If this case had come to your attention as a wage and salary administrator, what should you do — if anything? Why?

chapter 15

ESTABLISHING JOB PERFORMANCE STANDARDS AS A BASIS FOR EVALUATING EMPLOYEES

This chapter depicts the various methods that have been used by organizations for establishing the job performance standards that are necessary if employee performance is to be appraised satisfactorily. The idea of establishing job performance standards which can be measured is not a new one, but it seems that few companies have done little more than attempt to establish such standards for repetitive production jobs. The establishing of satisfactory job performance has always been a difficult task. There are those who believe that many jobs, especially managerial jobs, do not lend themselves to accurate measurement. For this reason the establishment of job performance standards has often been neglected or poorly executed. Let us look into the matter by first identifying the nature of job performance standards.

What are job performance standards?

Job performance standards are the various degrees of job results that are expected or associated with the success of a job. Job performance standards are derived from the various duties that are part of every job and found in the job description. Every job has some basic reasons for being in existence. These reasons are to perform certain duties. Each duty is a statement of *what* is to be done (goals to be achieved), *how* it is accomplished (method to use), and *why* it needs to be done (justification). For every duty or goal that is to be achieved, there is some acceptable performance that must be met if the duty (and in turn the job) is to be an asset to a firm. Performance on a job can vary greatly from unsatisfactory to outstanding performance.

Job performance standards indicate what job performances are considered unsatisfactory, satisfactory, and outstanding. Satisfactory job performance is most closely associated with what the average employee who is considered qualified to do the job performs while working at a normal (average) pace. This can be used to determine what is a fair day's work. Sometimes the standard for average job performance is more easily identified by noting what the average performance is for a large group of employees. The work of employees whose job performance is somewhat below the average performance (or is not sufficient for the firm to break even economically) is considered as the unsatisfactory standard. The work of employees whose performance is well above the satisfactory performance of the average employee and who approach an ideal performance is considered as the outstanding job performance standard.

Job performance standards may be described in terms of job quality or quantity or both. The more tangible these standards can be described, the better they can be identified and understood. For example, a satisfactory department store salesman may be expected to wait on 50 customers each day. He may also be expected to average $2 per sale. Thus, the quantity standard for the job is 50, while the quality standard is $2. Some combination of these two considerations should reveal the value of the satisfactory salesman to the company. Job performance standards then become the various performance markers or graduations on a yardstick that may be used to evaluate employee job performance.

The need for job performance standards

There is a definite need for developing job performance standards for each job if management expects to educate its employees on what good performance is and in turn wishes to motivate its employees to be productive and to reward them commensurate with their job results. If wage raises need to be earned, management needs to know what kind of job performance is making money, losing money, and just breaking even. It is through job performance standards that a company can determine whether its employees are marking time, sliding backward, or moving forward. Job standards, therefore, make it easier for management to identify the training needs of employees and in addition serve as a logical and objective basis for promoting one employee over another.

Employees and their supervisors have been known to work under false assumptions. The supervisor too often assumes that his subordinate understands what is expected of him and how well the job must be done. If the job performance standards have not been carefully explained to the employee, he will have to use his own ideas on what constitutes acceptable job performance. His ideas are not likely to coincide with those of the supervisor. In fact, the subordinate may only know that he is expected to do his best and thus have nothing more definite or concrete than this to guide him. Every employee, from the mail boy to the president, needs a knowledge of the job standards for his job in order to give him a realistic picture of his job performance, that is, to alert him on what his performance is and what it should be.

The establishment of job performance standards tends to reduce the guess-work in management. It is difficult to see how any employee can be correctly evaluated unless there is some yardstick of job performance against which to measure him. Thus, any firm that wants to pay a fair day's pay for a fair day's work must somehow first determine the job performance standards for every job in the company.

Basic methods used to set job performance standards

The hierarchy of jobs in an organization can be a complex one. It is the rare firm that is composed of one type of job or jobs containing a narrow range of duties. The more varied the duties and the jobs in a company, the more difficult it becomes to establish job performance standards. Some jobs consist of simple and repetitive tasks, while other jobs are noted for their complex and intangible duties. Since most jobs are a mixture or a combination of the two, having some routine and nonroutine tasks, we shall discuss the methods that are available for establishing job performance standards for both repetitive and nonrepetitive jobs. First, let us clarify the difference between repetitive and nonrepetitive jobs.

Those jobs that consist of a limited number of tasks (or operations) which are regularly repeated to perform work of a routine nature are sometimes re-ferred to as *repetitive* jobs. Assemblers, punch-press operators, sweepers, typists, clerks, and key-punch operators are typical examples of jobs in which the work sequence goes through a cycle or routine that is often repeated throughout the day or hour. These repetitive jobs lend themselves more easily to the establish-ment of concrete job performance standards than do nonrepetitive jobs.

Nonrepetitive jobs, such as maintenance, engineering, supervisory, and research, contain a variety of duties that are generally not performed in a fixed sequence. There is great latitude in performing the tasks according to the job circumstances and conditions which are usually changing and nonroutine. The higher one goes in the job hierarchy in a firm, the more nonrepetitive become the jobs. And the reverse is also true.

It is fundamental that, to establish a satisfactory job performance standard for any job, we must first ask the question "What is the purpose or goal of the job?" The answer to this question must be known by the supervisor and the employee and should be clearly stated in the job description. The lower a job in the job hierarchy of the firm, the less complex is the goal. No matter what the goal or goals of the job, it is necessary to translate it (or them) into some meaningful end results that the job must consistently produce to justify its existence. For example, if the goal of a typist is to "Turn out high-quality letters by typing them accurately and neatly so as to save the time of the department," establishing job performance standards means at least indicating what performance is considered as unsatisfactory, satisfactory, and outstanding. To set the standards for this job, such questions as the following have to be answered: What is a high-quality letter? Is it one with no mistakes or are a number of mistakes allowable? How many? What is the quantity of letters that should be produced each day to be considered as unsatisfactory, satisfactory, and outstanding?

When a job has more than one goal (several duties), it is necessary to identify what performance is unsatisfactory, satisfactory, and outstanding for each of the goals. Likewise, the various goals have to be weighted according to their relative importance and tallied so that an overall rating of the employee's performance can be obtained.

There are five methods commonly used as a basis for establishing job performance standards: (1) past records, (2) work measurement, (3) standard data, (4) work sampling, and (5) estimation. The first four methods are most often used to establish job performance standards for jobs that are basically repetitive, while the fifth method is most often used for nonrepetitive jobs. However, under the proper conditions, one or more of these methods may be used to advantage on a specific job. No one method need have a monopoly on a job. The theory, strengths, and weaknesses of establishing job performance standards by each of the five basic methods are discussed in the paragraphs that follow.

Past Records

Company records may often reveal the amount of satisfactory and unsatisfactory production that has been turned out in the past. By a study of the past performance records of the various employees, it may easily be determined what performance is associated with failure, satisfaction, and promotion. Many people believe that such past performance records on various jobs may, under certain circumstances, be used as a guide in evaluating present employee job performance. The advocates of this method believe that past records are an objective way of determining what an average employee can reasonably be expected to produce in order for the company to break even or to make a fair margin of profit.

Although past production records may be a simple way to set standards, there are some considerations that should not be neglected if this method is to prove a satisfactory basis for evaluating present employees. First, the company must have actual and accurate records. In many cases records have been kept in a slipshod or careless manner and do not reflect true data. Second, the method in which the job was performed should be known and it should be considered as an efficient one. No management should be expected to pay for present production results based on past performances that were achieved in an inefficient or wasteful manner. If the past method is unknown or believed to be obsolete, the production records should not be used unless the job performance standards can be updated according to modern circumstances. Converting past records to present job performance standards is a ticklish feat and might be impossible unless both employees and employer can agree on how this can be done.

Normally, past records are not used to establish job performance standards if other ways are available. When past records are used, they need to be accurate and based on known satisfactory methods of production. In the sales field, past records have been averaged with or combined with estimates of future sales to determine more realistic job standards for the immediate future.

Work Measurement (Motion and Time Study)

One of the most well-known and established methods of determining job performance standards is called *work measurement*. Because work measurement involves the use of *motion and time study*, the technique is often also known by that name.

The work measurement technique is an attempt to have a systematic, consistent, and efficient approach to the measurement and establishment of job performance standards according to good management. Such an approach, if carried out properly, can be explained and justified to the worker. The plant industrial engineer is usually well trained in this technique and is looked upon as the person who is best qualified to establish valid and acceptable job performance standards.

The theory of work measurement embodies the belief that in order to set fair job performance standards, the work of an average fully qualified employee, working at a normal pace, should be measured and used as the basis for comparing other worker performance. In other words, in setting fair job performance standards the average worker should be the model or standard of comparison. It is also a principle of management that a firm should not have to pay for an inefficient or wasteful method of producing goods and services. This means that before the industrial engineer attempts to measure the quantity of work that is produced, he should first ascertain that the method used for the job is a reasonable, efficient one. Usually the industrial engineer spends a reasonable amount of time attempting to find the best or the most efficient way to perform a job before he attempts to measure the time it takes to do the job. However, it is almost an impossible and impractical task to wait until the best method can be found before measuring the job. Thus, some method that is close to the best method is more than likely used. This method is almost invariably far superior to the original method that was first used to perform the job.

Finding the "best method" to perform a job first involves a breakdown of the job into its various tasks or component parts for study and analysis. A *motion study* of the work performed is made to determine whether the motions that the worker goes through are excessive, wasteful, or fatiguing. The industrial engineer attempts to question every motion being made as to whether it is necessary, whether it can be eliminated or shortened, whether it might be transferred to a machine, or done at a better time, or combined with another motion. This procedure thus makes it possible for the worker to eventually work smarter rather than harder. Throughout the years of industrial engineering, research on the motions of people has identified those motions that save time and are effective and productive. Worker motions that cause delays or useless spending of energy or effort are sought out and eliminated by the industrial engineer so that the employees do not become fatigued and ineffective. Worker motions that require the worker to reach unnecessarily or to perform complicated, jerky, or unnatural movements are eliminated. The motion economy laws that have been developed through research are used as a basis of appraising the worker's motions.

After the "best method" has been found for performing the job, the industrial engineer uses a stopwatch to measure the total length of time that the job requires. In this way the actual time to perform a task is found with some degree of accuracy and consistency. The actual time, however, is not used as the time for the work performance standard because most workers could not work at this pace all day without some interruptions and delays, or becoming fatigued. Then, too, the worker may need to wash his hands or attend to other personal needs. This means that a fixed percentage of time must be added to the actual performance time required to do the job in order to allow for the usual delays, fatigue, and personal time needed by employees.

The use of motion and time studies to measure work and establish job performance standards has many advantages when successfully accomplished. From the wage and salary administrator's viewpoint, the motion and time study arrives at a quantifiable or meaningful standard that can be validly used as a basis of pay. Thus, the study can be the basis for determining a fair day's work for a fair day's pay. Other advantages include its usefulness for estimating production costs, figuring delivery dates, and forecasting the number and kind of workers needed. Probably the biggest by-product or benefit resulting from work measurement is the elimination or reduction of ineffective worker motions. Thus, overall management efficiency is increased.

There are some obvious limitations connected with the establishment of job performance standards by the measurement of work through motion and time studies. It is expensive to conduct these studies and to keep detailed records. Unless the job being studied is a fairly repetitive one of at least six months' duration, the cost of the motion and time studies may be prohibitive if this cost is not paid for by comparable savings. Probably the most important limitation is the lack of worker acceptance of this technique, which has been subject to great controversy over the years. Much of the difficulty stems from management's early misuse and abuse of work measurement. In addition, some unions have not helped matters by their negative attitude.

It would appear that the establishment of job performance standards through work measurement and motion and time studies is an excellent method to use when the following conditions are present: (1) Jobs are of a repetitive nature and of long-range duration. (2) Union and management relations are cordial. The union respects management and management respects the union. (3) Management attempts to perform the studies with competency and is willing to listen to reasonable suggestions made by the union or other employees to make the standards acceptable. There can be little hope of success in establishing job standards if either employees or managers are unreasonable or unwilling to keep the common good of the firm and the customer's interest in mind. (4) Honest differences of opinion or disagreements are settled by an impartial umpire or committee.

Standard Data (Predetermined Time Values)

The standard data method is gaining momentum as a means of establishing job performance standards. This method might be thought of as an extension of motion and time studies since it draws entirely on data previously compiled by such studies and catalogued for easy reference. *Standard data,* also known as *predetermined time values,* are time values assigned to the various motions that the worker is expected to perform. By adding all the time values for the motions the worker uses and adding an allowance of time for local conditions (delay, fatigue, personal needs, etc.) a job performance standard can be established without the use of a stopwatch. There are several well-known methods available that have predetermined times established for the basic motions. The more common of these include Motion Time Analysis (MTA), Work-Factor (W-F), Methods Time Measurement (MTM), Methods Time Measurement — General Purpose Data (MTM-GPD), Dimensional Motion Times (DMT), Basic Motion Times (BMT), Universal Maintenance Standards (UMS), and Master Clerical Data (MCD).

To illustrate how standard data may be used to establish a time performance standard, we shall briefly describe the Work-Factor (W-F) method which has classified worker motions into the following eight elements:

1. *Reach or Move* — transporting an object or body member from one point to another.
2. *Grasp* — obtaining manual control of an object.
3. *Preposition* — orienting an object for a subsequent element.
4. *Assemble* — joining two objects together.

5. *Use* — processing time, manually or by machine.
6. *Disassemble* — disengaging two parts.
7. *Mental Process* — seeing, searching, inspecting, and remembering.
8. *Release* — losing manual control of an object.

Considering these eight elements, a Work-Factor analysis of a job consists of writing down the elements in the sequential order of job performance. Thus, the analysis of picking up a part and inserting it into a fixture is: Reach, Grasp, Preposition, Move, Assemble, and Release.

The Work-Factor Company has established time tables that list the time values in .0001 minutes for each of the eight worker movements or elements. To determine the job performance time standard for a job, it is necessary to know what motions the worker goes through, look up the time assigned for each motion, and then add all the times to obtain the total time allowed for the job or task. If a motion is not a difficult one, it is called a BASIC motion. When motions become difficult because they involve weight and resistance, they are listed (coded) as 1 W-F, 2 W-F, etc., with each W-F increasing in time value because more time is needed to perform the more difficult motion. (See Tables 15.1 and 15.2.) If an item is to be moved 12 inches without difficulty, the basic

TABLE 15.1
WORK-FACTOR MOVING TIME TABLE FOR ARM AND LEG
(Time in ten-thousandths of a minute)

Distance Moved, Inches	Basic	Work Factors				Distance Moved, Inches	Basic	Work Factors			
		1	2	3	4			1	2	3	4
(A) Arm — *Measured at Knuckles*						(L) Leg — *Measured at Toe*					
1	.0018	.0026	.0034	.0040	.0046	1	.0021	.0030	.0039	.0046	.0053
2	.0020	.0029	.0037	.0044	.0050	2	.0023	.0033	.0042	.0051	.0058
3	.0022	.0032	.0041	.0050	.0057	3	.0026	.0037	.0048	.0057	.0065
4	.0026	.0038	.0048	.0058	.0066	4	.0030	.0043	.0055	.0066	.0076
5	.0029	.0043	.0055	.0065	.0075	5	.0034	.0049	.0063	.0075	.0086
6	.0032	.0047	.0060	.0072	.0083	6	.0037	.0054	.0069	.0083	.0095
7	.0035	.0051	.0065	.0078	.0090	7	.0040	.0059	.0075	.0090	.0103
8	.0038	.0054	.0070	.0084	.0096	8	.0043	.0063	.0080	.0096	.0110
9	.0040	.0058	.0074	.0089	.0102	9	.0046	.0066	.0085	.0102	.0117
10	.0042	.0061	.0078	.0093	.0107	10	.0048	.0070	.0089	.0107	.0123
11	.0044	.0063	.0081	.0098	.0112	11	.0050	.0072	.0094	.0112	.0129
12	.0046	.0065	.0085	.0102	.0117	12	.0052	.0075	.0097	.0117	.0134
13	.0047	.0067	.0088	.0105	.0121	13	.0054	.0077	.0101	.0121	.0139
14	.0049	.0069	.0090	.0109	.0125	14	.0056	.0080	.0103	.0125	.0144
15	.0051	.0071	.0092	.0113	.0129	15	.0058	.0082	.0106	.0130	.0149
16	.0052	.0073	.0094	.0115	.0133	16	.0060	.0084	.0108	.0133	.0153
17	.0054	.0075	.0096	.0118	.0137	17	.0062	.0086	.0111	.0135	.0158
18	.0055	.0076	.0098	.0120	.0140	18	.0063	.0088	.0113	.0137	.0161
19	.0056	.0078	.0100	.0122	.0142	19	.0065	.0090	.0115	.0140	.0164
20	.0058	.0080	.0102	.0124	.0144	20	.0067	.0092	.0117	.0142	.0166
22	.0061	.0083	.0106	.0128	.0148	22	.0070	.0096	.0121	.0147	.0171
24	.0063	.0086	.0109	.0131	.0152	24	.0073	.0099	.0126	.0151	.0175
26	.0066	.0090	.0113	.0135	.0158	26	.0075	.0103	.0130	.0155	.0179
28	.0068	.0093	.0116	.0139	.0159	28	.0078	.0107	.0134	.0159	.0183
30	.0070	.0096	.0119	.0142	.0163	30	.0081	.0110	.0137	.0163	.0187
35	.0076	.0103	.0128	.0151	.0171	35	.0087	.0118	.0147	.0173	.0197
40	.0081	.0109	.0135	.0159	.0179	40	.0093	.0126	.0155	.0182	.0206
Weight Male (Pounds) Fem.	2 1	7 3½	13 6½	Up Up	- -	Weight Male (Pounds) Fem.	8 4	42 21	Up Up	- -	- -

Tables reproduced by permission of the Work-Factor Company, Inc., which holds the copyrights. "Work-Factor" is the registered service mark of the Work-Factor Company.

time value is .0046. If a 3 W-F difficulty is encountered, the motion value is .0102.

In order to find the time for the task of "moving a part to a punch-press die," the job analyst would need to know the code or abbreviations that are used for the various members of the body. He would have to measure the distance (in inches) that the worker's body moved, and he would have to decide (according to specific rules) whether the body motion was a basic one or whether it involved some difficulty (1 W-F motion, or a 2 W-F motion, etc.). Figure 15.1 illustrates how select times are obtained from the tables.

Time values in the tables are already *leveled*. *Leveling* means rating the operator's performance, that is, whether he is average, above average, or below average, in performing the job. However, allowances must still be added for delays, fatigue, rest, and personal time, which vary with company policy.

The advantages of using any one of the standard data methods to set job performance standards are as follows. The time standards are more consistent than those of time study because they do not vary as does the daily efficiency of a time study man. In other words, the standard time values for each motion have been empirically established and are not based upon a small sample or a possible

TABLE 15.2
WORK-FACTOR MOVING TIME TABLE FOR TRUNK AND FINGER-HAND
(Time in ten-thousandths of a minute)

Distance Moved, Inches	Basic	Work Factors				Distance Moved, Inches	Basic	Work Factors			
		1	2	3	4			1	2	3	4
(T) Trunk — *Measured at Shoulder*						(F, H) Finger-Hand — *Measured at Finger Tip*					
1	.0026	.0038	.0049	.0058	.0067	1	.0016	.0023	.0029	.0035	.0040
2	.0029	.0042	.0053	.0064	.0073	2	.0017	.0025	.0032	.0038	.0044
3	.0032	.0047	.0060	.0072	.0082	3	.0019	.0028	.0036	.0043	.0049
4	.0038	.0055	.0070	.0084	.0096	4	.0023	.0033	.0042	.0050	.0058
5	.0043	.0062	.0079	.0095	.0109	Weight Male ⅔	2½	4	Up	-	
6	.0047	.0068	.0087	.0105	.0120	(Pounds) Fem. ⅓	1¼	2	Up	-	
7	.0051	.0074	.0095	.0114	.0130	(FT) Foot — *Measured at Toe*					
8	.0054	.0079	.0101	.0121	.0139						
9	.0058	.0084	.0107	.0128	.0147	1	.0020	.0029	.0037	.0044	.0051
10	.0061	.0088	.0113	.0135	.0155	2	.0022	.0032	.0040	.0048	.0055
11	.0063	.0091	.0118	.0141	.0162	3	.0024	.0035	.0045	.0055	.0063
12	.0066	.0094	.0123	.0147	.0169	4	.0029	.0041	.0053	.0064	.0073
13	.0068	.0097	.0127	.0153	.0175	Weight Male 5	22	Up	-	-	
14	.0071	.0100	.0130	.0158	.0182	(Pounds) Fem. 2½	11	Up	-	-	
15	.0073	.0103	.0133	.0163	.0188	(FS) Forearm Swivel—*Measured at Knuckles*					
16	.0075	.0105	.0136	.0167	.0193						
17	.0078	.0108	.0139	.0170	.0199	45°	.0017	.0022	.0028	.0032	.0037
18	.0080	.0111	.0142	.0173	.0203	90°	.0023	.0030	.0037	.0043	.0049
19	.0082	.0113	.0145	.0176	.0206	135°	.0028	.0036	.0044	.0052	.0058
20	.0084	.0116	.0148	.0179	.0209	180°	.0031	.0040	.0049	.0057	.0065
Weight Male 11	58	Up	-	-		Torque M. 3	13	Up	-	-	
(Pounds) Fem. 5½	29	Up	-	-		(Inch-Pounds) F. 1½	6½	Up	-	-	

Work Factor Symbols		Walking Time				Visual Inspection	
W Weight or Resistance			30" Paces			Focus	.002
S Directional Control (Steer)	TYPE	1	2	OVER 2		Inspect	.003/point
P Care (Precaution)	General	.015	.026	.012 + .008/Pace			
U Change Direction	Restricted	.018	.030	.012 + .010/Pace			
D Definite Stop	Add .010 for 120° — 180° Turn at Start						

Tables reproduced by permission of the Work-Factor Company, Inc., which holds the copyrights. "Work-Factor" is the registered service mark of the Work-Factor Company.

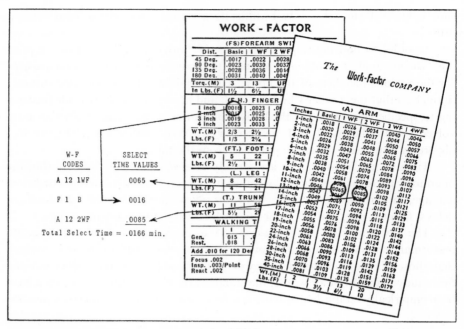

FIGURE 15.1 SELECT TIME TO REACH 12″, GRASP, AND MOVE A PART 12″ TO A
PUNCHER-PRESS DIE. From Work-Factor motion time-tables for
finger-hand and arm motions.

faulty time study. The standard data method focuses acceptance on standards that have been agreed upon previously. Another advantage is that the standard can be set quicker and with less equipment since it is rarely necessary for the industrial engineer to actually observe the job in order to set the time standard.

There are some limitations of the use of standard data as a method of establishing job performance standards. The method cannot be used until sufficient valid data have been previously collected, and therefore motion and time studies must first precede the standard data method. If workers frown upon motion and time studies, it may mean that they will not accept standard data standards. In spite of the apparent greater validity of standard data standards, some workers may feel that such standards are a sleight-of-the-hand trick or fail to see how time standards can be set without the use of a stopwatch. Thus, the method may be unacceptable to the less-educated employees.

Work Sampling (Random Time Sampling or Ratio-Delay)

Work measurement that is accomplished through stopwatch time study and elemental time values, although useful for measuring repetitive short-cycle labor operations, is very costly and not very efficient for measuring operations which have relatively long, irregular cycles. Work sampling can be used to advantage here. *Work sampling* is a technique for periodically observing (or sampling) job performance for the purpose of measuring work and establishing job performance standards. The observations can also be used for gathering data on work time elements, job delays, equipment and personnel utilization, and the like. The theory of work sampling is based on the fundamental laws of probability. Thus, if an adequate number of valid samples of work is taken, the findings can be relied upon to represent the results that would have been obtained if the whole universe were observed in a continuous 100 percent time study such as found in motion and time studies.

The advantages of establishing job performance standards through projections of valid work samples are many. The method frequently provides the information faster and at less cost (up to 50 percent less) than by the stopwatch or standard data methods because fewer calculations and equipment are required. The work sampling method also lends itself to most kinds of irregular work and is especially useful for establishing standards for work classified as repairing, clerical, and warehousing where gross units of work may be analyzed in preference to minute divisions as is the case in motion and time studies. Because an analyst can make instantaneous observations of a worker at random intervals throughout the work day, there is no need for making long continuous time studies. Some workers feel more comfortable when observed occasionally than when observed continuously for long periods of time as in motion and time studies.

The work sampling technique has a few limitations as a method of establishing job performance standards. The unsophisticated employee does not understand the sampling technique and is, in general, wary of statistical arguments. Some employees look upon those who take the samples as company spies and are therefore unwilling to accept the technique because it does not appear to be an honest one. Another disadvantage of the work sampling method is that the workers may change their performance (slow down) at the time the sample is being taken so that the job performance standard will be set on the low side. Such a sample would not be a valid one nor would the job performance standard that was established from it.

It would appear that the sampling technique of measuring work and setting job performance standards can prove satisfactory when the following conditions are present: (1) Employees understand the technique and believe it can be valid. (2) There are enough random samples taken over a long enough period of time to make the samples representative and valid.

Estimation

Estimation is a method of establishing job performance standards based on pure judgment or an educated guess. It may be used when substantial past records or statistics are generally not available to make use of one of the other methods previously described. In the past, this method was used only as a last resort when there were no other methods available. Recently, however, one application of estimation has become popularized under the label of "evaluation by objectives" (see pages 387 to 392) as a method of establishing job performance standards for nonrepetitive jobs. The reason for its apparent present popularity appears to be twofold. First, there is a general lack of satisfactory methods available for establishing job performance standards for nonrepetitive jobs. Second, as the educational level of employees has increased over the years, the employees and their bosses are reaching the stage where an educated guess is believed to have merit. This is especially true when the method is used at higher management levels or at any level where the boss and his subordinate are able to agree upon estimates that can be used as acceptable job performance goals or standards. More and more firms are attempting to pay employees on the basis of merit and job results, because the increased production will absorb the related higher labor costs. Likewise, more and more professional and white-collar workers would like to see their pay more closely based on results. Thus, the conditions would appear to be favorable to the use of this method of establishing job goals.

Another application of estimation as a method of establishing job performance standards is a technique that Elliott Jacques[1] has called the "Method of Successive Approximation." In this technique, the estimator is forced to make several estimates, starting with one extreme and then going to the other extreme and proceeding back and forth until an estimate is finally made that appears to be about right as the job standard for an average fully qualified employee working at a normal pace. As an illustration of how this technique may be performed, assume that you ask the office manager how many invoices he expects a clerk to check each day. He may reply that this is a very difficult question to answer because it sometimes takes only seconds to check an invoice, while other times it may take a half-hour or more if there are problems. He says that there are some 700 invoices to check each month and that it would be difficult to state how many a day would constitute slow work. You might ask him if one per day is slow. He says yes. Seven hundred per day? Impossibly fast. Five per day? Very slow. One hundred per day? Fast. Twenty per day? Slow. Fifty? Very good. Thirty? Would not want less. Thirty-five? Could not expect more! Thus, by the method of successive approximations, somewhere between 30 and 35 appears to be the office manager's job performance standard for satisfactory work. Consistently less than 30 is too slow and would constitute marginal performance, while consistently more than 35 would be above average performance.

The advocates of estimation as a means of establishing job performance standards point out the following advantages of this method. First, it is rela-

---

[1]Elliott Jacques, *Equitable Payment: A General Theory of Work Differential Payment and Individual Progress* (New York: John Wiley and Sons, 1961), p. 92.

tively simple to keep job standards up-to-date on jobs that change and on non-repetitive jobs in which new job performance standards may be established at every rating period. Thus, the method can be as flexible as needed to keep pace with changing technology. Second, the method is applicable to most all jobs and is especially useful for nonroutine jobs that heretofore appeared to defy the setting of performance standards. Third, when the employee has had a hand in the establishment of the estimates, it is a strong motivator of individuals as well as of teams. Fourth, the method lends itself to the establishment of a true merit rating system in which pay increases are tied to job performance results.

Limitations that the estimation method of establishing job performance appears to have are as follows. It takes time to gain the experience to properly relate job performance results with pay because every employee is an individual and a different case. Not every supervisor or member of management is proficient at making educated guesses. Thus, there is plenty of room for honest disagreements and increased grievances on job performance standards. The method will not work well where the overall general goals of the firm are unavailable or unclear, because good estimates need to be in keeping with centralized corporate goals.

In summary, estimation as a method of establishing job performance standards would appear always to be better than no method at all. It will become more valuable as employees and their superiors gain experience and learn to work together to establish realistic and acceptable job performance standards.

Establishing job performance standards for nonrepetitive jobs

The previous section mainly described various methods and bases that are chiefly used to determine job performance standards for repetitive jobs. Because it is much more difficult to establish job performance standards for nonrepetitive jobs, the following discussion is devoted to the ways and means that are available for establishing job performance standards for a variety of jobs which are basically nonrepetitive. These jobs, by their very nature, are quite complex and have a great variety of ever-changing factors that affect job performance results. This means that job results can be accomplished in a variety of ways, and therefore the job methodology is rarely the same for any period of time. This state of job flux makes it practically impossible to establish *one* set of job performance standards that will last longer than one employee evaluation period. We cannot expect to set job performance standards for nonrepetitive jobs in the same way as for routine jobs, nor can we expect that whatever standards are set will last for any length of time.

Too often companies have become frustrated because they could not establish job performance standards that would hold up for any period of time.

These companies failed to understand the underlying concept that nonrepetitive jobs are always changing and cannot be frozen long enough to establish permanent job performance standards. Once this principle is realized, it paves the way for considering how to evaluate a job that is ever moving. How then can a firm establish job performance standards for nonrepetitive jobs?

Factory Jobs

One manufacturer known to the authors has a rather unique method of handling the subject of job performance standards. This employer believes in a "fair day's work" policy in which employees are asked for a fair day's work (job standard) rather than for a production quota per hour or per day. Thus, employees do not have a job production performance standard but a standard involving worker effort in which the worker is expected to stay on the job and exert an honest effort.

The company in question defines a fair day's work as the normal effort of a properly selected, trained, and placed employee effectively using the facilities provided by management and continuously following the prescribed method throughout the specified working period. In the fair day's work concept, management has carefully spelled out the four components involved and the mutual responsibilities of management and employee. The four components are (1) normal effort; (2) properly selected, trained, and placed employee; (3) effectively using the facilities provided by management; and (4) continuously following the prescribed method or procedure throughout the specified working period. It is management's responsibility to properly select, train, and place the employee; to provide adequate facilities; and to designate the prescribed method. It is the employee's responsibility to exert normal work effort; to effectively use the facilities provided; and to follow the prescribed procedure throughout the day. The success of the fair day's work plan depends upon the willingness of both management and the employee to fulfill their obligations. The fair day's work policy is an operating philosophy based on *fairness* — to both the employee and the employer. This appeal to "fair play" is the key to the successful application of the plan.

The fair day's work policy is not limited to production employees. The management of this firm believes that this policy applies to *all* employees, productive or nonproductive, hourly or salary. Approximately two thirds of the firm's total employment is indirect labor. Since job performance standards are difficult to establish for indirect labor, it is necessary that these employees put forth a fair day's work. In keeping with this policy, there are no coffee breaks or other breaks condoned, and excessive personal time is investigated.

One might ask what the advantages are of the fair day's work plan over a plan having production standards or more concrete job performance standards. The more important desirable features appear to be:

1. Employees work the full day because they are expected to. There is no reason to stop working in order to hold down production because there is no official production quota. There is likewise no advantage to concealing production since only an honest day's effort is asked.

2. Employee dissatisfactions are reduced. "Speed-up" charges are eliminated because only normal effort is requested. Employees are not asked to work harder or faster. There are no reasons for grievances on the basis of time study or production figures, since production figures are not discussed. Emphasis is placed on using proper methods and staying on the job, not on a production quota.

3. More harmonious employer-employee relations develop because employees are placed on jobs for which they are best suited, they are paid for normal effort and get credit when they suggest job improvements or do their best, and they are not criticized for failure to attain a certain production quota.

Some limitations of the fair day's work policy appear apparent. There is less concrete and objective evidence to use as a basis for determining promotions and pay raises since normal effort is more difficult to measure than the amount of production produced. When only normal effort is expected of the employee, it may cause the better employees to work at reduced effort since there would appear to be little incentive for them to do their best. Job performance standards do have to be established if a firm is to know how efficiently it is operating and whether inefficiencies are due to machines, materials, or employees. When job performance standards are developed, it may be difficult to convince the employees that the standards are not being used against them.

Supervisory Jobs

A simplified method of establishing job performance standards for first-line supervisors, utilizing the evaluation by objectives approach, would be as follows. The supervisor's superior would first write out ten answers to the following question: "What specific conditions (end results) should exist at the end of the evaluation period if my subordinate carries out his duties and performs to my complete satisfaction?" Second, the supervisor would be asked to list five to ten specific conditions (in terms of quantity, quality, time, etc.) that should exist at the end of his evaluation period if he carries out his responsibilities to the satisfaction of his superior. The supervisor and his superior would then get together to compare their lists and agree upon a number of the specific conditions (five and their priority) to be attained. These specific conditions then become the end goals from which job performance standards are established to serve as the basis for evaluating the supervisor's performance.

The advantages and disadvantages of this technique have been previously spelled out in Chapter 14 in the discussion on "evaluation by objectives." Therefore, it is sufficient to say that the advantages far outweigh the disadvantages and that the technique works best when cordial relations already exist between the supervisor and his superior and when the supervisor is experienced, conscientious, and realistic.

Executive Jobs

Even though it may appear very difficult to set performance standards for some executive jobs, there are a number of different methods being used successfully to establish job performance standards for executive positions.

Self-Study. Although few executives would subject themselves to observation by time study men, many executives are aware of the advantages of personal time utilization analysis and are enthusiastic about analyzing their own activities. There is a self-study device available from the Meylan Stopwatch Corporation called an *Executrol*, which measures and records the time spent by an executive on his different activities throughout his workday. The use of the Executrol, shown in Figure 15.2, enables the executive to evaluate himself by examining a printed record on a time-graduated tape that reveals the "unplanned" as well as the expected activities of his workday. The visible record produced by this pushbutton device can be summarized by the executive, or his secretary, into a daily, weekly, or monthly time utilization analysis. From this analysis, job performance

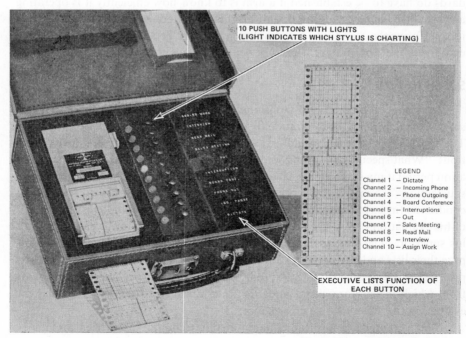

10 PUSH BUTTONS WITH LIGHTS
(LIGHT INDICATES WHICH STYLUS IS CHARTING)

LEGEND
Channel 1 — Dictate
Channel 2 — Incoming Phone
Channel 3 — Phone Outgoing
Channel 4 — Board Conference
Channel 5 — Interruptions
Channel 6 — Out
Channel 7 — Sales Meeting
Channel 8 — Read Mail
Channel 9 — Interview
Channel 10 — Assign Work

EXECUTIVE LISTS FUNCTION OF
EACH BUTTON

Meylan Stopwatch Corporation

FIGURE 15.2 "Executrol" — An Executive Self-Study Device

standards can be established. Of course, a similar analysis could be made manually by keeping a daily time log.

The Manager's Letter. Another technique that has been used to establish job performance standards for executives and managers is the *Manager's Letter*. In this technique, a top-level executive asks his subordinate to write him a letter once every six months or a year. The subordinate is instructed to define the goals of his boss's job as well as his own and then to draw up the job performance standards that the subordinate believes should be applied to him. Next, the subordinate is to outline what he proposes to do to attain his job performance goals and what he considers the main obstacles, within his department, to achieving these goals. Finally, he lists what his superior and the company do that both helps and hinders him in reaching the goals. If his superior agrees with the contents of the letter, the job performance standards outlined in it become the basis upon which the subordinate will be evaluated.

This technique would appear to have real merit where the subordinate and his superior see eye to eye on their jobs and responsibilities. Certainly the technique is flexible in that it allows for changing job performance standards that are in keeping with changing technology and company strategy. It may not work well in situations where the subordinate does not have adequate freedom to control the activities that govern the job performance results. If compensation rewards are tied to the attainment of the job goals, there may be some difficulties in determining the proper amount of compensation for performance that falls short of or exceeds the predetermined job goals.

Budgets. *Budgets* represent another medium that can be used in conjunction with the establishment of job performance standards. Accountants have strongly advocated and been most instrumental in seeing that job performance standards (in terms of budgets) have been determined for at least three areas of responsibility: direct materials, direct labor, and factory overhead. Every organization has these costs and should have records that can reveal what is an acceptable cost (or performance standard) for each of these items. The firm's accountant, or chief financial officer, can be most helpful in assisting supervisors, managers, and executives to use these or other cost items to establish at least the minimum standards of performance on budgets (what is unsatisfactory, satisfactory, and outstanding).

The advantages of establishing job performance standards for budgets as a means of evaluating employees are many. First, all organizations already deal with money and must spend it wisely if they are to be competitive and survive for any length of time. Budgets can represent a valuable method of evaluating performance if performance standards are set for the budgets. Second, budgets are like a common denominator in that they can be used at all levels of management from the first-line supervisor to the president of the firm. In fact, budgets should be used at all levels as one means of coordinating departments to reach corporate goals. Third, budgets are not only a uniform medium for establishing performance standards but are also flexible in that they can be tailor-made according to the various conditions and circumstances of each level of management. Fourth, since budgets deal with money, the performance standards can be quantitatively stated and easily measured. This can provide objectivity and a standard that is easily understood.

The limitations that budgets appear to have as a device for establishing job performance goals are as follows. Various members of management are not always enthusiastic or receptive to budgets because budgets tend to put pressure on supervisors and may place them under undue tensions. Budgets are also said to be traditionally based on past history, which is sometimes a poor indicator of future performance. Finally, achieving budget performance standards is not always a true measure of job performance because budgets can depend upon many factors, some of which may not be within the control of the supervisor. An employee could look bad if he does not meet his budget because of an uncontrollable factor.

Under what circumstances should budgets be utilized as a means of establishing job performance standards? It would appear that budgets are a satisfactory means of establishing job performance standards when the employee can participate in the setting of the standards, when the factors that control the performance standards are under his jurisdiction, when the standards are established according to the circumstances and conditions of his job, and when the standards can serve as a challenge and provide him with the satisfaction that meets his needs and abilities.

PERT. A rather unique method that can be utilized by firms to establish performance standards for a job is called *PERT* (Program Evaluation and Review Technique). PERT is a technique that identifies and establishes time standards for the various activities necessary to accomplish the goal of a project. Although the technique is also used as a planning, estimating, scheduling, and control tool of management, it requires that a time allowance (standard) be set for each activity that must be performed to accomplish a project or objective on time.

PERT was developed in 1958 as a time-cost-planning-measurement tool for the United States Navy by the management consultants of the firm of Booz, Allen and Hamilton. The aim was to develop, test, and implement a methodology for the scheduling of the Polaris missile program, because it was necessary to identify the various activities of this complex program so that the relationships of these activities could be seen to pave the way for properly planning and controlling them. Many complicated industrial projects today are so involved that no one really knows enough about them to coordinate their events or activities; thus, no one knows how long a project will take to complete nor can anyone do much to prevent delays because a person normally does not find out about these difficulties until after they have happened. Then it is too late. PERT then has served as a device for identifying, ahead of time, all the activities or events involved in a project and establishing realistic times (in terms of days, weeks, or months) for the completion of each activity as well as the total time needed for a project. The technique has been credited with enabling the United States Navy to make operational its ICBM — firing (Inter-Continental Ballistic Missile — more popularly called the Polaris program) nuclear submarine two years ahead of schedule. PERT has also proven so valuable that the United States government has been insisting that contractors submit a PERT proposal when they enter a bid on a government contract. With the success of the PERT technique has come a variety of similar techniques known as CPM (Critical Path Method), PEP (Program Evaluation Procedure), and others, each of which utilizes the PERT principle.

The operational theory of PERT is relatively simple. Once a project goal has been established, a list of all the necessary elements, events, or activities (called a network) involved in the program (which takes two weeks or longer to complete) must be identified. Next, time allowances (standards) must be established for each activity in order to know the day *when* the total project will be completed and to know at any time *whether each activity is on schedule* (this is the phase of PERT that relates to the establishment of job performance standards). The establishment of a completion time for each activity is, in reality, the establishment of a time performance standard that can be used to evaluate the employee or group of employees responsible for the activity. The establishment of the time standard for an activity is rather unique in that the employee or employees are asked to indicate three possible time lengths that the activity might take: the shortest possible time needed if everything goes well (most optimistic, t_o); the longest possible time needed under adverse conditions (pessimistic time, t_p); and the most likely time that the project will actually take (t_m). These three time estimates describe a distribution that is approximately Beta where the mode is t_m, the lower bound is t_o, and the upper bound is t_p. The expected time (t_e) is then found through the formula:[2]

$$t_e = \frac{t_o + 4t_m + t_p}{6}$$

Statisticians indicate that the computed result, t_e, is the point estimate of the time to accomplish the task. In order to establish the time performance standards for evaluating employees, the expected time could be considered as the standard performance expected (satisfactory). Anything longer than the most

[2]For a more detailed explanation of the formula, consult a standard text on Operations Research such as Frederich S. Hillier and Gerald J. Lieberman, *Introduction to Operations Research* (San Francisco: Holden-Day, Inc., 1967), p. 229.

pessimistic time could be considered as the standard of marginal performance (or unsatisfactory). Achieving the most optimistic time could be considered as the outstanding performance standard. Of course, each firm decides for itself what length of time it considers to be the standard for satisfactory, unsatisfactory, and outstanding performance.

The advantages of using the PERT technique as a means of establishing job time performance standards are as follows. It can be used to evaluate either individual employees or teams of employees or both. This means that the many employee performance evaluations can be related and integrated into a total company evaluation. The need for techniques to evaluate groups of employees and firms is becoming greater as technological progress tends to depend more and more on team and company efforts. Since the setting of a time standard involves the employee who is to be evaluated by his own standard, there is every reason to believe the project will be completed on time, if not sooner. The reason for this is that the employee is establishing a realistic goal which he believes he can meet. Thus, the employee not only understands the standard set but also is more likely to be motivated to do everything in his power to meet his own goal and thereby gain recognition and status from his friends who may be depending upon him. Another advantage of a PERT time performance standard is that there can be little doubt about the standard being considered reasonable and fair by the employee, since he has been mainly responsible for establishing it. Experienced and fully qualified employees who are close to the tasks to be performed and who are really concerned about the firm, its employees, and customers are most likely to be best qualified to set the standards. The degree to which an employee has erred in being either too optimistic or too pessimistic in his judgments furnishes an additional factor upon which the firm can evaluate his job performance.

Although PERT is still relatively new, there are a few limitations in its use in establishing job performance standards. First, the standard strongly emphasizes the time element. Most job performance standards need to consider both the quality and the quantity aspects. Firms are presently concerned with establishing both cost and quality standards in addition to PERT's present time standards. Second, PERT has been somewhat limited to narrow applications (one-shot projects). It has not been extensively tested across the board in broad areas of company operations. It has been pretty much restricted and tested in large-size companies because they are the only ones that get involved in the large-scale projects. However, there is reason to believe that the principle of establishing the three time values, as utilized in the PERT technique, can be used as job performance time standards in a small as well as in a large firm. This assumes, of course, that those who set the standards are experienced, fully qualified, and truly concerned about the common good of the employees, the firm, and the public.

Who should set job performance standards?

Sooner or later in establishing job performance standards, questions such as the following arise: Whose responsibility is it to set job performance standards? Who is best qualified to set job performance standards? Should the employees be consulted? The answers to these questions are discussed below.

The person charged with the responsibility for seeing that the work is performed is the one who should see that adequate job performance standards are established. This person is the immediate superior of the employees who hold the jobs for which the performance standards are being set. He should know the jobs well if he is in charge of them. For nonmanagerial jobs, this person is the supervisor or foreman or office manager. Although these superiors should be capable of establishing job performance standards for their employees, it is often desirable to call upon others in the firm for assistance and counsel. Most organizations have someone within the firm who has had special training in management efficiency. He is often called an industrial engineer, a methods engineer, or a time and motion study man. This person should be especially valuable in either recommending or actually establishing the job performance standards (with the supervisor's approval) for nonmanagerial jobs. He may also be of some assistance on some managerial jobs, although he is not often used at this level.

For managerial jobs, the person in charge of such jobs has the task of seeing that suitable job performance standards are established. At the managerial level, it becomes increasingly difficult to set standards, because of the variety of repetitive duties of these jobs. Standards therefore cannot be set with as much confidence and validity as at the lower levels. For this reason, they may be set by a committee of two or more persons in order to arrive at reasonably valid and acceptable standards. Sometimes the supervisor and his superior pool their judgment to arrive at job standards for the jobs of the supervisor's subordinates. This is recommended when the supervisor is not able to do it alone and when his subordinates are of no help. In other instances, the supervisor and his subordinates may be able to establish the standards. This is only desirable when subordinates are well educated, experienced, and motivated to establish standards that are best for the common good of the firm. If the subordinates are antimanagement, selfish, or unfamiliar with their jobs, they are not likely to be of much positive help in setting standards.

Problems connected with the establishment of job performance standards

One of the more important hurdles to the establishment of job performance standards for nonrepetitive jobs such as engineering, research, administrative, and executive is the resistance of the employees holding these positions. The very persons who endorse performance standards for rank-and-file jobs tend to resist the establishment of standards for their own jobs. There appears to be the general feeling by these employees that their duties are so complicated and intangible that performance standards cannot be set for their jobs. Although this feeling is understandable, it is based on a misconception of why they were hired and of the importance of standards to sound management.

Performance standards indicate how well a job should be done. Although they may be fixed or constant for repetitive production jobs, which are routine and constant, the standards can be as flexible and as changeable as the nonroutine position. Even dynamic jobs which are ever changing lend themselves to short-range and flexible standards that can be established by the "evaluation by objectives" method previously described in Chapter 14. Thus, new performance standards can be set periodically in accordance with the establishment of a new project or a changing assignment. It is only through job performance standards that an employee can ever know whether he is actually performing acceptable work. This is true of every job from the company messenger boy to the president.

There should always be a valid reason for hiring an employee whether a job is routine or nonrepetitive. The justification for every job should be clearly identified in the job description which spells out the goal of the job or the job performance results expected. This means that specific job performance standards have to be established in order to determine whether the job is an asset or a liability to the firm. No firm can justify the hiring of employees to perform jobs that prove to be handicaps to the firm. Employees in nonrepetitive positions need to be made aware of the economic considerations necessary for good management in order to overcome their resistance to the establishment of job performance standards. This phase of an employee's education should have been completed during the induction program when hired, if not sooner. It is much easier to prevent resistance to job performance standards than it is to try to overcome it after the standards have been established.

Useful criteria for setting job performance standards

This chapter has attempted to emphasize the need for establishing objective and acceptable job performance standards as an important basis for motivating, evaluating, and rewarding employee performance. The establishment of acceptable job performance standards is facilitated when the following criteria are kept uppermost in mind:

1. Company aims and goals must first be identified and communicated before various job performance standards can be properly established, because individual job performance goals and standards need to contribute to the achievement of the firm's central goals. Otherwise, individual job performance standards can become a meaningless collection of goals.

2. Job performance goals should be limited in number and well coordinated with other aspects of the job and the department as well as the firm. Five or six job performance goals are normally the most that can be reasonably attained during one evaluation period of time. The job performance standards for each goal can easily be derived from the job duties found in the job description. If the job duty has been properly described, it defines the end results or goals that the duty must consistently produce to justify its existence. No one goal should receive such emphasis that it becomes detrimental to the others. For example, if so much stress is put on attaining greater profit-as-a-percent-of-sales that inventories and receivables get out of hand, it will unduly cut into the returns on investment. It is highly desirable that the various job performance goals be cross-checked to see that they are harmonious with other jobs in the department, other departments, and other divisions, and with the firm's central goals.

3. Specific job performance standards should be set for each job goal that is expected on the job. Each job goal, in turn, should be described in both a quantitative dimension whenever possible in order to increase the objectivity of the standard and to facilitate its measurement. For example, a job goal may be to reduce metal scrap from 8 to 4 percent per hundred pieces. Thus, the job goal is to improve the quality of the product from 8 percent scrap to 4 percent while the quantity is held to a rate of 100 pieces. All too often job goals are poorly described, such as, "conduct scrap reduction program." Employees need to know whether the job goal represents just satisfactory, above average, or outstanding accomplishment. In addition, they need to know what is considered unsatisfactory accomplishment. In short, job standards should at least specifically indicate what job performance results are considered as unsatisfactory, satisfactory, and outstanding.

4. Job performance standards should be practical and challenging. They need to provide an incentive to the employee to work up to his capacity. The standards should not be set like old-fashioned sales quotas nor should they be set to insure easy achievement. They should not be too easy because employee interest may be quickly lost, with the result that the duty becomes either boring or routine. If a job performance standard is too difficult to attain, the employee may become discouraged and stop trying. The standards should be attainable in light of all the foreseeable conditions and call for full effort from the employee. Average results obtained by a qualified person working at a normal pace would generally be considered as satisfactory performance, while ideal results are considered as outstanding and below break-even results are considered as unsatisfactory.

5. Finally, job performance standards must be made known to the employees who hold these jobs. The standards must appear reasonable and be accepted by these employees. When employees have a hand in setting the standards, the standards are more likely to appear valid, be acceptable, and achieved by the employees concerned.

REVIEW QUESTIONS

1. Why are job performance standards necessary?
2. How can the shortcomings of work sampling be overcome?
3. What are the criteria that affect the establishment of acceptable job performance standards?
4. What type of work is best suited to setting standards by estimation? Why?
5. According to the authors, what constitutes satisfactory job performance?
6. Executives can be evaluated by the "Manager's Letter" and by budgets. What are the advantages and disadvantages of these two methods?
7. What are job performance standards?
8. Who should be responsible for setting the job performance standards? Why?
9. How can PERT be used to set standards for the evaluation of employees?
10. What are the advantages and disadvantages of each of the basic methods used to set standards for repetitive jobs?
11. Why is it more difficult to set performance standards for professional jobs?
12. Before any attempt is made to set standards for a particular job, what must be done?
13. Explain why you agree or disagree with the following statement: "Once job performance standards have been determined, they should never be changed."

RESEARCH OR SEMINAR QUESTIONS

1. Should the employees and/or their unions be allowed to participate in setting job performance standards?
2. What methods, other than those described in the chapter, are being used to set standards for nonrepetitive jobs?
3. Is it better to state job performance standards in terms such as "3 percent scrap is outstanding" or "97 percent usable pieces is outstanding"? Explain the reasons for your answer.
4. How can managers who have set different job performance standards for themselves be compared? Is it necessary to set standards for managers?

PRACTICAL EXPERIENCE ASSIGNMENTS

1. An employee's dexterity and mental ability tests consistently point to the fact that he is unsuited for a particular type of job. However, because of his repeated experience in this type of work, he proves that he can more than adequately handle this repetitive type job. How would you deal with this situation when considering pay increases and promotions for this employee?
2. A college student worked for the same nonunion company for two summers and during holiday vacations. His performance was considered above ordinary; in fact, he had supervisory capacity over five full-time employees. Due to company policy, he was considered as part-time help. The part-time employee policy of the company placed him in a lower hourly earning scale than his subordinates. This part-time employee confronts you, the wage and

salary administrator, with this situation and demands a raise in pay because of his performance and total amount of time with the firm. How would you attempt to resolve this case, keeping in mind the company's part-time help policy and the student's value to the firm?

3. The employees have heard that your company is planning to conduct time and motion studies to assist in setting performance standards. The union business agent, who has a great deal of respect for you, the wage and salary administrator, comes to you to get information about the effect that the proposed time and motion studies will have on wages. He appears to be against any time studies being made. Outline your plan for handling this situation.

CASE PROBLEM

15–1. THE FLAWLESS FOUNDRY COMPANY

Determining Job Performance Standards

In the Mixer Shop of The Flawless Foundry Company there are three foremen and 60 skilled workers. Each foreman supervises the work of 20 workmen. The company has a merit rating system in operation, and each foreman is required to rate each worker under him once every six months. In the opinion of the general foreman of the Mixer Shop, Mr. Bang, the men under foreman Quick are very efficient workers, while the men under foreman Smith are fairly typical, which means that some of them are very good, some of average standard, and a few of poor standard. In his opinion, the men under foreman Jones are generally of poor standard.

According to the existing merit rating procedure, the foremen are required to rate employees under them as very satisfactory, satisfactory, or not satisfactory. Foreman Quick used to rate his employees in a set pattern—25% "very satisfactory," 50% "satisfactory," and 25% "not satisfactory." Ratings were kept confidential and employees were never told of their ratings. Foreman Smith had a tendency to divide his men between the two classifications "very satisfactory" and "satisfactory." Generally, it was noticed that he was rating 40% of his men as "very satisfactory" and the rest as "satisfactory." Like foreman Quick, he also kept the ratings confidential. Foreman Jones used to discuss the individual ratings with the employees concerned. His ratings were usually all "satisfactory," except for one or two "very satisfactory." After a period of time, management noticed great dissatisfaction among the employees of the Mixer Shop over the rating system. Very soon the union officials demanded that merit rating should be discontinued and employees should be given fixed automatic raises every year.

Problem:

As the wage and salary administrator, you are asked to investigate the present merit rating system of the company and advise the management whether or not the company should agree to the union demand. If not, what measures would you suggest be taken to remove the causes of employee dissatisfaction over the merit rating issue? What factors do you think should be included in a merit rating form to ensure an unbiased employee evaluation?

chapter 16

ADOPTION AND INSTALLATION OF AN EMPLOYEE EVALUATION PLAN

In the preceding two chapters, the background and the fundamental concepts of employee evaluation and the establishment of job standards were presented. In this chapter we discuss the thinking and the considerations that are part of the procedures necessary for the successful adoption and installation of an employee evaluation plan.

Before adopting a program, special consideration must be given to what we seek to accomplish and what we aim for as the desired goal. The typical questions introduced at this point show the course to follow for an effective program and for the installation of an employee evaluation plan:

1. Shall our aims and policies be consistent, that is, based on a long-range view, or as a matter of expediency? What specific purpose should employee evaluation serve? Should a ready-made plan be adopted, or should an individualized plan be prepared to fit the specific organizational setup?
2. How will the employees react? Does the union favor employee evaluation? Shall union representatives participate in preparing the program?
3. Who should do the rating and how shall the inexperienced raters be trained? Shall a manual be prepared? What should it contain?
4. How often shall employees be rated?

5. Should rating be discussed with employees? How and where should the interview take place?
6. Which rating method should be used? Which type is best suited for our organization and conditions?
7. What will be the field of application? Which employee groups should be evaluated and rated first?
8. What type of employee evaluation forms shall we use? Shall weighting and scoring be done by the rater on the same form, or should it be delegated to someone else?
9. How should the rater approach objective rating? What should be done to make purely subjective rating more realistic?
10. Which specific factors are to be considered "basic"? Shall only the basic factors, as such, be used, or shall subfactors be considered to further facilitate rating according to degrees?
11. What system should be adopted for weighting and scoring?
12. What should be the procedure for preparing progress reports?

A discussion of these questions will be brought into focus by a treatment of the following topics, which may be used as the steps in setting up and administering an employee evaluation plan:

1. Deciding on the adoption of a plan.
2. Selecting a suitable plan.
3. Choosing suitable evaluation factors and their weights.
4. Determining the procedures of the plan.
5. Training the raters.
6. Handling the problems connected with employee evaluation.

Deciding on the adoption of a plan

If a plan of employee evaluation is ever to be established, someone must make a decision that a plan is needed. No plan is likely to amount to much unless this decision is either made by, or backed by, top management. When top management endorses a plan, authority is granted to proceed with its development, and employees become aware of the importance that management attaches to it.

Experienced managements know that an individual is the most important of the many ingredients that go into the makeup of a company. If a firm is to be highly successful or to compete satisfactorily with other firms, it must therefore utilize its labor force to its utmost. As discussed in Chapter 14, an employee evaluation plan is one of the basic vehicles for motivating and utilizing employees. Through the process of evaluation, employee strengths and weaknesses are discovered, and employees can be counselled and assisted in developing themselves after the evaluation results have been made known. The employees can also be rewarded commensurate with the contributions they are making to the company. Employee evaluation results can be beneficial to the company as well as to the employee. Any company that properly rewards the performance of its employees should have a highly motivated work force that will remain with the firm; thus, labor turnover costs will be less than otherwise. In addition, when employees are motivated and assisted in self-development, the company may enjoy increased productivity or efficiency. Finally, the evaluations identify the more qualified employees who become the key men of the future.

The continual evaluation of employees in every company is actually going on all the time. Ever since the beginning of time, man has been regularly making judgments about his fellow man. So, in reality, every firm does have an informal plan of employee evaluation whether it realizes it or not. However, an informal plan that operates without specific aims and a sense of direction is like a ship adrift on the high seas. It may never get anywhere and if it did, who would know about it?

Once a firm realizes that it already has an informal employee evaluation plan, the question may be raised as to how effective it is. This cannot be answered until some objectives are established as to what the plan is supposed to do so that an evaluation of it can be made.

Most informal employee evaluation plans, if appraised on the basis of how well they have aided the development of employees and rewarded them according to their merits, would fare poorly. Usually employees are unaware of any direct relationship between their productivity and pay, and they suspect that pay raises are granted mainly to the favorites of the supervisor. This poses the question as to whether the plan should remain on an informal basis or be put into writing and operate on a formal basis.

It would appear that very small firms of less than a dozen employees may be able to operate satisfactorily on an informal basis as long as an attempt is made to establish some goals for the plan and to evaluate the employee on a similar basis. The employees, of course, should be informed of any such evaluation plan. The larger a firm becomes, the greater the need for a formal plan of evaluation in order for employees to be assured of consistent treatment. It is highly desirable and practically necessary for the vast majority of firms to formalize their employee evaluation plans by putting them into writing and communicating their details to all employees concerned.

It is recommended that as soon as management makes the decision to adopt a formalized evaluation plan, the director of wages and salaries be appointed to take charge of seeing that the program is properly planned, established, and administered. A committee should be organized under the direction of the wage and salary administrator. It should be composed of employee representatives as well as operating executives and supervisors, preferably a joint labor-management committee as was recommended for the installation of a job evaluation program (page 207).

A formal evaluation program begins at the moment management makes the decision to adopt a formalized plan. Right from this beginning, it is important for management and supervision to be in full accord with the idea of starting and maintaining an evaluation plan and to commit themselves by word and action. Therefore, all parties concerned should be included in the planning as soon as feasible. The intent is that participation by management, supervisors, and employees will more readily bring about understanding and acceptance of the evaluation concept. During the early stages there may be apprehension, distrust, and fear by the planners and possibly by the participants, especially if evaluation and rating have failed elsewhere in the community or if similar organizational and managerial policies were unsuccessful within the company. Fairness, goodwill, honesty, and diplomacy can help overcome some misconceptions.

One of the first tasks for the employee evaluation planning committee is to formulate the aims of the program. It is not wise to expect a program to accomplish a multitude of goals. Few plans, no matter how ingenious, can effectively serve more than one or two goals. Since the various aims of employee evaluation were discussed in Chapter 14, let us assume that the decision has been made to appraise employees chiefly for two purposes: (1) to assist individuals in self-development, and (2) as a basis for salary considerations. The committee must next consider whether to select a ready-made plan or to tailor-make their own formal plan.

Selecting a suitable plan

The start of an employee evaluation plan invariably brings up questions like: To which employee group level or groups shall the rating plan apply? Who should be evaluated and rated first? Which forms and rating factors shall we select to realize the results expected from that particular group? Shall we start at the lowest level of employees, or at the top?

Establishing Evaluation Plans for Different Employee Groups

The trend in establishing employee evaluation plans has been to have a separate plan for whatever groups of employees appear to be sufficiently different because of their jobs and circumstances. The idea is similar to the reasoning used in establishing separate plans of evaluating jobs. The more common groups of employees for which a separate employee evaluation plan may be established are as follows:

Group 1. All shop employees working on an hourly wage-base rate, commonly called "day rate."

Group 2. Salaried employees in offices, clerical and nonexempt workers paid hourly wage-base rates.

Group 3. Supervisors, exempt salaried, and professional employees, such as designers, engineers, and accountants.

Group 4.   Sales personnel employed in stores or in a given territory, who are paid salaries and commissions.

Group 5.   Managerial, executive, and administrative personnel.

The five groups above are arranged according to the policy of most companies, which, however, is not always conducive to the best employee morale. Starting the evaluating and rating at the top instead of at the bottom is now viewed with favor and is practiced by some companies. The advantage is obvious for two significant reasons: First, by starting with the evaluation and rating of all executives as well as those in charge of administering the rating program, raters are more impressed with the importance of employee evaluation. The chief analyst and his committee are influenced to select effective methods, proper forms, scales, factors, and definitions. Secondly, the psychological reaction of the largest groups, namely, shop and office employees, is usually such that if rated last, they are convinced there is little, if any, discrimination against the "lower level" employees. For one reason or another, it may not be possible to set the good example by establishing employee evaluation plans starting from the top down. Consideration also needs to be given to the answers to questions such as the following. What group of employees has the most pressing need to be evaluated? Which groups of employees recognize the need to be evaluated? What group of employees is most enthusiastic or receptive to being evaluated? On what group of employees is the employee evaluation committee best qualified to begin? For what group of employees are there a great many ready-made plans of evaluation from which to choose? The answers to these questions should reveal the most promising group of employees for which to begin to select an evaluation plan. Usually it is best to select the group that is greatly in need of evaluation, where the need is recognized, where cooperation may be easily obtained, and where the committee has adequate background so that the employee evaluation program can get off to a good start and gain the respect of the employees.

Tailor-Made v. Ready-Made Plans

There are a vast number of employee evaluation plans in use today. Each one attempts to accomplish one or more specific purposes. As with many phases of scientific management, employee evaluation must be tailor-made according to the functional setup, the jobs and activities involved, as well as the organizational structure. There are possibilities for adopting a ready-made plan, however, if the functions and jobs of one company are identical with or similar to those of another company. This procedure has proved acceptable among employees in the same industries, such as the National Metal Trades Association, or the insurance companies represented by members of the Life Office Management Association. Even under these conditions management should follow a predetermined course and be cognizant of what the plan will accomplish. Each company has its own peculiarities to consider and problems to solve, thereby necessitating changes in the ready-made plan. Professor Joseph Tiffin, an authority on industrial psychology, made the following appropriate comments:

> If a management has installed a system because the charts were attractively printed, or because some other company was using it effectively, but has not definitely decided just what the system is supposed to accomplish and carefully analyzed the system to determine whether it will accomplish these stated objectives, there is danger that a great deal of time and money will be spent with little or no return on the investment. This is exactly what has happened in no small number of plants.[1]

Similarly, as early as 1942, a National Industrial Conference Board investigation proved:

> . . . that there is no such thing as the "one best type of rating form." Those that have been most successful have been tailor-made to suit the particular conditions, jobs, and objectives of the organization in which they were to be used.[2]

This does not mean, however, we should ignore what others have accomplished in a similar situation. A great deal of time, effort, and expense may be saved by making a survey of other employee evaluation plans to ascertain the extent of their success or failure.

To the question, "Which method of employee evaluation shall we choose?" an appropriate answer is difficult unless there is complete familiarity with all conditions. Claims and counterclaims about the advantages and disadvantages inherent in one or another employee evaluation method are abundant in the literature of psychology and personnel management. It should be remembered that an advantage for one company may be a disadvantage for another, or vice versa. After studying the various methods, however, one should be able to decide which method or methods are preferable to fit his organization, depending upon the kind of work performed, the level of personnel to be rated, and the scope of evaluation. Generally, some ready-made plan can be found that comes close to meeting the conditions and circumstances found in the company that is desirous of setting up an evaluation plan. However, each firm may find it advisable to make whatever changes are necessary in the ready-made plan so that the resulting modified plan better meets the company's individual needs. There may be occasions when a firm has to develop its own tailor-made plan because its employees are of a special type or because there has been no experience in

---

[1]Joseph M. Dooher and Vivienne Marquis, *Rating Employee and Supervisory Performance* (New York: American Management Association, 1950), p. 11.

[2]*Studies in Personnel Policy*, No. 39 (New York: National Industrial Conference Board, Inc., 1942), p. 5.

evaluating employees on a group of new jobs recently created as a result of technology. In such a case the committee must begin developing its own plan to meet its own objectives. This calls for the selection of a set of suitable factors for evaluating employees.

Choosing suitable evaluation factors and their weights

The shortcomings in the terminology of employee evaluation and rating, as previously discussed, are noticeable in the usage of terms to designate rating factors. The student may find such terms as "qualities," "items," "elements," "traits," "characteristics," "qualifications," and others equivalent to the term "factors." There are various descriptions for the same term, and conversely, the same description for various terms. In this text the all-inclusive term "factor" has been adopted since it is also used in job evaluation.

Factors serve as a yardstick in evaluating employees. The selection of suitable factors may be regarded as the backbone of a plan for evaluating employees. In order to assist those seeking to choose suitable evaluation factors, we shall discuss the criteria for selecting factors, objective and subjective rating, and a number of other considerations that relate to evaluation factors.

Criteria for Selecting Suitable Factors

It is essential that the factors selected to evaluate personnel fit the company needs and be applicable to the employees being evaluated. To obtain satisfactory and lasting results, we recommend that a committee be assigned the task of selecting a number of factors that will validly evaluate the employees and at the same time be mutually acceptable to both management and the employee representatives. Before the selection of factors can begin, the committee needs to know whether there will be only one plan established to evaluate all employees or a separate plan for each of the different groups of employees, such as clerical, factory, sales, supervisory, and executive. Small firms of less than two dozen employees may prefer to evaluate all of their employees under a single plan, while larger companies usually have more than one plan. In either case the criteria for selecting the factors remain the same, but the factors usually vary. The committee that is charged with selecting evaluation factors should adopt some criteria, such as the following, for selecting the suitable factors.

The first requirement for the selection of suitable factors is that the factors be common denominators; that is, they can be found within the item(s) to be appraised. Since we previously established two separate goals of an employee evaluation (appraisal of job performance and appraisal of employee for self-development), we must have common denominator factors that are part of each goal. Unless a factor runs through each of these items, there will be great difficulty in comparing job performances and employees and in reaching an agreement on a final evaluation. Two examples of factors that are a part of every job performance are Quality and Quantity. The performance of every job has both a quality and a quantity aspect that may lend itself to evaluation. These factors, then, would be useful in evaluating the first goal of employee evaluation. The other goal, appraisal of employee self-development, requires factors that are related to or are responsible for job improvement or promotion. These factors are commonly referred to as personal traits or qualifications. Ability to Learn would be an example of a common denominator factor that definitely affects the chances of improving an employee's present job performance and his promotional job prospects.

The second requirement for the selection of suitable factors is that each factor should be considered important, measurable, and acceptable. The answers to the following questions will help determine whether the factor meets these tests:

1. Is the factor *important*? An important factor is one that management and employees recognize as necessary for job success. For example, most everyone realizes that the factors of Quality and Quantity contribute to the success of a job. Important factors are those for which management is usually willing to pay money to those employees who have them or are willing to develop them. Important factors lend validity to the employee evaluation.

2. Is the factor *measurable*? For a factor to be measurable, it must be possible to determine or observe the amount or frequency of its use when evaluating job performance and employees. The factors of Quality and Quantity are both measurable when applied to job performance. The factor Job Knowledge may be measured by tests and observations when attempting to determine the prospects for an employee to improve his job performance or his promotional job prospects. If reasonable measuring or rating of the factor is debatable, the factor should not be used.

3. Will the factor be *acceptable* to the personnel evaluated? To be acceptable, the factor needs to be understandable, considered fair, and practical. Acceptability of a factor by the vast majority of employees concerned is more easily met when a respected committee (rather than a single individual appointed by management) is chosen to select the factors.

The third and final requirement for the selection of suitable factors is that collectively the factors will adequately evaluate the employee without overlapping each other. Too few factors may result in an inadequate evaluation of employees and cause the employees to doubt the validity of the evaluations. Too many factors may result in undue complexity and needless red tape in the administration of the evaluation plan. Sometimes too many factors cause overlapping of factors which results in a distorted weight being given to some of the factors in the evaluation.

Objective and Subjective Rating

Before the proper selection and description of the factors in evaluation and rating are discussed, it seems necessary to differentiate between objective and subjective rating.

Objective Rating. The aim of a well-organized evaluation plan should be to make the rating of employees as simple as possible and, at the same time, objective. In choosing such factors as Quantity, Quality, and Punctuality, we are immediately aware of something that is measurable. In other words, we deal with a quantitative rating, thus comprehending an *objective magnitude* or value. We can measure the employee's accomplishments in pieces completed or in value of dollars and cents. We know, in units of time, how often the employee was absent or how many hours per week he was late. If measurements and accurate records are not available, however, a completely defined factor is essential. A brief description of the factor Quantity in the statements, "This factor appraises the employee's output of satisfactory work" or "Consider the employee's ability to produce the amount of work expected," gives the rater a conception of what is expected. Furthermore, definition of the factor aids in checking validity and reliability.

Subjective Rating. In attempting to evaluate and to rate the traits of an employee's personality, such as adaptability, attitude, and interest, we are dealing with character ratings and are using purely *subjective factors*. It must be conceded that most character factors to be rated are of a subjective nature, yet experience has proven that subjective traits take on an objective aspect when the rater is trained to depend on critical observation and analysis, especially if he is assisted with adequate interpretations of the factors. Two of the aforementioned factors might then read: "Adaptability — this factor appraises the employee's ability to meet changed conditions and the ease with which he learns new duties." "Attitude — this factor appraises the employee's open-mindedness toward his work, company, and other employees; his willingness to cooperate with associates, and agreeableness in carrying out safety and other company policies." The factors Adaptability and Attitude now have fairly realistic meanings, and tend to be more objective.

Employee Rating Factor Considerations

There are a number of other considerations that relate to the selection and suitability of factors to be used in an employee evaluation or rating plan. A brief discussion on the more important of these considerations follows.

Number of Rating Factors. In examining over 300 forms covering various phases of commercial and industrial activities, the authors have found few forms that contain the same number of rating factors or the same descriptions and definitions, except in the forms distributed by commerce groups and trade associations to their members. This is as it should be, when viewed from the standpoint of organizational individuality, or when considering our previous discussion concerning the feasibility of tailor-made plans. There is no reason, however, why three large banks with practically similar activities and services in the same city, should have a large number of rating factors that differ in terminology, definition, and grading. It is also difficult to see the reason why one manufacturer uses 29 rating factors for nonexempt employees, while a competitor manufacturing the same products with similar equipment uses only 10 factors for a similar group of employees. These examples are brought to light mainly to point out the need for a comprehensive study and analysis of those rating factors that are significant and necessary for the successful rating of a specific group.

A survey of 164 companies, which was completed in 1953 by the management department of Northwestern University, shows that the largest number of factors used is 29; the smallest number is 3, applied to shop workers and nonexempt salaried groups. These figures are fairly close to those of Roland Benjamin's survey,[3] conducted among 75 companies ranging in size from 130 to 196,000 employees, wherein 114 rating plans are used and the number of factors range from 5 to 32. Walter Mahler's survey of 132 employee rating plans shows from 1 to 33 factors being used in industry.[4] Roger H. Bellows claims that the average number of 8 factors is used for "wage groups" (hourly rated nonexempt); 9 factors for "clerical and nonsupervisory employees"; and 12 factors for "supervisors and executives."[5]

It would appear that five to ten factors should prove satisfactory for most employee evaluation plans. Fewer than five factors may fail to cover all the necessary aspects of the evaluation, while more than ten factors runs the risk of overlapping factors or excessive proliferation of one or more factors. Administrative detail also increases as the number of factors increases.

Types of Factors to Adopt. Before deciding on which type of rating factors to adopt, consideration should be given to the possibility of establishing a relationship to job factors, if a job evaluation plan exists. Employee rating should not be used as a by-product of job evaluation, however. Employee evaluation, dealing as it does with the determination of human behavior, is a significant function of wage and salary administration; and it should be considered as a primary procedure even in a small company.

---

[3]Roland Benjamin, Jr., "A Survey of 130 Merit Rating Plans," *Personnel* (New York: American Management Association, November, 1952), p. 293.

[4]Walter R. Mahler, "Some Common Errors in Employee Merit Rating Practices," *Personnel Journal*, Vol. XXVI (1947), p. 69.

[5]Roger H. Bellows, *Psychology of Personnel in Business and Industry* (New York: Prentice-Hall, Inc., 1949), p. 255.

The success of the employee evaluation plan, to a great extent, is contingent upon the selection of suitable factors to fit a specific situation. For the sake of emphasis, let us repeat two statements:

1. The selection of employee rating factors depends upon the nature of the business and the type of work.
2. Only pertinent factors concerning the employee's activity in relation to his job and his personal progress are to be included.

The actual selection of specific employee evaluation factors that meet the criteria previously described becomes an individual matter for each firm according to its needs and desires. In other words, each firm must decide for itself what specific factors appear to best meet their needs according to the goals they have established for their employee evaluation plan or plans. Figure 16.1 contains an

---

VARIOUS FACTORS THAT ARE BEING USED FOR EMPLOYEE EVALUATIONS

ability	earnestness	perseverance
accuracy	effectiveness	personality
achievement	emotional	physical fitness
adaptability	enthusiasm	planning
aggressiveness	errors	poise
alertness	evaluating	potential
ambition	experience	productivity
analytical ability		progress
appearance	financial acumen	punctuality
application	friendliness	
aptitude	goodwill	quality of work
attendance	health	quantity of work
attitude	honesty	reliability
		resourcefulness
carefulness	industry	responsibility
character	initiative	
common sense	integrity	safety
communications	intelligence	sales ability
conduct	interest	self-reliance
conscientiousness	investigating	sincerity
consideration of others		skill
cooperation	judgment	sociability
coordinating	knowledge of job	speed
cost consciousness	leadership	stability
courage	learning ability	staffing
courtesy	loyalty	stamina
creativity		supervisory ability
customer relations	maintenance of equipment	
	manner	teaching ability
decisiveness	neatness	teamwork
dependability	negotiating	technical knowledge
dominance	organization	thoroughness
drive	output	versatility
		vigor
		vision
		volume of work
		workmanship

FIGURE 16.1 A Checklist of the More Common Factors Used to Evaluate Employees

alphabetical checklist of the more common factors that have been used in various employee evaluations. It can serve to suggest factors that may meet each company's goals. For example, to meet the goal of measuring employee job performance, any one or more of the following factors taken from Figure 16.1 might be used: achievement, errors, output, productivity, progress, quality of work, quantity of work, volume of work, and workmanship. Each separate plan for evaluating a different group of employees may require different words as the factors that best appraise the individual group of employees involved.

To meet the second goal of employee evaluation (that of assisting the employee to improve performance and develop himself), a firm may wish to select only those factors that have been found to relate definitely to job performance and individual development. On the other hand, there are firms that have not identified definite relationships between job performance and success factors. In fact, more people are beginning to believe that these relationships vary with individuals, and if job performance is to be improved and individuals developed, it may be an individual matter for each case. This could mean that a firm would have no official standard set of evaluation factors to evaluate everyone for the purpose of improving their performance or determining areas for self-development. Instead, the firm would have a comprehensive checklist of factors known to affect job performance, which a rater could use as a source for discovering individual areas for job improvement and employee improvement. This checklist idea would give flexibility in accomplishing the second goal of employee evaluation. Furthermore, the second goal does not really require as fine a degree of evaluation on each factor because its purpose is to assist employee self-development and improved job performance by an identification of the various factors that tend to handicap better job performance and promotional possibilities. An exact degree of evaluation on personal factors may be neither possible nor desirable. In fact, it may be looked upon by some employees as an overly critical evaluation and cause resentment, thereby defeating its purpose of motivating the employee to develop himself and improve his job performance. If a rating is desired, it could be used to check one of three categories: not suitable for promotion, possible promotion with further self-development, and appears to be ready for immediate promotion.

The next few pages will identify the specific factors that various organizations and persons believe are useful for evaluating specific groups of employees.

The National Metal Trades Association has since 1939 recommended six factors for evaluating the factory worker to determine what he has done, what he can do, and whether you can rely on him. Their factors are as follows:

1. Quality of Work   } What he has done
2. Quantity of Work   }

S & S CORRUGATED PAPER MACHINERY CO., Inc.   **PERFORMANCE REVIEW**   DATE_____

Name_____   Clock No._____   Dept._____   Job Title_____   Labor Grade_____

FACTOR	EXCELLENT	VERY GOOD	GOOD	NEEDS IMPROVEMENT	UNSATISFACTORY
Quality of Work	Work is consistently well organized, orderly and accurate. Makes a minimum of errors.	Work is usually properly organized, orderly and accurate. Few errors.	Acceptable performance; normal accuracy.	Occasionally careless; makes more errors than acceptable.	Makes many errors; requires frequent checking.
Quantity of Work	Amount of work produced is consistently outstanding.	Usually completes an above average amount of work.	Consistently completes an acceptable amount of work.	Somewhat slow; does not always complete an acceptable amount of work.	Generally slow; does not produce enough work.
Knowledge of Job	Outstanding knowledge of duties, responsibilities and objectives. Requires minimum supervision.	Knows duties well, thorough working knowledge, requires little supervision.	Has adequate knowledge of duties; requires normal instruction and supervision.	Not fully familiar with duties. May lack some prerequisite training or experience.	Slow to grasp duties and responsibilities. Insufficient training or experience.
Initiative	Always gives his best. Self-reliant. Frequently offers suggestions.	Shows interest. Prudently undertakes nonroutine situations.	Properly utilizes standard procedures.	Somewhat indifferent attitude.	Shows little interest or effort.
Cooperation	Goes out of his way to cooperate with supervisors and co-workers.	Generally gets along well with supervisors and co-workers.	Businesslike manner; gets along with others.	Occasionally causes friction or slow to follow instructions.	Disruptive, antagonistic manner toward supervisors or co-workers.
Attendance	Outstanding record. Virtually no absences or lateness.	Very few absences or lateness.	Acceptable attendance record.	Absences or lateness exceed normal.	Frequent absences or lateness impair dept. operation.

COMMENTS:

Present Hourly Rate:_____

Job Seniority Date:_____

Company Seniority Date:_____

Recommended Increase_____

Effective Date:_____

Rated by:_____

Approved by:_____

Personnel Dept._____

Next Review_____   Effective Date:_____

Employee Interviewed by:_____   F/U Date:_____

Date:_____

INSTRUCTIONS TO SUPERVISOR:

1. Rate each factor. Enter under "Comments" any significant information affecting rating.
2. Indicate recommended increase, where applicable.
3. Secure approval signature of divisional head.
4. Forward to Personnel for review and signature.
5. Upon return of Review, bearing Personnel signature, interview employee and sign in appropriate space. Record any pertinent comments made by employee during interview.
6. Return immediately to Personnel in order to permit prompt notification to Payroll Department of salary change.

FIGURE 16.2 PERFORMANCE REVIEW FORM FOR GRANTING MERIT INCREASES TO NONEXEMPT HOURLY EMPLOYEES

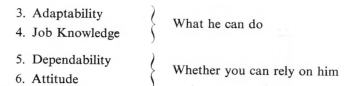

3. Adaptability

4. Job Knowledge   } What he can do

5. Dependability

6. Attitude   } Whether you can rely on him

The S & S Corrugated Paper Machinery Company, Inc., of Brooklyn, New York, uses a similar set of factors, shown in Figure 16.2, to determine which of its nonexempt hourly employees deserve a merit increase and how much that increase should be. Figure 16.3 shows an evaluation form containing 12 factors that are designed to evaluate two employee groups. The first 11 factors are used in the evaluation of nonexempt employees, while all 12 factors are used in the evaluation of supervisors.

The Northwestern Mutual Life Insurance Company of Milwaukee, Wisconsin, uses the following factors for appraising all their office staff employees: Quantity of work done and/or promptness in doing work, Quality of work, Personal Conduct as it affects work of others, Capacity and Adaptability, Cooperativeness, and Special Merit. The Special Merit factor is included to provide a way of giving special credit to the employee who makes a real contribution in areas that cannot be specifically recognized in other factors of the rating scale.

The research studies of the Management Development Laboratory of the Industrial Relations Center at the University of Minnesota have suggested the following measures of managerial performance: [6]

Planning	Supervising
Investigating	Staffing
Coordinating	Negotiating
Evaluating	Representing

The measurement of engineering and scientific personnel had been, for the most part, neglected by management until the late 1950's and the early 1960's. The Plastics Division of the Mobil Chemical Company is one of the companies that has established a formal rating program for these types of employees. [7] The plan divides employee performance into four overall levels that are subdivided into three degrees. The rater selects the statement that best fits or most accurately describes the employee (see Figure 16.4). The rating the employee receives determines his salary increase. There is no salary increase for Level 4, but there is a minimum or "normal" increase given for a level 3 appraisal, with successively higher amounts permitted for Levels 2 and 1. [8] The other side of the rating

---

[6]Thomas A. Mahoney and others, *Development of Managerial Performance — A Research Approach*, Monograph C-9 (Cincinnati: South-Western Publishing Co., 1963), p. 15.

[7]Irwin W. Krantz, "Evaluating the Technical Employee: A Results Approach," *Personnel* (January/February, 1964), p. 55.

[8]*Ibid.*

EMPLOYEE EVALUATION FORM				RATING FOR_____	

DEPT.   **CLOCK NO.**

INSTRUCTIONS

1. Disregard your personal feelings. Judge this employee on the qualities listed below.
2. Study the definitions of each factor, and the various phases of each before rating.
3. Call to mind instances that are typical of employee's work and actions.
4. Using your own careful judgment — check the phrase in each factor that is typical.
5. If employee performs no supervision — do not rate additional factor for supervisory ability.
6. Explain on reverse side any unusual characteristic not covered in regular factors.

	FACTOR	RANGE					RATING
1	**QUALITY** Performance in meeting quality standards	Careless — 4	Just gets by — 8	Does a good job — 12	Rejects and errors rare — 16	Exceptionally high quality — 20	
2	**JOB KNOWLEDGE** Understanding in all phases of his work	Expert in own job and several others — 25	Expert but limited to own job — 20	Knows job fairly well — 15	Improvement necessary — just gets by — 10	Inadequate knowledge — 5	
3	**QUANTITY** Output of satisfactory work	Turns out required amount but seldom more — 8	Frequently turns out more than required amount — 12	Slow — output is seldom required amount — 4	Exceptionally fast; output high — 20	Usually does more than expected — 16	
4	**DEPENDABILITY** Works conscientiously according to instructions	Dependable; no checking necessary — 20	Very little checking — 16	Follows instructions — 12	Frequent checking — 8	Continuous checking and follow-up — 4	
5	**INITIATIVE** Thinks constructively and originates action	Good decisions and actions but requires some supervision — 9	Minimum of supervision — 12	Thinks and acts constructively; no supervision required — 15	Requires constant supervision — 3	Fair decisions routine worker — 6	
6	**ADAPTABILITY** Ability to learn and meet changed conditions	Prefers old methods; does not remember instructions — 3	Learns slowly; reluctant to change — 6	Normal ability; routine worker — 9	Short period for mental adjustment; willing to change — 12	Learns rapidly — adjusts and grasps changes quickly — 15	
7	**ATTITUDE** Willingness to cooperate and carry out demands	Good team worker — 10	Cooperative — 8	Limited cooperation — 6	Passive resistance — 4	Poor cooperation; argumentative — 2	
8	**ATTENDANCE** Amount of excessive absenteeism	2 to 3 days normal or 2 days own accord — 6	1 to 2 days normal or 1 day own accord — 8	No days lost — 10	3 to 4 days normal or 3 days own accord —	More than 4 days absence — 2	
9	**SAFETY AND HOUSEKEEPING** Compliance with safety and housekeeping rules	Safe and orderly worker; equipment well cared for — 10	Workplace clean and safe — 8	Occasional warning about safety and orderliness — 6	Warned repeatedly about safety and cleanliness — 4	Area dirty; safety rules ignored — 2	
10	**POTENTIALITY** Potential ability to lead and teach others	Has no more growth — 2	Future growth doubtful — 4	Slow development ahead — 6	Bright future growth — 8	Exceptional possibilities — 10	
11	**PERSONALITY** Ability to get along with associates	Disagreeable — 2	Difficult to get along with — 4	Average or reasonable — 6	Well liked and respected — 8	Winning personality — 10	
12	**SUPERVISORY ABILITY** Additional rating for supervisors only	Poor organization and planning — 7	Inadequate supervision — 14	Nothing outstanding — 21	Good planning and effective organization — 28	Outstanding leadership — 35	

Date rated_____   Signed _____   TOTAL_____

USE SPACE ON REVERSE SIDE FOR REMARKS. EXPLAIN ANY RATING THAT IS ABNORMALLY LOW OR EXCEPTIONALLY HIGH

Factory Management and Maintenance

FIGURE 16.3   RATING FORM DESIGNED TO SERVE THE RATING OF TWO EMPLOYEE GROUPS

form is an integral part of the evaluation. It contains several open response questions that are used to substantiate the evaluation. It also contains a checklist of items that attempt to identify the employee's shortcomings which should be remedied to improve job accomplishment.

MOBIL CHEMICAL COMPANY
PLASTICS DIVISION

Engineering and Scientific Personnel   Employee _____
EVALUATION OF WORK ACCOMPLISHMENT   Clock No. _____ Dept. _____

Instructions

1. **The Evaluation of Work Accomplishment** should be made jointly by the employee's immediate supervisor and his supervisor, using all evidence or information available to them, including the most recent Management Development Appraisal.
2. Four generalized, composite statements of performance levels are shown below. It is not expected that any statement will precisely describe all facets of an employee's performance. The rating supervisor(s) should select the statement that *best fits* or *most accurately describes* the employee. Within this level, he should then select a point along the continuum which indicates how closely the statement describes the employee's achievements.

LEVEL 1	The employee and/or his unit have made some extremely valuable contributions. The results achieved far exceed those normally expected of the great majority of engineers or scientists with comparable education or experience. He and/or his people exhibit a high degree of creativity or ingenuity in producing useful, practical, often unique solutions to problems. He gets things done well within established deadlines and at minimum cost. He and/or his unit are consistently productive, handling unusual amounts of work and using their time effectively. He is careful and analytical, anticipating difficulties in advance, so that his work is almost always "right" on the first attempt His activities consistently encourage teamwork and enhance the efforts of other groups. Virtually all his superiors, peers, and/or subordinates have a very high regard for his ability. Any personal shortcomings are relatively minor and have virtually no effect on his ability to achieve results.
LEVEL 2	The employee and/or his unit have made some worthwhile contributions. The results achieved are better than one would normally expect of most professional engineers or scientists with comparable education or experience. The work produced exhibits a degree of creativity or imagination and is usually suitable to the problems at hand. The work is most often completed on time, at a reasonable cost and with a minimum of wasted effort. He is careful and uses foresight in anticipating difficulties so that his work seldom requires rechecking or redoing. His activities sometimes contribute to the efforts of other groups. Most of his superiors, peers, and/or subordinates respect his ability. He may have a few personal shortcomings that should be remedied, but they do not seriously interfere with his ability to achieve results.
LEVEL 3	The accomplishments of the employee and/or his unit are adequate or acceptable. The results achieved are those one would expect of most engineers or scientists with comparable education or experience. He and/or his people do what is asked or assigned, not typically leaving the beaten path in solving problems. His work usually meets its intended purpose, but his superiors may sometimes feel the job could have been done better, more quickly, or less expensively. He and/or his people produce a normal amount of work in a steady, almost predictable fashion, occasionally going off onto unproductive tangents. He is usually careful, but at times his work requires rechecking or redoing. His activities do not interfere with the efforts of other groups. His superiors, peers, and/or subordinates consider him competent. He may have a number of personal shortcomings, which, if remedied, would improve his ability to achieve better results.
LEVEL 4	The accomplishments of the employee and/or his unit have been limited. Work accomplishments tend to be erratic or inconsistent, sometimes meeting their intended purpose, at other times falling short of an acceptable level. Frequently, it is felt that too much time, effort, and money are devoted to projects. The employee and/or his unit seem to tackle jobs in an unimaginative, routine fashion. His and/or his people often go off onto unproductive tangents or blind alleys, which could usually be avoided by better analysis of problems or greater foresight. His work must often be rechecked or redone. His activities may cause some friction or interference with the efforts of other groups. His superiors, peers, and/or subordinates have some doubts about his competence. His personal shortcomings often interfere with his ability to accomplish results. Unless performance improves, there would be serious question concerning his continued employment.

FIGURE 16.4 Evaluating the Technical Employee Via Four Levels of Performance with Three Degrees Within Each Level. Front side of rating form for professional personnel.

From the discussion on the types of factors to adopt, it should be apparent that there are a number of factors available to fit most any situation or condition. In fact, many of the factors thus far mentioned are very similar in meaning and could pass as duplicates. Therefore, when the selection committee has made its decision on the factors to be used for evaluation, it should clearly define the factors so as to avoid misunderstandings.

Factor Definitions. In discussing job evaluation factors, the importance of accurate factor definitions was stressed. Here again we point to the need for adequately described and defined factors in employee evaluation and rating. Not only should descriptions and definitions agree with the unified concepts of those concerned in the same organization or entire company, but also every effort should be exerted to use definitions that conform with those of other companies in the same field of activity or industry. Thus, benefits will be derived from a uniformity of language in wage surveys, as well as in dealings with unions. The trend in union bargaining and union-management agreements is toward formalizing joint employer-employee rating plans that are industry-wide. As a result, the meaning of any factor will then be the same to all raters within the industry as well as within the company.

Factor Degrees and Descriptions. The number of degrees for each rating factor varies from three to eight. Most companies, however, use five degrees. Some start with "poor" as the lowest, ending with such adjectives as "excellent," "exceptional," or "outstanding" as the highest. It should be noted that the purely numerical, alphabetical, and percentile degrees shown in Figure 14.7 are now seldom used. But, combinations with adjectives or adverbs, as shown in Figures 14.6 and 14.8, are still utilized. Such combinations should be used only when the rating factors are fully defined and well described. The numerals then serve to indicate the weighting of the degree and scoring.

To minimize the likelihood of the rater being in the embarrassing situation of not using the "poor" or "excellent" degrees, the best procedure is to eliminate the adjectival "poor," "fair," "average," "good," and "excellent" entirely, and to use definitions, descriptions, or brief step phrases as shown in Figures 14.8, 14.9, and 16.3. Such definitions and descriptive degrees make it possible for all raters to adopt the same interpretation, thus establishing a uniform procedure and accurate rating.

In Figure 16.3 we find 11 factors (not considering Supervisory Ability) with five degrees assigned to each factor. Aside from the very effective manner in which the rater is assisted in rating each degree for the respective factor, each of the five degrees is briefly but clearly defined. Note the varying number of points assigned as the weight or importance to each factor and degree. The weighting, and eventual scoring, of each factor is generally tied in with the selection of factors. A discussion of these two considerations follows.

Weighting of Factors. There is no specific rule regarding the relative weights to be assigned to rating factors. The assignment of weights is contingent upon the selection and number of factors, kind of services rendered by the employees to be rated, and the pooled judgment of committee members. The committee generally assigns different weights to the subfactors according to the relative significance attached to the basic factors. One company might assign 25 points to the basic factor Ability and 50 points for Production, while another company might consider a relatively different percentage in number of points.

Sample rating forms actually used in various enterprises have been purposely introduced to bring to the attention of the reader the variations in approach and differences in setups. A reexamination of the rating forms will indicate the variations in the number of factors and degrees that are affected by weighting. The plan in Figure 14.9 provides six factors with eight degrees; Figure 16.2 has six factors and five degrees; while in Figure 16.3 there are 12 factors divided into five degrees. It is evident that the weighting differs according to the designed plan, type of rating form, and relative importance of each factor.

Generally, most plans provide for weighting in number of points based on the five adjectival scales "poor," "below average," "average," "above average," and "excellent," even though the actual adjectival descriptions are omitted. (See Figure 16.3.) For the degree "excellent," there are usually 100 points allotted, equaling 100 percent for the highest total score. However, to arrive at a more precise rating, to avoid overlapping, and for other reasons, the weighting of factors and the number of points are often assigned arbitrarily. For example, one company uses 10 factors and 5 degrees, allotting a total of 40 to 90 points for "poor," 460 to 760 points for "average," and from 920 to 1,000 points for "excellent." A proportionate number of points is assigned to degrees "below average" and "above average." The percentage for each factor is obtained by dividing the total score by ten. Thus, the lowest rating total may differ between 4 percent and 9 percent, the average total between 46 percent and 76 percent, and the highest total between 92 percent and 100 percent.

Some plans show a considerable departure from the usual five degrees. The points assigned to the six basic factors in the NMTA plan (Figure 14.9), are arranged to rate eight different degrees for each factor. The lowest degree (R-8) starts with 30 points, increasing by 10 points for each degree until the maximum total of 100 points is reached for the highest (R-1) degree. [9] The distribution of points for eight degrees of all six factors is shown in Table 16.1.

Weights should be assigned to all factors, in accordance with their importance, that represent job performance (Quality, Quantity, etc.) if the firm is desirous of relating pay raises to job productivity or efficiency. For those factors

---

[9] A. L. Kress, "How To Rate Jobs and Men," *Factory Management and Maintenance*, Vol. XCVII, No. 10 (October, 1939), p. 66.

TABLE 16.1

NMTA POINT VALUES FOR RATING NONEXEMPT WORKERS

Factor	R-1	R-2	R-3	R-4	R-5	R-6	R-7	R-8
1. Quality of Work.......	25	23	20	18	15	13	10	8
2. Quantity of Work......	20	18	16	14	12	10	8	6
3. Adaptability..........	15	13	12	10	9	7	6	4
4. Job Knowledge........	20	18	16	14	12	10	8	6
5. Dependability.........	10	9	8	7	6	5	4	3
6. Attitude..............	10	9	8	7	6	5	4	3
Totals..............	100	90	80	70	60	50	40	30

Source: Factory Management and Maintenance.

such as Initiative and Skill that pertain only to improving job performance and assisting the individual employee in developing himself, it would appear that assigning specific weights to them is not necessary because they are used only as a source in counseling and motivating employees toward self-development. However, an evaluation of such factors does need to indicate on which factors the employee is below and above average in his development.

Scoring of Factors. Psychologists have debated the advisability of scoring each factor, claiming that it is impossible to judge human values and to apply exact numerical figures to human traits. Similarly, opinions differ regarding the advisability of judging an employee by individual factor scores, or by an overall score only.

When a company wishes to reward its employees on the basis of job performance, only those factors that represent job results (Quality, Quantity, etc.) need to be scored and converted into a meaningful overall performance rating that is keyed to a predetermined schedule of rewards (financial and nonfinancial). Likewise, for each objective that an employee evaluation is expected to serve, there should be a separate appraisal consisting of only those factors that relate to that objective. There can be no single, global, comprehensive, or overall rating that can validly serve more than one purpose. Too many firms somehow expect an employee evaluation to produce a single score or rating that is useful for whatever purpose they wish. Nothing could be more misleading or invalid.

After the scoring for each individual objective of employee evaluation has been completed, it is necessary for employees to know what the score represents. If an employee receives a job performance rating of 75, his supervisor needs to know the answers to such questions as:

1. Does the worker deserve a raise within the same job range?
2. Should he be promoted to a higher job grade?
3. Shall he be transferred to a higher paid job?
4. Does he need counseling and guidance to improve himself?
5. Should he be demoted to a lower paid job? (This action is not recommended unless a mistake in placement has occurred.)

6. Should he be given special training?
7. Should he be discharged?
8. Should his status remain the same as it was before rating?

The supervisor will have the answers to the above questions only if predetermined actions have been keyed to the range of possible scores. For example, when an hourly employee of the S & S Corrugated Paper Machinery Company receives a rating score of "good," he is granted at least a 5 cent-per-hour pay raise. If his rating is "very good" or "excellent," he receives increases between 7 cents and 15 cents an hour.[10] At many universities, college students know that when they take a test and receive a performance score of 0–69 percent, it means an F or failure; that 70–77 percent means a D, which is passing but below average; that 78–84 percent is C or average; that 85–92 percent is B or above average; and that 93–100 percent is A or outstanding. Employees should know the basis for determining the various levels of performance. This is discussed in the next chapter.

Once suitable evaluation factors, weights, and scoring keys have been selected, there remains a number of procedures that need to be worked out before a plan of evaluating employees can be considered established.

Determining the procedures of the plan

Every employee evaluation plan requires certain procedures to stabilize the plan and make it practicable. Criticism has been levied at various procedures of evaluation plans. Some say that the plans are too time-consuming, too complicated, too difficult to administer, or are frequently misunderstood by management as well as the employees. Others complain of the timing of evaluations, the forms, and the rigidity of the plans, which fail to adjust to changing times.

Current company practices on a number of procedures will be discussed in order to offer some guidelines when one attempts to develop a tailor-made plan that will be relatively free of criticism.

Design and Contents of Rating Forms

When designing the rating form or "chart," one should remember its use as an instrument or tool in setting up the rating plan. It should be regarded as the "heart" in the functioning of the system. A thoughtfully designed form, with brief but clear instructions and properly defined factors, will minimize subjectivity and probable error. Only pertinent factors concerning the employee's activity in relation to his job and his progress should be included.

---

[10]"Simple Chart Determines Who Gets Merit Raises," *Employee Relations Bulletin*, Report No. 888 (January 8, 1964), p. 5.

Large and medium-size companies utilize separate and distinct forms for each of the employee groups that come under a different plan of employee evaluation. The General Electric Company, with its complex activities and thousands of employees, adopted an employee-rating system that uses two rating forms, one for shop workers and nonexempt salaried employees and one for supervisory, professional, and managerial employees. The selection of the two forms by General Electric, a pioneer in the development and use of employee-evaluation plans, is based on over 30 years of experience with employee evaluation and rating systems. Their rating form is small and simply worded so that the rater can definitely make up his mind to check one of the three descriptive grades. Instructions to the rater are brief, but thoroughly explained in a manual that also includes definitions of the three factors.

There is a general tendency among other companies to define the factors on the rating form, to exemplify the traits, and to include descriptive values as shown in Figure 14.9, used by members of the National Metal Trades Association.

Frequency of Rating

Repeat ratings depend upon economic conditions, supply and demand of labor, and wage trends. Whether supervisors can be burdened with repetitive rating is also an important factor. There is a danger that the rater may lose interest and make incorrect ratings if the frequency of ratings is too great or if the interval between ratings is too long.

New employees should be observed and rated biweekly or monthly over a certain period to determine whether the wage rates are equitable and whether the employees should be retained on the allotted jobs. Probationary employees should be rated within short periods to ascertain their improvement. Under normal conditions the older employees should be rated semiannually or annually. The tendency, however, is to rate employees quarterly to assume an objective rating and uniformly fair treatment. This is especially advisable during periods of rising prices and labor shortages.

Many companies make quarterly ratings a regular procedure of their wage and salary program, especially if wage-rate increments are due quarterly. Four times a year every foreman or office manager receives from the personnel department a form for each employee. The forms must be filled out and returned to the personnel department within 15 days. For a permanent individual record, the personnel department either copies the total score or calculates the total number of points earned by the employee. Thus, if the employee has been with the company over one year, there are four quarterly ratings in his record folder. Hence, every employee who undergoes evaluation and rating not only feels secure in his position, but is also aware that the supervisor and the personnel department will put him in line for a wage raise within the pay grade or promote him to a higher pay grade. Performance ratings on employees of the federal government are conducted at least every year for employees of grade GS-10 or below and at 18-month intervals for employees of grade GS-11 or above (with at least three months of mutual working experience between the supervisor and the employee).

Who Should Do the Rating?

Those persons who come in direct contact with the employee to be rated and have first-hand knowledge about him are usually the best qualified personnel to do the rating, provided they have had adequate instruction or experience in the rating process. These personnel would include the employee's immediate supervisor, the immediate supervisor's superior, the employee's co-workers, and other supervisors.

The common practice in most firms is to have the employee's *immediate supervisor* do the rating by himself. The advantage of the supervisor handling the rating is that he generally has the greatest knowledge of the employee and should be the most qualified to do the job. Other advantages in using the supervisor are that he can do the job with comparative ease, there is less total evaluation time required, and the process is less expensive. A disadvantage of using only the supervisor as a rater is that he can intentionally bias his ratings. He sometimes is also slipshod in evaluating his employees, especially if he is under constant pressures and is unable to devote adequate time to evaluate his employees properly. Having the immediate supervisor handle the rating is most desirable when the raters are thoroughly trained and when they have adequate time to perform the evaluation. This method also lends itself better to a firm whose leadership is more autocratic than democratic and when its employees are willing to follow that leadership.

To overcome the disadvantages of inadequately trained supervisors, those who are not free of biases, and haphazard evaluations, some firms use a committee system for rating employees. The committee may be composed of three or four people who know the ratee first-hand, such as the employee's immediate supervisor, his superior, a co-worker of the employee, or one or two other supervisors. The committee of raters can help eliminate the shortcomings of a faulty single supervisory rating by increasing the amount of knowledge that is available for discussion when evaluating the ratee. This helps to insure that the evaluation data will be interpreted more objectively.

The critics of the committee system of rating indicate that it is time consuming, cumbersome, and expensive if the evaluation is done well.[11] Some say that the committee often serves as a smoke screen for the employee's immediate superior by presenting his viewpoints as those representing the committee. Then, too, some committee members may not have the interest, the know-how, or

---

[11]William G. Rothstein, "Effective Appraisal Programs," *ILR Research*, Vol. VIII, No. 2 (1962), p. 11.

enough time to perform their committee assignments satisfactorily. The committee system, sometimes referred to as "peer ratings" when all its members fit this classification, has been recommended as an effective evaluation technique when a number of employees are rated in order to select one of them for an available promotion.[12] All other factors being equal, the committee method of employee evaluation *for promotion* is better than that of the supervisor alone because of the greater validity of the pooled judgment of the committee. The committee ratings of an employee would also be the more desirable method to use whenever a supervisor is incapable of doing the rating alone.

Sometimes the decision as to who should do the rating is determined by the appraisal method that the company chooses. In evaluating employees by the objectives method, the employee himself may make the appraisal or it may be done jointly by the employee and his supervisor. Some of the advocates of the method of evaluating employees by objectives believe that this method is best because when the employee sets his own performance standards, with or without the help of his superior, there can be no misunderstanding of the evaluated results. If any employee evaluation is to be most meaningful, the employee must know how he stands and the reasons for his performance. When the employee is part of the evaluation, he examines and appraises his own performance and thereby has a better understanding of it and what self-development he needs. It would appear that self-evaluation is the most desirable method of employee evaluation when the following circumstances prevail: (1) the employees are well educated, self-motivated, and have the interest of the firm as well as their own interests at heart (usually professional, technical, and managerial personnel); (2) the management is open-minded and willing to take the employees into their confidence by making known the company objectives and pertinent facts that have a bearing on these; and (3) the jobs are of a nonrepetitive nature.

Handling the Rating Results

As pointed out earlier, employee evaluation is equally advantageous to the employer and the employee. Consequently, it would be assumed that after the ratings are completed, the employee will be told "where he stands," favorably or unfavorably. This point of view is not shared by all administrators, however. Recent studies conducted by the Behavioral Research Service at General Electric have suggested that if the appraisal interview hopes to accomplish the two objectives of providing a written justification for salary action and motivating the employee to improve his work performance, the two purposes, which are in conflict, should not be handled in the same interview.[13]

---

[12]Gene S. Booker and Ronald W. Miller, "A Closer Look at Peer Ratings," *Personnel* (January/February, 1966), pp. 42–47.

[13]H. H. Meyer *et al.*, "Split Roles in Performance Appraisal," *Harvard Business Review* (January/February, 1965), p. 128.

Discussing Ratings with Ratees. Some authorities object to discussing the ratings with ratees on the premise that the supervisor who did the rating would not want his workers to know that he interfered with their advancement. Furthermore, it is feared that if the rating is unfavorable or if a mistake occurs, the employee will show ill will. It is also assumed that ratings should be kept secret so that misplacements, counseling, promotions, transfers, layoffs, and periodic wage increases can be handled confidentially by the personnel department.

Experience proves, however, that by discussing the ratings with employees, the mutual employer-employee benefits counteract the fears. Fears are usually unfounded if the ratings are based on facts and not on personal opinion. If a rating were unfavorable because of error, it should be rectified. The plan will then be regarded as just and fair. Most employees are eager to know "how they stand" and whether they are progressing. Hesitation to let workers know their status is contrary to sound and successful employee evaluation and rating plans, and then the purpose of the plans may be defeated.[14]

The Employee's Point of View. One of the reasons why workers, in some cases, are antagonistic to employee evaluation is that supervisors or raters are not taking the employees into their confidence to advise them of a low rating in order to correct the undesirable status. If the employee is informed of his low rating in a sympathetic and helpful mood, a situation is created where improvement may be expected. The worker, then, is anxious to improve his status, to receive a higher rating at the next review, and to express his desire to know "How am I doing?"

A favorable rating makes the employee feel more secure in his job. On the other hand, some employee's characteristics may need correction. A tactful heart-to-heart talk in a sympathetic atmosphere will normally bring about an improvement. In general, it may be stated that to obtain full value from evaluation and rating, *the immediate supervisor should always report the outcome of the rating to the ratee.* See Figure 16.5 for an outline of the possible topics that might be discussed in the interview.

The General Electric research studies[15] suggest that the motivation of employees to improve their performances should be more of a day-to-day type of coaching rather than a once-a-year activity. The reason for this suggestion is that each employee can only take so much criticism at any one time. This means that every employee has a tolerance level for the amount of criticism he can take. After this level is reached, it is increasingly difficult for the employee to accept responsibility for his shortcomings. Then, too, if the supervisor waits until the end of the appraisal period to present all the employee's shortcomings that he has saved up, it will be difficult to correct the shortcomings if they have become

[14]Clifford E. Jurgensen, "How'm I Doing?" *Personnel Psychology*, Vol. IV, No. 1 (Spring, 1951), pp. 49–62.
[15]Meyer *et al., op. cit.*, p. 127.

TOPICAL OUTLINE FOR AN EMPLOYEE EVALUATION INTERVIEW

I. **Discuss Job Performance Results (for pay increases) in terms of:**

	Below Standard	Meets Standard	Above Standard	Well Above Standard
A. Quality				
_____	___	___	___	___
_____	___	___	___	___
B. Quantity				
_____	___	___	___	___
_____	___	___	___	___
or Predetermined Objectives				
_____	___	___	___	___
_____	___	___	___	___

II. **Discuss Job Performance Improvement in terms of any of the following which may be appropriate:**

	What Needs Improvement?	What Are Strong Assets?
A. Employee Qualifications		
_____		
_____		
B. Job Conditions		
_____		
_____		
C. Other Circumstances		
_____		
_____		

III. **Discuss Possible Plans for Improving Job Performance (or helping the employee develop himself) in terms of:**

    A. What progress has been made since the last interview.

    B. What the employee can do by himself.

    C. What the firm and the supervisor can do.

FIGURE 16.5   Topics that Might Be Discussed in an Employee Evaluation Interview

deep-seated habits. Likewise, the feedback to the employee on his performance improvement will be less effective if only given once a year. On the other hand, the supervisor's criticism should not be given so frequently that it destroys the employee's self-respect and disrupts rather than improves his subsequent job performance. When job performance improvement is sought, it may be better for the supervisor to mold the discussions around the conditions and circumstances that can improve job performance rather than stressing the employee's personal traits.

How to Present Ratings to Employees. To avoid possible ill will on the part of some employees, a few pointers on how to present the ratings are:

1. *Plan the interview.* Decide on how, when, and where to discuss the rating. Have facts ready and discuss all details in strict privacy.
2. *Be prepared for the employee's reaction.* The employee who has a chip on his shoulder is usually antagonistic and hard to handle. Thoughtful preparation will ameliorate the situation. Be a good listener.
3. *Review the purpose of evaluation and rating.* Present the most important and attractive benefits. Explain that periodic ratings and interviews will occur in the future.
4. *Explain how the employee was rated.* After the employee is made to feel at ease, bring out the good points first. Then present those facts that specifically affect his performance and the other objective ratings. Explain his shortcomings sympathetically with the attitude that he can help himself but, at the same time, explain that you are willing to assist him in every way to progress and advance his status.
5. *Show a willingness to listen.* Handle the situation diplomatically. Have the employee express his reactions to the ratings and encourage him to be more competent and cooperative. By finding out his obstacles, you may discover unfavorable conditions that are the company's fault.
6. *Briefly review the strong and weak points.* Show the possibilities for improvement, especially in connection with personality shortcomings. Express your sincere interest in solving his problem.

Preparing an Employee Evaluation Manual

Training of the raters will be more effective if an employee evaluation manual is prepared in which the objectives, purpose, methods, and procedures of employee evaluation are detailed. The description of forms, factors, degrees, and the use of scales will serve as a guide for adhering to rules and standards. Besides helping the foremen and supervisors to grasp fully the details and procedures involved, the manual will be an equally valuable guide for stewards and joint union-management committee members who participate in preparing and maintaining the rating plan. The contents, format, and illustrations will differ with each company, depending upon whether one manual will be used for all, or at each, organizational level.

The Minnesota Mining and Manufacturing Company uses a neatly printed 8½″ x 11″ employee evaluation manual for evaluating all levels and types of employees. The manual is divided into two parts. Part One, entitled "Performance Appraisal," provides a background, describes general objectives and selection of factors, and gives the appraisal outline illustrated with forms. The "How to Make the Appraisal" section deals at length with frequency of rating, securing information, using the scales, establishing performance requirements, making recommendations, doing the overall rating, and preparing records for the future. Part Two covers the approach and describes progressively how to discuss the rating with employees and how to review the appraisal in order to encourage employees toward further development and promotion.

Training the raters

Rating requires skill that can be acquired only through proper training. Many unsuccessful rating plans are traceable to the limited formal education of the rater who has insufficient knowledge of what rating involves. Foremen who are promoted from the rank and file are generally biased and may oppose rating primarily because of prejudice, incompetence, and lack of proper judgment. Or, they may place undue emphasis on certain job duties. Few raters know how to observe and evaluate an employee's behavior apart from his job performance. It is often times difficult to get even supervisors and executives to review the employee evaluation ratings with their subordinates. Many of the above shortcomings and other difficulties connected with employee evaluations can be overcome by training all raters (and potential raters) on a select group of appropriate topics taken from Chapters 14, 15, and 16. Every rater who is not able to evaluate his subordinates accurately will not make effective use of their abilities and thus this will reflect poorly on his own performance.

A well-organized training course directed by the personnel manager or an industrial engineer will prepare the raters to base their findings on actualities. For example, production rating should be based on quantities actually produced per hour or per week. Similarly, quality rating should be based on the percentage of rejects by the inspection department, the number of items scrapped, or the quantity of material wasted over a certain period of time.

Proper training with the use of scientific aids, such as the various forms, checklists and scales, examples, illustrations, and participation in discussions, should caution the rater not to be influenced by petty details or by the judgment of others. A discussion of the rating form and the reasons for the different arrangements of scales and factor grades will help the rater to grasp the principles of factual and objective rating. If the supervisors participate in preparing the plan, training becomes merely practice in learning the procedural details and techniques of rating.

Once the plan of evaluating employees has been formally organized and installed, there remains its administration. Connected with these activities are problems that arise for one reason or another. The more important ones connected with employee evaluation will now be discussed.

Handling rating problems connected with employee evaluation

When raters have been well trained to evaluate employees, only a minimum number of minor problems are likely to arise because the raters have been taught to prevent the big problems and to correct the small problems. However, it appears that only the better managed companies have been able to instruct raters adequately. Thus, there are a number of problems connected with the evaluation of employees. Three of the more common problems, known as rating errors, are the halo effect, the horns effect, and the central tendency.

The Halo Effect

When a rater tends to rate an employee too high, either because of a general impression or because of some outstanding characteristic that influences his judgment, the tendency is called the *halo effect*. For example, John Miller is known to his foreman as a fast worker, always completing his jobs in considerably less than the allowed standard time. The foreman is so captivated by this achievement that he rates Miller very high in such factors as quality, adaptability, dependability, ingenuity, and cooperativeness; yet Miller does not deserve the high rating for all factors.

There are a number of ways for minimizing or possibly avoiding the halo effect. In the graphic scale method, descriptive phrases may be reversed so that the "poor" grade is at the right on one line and at the left on the next line, as may be seen in Figure 16.3. Thus, the rater is alerted and should proceed cautiously. Some personnel managers insist upon all employees being rated on one factor at a time before proceeding to rate any employee on the next factor, thereby minimizing the influence of an overall impression.[16] The Lincoln Electric Company of Cleveland, Ohio, which employs this method, uses the four factors of Supervision Required, Contribution to Improvement, Workmanship and Attitude Toward Quality, and Output. A separate and different colored rating form is used for each of these factors.

The Horns Effect

When a rater tends to rate an employee lower than circumstances justify, the rating error may be called the *horns effect*. The horns effect is the opposite of

---

[16]For a more complete discussion of the halo effect, see R. S. Driver, "A Case History of Merit Rating," *Personnel* (May, 1940), pp. 137–162.

the halo effect. Raters are often guilty of the horns effect because they lack training in rating or have some bias. Odiorne indicates that the horns effect may be due to the rater being a perfectionist or a contrary person, or the employee being a maverick or a nonconformist.[17] Or, the employee may be the victim of being on a weak team or associating with the wrong crowd or boss. Sometimes the employee receives a low rating because one recent error is all the rater remembers about the employee.

The horns effect can be minimized in a manner similar to that recommended above for the halo effect. Both the halo effect and the horns effect will tend to be reduced if the rater is forced to establish predetermined objective job performance standards as a measuring yardstick of performance. Of course, there is no substitute for the proper training of raters to avoid the pitfalls of the various rating errors. To require raters to use a frequency distribution of some type is not an adequate substitute for training nor a long-range solution to rating errors.

The Central Tendency

Both the halo and the horns effects described above are rating errors that primarily relate to the individual. The *central tendency* is a different type of rating error, for it relates to a group of employees rather than to one individual. In this error the rater tends to rate or classify all of his subordinates in the same category, which is usually average. Raters who fall into this error of grouping or bunching all their employees in the average category are sometimes accused of being weak and not having a mind of their own. This may be true where the supervisor is afraid that if he rated someone high or low, he would be asked to justify the rating. When the supervisor places all his employees in the same rating group, he may erroneously feel that everything is fine because he is not discriminating against anyone. Even though all employees may sometimes fit into the same rating category, there are differences among employees; therefore, the employee evaluation should reveal rankings within a category.

The central tendency error can be the result of raters not understanding that individuals and their performances do differ and that evaluating employees brings out these differences. Every department usually has employees who fall into more than one rating category for several reasons. New employees are continually coming into a department while others are leaving. Some workers within the department are regulary developing themselves for promotion while others are just marking time or coasting. By the very nature of people, they differ physically and in temperament, likes, dislikes, intelligence, ambitions, drives, aptitudes, interests, motivations, etc. Thus, it would be the exceptional situation where all the employees in a department, or its subsection, fall into the same rating category.

---

[17]George S. Odiorne, "What's Wrong with Appraisal Systems?" *Personnel Policy: Issues and Practices* (Columbus, Ohio: Charles E. Merrill Books, Inc., 1963), chap. 13.

The central tendency effect may be minimized by having the raters take a training course in rating. When this long-range solution is not possible, management sometimes resorts to the short-range solution of forcing raters to differentiate between employees by requiring them to rank their subordinates in the order of their value to the department or to the company, or to separate their employees into separate categories or groups such as the top 10 percent, next 20 percent, next 40 percent, next 20 percent, and lowest 10 percent.

REVIEW QUESTIONS

1. What are the *main* disadvantages of an informal employee evaluation plan?
2. What group of employees should be evaluated first? Why?
3. What type of factors should be included in a successful employee evaluation plan?
4. Who is the best qualified person to rate employees?
5. When should an employee's rating be discussed with him?
6. What are the advantages that the company derives from the information gained through employee evaluation?
7. Is there a place for informal plans in employee evaluation? Explain your answer.
8. Why is top management's endorsement necessary before adopting a formal plan of employee evaluation?
9. Which employees should be allowed to participate in the establishment of a formal plan of employee evaluation?
10. How can one go about making an employee evaluation more objective?
11. What are some problems that are connected with employee evaluation? How might they be overcome?
12. Under what circumstances should an employee evaluation plan be tailor-made? ready-made?
13. How often should employees be evaluated? Explain your answer.
14. When might it be advantageous to have the employee evaluate himself?
15. What are the criteria for selecting suitable factors for an employee evaluation plan?
16. What advantages and disadvantages does the committee form of employee evaluation have over the single man evaluation?

RESEARCH OR SEMINAR QUESTIONS

1. Has the evaluation of employees become more objective or subjective during the last 10 years?
2. Should a person who has been at the top of his rate range for the past 10 years continue to be evaluated along with the rest of the employees or is evaluating him a waste of time?
3. How can the areas of personnel, other than wage and salary, make use of the information gained from employee evaluation?

PRACTICAL EXPERIENCE ASSIGNMENTS

1. Outline a procedure for instructing employees on what you think they should be told about the company's employee evaluation program.
2. Prepare a topical outline covering the contents of a training course that you would recommend for the training of merit raters.
3. It was company policy that the immediate supervisor should do the rating of employees. One particular supervisor had the tendency to rate all his employees in the mediocre range (central tendency). He explained that "all my subordinates are just average. I ought to know — I'm in daily contact with them." How would you tactfully relate to him that his central tendency attitude could be harmful to his department and the overall employee evaluation plan?
4. Design a rating form for evaluating either the officers or the personnel of a club, a union, or an organization with which you are familiar.

CASE PROBLEM

16–1. THE PROGRESSIVE MANUFACTURING COMPANY

Inconsistencies in Employee Evaluation

Jay Don and Michael Ray, two promising and experienced workers in different sections of the production department of The Progressive Manufacturing Company, were both interested in becoming the new supervisor of a small group of inspectors recently hired. Each man appeared to be qualified for the job. In practically all respects — age, education, seniority, marital status — there was little noticeable difference in the men. It was secretly decided by those in charge of the situation that whichever man received the higher annual employee rating would be promoted to the supervisor's position.

Each man was to be evaluated by three of his supervisors who knew him very well. The raters did not know that their ratings were to be used as the basis of a promotion. As it happened, no one rater knew both Jay and Mike.

All ratings were made on the standard company employee evaluation form. When the ratings were turned in, the results showed that Jay Don received ratings of 73, 75, and 77. Michael Ray received ratings of 55, 75, and 95. These ratings were turned over to the wage and salary administrator to decide who should receive the promotion.

Problems:

1. What are some possible causes of the inconsistency of ratings on Mike?
2. What action would you take to get a more reliable rating on Mike?
3. How can such inconsistent ratings of personnel be reduced or eliminated in the future?
4. Can you be sure that the final ratings are valid? Why?
5. How would you go about deciding who is to be promoted?

chapter 17

BASIC METHODS OF COMPENSATING EMPLOYEES

The first 16 chapters of this book have presented a framework of compensation by stressing the job and man relationship and the values that can be attached to each of these two components. Chapters 17 through 23 examine the various methods and plans that are available for compensating employees after the job worth and the man worth have been determined. Chapters 17 through 21 deal primarily with the basic methods of paying employees, while Chapters 22 and 23 deal with the supplemental methods of payment. A study of the various methods of compensating employees is important from the standpoint of keeping costs at a minimum and of finding the best ways and means of motivating and rewarding employees for their efforts.

The purpose of this chapter is to identify and classify the basic methods of compensation that are available for paying employees so that a meaningful framework is established for Chapters 18 through 23.

Classification of compensation methods

For proper distinction and practical application purposes, the principal methods of compensating employees may be divided into three classes:

1. Compensation on the basis of time.
2. Compensation on the basis of productive efficiency.
3. Supplementary compensations.

451

Compensation on the Basis of Time

Under the method of compensating the employee on the basis of time, the value of work performance has little or no specific rating. *The employee is paid primarily according to the time he spends at work*. The employer accepts the responsibility for all worker losses, and he receives all the worker's gains.

Compensation on the Basis of Productive Efficiency

Under the method of compensating the employee on the basis of productivity or results, the job to be performed is given a definite monetary value. *The worker is paid a specific amount of money for performing a job or an operation or for producing a completed item, part, or piece*. The worker may take all the gains or losses, according to the differences in the quantities he produces, or he may agree to share these with the employer.

Supplementary Compensations

A third method of compensating employees is called supplementary compensations. Because both of the first two methods by themselves are generally inadequate as a form of total compensation, it is necessary to supplement them to more fully meet the needs of the worker and his employer. Supplementary compensations may be of a financial or a nonfinancial nature and are commonly granted on the basis of such criteria as the time the worker has spent on the job, his productivity, his pay, a percentage of profits, a law, or the needs of the worker or his employer.

Supplementary compensations may be subdivided into two subdivisions or categories: (1) those that are intended to directly pay their way (such as suggestions and efficiency bonuses) and thus primarily benefit the employer, and (2) those supplementary compensations, more commonly called fringe benefits, which primarily benefit the employees and are not expected to directly pay their way (vacations, insurances, etc.).

In this chapter, we shall describe the standard traditional compensation methods and incentive plans indicated in Figure 17.1 under classes (1) and (2). We shall also explain the formulas for their wage calculations and the major differences between the plans. Chapters 18 through 21 will deal with the most modern concepts of these classes. Supplementary compensations (class 3), representing over one fourth of total compensations paid, will be treated separately in Chapters 22 and 23.

Symbols and Tables Used to Illustrate Compensation Methods

For a better understanding of the wage plans to be described, the symbols explained in Table 17.1 will be used for all algebraic formulas presented throughout this chapter.

CLASS	SPECIFIC NAMES OF SAMPLE PLANS FOR EACH CLASS
(1) Time Class	Straight Hourly Rate, Day Rate, Weekly Wage Rate or Salary Plan
(2) Productive Efficiency Class	Straight Piece Rate, Taylor Differential Piece Rate, Manchester Piece Rate
	Standard Time, Multiple Time Rate
	Halsey Premium, Rowan Premium, Gantt Task and Bonus, Automatic Sliding Scale, Emerson Efficiency Bonus, Measured Day Rate, 100 Percent Time Premium (Estes), Standard Hour
(3) Supplementary Compensation Class	Profit Sharing, Stock Distribution, Anniversary Checks, Pensions, Annual Vacations, Life Insurance, Unemployment Compensation, Dismissal Compensation

FIGURE 17.1   Classification of Compensation Methods

To facilitate the solution of specific problems and to clarify the described wage plans, example tables are used to illustrate most plans. For the sake of simplicity and uniformity, the following data are assumed for all examples and tables throughout this chapter:

1. The hourly wage-base rate (Rh) in all examples is $3.
2. Production items are "Gears." Two gears per hour, or 16 per eight-hour day, is the accepted standard.
3. The assumed working hours are eight per day.

The reader should remember, however, that *all examples, figures, and computations are presented only for illustrative purposes.*

TABLE 17.1

KEY SYMBOLS USED IN WAGE FORMULAS

Key Symbols	Explanation	Key Symbols	Explanation
E	= Earnings in dollars	Q	= Quantity or number of pieces produced
Ha	= Actual hours worked		
Hc	= Credited hours	Rh	= Wage-base rate per hour (Day rate = $3)
Hst	= Standard hours allowed per unit		
Hsd	= Hours saved	Rhh	= High wage rate per hour
Pe	= Percent efficiency	Rp	= Money rate per piece (Piece rate = $1.50)
		Rph	= High money rate per piece

Compensation on the basis of time

Paying a worker on the basis of time is the oldest method of compensating labor. In the early days of employer-employee relations, laborers and craftsmen were hired to perform work over a certain season or a definite time period. Since the employer and employees worked together, and each employee performed his work under the employer's instructions and supervision, there was no problem of either measuring his output or evaluating the time he spent on the job. The worker's presence on the job was sufficient for him to receive what later became known as a "worker's time wage."

As trade and industry developed, all laborers and shop workers were then hired by the day or week. Thus, "straight-time rate" or "day rate" gradually evolved as the method of remunerating employees for the time they spent at work. The employer assumes the entire responsibility for the quantity and quality of work the employees have to perform.

More recently there has been a trend to pay hourly employees on a longer basis of time such as a week (or longer) and to consider the employees as being on a salary basis. International Business Machines, Texas Instruments, and Motorola were among the first companies to place their hourly employees on a salaried basis. There is the belief that when an employee is put on a salary basis, he is more closely identified with the company and has a greater degree of security. Although unions have for years been pressing for compensation on a salary basis, the three firms above who have adopted the salary scale are nonunion.

Straight-Time Plan

The terms "day work" and "day rate" are inherited from the early industrial period when a day's time spent in doing a day's work was the standard, as explained above. However, the terms have partially lost their original meaning. "Day work" and "day rate" are now synonymous with "straight hourly rate," which is also known as "straight day rate" and "straight-time rate." In civilized countries the hourly wage-base rates prevail. Even women employed in domestic service are now paid by the hour because of the social security deductions demanded by law since January, 1951.

Workers in industry are predominantly hired by the hour, while executives, office workers, and salesmen are employed by the week or by the month, and are paid a definite sum per week, or per month. As is still the custom in many industries, the hourly rate ("day rate") is paid regardless of the quantity or quality of work performed. Usually, there are neither individual performance standards to follow nor financial incentives, other than the hourly production rate established by predecessors, to spur workers on to higher production. Very often, however, a negative incentive exists in that the foreman is constantly alerted to keep the workers from "loafing." In other words, the "driving method" is employed to obtain a day's work.

Straight-Time Formula:[1]

E = Ha × Rh: (Earnings = Actual hours worked × wage-base rate per hour)

Assume Ha = 8, and Rh = $3; then E = 8 × $3 = $24

The straight-time rate is the only plan of compensation whereby a worker's earnings remain constant regardless of his daily output. Table 17.2 shows that under the straight-time pay plan, the worker's earnings would be a constant $24 per day (8 hrs. × $3 per hour). It also shows how the labor cost per gear drops as the worker's productivity rises.

TABLE 17.2

STRAIGHT-TIME PLAN

Gears Per Day	Worker's Earnings	Labor Cost Per Gear
8	$24	$3.000
12	24	2.000
16	24	1.500
20	24	1.200
24	24	1.000
28	24	.857
32	24	.750
36	24	.667

Selecting the Straight-Time Payment Method

The straight-time rate is the simplest method of wage payment to use in compensating the worker for his time spent on the job. Hourly, weekly, or monthly earnings remain constant regardless of performance. In most cases there is little or no relationship between earnings and the output. The general consensus is that *under a day-rate compensation method, workers tend to produce only about 50 percent of what the average* |*incentive worker produces.* In other words, worker productivity under nonstandardized day-work conditions is estimated to be only one half of the production that a motivated incentive worker can produce under standardized conditions and measured production. Often the output of the least efficient day worker, who may be the one that sets the pace, is equivalent to only 38 percent of the average incentive worker's production. Furthermore, with no definite production goals, the day workers are unperturbed by work interferences and inefficient indirect labor. Thus, *losses as well as gains concern the employer more than the employee.*

---

[1]For explanation of symbols, see Table 17.1, page 453.

Reasons for Selecting Straight-Time Wage Payments. Many enterprises use only straight-time rates partly because the setting of standards for incentives is not understood and partly because management is either indifferent to production control or because its attitudes toward labor costs are haphazard.

Certain groups of workers are compensated only by the straight-time rate because their diversified work renders the setting of standards impractical. For instance, jobs with short work cycles, employees doing experimental and research work, and supervisory activities are usually paid on a time basis because such activities may cost more to measure than the savings that can be obtained. Therefore, the combination of time-rate payments and supplemental payments (profit sharing or plant-wide bonuses) may encourage the best performance. Similarly, time payments are advocated where machine production sets the pace because the workers do not have direct control over production. The advantages and disadvantages of a straight-time wage payment method should be carefully studied before it is adopted.

Advantages of the Straight-Time Payment Method. Since no special formula is involved, workers can easily compute their earnings by multiplying their wage-base rate by the number of hours worked. The administration of the straight-time wage payment method is a simple payroll department procedure. Under proper supervision and fairly standardized working conditions, an employer has the added advantage of raising production without incurring additional unit costs. The day-rate payment is well adapted for jobs where unavoidable delays are constantly occurring. Also, it is claimed that under the day-rate method, the workers are not pressured to sacrifice quality for quantity. This claim may be justified if quality control is maintained through proper inspection.

Disadvantages of the Straight-Time Payment Method. The most common objection to the straight-time rate is that there is no motivation for the worker. If the worker does not share the gains from increased production, he will produce only enough to hold his job. Hence, production costs are higher than under an incentive plan, and they are so unpredictable that the employer is unable to anticipate his labor costs.

Inasmuch as under the straight day-rate method the least efficient worker generally receives the same amount per hour as the most efficient worker doing the same job, the workers become dissatisfied. The injustice of not giving recognition to individual differences usually causes unrest among the workers. The employer, in turn, is always apprehensive that the prolonged production overly increases the labor cost. Moreover, the most efficient workers may be lured away by a competitor's wage incentive plan, while the inefficient workers are inclined to remain with the employer who pays straight day rates. Furthermore, since supervision is compulsively striving to maintain a fair degree of efficient production — often resulting in pressuring and driving the employees — industrial relations may be strained by various grievances that arise.

Compensation methods on the basis of productive efficiency

A variety of plans have been devised for paying a worker primarily on the basis of his productive efficiency or individual merits. The theory underlying these plans is that such compensation will motivate him to be as productive as he can be, because in this way the worker can earn more money for himself. Some of the payment plans attempt to pass along to the worker all the rewards for production increases for which he is primarily responsible. Other plans call for a sharing of rewards between the worker and the employer. Some plans are designed to pay the worker according to the specific length of time it takes him to produce a given amount of work, while other plans compensate him directly for the number of pieces he produces, or for a whole project completed. Since many of these plans have been referred to by various names, they have caused much confusion. An attempt will be made in this chapter to spell out the theory and concepts of the traditional plans that are in use and that primarily pay employees on the basis of their productive efficiency or results. Later chapters will discuss the very latest concepts and plans. Before discussing any wage payment plans based on productive efficiency, it is first necessary to present the general concept of what is meant by productive efficiency.

The Concept of Productive Efficiency

When workers are to be paid according to their productivity, or the work they produce, there must be some measuring stick or means of gauging the production results to determine how efficient each worker is. Chapter 15 discussed the methodology of establishing job performance standards as a basis for evaluating employees. It suggested a minimum of three categories of performance efficiency, namely: unsatisfactory, satisfactory, and outstanding. In general, when an employee is compensated on the basis of his productivity, the real gauge of efficiency is the *number of acceptable pieces* that the worker can produce within some unit of time (an hour, day, or week). Whether the number of acceptable pieces produced is given a high, low, or average rating of efficiency depends on how this number compares with the number of acceptable pieces that a typical fully qualified worker can turn out working at a normal or average pace. In other words, the production that an average fully qualified worker can turn out is used as the acceptable standard of satisfactory efficiency. The emphasis is on quantity, and only a minimum degree of quality is necessary. Within this general framework of productive efficiency, we can now proceed to observe how productive efficiency has been used with the traditional individual compensation methods of payment in use. We shall later show how production standards and performance levels are specifically related to productive efficiency.

Traditional Individual Incentive Plans

Earlier in this chapter, it was pointed out that compensation on the basis of productive efficiency has many forms. We shall discuss those plans that pass along *all* the rewards of increased production to the worker under the heading, "Traditional Individual Incentive Plans." Those plans that *share* the rewards for increased productivity with management will be discussed under the heading, "Traditional Gain Sharing or Bonus Class Incentive Plans."

Compensation on the basis of productive efficiency is the second oldest compensation method for production workers. With the advent of mass production, employers began to realize that both employer and employee could benefit by the adoption of piece work instead of paying for the amount of time spent on the job. In principle, then, payment under a piece-rate method is contrary to that of the straight time-rate method. A more creative interest in the job is fostered under piece rate than under straight-time rate. The research of Wyatt and Fraser has indicated that piece-rate systems lead to fewer symptoms of boredom than does straight hourly pay.[2] Whyte has indicated three other sources of reward (in addition to money) found in piece-rate systems: escape from fatigue, because the worker has a meaningful goal to shoot at; escape from management pressure and gain of control over one's own time; and "playing the game" of trying to attain quota.[3]

Under the piece-rate method, the worker gains by his increased productivity since he is paid a definite amount for a given operation or a unit of product; and the more he produces, the larger are his earnings.

When piece-rate plans were first substituted for time-rate plans, the price per piece was generally determined on the basis of the straight time-rate production, estimating what the straight piece rate should be according to the output of the most efficient day-rate worker. Thus, the "ordinary" or "straight piece rate" as a method of wage payment evolved.

Ordinary or Straight Piece Rate. Under this method the worker is paid for the number of pieces or jobs completed *regardless of time spent*. He earns the established money rate per piece. Any interference in his work is detrimental to the worker since he may earn less than his hourly base rate. On the other hand, the employer may lose because of the worker's "holding down" in fear that increased earnings may result in a sharp cut in the rate per piece.

---

[2]S. Wyatt and J. S. Fraser, *The Comparative Effects of Variety and Uniformity in Work,* Industrial Fatigue Research Board Report No. 52 (London: His Majesty's Stationery Office, 1929).

[3]W. F. Whyte *Money and Motivation: An Analysis of Incentives in Industry* (New York: Harper & Brothers, 1955).

Under the old method of straight piece-rate setting, the superintendent or foreman usually established the rates haphazardly. As soon as a worker began to increase his output and earnings, a rate cut usually followed. If a worker continued to earn more than was deemed proper according to the superintendent's or foreman's judgment, further cuts would be made until earnings showed that the piece rate was "struck about right." There were no guaranteed base rates. Under standardized conditions, where performance rates are set by time study, piece rates are usually static until conditions change drastically.

Straight Piece-Rate Formula:

$E = Q \times Rp$

Straight Piece-Work Earnings = Number of Pieces $\times$ Rp

Assume Q = 32 and Rp = $1.50; then E = 32 $\times$ $1.50 = $48

Table 17.3 shows that under the ordinary or straight piece-rate pay plan, the worker's earnings increase in direct proportion to his production increases and the labor cost remains constant.

TABLE 17.3

ORDINARY OR STRAIGHT PIECE-RATE PLAN

GEARS PER DAY	WORKER'S EARNINGS	LABOR COST PER GEAR
8	$12	$1.500
12	18	1.500
16	24	1.500
20	30	1.500
24	36	1.500
28	42	1.500
32	48	1.500
36	54	1.500

Taylor Differential Piece-Rate Plan. For many years the day-rate and straight piece-rate methods of compensation were the only plans in existence. In 1884, however, Frederick W. Taylor installed the first incentive plan, called the *Taylor differential piece-rate plan,* at the Midvale Steel Company, Philadelphia, Pennsylvania. Taylor's plan was one of the most revolutionary ideas in the establishment of scientific management.

Under the Taylor differential piece-rate plan, all standards are scientifically established. Dr. Taylor felt that a strong incentive in the form of a higher piece rate should be offered those willing to exert special efforts to attain or exceed the set standard output. Those producing quantities below the set standard should be considered less efficient, and should receive a normal piece rate. For example, if the standard is set at 16 pieces per day, those producing 16 pieces or more per day receive the higher piece rate, while those producing less than

16 pieces per day get the normal piece rate. Under Dr. Taylor's plan no day rate was guaranteed. In other words, if a worker could not come up to standard, he had to be satisfied with whatever he earned, thereby "attracting the best men for each class of work, and developing many first-class men who would otherwise remain slow and inaccurate."[4]

Aside from the scientifically established rate that was assumed to be fair to both worker and employer, the significance of the new plan was the guarantee that no rate would be cut unless radical changes in the structure of parts or surrounding conditions, including new tooling equipment, were made.

New methods of establishing rates and new kinds of compensation methods, which included an incentive for larger production or higher attainments, came into existence with the Taylor differential piece-rate plan. The formulas, examples, and Table 17.4 show workers' earnings and cost per piece under the below standard, standard, and above standard rates.

Taylor Differential Piece-Rate Formulas:

(1) Output below standard: $E = Q \times Rp$

(2) Output at standard or above: $E = Q \times Rph$

Assume: In (1) Normal rate $1.50 per piece and $Q = 15$, and
        In (2) High rate $1.80 per piece and $Q = 18$, then,

(1) E = Number of pieces $\times$ normal rate per piece: $E = 15 \times \$1.50 = \$22.50$

(2) E = Number of pieces $\times$ high rate per piece: $E = 18 \times \$1.80 = \$32.40$

TABLE 17.4

TAYLOR DIFFERENTIAL PIECE-RATE PLAN

Gears Per Day	Worker's Earnings	Labor Cost Per Gear
8	$12.00	$1.500
12	18.00	1.500
16	28.80	1.800
20	36.00	1.800
24	43.20	1.800
28	50.40	1.800
32	57.60	1.800
36	64.80	1.800

---

[4]F. W. Taylor, "A Piece Rate System," *Transactions* (American Society of Mechanical Engineers, 1895), Vol. XVI, p. 858.

The Manchester Plan (Piece Rate with Guarantee). The Taylor differential piece-rate plan was hailed as the most progressive method of compensation because of its incentive possibilities. It was also held in disfavor, however, on account of the penalty imposed upon the beginner, who earned less than his wage-base rate before attaining the standard output.

A new piece-rate plan containing a guaranteed day-wage rate was therefore formulated which, because it originated in Manchester, is known as the *Manchester plan*, or *Manchester piece rate with guarantee*. The worker is *guaranteed a day-wage rate regardless of his output*. This piece-rate plan is different from the old so-called straight piece-rate plans whereby a worker carried the entire burden while he went through the necessary period of apprenticeship or training.

Manchester Formulas:

    (1) Output below standard: $E = Ha \times Rh$

    (2) Output at standard or above: $E = Q \times Rp$

       If $Q = 28$, then $E = 28 \times \$1.50 = \$42$

Table 17.5 shows that under the Manchester plan, the worker is guaranteed a fixed amount ($24) for all production below standard and that his earnings rise in direct proportion to his increased production above standard. On the other hand, labor costs increase with decreased production below standard and become constant above standard.

TABLE 17.5

MANCHESTER PLAN

Gears Per Day	Worker's Earnings	Labor Cost Per Gear
8	$24	$3.000
12	24	2.000
16	24	1.500
20	30	1.500
24	36	1.500
28	42	1.500
32	48	1.500
36	54	1.500

Standard Time Plan. The *standard time plan* is also known as the *differential day-rate plan* and the *differential time plan*. As the term "standard time" implies, the working time is standardized. The plan includes two day-rate standards. One is the wage-base rate paid for producing quantities below the set standard time-rate of production or task; the other is a higher wage rate that is paid if the worker reaches or exceeds the set standard. He receives the same amount, however, regardless of how much above task his increase of production may be. Two constant earnings are thus possible.

Standard Time Formulas:

    (1) Below standard: $E = Ha \times Rh$
        If $Ha = 8$, then $E = 8 \times \$3 = \$24$
    (2) Standard and above: $E = Ha \times Rhh$
        If $Ha = 8$, and $Rhh = \$3.60$, then $E = 8 \times \$3.60 = \$28.80$

Table 17.6 shows that under the standard time plan, the worker's earnings are the same for all production below standard and that above standard they are higher but uniform. Labor costs decrease as production increases.

TABLE 17.6

STANDARD TIME PLAN

GEARS PER DAY	WORKER'S EARNINGS	LABOR COST PER GEAR
8	$24.00	$3.000
12	24.00	2.000
16	28.80	1.800
20	28.80	1.440
24	28.80	1.200
28	28.80	1.029
32	28.80	.900
36	28.80	.800

Multiple Time-Rate Plan. The *multiple time-rate plan*, like the standard time plan, has more than one hourly rate. As the term "multiple" indicates, several hourly rates are established for different production ranges. A worker is paid in accordance with the "zone" of production where his particular accomplishment for the pay period is classified. In some cases a definite wage-base rate is established and additional percentages are added for levels of accomplishment that fall within the various established production zones, which are divided on percentages of efficiency.

Thus far, we have discussed the traditional individual incentive compensation payment plans that passed along all the rewards of increased production to the worker. We have seen that the meaning of productive efficiency was rather loosely used. This caused worker grievances and dissatisfactions and eventually forced an improved interpretation of productive efficiency in terms of production standards and performance levels, which will be discussed next.

The Concepts of Performance Levels and Production Standards

In order to make the term productive efficiency more meaningful, it is necessary to know how efficient a worker can be considered who performs at a certain level of production. This requires the setting of production standards for various levels of performance. Sometime during the early history of the piece-rate method of wage payment, industrial engineers, foremen, and union leaders came to refer to various levels of production as *tasks*, since a task was thought of as a standard of accomplishment in units of time and quantity. There were five production levels or tasks that developed; namely, low task, medium task, 100 percent standard task, high efficiency task, and top task. These performance levels and standards were originated by those who tailored wage incentive plans either to suit the policy and objectives of an enterprise, or to comply with their philosophies of worker motivation and compensation of workers at different production levels. Although the use of the word task is not commonly used today, the five levels of production give us a frame of reference as to worker efficiency. We cite this background of events mainly to acquaint the reader with some differences in terminology that he can find if he researches the early incentive plans.

To avoid confusion, the term production will be generally used instead of task because the term is presently more commonly used and is therefore more meaningful. A worker's production today usually refers to the number of pieces, units, or parts that he completes within some unit of time. Each unit of production must have an acceptable degree of quality so as to be counted as part of the worker's production. No company can afford to pay for unsatisfactory production. It is also important to bear in mind that to be paid for productive efficiency means to be paid for productive results, and not for worker efforts. Worker efforts can only be compensated for when they are meaningful and result in concrete productive results. The theoretical relationship between worker efforts and worker productivity is shown in Figure 17.2 according to the following five production efficiency levels:

1. Low production efficiency level.
2. Medium production efficiency level.
3. 100 percent standard production level.
4. High production efficiency level.
5. Top production efficiency level.

Low Production Efficiency Level. The *low production efficiency level* usually refers to the production of a day-rate worker operating with minimum effort *under nonstandardized conditions.* (See Figure 17.2 at circled No. 1.) Because the worker is not being motivated by a financial incentive, he produces just enough to be steadily employed. Experience has proven that the low-task production level of the qualified day worker is only 50 percent of the production turned out by the typical average incentive worker. The low production efficiency level is only 62.5 to 66.7 percent (two thirds) of the production standard that most engineers have set as the beginning point of incentive earnings. Union men frequently refer to the 66.7 standard as their "normal average." Also, it is this production level that usually coincides with the standards obtained from past performances of day-rate jobs. The past performance rates are considered in

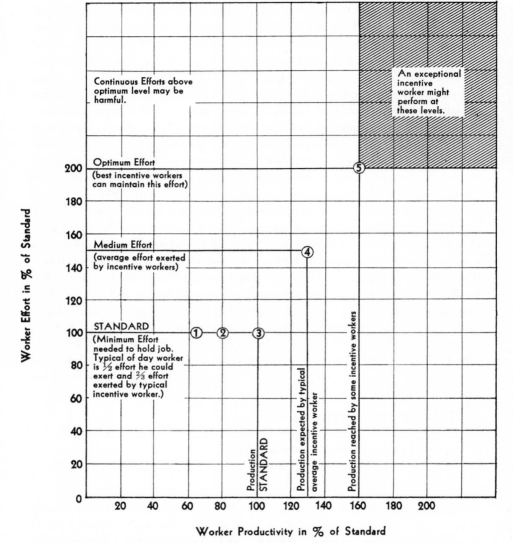

FIGURE 17.2 The Theoretical Relationship Between Worker Effort and Worker Productivity

Key:

① Low-level day-worker production, Minimum Effort, nonstandardized conditions.

② Medium-level day-worker production, Minimum Effort, standardized conditions.

③ 100 Percent Incentive Standard-level day-worker production, Minimum Effort under standardized conditions and measured production.

④ High-level incentive worker production, Medium Effort under standardized conditions, measured production, and motivation.

⑤ Top-level incentive worker production, Optimum Effort under standardized conditions, measured production, and strong motivation.

general to be "loose," which simply means that under nonstandardized conditions, even inexperienced workers can earn more than is justified, and experienced workers can "run away with the job."

Medium Production Efficiency Level. The *medium production efficiency level* applies to the productivity of a day worker while exerting minimum effort *under standardized conditions*. (See Figure 17.2 at circled No. 2.) By standardized conditions, it is meant that the tools, general equipment, materials, and surrounding conditions are standardized. In the medium-task production level, the worker has not been motivated to increase his efforts over the low-task productivity. However, since he works under good supervision and with better tools, equipment, etc., greater output materializes without increased effort. Experience has proven that under standardized conditions, a worker will usually produce 15 to 20 percent more without extra effort. Since management was primarily responsible for the increase in output, some managers and engineers feel that the worker is not entitled to incentive pay, because *incentive pay is based on output resulting from increased worker effort.* Others are convinced, however, that incentive payments starting at this level of production encourage the worker to strive for output over the 100 percent production standard.

100 Percent Standard Production Level. The *100 percent standard production level* describes the accepted standard level of effort and productivity that most designers of incentive plans consider as *the* beginning point of incentive earnings. (See Figure 17.2 at circled No. 3.) Performance is accomplished at the day-rate effort under standardized conditions and measured production, which has been based on motion and time study with due allowances for leveling. The standard daily output can be accomplished without physical or mental impairment to the worker. Industrial engineers and managers have accepted this production standard as the "true normal" under sound management. Hence, the meeting points of 100 percent wage-base rate and 100 percent production standard (circled in Figure 17.2), are accepted as *the standard for comparing the wage incentive earning curves of all incentive plans.* This standard is regarded as the starting point of the high incentive production efficiency.

High Production Efficiency Level. The *high production efficiency level* signifies that the day worker is being paid for *extra efforts which result in productivity over and above the 100 percent standard.* (See Figure 17.2 at circled No. 4.) When the worker performs under standardized conditions, measured production through time and motion studies, and is motivated to produce above the 100 percent production standard, he is considered an *incentive worker.* Through the years sound incentive plans have proven that the average qualified incentive worker who diligently attends to his job can usually reach 120 to 130 percent productivity. Management engineers have, therefore, adopted 120 to 130 percent as high-task productivity.

Top Production Efficiency Level. The *top production efficiency level* signifies that the incentive worker is strongly motivated and is being paid for *optimum efforts that result in productivity over and above the 120 to 130 percent level at which average qualified incentive workers produce.* Some of the more efficient incentive workers who exert optimum effort may reach an output of 160 percent production, and outstanding workers may reach even greater heights. (See Figure 17.2 at circled No. 5.) However, when the worker is exerting effort beyond the optimum level, it may be a "killing effort" and thus be injurious to his health. This should not be the signal for rate-cutting, but rather for taking steps to protect the worker's health.

The five production efficiency levels discussed in the preceding paragraphs will become more meaningful to the reader as he sees how they relate to the traditional gain sharing and bonus class incentive plans that follow.

Traditional Gain Sharing or Bonus Class Incentive Plans

According to the traditional concept of industrial engineers and management authorities, premium and bonus incentive plans are referred to as *gain sharing* plans. The term gain sharing seems to be appropriate since in premium and bonus plans both employer and employee share in the results. Day-rate wage plans burden the *employer* with losses and favor him with all gains, while piece-rate plans shift losses and gains to the *employee*. However, not all premium and bonus plans offer equal gain sharing, as will be explained later. Similarly, only plans such as the Halsey and Rowan plans are traditionally considered gain sharing, while such plans as the Emerson efficiency and a few other plans are known as empirical. For practical purposes, however, we shall place all premium and bonus plans in the category of gain sharing.

Old and New Meanings of the Words Premium and Bonus. Traditional premium and bonus pay plans have been regarded as compensation methods whereby a special reward is offered for extra employee efforts. It is necessary to keep this in mind when reading about the remaining traditional incentive plans in this chapter. However, before discussing these traditional plans we shall try to clarify the present meanings of the words *premium* and *bonus.*

Premium. The meaning of the two terms — premium and bonus — has changed considerably since the Fair Labor Standards Act of 1938 became a governing factor in labor-management contract provisions. The term premium is seldom used for bonus. According to the United States Department of Labor, *premium* is now generally used to designate *extra payments to compensate employees for conditions of work that are considered disadvantageous or burdensome.*[5]

---

[5]See *Labor Management Contract Provisions 1950–51*, Bulletin No. 1091, and *Premium Pay in Private Industry* (United States Department of Labor, Bureau of Statistics, 1951).

Premium is also used to indicate a supplementary wage or fixed payment in addition to wage-base rates for differential shifts, overtime payments, and extra compensation for Saturday and holiday work, or for any jobs that cause inconveniences to the worker.

Bonus. The term bonus is used for different types of incentive payments and for deferred incentive payments such as a "Christmas Bonus," "End-of-the-Year Bonus," and "Continuous Service Bonus." All production bonuses are based on a standardized time that determines how long it should take an average qualified worker to perform a job. For that reason, the production bonus is often termed a *time bonus.* The amount of payment is equal to the standard wage-base rate for the actual time consumed (which is usually less than the time allowed), plus an additional reward for any one of the following:

1. All the time saved, for which the total value is given to the workers. This is the principle of most bonus plans.
2. A fixed portion of the time saved, which is the basis of such plans as the Halsey premium plan.
3. A portion of the time saved, which varies with the ratio of the time taken and the time allowed. This is the basis of the Rowan plan.

Halsey Premium Plan. Of the many premium and bonus plans, the first to come into existence was the *Halsey premium plan.* It was devised in 1890 by F. A. Halsey, a mechanical engineer, while he was superintendent of the Rand Drill Company, Sherbrooke, Canada.[6] Halsey was the first to break away from the traditional day-rate or piece-work method of compensation.

The Halsey premium plan provides for payment of an hourly wage-base rate regardless of the job's outcome. The standard for a task is based upon past performance records. The time previously spent to do a certain job, or the average time for a group of previous jobs, is the standard time. In other words, no preliminary time studies or job specifications are necessary. If the worker completes his task in less than the allowed standard time, he receives his hourly wage for each hour worked and, in addition, a definite percentage of the savings between the actual and the standard time of direct labor.

If a certain job has an established standard time of eight hours, and the worker reduces the time to six hours, the management splits with the worker on a 50-50 basis. That is, of the two hours saved, the worker is paid for one additional hour, while one hour is retained by management. Although the 50-50 plan was originally used, it was later changed to also include a $33\frac{1}{3}$–$66\frac{2}{3}$ plan. That is, on jobs regarded as easy or simple to manipulate, the worker receives $33\frac{1}{3}$ percent of the savings, while $66\frac{2}{3}$ goes to management. The following table clearly indicates differences in the worker's earnings and labor cost per item.

---

[6]F. A. Halsey, "Premium Plan of Paying for Labor," *Transactions* (American Society of Mechanical Engineers, 1891), Vol. XII, p. 755.

Halsey 50-50 Formulas:

(1) Production up to task: $E = Ha \times Rh$

(2) Production above task: $E = (Ha + \dfrac{Hsd}{2}) \times Rh$

If $Ha = 8$ and $Hsd = 3$, then $E = (8 + \dfrac{3}{2}) \times \$3 = \$28.50$

TABLE 17-7

HALSEY 50-50 PREMIUM PLAN

Gears Per Day	Savings	Worker's Shares	Worker's Earnings	Labor Cost Per Gear
8	. . .	. . .	$24	$3.000
12	. . .	. . .	24	2.000
16	. . .	. . .	24	1.500
20	2 hrs.	1 hr.	27	1.350
24	4 hrs.	2 hrs.	30	1.250
28	6 hrs.	3 hrs.	33	1.179
32	8 hrs.	4 hrs.	36	1.125
36	10 hrs.	5 hrs.	39	1.083

Rowan Premium Plan. The *Rowan premium plan* was originally installed by James Rowan[7] at the works of David Rowan and Company, Glasgow, Scotland. The plan is similar to the Halsey plan in its guarantee of hourly wage rates. Production standards are based on past performance and no time studies are involved. The Rowan plan differs from the Halsey plan in the method of calculating earnings, however. In time saved, the Rowan plan adds to the amount earned for actual working time, a percentage computed by the fraction, "hours saved divided by standard hours allowed (hours saved ÷ standard time)."

Rowan Premium Formulas:

(1) Production up to standard: $E = Ha \times Rh$

(2) Production above standard: $E = Ha \times Rh + (Ha \times Rh \times \dfrac{Hsd}{Hst})$

If $Ha = 8$, $Hst = 10$, and $Hsd = 2$,

then $E = 8 \times \$3 + (8 \times \$3 \times \dfrac{2}{10}) = \$24 + \$4.80 = \$28.80$

[7]James Rowan, "Premium Plan at the Works of David Rowan and Company," *American Machinist* (1902), Vol. XXV, pp. 49–53.

Gantt Task and Bonus Plan. Henry L. Gantt, a co-worker of Dr. Frederick W. Taylor, designed a plan that he termed *task-work with a bonus*.[8] Mr. Gantt first introduced his plan at the Bethlehem Steel Works in 1901. To achieve the desired results, he standardized shop conditions, improved methods, and maintained all machines in their best condition. The standard time (task time) was determined by a time study similar to that used in Taylor's piece-rate plan. The Gantt plan differs from the Taylor plan in that the beginner is encouraged by the payment of a guaranteed day rate if the actual working time is longer than the task time. A worker who completes his job in standard time or less receives the day rate multiplied by allowed time (credited hours) plus a fixed percentage of this amount as a bonus. To stimulate the worker's best efforts, the bonus varies from 20 to 50 percent, depending upon the kind of work and the incentive.

To insure the largest output without loss in quality, and to make it possible for all workers to earn a bonus, Gantt conceived the idea of paying foremen a bonus in proportion to the number of men they supervise who complete their jobs in task time or less. Thus, foremen were always on the alert and eager to maintain efficiency.

Gantt Task and Bonus Formulas:

(1) Production up to standard: $E = Ha \times Rh$

(2) Production at and above standard: $E = Hc \times (Rh + \text{fixed } \% \text{ of } Rh)$

If fixed $\% = 30\%$, then $E = Hc \times (Rh + 30\%)$

Assume $Hc = 15$, then $E = 15 (\$3 + 30\%) = 15 \times \$3.90 = \$58.50$

Table 17.8 shows that under the Gantt task and bonus plan, the worker's earnings are based on a fixed rate (\$3) for each credited hour earned plus a 30 percent bonus after standard is reached.

TABLE 17.8

GANTT TASK AND BONUS PLAN

Gears Per Day	Credited Hours	30% Bonus	Worker's Earnings	Labor Cost Per Gear
8	4	. . .	$24.00	$3.000
12	6	. . .	24.00	2.000
16	8	$7.20	31.20	1.950
20	10	9.00	39.00	1.950
24	12	10.80	46.80	1.950
28	14	12.60	54.60	1.950
32	16	14.40	62.40	1.950
36	18	16.20	70.20	1.950

[8]H. L. Gantt, "A Bonus System for Rewarding Labor," *Transactions* (American Society of Mechanical Engineers, 1902), Vol. XXIII, p. 343.

Automatic Sliding Scale. The *automatic sliding scale wage plan* may be considered gain sharing due to its tie-in between wages and the increase or decrease in the sales and profits of a business venture, especially of certain manufacturing industries. This method of wage payment originated in British coal and metal mining industries. It began with the collective agreement between trade unions and employers in an effort to withstand the fluctuations and changes of wholesale prices. A specific wage rate was determined at the beginning of a contractual agreement, and then increased or decreased within six-month periods in direct ratio to the degree of change in the sales price.

In the United States, the automatic sliding scale method of compensation has been used predominantly since World War I as a cost-of-living bonus. Wage-base rates have been automatically changed in accordance with cost-of-living indexes. During the 1930–1933 depression years, wages dropped as much as 50 percent, but began to increase rapidly during the recovery. In 1936 some companies, such as the General Electric Company and the United States Steel Corporation, established automatic sliding scales. Wages were adjusted automatically upward or downward 5 to 10 percent according to fluctuations in living costs. The principle of automatic sliding scale adjustments was the outstanding bargaining factor between the General Motors Corporation and the United Automobile Workers-CIO in 1950.[9] The annual improvement factor and the cost-of-living adjustments included in the famous escalator clause were subsequently adopted by a majority of other unions.

Some sliding scales are based on efficiency ratings somewhat similar to efficiency bonuses, although they are erroneously termed "Day-Rate Sliding Scales." Assume that the wage-base rate for a certain job is $3 per hour and the standard production efficiency is 70 percent. At that rate the wage increase will automatically become effective in direct ratio to the increase in production efficiency, depending upon the established sliding scale. Table 17.9 shows wage-base rates in relationship to efficiency as used in a hand screw machine department. In this case, a four percent increase in hourly wages is provided for each five percent increase in production efficiency. The efficiency rating and wage percentages may be arranged to suit the type of work and the working conditions.

Emerson Efficiency Bonus Plan. Harrington Emerson, a professional industrial engineer who, like Dr. Taylor, made analytical studies of scientific management, pioneered the *efficiency bonus plan*. Knowing some of the unfavorable results obtained through plans installed by Dr. Taylor and his associates, Emerson tried to improve his method by establishing a high standard level with very accurately analyzed job specifications and time studies. Under

---

[9]See Chapter 5.

<table>
<tr><td colspan="2" align="center">*TABLE 17.9*</td><td colspan="2" align="center">*TABLE 17.10*</td></tr>
<tr><td colspan="2" align="center">AUTOMATIC SLIDING SCALE
PLAN
Wage increase 4% for 5% efficiency</td><td colspan="2" align="center">EMERSON EFFICIENCY BONUS
PLAN
For increase above 80% of standard</td></tr>
</table>

PRODUCTION EFFICIENCY	WAGES PER HOUR	% EFFICIENCY	% BONUS
70%	$3.00	79	...
75%	3.12	80	...
80%	3.24	81	1
85%	3.36	82	2
90%	3.48	83	3
95%	3.60	84	4
100%	3.72	89	9
105%	3.84	90	10
110%	3.96	91	11
115%	4.08	99	19
120%	4.20	100	20
125%	4.32	105	25
		110	30
		115	35
		120	40

the original Emerson plan, first installed in 1904, the worker received his hourly base rate for accomplishments up to 66 percent of production standard. From there on, there was a differential increase of bonus in accordance with the worker's efficiency, which was plotted on a hyperbolic curve. Starting with 0.01 percent bonus at 67 percent efficiency, there was an increment up to 10 percent bonus at 90 percent efficiency. From that point, 1 percent bonus was paid for each 1 percent gain in efficiency.

The plan underwent a complete revision by The Emerson Engineers to further simplify it according to the progressive changes in commerce and industry. In accordance with present practice, wage-base rates are paid up to 80 percent of standard instead of 66 percent. From there on, as shown in Table 17.10, an additional 1 percent is paid for each 1 percent gain in efficiency. At 100 percent efficiency (production standard), the worker receives 20 percent bonus and his earnings increase 1 percent for each 1 percent efficiency.[10] As was originally intended, the less skilled are able to earn a bonus sooner, and are thereby induced to increase their proficiency more quickly. In the present use of the Emerson efficiency bonus plan, it has in most cases been revised to conform to the latest union-management agreements.[11]

---

[10]Information about the revised plan received by the authors from The Emerson Engineers, April, 1960.

[11]Information received by the authors from William R. Sorensen, President of The Emerson Consultants, Inc. (formerly The Emerson Engineers), August 15, 1967.

Emerson Formula According to the Revised Plan:

Up to 80% of standard: $E = Ha \times Rh$

81% of standard to any point above 100% efficiency: $E = Ha \times Rh + (Ha \times Rh \times [Pe-80])$

Assume standard hours are 9.2

% Efficiency $= \dfrac{9.2 \times 100}{8} = 115\% = Pe$

From Table 17.10, Bonus $= 35\%$

Then, $E = 8 \times \$3 + (8 \times \$3 \times 35\%) = \$24.00 + \$8.40 = \$32.40$
Earnings

In reality, there is no need for using a table to calculate earnings according to the revised plan. The workers, as well as the payroll department, need only to know the percentage of efficiency (Pe). If the production has reached 81 percent efficiency, it is simply a question of adding 1 percent of the wage-base rate as a bonus for each percent of efficiency. Table 17.11 shows earnings and labor cost according to the revised plan.

TABLE 17.11

EMERSON EFFICIENCY BONUS PLAN

Gears Per Day	Production %	Bonus %	Bonus	Worker's Earnings	Labor Cost Per Gear
8	50	...	...	$24.00	$3.000
12	75	...	...	24.00	2.000
16	100	20	$4.80	28.80	1.800
20	125	45	10.80	34.80	1.740
24	150	70	16.80	40.80	1.700
28	175	95	22.80	46.80	1.671
32	200	120	28.80	52.80	1.650
36	225	145	34.80	58.80	1.633

Measured Day Rate (Measured Day Work). The *measured day-rate plan* became popular in the early depression years when labor unions opposed incentives. The plan consists of two parts, the usual wage-base rate and an incentive rate. Performance standards are established by time study to determine the worker's efficiency. A wage-base rate is established for each classified job by means of job evaluation and employee rating, using the rating factors discussed in Chapters 9 through 16.

It is in the application of a worker's efficiency to his earnings over a long period (two to three months), however, that the measured day-rate plan differs from other bonus plans. In addition to a bonus reward for increased production, calculated in terms of productive efficiency, the worker receives small percentages of his base rate as supplemental bonuses for punctuality, regular attendance, quality, versatility, length of service, and cost of living. While the wage-base rate remains constant, the measured day rate or the incentive rate varies, depending upon the average efficiency obtained over a certain period. This rate may be revised either up or down.

For example, consider four periods of two months each. A certain job is evaluated at $3 per hour for the employee whose expected productivity is 80 percent efficiency (80 percent of standard time). Increases in measured day rates are then based on an efficiency scale similar to that shown in Table 17.9 (page 471). The wage rates increase in relation to percentages of efficiency. Assume that one percent of the wage rate equals one percent efficiency, and that the worker achieves an additional average efficiency of 10 percent during the first two-month period. His measured day rate will then be increased to $3.30 for the second two-month period. Similarly, if the worker's efficiency increased another 15 percent in the second period, he would be credited with an average of 25 percent for two months and would receive an adjusted base rate of $3.75 per hour for the third period regardless of his productivity. If, within the third period the average efficiency were to drop 10 percent, the adjusted rate would then be reduced to $3.45 for the fourth period. As a rule, the workers' efficiency ratings are posted daily or weekly to inform them of their status for the forthcoming period.

TABLE 17.12

COMPUTATION OF MEASURED DAY RATE
For March–April

	%	Amount
Wage-Base Rate......	...	$3.00
BONUSES		
Productive efficiency...............................	25%	.75
Versatility...	5	.15
Punctuality..	3	.09
Attendance..	2	.06
Quality..	2	.06
Seniority*...	...	
Cost of living......................................	3	.09
TOTAL for May–June.............................	40%	$4.20

*The seniority bonus is not included in the computation since the worker had not been employed 4 years, at which time the seniority bonus begins.

100 Percent Time Premium Plan. The *100 percent time premium plan* in reality belongs in the piece-rate-with-guarantee classification of compensation methods. The 100 percent time premium plan differs from the Manchester plan, however, in that the standard of the former is established in terms of time required per piece instead of price per piece. Also, in the 100 percent time premium plan, the worker's efficiency is considered when earning calculations are based on the standard hour. Thus, the 100 percent time premium plan may be termed a bonus plan even though there is no direct gain sharing.

The 100 percent premium plan was devised by L. V. Estes,[12] with the idea in mind of setting a definite time performance standard for each job. The worker receives a guaranteed wage-base rate if his performance is below standard and is paid a bonus for every hour saved.

Standard-Hour Plan. The *standard-hour plan*, while differently described[13] has the same features as the 100 percent time premium plan. Both plans are based on the standard time allowance for a given quantity of work or operations. The same plans are also known as the *100 percent bonus plan, hour-for-hour plan, standard-hour bonus plan,* and by many other names.

From Table 17.13 it will be noted that the 100 percent time premium plan and the standard-hour plan are identical to the Manchester plan (Table 17.5) from the standpoint of workers' earnings and labor cost per item. In each case earnings up to task and higher earnings above task are the same.

100 Percent Time Premium and Standard-Hour Plan Formulas:

(1) Up to standard: $E = Ha \times Rh$

(2) Above standard: $E = Hst \times Rh$

If $Hst = 14$, then $E = 14 \times \$3 = \$42$

TABLE 17.13

100 PERCENT TIME PREMIUM AND STANDARD-HOUR PLAN

GEARS PER DAY	PREMIUM	WORKER'S EARNINGS	LABOR COST PER GEAR
8	...	$24	$3.000
12	...	24	2.000
16	...	24	1.500
20	$ 6	30	1.500
24	12	36	1.500
28	18	42	1.500
32	24	48	1.500
36	30	54	1.500

[12]L. V. Estes, "Comparison of Wage Incentives and the 100% Time Premium," *Industrial Management* (September, 1920), pp. 210–216.

[13]M. E. Merriam, "The Standard-Hour Plan of Wage Payment," *Management Engineering* (May, 1923), p. 315.

Selecting a Productive Efficiency Compensation Method

At the outset, it should be realized that no one specific incentive wage payment method is universally suited for all industries. There are, however, several different plans that lend themselves for application in the same or similar industries. The company objectives, the attitudes of the workers or the union leaders, and the local conditions should be considered before selecting a plan. Incentive payment methods within the same or different industries may vary from piece-rate methods to several types of gain sharing or bonus payments *based on a percentage of measured production efficiency.*

The reader should be ever mindful that the main purpose of an incentive wage payment is to stimulate higher productivity by rewarding workers for increasing their efforts to increase the output. There are, however, other reasons for selecting specific incentive wage payment plans. Some employers prefer the use of a piece-work rate in order to simplify cost computing and payroll upkeep so as to be in a better position to estimate costs for bids. On the other hand, as explained later, others favor bonus arrangements as a means of stimulating workers to perform at certain levels of production. Similarly, some unions prefer piece work because it is the traditional trade wage payment; some favor day rate for bargaining and contractual agreements; while others agree on formal bonus plans at low production levels. Consequently, it should be realized that selecting the proper incentive plan for a particular industry is highly important.

The selection of a wage incentive plan invariably evokes questions such as: Which plan or method should be adopted? What factors or governing conditions will have to be considered regarding the wage policies and objectives of the specific enterprises? At what percent of production efficiency shall the incentive wage payment begin? How much should the incentive payment be? The answers to these questions are partially found in the wage incentive curves of commonly used plans whereby the contrasting differences can be collated and discerned. For comparison purposes, the 100 percent time premium plan, also known as the standard hour plan, has been chosen. This wage incentive plan is being increasingly favored by outstanding companies. Under this plan, employees are rewarded in direct proportion to their output. The plan is methodically formulated on the basis of 100 percent measured production efficiency, that is, the measured production produced by the average qualified worker performing at minimum effort under standardized conditions and motion and time studies.

The chart in Figure 17.3 shows *incentive earning curves in relation to the production of the 100 percent measured efficiency standard.* The curves also indicate the production levels (percentages) where incentive wage payments start. Note that the earnings in percent of the base rate are shown on the scale of the vertical axis, and the production in percent of the measured efficiency standard is given on the scale of the horizontal axis. The day-rate earnings curve is the straight, heavy, solid line (paralleling the abscissa) and is labeled base rate. It represents a fixed wage rate. That is, an employee receives the same earnings — per hour, per day, or per week — regardless of how little or how much he produces. The day-rate line also denotes the guaranteed base rate for all the incentive plans shown above it.

Major Differences Between the Traditionally Used Incentive Plans

Since Taylor pointed the way to a systematically designed wage incentive structure, 40 or more plans have appeared on the industrial scene. Each has claimed some advantage over others, but all have attempted to serve the specific purpose of providing additional earnings as a reward for increased efforts which result in increased productivity. From the standpoint of practical application, however, it is felt that a discussion of the major differences between the most commonly used plans will be of sufficient aid in selecting a well-suited plan for a particular industry. The plans to be discussed are:

1. Piece rates.
2. 100 percent time premium.
3. Halsey premium.
4. Rowan premium.
5. Gantt task and bonus.
6. Emerson efficiency bonus.

Piece-Rate Compensation Methods. In most small and medium-size companies, the foremen or supervisors set the piece rates arbitrarily under nonstandardized conditions and without establishing time standards. Thus, a foreman's estimated rates often are so far out of line that unusually high earnings may induce rate cutting. Workers generally realize this, and to avoid the rate cutting, they curtail production, thereby effecting what is known as "restricted output."

When establishing piece rates in progressive companies — small, medium-size, or large — the production standard for the average incentive worker is obtained through motion and time studies. The time rate per piece or per job is then applied against the wage-base rate of the evaluated job to determine the money value per piece or per job.

Guaranteed Day Rate. It is indicated in Figure 17.3 that originally the straight piece-rate plan and the Taylor differential plan did not guarantee day rates. However, all currently used incentive plans pay a guaranteed day rate up to the production level points where the incentive payments start. Hence, it should be understood that the guaranteed day rate, or at least the legal minimum rate, is paid under all incentive plans when the jobs involve interstate commerce.

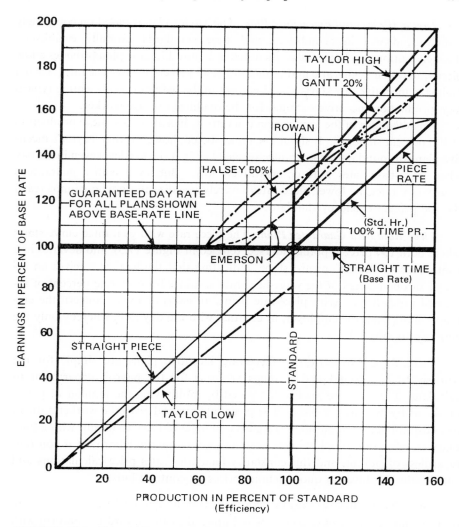

FIGURE 17.3 CHART COMPARING PRODUCTIVITY AND EARNINGS OF VARIOUS WAGE PLANS

Straight Piece-Rate Plans. Straight piece-rate plans no longer exist in the strict sense of the term. Under the Fair Labor Standards Act, payment of a specific minimum wage is mandatory. This Act refers to all modified piece-rate plans, including the Taylor differential plan. Note in Figure 17.3 that the straight piece-rate earning curve starts at the 0 point of production and wage earnings, cuts through the 100-100 point, and continues the upward slope to present a one percent increase of wage-base rate earnings for each additional one percent of increased production.

Taylor Differential Piece-Rate Plan. The Taylor plan is based on completely standardized working conditions and time standards carefully established through motion and time study. As noted in Figure 17.3, the plan provides a low piece rate which begins at 0 and terminates at 83 percent of the base rate. Then a high-step incentive rate starts at 125 percent of the base rate, representing typical high production incentive earnings for the qualified average worker.

An advantage of the Taylor plan is its strong incentive to achieve production at 100 percent standard. It should be remembered, however, that Taylor's incentive plan without day-rate guarantee seemed harsh at the low level even in his day when wage-base rates were comparatively low. But, even with a guaranteed hourly day rate, the lower piece rates severely penalize those who cannot reach the 100 percent efficiency standard.

Piece Rate with Guarantee Plan. The piece rate with guarantee curve starts where both 100 percent points intersect (circled in Figure 17.3), and deviates in a continuous 45 degree upward slope, indicating that the worker receives an increase of one percent of the wage-base rate earnings for each one percent of increased production. With piece-rate plans, all gains or losses concern the employee more than the employer, in contrast with the day rate, whereby only the employer is affected.

PIECE-RATE ADVANTAGES. Piece-rate incentive plans are simple for the workers to understand and earnings are easy for the payroll department to calculate. Earnings are readily computed by multiplying the number of pieces produced by the rate per piece. The piece-rate method gives the worker a direct incentive for action at all times since his earnings continue to mount with higher output. Piece rate simplifies cost accounting because the labor cost is constant regardless of output, and this constancy facilitates sales price calculations and enables the employer to quote definite prices on contract bids.

PIECE-RATE DISADVANTAGES. Since piece-rate standards are expressed in terms of money, they have to be revised upward or downward to conform with the fluctuating hourly wage rates, although the time required to do the job remains the same. It is claimed that workers often become confused in calculating new rates.

Assume that during two years, readjusted or negotiated wage increases netted the worker four raises each of 10 cents per hour, thus increasing his wage-base rate from $3.00 to $3.40 per hour. The piece rates likewise had to be changed four times to equal the four wage raises. On the other hand, if wage-base rates are changed under a time-rated bonus, the incentive rates need no revisions. This may not be a serious disadvantage, however, since there are foremost manufacturers such as the Lincoln Electric Company and Allis-Chalmers Company who have successfully used the piece rate with guarantee plan for many years.

100 Percent Time Premium Plan. The 100 percent time premium plan, also known as the standard hour plan, compensates the worker in direct proportion to his output. The plan provides a guaranteed day rate for production up to the 100 percent measured production standard. At that point the bonus payment, based on the number of standard hours earned, starts. The bonus curve in Figure 17.3 shows that the incentive operator receives an increase of one percent of wage-base rate earnings for each percent of increased production.

Many companies have replaced piece-rate plans with the 100 percent time premium plan mainly because the standards are expressed in time units. Related performances by employees in different departments can easily be compared. The motion and time study department is concerned only with the setting of time standards. Since the bonus is paid in percent of wage-base rate for an equal percent in time saved, there is no need to translate time into piece rates.

Halsey Premium Plan (Gain Sharing). In 1890, when F. A. Halsey introduced his premium plan (also known as the *Halsey constant sharing plan*), he replaced the traditional piece rates with the new philosophy of compensating a worker for performing a task in less than the prescribed time. His was the first plan whereby the employer and the employee share the gains from the time saved. Moreover, it was the first plan to pay a guaranteed day rate and a bonus for a comparatively low output.

Compare the Halsey 50 percent plan with the 100 percent time premium plan in Figure 17.3. Note that the Halsey incentive earning curve starts on the base-rate line at the 63 percent production point, while the 100 percent time premium curve starts at the 100 percent production point.

There are specific reasons for Mr. Halsey's incentive payment beginning some 37 percent lower than the production point of the 100 percent time premium plan. His plant had neither standardized conditions, nor production standards established through motion and time studies as is the case with the 100 percent time premium plan. He used production standards based on past performance records mainly to avoid additional expenditures. It has been previously emphasized that such a method results in "loose rates." Halsey realized this condition and, anticipating that a worker might "run away with the job" and earn what appeared to be excessive earnings, he introduced the gain-sharing plan whereby only one half (or any other fraction of the time saved) is earned by the worker. The company retained the other part of the earnings. Thus, as long as the worker was highly motivated, it did not matter how much he earned since the company shared his earnings.

Advantages of the Halsey Plan. The plan motivates even a relatively low producer and is very attractive to beginners. Some experienced workers also consider it to be acceptable. Since the standards are expressed in time units, the disadvantages of the piece-rate plans are eliminated. Where conditions are unusually variable (nonstandardized), past performance records may be used to establish standards even though, theoretically, they are not always desirable. Although workers earn more bonus at a comparatively lower production pace than under any other plan, both employer and employee are somewhat protected. The Halsey premium formula can be adapted to any condition where "loose" standards exist by adjusting the percentage of the worker's share.

Disadvantages of the Halsey Plan. The fact that the plan is acceptable to low producers (the inexperienced and inefficient workers) makes it unacceptable in some plants where maximum productivity and standard time are the major considerations. The sharing feature is its main disadvantage because the majority of workers and union leaders resent a condition whereby "management takes away a part of their hard-earned incentive wage."

Rowan Premium Plan. The characteristics of the Rowan and Halsey plans are similar. As shown in Figure 17.3, the Rowan incentive earning curve starts at the base-rate line and the 63 percent production point, the same as the starting point for the Halsey plan. As with the Halsey plan, the standards under the Rowan plan are based on past performance records and the premium (bonus) is paid for time saved. However, the Rowan plan differs somewhat in the calculation of the premium, since it involves a percentage of the *time worked rather than the time saved.* The Rowan plan pays a larger premium than the Halsey plan for small savings up to the calculated production efficiency of 125 percent, but thenceforth the premium is proportionately smaller as the time savings increase.

The Rowan plan is suitable for enterprises wherein working conditions are partly standardized and partly "loose." Its use has proved favorable where a wide variety of working conditions must be covered by one plan.

Gantt Task and Bonus Plan. The Gantt plan is one of the early bonus plans engineered to eliminate the punitively low Taylor piece rate, while retaining an equivalent of the high Taylor piece-rate plan. Like the 100 percent time premium plan, the Gantt plan guarantees the day rate for production below the 100 percent measured production standard. Based strictly on accurate motion and time study, it requires the standardization of every phase in the organization that may affect high-task earnings.

Unlike the 100 percent premium, which starts the bonus at the 100-100 percent point, the Gantt plan pays a step bonus of 20 percent of the wage-base rate when the 100 percent standard task is reached. For production efficiency ratios at and above 100 percent efficiency level, the worker receives the full share of time saved multiplied by 120 percent of the wage-base rate.

Inasmuch as the step bonus is relatively high, management must standardize methods, tools, materials, and working conditions, as well as maintain a steady flow of work and materials, to make it possible for the worker to earn a bonus.

The step bonus is an attractive incentive for the worker to exceed the 100 percent production standard. This leads to increased productivity that helps to distribute the high overhead costs over a larger volume of output per day, thereby reducing the total cost per item.

Frequently the thought is evoked that maintaining the accurate standardized conditions — an absolute requisite for the Gantt bonus — is costly and somewhat of a disadvantage. The authors disagree with this trend of thought. In an era of high wages, skilled-labor shortage, and high overhead costs, production control and all means of maintaining precise or at least accurate standards at all levels of organization and management are significant.

Original Emerson Efficiency Bonus Plan. The original Emerson efficiency bonus plan was used successfully from 1904 until World War II, when it was slightly modified to suit current conditions. Since the wage and salary administrator will benefit from Mr. Emerson's philosophy and concept of what a wage incentive should accomplish, both the original and the modified forms of his bonus plan shall be discussed.

The Emerson 100 percent efficiency standard is based on a well-planned organization, standardized plant conditions, and accurate motion and time studies. As shown in Figure 17.3, however, the Emerson plan differs from the 100 percent time premium plan in that on the base-rate line at 66⅔ percent production efficiency, the Emerson plan starts to pay a small bonus — a fraction of one percent of the base-rate — for each percent of increased production. The bonus gradually increases with *accelerated increments* until it reaches the 100 percent measured production standard at the 120 percent level of base-rate earnings.

The starting curve, resembling the part of a hyperbola, was established *empirically* up to the 120 percent point of base-rate earnings at the 100 percent production standard line. From that point on, a straight-line bonus curve slopes upward paralleling the 100 percent time premium bonus.

Emerson's plan is frequently termed *empiric* or *accelerated* because of its original construction as explained above. However, it is more often known as an *efficiency bonus plan* because the bonus is computed for the period of a whole week rather than for each operation, and is *paid on the basis of the worker's efficiency rating for that period.*

A table constructed empirically is used with the original plan to indicate the bonus for each percent of increased production efficiency. At 66⅔ percent efficiency, the bonus is 0.01 percent of base earnings; at 70 percent efficiency, 0.22 percent; at 80 percent efficiency, 3.27 percent; at 90 percent efficiency, 9.91 percent; and at 100 percent efficiency, 20 percent bonus.[14] From there on,

---

[14]For a complete analysis of the original Emerson plan and the entire table, see Charles Walter Lytle, *Wage Incentive Methods* (New York: The Ronald Press Company, 1942), pp. 268–80.

in addition to the 20 percent, one percent bonus is paid for each additional one percent of increased production efficiency.

Advantages of the Emerson Plan. The plan is based on Emerson's philosophy that it is unethical to penalize a worker who cannot reach 100 percent measured production standard. He repeatedly professed his philosophy predicated on the theory that if a worker is offered a bonus at the low production level and the bonus gradually increases until it reaches the medium level of 80 percent, the worker is spurred on to reach the 100 percent normal production standard and the high-task efficiency of 120 to 130 percent above that standard.

Disadvantages of the Emerson Plan. The strongest criticism against the original plan is that it is somewhat costly to administer, since it involves calculation of the fractional bonus rates according to tables. Furthermore, the plan with its empiric incentive calculations seems complicated and incomprehensible to the workers since they are not always able to ascertain the amount of their incentive earnings.

Modified Emerson Wage Incentive Plan. The modified Emerson plan retained the original principles and philosophies except for a change in the production level where the bonus starts. The worker is paid full day rate for his performance *up to and including 80 percent production efficiency*, which is considered a reasonably attainable incentive performance. Thereafter, for every one percent increased production, the worker's hourly pay is increased by one percent of his wage-base rate, thus offering an incentive which makes for consistent and lasting improvements in performance. Thus, as noted in Figure 17.3, the incentive curve starts along the base-rate line at the point of 81 percent production and in a straight line slopes upward, cuts through 120 percent of wage-base rate earnings at the 100 percent standard production line, the same as the original curve.

The objection to efficiency tables is avoided. All the worker needs to know is how to calculate his efficiency at the end of a workweek. His efficiency is determined by dividing the sum of standard times by the total actual time taken. The modified plan has all the advantages of the 100 percent time premium plan plus an incentive for the worker to improve his production efficiency at the medium production level. Hence, at the 100 percent standard production efficiency level, the worker is paid 120 percent of base earnings and continues to receive an increase of one percent of the wage-base rate for each one percent of increased production as in the original plan.

In drawing this chapter to a close, we remind the reader that this chapter attempted to identify and clarify the basic classes of compensation methods that are available and to describe the more traditional ones that have been successfully used over the years. Although many of these plans are still in existence, there is a great deal of controversy today about their future and the direction that compensation methods, particularly incentive plans, should take. The next chapter describes the latest thinking of practitioners and social scientists on this subject.

REVIEW QUESTIONS

1. List the basic principal methods of compensating employees and identify how the methods differ.
2. (a) Differentiate between wage-base rate, hourly rate, and day rate. (b) How did the term day rate originate?
3. What are some of the factors to consider in deciding whether to pay by the straight-time payment plan or on the basis of productive efficiency?
4. (a) Explain the theory of the straight piece-rate system, which does not make use of job studies. (b) Under what circumstances is this payment system advantageous? (c) What are its disadvantages?
5. (a) Briefly outline the basic concept of the Taylor differential piece-rate plan. (b) How does it differ from the Manchester formula?
6. In an incentive plan of compensation, what does the term "standard" time imply?
7. Define the concepts of low task, medium task, 100 percent standard task, high task, and top task.
8. (a) In regard to pay, what does the word premium mean to you? (b) How does the United States Department of Labor define it?
9. What is the underlying principle involved in most bonus plans?
10. Are the Halsey and Rowan premium plans truly premium plans? If yes, why? If not, what are they?
11. What are the basic differences between Taylor's differential piece-rate plan and the Gantt task and bonus plan?
12. (a) Describe the automatic sliding scale plan of wage payment. (b) Under what conditions can it be used as a bonus?
13. (a) What is the basic concept of the Emerson efficiency bonus plan? (b) What are its advantages and disadvantages?
14. Is the measured day rate actually a day rate? If it is, why is it classified among the gain sharing and bonus plans? Explain.
15. (a) How are the 100 percent time premium plan and the standard hour plan the same as the Manchester plan? (b) How do they differ from the Manchester plan?
16. Why has the 100 percent time premium plan been adopted by some outstanding companies?
17. Enumerate some of the major differences between the traditionally used incentive plans.

18. After studying Figure 17.3, under what conditions or circumstances would the adoption of a set wage be preferable to that of an incentive system?

19. What are the advantages and disadvantages of the piece rate with guarantee plan?

20. Compare the Halsey premium plan with the 100 percent time premium plan in Figure 17.3. What are the reasons why the Halsey premium plan begins lower than the 100 percent time premium plan?

21. The Gantt task and bonus plan has been criticized because it requires the maintenance of accurate standardized conditions, which is costly. Why do the authors disagree with this trend of thought?

22. What are the basic differences between the original and the modified Emerson wage incentive plan?

RESEARCH OR SEMINAR QUESTIONS

1. It is widely known that when workers are paid according to a production efficiency system, some of them may disregard safety devices because they contend that such devices "slow down" their production. How would you attempt to point out the necessity of such safety devices to the workers?

2. What are some of the various factors that must be considered when attempting to determine how much the incentive remuneration should be?

3. How do you account for the fact that some companies have more than one type of incentive program? Do you feel that this is desirable?

4. Comment on the statement "Theoretically all wage payments are incentives."

PRACTICAL EXPERIENCE ASSIGNMENTS

1. The Ray Allin Condenser Company had a bank of 5 eyeletting machines where the operator eyeletted a prelooped wire to each of three metal strips. The established performance standard was set at 400 units per hour. At the end of an 8-hour day, 5 operators, A, B, C, D, and E, reported their production in units as follows: A — 2,800; B — 3,000; C — 3,200; D — 3,600; and E — 4,000.

   For each of the following compensation methods, indicate the formulas and calculate the hourly earnings, daily earnings, and the labor cost per unit. The wage rate is $3.20 per hour.

   (a) Straight time plan (day rate).
   (b) Straight piece-rate plan, 80¢ per 100.
   (c) Piece rate with guarantee.
   (d) Halsey 50-50 plan.
   (e) Gantt task and bonus plan (30%).
   (f) Emerson efficiency plan.
   (g) 100 percent time premium plan.

2. Contact a company which uses a wage incentive plan for its production workers. Find out at what percent of production efficiency the wage incen-

tive payment begins and how much the plan pays as production is increased. Be prepared to tell the class about your findings and to answer any questions they may have about the plan.

3. Your plant has a potentially excellent incentive pay plan which will result in greatly increased take-home pay for employees as well as reduced production costs. You learn that there is an "unofficial limit" on earnings and that the union leaders are cautioning employees to stretch out the work. What action do you recommend?

CASE PROBLEM

17–1. THE MODERN EQUIPMENT COMPANY

Part-Time Employees on Premium Equipment

The Modern Equipment Company, a small manufacturing concern located in the Midwest, began to experience difficulties with its unskilled labor in the shop. There had been a series of annoying delays and persistent complaining among the plant's regular workers.

The complaints stemmed from the company's policy of hiring part-time summer help at substantially lower rates and placing the part-time workers in jobs similar to those held by the regularly employed workers at the plant. The regular full-time employees at The Modern Equipment Company did not belong to a union. Their rate of pay was $3.25 per hour with an extra bonus of between 10 and 35¢ per hour for running certain types of machinery. The general pay rate for the summer help was between $2.25 and $2.37 per hour. The part-time employees could be trained in three to four weeks to work alongside the regular workers as the jobs required relatively little skill. Added to this was the fact that many of the part-time workers were college students who returned three or four summers and could step right into a job with no retraining. The part-time help could not earn the premium rate on the equipment, so the company, in order to reduce labor costs, would place these workers on premium-rate equipment whenever all the regular workers were on premium-rate equipment. The regular workers complained that the part-time help should never work on premium-rate equipment because it denied the regulars the chance to earn the rate on other days when there was not enough work to keep all the premium-rate equipment going.

The situation led many of the regular workers to split the rates among themselves. This could be done relatively easy by "doctoring" the time cards to show that two workers worked four hours apiece on rated equipment, when actually the equipment was run only six hours that day by one man. The company could check the actual running time of the equipment but was lax in doing so. The part-time help would also "donate" their equipment time to the regulars. When any machinery was damaged, it was almost impossible to tell who was running the machine at the time of the breakage.

The problem came to the attention of Bob Johnson, a supervisor. After reviewing the situation, he informed the regular workers that the present set-up would continue for the following reasons: (1) the company could save a considerable amount of money on production costs, (2) the only time that the part-timers used premium-rate equipment was when all the regulars were already working on premium-rate equipment, and (3) the regular workers should have nothing to complain about because they were already earning almost a dollar more than the part-timers. The workers contended that there was no rush to the work, and that even though all the regulars were working on premium-rate equipment one day, the next day there might not be enough work to go around. They said that the company should save the premium work for the next day. Besides, they explained, "We have families to support."

Problems:

1. What should the company do in this case?
2. Did the supervisor err in his explanation to his men? If so, how? What should he have said?
3. How should the company handle the problem of rate-splitting?

chapter 18

THE INFLUENCE OF THE BEHAVIOR SCIENCES ON COMPENSATION

There is considerable evidence [1] that employee incentive compensation plans usually result in greater output per man-hour, lower unit costs, and higher wages when compared with straight-time compensation plans. The best managed companies have long known that employees are the key factor that makes the big difference in the success of one company versus another. Most all well-established companies have enough money to buy the same machines, materials, and other facilities needed to produce products. The real difference in companies is the effectiveness or efficiency of the workers. Much of the effectiveness of both the workers and their companies is due to the degree that the workers are motivated. It is therefore important that due consideration be given to the human factor in compensation plans. The job of managing people has usually been considered more an art than a science. Thus, if management is to do its job well, it needs to attract, hire, motivate, reward, and retain the best employees. As a part of this task, the various methods of compensating employees should be examined in light of their effects on the employees to whom they are applied. The various techniques and principles of management, important as they are,

[1] J. Dale, "Increase Productivity 50% in One Year with Sound Wage Incentives," *Management Methods*, No. 16 (1959), pp. 38–42.

A. A. Rath, "The Case for Individual Incentives," *Personnel Journal*, No. 39 (1960), pp. 172–175.

M. S. Viteles, *Motivation and Morale in Industry* (New York: Norton, 1953).

would be of little value without due regard for their human aspects and an understanding of employee needs, desires, and motivations. The purpose of this chapter is to examine the latest thinking about employees and their jobs and to explore the basis for employee compensation incentives as they relate to the needs, desires, and motivations of employees according to the recent research findings of social scientists (primarily psychologists, sociologists, anthropologists, and economists.)

The need for incentives

Human life and progress are strongly affected by various stimuli. Human resources are the key to economic development. How people think about work and what they consider to be important goals in life will determine whether their company and country will develop or not. Any human system that hopes to progress must be motivated or have an incentive. *The Random House Dictionary of the English Language* (unabridged edition) defines the word *incentive* as that which incites to action, and the term *incentive wages*, as a wage paid to promote the productivity of an employee. We shall therefore consider an incentive as some form of an agreed-upon financial or nonfinancial inducement or reward that prompts an employee to act so as to achieve some specified job performance or goal of the firm.

We would also like to use a broad interpretation of incentive to include any kind of wage or salary incentive that promotes efficiency or productivity, in terms of quality and quantity. This would include methods changes, new tools, new ideas, improved products, plant layout, innovations, etc. An incentive attempts to obtain cooperation on the part of employees in the attainment of the goals of the organization. In other words, we want to stress that incentives should not be narrowly considered to mean only working the employee harder physically. Incentives must also concentrate on mentally motivating all employees to work more intelligently and as an integral part of a team. This is especially important now and will be more so in the future. The greatest achievements in art, science, and industry result from some kind of incentives. For each man-hour of work performed today we turn out three times as much goods and services (GNP) as we did 50 years ago. In the coal mines 150,000 men can handle the same amount of work that formerly required 700,000 men. [2] One hundred and fifty years ago it took 20 days to travel from Washington, D.C., to Chicago by horseback. Fifty years ago it took 24 hours by train. Twenty-five years ago it took five hours by airplane. Today, it takes about only one and one-half hours by plane. [3] In 1900 the average worker put in 60 hours of work a week.

---

[2]*Saturday Evening Post* (October 12, 1963), p. 12.
[3]Leon Greenberg, Bureau of Labor Statistics, U.S. Department of Labor, "Productivity and Technological Developments in the United States" (From a speech to the 13th Annual Meeting of the National Council on the Aging, Edgewater Beach Hotel, Chicago, February 11, 1964), p. 4.

Today he works approximately 40 hours and in addition has paid vacations, sick leave, and holidays.[4] Without some type of incentive these accomplishments would not have been possible. Leading companies such as General Motors and Lincoln Electric are strong advocates of incentive systems and readily acknowledge that much of their success has been due to such systems.

Clarence Francis, former chairman of the board of General Foods Corporation, has said:

> You can buy a man's time, you can buy a man's physical presence at a given place, you can even buy a measured number of skilled muscular motions per day or per hour, but you cannot buy enthusiasm, initiative, loyalty, nor the devotion of hearts, minds and souls. You have to earn these things.[5]

This means that management somehow needs to gain the respect of its employees so as to pave the way to receive the above benefits. Certainly a company generally pays the same for labor whether it is managed well or not, but what it gets from its labor depends to a large extent upon whether the employees work with a will. We believe that there are several reasons why managements should offer a number of financial and nonfinancial incentives to employees so that they will work with a will that will prove advantageous to the company and the employees.

To Attract and Motivate the More Talented Employees

First, it is generally recognized by most management authorities and behavior scientists that employees rarely, if ever, work up to their capacities. It is believed that the average rank-and-file worker in a factory puts forth only the minimum amount of effort needed to hold his job. In other words, there is much wasted manpower and a need to increase industrial efficiency. William James, the father of American psychology, said that the average American uses only about 10 percent of his abilities.[6] Other psychologists believe that few, if any, people have ever developed as much as 50 percent of their abilities.[7] The late Dr. Butler, president of Columbia University, said that the average American dies at age 35 (intellectually) and is buried at 65, and that the only difference between a rut and a groove is their dimensions.[8] Psychologist Wechsler has indicated that the range of human abilities and capacities is at least 3 to 1.[9] This means that the most efficient worker can do three times more work than the

[4]*Ibid.*, p. 3.

[5]F. G. Lesieur (ed.), *The Scanlon Plan* (New York: Wiley; and The Technology Press of the Massachusetts Institute of Technology, 1958), p. 124, copyrighted by the Massachusetts Institute of Technology.

[6]*Industrial Relations — Here and Now*, Report No. 34 (New York: American Management Association).

[7]J. F. Lincoln, "Organizing Business for Increased Productivity" (From a speech to the Symposium on Solving Problems of Productivity in a Free Society at Winspread, Racine, Wisconsin, November, 1961), p. 67.

[8]*Industrial Relations — Here and Now, loc. cit.*

[9]David Wechsler, *The Range of Human Capacities* (Baltimore, 1935), chap. 8.

least efficient. Thus, appropriate incentives could attract and motivate the more talented employees.

To Improve the Efficiency of Employees

According to management consultant, Bruce Payne, approximately 20 to 40 people out of every 100 office workers in America produce nothing.[10] He believes that the efficiency of the average office is seldom higher than 80 percent and may be as low as 60 percent. Harold W. Nance, president of Serge A. Birn Company, Inc., management consultants, has indicated that the productivity of clerical and office workers is at a low ebb. Mr. Nance estimates the average office worker operates at about 50 percent productivity.[11] Others believe that we are getting an efficiency as low as 30 percent (from some clerical people) and rarely more than 80 percent (from some production workers).[12] Another person has indicated that in the average metalworking plant, ten clerical employees are probably doing the work of four, ten maintenance people are doing the work of five, four engineers are doing the work of three, and six production workers are doing the work of five or less.[13] One president of a well-known, large corporation believes that the best managed companies are probably no more than 10 percent overall efficient. Professor Ginzberg of Columbia University, after nearly 20 years of studying man, has concluded that only a small minority of people are work oriented and really interested in working very hard and that the world's work is always carried on by a small minority.[14] This may explain why most employees never seem to reach their maximum degree of efficiency.

It is easy to understand how inefficient workmen and organizations can be. Anyone who has observed outside construction projects can usually see a large number of workers standing around watching others or engaging in some idle conversations. Some offices are similar. Taxpayers often complain of the slowness or idleness of city employees. Table 18.1 shows the cost of idle minutes in companies of various sizes and paying varying hourly rates of pay.

It would appear that the offering of financial and nonfinancial incentives can do a lot to improve the efficiency of employees, especially when they are responsible for the differences in efficiency between companies in a very competitive market. Mr. Crawford H. Greenwalt, chairman of the board of E. I. duPont de Nemours and Company, shows how critical he feels employee performances can be when he said:

---

[10]Bruce Payne, "Controlling White Collar Labor Costs," *Michigan Business Review*, Vol. 19, No. 1 (January, 1967), pp. 10–19.

[11]"Puncturing Myths About Office Managing," *Iron Age*, Vol. 196, Part 2 (October–December, 1965), p. 87.

[12]"People Power," *Steel*, Vol. 148, No. 1 (January 2, 1961), p. 89.

[13]"Your Most Wasted Resource," *Steel*, Vol. 148, No. 1 (January 2, 1961), p. 93.

[14]Eli Ginzberg, "Man and His Work," *California Management Review*, Vol. V, No. 2 (Winter, 1962).

TABLE 18.1

THE COSTS OF IDLE MINUTES IN COMPANIES
OF VARIOUS SIZES FOR VARIOUS RATES OF PAY

Minutes Are Money: What "Only Five Minutes" Lost Time Each Day*Costs!

HOURLY RATE	NUMBER OF EMPLOYEES					
	5	10	25	50	100	500
$1.40	$297.50	$ 595.00	$1,487.50	$2,975.00	$ 5,950.00	$29,750.00
1.60	340.00	680.00	1,700.00	3,400.00	6,800.00	34,000.00
2.00	425.00	850.00	2,125.00	4,250.00	8,500.00	42,500.00
2.50	531.30	1,062.50	2,656.50	5,313.00	10,626.00	53,130.00
2.75	584.40	1,168.80	2,922.00	5,844.00	11,688.00	58,440.00
3.00	637.50	1,275.00	3,187.50	6,375.00	12,750.00	63,750.00
3.50	743.80	1,487.60	3,718.80	7,438.00	14,876.00	74,380.00
4.00	850.00	1,700.00	4,250.00	8,500.00	17,000.00	85,000.00

*Based on 8-hr. day, 5-day week, 255 working days per year, overhead cost taken equal to hourly rate.

Source: Cincinnati Time Recorder Co.

The difference between the notably successful institution and one whose record is simply run-of-the-mill is seldom very great. It does not consist of brilliant and inspired flashes of genius . . . certainly not over a considerable period of time. The difference rather is in the small increment of extra performance diffused over a very large number of individuals at all levels of the organization. [15]

There is a pressing need today to continue to improve industrial efficiency or productivity. The advancement of society is dependent upon this. There is such great concern today over how to increase productivity that "productivity centers" have been established throughout the Western countries of the world to study the problem. In the United States, a good example is the Center for the Study of Productivity Motivation, which was established in 1961 by the Johnson Foundation (Trust) at the School of Commerce at the University of Wisconsin for the purpose of encouraging educational and research activity in the newer forms of productivity-oriented socioeconomic concepts (especially total system incentives). As employees continue to demand increased wages and a higher standard of living, it is necessary for them to be more efficient in order to pay for these benefits. Then, too, for every percent increase in population there must be a corresponding increase in productivity just to maintain our present standard of living. Most workers want to improve our standard of living, which means that the increase in productivity or efficiency must exceed the increase in population. Finally, there are the customers who want higher quality products and

[15]B. L. Metzger, "Profit Sharing: A Cybernetic Response to the Challenge of Cybernation," *The Personnel Administrator* (March–April, 1965), p. 26.

services, whether these be safer automobiles or higher quality medical care. Thus, through appropriate incentives, employees can be motivated into becoming more efficient and valuable so as to qualify for greater responsibilities, promotions, and rewards. The company, in turn, can benefit as it finds itself more competitive and secure as inefficiency is reduced.

To Help Satisfy the Needs That Cannot Be Met by a Wage or Salary Alone

Another reason management needs to offer its employees a number of financial and nonfinancial incentives is that a wage or salary alone is inadequate to meet fully either the needs of the employees or the company. Behavior scientists tell us that man's wants and needs are never ending. As soon as one of man's needs is satisfied, another comes to the surface. Some religions hold that man can never be fully satisfied on earth but only in heaven. This would mean that a number and variety of flexible financial and nonfinancial incentives could help to satisfy those needs that a fixed wage or salary cannot. Since a company is composed of employees, its needs and desires are likewise continuous and never static. Appropriate incentives for its employees are needed to assist a wage or salary in meeting the employees' as well as the employer's goals.

To Reduce Costs

Finally, incentives which pay their way can reduce costs, while at the same time increasing productivity and workers' wages. Cost reduction is important if a firm is to remain competitive and to enlarge its sales. McKersie has pointed out that during the past 10 to 15 years, important changes have taken place in wage and salary structures which have tended to reduce the effectiveness of certain compensation techniques that in the past were good motivators.[16] For example: many promotional increments have been eliminated as classification structures have been streamlined; merit systems have given way to the emphasis on seniority; wage and salary structures have been compressed so there is less money spread and motivation to seek advancement; and the growth of fringe benefits, which are unrelated to performance, have further leveled out compensation differentials and employee motivation. In addition, the use of discipline and layoff to "weed out" inefficient employees has been constrained by the pressure of unions, the limitations of the collective bargaining agreement, and the decisions of arbitrators. In view of these past developments, it is not surprising that the subject of how to motivate and reward people is now receiving an increasing amount of attention. The consequences of failing to motivate employees is well expressed by J. W. Gardner of the Carnegie Foundation in his

---

[16]Robert B. McKersie, "Wage Payment Methods of the Future," *British Journal of Industrial Relations,* Vol. 1 (1963), pp. 191–212.

book, *Excellence*: "Whatever the reasons for lack of motivation, the consequences are apt to be devastating. Nothing — neither wealth nor technology, neither talent nor wisdom — will save a society in which motivation continues to deteriorate." [17]

In short, appropriate wage and salary incentives are needed and can serve to reward all the key components of an industrial enterprise: employees, owners, and customers. Incentives can increase efficiency and production, which in turn make it possible to pay higher wages and dividends while at the same time reducing customer costs. Thus, the employees, the employer, and the customer can share in the fruits of incentives. To understand more fully the importance, the place, and the impact of incentives, we shall now examine the psychological, social, and economic effects of incentives on the employees and their employer.

Psychological effects of wage and salary incentives

If it is conceded that a financial incentive must be continuous, we must then search for basic principles that will verify our assumption. Every project devised to promote the welfare of man must have a sound psychological, economic, and sociological basis if it is to have stability and endurance. The psychological effects of incentives deal with the manner in which wage and salary incentives affect the mind or mental behavior of individual employees.

Psychologists remind us that if management is to make a man's work effective, it must consider each worker from the standpoint of Capacities, Interests, Opportunities, and Personality.[18] If it were possible to balance these four factors perfectly, we would reach the ideal in human and industrial relations. We realize that such perfection is — for the present at least — not always possible. However, there is no reason for not endeavoring to approach this ideal if we know which means to utilize and what channels to follow.

Of the aforementioned four factors, Interest predominates. Therefore, it is important that incentive plans based on compensation in proportion to a worker's output comprise all the elements that awaken and keep the worker's interest in constant acceleration. It takes very little imagination to realize the attainment potential of men and women who are interested in their work. Any capital outlay applied to arouse the worker's interest is a wise investment.

James F. Lincoln proved conclusively (by actual application) that development of the worker's mental capacities is a strong influence toward acquiring financial rewards. In Mr. Lincoln's philosophy we find that development of the worker's interest, capability, clear judgment, and pride in cooperation are means toward the end of obtaining the largest mutual financial rewards for labor,

---

[17]John W. Gardner, *Excellence* (New York: Harper & Row, 1961), p. 96.
[18]Walter Dill Scott, Robert C. Clothier, and William R. Spriegel, *Personnel Management* (6th ed.; New York: McGraw-Hill Book Company, Inc., 1961), p. 7.

capital, and the consumer.[19] Incentives, therefore, offer a dual motive in providing a monetary stimulus to satisfy the acquisitive desire, and a psychological stimulus of self-satisfaction in the performance of a given task.

Incentives and Opportunities for Employees

In Chapter 2 we emphasized the close employer-employee relationship of early industrial development. The employee was imbued with his employer's spirit of frugality and efficient productivity. He was continually motivated and inspired by the opportunities ahead of him and by the hope of emulating his employer to achieve a high standing in the community.

With the coming of the machine age and the insistency of industrial progress through division of labor and mass production, the worker's aspirations and outlook in life changed drastically, however. The majority of present-day industrial workers are neither inspired by their employers' accomplishments nor are they self-reliant in their outlook for future security.

It may be stated that, in general, the legal status of equality and equal opportunity are the same today as they were in the early days of industry. Executives, inventors, engineers, designers, craftsmen of unusual ability, and successful businessmen still have the opportunity to gain fame or high social standing in the community by exercising their potentials for achievement. It cannot be denied, however, that very few of the skilled and unskilled laboring men performing manual tasks have the same opportunities. Specialization, mass production, and small routine jobs have combined to take away the opportunities which were a source of satisfaction in the early days. As Mr. James F. Lincoln states:

> We are now allowing millions of latent geniuses to go to their graves with their abilities undeveloped and unknown because the incentive and desire are not sufficiently urgent in our present industrial system.[20]

The well-known phrase, "All men are created equal," applies to a man's birthright and legal status as a citizen. But, "equal opportunity" does not apply in the same sense. The exceptional individual will generally forge ahead in spite of difficulties, but for the majority of workers, opportunities for self-expression and advancement must come through the medium of their labor. If a normal standard of production is set as a goal, and a financial incentive is provided as a reward for output above standard, the average worker will strive to attain it. *He measures his success by comparing the percentage of his output in relation to his skill, effort, and increased earnings.* He realizes that in this way an opportunity for self-expression is provided. A worker's aspiration to self-expression, even in simplest form, appears to be a means of solving our labor problems.

---

[19]James F. Lincoln, *Lincoln's Incentive System* (New York: McGraw-Hill Book Company, Inc., 1946), p. 28.

[20]James F. Lincoln, *Incentive Management* (6th printing, 1963, Cleveland: The Lincoln Electric Company, 1951), p. 64.

Ineffective Negative Incentives

Prior to World War I, immigration problems had a disturbing influence upon the stabilization of compensation because manpower was plentiful. The problem was not so much how to select and utilize properly the right man for the job, but rather how to supervise and control him. Supervisors often adopted and practiced driving methods in the belief that the fear of losing one's job would induce a worker to produce more. But driving methods did not achieve the desired results then as they do not now under similar conditions. Workers are prone to loaf so as to stretch out the job over a long period, performing only under surveillance. Driving is not leadership. It is bossing of the worst type, being costly and very unsatisfactory to the employer, the employee, and the consumer.

Psychologists, sociologists, and authorities on "human engineering" agree that coercion is wasteful. It not only has destructive effects upon the individual's work-spirit, but also adversely influences his social and moral life. Instead of inspiring a worker to increase his pace, the unrelenting pressure of fear will eventually cause him to lag behind his normal capacity in the quality and quantity of his output. Satisfactory results can be expected only when all the motives governing human activity are influenced by an incentive. No strings should be attached to an incentive plan. A worker will do his best when his mind is at ease and he is confident that his voluntary efforts will be rewarded.

A study of the most successful financial incentive plans in various companies will reveal that a cooperative spirit permeates the entire organization, creating a sense of security and confidence. On the other hand, organizations attempting to obtain results by the cudgel of fear and by driving methods are certain to suffer losses through high labor turnover, as well as through a waste of time and materials with the inevitable low productivity.

Incentives and Repetitive Work

For some time, there has been considerable speculation about the effects of repetitive tasks on workers. Arguments are prevalent that modern production methods and wage incentive plans create monotony. It would appear that the traditional piece-rate factory production work is considered repetitive and monotonous to most workers. However, if workers are selected carefully, repetitive work is not necessarily as monotonous to the less educated worker. All too often, many workers have been hired who were overqualified or overeducated for this level of work.

New incentives have come upon the scene as workers have become better educated and more capable of contributing in work areas formerly thought to be the domain of management. For example, there is no reason why the better educated workers cannot be offered incentives to invent new methods, improve plant layouts, devise new tools, suggest new products and ideas, etc. This means that incentives of the future need to be geared to employee development and capabilities. This would suggest more emphasis on the qualitative aspects of the product (or business) which chiefly rely on mental effort rather than the quantitative aspects which rely heavily on physical effort. As increased mechanization and automation take over in an organization, they perform most of the physical effort and prevent the worker from setting his own physical pace. Thus, if future incentives are to motivate the worker and not appear monotonous, they must be designed to interest the mind!

Other Psychological Effects of Incentives

When incentive plans are properly established and adequately maintained, they can be very satisfying to those workers who have a high ego or self-fulfillment need or to those employees who are seeking more freedom to control their job conditions such as work pace and earnings. Likewise, incentives are looked upon very favorably by those employees who are seeking prompt recognition and dependable rewards according to their productive efforts (merits). Individual incentives can provide an employee with a sense of personal worth and dignity. To some employees, even a small difference in pay can have a psychological significance that far exceeds the monetary difference. Incentives can also prove very satisfying to management because employees become receptive to self-development and greater efficiency. This, in turn, may reduce the amount of supervision needed.

When an incentive system is not set up properly or adequately administered, these negative effects tend to develop: workers set production ceilings on their efforts when they feel that high performance would jeopardize their job security or high earnings; workers develop undue anxiety and friction among themselves or their departments if distorted wage structures appear; employees cannot agree on the fairness of the job performance standards that are set; and distrust, suspicion, hostility, and grievances may appear. Finally, employees may dislike incentives because of their ill effect on their social relationships with other employees.

Sociological effects of wage and salary incentives

The sociological effects of incentives deal with the manner in which wage and salary incentives affect society or social groups of employees (in contrast to the psychological effects that primarily deal with employees as individuals). One social effect of incentives is that they can draw people together into cliques and various size social groups and thus serve as group motivators. Some better known examples of group incentives that utilize sociological concepts are the following types of compensation plans: Lincoln Electric, General Motors, Kaiser Aluminum, Scanlon, Rucker share-of-production, profit sharing, stock ownership, and zero defects.

Not enough is yet known about the circumstances under which norms of a social system support the drive toward productive results.[21] However, it would appear from the results obtained from the use of several of the above plans that there is a motivational relationship between the social needs of employees and the performance needs of an organization. The majority of employees have social needs that are expressed in the employee's desire to belong, to find acceptance, to be part of a group, and to associate on a friendly basis with others. Certainly, most employees at least want to be accepted and feel that they really belong to the organization which employs them. The more famous the firm, the more likely an employee wants to be identified as "on the team." Group incentives have been known to satisfy this desire to be identified and accepted by the firm. Thus, group incentives have a way of acknowledging that the employee has been accepted as a worthwhile member of the team. This of course promotes teamwork and cooperation among the group members. Montagu, a cultural anthropologist, has pointed out that men prefer to survive through cooperation rather than through competition and that the principle of cooperation is the most dominant and biologically the most important.[22] The social pressure of the group also tends to discourage marginal performance on the part of those team members who might have the temptation to loaf. It also tends to discourage the less efficient workers from joining the team. There are other positive sociological effects of group incentives. There is less likelihood of complaints regarding discrimination because group incentives allow more employees to participate. When the whole plant participates as in profit sharing, there can be no complaint of discrimination. Group incentives tend to reduce individual rivalry and yet can promote friendly team rivalry.

There are some negative sociological effects of group incentives. It is almost impossible to reward all group members equitably. The more able employees of the group team have to carry the less capable. As long as these differences in ability are not too great, it generally does not cause much fuss. However, when differences are great, the less efficient are likely to be pressured into being dropped or transferred. The most efficient are likely to leave the group unless other compensating factors (recognition or pay) prevail. In addition, group incentives as total motivational systems may be more difficult to carry out than individual incentive systems because it is not easy to reward each employee equitably. Then, too, whenever management is vague about its policy on high earnings, loose standards, unemployment, rate-cutting, etc., the social pressure of the employee groups may force informal ceilings on production or earnings. "Rate busters" are not popular in the group and are often ostracized or penalized in some way by other employees.

---

[21]William F. Whyte, *Men at Work* (Homewood, Illinois: The Dorsey Press, 1961), pp. 551.

[22]Ashley Montagu, *Man in Process* (New York: New American Library, 1962), p. 50.

Economic effects of wage and salary incentives

The economic effects of wage and salary incentives deal with the manner in which incentives affect the production, distribution, and consumption of wealth, and with the various related problems of labor, finance, employment, etc. Statistical data issued by governmental sources and independent agencies definitely indicate that greater productivity lowers consumer cost. It raises the standard of living for wage earners and society as a whole. Greater purchasing power and a higher standard of living go hand in hand. They stem from the same source, namely, greater productivity, which is based on consumption or the utilization of goods to satisfy human wants. What can happen to a society when labor and management lose their economic motivation is described in a book by F. R. Bentley, a business consultant in England. He points out that where the motivation to increase productivity is lacking, a worker attitude of "I'm all right, Jack," takes place, which results in reduced productivity and far-reaching negative effects throughout their economy.[23]

Effects of Wage and Salary Incentives on Consumption and Production

In the existing economic order, consumption problems are closely related to the problems of production, since mass production and mass consumption are interdependent. Consumption, in turn, depends on purchasing power, especially mass purchasing power, in a progressive society. Economic conditions prevalent in the United States since the beginning of the twentieth century substantiate the theory that large consumption is synonymous with a high standard of living.[24] The term *standard of living* is often used to indicate the actual level of consumption that has been attained by individuals. Furthermore, economists now generally agree that, "The final end of all economic activity is consumption, and since it is possible to produce far more than we consume, consumption regulates production."[25] This thought is further stressed by contemporary economists who share the conviction that:

> Consumption is not only the ultimate goal of all economic endeavor but also the clearest test of its effectiveness . . . . Only during the past generation has the study of consumption been developed to a point where it is clear that a high level of consumption is necessary to the continued satisfactory operation of the whole economy.[26]

---

[23]F. R. Bentley, *People, Productivity and Progress* (London: Business Publications, Ltd., 1935).

[24]W. T. Foster and W. Catchings, *The Road to Plenty* (Newton, Massachusettes: Pollak Foundation, 1928).

[25]William T. Foster and Waddil Catchings, *Progress and Plenty* (New York: Houghton-Mifflin Company, 1930), p. 81.

[26]James Harvey Dodd and C. W. Hasek, *Economics: Principles and Applications* (3d ed.; Cincinnati: South-Western Publishing Company, 1957), p. 146.

Mass production and consumption cannot create high standards of living without the steady and progressive interaction of capital and labor cooperating to achieve this important aim for society as a whole. Only then can a greater quantity of goods be made available to the masses by means of high earnings gained through incentive wages.

Today, through the proper use of incentives, the employee can be one of the most important factors in increasing productivity. However, this is not primarily through the medium of increasing his manual skill or physical efforts, but through his mental efforts in finding more economical ways of doing the job. Each employee, with his job knowledge, can assist management in increasing production by offering suggestions to improve manufacturing operations and discovering different tools, methods, machines, and materials that make the production of goods and services more efficient.

In 1914, Henry Ford I, established the minimum wage of $5 a day — 100 percent more than his competitors — based on the theory that "more wages mean more purchasing power which, in turn, means more prosperity." This theory was then adopted by some leading industrialists and successfully applied during the last five decades.[27] From the standpoint of highly profitable incentive management, it is no longer a speculative theory. It has become a reality to some contemporary industrialists in successful enterprises, such as the Lincoln Electric Company of Cleveland, Ohio, where highest incentive wages, lowest costs to consumers, and high profits have existed for over 40 years. Its management has proven that:

> High wages are necessary for low production cost. Only so can the worker have the standard of living and the pride in his ability to make him an outstanding producer.
> . . . It is the industrialist's job to pay these higher and higher wages and still give more and more to the customer for less and less. His success in doing that determines how good an industrialist he is.[28]

Table 18.2 clearly indicates Lincoln Electric's outstanding record of employees' earnings that amount to over twice the average amount earned in all manufacturing industries. This achievement is due to the:

> . . . adopted incentive management philosophy and the prevailing spirit which — from top management down to the sweeper — stimulates each one to give his best to the whole organization, an organization of people who work as a team. Incentive management is not theoretical, it is a matter of opportunity given to all workers. The rewards of individual

---

[27]See Eugene G. Grace, President, Bethlehem Steel Corporation, "Some Builders of Prosperity," *The Review of Reviews* (January, 1929). Also, J. D. Cox, President, Cleveland Drill Company, "Prosperity and Fair Wages," *Machinery* (August, 1928).
[28]Lincoln, *Incentive Management, op. cit.*, p. 49.

TABLE 18.2

AVERAGE HOURLY EARNINGS OF PRODUCTION WORKERS AND NONSUPERVISORY MANUFACTURING PERSONNEL OF THE LINCOLN ELECTRIC COMPANY AND ALL MANUFACTURING INDUSTRIES

	AVERAGE HOURLY EARNINGS OF:	
YEAR	THE LINCOLN ELECTRIC CO. [a]	ALL MANUFACTURING INDUSTRIES [b]
1956	$4.59	$1.95
1957	4.43	2.05
1958	4.22	2.11
1959	4.76	2.19
1960	4.87	2.26
1961	4.93	2.32
1962	5.35	2.39
1963	5.79	2.46
1964	6.58	2.54
1965	6.64	2.61
1966	6.84	2.72
1967	6.95	2.83
1968	7.20	3.01

[a]Computed from company records through the courtesy of Mr. Charles G. Herbruck, Assistant Secretary of the Lincoln Electric Co. The earnings include overtime premium, bonus, and vacation pay. (They do not include retirement, annuities, or other fringe benefits.)

[b]Obtained from the Employment and Earnings Statistics for the United States Bureau of Labor Statistics Bulletin No. 1312-2 and the *Statistical Abstract of the United States*, 1968, p. 230. Earnings represent gross earnings less social security and federal income taxes.

recognition through wage incentives provide encouragement and stimulates in all members of the team a strong desire to develop their latent abilities.[29]

If prosperity is governed by purchasing power for consumption, and regulated by production, it appears that the problem is how to induce interest in greater production. Such interest can be lasting only if the latent capacities in every worker are awakened to efficient activity.

Effects of Wage and Salary Incentives on Employers and Profits

The employer is in business to make a profit. To accomplish this objective, he attempts to reduce production costs to a minimum. In ascertaining his profits he discovers that material and overhead can be measured closely, but labor, compensated on an ordinary hourly day rate, cannot be measured as accurately. The day rate is purely a time payment to a worker who usually is indifferent to his total daily output. It is difficult to predict labor costs since productivity on

---

[29]James F. Lincoln, "Wage Incentives at Lincoln Electric Company" (From a speech to the American Institute of Industrial Engineers, March 8, 1960).

day work is unpredictable. Without an incentive, day workers do just enough to keep their jobs, and unit labor costs fluctuate from day to day. Therefore, the use of predetermined wage incentives facilitates the establishment of accurate labor costs, and profits can be definitely ascertained. This information is also useful in the preparation of contractor's bids.

During 1928 the New England textile industry suffered highly unfavorable and prolonged strikes. In their aftermath, chaos and staggering losses were caused by wage reductions in an attempt to lower costs. By contrast, increased productivity, high wages, and satisfactory industrial relations continued in the automobile industry during 1918 to 1929. Eighty percent of the workmen in the automotive industry were compensated on the basis of incentive plans. Most of them increased production 200 to 220 percent per man-hour. [30]

If a normal (average) time-base rate is established and the employer convinces his workers, *through financial incentives*, that they can obtain increased earnings in proportion to their output without restrictions, output may increase from 100 to 150 percent. This is conclusive evidence that a properly installed incentive plan benefits the employer as well as the employee. Since the fixed overhead cost remains the same, the labor unit cost is reduced according to increased output, thereby increasing profits.

It is common knowledge that General Motors has been one of the most profitable and successful corporations in America. Alfred P. Sloan, in his book *My Years with General Motors*, relates how their salary bonus plan (started in 1918) has had an important effect in creating an identity of interest between management and shareholders and how it established the concept of corporate profit in place of divisional profits. [31] More important, though, their incentives have been so successful in creating profits for the firm that in 1962, for example, some 14,000 employees were awarded bonuses totaling $94,102,089. [32]

Effects of Wage and Salary Incentives on Industrial Relations

Frequently, workers employed on incentive jobs experience interferences or delays because of faulty equipment, shortage of material, or lack of production standards. Thus, their earnings are affected, and they suffer a loss of income. In such cases they usually watch closely to see that standards of procedure and maintenance are consistently maintained. Invariably, they will report conditions which would lead to unhealthy industrial relations. Generally, favoritism and other irregularities displayed by minor executives are not overlooked. Therefore, the installation of an incentive plan induces top management to exercise greater

---

[30]H. P. Dutton, "Is Wage Reduction the Best Way to Lower Costs?" *Factory and Industrial Management* (January, 1929), p. 51.

[31]Alfred P. Sloan, Jr., *My Years with General Motors* (New York: Doubleday & Company, Inc., 1964), pp. 408–409.

[32]*Ibid.*

control and coordination of all activities, especially at the first-line managerial level.

Compensating workers by means of a financial incentive plan tends to remove barriers that were raised by the "conflict" between employer and employee. Establishment of just and equitable standards permits management and workers to approach each other on the basis of practical human-labor relations and mutual understanding. The former predominant wish of each side to be "victorious" yields to an attitude of compromise. Compromise then leads to a composite of mutual and permanent objectives with beneficial results to employer, employee, and the general public. It enhances industrial labor relations and stabilizes employment.

On the other hand, if incentive systems are not administered well or are allowed to go to seed, there can be industrial relations troubles. General Electric Company, at their Schenectady plant, found in 1965 after many years in operation that incentive workers were not turning out greater productivity than day workers. Yet the incentive employees were more highly paid. General Electric was faced with the admission of the failure of their plan and the need to make a change or go out of business. After much negotiation the employees reluctantly accepted some necessary changes as the lesser of two evils. George W. Taylor has indicated that obsolescence in many plans of some of the incentive wage systems constitutes virtually the number one operating problem in the field of industrial relations.[33]

Effects of Wage and Salary Incentives on Technological Employment

The tremendous increase in production and the standard of living during the first half of the twentieth century is traceable to technological methods (machine production). Literally millions of professional, skilled, and unskilled workers gained employment to maintain and further increase technological productivity. In most parts of the world, mechanization has meant a rise in the standard of living, an improved status, and greater political power for humble people. It has improved health, increased life span through advanced medical knowledge and health care, lessened laborious toil, and given us greater leisure. The working man of today enjoys comforts that were merely fairy tales to princes and barons of 300 years ago.[34]

There has been some fear by labor unions that automation creates much unemployment. Robert Theobald, a British-educated economist and author, also believes that the effect of automation is only beginning to be felt and that

---

[33]George W. Taylor, "Some Problems Facing Union and Management Negotiators," *The Changing Character of American Industry* (Washington: AFL-CIO, 1958), p. 43.
[34]"Some Human Consequences of Our Increasing Industrialization," *The Royal Bank of Canada Monthly Letter*, Vol. 42, No. 8 (October, 1961), p. 2.

unemployment will be a real problem.[35] On the other hand, Laughlin McHugh, economist for the Committee for Economic Development, has said that his organization has reviewed the literature on the effects that technological change has had on employment and concluded that employment seemed to increase with increased automation.[36] The record in the United States does not confirm the fears of those predicting unemployment. The United States Department of Labor estimates that possibly 200,000 jobs a year have been affected by automation (less than one half of one percent of the labor force). Meanwhile, we are creating three new jobs for every two being lost from all causes.[37]

There is no doubt that some temporary displacement of workers is experienced as new machines and methods are introduced. A certain amount of unemployment, distasteful as it may be, will always be with us because of seasonal industries and employees seeking a change of jobs. This is a necessity if a firm or a country expects to make progress. There can be no progress without some temporary unemployment while firms are converting over to new machinery and models. If the auto industry had not over the years used new and modern machines, a new car today would cost $65,000 to manufacture. If the United States went back to the farming methods of 1910, it would take every man and woman in our country working 48 hours a week just to feed us in the style to which we have become accustomed.[38] Without mass production today, we could not produce enough goods to satisfy the elementary wants of people.

If mechanization creates vast unemployment, the United States would have greater unemployment today than in the past. E. L. Hazard has indicated that since 1850, the population of the United States has grown about eight times, jobs have increased more than nine times, and goods and services 75 times. With the technology fostered by a free economic system, jobs multiply faster than people, and goods and services multiply faster than jobs.[39] Today, there are more auto workers and mechanics than there ever were buggy makers and blacksmiths, more electrical workers than there ever were candlemakers, and more people making refrigerators, freezers, and air conditioners than there ever were ice men. A recent record shows that unemployment has remained fairly steady over the past quarter of a century. This is true in spite of the fact that the annual increased efficiency of industries would normally have reduced the need for the same number of workers each year. Wiener indicated in 1964 that at 3 percent increased productivity, some 1.8 million jobs would be eliminated for that year

---

[35]*The Wisconsin Productivity Letter* (Madison: Center for Productivity Motivation, University of Wisconsin, January, 1965), p. 3.

[36]*Ibid.*

[37]*Notes and Quotes*, No. 337 (Hartford, Conn.: Connecticut General Life Insurance Co., June, 1967), p. 1. Reprinted from *Management Information* (Mt. Vernon, N.Y.: Elliott Service Co.).

[38]Ellison L. Hazard, President of Continental Can Company, "The Real Danger in Automation" (From a speech to the Executives' Club, Chicago, October 9, 1964, and the Rotary Club, Los Angeles, October 30, 1964), p. 3.

[39]*Ibid.*

alone.[40] Another revealing fact in the employment picture is that, since 1940, 11 percent more women have been added to the work force than formerly. In other words, in 1940 only 25 percent of the labor force were women. Today women account for 36 percent of the labor force. If the labor force had not added or absorbed this 11 percent of women, there would actually be a 6 to 7 percent shortage of employees (even in spite of the 4 to 5 percent of so-called unemployment that exists today).

Some people seem to think that there is only just so much work to be done and that if a machine can do the work quicker or better, it will replace the man and create unemployment. Machines should do the backbreaking, monotonous, and repetitive work that men detest and free men to do the work that machines cannot do. However, there will always be more work available than man can do, as there are endless wants of society to be satisfied; therefore, machines should not be feared by employees. In short, mechanization does not create long-term unemployment except when employees (or unions) insist upon keeping outmoded jobs (railroad firemen, stand-by motion picture operators, etc.) and show little willingness to improve society by training for (or accepting) other work that is available. Management must likewise be willing to assist displaced persons until they have obtained other satisfactory jobs.

Improved technology and mechanization does bring with it certain environmental changes and problems that affect employment and incentives in the factory. Continuous machine operation (often on a 24-hour basis) is part of the new technology. The design of incentive systems must allow for rapid changes and new developments. Existing incentive plans, especially piece-rate systems, will be superseded by new plans that pay on a constant or prolonged production basis. Future incentive plans will need to focus attention on all factors of production, not just labor. Many cost items are controllable in the sense that people can utilize raw materials more efficiently; they can conserve fuel, supplies, etc. Incentive plans that overlook these and similar items are missing important opportunities for cost reduction. The rapid change of technology also brings with it the need for employees to accept rapid and extensive change. Equipment becomes obsolete more rapidly. Firms experiencing rapid technological change are likely to find that wage incentives increase resistance to change, especially when it raises doubts about future employee earnings or the amount of effort that will be required. Modern technology is also making individuals and functions within the firm more dependent upon each other. This will require greater employee cooperation and a group incentive or "systems approach" that embodies both qualitative as well as quantitative requirements.

James F. Lincoln, the late well-known industrialist, with some 40 years of successful experience with incentives, made this observation:

---

[40]Norbert Wiener, "Technological Change, Productivity, and Employment," *Occupational Outlook Quarterly*, Vol. 8, No. 3 (September, 1964), p. 3.

Incentive management is becoming of progressively greater importance as our mechanization of productive operations advances. . . . As mechanization of industry progresses, the desire of the worker to make the machines work and their skill in using and caring for these machines is of progressively greater importance. Lack of skill and proper desire to use such skill is many times more harmful to efficiency now than before present mechanization of manufacturing operations.[41]

Effects of Wage and Salary Incentives on Restriction of Output and Unionism

There is no uniform official union attitude toward incentives today because individual union policies have varied too much over the years. Kennedy pointed out in 1945 that most unions opposed wage incentive plans.[42]   However, within the last 10 to 15 years most unions have altered their attitudes. Yet, it is still probably true that most unions oppose incentives in principle, but in practice the unions accept incentives and are often the first to object when management wants to abandon them. The main objections that unions seem to have regarding incentives is with incentive abuses such as speed-ups and tight standards, and uncertainties about normal pace ratings, employee job security, earnings, and the like. When the union has some objection to the incentive plans, employee group standards and social pressures are likely to restrict output. When incentive plans are established on just and fair principles that afford workers full and unrestricted opportunities to improve themselves and their earnings, unions do not generally oppose the incentives nor do they restrict their output.

As safeguards against management abuses of incentives, most large unions train or employ industrial engineers and publish considerable material on wage payment matters. Some unions conduct time study training sessions for union personnel. A few even agree to designate some stewards as "time study stewards." Many companies indicate that incentive disputes today are being discussed more on technical grounds rather than on tactical grounds.[43] From time to time, some researchers voice their criticisms on the restriction of output and the negative results of certain incentive systems.[44] There have been and still may be managers with outmoded administrative skills and points of view which are incompatible with current problems of industrial human relations. Their deeds — or rather misdeeds — counteract the philosophy of those who have accepted the use of financial incentives.

---

[41]Lincoln, *Incentive Management, op. cit.,* p. 78.
[42]Van Dusen Kennedy, *Union Policy and Incentive Wage Methods* (New York: Columbia University Press, 1945).
[43]Robert B. McKersie, "Wage Payments of the Future," *British Journal of Industrial Relations,* Vol. 1 (1963), p. 204.
[44]See William F. Whyte and others, *Money and Motivation, an Analysis of Incentives in Industry* (New York: Harper & Brothers, 1955).

The nature of employees and their motivations

Now that we have discussed the need for some type of incentive and the various psychological, sociological, and economic aspects that affect the incentives, we are ready to study the makeup of employees to learn about their various motivations in order that an employer can more fully motivate his employees to the mutual satisfaction of employer, employee, and the public.

The Nature of Employees

If management is to motivate employees to produce beneficial results to the employee and the employer, management needs to have a thorough understanding of employees in general. Let us examine some of the thoughts that behavior scientists and others have about people.

The idea has finally crystallized that employees are more than agents of production (like machines) and are also human beings who share the risks and may get involved in the company's problems and decisions. They are alike in many ways, and they are likewise different in a number of ways. All employees are born with a set of basic drives and instincts, and each has his own individual innate abilities, capacities, interests, personality, and set of values. Since man believes he is of the highest order of creatures on earth, it is only natural for him as an employee to expect to be treated with human dignity. This implies fair treatment and respect, and in a democracy as much control over his life as possible with a minimum amount of authority over him. Brown has indicated that people have three motives for working, each related in varying degrees to the work itself: (1) the work may be done as an end in itself; (2) the work may be carried out willingly for other motives directly associated with the work situation (comradeship, status, power); (3) the work may be carried on for genuinely extrinsic motives (money for a variety of purposes).[45]

All employees also have a variety of needs, wants, and desires of some sort that man strives to satisfy. Man's needs are continuous and never seem to be completely satisfied because as soon as one need is satisfied, another seems to appear on the surface. Thus, employees go through life constantly trying to satisfy one need after the other. Man's needs must be satisfied to a reasonable degree for him to exhibit normal behavior. Needs may be satisfied on the job, off the job, or on and off the job. Most employees have to work to earn a living and to help satisfy certain needs. Each need that an employee has may have a different value or degree of importance attached to it by the employee. Because employees differ in many respects (age, sex, religion, national descent, parents, culture, economic level, living location, abilities, capacities, etc.), they are most likely to have a variety of different values, interests, ambitions, personalities,

---

[45]J. A. C. Brown, *The Social Psychology of Industry* (Baltimore: Penguin Books, Inc., 1954), p. 206.

wants, etc., and should therefore be dealt with as individuals as well as in groups. Every employee, at every level of the firm, brings to his job his own expectations and needs and some ideas on how he hopes to fulfill them. Temple Burling, a psychiatrist, has pointed out that when employers hire a person, they do not just hire his pair of hands but are in reality hiring the whole person with his needs and wants, personality, strengths and weaknesses, his family problems, and so on.[46]

From psychology we learn that all human behavior is *caused* by something. Generally, behavior reflects the nature of the various relationships that have been developed since the time of a person's birth, with people who were important to him. If management wishes to influence the employee's behavior, and thus motivate him, it must consider his background and present needs and wants. If employees are to be reasonably satisfied with their work, they need to possess a philosophy of life within which their job or work "makes sense." They need a sense of purpose, the will to achieve, and the feeling of being needed and accepted. Most people get satisfaction out of meeting job challenges successfully. They should not have their self-esteem injured by any action that would lower their status in the eyes of other employees. Cooperation, high morale, and job satisfaction follow when management has done a good job of meeting the major needs and expectations of its employees. Blauner's research[47] indicates that there has been a remarkable consistency in the findings that the vast majority of workers, in virtually all occupations and industries, are moderately or highly satisfied, rather than dissatisfied, with their jobs. Gross[48] says it is possible to generalize on the basis of the evidence that the greater the degree of control that a worker has over the conditions of his work either in a single dimension or as a total composite, the greater his job satisfaction.

Increasing Efficiency or Productivity

The various types of compensation incentive plans that a firm has at its disposal are intended to motivate the employee to increase his efficiency or his productivity. Figure 18.1 shows the basic methods of increasing productivity and the assumptions upon which they are based. Some people have indicated that most productivity increases have come through technology — new tools, machines, materials, or methods. This is no doubt true. However, such improvements do require a creativity and a willingness *by people* to create, finance, and adopt these. It would appear that employees are not entitled to claim the whole credit for increased technological productivity unless they have *created, financed,*

---

[46]Temple Burling, *You Can't Hire a Hand*, Extension Bulletin No. 2 (Ithaca: New York State School of Industrial & Labor Relations, Cornell University), p. 3.

[47]Robert Blauner, *Work Satisfaction and Industrial Trends in Modern Society*, Reprint No. 151 (Berkeley: Institute of Industrial Relations, University of California, 1960), p. 353.

[48]Edward Gross, *Work and Society* (New York: Thomas Y. Crowell Company, 1958), p. 428.

and *paved the way* for their adoption. They are no doubt entitled to receive some share of the overall company prosperity that they have helped make possible. In any event, it takes people (directly or indirectly) to improve productivity, and employees should accomplish this rather than people from outside the firm. Figure 18.1 shows that the employees must of course have the ability to improve productivity. If unqualified or inferior employees have been hired, there can be little hope of increasing productivity unless the employee happens to have undeveloped abilities that can be developed through training. Even then, the employee needs to be motivated to develop himself.

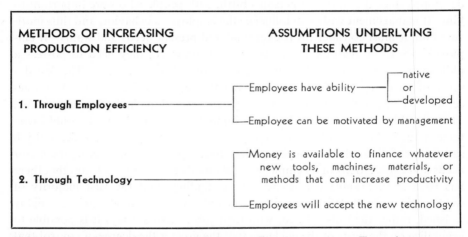

FIGURE 18.1 Basic Methods of Increasing Productivity and Their Assumptions

Increasing productivity or efficiency can be accomplished by the human factor or the technical factor or by a combination of these. In the past, the technical factor was thought to be the main job of management, but there is no reason why employees should not be encouraged and rewarded for technological improvements. As the level of employee education continues to rise, employees should be able to make a greater contribution to increased productivity through the technical factor if they are encouraged and adequately rewarded by management. Incentives of the future should offer more opportunities along this line. In short, the key to successful incentive plans that contribute to increased productivity, reduced costs, and increased employee compensation is dependent upon the degree to which employees are motivated. What then are the modern theories of motivating employees?

Theories of Motivating Employees

The secret of how to motivate people to work as efficiently as they are capable is a problem as old and as complex as society. There are no universal or simple answers. The principles of motivation are psychological concepts related to human behavior, and, because human behavior is not always predictable, there are no "laws" of motivation, only theories.[49] These theories and principles need to be adopted and individually applied much in the same manner that a physician goes about improving the health of his patient. The following are a few examples of the more promising theories that have been advanced on the motivation of employees.

Maslow's Need-Hierarchy Model.[50] Dr. Abraham Maslow, a psychologist at Brandeis University, has theorized that man is a wanting creature always having personal needs from birth to death and that man works to satisfy his present needs according to their importance in an organized series of levels. He believes that in order of importance man has the following five categories of needs: (1) physiological, (2) safety, (3) social, (4) ego, and (5) self-fulfillment.

Man's most basic need is the physiological, i.e., food, clothing, shelter, rest, air, water, etc. This is a need of self-preservation or survival and is the most important to him until it is reasonably satisfied. Once the physiological need has been thus satisfied, it no longer is a motivator of behavior. This need is mainly satisfied through money. When this need is satisfied, man's next most important need and motivator is safety, that is, protection against danger, threat, unemployment, discrimination, and favoritism. Some people refer to this as the need for security. When the employee is confident that he has job security and is reasonably safe and protected against arbitrary, unfair, and inconsistent management actions and decisions, he then becomes concerned about his social needs, which then become his strongest motivator.

Social needs are represented by man's desire to "belong" and to "be accepted by others." Social needs include such group needs as the desire for friendship, identification with the group, teamwork, helping others, and being helped.[51] Social needs are satisfied by contacts with others such as with fellow employees, the union representatives, management personnel, and friends on and off the job. If management thwarts these needs or tries to control them unduly, the employee's behavior may become resistant, uncooperative, and even antagonistic. Many employees may have their social needs already satisfied off the job. When this is true, any further attempt to satisfy the social needs on the job is not likely to serve as a strong motivator.

Once man's social needs are reasonably satisfied, his ego needs become important motivators of his behavior. Egoistic needs are those that enable a person

[49]Charles M. Whitehead, "Motivation or Manipulation," *Production and Inventory Management* (January, 1966), p. 26.
[50]A. H. Maslow, *Motivation and Personality* (New York: Harper and Bros., 1954).
[51]Strauss and Sayles, *Personnel: The Human Problems of Management* (Englewood Cliffs, New Jersey: Prentice-Hall, Inc., 1960), p. 8.

to be highly satisfied with himself. Most people need self-respect, want to achieve status, be honored or recognized, and be a master of something. To maintain a high estimate of ourselves, most of us regularly need reassurance that we are held in esteem by others.[52] This means that we continue to seek daily satisfaction of our egoistic needs, in spite of the fact that they may have been satisfied quite well the day before. Thus, ego needs are continuous and never seem to stop motivating. This differentiates egoistic needs from physiological, safety, and social needs which, when satisfied, cease to motivate. It would appear to us that the typical organization offers very few opportunities for the satisfaction of these egoistic needs to employees who work at the low-level jobs in the firm.

If the ego needs become reasonably satisfied, the self-fulfillment needs then become the most important motivators of an employee's behavior. The self-fulfillment needs are those needs for continued self-development to reach one's own potentialities. It appears that very few jobs offer more than a limited opportunity to fulfill this need completely.

The above categories of needs are interdependent and overlapping, each higher need level emerging before the lower needs have been completely satisfied. Most people tend to be partially satisfied and partially unsatisfied in each area, and there is higher satisfaction at the lower need level than at the higher need levels. Maslow pictured the average citizen as (for illustrative purposes) 85 percent satisfied in his physiological needs, 70 percent satisfied in his safety needs, 50 percent in his belonging needs, 40 percent in his egoistic needs, and 10 percent in his self-fulfillment needs.[53]

In summary, the Maslow theory presents an orderly framework of important employee needs that can motivate employee behavior to achieve satisfaction of these needs. This concept has led some people to feel that the worker can never be completely satisfied with his job because as soon as one need is satisfied, another is created and thus there is a continuous revolving set of needs. However, it is probably more important to the worker to know that management is interested in him and is trying to satisfy his needs than it is to satisfy what appears to be the impossible (a continuous set of needs). Since each worker may present at any one time a different set of needs, it brings out the importance of each supervisor being aware of the most current needs of his employees and of the difficulty of seeking universal satisfiers for employee needs.

McGregor's (THEORY X and Y) Model.[54] The late Douglas McGregor, a professor of Industrial Management at Massachusetts Institute of Technology,

---

[52]R. A. Sutermeister, *People and Productivity* (New York: McGraw-Hill Book Co., Inc., 1963), p. 14.
[53]James A. Clark, "Motivation in Work Groups: A Tentative View," *Human Organization,* Vol. 19 (Winter, 1960–61), p. 199.
[54]Douglas McGregor, *The Human Side of Enterprise* (New York: McGraw-Hill Book Co., Inc., 1960), chaps. 3 and 4.

believed that to motivate employees, it was necessary to understand human nature and behavior. He attempted to pull together the traditional assumptions about human nature and, for the want of a name, he called them THEORY X. According to this theory, the average human being has an inherent dislike of work and will avoid it if he can. Because of this human characteristic of dislike of work, most people must be coerced, controlled, directed, and threatened with punishment to get them to put forth adequate effort toward the achievement of organizational objectives. The average human being prefers to be directed, wishes to avoid responsibility, has relatively little ambition, and wants security above all.

This theory provides an explanation of some human behavior. Since the beginning of Christianity, most Christians have believed that because of the fall of Adam and Eve, man has been forced to earn his living by the sweat of his brow. This was a punishment passed along to man because of the sin of his first parents. Thus, it is not any wonder then that most employers in the past have followed THEORY X and used a negative means of motivating employees through threats of punishments, discipline, withholding awards, layoffs, etc. McGregor believed that this treatment often squashes the employee's ego motivation; and when employees are paid to do what they are told and management is paid to tell them what to do, a feeling of psychological failure is created, which leads to passivity. This treatment also fails to make use of the challenging opportunities inherent in every industrial organization for people to assume responsibility, acquire new skills, achieve status, and above all, to learn, develop, and be creative.

McGregor indicated that the growth of knowledge in the social sciences has brought into question some of the assumptions about human nature contained in THEORY X. The social scientists (especially Maslow) have indicated that man is a wanting animal — as soon as one of his needs is satisfied, another appears in its place. Man continuously works to satisfy his needs according to an order of importance to him. As needs are satisfied, they cease to be motivators of behavior. Therefore, McGregor believed there were some new assumptions about man that should provide a basis for the management of human resources. He referred to these assumptions in his THEORY Y. According to this theory, the expenditure of physical and mental effort in work is as natural as play or rest. External control and the threat of punishment are not the only means for bringing about effort toward organizational objectives. Man will exercise self-direction and self-control in the service of objectives to which he is committed. Commitment to objectives is a function of the rewards associated with their achievement. The average human being learns, under proper conditions, not only to accept but also to seek responsibility. The capacity to exercise a relatively high degree of imagination, ingenuity, and creativity in the solution of organizational problems is widely, not narrowly, distributed in the population. Under the conditions of modern industrial life, the intellectual potentialities of the average human being are only partially utilized.

In essence, THEORY Y implies that management should persuade rather than bribe workers to change their behavior and that management's methods of organizing and controlling the firm are the key to employee motivation. The theory suggests creating employee opportunities that will release their energy and potential and remove obstacles to employee growth while at the same time providing the necessary guidance. In other words, management needs to organize the firm properly and to establish the right working climate so that employees can actively participate and thus be encouraged to give their best. This theory implies that employees can be strongly motivated to exercise a surprising amount of self-direction and self-control when they are committed to goals that have meaning to them, i.e., when they can integrate their goals with those of the organization. Managements should then provide as much opportunity as possible for employees to exert self-direction and self-control. Lincoln Electric in Cleveland, Ohio, is an excellent example of a firm utilizing the THEORY Y approach. The Scanlon plan is a good example of an incentive plan that embodies the THEORY Y philosophy.

It would appear dangerous to accept either THEORY X or Y alone because all employees cannot be placed in one category unless they are handpicked at the time of hiring. This means that management must be aware of the differences in employees, their beliefs, and motivations. In any event, if management is to be efficient, it needs to study their employees to be able to motivate them as fully as possible. This does not mean manipulation, i.e., tricking them into doing tasks by gimmick or insincerity. It means understanding employee aspirations, abilities, satisfactions, etc., so that employees can get adequate enjoyment out of doing their jobs, which in turn should accomplish the goals of the firm.

Herzberg Motivational-Maintenance Model. Frederick Herzberg and a group of colleagues[55] have theorized that motivation results primarily from employee job conditions. According to this theory, there is one set of factors (called motivational factors) that motivates a person to be more productive or creative; a second set of factors (called maintenance factors) that prevents the employee from becoming dissatisfied to the point that he contemplates or actually quits his job. The set of "motivational factors" is concerned with the job itself and the satisfaction the employees get out of doing it. The motivational factors are achievement, recognition, the work itself, opportunities for advancement, and the level of responsibility the person has. When these factors are present on the job, they motivate the employee by satisfying his higher needs; when

---

[55]Frederick Herzberg, Bernard Mausner, and Barbara Synderman, *The Motivation to Work* (New York: John Wiley & Sons, Inc., 1959).
    Frederick Herzberg, *Work and the Nature of Man* (Cleveland: The World Publishing Co., 1966).

these factors are absent from the job, they do not cause much dissatisfaction. The set of "maintenance factors" is also known as satisfiers or dissatisfiers and has a strong bearing on the person's morale by satisfying his lower needs. They do little to motivate the employee to be more productive or creative. The maintenance factors include company policy and administration, technical supervision, interpersonal relations with peers and supervisors, and working conditions. When these factors are satisfactory, they keep the employee from becoming dissatisfied with the job. When these factors are unsatisfactory, they cause dissatisfaction, low morale, and the employee may quit.

This theory tends to point out that the chief motivational factors of productivity and creativity might be considered internal since they are mostly job centered in that they are closely related to the content of the job itself and what the employee does in performing it. Thus, the real employee motivation comes from drives fostered by the need for esteem and self-actualization. The maintenance factors appear to be external because they are more closely related to the environment or outside conditions that surround the job. It would appear that the employee is more strongly motivated from within (internally) when he is involved and is on his own a good deal of the time rather than from without (externally) when he is chiefly directed by the conditions surrounding the job.

There is some parallel between the internal and external motivational factors and what in the field of psychology are called intrinsic and extrinsic motivators. Intrinsic motivators are those that take place *while performing* the work. This means that the work itself is the motivator because it is so rewarding. Extrinsic motivators are rewards to be obtained *after* the work is completed. The work itself may be very dull but the bonus, holiday, or award to be received afterward is supposed to motivate the employee sufficiently so that he completes the work. Intrinsic motivators are considered more effective than extrinsic motivators because the employee is actually enjoying his work all the time he is performing and does not have to run the risk of becoming bored or discouraged because he has to wait until the work is completed before he can enjoy the results.

A Summary of Guidelines on Employee Motivation

Based upon the motivational theories above, the research of the social scientists, and the authors' personal experiences, the following observations are offered as guidelines in motivating employees through compensation.

1. Every organization must make continuous progress to survive. There must be some form of continuous incentive for the organization to make continuous progress. Employees are the most important single ingredient in the makeup of any organization. The competency and efficiency of employees make the big difference between the progress and success of one company versus another. Much of the employee effectiveness is tied to the degree that he has incentive and is fully motivated.

2. Employee incentive and motivation are tied to the everchanging needs and wants of employees. Human nature is such that employees rarely ever fulfill all their needs and wants. Economists and psychologists have established that the satisfaction of one human want automatically creates another want.

3. Employee needs are diversified, and each need has a different value or degree of importance attached to it. Most employees' needs can be grouped into one of five levels or categories. Most employees consider the following as their order of importance of their needs: (A) physiological, (B) safety, (C) social, (D) ego, and (E) self-fulfillment. The motivation of an employee is an individual matter and is based upon his individual circumstances and makeup. The motivation of several employees or groups of employees is based upon the assumption that these employees will be motivated by some common element that will move them to action.

4. Employee behavior is caused by some stimulus. Behavior that seems to lead to reward tends to be repeated, and behavior that leads to punishment tends not to be repeated. Knowles and Saxberg[56] have suggested that if management assumes that man is basically "good," then any misbehavior is a reactive response rather than a manifestation of character and that management should therefore search for causes of misbehavior in man's experience (outside the offender) rather than in his nature. If management assumes that man is basically "bad," then any misbehavior is caused by something within him which cannot be altered directly and so management can then only limit the employee's freedom to choose and to act so as to curb or control misbehavior.

We believe that man is basically good and that employee behavior can be influenced when it is related to each person's needs and desires. The key to the strongest motivation of an employee is to provide the job or the job climate which provides the opportunity to grow and mature continually so that he is best able to realize his own goals by working for the success of the firm that employs him. Employees tend to resist change because people are creatures of habit and because people like to feel that they are the owners of their own behavior and therefore should have free choice to control their own destiny. If employees are to be motivated to change their behavior, the appropriate job conditions or circumstances must be established so that the employee will change himself because he wants to. When the goals and aspirations of the employee are in agreement with the company goals, optimum performance should result. However, managerial personnel first have to determine somehow what needs are currently most important to the employee so as to provide the appropriate job climate to satisfy the various needs.

5. It would appear that: (A) physiological needs are mainly satisfied by money; (B) safety needs are satisfied by job tenure, safe machinery and equipment, and management assurances of fair and equitable treatment

---

[56]Henry P. Knowles and Borje O. Saxberg, "Human Relations and the Nature of Man," *Harvard Business Review* (March–April, 1967), p. 178.

among employees; (C) social needs by joining groups such as the union, social clubs, athletic teams, and associating with various levels of employees, friends, etc.; (D) ego needs are satisfied by praise for work, job titles, awards, status symbols, free time, new responsibilities, added authority, and a maximum amount of control over one's job activities; (E) self-fulfillment is satisfied by being placed in the job that the employee enjoys, allowing him to work up to his capabilities, and giving him the opportunity to make an important contribution to the company or society.

6. Brown[57] takes the position that: (A) there is no one ideal incentive — incentives vary from one culture to another, one firm to another, one individual to another; (B) the law of diminishing returns applies to all material incentives; (C) incentives may conflict with other motives; (D) money is of less significance than has been supposed; (E) but in our culture motives tend to become monetized. People have been taught that money is the key to satisfaction; so when they feel something is wrong with their lives, they naturally ask for more money.

7. Surveys about people tend to indicate which needs in the hierarchy of needs have been satisfied and which have not, i.e., where the employee has been satisfied on the Maslow scale of needs. At present, the two most basic needs — physiological and safety — are not too difficult to gauge or fulfill. However, until more concrete measuring devices of social, ego, and self-fulfillment needs are available, it will be difficult to measure the degree of these satisfactions.

8. We believe that motivating the employee lends itself to a positive or a negative approach. In the positive approach, the benefits the employee can gain internally or externally by desirable behavior are emphasized. In the negative approach, the losses the employee will encounter internally or externally if he does not exhibit desirable behavior are emphasized. It is generally believed that the positive internal approach is more effective on most employees than the negative external approach. However, there are some employees whose behavior is influenced only by a negative and external approach. The choice of any approach is determined by the individual circumstances.

9. A major issue that appears to be on the horizon which must be dealt with before management can hope to motivate employees strongly is the apparent dilemma between the new philosophy of management, as advocated by the behavior scientists, and the new technology of automation and systems, as advocated by the engineers. It would appear that the behavior scientists are calling for a more human approach in managing employees while the "systems advocates" are calling for a total systems approach that fits men and machines together in an impersonal system.[58] Management will somehow have to discover how to integrate the two in

---

[57]Brown, *loc. cit.*
[58]John A. Beckett, "Motivation and Systemation — New Realities for Industrial Management" (From a speech delivered on January 9, 1963, and published by The Whittemore School of Business and Economics, University of New Hampshire), p. 17.

order to take advantage of the efficiency produced by the systems approach and the job satisfaction and motivation generated by the humanizing approach. Possibly the key to this integration is the most careful recruitment, selection, placement, and training of employees for the available jobs within the total systems approach. This means that management personnel must be fully aware of the company job opportunities and requirements and the various employee needs, desires, and motivations that relate to the job conditions.

Analyzing employees for their motivations and incentive preferences

Before bringing this chapter to a close, a word should be said about how members of the management team might learn more about their employee motivations and incentive preferences. Mr. Penney, president of J. C. Penney Company, explained the need for this when he said:

> To be worthy of management responsibility today, a man must have insight into the human heart, for unless he has an awareness of human problems, a sensitivity toward the hopes and aspirations of those whom he supervises, and a capacity for analysis of the emotional forces that motivate their conduct, the projects entrusted to him will not get ahead.[59]

Thus, a part of management's job is to understand all the factors that motivate employees and to arrange conditions and methods of work so that employees can best achieve their own goals, and in turn, the firm's goals through their own efforts. Too often managements think that rank-and-file employees have the same needs as and are motivated by the same incentives as managers. Nothing could be further from reality, for rank-and-file employees look at conditions differently. Managers sometimes complain that employees do not act in a rational or reasonable way. This is often because managers are thinking in terms of their point of view and do not realize that employees act with a purpose that makes sense according to their goals, needs, and motives. A study of an employee's motivation requires an understanding of his attitude toward work, his goals and desires, and the means that are available in achieving these.

If the members of the management team hope to motivate fully their employees, it is absolutely necessary that they somehow become aware of each employee's needs, the opportunities there are on all the jobs under their jurisdiction, and the type of person or persons who are needed for them. Furthermore, managers need to be able to select and place capable employees in these assignments so that they are highly motivated to top performance. Since this is a dynamic situation, with changes constantly taking place in people, business, and environment conditions, it requires a continuous effort on the part of each manager.

---

[59] J. C. Penney, from *Business Management* (October, 1964), p. 63.

Although this is not easy to do, there are a number of tools and devices for gathering such data and for keeping one's fingers on the pulse of employee motivations and incentive preferences.

Earlier in the chapter an attempt was made to identify the various needs, goals, and desires that most employees have. Maslow's theory of motivation categorized these needs into levels of importance, while McGregor and Herzberg added to the use of these. It would appear that one of the first tasks of the immediate supervisor is to identify just where each of his employees is in the hierarchy of needs and what specifically are his long- and short-range goals and needs. To do this, managers must first get to know their employees and establish rapport so that they are at least on a friendly basis and can, at most any time, engage the employees in conversations. By informal chats, observations, and discussions managers can learn a great deal. A sensitive and observant interviewer can pick up many clues about employees. There is nothing wrong about asking subordinates what they are hoping to achieve and what their short- and long-range goals, ambitions, and immediate needs are. Employees do not always know themselves what they seek. However, such inquiries and interest by managers will spark employee thoughts on these subjects, which can lead to a much better understanding of what motivates the employee. It may often appear that the employee says his needs are one thing when in reality they are another. When this happens, it means that what the employee said his needs are, may be in reality the means to obtain his real need. Thus, if the worker says his needs are money, it may mean that what he wants the money for (car, house, etc.) is his real need and the money is the means to achieving this end.

Some firms utilize exit interviews and make periodic morale or attitude surveys to obtain valuable information on the views and goals of the employees. Other firms utilize consultative management, suggestion systems, and the union as valuable sources. Edward N. Hay and Associates, management consultants, have developed an aspiration guide as an aid in the analysis of employee aspirations. Informal departmental and group meetings can also reveal some indications on overall employee needs. Informal chats and private conferences are very good. In short, each member of management must have one or several ways of somehow determining those needs that employees are most concerned about and know what the chief media for satisfying these needs are. Let us examine some of the means that may act as motivators of employees and satisfiers of their needs.

Money as a Motivator of Employees

The use of money as a form of incentive to motivate workers to work harder to produce more was first put into practice in the United States by Frederick W. Taylor in the last few decades of the nineteenth century. Taylor's ideas were copied by others and became the accepted manner of motivating people until the late 1920's when the Western Electric Studies of Elton Mayo brought to light that employees can be motivated by ways other than just money. Since that time, there has been a great deal of confusion and controversy about the role of money as a motivator of human behavior. There are various articles to support a number of different viewpoints. Opsahl and Dunnette of the University of Minnesota have made a comprehensive study of the role of financial compensation in industrial motivation.[60] They have concluded that at the present time there are only theories about money and that very little has been done to test these theories adequately. Thus, the real value of money as a motivator is still unknown. However, we shall attempt to cite our views and the ideas of others in order that a better understanding of the use and place of money as a motivator can be obtained until researchers can validly appraise the real role of money as an employee motivator.

It would appear that if only one reward were available to employees in return for performing a job, pay would be by far the overwhelming choice. An employee must have pay before he seeks other rewards. This is another way of saying that pay is initially the most important reward to the employee because it is absolutely necessary to have money to buy the food, clothing, and shelter that are needed to satisfy his most basic needs. The only alternative is to have the employer furnish the food, clothing, and shelter; and who would prefer this? If it can be assumed that, of all the single rewards possible, pay is the most important, the question that comes to mind is: When does pay cease to be the most important motivator of employee behavior? At present, no one seems to know. However, it would appear that money generally ceases to be the number one motivator of an employee *after* he has reached the standard of living that he has set for himself. A person's ambition or level of aspiration (or achievement) can indicate what standard of living the employee has set as his immediate goals. Since money is the most flexible and accepted medium or symbol for attaining those material goods that are identified with a standard of living (house, car, clothes, food, etc.), it continues to motivate the employee until he has obtained those goals that only money can buy. It is easy to observe that young workers prefer cash to other benefits because they want to buy those things that will give them a more comfortable living. If an employee strongly desires to become a millionaire, money would probably be his strongest incentive until he reaches his first million, which may be near the end of his career.

In Frederick W. Taylor's day, most employees were struggling for survival and earned barely enough to meet their most basic needs. This is why money incentives were such a success in motivating those employees. Today, most em-

---

¶ [60]Robert L. Opsahl and Marvin D. Dunnette, "The Role of Financial Compensation in Industrial Motivation," *Psychological Bulletin*, Vol. 66, No. 2 (1966), pp. 94–118.

ployees in the United States already have their basic needs well satisfied and are more likely seeking vacations, hospitalization, and other benefits in place of pay. However, as employees seek those satisfactions above their basic needs (safety, social, ego, and self-fulfillment) there are times when money can assist the satisfaction of these needs and thus money may again become a strong motivator (temporarily). For example, if a person wants to join an exclusive country club, he must have enough money to meet the membership fees. If he wants to "put on the dog," he has to have money to buy the goods or services that impress others. Buying an expensive car, a boat, or airplane may give an employee that status that feeds his ego. Some employees might gain stature by financing some civic or church project. In the business world, an employee's pay is an important measuring gauge that applies to all employees. It can measure the employee's self-progress and how well he has done in comparison to other employees. It can measure his success by the standard of living he is able to provide for his family and his contributions to his community. Money can also serve as one form of recognition that satisfies the employee's higher needs. The employee who moves into the five- or six-figure pay bracket, or who gets a substantial pay raise, is being given real recognition of his value to his firm. How many employees would think management is insincere if their recognition is not backed up by appropriate compensation treatment? Increased pay can be one of the more significant rewards that an employee receives in return for assuming the responsibilities and work connected with higher level jobs; therefore, it can be one of the important incentives for motivating employees to work for advancement. In short, *money is a multipurpose motivator and can be the strongest motivator of employee behavior at a number of different times in the span of his career.* Usually it is the strongest motivator when workers are young and just getting started in a career. It is always the number one motivator when employees are struggling to meet the most basic needs of survival. It would appear as the United States labor force becomes larger, due to the influx of youth, that money will generally tend to become of greater importance to the labor force as a whole. According to a study of the National Committee on Pockets of Poverty, one tenth of all Americans still live in abject poverty.[61] Herman Miller, Census Bureau economist, estimates that even by 1980 there will still be close to 12 percent of the United States families who will have incomes of less than $3,000 a year.[62] A study by the Food and Agriculture Organization of the United Nations (FAO) confirmed that at least one third to one half of the world's people suffer from hunger and malnutrition.[63] Until these people get beyond the survival level, it would appear that money is their strongest motivator.

---

[61]Industrial Union Bulletin, AFL-CIO, Vol. 9, No. 1 (Washington, D.C.: January, 1964), p. 1.

[62]IUD Bulletin (October, 1963), p. 11.

[63]*The Royal Bank of Canada Monthly Letter*, Vol. 45, No. 6 (Montreal: June, 1964), p. 1.

Lawler has found that the misunderstanding of how pay functions as a motivator has caused some managers to become disillusioned with pay as an incentive to increase productivity at the managerial level. [64] He claims to have considerable evidence that many managers who work under systems which claim to tie productivity to pay, simply do not feel that better performance will lead to higher pay. In other words, if most of the proper conditions do exist for money to be used as a suitable motivator to increase productivity, there will be little increase in productivity until the managers see that management is actually relating pay to productivity. When management gives lip service to pay based on productivity and reneges on pay rewards related to productivity, there can be little criticism of the concept that money motivates, but only criticism of management's failure to administer properly such a concept.

Status Symbols as a Motivator of Employees

Business Management reported what 76 company presidents said about their attitudes toward status symbols and the special privileges they give some of their executives:

> Most of the presidents give special privileges to executives who are nearing the top of the corporate ladder. Most of the presidents believe in the use of status symbols . . . as practical useful devices that are here to stay. Few . . . believe that status symbols have a negative impact on their companies or on their employees' morale. . . . most of them favored at least limited use of such symbols . . . to acquire and keep capable people.[65]

Business Management asked Dr. Charles L. Hughes, an industrial psychologist and author of the book *Goal Setting,* to comment on status symbols. He indicated the following:

> Status symbols hold more potential for dissatisfaction than satisfaction. Status symbols are confusing. They are not status in and of themselves. . . . they have no inherent motivational value. They are an incentive only when employees have been conditioned to respond to them, like Pavlov's dogs. Status symbols are obsolete in light of current knowledge. Use of them is a prime example of how we still attempt to pattern today's business organization in the light of traditional assumptions about people. We assume people must be ordered to work by an authority. We should assume that they will work for goals they see as their own. . . . management must take steps to minimize symbols that serve no purpose. . . . When a person is truly important to the achievement of company objectives and when he actually feels a commitment toward his personal goals and those of the company, then his work itself will be his status.[66]

---

[64]Edward E. Lawler, III, "The Mythology of Management Compensation," *California Management Review,* Vol. IX, No. 1 (Fall, 1966).

[65]"What Your Peers Think About Status Symbols," *Business Management,* Vol. 29, No. 7 (April, 1966), pp. 23–27.

[66]*Ibid.*

We believe that status symbols can and do impress and motivate some employees. However, it is necessary to be aware of those employees who regard them highly because there are some employees who are not motivated by them.

Utilizing Surveys to Determine Employee Motivations

Employee surveys are often utilized to throw light on employee attitudes, wants, and desires. Surveys can indicate various group or class needs. For example, Best,[67] Research Director of Opinion Research Corp., in a study of 622 professional scientists and engineers reports that they are work oriented and primarily seek greater individual recognition in their profession. Satisfaction in their work and discovery of new knowledge are their main goals. They seek freedom from job pressures and work rules, and a chance to do outside consulting, university teaching, attend important meetings, and publish their work in professional journals. Such research can provide valuable clues on the common needs of a particular class or group of employees. Extreme caution must be taken in interpreting such results because the results indicate the personal preferences only for those surveyed and at that point in time. Such results do not mean that these employees will be motivated in the future by the same needs, any more than a picture taken of the group today will be a typical likeness of them a year or two from now. Certainly employee needs of the future will be different from those of today. In other words, one must be very careful in projecting survey results to other or even similar categories of people. They may be different and most likely will vary. What the survey really indicates is the common need of that group of employees polled and where they might fit on Maslow's hierarchy of needs. A similar group of engineers (or any other category) would probably have different needs than those surveyed, especially if they differed in age, sex, or any number of other factors that may affect compensation preferences in a career. Attitude survey data on groups are especially valuable for planning and establishing group incentives for whatever group is surveyed, since the data represent this group's preferences. The data may prove useful for other similar groups, but it must first be ascertained that the other groups have the same needs and desires and would recognize that the planned group incentive would satisfy their needs.

In order to give the reader some clues as to what to look for regarding the various types of needs, wants, and motivations of different groups and classes of employees, the following research findings are offered as guidance.

Motivation of Research and Development Personnel. Rosen[68] reports that Research and Development (R & D) personnel demand a salary that will

---

[67]Robert D. Best, "The Scientific Mind vs. the Managerial Mind," *Industrial Research* (October, 1963).

[68]Hjalmar Rosen, "Occupational Motivation of Research and Development Personnel, *Personnel Administration*, Vol. 26, No. 2 (March–April, 1963), p. 39.

permit comfortable living, is based upon merit, and is equitable. They are highly concerned with the potential to increase earnings. They feel strongly that both salary and promotions should be based on merit. They want job challenge — that is, work that is interesting, permits creativity, is challenging, and is commensurate with their abilities. They are highly concerned with competent and trustworthy supervision (fairness, objectivity in evaluation of employee, and reliance). Factors having little motivational importance included seniority, routine work, pressure to produce, travel, and elaborate fringe benefits. Social status derived from their positions appeared unimportant to them.

These results suggest that, in general, the chief occupational motivators of R & D personnel include a broad range of job conditions rather than narrow limits. For instance, there was little evidence that salary and remuneration are the dominant values, although there was little doubt that R & D personnel were concerned with salary and promotion in terms of job level and merit. This suggests that the efficiency and job stability of R & D personnel are tied in with material benefits, although these are not the only important factors.

Motivation of Salesmen. According to a panel of 16 senior executives in a National Industrial Conference Board study, there is a strong consensus that money, in the form of extra pay for extra performance, is the most powerful incentive for salesmen.[69] However, there was an equally strong feeling that money alone will not fully motivate salesmen, since a number of successful incentive programs blend cash and noncash elements. Sales contests, for example, are widely used, with the winners receiving merchandise and expense-paid trips to exotic places. Among other noncash incentives were company autos, additional life insurance, and corporate stock. The participants in the study stressed that the primary task in designing an incentive program is to provide a combination of as many motivators as possible, of which money is just one. Programs must appeal to the salesman's need for security and recognition, to his competitive spirit, and to his desire for advancement.

Motivation of Scientists. According to a study sponsored by the Center for Productivity Motivation at the University of Wisconsin[70] and conducted by Dr. Albert Chalupsky, a psychologist with the Philco Corporation in California, there was considerable agreement between research management and scientists on the success of *merit salary increases, promotions,* and *increase in complexity and challenge of assignments* to motivate scientists. These three incentives were valued highly by both the productive scientists as well as their less productive colleagues.

---

[69]*Incentive for Salesmen: Experiences in Marketing Management,* No. 14 (New York: National Industrial Conference Board, 1967).

[70]*The Wisconsin Productivity Letter* (Madison: Center for Productivity Motivation, University of Wisconsin, July, 1964), p. 2.

The more productive scientists considered the incentives of *greater freedom to come and go,* and *time off for attendance at professional meetings* to be influential in motivating research output. However, neither of these incentives was ranked highly by the managers nor by the less productive scientists.

The younger scientists appeared to value *educational assistance* more than did their elders, while *commendations for superior performances, stock options and purchases,* and *participation in company seminars or meetings* made a greater impression on the older group. *Recognition of performance* received the greatest number of write-in comments from both managers and scientists as the most effective nonfinancial incentive. Scientists, however, placed more stress upon the role of the supervisor in appraising and recognizing research performance.

Danielson[71] in his study of engineers and scientists found that the recent college graduate is different from those of the past in that ". . . he is no longer satisfied with prestige symbols as the key to the executive's washroom but instead is seeking job status — and he is impatient to achieve it. . . ." The young scientists want more freedom of action, more individualized assignments, more challenge, and more evidence of appreciation for work well done. While scientists and engineers are intensely interested in their work, they do not always regard a job well done as its own reward and thus are equally concerned with personal advancement, recognition, and financial reward for their efforts.

Caution should also be taken on the various research reported on human behavior and motivation in that some of the findings and conclusions are based on studying animals and under circumstances and situations not typical of people. Such research may lead to valid theories about human behavior, but such findings should not be considered as valid for human beings until the theories have been tested on human beings and proven to apply to them.

In closing this discussion on motivators of employees, the student should be reminded that motivation is seldom due to just one reward, cause, need, or desire. Since most employees are seeking several rewards and have many needs, they are more likely to be motivated by a combination of rewards that satisfy one or more of their needs. We have limited our discussion to the relationship and strength of a number of individual motivators because of the complexity of treating them in combinations and because one motivator is often strong enough to influence behavior.

After managers have been able to determine employee motives, desires, goals, ambitions, and the like, it is necessary to determine the appropriate satisfiers of these needs in terms of those financial or nonfinancial incentives that are available to motivate employees to their peak efficiency. The next three chapters will deal with the various facets of those financial and nonfinancial incentives that are available and have been used successfully.

---

[71]Lee E. Danielson, *Characteristics of Engineers and Scientists* (Ann Arbor: Bureau of Industrial Relations, University of Michigan, 1960).

REVIEW QUESTIONS

1. What is the chief factor that accounts for the real differences in productivity among well-managed companies?
2. Define (a) incentive and (b) incentive wage.
3. For what reasons should management offer financial incentives?
4. If employees expect the standard of living to rise, why must productivity increase at a faster rate than population growth?
5. Explain how an employee can benefit, other than financially, from an incentive.
6. What are some changes that have taken place in wage and salary structures in the last decade that have tended to reduce the effect of compensation as a motivator of employees?
7. How do the employees, the employer, and the customers share in the benefits of successful incentives?
8. What are the psychological effects of incentives, especially with regard to interests and capacities?
9. (a) How have specialization and mass production methods of today taken away the opportunities that were a source of satisfaction to craftsmen of earlier years? (b) How can modern man be compensated for this lack of self-expression?
10. What is the effectiveness of negative incentives?
11. Why should future incentives be designed to challenge the mind of the employee?
12. What are some of the positive sociological effects and the negative sociological effects of group incentives?
13. How are consumption and productivity related in the economic sense?
14. What does the Lincoln Electric Company regard as the key concept responsible for the success of its incentive program?
15. How do incentives tend to remove the barriers between employer and employee relations?
16. Is there a justification in the statement that machines have increased employment? Explain in detail.
17. Explain the effect of mechanization on long-term unemployment.
18. What are the effects of incentives on the restriction of output and unionism?
19. According to psychologist J. Brown, what are the motives for working?
20. Should the employees share in the increased productivity due to technological advances? Why?
21. (a) Briefly explain Dr. Abraham Maslow's Need-Hierarchy Model of motivation. (b) How do these needs relate to incentive compensations?
22. What are the main differences between Douglas McGregor's THEORY X and THEORY Y models?
23. Describe the motivational and maintenance factors in the Frederick Herzberg model.

24. (a) Define intrinsic and extrinsic motivators. (b) Which is considered more effective and why?
25. How should management deal with its employees when it assumes that people are (a) basically unwilling to work and (b) basically willing to work?
26. In our culture why do employee motives tend to become monetized?
27. (a) Why is it essential that a manager become aware of the employee's needs? (b) Are the manager's motivational needs the same as those of his employees?
28. How can a manager identify the various needs of the individual employee?
29. Under what circumstances is money considered to be the strongest single motivator of employee behavior?
30. Under what circumstances are status symbols considered to be an important motivator of employees?
31. What precaution must be taken when utilizing sample surveys to indicate employee motivational needs?

RESEARCH OR SEMINAR QUESTIONS

1. Why should management be concerned with the human aspect when it is considering employee compensation?
2. Psychologist William James has said that the average American uses only about 10 percent of his abilities. Explain why you disagree or agree with this statement.
3. Cite some examples to show how group pressure can force an employee to conform to group standards.
4. Discuss the effect of the increasing introduction of machines on worker motivation.
5. Trace the influence that incentives have had on industrial relations.
6. Read some magazine articles concerned with industrial relations problems. What effect do incentive plans have on such problems?
7. Are the activities of a business solely profit motivated?
8. Discuss how management, generally, should go about the task of satisfying the needs and wants of an employee.
9. What are the most effective methods available to the supervisor for learning of the needs and goals of his employees?
10. Select one of the five basic needs in Dr. Maslow's theory of motivation and discuss how management could fulfill this need once management is aware of it.

PRACTICAL EXPERIENCE ASSIGNMENTS

1. As a wage and salary administrator, in one of your plant tours you notice a number of employees wasting time in performing their jobs. The idle time was not of significant proportion to necessitate direct disciplinary action. However, you are concerned over this lost time. How would you handle the situation?

2. Conduct an informal interview with a production worker to determine what his basic needs and goals are. Be prepared to relate your findings to the class.
3. Interview a union official to find out why his union would oppose a wage incentive plan. Discuss, specifically, how management should respond to overcome each objection that the union official has to a wage incentive plan.

CASE PROBLEM

18–1. THE PROGRESSIVE MANUFACTURING COMPANY

Paying for Supplemental Services

John Archer, one of the best machine operators in the Milling Machine Department of The Progressive Manufacturing Company, approached his foreman for a raise. The foreman, knowing he was paying John the top rate for his job, told him that he recognized he was one of the best men on the job, but he felt that his rate was in line and that he could do nothing for him at this time.

John immediately took a defensive attitude and said he knew that his coworker, Mike Riley, who was doing the same type of work, was getting the same rate. The foreman knew that the rates of both men were identical. He indicated to John, however, that it may or may not be true that Mike was getting the same rate, but countered with the appeal that if John would stop and think about it, he would probably admit that Mike was also a very good man who, when he came to the company, had a long background of lathe experience. John admitted that Mike was a good man, but he made a definite point that Mike had only about three years of service with the company as contrasted with his own fifteen years of service. John also claimed that he was more versatile than Mike and that he was always punctual in his attendance.

The foreman, sensing a great deal of tension building up in John and recognizing this as a difficult problem to which he wanted to give some thought, told John he would check Mike's rate and give his request consideration. He then told John he would talk to him further about his request the next day.

Problems:

1. As the foreman, what course of action would you take on the request?
2. What would you tell John the next day?
3. As a wage and salary administrator, what could be done? What should be done?

chapter 19

INDIVIDUAL FINANCIAL INCENTIVE PLANS

There appear to be a number of conflicting views and writings in recent years concerning the prevalence, success, and even the future of individual financial wage incentive plans in the United States. The purpose of this chapter is to attempt to appraise the present and future status of individual financial wage incentive plans. To do this, we shall cover the scope over which nonmanagerial individual incentive plans are being used today and describe a variety of recent plans that will give the reader a wide background on their use, theory, and the conditions which have tended to make these plans a success. The reader may remember that the older and more traditional plans were treated in Chapter 17. We shall limit this chapter to a discussion of individual incentives at the non-managerial level. Group and plant-wide incentives will be covered in Chapter 20, while Chapter 21 will deal with the adoption, installation, and maintenance of incentive plans.

Background perspective on individual financial wage incentive plans

Individual financial wage incentive plans are generally designed to do several things: (1) relate the level of earnings to the level of job performance or output; (2) increase productivity, efficiency, or job performance; (3) increase wages or earnings; and (4) decrease costs so as to improve net profits. If the incentive plan proves successful, the employer gains higher output, greater use of plant equipment, and lower unit costs. The customer benefits in either lower costs or, when prices are rising, in the firm maintaining the same costs. Stockholders benefit in greater dividends as profits are increased through either lower unit costs or increased sales. Employees are generally rewarded through increased earnings. They may be also rewarded by increased leisure or a combination of increased earnings and leisure.

Scope of Wage Incentives

Individual wage incentives began with Frederick W. Taylor before the turn of the century and have been primarily applied in manufacturing industries. By 1929 eighty percent of the workmen in the auto industry were compensated on the basis of incentive plans. Incentive plans may have reached their peak sometime before the depression of the 1930's.

In a 1935 study, the National Industrial Conference Board (NICB) found that 75 percent of the firms they polled used some form of wage incentive. In 1939, in another study by the NICB, 52 percent of the firms polled were using some form of wage incentive. In two separate Bureau of Labor Statistics (BLS) studies (1945–46, 1951–52) of manufacturing workers, 30 percent were reported using incentives.[1] According to a BLS study published in May of 1960, some 27 percent of production and related workers who were employed in manufacturing (as of May of 1958) were paid on an incentive basis.[2] In a 1959 survey of 785 plant and 21 industrial categories, *Factory* magazine (now *Modern Manufacturing*) reported that some 51 percent of the plants were using wage incentives for nonmanagement employees.[3] In June of 1964, BLS reported in another study that 26.2 percent of the workers in manufacturing plants (for 1962–63) were paid on an incentive basis.[4] In a survey report of September, 1964, the American Association of Industrial Management and the National Metal Trades Association (AAIM/NMTA) surveyed 512 plants and found that 38 percent of them were using one or more types of incentive plans.[5] In a similar survey of 619 plants in 1959, 37 percent of the plants were using incentives; thus, the AAIM/NMTA findings would indicate no significant trend in incentives. In another survey of plants by *Factory* magazine in 1965, some 41 percent were reported to have wage incentive plans in their plants.[6] Individual financial incentive plans for office

---

[1]Otto Hollberg, "Wage Formulation in Major Labor Markets," *Monthly Labor Review*, Vol. 76 (January, 1953), p. 26.

[2]L. E. Lewis, "Extent of Incentive Pay in Manufacturing," *Monthly Labor Review*, Vol. 83 (May, 1960), pp. 60–63.

[3]"The Truth About Wage Incentives and Work Measurement Today," *Factory*, Vol. 117 (April, 1959), pp. 74–84.

[4]"Wages and Related Benefits," *Monthly Labor Review*, Vol. 87 (June, 1964), p. 678.

[5]American Association of Industrial Management and National Metal Trades Association, *Wage Incentive Practices — A Survey Report* (Jenkintown, Pa., September, 1964), p. 1.

[6]Gregory V. Schultz, "Plants' Incentives Slump Badly Over Last 6 Years," *Factory* June, 1965), pp. 68–79.

workers have never approached the popularity of those in manufacturing. In fact, individual incentive plans for clerical workers are more likely to supplement their pay rather than being the primary source of it. In a study of clerical incentives by the University of Wisconsin and the National Office Management Association (now the Administrative Management Society), it was found that only 2.6 percent of some 648 firms polled were using individual clerical incentive plans in the office.[7]

Although the various studies cited above represent different samples of plants, industries, and employees, it appears that since 1959 there has been a leveling off and some decline in the use of incentive plans in manufacturing industries. The two studies by *Factory* are comparable enough to conclude, as their studies show, that there has been a 10 percent decrease in the number of *plants* having wage incentive plans.[8] Table 19.1 compares the two surveys by plant size, number and percent of plants, and the trend from 1959 to 1965.

TABLE 19.1

TREND IN PLANTS WITH WAGE INCENTIVES

SIZE OF PLANT (BY NO. OF EMPLOYEES)	PLANTS WITH WAGE INCENTIVES			NO. OF PLANTS	
	1965	1959	CHANGE	1965	1959
50– 99	20%	20%	0%	71	5
100– 249	33	45	−12	291	88
250– 499	40	45	− 5	174	312
500– 999	58	52	+ 6	122	215
1,000–2,500	55	63	− 8	65	114
over 2,500	69	69	0	28	51
Average	41%	51%	−10%	751	785

Source: Factory magazine (now *Modern Management*).

Although the various BLS studies cannot be compared to the *Factory* surveys because the BLS studies were of numbers of *employees* while the *Factory* surveys were of numbers of *plants*, it would appear that the latest BLS survey showed a slight decline in the number of employees being covered by wage incentives. The fact that the BLS survey also included commissions and group incentive plans (Rucker and Kaiser plans) may be an indication of a shift away from individual incentive plans to group and plant-wide incentive plans. At one time, 80 percent of the autoworkers (1929), 70 percent of the steelworkers (1959), and 80 percent of the rubber industry (1959) were on incentive plans. Today the figures are much lower. Table 19.2 shows the percent of various industry groups of production (or related) workers who are paid on an incentive basis. The industry groups

---

[7] J. J. Jehring, "Financial Incentives in the Office," NOMA Management Bulletins, *Personnel*, Unit 12 (National Office Management Assn., Willow Grove, July, 1963), p. 3.
[8] "Fein vs. Schultz," *Factory*, Vol. 125, No. 7 (July, 1967), p. 85.

TABLE 19.2

PERCENT OF PRODUCTION AND RELATED WORKERS PAID ON INCENTIVE BASIS, BY INDUSTRY GROUP, IN ORDER OF INCREASING LABOR COST AS PERCENT OF VALUE ADDED

SIC CODE	INDUSTRY GROUP	LABOR COST AS PERCENT OF VALUE ADDED	PERCENT PAID ON INCENTIVE BASIS
331	Blast furnaces, steel works, and rolling mills.	7.3	60
211	Cigarettes.	11.8	3
283	Drugs and medicines.	11.8	17
289	Miscellaneous chemicals.	14.9	12
209	Miscellaneous food products.	18.1	5
285	Paints, pigments, and fillers.	19.1	13
204	Grain-mill products.	19.5	7
208	Beverages.	19.8	5
282	Industrial organic chemicals.	21.9	5
281	Industrial inorganic chemicals.	22.7	8
324	Cement, hydraulic.	23.5	2
386	Photographic apparatus.	25.6	46
288	Vegetable and animal oils and fats.	25.9	5
205	Bakery products.	27.1	5
207	Confectionery and related products.	28.0	31
203	Canning and preserving.	30.1	12
271	Newspapers.	30.8	7
329	Miscellaneous nonmetallic mineral products.	31.2	22
382	Mechanical measuring and controlling instruments.	31.3	32
327	Concrete, gypsum, and plaster products.	31.5	14
352	Agricultural machinery and tractors.	31.6	32
358	Service industry and household machines.	32.6	33
361	Electrical generating, transmission, distribution, and industrial apparatus.	33.2	38
356	General industrial machinery.	33.4	32
353	Construction and mining machinery.	33.6	12
394	Toys and sporting goods.	36.5	24
227	Carpets, rugs, and other floor coverings.	36.6	40
381	Laboratory, scientific, and engineering instruments.	36.7	7
335	Rolling, drawing, and alloying of nonferrous metals.	36.8	33
	Motor vehicles and equipment.	36.8	13
391	Jewelry, silverware, and plated ware.	37.1	35
343	Heating apparatus (except electric) and plumbers' supplies.	37.7	31
342	Cutlery, handtools, and hardware.	38.1	44
212	Cigars.	38.2	66
364	Electrical equipment for vehicles.	38.4	53
372	Aircraft and parts.	38.6	4
349	Miscellaneous fabricated metal products.	38.7	18
234	Women's and children's undergarments.	39.9	52
344	Fabricated structural metal products.	40.0	14
396	Costume jewelry, buttons, and notions.	40.3	17
339	Miscellaneous primary metal industries.	40.9	42
267	Paperboard containers and boxes.	41.1	20
357	Office and store machines and devices.	41.2	31
322	Glass and glassware, pressed or blown.	41.5	45
359	Miscellaneous machinery parts.	42.1	19
201	Meat products.	42.3	18
239	Other fabricated textile products.	43.4	23
238	Miscellaneous apparel and accessories.	43.5	50

TABLE 19.2 (concluded)

SIC CODE	INDUSTRY GROUP	LABOR COST AS PERCENT OF VALUE ADDED	PERCENT PAID ON INCENTIVE BASIS
387	Watches and clocks.....................	44.2	24
346	Miscellaneous stamping, coating, and engraving...............................	44.5	22
233	Women's outerwear......................	44.8	63
251	Household furniture.....................	44.9	25
354	Metal working machinery................	45.6	24
317	Handbags and small leather goods........	46.2	15
249	Miscellaneous wood products.............	46.3	13
325	Structural clay products.................	46.4	31
236	Children's outerwear....................	46.8	48
225	Knitting mills..........................	47.1	64
275	Commercial printing....................	47.3	1
243	Millwork, plywood, and prefabricated structural wood products...................	48.0	7
311	Leather: tanned, curried, and finished.....	48.2	51
	Wool textiles..........................	49.4	29
326	Pottery and related products.............	49.5	26
314	Footwear (except rubber)................	49.8	70
	Dyeing and finishing textiles.............	50.0	14
231	Men's and boys' suits and coats..........	50.3	71
232	Men's and boys' furnishings and work clothing..............................	50.4	71
336	Nonferrous foundries....................	50.7	23
332	Iron and steel foundries.................	51.6	27
242	Sawmills and planing mills...............	54.5	5
	Synthetic textiles.......................	55.4	29
373	Ship and boat building and repairing......	60.5	20
	Cotton textiles.........................	61.5	36

Source: United States Department of Labor Survey as reported in *Monthly Labor Review* (March, 1964), p. 272.

that have the highest percentage of incentive workers include: men's and boys' suits and coats (71%), men's and boys' furnishings and work clothing (71%), footwear (70%), cigars (66%), knitting mills (64%), and women's outerwear (63%). Those industry groups that have the lowest percentage of incentive workers include: commercial printing (1%), cement, hydraulic (2%), cigarettes (3%), and aircraft and parts (4%).

It would appear that as technological change increases the use of mechanization and automation, more production processes become machine paced. This means that as workers lose control of the work pace, traditional individual incentives, which were strictly based on productivity resulting from increased worker efforts, are on the decline. However, there is no reason why new incentives (individual or group) cannot be developed to keep machines producing as close to 100 percent of the available time as is possible. In other words, the employee's earnings would be related to the productivity of one or more machines (through the employee's ability to keep them functioning smoothly) rather than the employee's physical efforts to manufacture the pieces himself.

Incentive Earning Guidelines

Most individual wage incentive plans are designed by industrial engineers who believe that the average nonmanagerial employees should be provided with an incentive that permits them to earn an extra 35 percent above their hourly base rates. However, extra earnings of anywhere from 15 to 35 percent (above the hourly rates paid to day workers on similar jobs) are generally considered to be an acceptable range of incentive earnings. Individual wage incentive plans that provide most incentive workers with less than 15 percent extra earnings are usually considered to be too low to motivate workers effectively to perform to the higher levels at which they are capable. When incentive plans provide most incentive workers with earnings over 35 percent, there is a strong tendency for management personnel to believe that the earnings are too high (out of line). Many incentive workers believe that such high earnings will cause management to take some form of action which will ultimately reduce earnings or bring them more in line. Thus, incentive workers often "restrict" or hold back their productive efforts whenever they believe that either their productivity or their earnings are as high as management will permit.

There are a number of sources that have tended to influence and establish precedent on incentive earnings. During World War II, the War Labor Board recommended a range of 20 to 25 percent for incentive earnings. During the Korean War, the Wage Stabilization Board established a minimum of 15 percent but no maximum.[9] Books on wage incentives more often recommend a minimum of 20 percent and a maximum of between 30 and 40 percent. The basic incentive plans in the steel industry consider 35 percent as their goal.

The pros and cons of individual financial wage incentives

The various writings in recent years on individual financial wage incentives present a variety of views. Some of these views, as shown below, are not only contradictory but also confusing as to the future of this type of incentive.

The Pros of Individual Financial Wage Incentives

When individual financial wage incentives are properly planned, installed, and maintained, the following points support the proposition that these incentives will be around for a long time to come: (1) An individual incentive is one of the most sound and valid methods of rewarding an employee for his merits because it can be tied more directly to his output. (2) An individual incentive comes closest to paying the employee a fair day's pay for a fair day's work.

---

[9] Garth L. Mangum, *Wage Incentive Systems* (Berkeley: Institute of Industrial Relations, University of California, 1964), p. 16.

(3) Individual wage incentives result in providing objective and useful information about a worker's ability and his qualifications for promotion, transfer, demotion, etc. (4) Individual wage incentives provide more accurate control and data on costs than other wage payment methods. (5) Individual incentives are one of the most powerful means of motivating each individual to work up to his capabilities when the incentives are tailored to meet his individual needs. They can offer him a challenge, a chance to escape unwelcome pressure by the supervisor, an opportunity to increase his earnings, and more control over his work pace. (6) The record shows that sound individual wage incentives can increase productivity, wages, and profits while lowering costs. They therefore have all the potential for rewarding the important segments of any successful concern — the employees, the stockholders, and the customers. There has been some good that has come even from incentive plans that have had serious shortcomings. Most managers and their employees have somewhere along the line been forced to rethink through their job performances and have come up with new and better ways to accomplish the tasks at hand.

The Cons of Individual Financial Wage Incentives

The following arguments tend to support the proposition that individual wage incentives are on the decline and may be on their way out: (1) Technological change appears to handicap the traditional future use of individual wage incentives. Technological pace is becoming so rapid that there is hardly adequate time to properly plan, develop, install, and maintain a sound system long enough to pay its way, to say nothing of the proper training of those who are expected to manage it. Then, too, technological change is resulting in more mass production through increased mechanization and automation and causing greater machine pacing of work. This reduces or eliminates the opportunity that the worker has to control his production and thus tends to destroy the traditional concept of individual financial incentives which rewarded an employee for increased physical effort that resulted in increased productivity. (2) Individual wage incentives are often resisted because either the company or the persons who are responsible for them are not completely trusted nor held in high esteem. (3) The installation and the administration of individual wage incentives are time-consuming, expensive, and a source of irritation that appears to intensify as individual incentives become more complex. The task increases in complexity as product variety becomes greater, production runs become shorter, and more workers have nonrepetitive tasks as part of their jobs. (4) Employees and unions have not accepted their responsibility to make individual incentives work according to the rules of the game. Employees have been known to try to outsmart management so that they can gain a larger share of money than they are entitled to. Employee abuses include false production reports, faking a normal working pace when production standards are set, complaining that fair standards are too tight, and not reporting changes that make standards loose. (5) Rightly or wrongly, there is a large number of people (managers, employees, stockholders, and others) who are beginning to wonder whether individual incentives are worth all the trouble they create. The cost of establishing and administering incentive plans plus possible problems of inferior product quality, customer discontent, lower employee morale, more grievances, and increased accident insurance rates may more than offset whatever savings and advantages the plans are supposed to have. A *Factory* magazine survey indicated that twice as many of the survey respondents said they planned to discontinue existing wage incentive plans as those that planned to institute new ones.[10]

The Future of Individual Wage Incentives

Although many of the traditional individual financial wage incentive plans for manually controlled operations will be discontinued for one reason or another, many such plans will continue to be relied upon as motivational tools in those industries requiring substantial manual effort and having a high percentage of labor content. Most of the current traditional plans will need to be revised or improved if they are to survive for any length of time. New plans will need to be developed in undeveloped nonroutine areas (maintenance, clerical, housekeeping, etc.) as pressure is placed on industrial engineers to develop practical ways to measure nonroutine work and to design incentives that will make employees more efficient. As manually controlled production operations become machine controlled, there will have to be more individual incentive opportunities that will encourage employees to work more intelligently rather than physically if incentives are to keep from declining. Traditional-type individual wage incentives of working the man harder physically will be on the decline. However, there may be opportunities to establish individual incentives based on the percentage of machine utilization. The reason for this is that the cost of an idle process or equipment hour is usually many times the cost of a similar operator idle hour. Suitable incentive plans will also need to be designed to reward workers for suggesting better tooling or planning their own methods improvements. This type of incentive would be especially desirable for those workers who are looking for new challenges and who are interested in being creative. Keener competition among firms will require greater labor utilization and efficiency and keep pressures on management to find untapped areas that will lend themselves to various types of incentive plans. Other forms of motivation will probably be necessary in the automated or process-controlled industries. Present individual financial wage incentive plans are not adequate for those jobs because they are highly mental or mostly nonskilled in nature, and therefore do not

---

[10]"Fein vs. Schultz," *loc. cit.*

offer much opportunity to increase earnings through extra physical effort. Such jobs may better lend themselves to new incentives of the type that rewards employees for the absence or prevention of machine downtime.

If the new types of individual incentive plans are to work satisfactorily and be of lasting value, they need to be very cognizant of two important requirements: (1) The plan should be able to react easily to change and thus keep up with the times. Today, dramatic change is the way of life in a technological age. Possibly, future incentive plans should be set up like a contract and guaranteed for a certain job or a specific length of time (say 6, 9, or 12 months), and at the end of that time the plan should be automatically dropped unless the employees and the employer both agree to continue it "as is" or to modify it. This would allow the necessary changes to be made, if needed, or the plan dropped if it were found to be unsatisfactory from either the worker's or the employer's viewpoint. Such a stipulation or clause in an incentive plan would permit management to drop the incentive if it did not work out as well as planned. For example, sometimes the quality of work produced over a period of time by incentive workers tends to deteriorate; in other cases incentive standards become loose, and eventually management may find itself legally forced to pay incentive bonuses for either defective work or productivity that is no higher than that of day workers. On the other hand, employees may likewise become disillusioned with the plan for one reason or another. In short, the contract or termination concept would not only permit the opportunity for a more valid appraisal of the plan but also pave the way for the continuance of those plans that have the potential to be successful over the long run. (2) The plan should be designed, installed, maintained, and used by only those people who want it, believe in it, and are willing to work with it to succeed. Incentives are doomed to failure if they become a game in which employees and managers each try to outdo the other. Incentives will not work well if they are used on employees who do not respect management or vice versa. This means that the future of incentives may depend on the ability of management to employ competent personnel and to train them to handle incentive plans successfully. This is a real test of how adequate a firm's management is. This also means that potential incentive employees must become involved in the plan and accept their share of responsibility to see that it succeeds and is not abused by fellow employees.

Examples of successful individual financial wage incentives

Within the framework of the strengths and shortcomings of individual financial wage incentives, we would now like to present some successful examples that illustrate the various activities in a firm in which individual incentives can be used.

Brickyard Incentives

The Guignard Brick Works in Cayce, South Carolina, has an incentive plan for most all of their employees because the firm believes that employees work better when they are "in business for themselves." Each employee incentive plan attempts to convert the employee's goals to those of the company. A few examples of their incentive plans will be cited to illustrate the essentials involved, since these ideas could be used in other firms.

Heavy equipment loading operators receive 2¢ per hour bonus for each extra truck load of shale that they load. The standard work load is one load of shale per hour per truck. When 15 extra truck loads are hauled in a 40-hour week, the operator earns a 30¢ an hour bonus or $12 for the week.

Truck drivers receive a bonus of 4¢ per hour for every hour worked in the week for each extra load they haul in the week. In the clay pits, a standard hauling is 2 loads every 3 hours. If a driver were to haul 38 loads in 45 hours (8 loads over standard), he would receive 32¢ per hour bonus (8 loads × 4¢) for each of the 45 hours. Thus, the incentive bonus for that week would be $14.40.

A part-time supervisor in the grinding department is paid 10¢ per hour more for each 1¢ per thousand bricks that the grinding cost goes below the standard cost of 30¢ per thousand. To illustrate, if the grinding cost were to be reduced to 26¢ per thousand bricks for the week, the supervisor would have earned $16 incentive bonus [10¢ (per hour) × 4 (lower cost of 4¢ per thousand) × 40 (hours worked)]. Richard Winchell[11] reports that before this incentive plan was put into effect, the average grinding costs were over 70¢ per thousand bricks and that in the most recent six-month period they have averaged 41¢ per thousand, or a 56 percent reduction in costs.

Not only does the Guignard firm have incentives for these and most other jobs, it also has incentive bonuses (based on simple formulas)[12] for their foremen in the mining, extrusion, tunnel kiln firing, and tunnel kiln unloading departments. Even the superintendent has a bonus formula. The company believes that the bonuses and incentives have encouraged their employees to make more and better bricks at lower costs, while at the same time providing the employees with respectable incomes. There is no reason why the incentive concepts utilized in the brickyard operation could not be adapted to other small business enterprises such as lumber yards, quarries, and contracted construction projects.

Sales Incentives

Most companies have special compensation plans for their salesmen, just as they have separate plans for executives, factory, and clerical personnel. Incen-

---

[11]Richard Winchell, "Incentives for Brickyard Supervisors," *Ceramic Age* (July, 1967), pp. 34–35.

[12]*Ibid.* (The article describes the criteria used to determine various other bonuses.)

tive pay plans for salesmen have a long history in the United States. The wage surveys of the American Management Association show that in every product category in which AMA surveys, at least 50 percent of the companies pay salesmen on some basis other than straight salary.[13] However, the trend is away from paying salesmen completely on straight commission or solely on an incentive basis.

The typical reasons given by firms for paying their salesmen on an incentive basis are as follows: (1) less supervision is required because the salesman has an incentive to produce, rather than to loaf, on the job; (2) sales work especially lends itself to incentives when salesmen can work alone, because a salesman can produce and control job results to a greater degree than people who have to work as a team or depend on each other; and (3) it puts new life into a sales force, and extra sales are produced when competent salesmen are adequately rewarded for their extra efforts. Whether these reasons justify offering incentive pay plans depends upon each firm determining for itself whether these or other advantages are worth their cost to that firm. Straight commission incentive plans may be used when short-range objectives such as immediate sales are desired. When long-range plans are more important, a firm offers both a salary and a bonus incentive or commission.

In developing an incentive plan for salesmen, it is necessary to be able to identify and measure job performance and to decide on a basis of reward. This requires that management determine what goal it is seeking and have available accurate data on sales and market conditions that will enable them to establish proper sales performance standards. If management is not able to read the economic conditions properly, it may establish impractical sales incentive standards that can result in either too small a payout for the salesmen or too high a sales expense. The larger percentages are paid only when there is a direct relationship between the salesman's effort and sales results. In a straight commission incentive pay plan (with no base pay), the incentive reward is usually expressed as a percent of the sales dollar. The reward may also take the form of a fixed amount per sale. In any event, the commission is the same for the first as well as the last unit sold. A variation of the straight commission incentive plan would be to increase the reward as the sales volume increases. Sales expenses vary and sometimes are included in the commission and at other times are treated separately. Some managements do not subscribe to straight commission incentive pay plans because they believe that such plans reduce their control of a sales territory and thus interfere with their long-range plans to cultivate a sales territory. When this is the case, management might subscribe to some modification of the straight commission plan.

---

[13]William F. Dinsmore, "Sales Incentive Plans," *Sales/Marketing Today* (June, 1965), p. 8.

One modification of the straight commission incentive plan would be to provide a base salary with a commission arrangement that begins at some pre-determined performance point, such as normal performance. This type of incentive plan requires that normal performance be identified and easily measured. In a study of over 16,000 salesmen, Richard C. Smyth reports that the average salesman receives incentive pay that amounts to 26 percent of his annual base salary, or 21 percent of his annual gross compensation.[14]   He also points out that the average salesman's bonus or commission earnings ranged from a high of 82 percent to a low of 4 percent of annual base salary.[15]   If a sales incentive plan is to be successful, it would appear that the average salesman needs to have the opportunity to earn, through commissions or bonuses, some 25–30 percent of additional income beyond his regular salary. Management may reward the salesman who performs above normal in any one of a number of ways — by management discretion, by overall ranking of salesmen, or according to his performance measured against a quota.

Rewarding a salesman at the end of the year by management discretion is a very simple but difficult to justify method. The reward is based on management's judgment and could be subject to criticism when the awards are not based on some predetermined qualitative and quantitative criteria. The method will receive less criticism when used in small firms or when it is common knowledge which salesman is best, poorest, etc.

The ranking method of rewarding salesmen for their extra efforts consists of overall management rankings of salesmen according to some range, say 0 to 10 or 0 to 20. Management can use the forced method of ranking as utilized in job evaluation or devise its own system of ranking. After the rankings have been made, the best salesmen may get 20 percent of their base pay as a bonus or reward. The rewards decrease with the rankings of the remaining salesmen until the relatively low performing salesmen either get nothing or a token amount. Another way to reward the performance of the ranked salesmen would be to find an average value of their performances and then reward each salesman according to the relationship of his performance with the average value. This latter method of incentive reward is most appropriate when the various salesmen's selling conditions are pretty much the same.

Compensating a salesman according to his performance, when compared with an established quota, is one of the more popular incentive plans being used. In this method management has to determine the goal or quota upon which rewards will be based. The compensation rewards are made on the basis of either a fixed amount for each unit sale over the quota, or according to some percentage

[14]Richard C. Smyth, "Financial Incentives for Salesmen," *Harvard Business Review,* Vol. 46, No. 1 (January–February, 1968), p. 114.
    [15]*Ibid.*

by which results exceed the quota. For example, the sales that result in the salesman earning his base pay could be considered the 100 percent level or standard. The salesman may have a quota of 10 percent over this standard and be given a fixed cash reward (equivalent to 1 percent of the base rate) for each percent that his sales exceed the standard. Under some circumstances, the fixed cash reward for each extra sale may create an inequity between two salesmen. Even though salesmen's efforts may be equal, it is more likely that a large active sales territory will result in more sales than a smaller, less active area.

A sales incentive reward can be also geared completely to percentages that are either fixed or varying. For every percent of sales above standard up to the 10 percent quota, the reward would be one percent of salary. For each percent over quota, the reward could be one and one-half percent of salary. Such a variable reward for extra effort would keep a salesman working hard, without let-up, to the end of each evaluation period.

Many variations in these basic incentive plans are found today because each plan is designed to cope with conditions that differ from one firm to another. For example, where there are two products with different profit margins and one sells more easily than the other, an incentive plan needs to take these conditions into consideration. One method of doing this would be to establish separate product rewards, with the more desirable product having the higher reward. Another method would be to equate a number of the easier sold products to equal one of the more difficult-to-sell products. Still another method would be to design the incentive plan so that the volume of sales must include a certain percentage of the more desirable product. It is easy to see that an incentive sales plan which has a number of modifications could become complicated to the point that it is not acceptable to the salesmen. It may be better to keep the incentive pay plan simple by not trying to differentiate between too many products and leave the decision on product mix up to the first-line sales management. Simplicity of incentive plans also means less administrative costs. Sales incentive pay plans that are tailored to a specific set of conditions need to be reviewed periodically to determine whether the conditions have changed enough to alter the incentive plan.

Some firms use nonfinancial incentive programs as a means of increasing sales. In 1964, $325 million was estimated to have been spent on merchandise-based sales incentive programs.[16] However, many firms are taking a close look at these programs, which appear to some as gimmicks and to others as programs of short duration. It would appear that they do have a place and are not going to disappear as long as the increase in sales more than pays for the sales contest. One of the problems which arises when a firm promotes a sales contest is to

---

[16]Lassor A. Blumenthol, "Are Sales Incentives a Waste?" *Dun's Review and Modern Industry*, Vol. 86 (October, 1965), p. 66.

assure that all salesmen are treated equitably. Figure 19.1 describes how one firm claims it has successfully handled the problem.

SALES CONTESTS: FAIR DEAL FOR ALL

To win a prize in a sales-incentive contest, a salesman usually has to increase his volume by a certain amount. This is normally done on the basis of either a dollar or a percentage increase.

Both systems, however, contain built-in inequities. When the increase is based on dollars, it militates in favor of the more successful salesman, who needs to increase his sales by a much smaller proportion than his less fortunate colleague. In contrast, a percentage-based increase favors the latter, who needs to sell considerably less than a more successful salesman in order to achieve the same percentage improvement.

Porter Henry, head of the New York-based sales-training organization Porter Henry & Co., claims that he has the solution to this dilemma. The use of square roots, he says, will put all salesmen on an equal footing. Henry's system: Take the square root of each man's previous annual sales. Add all the square roots and divide the total into the budgeted sales increase. Multiply this "unit" by the square root of the man's sales to give him his target in dollars.

To illustrate, last year, a division's sales were $520,000; this year's new goal is $600,000:

Salesman A's sales last year: $160,000
Salesman B's sales last year: $360,000
The square root of A's sales: $400
The square root of B's sales: $600
Total of the square roots: $1,000
1,000 divided into the increase of $80,000: 80

A's required increase, $400 x 80: $32,000
B's required increase, $600 x 80: $48,000

Dun's Review and Modern Industry

FIGURE 19.1 How One Firm Attempts to Assure That All Salesmen Are Treated Fairly in a Sales Contest

Incentives for Cashiers in Retail Stores

A department store in Milwaukee, Wisconsin, has a simple individual financial incentive plan for cashiers. For each error the cashier discovers regarding price tags (underpriced or overpriced) when ringing up sales at the check-out counter, the cashier earns 9¢. In other words, whenever a cashier discovers that the ticket on merchandise does not have the correct label or selling price, the cashier earns a bonus of 9¢. This is intended to insure that the customer pays the correct price (and also avoids cheating by customers who sometimes change labels).

This incentive keeps the cashiers alert. The 9¢ incentive award can also be earned whenever cashiers discover mismatched merchandise. For example, if a woman's suit has a size 12 jacket and a size 14 skirt, the customer will be displeased because the two do not match. Cashiers who discover any such irregularity or mismatch of such items also earn a 9¢ bonus for each discovery.

This incentive idea could apply to cashiers or salesmen in a variety of stores, such as shoe stores, supermarkets, clothing stores, and discount stores. The incentive amount would need to be tailored to the type of store and the nature of the merchandise or sales that are made. For example, in a 5¢ to $1 item store, a fixed amount (say 5¢) per error discovered might be an adequate incentive and reward for errors discovered on small purchases. In a department store, where sales may be $5, $10, or $20, it might be more satisfactory if a percentage incentive were awarded for price-tag errors. Each kind of store utilizing this form of incentive would need to appraise its own situation as to the type and number of errors that are excessive and need to be reduced. The monetary incentive should be established so that it is worthwhile for the salesperson or cashier to discover such errors and thereby reduce them to a minimum level without having to pay more to correct the error than it is worth to the store or the customer.

Office and Clerical Incentives

There is no specific or ready-made pattern to follow in setting standards and applying incentives to office work. Most companies employing successful incentives analyze the job in order to separate and measure those job tasks that lend themselves to job standards. Figure 19.2 shows a typical example of how time standards have been established for some office operations. Measuring job tasks and setting standards needs to be tailored to suit the activities and conditions of each particular enterprise and the kind of work performed. Clerical incentive plans become more effective when office workers understand how their performance is to be measured and how they can readily calculate their earnings. It is important that supervisors be thoroughly conversant with and in favor of any adopted incentive plan so that they can instruct office personnel on how to achieve the best results and how to compute incentive wages.

Measuring Transcription and Other Typewritten Work. Some office managers claim that it is sufficient to take the average of past performance records or to adopt a certain daily number of transcribed discs or pages typed for use as a standard in determining a wage incentive. Others are satisfied with counting the lines typed by a group of operators during a certain period to obtain the average standard output. These measurements, although not precise, may be satisfactory if the quantity of work is relatively small. However, where the work is repetitive and in comparatively large quantity, more accurate measurements are needed to establish satisfactory standards. For example, in setting standards for typing statistical or tabulated material, the output could be measured by determining the number of square inches typewritten per hour.

Description of Operation	Time Standards in Minutes	Units of Production Per Hour
OPEN SEALED ENVELOPES		
Slit envelopes on opening machine (one side only)......	.010	6,000
Slit sides of opened envelopes by hand...........	.063	952
Open envelopes by hand — single operation......	.110	545
SEALING ENVELOPES		
Seal ordinary envelopes........................	.070	857
Apply tape postage to envelopes................	.090	667
Seal bulky envelopes...........................	.160	375
FILING		
File item into readily apparent positions in small file..	.038	1,579
File item into readily apparent positions in large file..	.073	822
File small quantity of items into banded group..	.104	577
Return single item to marked "Out" position in file — four paces walking each way...........	.139	432
File items alphabetically, little selection of position, file conveniently located, largest item 5 by 7 inches..................................	.147	408
File items alphabetically, little selection of position, file conveniently located, items letter size or over.......................................	.191	314
File items numerically by date, difficult selection of position, items 3 by 5 inches...............	.198	303
File items numerically or alphabetically, extended selection of position, files cover many drawers......................................	.287	209
File items alphabetically by classification, and alphabetically by customer within classification, difficult selection of position.............	.464	129
File extremely bulky batch into vault files.......	1.226	48

American Business Magazine

FIGURE 19.2   A TYPICAL EXAMPLE OF TIME STANDARDS APPLIED TO VARIOUS OFFICE OPERATIONS

For ordinary straight-copy typing, the best results are obtained by attaching to the typewriter a counter (cyclometer) that indicates the number of strokes made per hour. A bonus may then be paid for the number of strokes produced above the normal standard. Apparently most incentives for typing are based either on the number of lines or the number of strokes typed per hour, which are then translated into points. A point is equivalent to 240 strokes, and an average line equals 60 strokes to the line. Due to the difference in line lengths, the number-of-strokes method is preferable to a plan based on the number of lines typed.

An Example of Standardizing Office Work. A manufacturer of drugs and medicines employs about 600 office workers. Although shop production has been measured and payments based on an incentive plan have been in existence since 1914, office production was not measured until 1947. Incentives for office work were introduced for the same purpose as those that were established for shop labor, namely, to fully reward employees for increasing their output.

Despite rapidly changing products and seasonal demands, the company avoided layoffs and labor turnover. Employees were kept abreast of forthcoming changes, company intentions, policies, and results expected; thus, management instilled the confidence, understanding, and goodwill among its workers. When work measurement was introduced in the offices, the employees accepted the new policies and changes with the knowledge that they as well as the company would benefit. The main problem was how to obtain standardization and measurement units economically. Analytical studies indicated that most office operations were interrelated and largely interdependent. Most activities in all offices could be related to the measurement of comparatively few major units. The procedure for establishing standards was relatively simple:

1. Flow charts were made to show the relationship of activities.
2. Method studies were made and time values were established for the various operations and suboperations.
3. Standards were established for each major unit of measurement so that each standard contained time for all suboperations that were directly related to the unit. For example, the standard for preparing a shipping order would contain some time for filing, preparing a report, and making up a related form when required.

An Incentive Plan for Letter Opening. A large department store has established an incentive plan for the opening of incoming mail. The job consists of removing the contents of envelopes and then sorting the material. As was done for many of its other office activities, a careful time study determined the proper time and bonus percentage. The method of incentive wage payment used is called a "Standard Hour Plan." In reality, however, the plan is a modification of the Emerson efficiency plan, arbitrarily calculated inasmuch as the bonus is based on the percentage of efficiency attained each week. The task of opening the mail is divided into the following operations:

1. Slit two sides of envelope.
2. Remove contents.
3. Unfold letters, order blanks, and remittances.
4. Fasten contents.
5. Place in piles according to classification.

The standard time allowance for this task is established at 0.17 minutes per letter. Figure 19.3 shows how the bonus is calculated for an operator who has an efficiency rating of 89 percent for the week.

$$\frac{\text{Standard minutes allowed}}{\text{Actual minutes on operation}} = \% \text{ of Efficiency}$$

1. Number of letters opened during the week 11,280
2. Standard minute allowance per letter . . . . 0.17 Min.
3. Actual minutes on operation 2,160

11,280 × .17 = ... 1,918 Std. Min.

1,918 ÷ 2,160 = ... 89% Efficiency Rating

Bonus rate paid at 89% efficiency is $7.17. (In this system a bonus payment commences at $66\frac{2}{3}\%$ of efficiency.)

FIGURE 19.3   EFFICIENCY RATING AND BONUS OF A MAIL-OPENER

The salary-base rate for the job of mail-opener is $60 a week. The bonus efficiency scale per week starts with a fraction of one percent, ascends in certain steps, and ends with $10 at 100 percent efficiency. When the operator increases efficiency above 100 percent, the increment is $.25 for each point of efficiency until 110 percent is reached; then an increment of $.35 is paid for each point of efficiency above 110 percent efficiency. Salary rates are always paid in full whether or not the operator earns a bonus. The entire amount of the weekly salary plus the bonus is included in one check. A small box printed at the top of the check reads: "Amount of earned bonus is————." Thus, in this example the amount included as bonus is $7.17 and the total amount earned is $67.17. Although the regular salary and the bonus are combined in one paycheck, the operator can readily distinguish the bonus from the regular salary payment.

Incentives for Quality Control Inspection

Inspection is the art of comparing the quality and the quantity of materials, products, or performances with established standards. Thus, in manufacturing, inspection is a comparison of products with known standards. Inspection of a product may involve shapes, sizes, smoothness of finish, and color of parts or complete products. It is a quality-control procedure to ensure that a manufactured product conforms to specifications acceptable to the customer. In general, inspection is regarded as an indirect-labor function requiring a specific approach to establish wage incentives.

Function of Inspection and Its Work Measurement. The measurement of inspection work is governed by three different types of inspection: (1) centralized inspection, (2) floor inspection, and (3) line inspection. *Centralized inspection*, as the name implies, is usually performed in a centralized room of the inspection department. *Floor inspection*, also known as "local inspection" and "roaming inspection," involves inspection of parts, or operation of parts, in the department where an item is processed. The inspector moves from machine to machine or from bench to bench to perform his duties of process inspection. In *line inspection,* the inspector begins with the very first operation and follows through a complete cycle of operations in a line until the product is completed.

Centralized 100 percent inspection work can be measured by the same techniques that are employed in measuring and setting standards for direct-labor production jobs. Since there are no definite units to measure in "roaming" or patrol inspection, however, a different approach is necessary. In this case, the time-study analyst makes several all-day studies to obtain a representative sample. A time standard is arrived at by recording the covered area, operations, and time consumed. If direct-labor group incentives are used, the inspector's incentive may be included. Or, a ratio method may be used to compute the inspector's incentive percentage.

Reaction to Incentives for Inspectors. Modern inspection methods are applied in manufacturing to safeguard quality, especially when incentive wages are paid for efficient direct-labor production. For years, inspectors were considered indirect-labor workers and were compensated on a day-work basis because of the prevalent and still persistent opinion that if inspectors are motivated to earn incentive wages, speeding up is inevitable, which, in turn, may cause them to pass defective work and to receive rejections from customers. The excellent results of paying incentive wages to inspectors disprove this theory, as shown in the following example of a company in which inspection operations on an incentive basis have existed for many years. Individual inspection work increased over 50 percent; customer complaints as well as credit allowances were substantially reduced; and the company has been able to maintain a closer adherence to quality standards.

Incentives for Inspectors. This example presents the experiences of the Norton Company, Worcester, Massachusetts, manufacturers of grinding wheels, refractories, and grinding machines. The example mainly concerns the intricate manufacturing process of grinding wheels, fabricated under exacting specifications and standards of operation. Literally thousands of orders are in the process of manufacture at all times. Men and women work on inspection, with the heavier work being done by men.

Inspection Procedure. The overall requisite of inspection is to make sure the product will meet customers' requirements. The inspection process involves examination for (1) operational safety (since grinding wheels revolve at high speed, they must be inspected for possible breakage to prevent serious accidents); (2) dimensional and shape requirements; and (3) grinding performance. Grinding performance implies meeting requirements for (1) removing a definite quantity of material when grinding certain items; (2) pieces ground per hour; (3) total production during the life of the grinding wheel; and (4) grade of finish.   Therefore, inspection involves an examination of the product for a particular property under a specific test.

Although the incentive system has been in effect for many years, the approach has not varied except that inspection methods were changed to the acceptance sampling plan (statistical quality control).   A rate per 100 pieces has been established for work performed in a detailed inspection of the sample quantity.   If the sample is defective, the entire order is inspected for that particular defect.

Piecework Incentives.   The straight piecework incentive system and method of payment for inspection has remained unchanged from its inception.   The rate per order (called the setup) compensates the inspector for time spent in reading the manufacturing record; obtaining necessary tools, gauges, and templates; and signing the order when inspection is completed.   In addition, the inspector receives a definite amount for each manufacturing order at a rate per 100 pieces inspected.   To ensure continued quality standards and accurate inspection, check inspectors (also known as "reinspectors") reinspect a certain percentage of work passed by the piecework inspectors.

Established piece rates are based on time studies with the usual allowance for personal time, fatigue, and delays.   The earnings of most inspectors working under normal conditions are 30 percent above the wage-base rates.   Some inspectors exert more than average effort and thereby earn considerably more. It is Norton's experience that piecework rates provide the incentive to do a reasonable day's work, and they reward the inspector for increased efficiency.

Material Handling Incentives

Material handling pertains to methods and equipment for facilitating direct-labor production in shops, and for maintaining orderly inventories in storerooms and warehouses.   It involves transportation, storing, and packaging for shipping purposes.   Of the numerous jobs and functions included in material handling, we shall concentrate on (1) trucking jobs and (2) warehouse jobs.

Trucking Jobs.   Work measurement and incentive plans for trucking may seem complicated because of interdepartmental and interplant activities that involve long-distance travels and the manipulation of various items.   By making ordinary observations, analyzing and recording starting points, describing loads, registering points of destination, and utilizing predetermined time values, however, measuring and incentive setting become relatively simple.

One medium-size company discovered that only 50 percent of its trucking time was used for transporting goods.   The balance of time was wasted in waiting, looking for empty skids and pallets, obtaining gas, oiling, and getting and returning trucks.   After standardized material-handling operations were installed, efficiency increased 100 percent within six months. Over $200,000 in labor costs were saved each year by introducing a 100 percent time premium incentive plan. Truckers' earnings increased 30 to 40 percent above their wage-base rates.

In some industries, trucking includes transporting materials from storage locations to production machines; moving finished products to weighing scales; and finally transporting materials to warehouses or shipping departments. The equipment is usually classified into hand-operated lift trucks, electric lift trucks, gas or electric power-driven trucks, flat trucks, hoist trucks, and interplant trailer trucks. Further analysis entails the division of jobs into eight basic characteristics: (1) starting point of trip with or without moving ticket, (2) description of load contents, (3) quantity and weight of load, (4) destination of trip, (5) number of trips made within a specified time, (6) distances traveled with or without loads, (7) description of work performed by trucker, and (8) handling time at all stages.

At the Advanced Manufacturing Company,[17] trucking is controlled from industrial truck dispatch stations that supply service to all points in the plant. Each station operates from 8 to 10 trucks and is supervised by a dispatcher and station clerk whose time is spent partly on a truck and the remainder at the station. Each station is responsible for all trucking requests (by phone) within a certain area. The time when the request is made, the points between which material is to be transported, the truck number, and the time it takes to make the trip are recorded on dispatch tags, which are then filed according to the time requested. This plan keeps a close check on the operations of each trucker.

Time-study analysts made studies to determine the time required in transit, loading and unloading material, crane and elevator delays, and unavoidable delays. Studies revealed that hoist trucks could make more trips than flat trucks. Therefore, separate time limits were set for each. Because of the differences in work performed by each station, it was deemed necessary to study each group of truckers separately. Each group included the dispatcher and clerk of the particular station.

Information concerning the number of each trucker's deliveries emanates from the storerooms and shipping sections on industrial truck requisitions that are signed before the material is moved. Since the group includes the dispatcher and station clerk, it is necessary to authorize the issuance of requisitions by someone outside the group.

Each worker is paid the guaranteed wage-base rate. If group members perform their work in less than standard time, the group receives full credit for the time gained.

The following formula was derived for computing the earnings of each group:

---

[17]Fictitious name. Manufacturer prefers anonymity.

Time allowed = (0.460 × NF) or (0.317 × NH)

Earning Efficiency = $\dfrac{STA}{ATT}$ expressed in percent

0.460 = Time allowed per delivery for flat truck
0.317 = Time allowed per delivery for hoist truck
NF = Number of deliveries made by flat truck
NH = Number of deliveries made by hoist truck
STA = Standard time allowed
ATT = Actual time taken

Warehouse Jobs. The Logan Company, Louisville, Kentucky, manufactures a large variety of metal products including conveying machines, metal furniture, ornamental iron work, and other similar products. A steadily increasing business necessitated the expansion of the warehouse from a small building to one of 60,000 square feet. Methods in the shop were constantly improved, but storage and order-filling remained unsystematic and inefficient.

Although direct labor in the shops was performed on standardized time and on an incentive basis for many years, the warehouse force and other indirect laborers received wage-base rates only, thereby losing some of the gains that were obtained through incentives for direct labor.

Management authorized time-study analysts to undertake standardized procedure for warehouse workers, a task that seemed impossible. By applying predetermined standards (MTM), however, all work was measured and methods were improved within a comparatively brief period.[18]

Work measurement involved the usual setting of time standards such as: trucking time plus allowance for moving around the truck; labeling and stenciling time; loading time; and designating areas with constant-time allowances for work that must be performed regardless of distances traveled and materials handled.

A route sheet (Figure 19.4), prepared after receiving shipping orders, lists the orders for which the warehouseman has to pick up items and presents a complete summary for processing as well as for time standards used in the warehouse incentive plan. Time allowances and total time are recorded to conserve the warehouseman's time.

Day-rate payments for warehouse labor were converted to incentive wages by installing piece rates with guaranteed hourly base rates. Indirect-labor cost decreased 40 percent, while earnings increased over 25 percent. Shipping time was improved 10 percent, in addition to securing better utilization of the material-handling equipment.

---

[18]"Incentives in the Warehouse," *Factory Management and Maintenance*, Vol. III, No. 9 (September, 1953). Tables reproduced by permission.

ROUTE SHEET

ORDER NUMBERS A 3042   A 3043   C 3192   B 3274

DATE 7-37 _____ ROUTE SHEET NO. 1

WORKING FACTOR (CONSTANT ALLOWANCE) 4.71

QUANT.	ITEM	AREA	TRAVEL TIME	LOAD TIME	TOTAL TRAVEL & LOAD TIME	MARKING TIME
3	#611 Screens	C-4	.30	.45	.75	
1	#4025-38" Screen	C-4	—	.15	.15	} 1.26
2	#331 Andirons	C-6	.27	.30	.57	
2	#1425 Fire sets	C-6	—	.30	.30	
	To	C-1	.48	—	.48	
5	#346 3/3 beds	B-2	.19	1.71	1.90	.86
2	#346 4/6 beds	B-2	—	.68	.68	
1	#350 Chair - G	B-7	.44	.15	.59	
1	#350 Chair - R	B-7	—	.15	.15	
	To	B-1	.43	—	.43	} .72
1	#950 Glider - G	A-10	.38	.41	.79	
1	#950 Glider - R	A-10	—	.41	.41	
7	Bell-Metal Bed					
	Rails	A-11	.63	1.38	2.01	.86
	To	A-15	.34	—	.34	
	Open & close gate 3rd fl.	—	—	.40		
		Total			14.66	3.70
					3.70	
	Total	allowed time			18.36	

FIGURE 19.4 SCHEDULE SHEET FOR SEVERAL ORDERS

Housekeeping Incentives

The maintenance department usually supervises housekeeping duties in industrial enterprises where tools, supplies, materials, lighting, and sanitation for direct-production workers must always be in readiness. Where housekeeping comes under the jurisdiction of the maintenance department, the proper layout for trucking and temporary storage, cleaning of equipment, building maintenance, cleanliness and orderliness around machines and on floors, orderly arrangement of work in process, clean offices, and general upkeep of safe and pleasant surroundings are all carried out by that department.

Generally, however, housekeeping is combined with sanitation, and is usually referred to as *sanitation housekeeping* or janitorial work. It comprises the work of cleaners, janitors, porters, sanitation workers, sweepers, painters, watchmen, window washers, and other housekeeping attendants.

In order to maintain satisfactory work schedules and standards, as well as an incentive system, it is necessary to formulate a quality control system based on some rating scale with descriptions of how the work should be performed and what is to be expected. Obviously, sanitation housekeeping in metal or woodworking plants will differ from that in pharmaceutical laboratories and food plants or other enterprises. Therefore, it is advisable to prepare a manual of procedures and quality control ratings for reference purposes.

Where housekeeping jobs are centrally supervised, job orders and standards are issued for all departments by one sanitation supervisor. Cleaning and removing waste around machines is generally directed by departmental supervisors and usually becomes part of direct production. Standards and incentives then become part of the direct-production group.

Work standards and incentive programs for housekeeping may be readily established and effectively administered if the jobs are analyzed and measured, and if performances are standardized in accordance with predetermined procedures. Simplified work measurements and operational (differentiated from elemental) time studies suffice to determine how long it should take to sweep and mop a given area of floor space, wash windows, empty wastebaskets, clean washrooms, etc. Once a pattern and time values have been established on repetitive work, standard data and performance rates can be built up for similar operations. Either individual or group incentives may be used, depending on the size of the plant, the number of direct workers to be serviced, and the quality of work required.

Housekeeping in a Rubber Manufacturing Plant. A successful wage incentive plan for plant housekeeping has been in effect for over 25 years at the United States Rubber Company, Passaic, New Jersey, manufacturers of rubber goods. Among the advantages claimed are improved housekeeping, reduced cleaning costs, and increased income for sanitation workers. The plan is divided into 32 areas, each area being serviced by an individual or a small group.

The whole plant's sanitation service is centralized and managed by the plant engineer. One foreman and several group leaders comprise the supervisory force for day and night shifts. Very little supervision is necessary, however, since each worker is trained to do an expert job, and his duties as well as responsibilities are clearly defined in the job description. Nonrecurring or "unpredictable" jobs such as snow and ice removal are performed by a special group of from three to five employees who are paid on a day-work basis.

Time studies and standard data are used to prepare schedules for approximately 60 jobs performed in each area. The schedule describes the job to be performed, materials and equipment to be used, and the standard time it should take a trained worker to perform the whole operation. Every employee or group in a sanitation department receives a schedule before commencing work. At the close of a day's work, the schedule together with time cards is turned in to the timekeeper who calculates the wages.

Time standards are set on completely finished jobs. For example, the standard time for cleaning a certain size shower room is 0.65 hours; and for cleaning dust collectors, 0.528 hours. If it takes longer than the scheduled standard time to complete a job, the workers receive as gross earnings the wage-base rate multiplied by the number of actual hours worked. If the job is completed in less than the scheduled time, an extra amount is paid for each percent of efficiency.

Assume that each of three workers in a group is paid an hourly wage-base rate of $2. The schedule indicates that all operations should be completed in a total *standard time* of 28.05 hours. If the operations are completed in 24 hours, that is, each of the three workers completed eight *working hours*, their earnings are computed according to the following formulas:

Efficiency = Assigned standard hours divided by the number of actual worked hours.

Total earnings = Number of actual worked hours times the wage-base rate multiplied by attained efficiency.

Earnings for each group worker = Total earnings of the group divided by the number of group workers.

Applying the figures of the assumed conditions indicated above:

$$\text{Efficiency} = \frac{28.05 \text{ Standard hours}}{24.00 \text{ Actual working hours}} = 116.9\%$$

Total earnings = 24.00 × $2 × 116.9% = $56.11

Earnings for each group worker = $56.11 ÷ 3 = $18.70

The company budgets all expenditures including housekeeping expenses. At the close of each month a report of activities and expenditures is prepared for the plant engineer, who compares budgeted with actual costs of sanitation. The report also aids the plant engineer to control departmental efficiency and enables him to ascertain how much "emergency" work had to be completed during the month.

Housekeeping in a Pharmaceutical Manufacturing Plant. Another outstanding example of measurements applied to housekeeping work is found at the plant of Merck, Sharp & Dohme, Inc., Philadelphia, Pennsylvania, manufacturers of pharmaceutical chemicals. For some time, managerial executives were concerned with the problems of obtaining efficient sanitation work at reasonable costs. The problems were easily solved, however, after forming a plant housekeeping committee composed of supervisors from production, maintenance, quality control, industrial relations, and industrial management departments, including union members appointed as work-group leaders. After outlining a program, including quality standards, the committee established improved cleaning methods and time standards; calculated overall manpower needs; prepared work schedules; trained workers in new methods; checked worker performance; and inspected each area periodically in accordance with specific rating procedures.

Standardization and work measurement saved over $24,000 yearly by reducing the work force and at the same time increasing the work load by 40,000 square feet. Those workers who were taken off their old jobs were transferred to other profitable jobs. Additional benefits were: employees maintained cleaner work areas; proper cleaning preserved surface finishes and cut painting costs; cleaner work places and evenly distributed work loads improved employee morale.

One reason for the success at Merck, Sharp & Dohme is that group leaders cooperate with time-study analysts to work out new methods standards. An example of one method improvement that saved 40 percent of the working time was the adoption of a scaffold to replace a ladder for cleaning light fixtures. This change saved time in cleaning pipes and painting walls and other small areas.

Time studies are made of complete operations, and times are established in minutes for a whole group of operations required for one job, as shown in Figure 19.5. A master list containing operation details and standard time data, including a 10 percent fatigue and personal allowance, was established for 29 housekeeping jobs, as shown in the partial list in Figure 19.6.[19]

Sample Time Study

To clean office area and furniture items listed:

Items	Time
Desks, 12	5.46 Min.
Chairs, 27	10.26
Cabinets, 32	7.04
Tables, 1	.33
Partitions — 48 ft	3.00
Walls — 112 ft	5.00
Pick up trash	4.10
Sweep floor	15.00
	50.19 Min.
Getting material and returning same	15.00
Total minutes allowed for job	65.19 Min.

FIGURE 19.5   SAMPLE TIME STUDY WITH TIME ALLOWANCES FOR JANITORIAL JOBS

---

[19]Mr. Daniel Granata, Service Manager, supplied the detailed information.

OPERATIONS	MIN. PER UNIT	UNIT
SWEEP FLOORS		
Office area, semicongested	1.4	100 sq. ft.
Production area, semicongested	1.5	100 sq. ft.
Congested area	2.0	100 sq. ft.
MOP FLOORS		
Damp mop, semicongested area	1.3	100 sq. ft.
Damp mop, congested area	2.0	100 sq. ft.
Wet mop, semicongested area	2.2	100 sq. ft.
Wet mop, congested area	2.7	100 sq. ft.
Strip mop, semicongested area	4.0	100 sq. ft.
Strip mop, congested area	6.7	100 sq. ft.
VACUUM FLOORS		
Wood floor	1.8	100 sq. ft.
Rugs	5.0	100 sq. ft.
SCRUB FLOORS		
Once over (2-man team — total)	10.6	100 sq. ft.
Twice over (2-man team — total)	18.7	100 sq. ft.
BUFF FLOORS	1.6	100 sq. ft.
WAX FLOORS		
One coat, semicongested area	1.4	100 sq. ft.
One coat, congested area	2.1	100 sq. ft.
Two coats, semicongested area	2.5	100 sq. ft.
WASH WALLS		

WASH VENETIAN BLINDS		
Wood blind	50.9	blind
Metal blind	36.7	blind
VACUUM VENETIAN BLINDS		
Wood blind	13.8	blind
Metal blind	16.3	blind
DUST VENETIAN BLINDS		
Wood blind	11.7	blind
Metal blind	12.0	blind

FIGURE 19.6 STANDARD TIME SCHEDULE FOR VARIOUS JANITORIAL JOBS AT MERCK, SHARP & DOHME, INC.

All jobs and operations are fully described for specific areas on instruction cards as illustrated in Figure 19.7. Besides serving the purpose of instructing each worker where and how to perform the job, the instruction card clearly describes what equipment and materials to use, and the standard time allowed. Each group leader carries a set of instruction cards in a pocket-sized manual for checking operations and for training new workers.

INSTRUCTION CARD

OPERATION: Daily Office   AREA: 9th floor, all offices on the
            Cleaning   Mount Vernon Street side

Obtain mobile trash container. Go through entire area emptying waste baskets, pencil sharpeners, ash trays. Wipe out ash trays with a damp cloth. Wheel trash container to freight elevator. Sweep area thoroughly, under desks, tables, etc.

Vacuum rugs nightly; give special attention under desks.

Damp-dust tile floors after the buffing operation.

Go through entire area each night. Dust desks, cabinets, window sills, partitions, baseboards and chairs. Also dust table in engineering department with a cloth. Dust all equipment on desks, moving when necessary. Wash glass covers on desks with a damp cloth and dry thoroughly. Pay special attention to back slats, legs, and arm rests of chairs when dusting.

PRECAUTIONS: Do not disarrange papers left on desks. Do not spill ink. Do not scar or mar furniture.

EQUIPMENT: Broom, dust cards, dust cloths, dust mop, radiator brush, feather duster.

TIME ALLOWANCE: 8.0 hours.

RETURN THIS CARD TO GROUP LEADER

FIGURE 19.7   Daily Instruction Card Describing Jobs for Specific Areas

Maintenance Worker Incentives

Plant maintenance, the primary category of indirect labor, is a requisite in most enterprises, especially in manufacturing. The overall function, also known as *plant engineering*, combines various subfunctions. Maintenance work has a marked influence upon the entire organization, affecting managerial and production control as well as investment in equipment. The principal function of maintenance is to assist direct production by keeping the plant and production equipment in perfect working condition. Maintenance work comprises the crafts of carpenters, electricians, inspectors, maintenance machinists, millwrights, oilers, painters, pipe fitters, plumbers, power plant personnel, sheetmetal workers, toolmakers, and toolsetters. In steel mills, the maintenance class also includes blacksmiths, boilermakers, bricklayers, furnace rebuilders, and welders.

Maintenance work is divided into two types: *preventive* and *corrective*. Both types maintain effective direct-labor production.

Preventive Maintenance. The function of eliminating deterioration and breakdowns of plant activities is known as *preventive maintenance*. It entails the work of inspecting plant and equipment, lubricating, eliminating vibration, maintaining lighting equipment, controlling corrosion, eliminating dust from motors, correcting electrical connections, testing automatic controls, and inspecting safety devices. Efficient preventive maintenance generally reduces the cost of corrective maintenance.

Corrective Maintenance. The second type of maintenance work, *corrective maintenance*, consists of repairing worn equipment, replacing old machines, and introducing new and more effective materials or supplies. The corrective maintenance crew also makes alterations for efficient production by replacing, repairing, or overhauling material-handling equipment.

Maintenance Incentives, UMS Application. The predetermined time values introduced under the name of Universal Maintenance Standards (UMS) found favorable acceptance. Significantly, this type of work measurement was applied at the United States Navy's Bureau of Yards and Docks as well as in 25 Navy supply depots, where time studies or similar work measurements were prohibited before 1950.

UMS was first applied at the Bayonne (New Jersey) Depot, where 200 maintenance workers represent all the crafts normally found among indirect-labor groups in manufacturing industries. The Navy's maintenance jobs were always estimated on the basis of past performance, averaging about 50 percent efficiency. The introduction of UMS boosted efficiency to about 100 percent, convincing the navy engineers that "*with adequate piece-work incentives 125 percent efficiency can easily be achieved.*"[20]

Besides increased performance, UMS application brought about the following advantages: increased methods- and time-consciousness among maintenance crews; better supervision for all levels; transferability of standards from one location to another; and reasonable installation and administration cost.

A Navy time-standards analyst developed time formulas for operations occurring in each specific maintenance job. A table showing the time standards for a range of variables is compiled for each formula. Emphasis is placed on average conditions that are based on UMS standardized times.

For the purpose of illustrating a UMS application, a pipefitting job has been selected as an example. The seemingly plain task required 25 formulas, each numbered and described for reference purposes. Figure 19.8 illustrates a table of time standards for formula number PW-16-2. It describes operations for straight and bent tubes; variable ranges occurring in tube lengths; and a time value for each of six variables. Time values are averaged according to variable ranges. It is worth repeating that all tables derived from the UMS time standard are based on the principle of time averages.

---

[20]"Slicing Maintenance Labor Costs at Navy's Bayonne Depot," *Factory Management and Maintenance*, Vol. CXV, No. 5 (May, 1957), pp. 81–84. Tables reproduced by permission.

TABLE OF TIME STANDARDS (in hours)
for Formula PW-16-2

Operation: Assemble and install copper tubing with soldered joints. Tubing may be soldered to a threaded fitting which is screwed into place, or soldered directly to previous work.

Col. 1 Length of Tube	Straight — No Bends			One or Two Bends		
	Col. 2 Tube soldered to threaded fitting, screwed into place, both ends	Col. 3 Tube soldered to threaded fitting one end, and directly to existing work on other end	Col. 4 Tube soldered to existing work, both ends	Col. 5 same as 2	Col. 6 same as 3	Col. 7 same as 4
3' or less	0.298 hrs.	0.265 hrs.	0.232 hrs.	0.310 hrs.	0.277 hrs.	0.244 hrs.
3+ to 10+	.410	.377	.344	.422	.389	.356
10+ to 20+	.522	.489	.456	.534	.501	.468

FIGURE 19.8   Average Time Standards for Formula PW-16-2

Another innovation in the Navy's use of UMS is the compilation of *summary values for each repetitive job.* Figure 19.9 illustrates task-time standard No. PFT-82, a comparatively short repetitive job of 4.187 hours. Although compact, the figure gives information regarding formula reference numbers, operations involved, unit time, number of units, total time for number of units, and total time for the complete job. Because task-time standards are compiled for all repetitive maintenance jobs, the administrative procedure is vastly simplified. Whenever an order for a repetitive job is issued, the applicator (standard time-setter) simply releases the already compiled standards for that specific job.

For longer jobs, a Job-Standard Calculation Sheet is issued containing the order number and all pertinent information including percentage allowances, as shown in Figure 19.10. Note that this long job of pipe-work installation is partly composed of task-time standard No. PFT-82 requiring 4.187 unit time, which is obtained from the formulas shown in Figure 19.9. The balance is obtained from other formulas. Thus, the allowed time of 16.70 hours for job order No. 0857 is computed from the total "raw time" of various formulas plus allowances for fatigue, personal, and other variable interferences.

TASK-TIME STANDARD   No.___PFT-82___

Description: Install hot and cold water pipes connecting one sink (copper tubing)

Reference No.	Operation	Unit Time, Hours	No. of Units	Total Time, Hours
PW-16-2 PW-16-2	Install pipes Install fittings	.232	16	3.712
PW-3	Measure	.015	6	.090
PW-4	Fit up pipe	.014	4	.056
PW-12	Inspect	.008	1	.008
PW-18	Cut and thread pipe	.015	4	.060
			Total	4.187 hours

FIGURE 19.9   TASK-TIME STANDARDS FOR REPETITIVE JOBS

JOB-STANDARD CALCULATION SHEET

Order No.:___0857___
Building:___321___

Work Center:___50___

Date:___4/4/--___

Description: Install copper tubing connecting two sinks with main line (one man required)

Operation or Task	Reference	Unit Time	Occurrence	Total Time
Install pipework	PFT-82	4.187	2	8.374
Travel	PW-1	.400	4	1.600
Job preparation	PW-6	.589	2	1.178
Extra job preparation	PW-6	.265	2	.530

(1) Total Raw Time Required, hours	11.68
(2) % Allowance — as determined for application 43% x (1)	5.02
Total Allowed Time	16.70

FIGURE 19.10   JOB-STANDARD CALCULATION SHEET.   Combined formula standards for long jobs.

Indirect Production Worker Incentives

The following example describes the methods used to measure the work of combined indirect-labor categories as a group in one special department of the American Seating Company. The company manufactures public seating, varying from ordinary folding chairs to theatrical seats, and from plain school desks to church pews.[21]

The manufacture of multifarious seating products requires a variety of activities and operations for *direct production* and covers about 400 job titles, which are manned by over 1,100 workers.

Various parts are produced in the gray iron foundry and scheduled through numerous processing departments and machining sections. Other parts consisting of thousands of stampings in steel, brass, and aluminum are produced in stamping departments on shearing machines, punch presses, and forming and trimming machines. Wood processing, cabinet making, and wood carving are carried out in woodworking departments on specialized machines. Other departments produce and fabricate plastics, nonferrous die-castings, upholstering, and complete metal and wood assemblies.

The wage payments for direct labor comprise guaranteed wage-base rates plus bonuses — group incentives — based on the standard hour plan (100 percent time premium). Direct-production workers are assisted by about 200 to 300 indirect-labor workers who are divided in 25 groups. Some of these group activities and incentive payments are described below.

Indirect-Production Workers. Standardization and incentive payments for indirect production are the outcome of management's desire to maintain the lowest direct- and indirect-production costs, to increase the weekly incomes of indirect labor, and to lower the cost of products in general.

Detailed studies of all indirect-production operations were made in an effort to establish incentives that could be administered economically. It is noteworthy that the analysts developed a simplified but successful procedure: (1) to combine several indirect-production categories in one group, (2) to set time standards for all categories as a group, (3) to pay incentive wages for indirect production in a certain ratio to direct production, and (4) to compute incentive wages for indirect labor.

Combined Indirect-Production Categories. In this example case, we are concerned with the work of maintenance, material handling, and housekeeping categories. Indirect-production categories consist of six groups: die setters and trouble shooters, crane operators, hi-lo (lift truck) operators, electric truckers,

---

[21]We are indebted to Mr. Margin J. Geerling, Chief Industrial Engineer of the American Seating Company, Grand Rapids, Michigan, for the information and data discussed in this example.

housekeepers, and rattlers (tumblers). These six indirect-labor groups service over 100 metal shears and various presses in the stamping department, designated as No. 27. In other words, all indirect-production workers are combined into one departmental organization to assist in eliminating idle time and in maintaining high production by direct labor.

Setting Time Standards for Indirect-Labor Groups. Work contents were determined separately for each of the above-mentioned six groups. Table 19.3 shows an example of time analysis for die setting on varied tonnage presses obtained from time studies.

TABLE 19.3

CLASSIFICATION AND TIME STANDARDS

118 Die Settings Plus 120 Trouble Shootings in Department 27

Indirect-Labor Groups and Activity	No. of Jobs Performed	Std. Min. Per Job	Total Min. Per Week
Die Setting, Heavy Level Press....	15	275	4,125
Die Setting, Medium Level Press..	29	180	5,220
Die Setting, Light Level Press.....	49	45	2,205
Die Setting, Inclined Press........	25	75	1,875
Trouble Shooting...............	120	5	600
Miscellaneous Allowances........	...	...	500

Allowed Minutes (Standard) per week......................... 14,525

14,525 ÷ 60 = 242 standard hours for all die setters per week

A total of 242 hours per week for die setting and trouble-shooting groups became the standard time required to serve direct-production groups whose output averaged 4,175 standard hours during the week when indirect-labor jobs were studied. Independent studies of the other five indirect-production groups were completed during the week in the same manner as for die setting. As shown in Table 19.4, a total of 835 indirect-labor standard hours is required to service the output of 4,175 direct-labor standard hours.

At the American Seating Company, *every indirect-labor incentive plan is designed to reflect the relationship between direct and indirect production.* Increases in direct-labor output compel indirect labor to increase production, thereby gaining proportionate incentive-wage increases. Conversely, if either one slows down, proportionately reduced incentive earnings ensue.

TABLE 19.4

TOTAL INDIRECT-LABOR STANDARD HOURS ALLOWED
For 4,175 Direct-Labor Standard Hours in Department 27

INDIRECT-LABOR GROUPS	STANDARD HOURS PER WEEK
Die Setters................	242
Crane Operators............	102
Hi-Lo Operators............	59
Electric Truckers...........	231
Housekeepers..............	50
Rattlers...................	151
Total Standard Hours.......	835

Allowance Ratios for Indirect Labor. A proportionate balance between direct and indirect production is maintained by applying allowed percentage ratios which also determine incentive pay for indirect labor.

The determination of allowance ratios necessitated an analysis of the high and low output levels under various conditions over a certain period. The percentages shown in Table 19.5 were then arrived at by time-study analysts in cooperation with supervisors. Thus, the allowed indirect-labor percentile ratios vary in proportion to the output of direct-labor groups.

TABLE 19.5

ALLOWED RATIOS FOR INDIRECT LABOR

DIRECT-LABOR OUTPUT	ALLOWED RATIO FOR INDIRECT LABOR
3,800 Hrs. and over.............	20%
3,200–3,799.....................	21%
2,600–3,199.....................	22%
2,000–2,599	23%
1,400–1,999....................	24%

It was comparatively simple to compute percentages after a number of allowance studies were made by time study. As stated before, the direct-labor group output in Department 27 was established as 4,175 man-hours during the same week when time studies of indirect labor disclosed that a total of 835 hours per week must be allowed the combined groups of indirect-labor categories to serve the direct-labor producers. To arrive at the allowed ratio, the number of indirect-labor man-hours is divided by the number of direct-labor man-hours. In this case, 835 ÷ 4,175 equals a 20 percent allowed ratio. All other percentages were arrived at in a similar manner.

Computing Incentive Earnings for Indirect Labor. Applying the percentage ratios shown in Table 19.5, the allowed indirect-labor standard hours are obtained by the simple formula: (direct-labor output) $\times$ (percentage constant) = allowed indirect-labor standard hours. Or, as in this case, 4,175 $\times$ 20% = 835.

Assume that the six indirect-labor groups complete their jobs in 630 hours per week; then incentive earnings would be computed as follows: Allowed indirect-labor hours = 835. Actual labor hours worked = 630. To obtain incentive earnings, divide allowed hours by actual worked hours: (835 ÷ 630) = pay ratio of 132.5%.

Let us say that direct-labor production increased to 4,500 standard hours per week, and indirect-labor workers spent 650 working hours. Then (20% $\times$ 4,500) = 900 allowed indirect hours. Dividing allowed hours by actual worked hours (900 ÷ 650) = 138.4% as the pay ratio.

Supervisors use allowance ratios and guide charts to decide the number of workers needed for various in-work loads. To afford indirect-labor workers every opportunity to earn incentive wages, foremen transfer them to different incentive jobs if sufficient full-time work of their own is not available.

Federal Employees' Incentive Awards Program[22]

The primary objective of the United States government employees' incentive awards program is to improve the efficiency and effectiveness of federal government operations by encouraging full use of employee skills and ideas. Through this program, the federal government attempts to underscore its desire to recognize and reward employees for their special contributions in improving the efficiency and effectiveness of the federal government. However, the incentive awards program is intended as only a part of the government's overall personnel policy designed to make careers in the federal service more attractive.

The program provides for the earning of individual or group awards (cash or honorary, or both) for such employee contributions as offering useful suggestions or inventions, for doing assigned work significantly better than required over an extended period, for overcoming unusual difficulties, for excellence of work in science or research, for outstanding professional achievement, or for the courageous handling of an emergency situation which is connected with the employee's employment.

---

[22]U.S. Civil Service Commission, *Federal Employee Facts No. 1* (Washington: U.S. Government Printing Office, July, 1964).

The cash awards may be for contributions of intangible value as well as for those which result in measurable benefits. Cash awards for adopted suggestions and superior accomplishments are based on the estimated first-year measurable benefits, or they are based on the value of intangible benefits. For example, benefits that can be measured in dollars, such as savings in production time, man-hours, supplies, equipment, and space, receive an award of $15 for measurable benefits of $50 to $300 ($100 is received for benefits of $2,000, and $500 for benefits of $10,000). Awards can be as high as $25,000 for a single contribution. For benefits such as better service, improved quality, and safer working conditions, that cannot be expressed in terms of dollars, the amount of the award is determined by the importance of the program affected by the contribution and its impact on that program.

Results of the awards program reveal that approximately 100,000 employees each year receive awards for adopted suggestions. Cash awards for suggestions have ranged from $15 to $5,000, with an average award of approximately $142. Approximately 75,000 employees each year receive awards for superior on-the-job performance or for special achievements. These cash awards average about $146. All too often people think that the various financial incentive plans are only applicable to industry. The above results would indicate otherwise. There is no reason why the federal employees incentive awards program cannot also be used successfully at the local and state governmental levels.

This chapter has attempted to discuss the present and future status of individual incentive plans. It has described a variety of successful plans that are presently being used. Today, there is also a keen interest in the application of incentives to small and large groups. This is the subject of the following chapter.

REVIEW QUESTIONS

1. Why do firms offer individual financial wage incentive plans to employees?
2. In what ways is the customer affected by individual financial wage incentive plans?
3. What is the trend in the use of individual wage incentive plans?
4. What arguments can you advance which would tend to support the proposition that individual wage incentives are on their way out?
5. Which industries employ the highest and the lowest percentages of individual incentive workers?
6. Do you believe that a ceiling should be established on incentive earnings above which an employee must not go or the standard will be cut? Why?
7. What arguments can you advance which would tend to support the idea that individual wage incentives are here to stay?
8. Give some examples of office work that lends itself to measurement and the application of wage incentive systems.
9. What are the chief reasons a firm may have for paying its salesmen on a commission basis?

RESEARCH OR SEMINAR QUESTIONS

1. Find out why unions oppose or are in favor of wage incentive plans. Be prepared to cite the specific source of reference of your information and to indicate why you agree or disagree with the union viewpoint.
2. What is the future of individual wage incentives?
3. Read a recent magazine article on the subject of wage incentives. Be prepared to present to the class the following:
   (a) Name and date of magazine.
   (b) Title and author of article.
   (c) Main conclusion(s) of article.
   (d) Why you agree or disagree with it.
4. Industrial engineers usually design individual incentive plans to pay a certain percentage above the regular pay of the employee. Evaluate whether this is a sound concept and justify your evaluation. Identify what percentage figure the industrial engineer should use if you agree with his concept.
5. What disadvantages can accrue to a firm that pays its salesmen on a straight commission basis?
6. What is your opinion concerning wage incentive plans in terms of their value in stimulating output and their effects on employee attitudes toward the employer, the job, and the work group?

PRACTICAL EXPERIENCE ASSIGNMENTS

1. Interview an employee who works under an individual incentive wage plan to determine the reasons he likes or dislikes the system and how it could be improved to benefit both the employer and the employee. Be prepared to give a brief report to the class on the highlights of the interview.
2. Company Y has its production workers on a piece-rate incentive plan. Productivity is excellent, but there still seems to be considerable difficulty in meeting production schedules. A wage survey reveals a wide disparity between direct labor and indirect labor, such as truck drivers and expediters. A general wage increase is granted but does not seem to help. The problem is to increase service personnel productivity. Make a recommendation how it should be accomplished. Explain how your proposal would work.
3. Contact a company which uses a wage incentive plan for its production workers. Find out at what percent of production efficiency the wage incentive payment begins and how much the plan pays as production is increased. Be prepared to tell the class about your findings and to answer any questions they may have about the plan.
4. Your plant has a potentially excellent incentive pay plan which will result in greatly increased take-home pay for employees as well as reduced production costs. You learn that there is an "unofficial limit" on earnings and that the union leaders are cautioning employees to stretch out the work. What action do you recommend?
5. Recently a union issued "friendly warnings" to 80 of 103 of its members who were found to be exceeding the union's piecework quotas at a manufacturing plant. The remaining 23 members may be tried by a union board on charges

of persistently exceeding piecework quotas. The union plans to fine guilty members $100 each. What does this incident tell you about the relationship between the union and its members? Between the union and the management of the firm? What appears to be the problem? What suggestions do you have to offer that would help to alleviate the situation?

CASE PROBLEM

19—1. THE COOPERATIVE MACHINE TOOL COMPANY

Defective Work Under an Incentive Wage Plan

The Cooperative Machine Tool Company produces a mechanical device which includes parts consisting of shafts, bearings, and housings for bearings that are manufactured and completely finished in one large department (Manufacturing Dept. #15). The workmen are compensated on the "Straight Piece Rate"; that is, the employee is paid for his work at an estimated rate per piece. Mr. John Kraemer, the foreman of the department, sets the piece rates by estimating the time. Sample parts are used for comparison, checking, and inspection during and after the manufacturing processes.

The workers in the Assembly Room (Dept. #32) received a lot of imperfect parts. They too are working on a "Straight Piece Rate." The shafts were supposed to have a "sliding fit" in the bearings, while the bearings were to have a "press fit" for the housing. But, the shafts fitted too tight in the bearings, while the bearings fitted entirely too loose in the housings. All parts were returned to the manufacturing department. The foreman of Dept. #15 immediately asked the mechanics to repair the parts and also proceeded to deduct from the workers' wage earnings an amount equivalent to the cost of the repairs. The workers of Manufacturing Dept. #15 refused the deduction, which amounted to one half of their weekly base-rate earnings. The workmen furthermore demanded that management "do something" to avoid such wasteful conditions.

Upon investigation, you as the wage and salary consultant found that the parts of the last lot fitted properly, because there was an understanding among the workmen what the dimensions should be before the parts were produced. The last lot of parts was made by some new employees.

Problems:

1. Which of the following solutions for repairing the defective parts do you recommend? Fully explain the reasoning behind your choice.

   (a) The workers should bear the entire cost of repairs.
   (b) The company should bear the entire cost of repairs.
   (c) Both the company and the workers should equally share the cost of repairs.
   (d) Some other solution. (Fully explain it.)

2. Suggest how the manufacture of defective parts can be avoided in the future. Outline a procedure that would make it possible for the workmen to obtain perfect work, and at the same time have the opportunity to increase their weekly and yearly incomes.

chapter 20

GROUP AND PLANT-WIDE
INCENTIVE SUPPLEMENTARY
COMPENSATION PLANS

The purpose of this chapter is to acquaint the reader with the possibilities of applying group and plant-wide incentives as a means of supplementing the regular compensation of employees.

Nature and scope of group and plant-wide incentive plans

A *group incentive* refers to the additional rewards that are paid to a specific group of employees who are working as a unit to produce more than their expected efficiency. The group incentive might be known by any one of a number of terms such as *group bonus, group premium, group piece rate, profit sharing, production sharing,* and *cost sharing.* Group incentives may consist of small groups (2–40 employees) or large groups that include whole departments or the entire plant. The human element and personal attitudes are prime factors in the group incentive structures.

Group incentives are sometimes looked upon as an attempt by management to create an industrial organization in which both the social and the economic systems are compatible and in harmony with one another. Group incentives, like individual incentives, can not only motivate workers to greater productivity and lower costs but also direct labor relations into more productive channels, which can result in increased teamwork, more security, and general acceptance of new technology.

There are many different types of group incentive plans available today. Many of these plans differ only in small details, which often causes confusion between the plans. Most plant-wide incentive plans fall into a category that is usually based on the sharing of profits, production value, sales value, or cost savings. These categories have much in common, when contrasted with individual incentive plans. Most group incentive plans have several general likenesses. They are based on a monetary performance standard (savings, costs, profits, etc.) rather than on a quantity production performance standard as is typical of individual incentives. They present a wide range of opportunities for improving performance through decreasing material, labor, and administrative expenses, and increasing product quality and customer services. They are influenced in different degrees by product price changes; raw material costs; changes in wages, salaries, and fringes; and in customer reactions. There are so many factors that influence the monetary performance standard that the employees rarely have direct control over all the governing factors. This means that group incentive plans are exposed to the unpredictables in a business and are related to the general welfare and goals of the firm. This tends to make company goals the goals of employees, which in turn results in teamwork and cooperation among all employees in the plan.

Most any number of employees can participate in most any group-type incentive plan because of the wide opportunities included in group plans. This contrasts drastically with individual incentive plans in which only certain employees and jobs are suitable to the individual incentive (as an average, no more than about 50 percent of a plant's man-hours). Individual incentives most often require extensive preliminary preparations in terms of work simplification, time studies, and training employees before they can be put into operation, while most incentives use "as is" conditions as a basis for incentive improvements. Thus, initial and maintenance expenses of group plans are considerably less than individual expenses and there is also less lead time needed to get started.

Development and growth of group incentive plans

All original wage incentive plans were developed principally to motivate individual workers to greater productivity. It has been found, however, that on many jobs individual work measurement was impractical because group work units were formed to complete the combined operations. In highly integrated and mechanized processes where the worker neither performs operations directly on the product nor controls the production rate, it becomes impossible to identify output units with individual efforts. [1] Other limitations of individual incentives that spur on the movement to group incentives include the fewer number of

---

[1] Barry M. Ginsburg, "The Impact of Automation on Wage and Salary Administration," *ILR Research*, Vol. IX, No. 1 (1963), p. 4.

employees who can be included in individual incentives (as indirect labor makes up a greater portion of the labor force) and the continued resistance to individual incentives by a large portion of employees and unions.

Much of the administrative cost of an individual incentive plan can be reduced by setting time standards for an entire group. Similarly, high clerical work cost and some payroll calculations may be reduced. Consequently, group incentive plans were developed and have been operating successfully in certain industries.

Plant-wide incentives appear to be a relatively new phenomenon on the American scene. Few, if any, were known before 1935 and only a handful were visible by 1948. Their real growth began to get underway in the mid-1950's. By 1960 they were being used by approximately 7 percent of the companies in the United States. [2] Group and plant-wide incentive plans are today popular in small and medium-size plants where employee communication has not become a problem and where employer-employee relations are on a friendly basis. It appears as if a large number of managements are in the process of shifting emphasis from individual incentives to group incentives. There are probably over 150,000 businesses that have installed some form of a group incentive, and these programs cover over five million employees.

Advantages of Group Incentives

The gregarious instinct holds group units together, and each worker has a stake in high output. Group pressure spurs the slackers and influences the conscientious workers. Furthermore, management gains by smaller administrative costs because less inspection, clerical work, supervision, and daily checkup are required under the group incentive plans than under the individual incentive plans. Then, too, group decisions on how to increase productivity are generally superior to individual decisions; thus, teamwork and greater overall plant productivity are often the rule rather than the exception. Under a group incentive, there is the free and continuous opportunity for all employees to make constructive suggestions of new methods and machinery when they share in the increased productivity that results. Group incentive performance standards are much more simple and objectively established than individual performance standards that often require expensive preparations in the form of motion and time studies, employee training, etc.

Disadvantages of Group Incentives

Dissatisfaction with the group incentive plan grows when numerous experienced workers quit and are replaced with inexperienced workers. Another good

---

[2] R. C. Scott, *Incentives in Manufacturing*, Vol. 2, Parts 6–11 (Cambridge, Mass.: The Eddy-Rucker-Nickels Co., January, 1967) p. 41.

argument against group incentives is that a highly skilled individual is not inclined to perform as efficiently in a group as he would under an individual incentive plan whereby he gains the full benefit of his own productivity.

Theory of group incentive plans

The spirit of teamwork and joint cooperation among employees appears to be the underlying factor that explains why group incentive plans are effective. When employees are so organized into appropriate groups, the selfishness of an individual can work to the advantage of the group as well as to the individual. For example, if an individual employee in a group incentive plan is selfish and works harder or more efficiently to obtain a larger reward for himself, he automatically becomes unselfish because he is really creating a larger reward for everyone included in the group plan. The opposite is also true, for if the employee is unselfish in his behavior so as to earn a greater reward for his fellow employees, he automatically obtains a greater reward for himself. This concept has been referred to as *Synergy* by a number of behavior scientists who have studied organization theory. The idea was developed from the work of Ruth Benedict, the noted anthropologist, and has more recently been treated by the well-known psychologist, Dr. Abraham Maslow, in his approach to the motivation of employees. Thus, the Synergy concept refers to the group's ability, through the simple use of certain types of organizational structure, to destroy the polarity between selfishness and unselfishness among the individuals in the organization. This means that it is possible to so structure a producing organization that, so far as the social and economic goals are concerned, an individual's selfishness can be converted to unselfishness.

It has also been said that group incentives tend to cause all employees to look at the needs and goals of a firm in a similar light. Thus, group incentives can get hourly and salaried employees pointed in the same direction, working together with the same purposes and criteria for measuring success, and acting as if they owned a piece of the firm. Individual incentives have been known to create friction among management specialists, such as the industrial engineer, the quality control manager, and the industrial relations director, because each of the specialists is often looking for different results that do not necessarily complement each other in attaining the overall company goals.

Models of group financial incentive plans

Many incentive programs have been created when competition among firms has brought about pressure for greater efficiency, higher quality, and newer methods. In order that the reader may glean ideas and knowledge of the variety of group and plant-wide financial and nonfinancial incentive plans that are being used successfully, the following sampling of the more popular ones is briefly described.

Profit Sharing

The Council of Profit Sharing Industries in Chicago developed this definition of *profit sharing:* "Any procedure under which an employer pays or makes available to regular employees subject to reasonable eligibility rules, in addition to prevailing rates of pay, special or deferred sums based on the profits of the business."[3] Although the word incentive is not mentioned in this definition, it is the substance of the concept of profit sharing. A distinguishing feature of profit sharing is its variability in that it fluctuates with current profit levels.

Nature of Profit Sharing. Profit sharing is a supplementary group-type of incentive compensation plan used by employers to stabilize employer-employee relationships. It is only one of a number of basic group incentive plans that a firm can establish. It is a method of sharing the profits of an enterprise with employees on the theory that the employee will be thus motivated to work more efficiently to increase both the company's overall profit and the amount it has to share. When this happens, employees tend to remain as employees with the firm and labor turnover is thereby reduced. It should be pointed out that profit sharing is not a substitute for a firm having a pension plan. Most people believe a pension plan must be established before a profit-sharing plan will be accepted by a union.

Profit sharing is a means of remunerating employees at periodic intervals according to a prescribed formula. Ordinarily, in the past, profits were distributed exclusively among managerial supervisors and executives. Commencing with the World War II period, however, there was a growing tendency to include shop and clerical workers. Profit sharing gained acceptance as a specific kind of supplementary compensation method mainly because it is of a deferred nature, serving several other purposes in addition to production incentives. As the Industrial Revolution and technology came into this country, the individual employee became a number and his individuality seemed to have gotten lost. Profit sharing has tended to restore the importance of the individual by giving him opportunities to become involved in the fortunes of the enterprise. Profit sharing might be thought of as the dynamic ingredient of production, the yardstick of efficiency, and the driving force for both capital and labor alike.[4]

Profit-sharing plans are sometimes confused with production bonuses, Christmas bonuses, earnings based on group efficiency, and savings (thrift) plans

---

[3]Council of Profit Sharing Industries, *The Constitution and Bylaws of the COPSI* (Chicago: COPSI, as amended October 17, 1962), p. 1.
[4]B. L. Metzger, *Profit Sharing in Perspective* (2d ed.; Evanston, Ill.: Profit Sharing Research Foundation, 1966), p. 18.

that are not related to actual profit sharing. This may be traceable to the various titles of well-known established plans based on actual profit sharing,[5] such as: "Wage Dividend Plan" (Pitney-Bowes, Inc.); "Joint Earnings and Trust Plan" (Geo. D. Hormel & Company); "Savings and Profit-Sharing Plan" (Sears, Roebuck & Company); "Combined Trust and Bonus Plan" (Daisy Manufacturing Company); "Bonus Plan" (The Lincoln Electric Company); "Cost Savings Sharing Plan" (Bunding Tubing Company); and the "Production Sharing Plan" (Continental Paper Company).

Robert W. Galvin, president of Motorola, Inc., has succinctly indicated what he thinks of profit sharing:

> . . . it will, in time, become a great thing for many, many people without it today. It is amazing what a great variety of things profit sharing can be to different people. It is incentive. It is loyalty-building. It is a sense of responsibility. It is a device for communication; it is communication itself. It is a platform on which you can build your whole company story, attitudes, and objectives. It is savings for your people. It is periodic rewards. It is a retirement pay plan. It is a termination pay plan. It is a vehicle for providing loans in distress. Profit sharing is the most versatile concept and tool available to business management for expressing its sense of responsibility to its people.[6]

Purpose and Objective of Profit Sharing. The main purpose of profit sharing is to imbue the whole organization with the teamwork spirit of working together in a business of their own — in other words, to identify all the employees, from the sweeper up to the top manager, as part owners of a closely knit organization. Profit sharing should mean more than sharing money. It should mean sharing in the "caring" of the business.

Although profit sharing is regarded as a supplemental reward, it is, nevertheless, designed for the purpose of encouraging employees: to eliminate waste of time and material; to have an active interest in the company's affairs; and, above all, to offer suggestions for reducing the labor cost. Several surveys indicate that by offering employees a share of the profits that come from their own production, they are motivated to increase efficiency by as much as 50 to 60 percent, even if they already work on a piece-rate or production-bonus system. This has been proven year after year under the Lincoln Electric Company profit-sharing (yearly bonus) system.

Mr. Norgren, president of the C. A. Norgren Company of Denver, Colorado, which manufactures pneumatic products and employs 270 people, has had a profit-sharing plan since 1945. He reports that his productivity per man-hour

---

[5]See "Profit Sharing Plans in Industry," *Factory Management and Maintenance* (November, 1948), pp. 94–102.

[6]B. L. Metzger, "Profit-Sharing Plans" (From a speech to the Industrial Relations Association of Chicago, January 4, 1962).

is over twice the national average and that in less than 20 years, employee productivity has increased 350 percent. Profit sharing has enabled them to absorb wage increases of 297 percent and material price increases of 140 percent, while raising prices to their customers by only 25 percent.[7]

The objectives and reasons for offering profit sharing are:

1. To instill a sense of partnership. Management shows it is treating the employee as a human being.
2. To serve as a group incentive. This should raise production and lower unit costs.
3. To provide employee security. Employees will not have to fear unemployment or old age.
4. A desire to give greater benefits to employees without incurring fixed commitments. Profits are shared only when they are available; otherwise there is no additional cost or commitment.
5. A desire for a flexible wage policy. During inflation and prosperity the employee shares prosperity.
6. A desire to attract better employees and reduce turnover. Employees take a greater interest in the firm and may decide to make a career with the company.
7. A desire to promote thrift. Employees will thus become more stable and dependable.
8. A desire for better employer-employee relations. Profit sharing does not discriminate against older employees as do pension plans. This helps to remove employee fears and distrust and develops mutual confidence between the firm and its employees.

Growth of Profit Sharing. Profit sharing in the United States had a rather slow growth until the 1950's. In 1940, there were only 37 qualified deferred profit-sharing programs in existence.[8] Some of the earliest profit-sharing plans (based on the principle of corporate partnership between management and labor) are still operating. Procter and Gamble (the oldest plan still in existence in the United States) started its profit-sharing program in 1887; Dennison Manufacturing Co. started in 1911; Eastman Kodak Co., in 1912; Harris Trust and Savings Bank, in 1916; Sears, Roebuck & Co., in 1916; and S. C. Johnson & Sons, Inc., in 1917. However, not too many companies adopted profit-sharing plans before the middle of the twentieth century and some who did had to drop them. Many cash profit-sharing plans were discontinued during the depression in the 1930's. At that time, interest in profit sharing was at a low ebb. It was not until 1939 that interest in profit sharing picked up because of a Senate report by the Vanderberg-Herring Subcommittee on Finance. Encouragement was given to companies through favorable tax legislation to initiate deferred profit-sharing

---

[7]"What You Pay Out of Profits Is Returned 100 Times," *Profit Sharing*, Vol. 12, No. 2 (Chicago: Council of Profit Sharing Industries, March–April, 1964), p. 15.
[8]Metzger, *Profit Sharing in Perspective, op. cit.*, p. 17.

plans for employees. These tax advantages benefitted stockholder-employees, higher paid management personnel, and lower paid management. The number of profit-sharing plans rose from 37 in 1940 to 2,113 in 1945 and to 3,565 in 1950.[9] Since then, there has been a rapid rate of growth.

It has been estimated that since 1951, the annual rate of growth of new profit-sharing plans has doubled every five years.[10] In 1951, about 1,000 new plans were established. In 1956 the number of new plans had grown to 2,000, by 1961 to 4,000, and by 1966 to 8,000. By 1976 it is expected that one of every two companies (having 12 or more employees) will have some type of profit-sharing plan.[11] The rapid growth of profit sharing appears to be due to its tendency to satisfy the various segments that affect the enterprise — the employer, the employee, the government, and the public. The employer believes that profit sharing gets employees to cooperate, the employees like the chance to earn extra money, the government likes its effect in helping to keep wage increases in line with productivity increases, and the public appreciates its tendency to reduce strikes that affect them.

The current number of profit-sharing plans in existence is not exactly known. However, it has been estimated that there are some 125,000 plans in the United States.[12] This would amount to almost one fourth of the half-million companies that have 12 or more employees.

B. L. Metzger, director of the Profit Sharing Research Foundation,[13] has indicated that seven of every ten profit-sharing plans have broad coverage in that they include a majority of the regular employees. Only one fourth of the plans are limited to special employee groups. More than 80 percent of the firms consider their plans successful or very successful in meeting the goals of their plan. Only about 15 percent of the firms consider their plans as so-so, and only one to two percent are disappointed with their plans.

Methods of Payment (Distribution). Profit shares are generally distributed either under a cash-payment plan, under a deferred-payment plan, or under a combination-payment plan. The current or cash payments may be in dollars and cents or, as in some plans, the shares are converted into company stock and distributed directly to employees. The deferred payments are usually turned over to a trustee for later distribution. The combination-payment plan simply means that cash and deferred payments are combined. Cash plans tend to predominate in firms having fewer than 20 employees, while deferred plans are the more popular in the larger size firms.

---

[9]*Ibid.*
[10]William J. Howell, "A New Look at Profit Sharing, Pensions, Productivity Plans," *Business Management*, Vol. 33, No. 33 (December, 1967), p. 27.
[11]*Ibid.*
[12]*Ibid.*
[13]B. L. Metzger, *Profit Sharing, Poverty, and Automation* (Racine, Wisconsin: The Johnson Foundation, 1966), p. 25.

Cash-Payment Plan. *Cash-payment plans* provide for the distribution of shares at regular frequent intervals. By making monthly or quarterly payments, the employees, being aware of the current company earnings, can appreciate the results of their efforts because the incentive payment follows shortly after the jobs are completed. On the other hand, if the shares are distributed annually or even semiannually, the employees do not seem to relate the incentive reward to their own efforts due to the time lapse between payments. It has been estimated that the average employee under the cash plan receives about $10,000 over a 25-year period, or about $400 a year.[14] The cash-payment plans make up about 40 percent of the present profit-sharing plans in existence. It is believed that there are some 50,000 to 60,000 cash plans in the United States.[15] The cash plan is especially popular with managements in very small firms because it is easy to understand and administer and does not require a lot of time and staff. Employees like it because they can realize immediate cash benefits. Some 36.4 percent of cash plans yield an average of 10 percent extra annual compensation for their employees.[16] The chief limitations of cash plans appear to be their vulnerability in nonprofit years, their lack of tax advantages for employees, and their lack of provision for future financial security.

Deferred-Payment Plan. In *deferred-payment plans*, either a part or all of the employee's share is turned over to a trust fund, to be credited to his account and invested on his behalf. The amount is held in trust for release either in installments or for income or periodic payments after retirement. Upon termination of employment, the employee receives the vested part of the fund. In case of death the accumulated credits are paid to the designated beneficiary. A deferred-payment plan is preferable to the cash-payment method in view of the income tax advantages for the employee. This can provide a flexible security fund and develop long-term incentive as an employee's account grows. Employees can even become stockholders. Some 34.7 percent of the deferred plans yield 15 percent of compensation beyond the employee's annual wage or salary.[17]

William Howell, a principal of Howell & Sisler of Chicago, a firm that specializes in deferred profit-sharing plans, has estimated that there are approximately 60,000 deferred plans in the United States.[18] In close to half of the deferred plans, employees have the opportunity to add to their trust fund by making contributions out of their pay. If the employee would normally receive $10,000 from the profits shared and he contributes $5,000 over the 25-year period, this would mean that the $15,000 that was invested for him in the trust fund could at the end of the 25-year period amount to anywhere from $25,000 to $50,000.

---

[14]Howell, *op. cit.*, p. 28.
[15]Metzger *Profit Sharing, Poverty, and Automation, loc. cit.*
[16]Metzger, *Profit Sharing in Perspective, op. cit.*, p. 17.
[17]*Ibid.*
[18]Howell, *op. cit.*, p. 28.

This is due to the tax advantage of the plan and the effect of compound interest on the money invested. About 50 percent of all profit-sharing plans are of the deferred-payment type. Popularity of these plans will increase as provisions are made to allow employees to borrow or to withdraw funds for important reasons. Undesirable features of deferred plans include the added communications and administrative details that are involved and a longer waiting period to receive the funds.

Combination-Payment Plan. The *combination-payment plans* — as may be surmised — are a combination of the cash-payment and the deferred-payment plans. The Pitney-Bowes wage dividend plan mentioned before is a combination type plan. This company extends the privilege to employees of investing about 10 percent of their profit share in company stock; another specified percent in the pension fund; and the balance is immediately paid in cash. About 10 percent of all profit-sharing plans are of the combination-payment type.

Amounts of Profits to Be Shared. The profits that are shared with employees usually depend on the conditions existing in the firm and the philosophy of those managing it. Two out of three firms establish a definite formula for calculating the amount of profits to be shared, while the other third determine it yearly by a discretionary decision of the board of directors. [19] Approximately 85 percent of those firms that have a formula for sharing profits do so on a "before-tax" basis. When the firm's profit-sharing contribution is deducted "before taxes," fewer calculations are required than when it is computed "after taxes." The reason some firms use the "after-tax" basis is the belief that a firm does not really have profits until taxes have been paid. There is also the argument that this method may place the profit-sharing employees on the same basis as that which the stockholders enjoy.

The amount shared with employees varies from 10 to 50 percent of net profit. Generally, the majority of companies pay 10 to 15 percent of the annual base pay under the deferred-payment program due to restrictions of the Internal Revenue Service that do not permit tax deductions for payments in excess of 15 percent of annual compensation. Some plans, like the Lincoln Electric Company's annual bonus, base the amounts to be paid on yearly merit rating related to earnings and production.

The Advantages and Limitations of Profit Sharing. All types of incentive plans have their strong and weak points. The following represent the chief advantages and limitations of profit sharing as a group incentive.

Advantages of Profit Sharing. The more common advantages of profit sharing are as follows:

---

[19]Metzger, *Profit Sharing in Perspective, op. cit.*, p. 74.

1. Rewards are directly related to the profitability of the firm. Therefore, a few employees cannot be a big success at the expense of the firm. The company and the success of the employees are therefore tied together.
2. Profit sharing tends to reduce employee turnover because employees are made to feel part owners of the firm and are generally satisfied to remain in a prosperous firm. This is especially true when some of the profits are deferred into an employee pension plan that pays off upon retirement.
3. The deferred-payment plan of profit sharing has a tax advantage for employees, thus giving them a greater dollar benefit in this type of incentive plan.
4. Profit sharing is relatively inexpensive to install and generally requires less effort to maintain the plan.
5. Profit sharing appears to be more adaptable to a larger number of firms than most other types of group incentives because it includes a wider range of factors that influence efficiency (and profits).
6. Profit sharing puts management in a strong position to argue against granting wage increases that exceed productivity gains because this would cut into the profits and company security.

Limitations of Profit Sharing. The more common limitations of profit sharing are as follows:

1. Many companies do not have a steady record of making profits; consequently, if the firm and its employees have a few profitless years, the plan may lose momentum.
2. Some employees believe that either deferring awards to a pension plan or providing only annual rewards is too long a delay between job performance and rewards. Thus, employees will not be strongly motivated. Other employees feel that, at times, there is a weak relationship between present plant efficiency and profits because of external conditions beyond the control of the firm. This results in discouraging some employees on a profit-sharing plan because they cannot see, or do not fully understand, this relationship.
3. Employees may not get behind the profit-sharing idea if they believe that the firm spends excessive amounts on executive salaries, expense accounts, advertising, etc. (and nothing can be done about such costs).
4. In time, profit sharing may lead unions into bargaining over an endless number of factors that management may be unwilling to yield on, such as control of prices, the profit-sharing formula, and various administrative features.

Requirements for a Sound Profit-Sharing Plan. A successful profit-sharing plan like other incentive plans calls for hard work and a willingness to make it work. Its success does not come automatically. The success of a profit-sharing plan is predicated upon the following prerequisites:

1. Design an appropriate plan and define its objectives and aims. Dispel any skepticism; assure stockholders that their due share of dividends will not

be curtailed. Any plan which hopes to motivate employees will need to share enough profits so that employees will receive at least 8, 10, or 12 percent benefit beyond their annual wage or salary.

2. The plan must be tailor-made to suit the needs of the enterprise in keeping with the philosophy and the principles of the employer or the board of directors, after approval by the stockholders.

3. The fully described plan should contain definite provisions regarding eligibility, method of distribution, time and formula for payments, administration, and any other matters that may be open to question or misunderstanding. Employees should also be aware of the state of the company's business: sales, trading, backlog, and projected growth. Employees should be kept aware of current plan investments and of the necessity for keeping up with research and new product development. They must understand how and why all these factors have an effect on the company's profits and the fund's growth this year and next year. This does not mean that total disclosure of all a company's innermost secrets to all employees is essential to profit sharing.

4. In a unionized plant, every effort should be made to have union members participate in setting up the plan. Unions may challenge the adequacy of the plan, especially in connection with deferred pensions.

5. The plan should be set up on the basis of mutual responsibility by management and first-line employees. Thus, loyal enthusiasm will not wane in profitless years, or even if losses occur.

6. The plan should be sufficiently flexible to allow for occasional changes or new ideas. No compensation plan should be static. This applies equally to profit sharing.

A profit-sharing program is useless in an enterprise without sound employer-employee relations, acceptable working conditions, equitable wage-base rates, and fair incentive wages. In other words, a company must "put its house in order" before attempting profit sharing.

The procedure of administering a profit-sharing plan depends upon whether the plan provides for individual cash payments only in addition to production bonuses, or whether it is designed for deferred payments in addition to various types of insurance and pensions. The latter would have to fulfill certain Internal Revenue Service regulations, especially if the deferred distribution necessitates a profit-sharing trust. One legal requirement is a full description of the fund with explicit information regarding the formulas for contributions to the fund and the distribution of profit shares. It should be noted that the National Labor Relations Board has held that profit sharing is a proper subject for collective bargaining.

The best procedure is to appoint a committee of three to five representatives, officers and employees, who may become trustees and custodians of the profit-sharing fund. They would be responsible for making all decisions relative to the plan. However, it is more practical that a bank or trust company take over the trusteeship and become custodian of the fund since it has all the necessary talent to select proper investments for the fund, and to attend to all matters of distribution.

The Scanlon Plan

The Scanlon plan has been a popular cost-saving incentive-sharing plan since the 1940's. Because the extra earnings that employees receive under this plan are related to sales income, the Scanlon plan is sometimes referred to as a sales value incentive-sharing plan. Mr. Scanlon was a staunch supporter of capitalistic free enterprise with its management of human effort. He insisted, however, that management must realize its responsibility and social obligations to raise the standards of living for its employees. Likewise, he urged workers to recognize their duty of doing "an honest day's work for an honest day's pay."

Mr. Scanlon's incentive philosophy began to crystallize in a steel mill where he was employed as a cost accountant and as an open-hearth worker in the shop. In the early 1930's the steel company had just emerged from bankruptcy when a local union was formed to demand higher wages for shop employees who were working with obsolete equipment under nonstandardized conditions. Scanlon became their spokesman and persuaded them to be more concerned with the company's survival which, he convinced them, could be accomplished by eliminating waste and by improving production efficiency. Even with obsolete equipment, costs were reduced and within a short period, wages were raised. Thus, through employer-employee teamwork the company survived, and a new type of incentive plan, the *Scanlon Plan of Participation*, had its inception.

Mr. Scanlon was dedicated to the principle of teamwork and union participation, but he was not opposed to individual incentives. In his discussion of "what the Scanlon plan isn't and what it is," Frederick G. Lesieur, an associate of Mr. Scanlon states:

> This plan doesn't mean turning the plant over to the union. . . . It means management makes decisions on what is good for the company and not on what's good for some personality down in the plant. This plan doesn't mean giving people a "sense of participation"; workers don't want that. This plan means giving them real participation.[20]

Conditions for Participation and Compensation. The Scanlon plan is based on incentive wage sharing in proportion to higher productivity and sales profits. The following conditions, while different from traditional thinking, are common under the Scanlon plan and acceptable to labor and management:

---

[20]Frederick G. Lesieur, Editor, *The Scanlon Plan* (New York: The Technology Press of Massachusetts Institute of Technology and John Wiley & Sons, Inc., 1958, copyrighted by the Massachusetts Institute of Technology), pp. 38–39.

TABLE 20.1

DEVELOPMENT OF AN ANNUAL RATIO BY ONE COMPANY FOR ONE YEAR

19___	Net Sales (1)	Changes in Inventory (In Process and Finished Goods) (2)	Sales Value of Production (3)	Factory Payroll (4)	Office and Salary (5)	Reserve for Vacations and Holidays (6)	Total Adjusted Payroll (7)	Ratio of 7 to 3 (7) ÷ (3)
January	$ 846,349	$ 15,365	$ 861,714	$ 185,796	$ 79,627	$ 12,402	$ 277,825	32.2
February	855,555	78,532	934,087	204,949	87,836	12,402	305,187	32.7
March	795,326	−9,856	785,470	194,916	83,535	12,402	290,853	37.0
April	682,540	11,363	693,903	200,547	85,949	12,402	298,898	43.1
May	754,430	61,337	815,767	216,148	92,635	12,402	321,185	39.4
June	863,115	−6,542	856,573	225,032	96,442	12,402	333,876	39.0
July	462,867	20,853	483,720	132,861	56,941	12,402	202,204	41.8
August	921,173	12,624	933,797	218,231	93,527	12,402	324,160	34.7
September	950,161	−3,009	947,152	217,834	93,357	12,402	323,593	34.2
October	851,333	8,751	860,084	239,100	102,471	12,402	353,973	41.2
November	826,551	17,883	844,434	254,094	108,898	12,402	375,394	44.4
December	703,158	10,767	713,925	210,704	90,301	12,402	313,407	43.9
	$9,512,558	$218,068	$9,730,626	$2,500,212	$1,071,519	$148,824	$3,720,555	38.2

1. Production and management problems are solved during monthly discussions between joint employer-employee committees. All departments and top management, equally represented, decide on matters pertaining to improvements submitted through the suggestion system. No cash awards are offered, yet more suggestions are submitted than under any other plan.
2. All essential matters involving the plan are incorporated in collective bargaining agreements to forestall grievances and friction among union members.
3. Fringe benefits, overtime bonuses, and similar additional compensations are generally eliminated.
4. Labor expenses related to sales value of production usually consist of all wages and salaries paid to direct and indirect labor, line-and-staff employees, executives, and administrators of the enterprise.
5. *All employees, including executives — in many cases including top management — engineers, accountants, office personnel, maintenance workers, and janitors participate in sharing any incentive bonus,* computed by a committee comprising management and employee representatives.
6. Incentive payments are made monthly or bimonthly. Thus, the principle of deferred payment does not impede the motivating effect on the employees.

Method of Calculating Scanlon Bonus Payments. The method of calculating bonus payments under the Scanlon plan is based on a ratio of the total labor cost to the total production value. The production value, in turn, equals the monthly sales, plus or minus the inventory changes. Table 20.1 gives one company's monthly ratio figures for an entire year. The annual ratio of 38.2 percent is determined by dividing the total adjusted yearly payroll ($3,720,555) by the total yearly sales value of production ($9,730,626).

Figure 20.1 shows another company's method of calculating the monthly bonus from an established production ratio of 44.06 percent for the previous year.[21] Note that 25 percent of the bonus pool reverts to the company in reserve for unexpected deficit months during one year. If the reserve exceeds the incurred deficits, the difference is paid out proportionately the same as the monthly bonus, namely, 75 percent to the employees and 25 percent to the company. The example in Figure 20.1 describes how the individual bonus percentage is calculated and prorated.

The monthly bonus payments remunerate employees close to the period of their accomplishments, which is a recognized psychological factor not associated with traditional profit sharing. Also, the bonus payments serve as a desirable element of checkup and close control. The employees are vitally concerned about the monthly profits. An unprofitable month draws labor and

---

[21]Table 20.1 and Figure 20.1 are reproduced with permission, Lesieur, *ibid.*, pp. 68 and 130.

METHOD OF BONUS CALCULATION AND DISTRIBUTION
FOR THE MONTH OF JANUARY

Example

1. Assume that in the 12-month *base period* the payroll cost of each dollar's worth of production value was 44.06 cents. This estabishes a *productivity norm* or ratio of 44.06 percent against which to measure the performance in each month of the following year, governing the bonus distribution.

2. Assume that during the month of January the *sales value of production* is . . . $87,837.00

3. If performance had been no better during this month than the average for the base period, the allowed payroll would have come to $38,701.00

(Allowed payroll = 44.06% × 87,837)

4. Assume, however, the *actual payroll* for January figured out to be $30,985.00

5. This would mean an improvement over the norm amounting to . . . . $ 7,716.00

($7,716.00 is the BONUS POOL.)

6. Setting aside 25 percent of the bonus pool as a *reserve* . . . . $ 1,929.00

7. Leaving *for immediate distribution* the sum of . . . . $ 5,787.00

8. Deducting the company's share (25 percent) . . . . $ 1,447.00

9. Making the employees' share (75 percent) . . . . $ 4,340.00

10. In percent of the actual payroll, the share for the employees is:
(4,340.00 ÷ 30,985.00) . . . .   = 14.0%

(14% is the *Bonus Percentage to be Paid* to each employee.)

11. An individual employee's pay record for the month of January may be as follows:

Name	Total Hours Worked	Including Overtime Hours	Hourly Rate	Total Pay	Bonus Per-cent	Bonus	Total Earnings
John Doe	200	20	$3	$660	14.0	$92.40	$752.40

FIGURE 20.1   METHOD OF INDIVIDUAL BONUS CALCULATION ACCORDING TO THE SCANLON PLAN

management together to ferret out the reasons for the poor results and to correct them.

The Scanlon Plan of the Parker Pen Company.[22]   A strong advocate of the Scanlon plan is Philip Hull, vice-president of the Parker Pen Company in

---

[22]Adapted with permission from a speech on the Scanlon plan by Mr. Hull at the 31st Annual IMS Industrial Engineering and Management Clinic at the Pick-Congress Hotel, Chicago, November, 1967.

Janesville, Wisconsin, who has had 13 years of successful experience with the plan. He believes that many companies face the critical problem today of trying to get every employee thinking and acting as though he owned the company and of recognizing and accepting his responsibility toward its goal, because in the long run the employee's interest is best served in that way. The Scanlon plan is doing this for the Parker Pen Company.

The Scanlon plan was installed in August, 1954, because the firm was interested in upgrading productivity and in getting rid of an individual incentive plan which was not working and which did not include a third of the employees in the manufacturing division. The firm was not in financial trouble nor was it looking for a substitute for good management. It was essentially interested in getting all employees in the manufacturing division involved to solve the problem of how to produce more of a better product and to put it on the shipping dock at a lower cost. The Scanlon plan was chosen over a number of group-type incentive plans because it seemed to offer an opportunity to resolve the question of how one might go about pointing all people within the division in the same direction and locking them in on the same objective.

After reaching an agreement with its unions, the Parker Pen Company established production committees and got an agreement on the measurement or standard (ratio) that would be used as the basis for the plan. The firm arrived at its ratio by totaling all payroll costs involved in producing everything that was made during the last 12 months prior to the installation of the plan. It then said to the employees, "You can have 75 percent of any reductions that result during the coming year from your efforts to eliminate every form of inefficiency." The remaining 25 percent of the reductions went to the firm. This meant that all factors that determine product cost became targets for examination. Company performance is computed monthly, and bonuses are distributed monthly.

Results of the plan have been very satisfying. Participation of employees in the effort to produce more and better pens at a lower cost has been on a broad scale. Mr. Hull says the plan has produced the best two-way communications flow that he has ever seen in factories. In 13 years, Parker Pen has received 5,394 suggestions, with an acceptance rate of 80 percent. Extra monetary rewards totaled $7,230,291 (employees, 75 percent) during that period for an average across-the-board incentive earning of about 15 percent each year to all participating employees. At the same time the firm has benefited some $1,800,000 (its 25 percent). Another benefit which has developed is that over 90 percent of its production now comes from within its own plant as against only 55 percent in 1953. The firm is also able to produce millions of parts for foreign-based operations of the corporation because its costs are lower than in the foreign countries, in spite of the fact that the foreign labor rates are substantially below those paid in the United States. In short, Mr. Hull feels that before the Scanlon plan it seemed that year after year *they were spending more and more time talking with everybody about more money for less work — now, the Scanlon plan has opened the door for them to get together to talk about more money for more work.*

Experience with the Scanlon Plan. In a study by Industrial Relations Counselors, Inc., of six companies which have used the plan,[23] it was found that two of the six companies abandoned the plan after two years' experience with it, two firms have used it from eight to ten years, and two had recently adopted it with certain modifications. The two chief reasons for a company's adopting the plan have been (1) financial difficulty and (2) dissatisfaction with an existing incentive system. The companies that used the plan were small or medium size, without a regular industrial engineering staff. They were controlled by one individual or a family group, with one person giving the plan enthusiastic support. The firms were in a poor financial position and in a branch of manufacturing in which labor costs represent a large proportion of total cost. The employee groups of the firms tended to be fairly highly skilled men, unionized by a single union with the local characterized by a fair degree of autonomy and internal democracy.

Some of the companies in the IRC study reported that the Scanlon plan encouraged the offering of valuable suggestions and contributed to high morale, favorable employee attitudes, and a resulting team spirit and atmosphere of cooperation. Some said it also reduced labor costs, increased employee earnings, and made improvements in deliveries, reduction in waste, and more efficient training of new employees.

The IRC study points out these limitations of the Scanlon plan: (1) It may limit company flexibility if outside consultants have to administer the plan or if necessary expansion or diversity is curtailed because bonuses are paid monthly instead of yearly. (2) The plan may be unwieldy to administer in large companies where time consumed in operating the plan may be disproportionate to the savings gained in labor costs or where firm bigness stifles two-way communications. (3) The standard incentive payroll ratio may not be suitable in those companies whose product line is constantly changing. (4) Management thinking and philosophy would need reorientation where management looks upon union participation as an encroachment upon management's prerogatives. Likewise, if the union believes that participation with management would undermine the union, the plan could only have limited success.

The study pointed out that before a firm should consider the adoption of the Scanlon plan, the following conditions should exist: (1) The firm must be able to pay a regular bonus continually. (2) The firm must have a basic need for the plan. (3) The firm's top officers, management, and union officials must share an

---

[23]For complete details of the study, see *Group Wage Incentives: Experience with the Scanlon Plan*, IRM No. 141 (New York: Industrial Relations Counselors, Inc., 1270 Avenue of the Americas, February 2, 1962).

enthusiasm for the basic concepts and principles of the plan. (4) The plan must have the complete cooperation of all employees.

The Kaiser Steel Long-Range Sharing Plan[24]

A unique and much-publicized long-range "economic" sharing plan is that of Kaiser Steel of Fontana, California. A 104-day steel strike by the United Steelworkers of America (USWA) in 1959 was the impetus that led Kaiser and the USWA to seek a lasting solution to eliminate the threat of strikes and to reduce employee grievances. In searching for a solution, a nine-man Kaiser-Labor-Public committee was formed. This long-range planning committee, after much deliberation, adopted the present sharing plan for the approval of the local USWA members in January, 1963. The plan was ratified by union members by a 3 to 1 vote margin and went into effect in March, 1963.

The plan as it was originally conceived is somewhat similar to the Scanlon plan. Both plans attempt to increase employee interest and, in so doing, generate increasing productivity at a lower cost. Also, both plans give rewards, in bonus forms, to the extent that cost-saving production is increased. Unlike a profit-sharing plan, the Kaiser plan proposes that the employees receive bonuses from production savings regardless of the level of company profits.

Generally, the Kaiser plan attempts to deal with two major aspects: first, a "better way" to solve the mutual problems of Kaiser and the USWA, and second, to create employee cost-saving productivity at Kaiser. More fundamentally, the sharing plan is designed so that Kaiser would be able to introduce technological changes and varying work practices with minimal employee-union grievance and resistance. To accomplish the above goals, the plan, though rather complicated and detailed, concisely provides that (1) there is greater job security and protection for Kaiser employees, (2) Kaiser workers are to receive a 32.5 percent[25] share of savings made by increasingly efficient production, and (3) if the steel industry grants a wage and/or benefit increase, the Kaiser employees are to receive payments at the same level or possibly greater than the rest of the steel industry.

Why Kaiser? At a glance, the production-sharing plan seems as though it could be a "do-all" solution for the introduction of technological change and the elimination of strikes.

It first must be noted that this plan was feasible at Kaiser because of certain unparalleled characteristics that Kaiser exhibits. Kaiser is relatively new to the

---

[24]We are indebted to Mr. Robert S. Anderson, Division Superintendent, Industrial Relations, of the Kaiser Steel Corporation for confirmation and revision of ideas and figures in this discussion.

[25]The 32.5 percent figure is based on the ratio of labor costs to total manufacturing costs at Kaiser in 1961; it is also the historical ratio of these cost factors. However, since its conception, the 1961 base-year production figures have been modified and updated, but the 32.5 percent figure is still in effect.

steel industry — it grew out of World War II. Therefore, because of its infancy to the industry, plant modifications to introduce technical changes are quite practical. Being a large single-plant operation in the highly volatile southern California labor market also lent itself to the feasibility of the plan. The growing optimism of being in an expanding economic area and at a competitive advantage in the Far West was favorable for the introduction of something "new" in labor relations. Also to be noted were the dynamic leadership personalities of Edgar F. Kaiser, chairman of Kaiser Steel, and David J. McDonald, former president of the USWA, who were instrumental in the formation and adoption of the plan.

To Eliminate the Old Incentive System. One of the major underlying objectives of the plan was the elimination, or least the reduction, of their incentive system as it existed in 1959. This incentive system as it existed was inequitable. In fact, some incentive workers earned more than some employees who were in higher job classifications but not covered by incentives. For this reason, Kaiser officials felt that incentive payments should be minimized.

The sharing plan was to take the place of the incentive system. The plan, to induce (but not force) workers off incentives, was regarded as equitable and most important, practical. For instance, an incentive employee would receive a lump sum of ten times the difference between his incentive earnings and his base rate for all hours worked over the preceding 13 weeks. For a 40-hour week the incentive worker would receive the lump sum difference of 5,200 hours (13 weeks × 40 hours = 520 hours × 10 = 5,200) for the 13 weeks worked. "If his regular rate was $3 and his incentive earnings $1.50, the lump sum would be $7,800 (5,200 hours × $1.50 = $7,800), which he would get no later than two weeks after the incentive plan for his unit is scrapped." [26] By the end of the second year of the plan, it was reported by Kaiser officials that the number of employees covered by incentives had decreased by one third. The advocates of the plan regard this one-third figure as quite satisfactory.

The 32.5 Percent Bonus. The 32.5 percent bonus based on productive efficiency, to be shared by the employees, deserves some consideration. The 32.5 percent figure is made up of labor and material costs that are saved through more efficient productivity. Part of the 32.5 percent figure is set aside for wage and benefit increases that are adopted by the industry or that the Kaiser employees may choose. The remainder is distributed in the form of monthly bonuses.

Under the plan the Kaiser employees get 32.5 percent of the savings on the cost of producing one ton of finished steel compared to the 1961 base-year cost. In 1966 the 1961 standards were raised through the substitution of the Bureau of

---

[26]National Industrial Conference Board, *The Kaiser Steel Union Sharing Plan*, Studies in Personnel Policy, No. 187 (1963), p. 27.

Labor Statistics Metal and Metal Products Price Index for the BLS Steel Price Index. Union and Kaiser officials regarded this change as necessary for the plan to remain equitable for all concerned.

All the employees who were originally covered by the plan were placed into five groups and factor points were assigned to each group. A sixth group was established for those employees electing to remain on incentives. The percentage figure of a particular group is calculated between that group and the whole. This figure determines the share of the gains to be made available in the form of a monthly bonus to that group. In January, 1966, this method of distributing the sharing-plan earnings was revised. The original five groups were combined to form two groups. According to Kaiser figures, the total cash distribution in the first four-year period was $10.9 million, which averaged a $2,100 bonus take-home per employee. Another $8.2 million has gone into a wage and benefit reserve fund. [27]

The Employee Guarantee. Another feature of Kaiser's plan is the employment reserve clause. This clause guarantees the reduction of the current (1963 employment figures) total number of employees below the number required to produce an equal number of tons of steel in 1961 only to the extent that attrition or increased production can absorb those displaced. [28] This takes into consideration changes in work practices, methods, or technology.

In effect, Kaiser may have a number of workers displaced because of a technological innovation, but these workers are guaranteed employment. For instance, they may be temporarily placed in another department, as in maintenance. The alternative to this placement is that a worker is placed on an "employment reserve" list and he does receive compensation. One's position and level of pay while on this employment reserve shall be at least as high as the job from which displaced.

How the Plan Has Worked. The preceding paragraphs have outlined what constitutes the Kaiser-USWA sharing plan of material and labor costs saved in production. This leads to an examination of the actual results of the plan.

Table 20.2 gives an excellent dollar-and-cents summary and monthly comparative analysis of employee gains for the first term of the Kaiser Steel long-range sharing plan. Upon close examination of the table, one can conclude noticeable trends in some of the figures. First, total gains have been steadily increasing, with the exception of the second year. According to Kaiser officials, this decrease in gains in year two was due in part because of a large upswing of new employees hired to replace older employees taking 13-week extended vacations and to fill employment needs created by an increase in volume. Another

---

[27]"New Slices for Kaiser's Melon?" *Business Week* (March 4, 1967), p. 149.
[28]National Industrial Conference Board, *op. cit.*, p. 13.

TABLE 20.2

MONTHLY COMPARATIVE ANALYSIS OF EMPLOYEE GAINS FOR THE FIRST TERM OF THE KAISER STEEL LONG-RANGE SHARING PLAN

FOURTH YEAR 1966-67*

	FIRST YEAR SUMMARY*	SECOND YEAR SUMMARY*	MAR.	APRIL	MAY	JUNE	JULY	AUG.	SEPT.	OCT.	NOV.	DEC.	JAN.	FEB.
TOTAL EMPLOYEE GAINS	$3,988,000	$3,632,000	574,000	604,000	672,000	655,000	709,000	665,000	619,000	582,000	644,000	518,000	510,000	509,000
Avg. Cents Per Hour Worked	53¢	39¢	69¢	77¢	85¢	83¢	93¢	85¢	80¢	70¢	81¢	68¢	62¢	67¢
Avg. % of Hourly Rate	21	15	27	30	33	32	36	33	31	28	31	26	24	26
CASH DISTRIBUTION	$3,725,000	$2,257,000	265,000	292,000	339,000	315,000	350,000	298,000	264,000	274,000	279,000	133,000	123,000	118,000
Avg. Cents Per Hour Worked	50¢	24¢	32¢	37¢	43¢	40¢	46¢	38¢	34¢	33¢	35¢	18¢	15¢	16¢
Avg. % of Hourly Rate Paid	17	8	11	12	13	14	13	13	11	11	12	6	5	6
WAGE & BENEFIT RESERVE	$ 263,000	$1,375,000	309,000	312,000	333,000	340,000	359,000	367,000	355,000	308,000	365,000	385,000	387,000	391,000
Avg. Cents Per Hour Worked	3¢	15¢	37¢	40¢	42¢	43¢	47¢	47¢	46¢	37¢	46¢	50¢	47¢	51¢
PARTICIPATING EMPLOYEES	4,600	5,200	5,300	5,500	5,600	5,500	5,900	5,600	5,800	5,700	5,800	5,800	5,800	5,800
Avg. Cash Distribution	$810.00	$434.00	50.00	53.00	61.00	57.00	59.00	53.00	46.00	48.00	48.00	23.00	21.00	20.00

FIFTH YEAR 1967*

	THIRD YEAR SUMMARY*	FOURTH YEAR SUMMARY*	MAR.	APRIL	MAY	JUNE	JULY	AUG.	SEPT.	OCT.	NOV.	DEC.	JAN.	FEB.
TOTAL EMPLOYEE GAINS	$4,563,000	$7,261,000	462,000	564,000	547,000	543,000	576,000	584,000	692,000					
Avg. Cents Per Hour Worked	46¢	77¢	57¢	72¢	66¢	67¢	74¢	73¢	88¢					
Avg. % of Hourly Rate	18	30	22	28	26	26	29	28	34					
CASH DISTRIBUTION	$1,787,000	$3,050,000	99,000	149,000	103,000	130,000	131,000	127,000	221,000					
Avg. Cents Per Hour Worked	18¢	33¢	12¢	19¢	12¢	16¢	17¢	16¢	28¢					
Avg. % of Hourly Rate Paid	6	11	4	6	4	5	5	5	9					
WAGE & BENEFIT RESERVE	$2,776,000	$4,211,000	363,000	415,000	444,000	413,000	445,000	457,000	471,000					
Avg. Cents Per Hour Worked	28¢	44¢	45¢	53¢	54¢	51¢	57¢	57¢	60¢					
PARTICIPATING EMPLOYEES	5,600	5,700	5,900	5,700	5,800	5,600	5,900	5,500	5,900					
Avg. Cash Distribution	$319.00	$535.00	17.00	26.00	18.00	23.00	22.00	23.00	37.00					

*Figures rounded.

Source: Reprinted with permission from the Kaiser Steel Corporation, Fontana, California.

significant observation is that more of the total gains have been placed in wage and benefit reserve. This reserve is used to meet industry wage and/or benefit increases, or the Kaiser employees can elect to put it to some other future use.

Other Results of the Plan. For 1963 the company reported a net profit of $11.3 million, as compared with a 1962 net loss of $5.2 million. A word of caution, however, for 1963 was a remarkable year for Kaiser and how much of this net profit that can be attributed to the plan itself, is not testable. It should be remembered that profits, as such, do not enter into calculations of employee bonuses.

After a full year's operation, the plan diminished the number of employee grievances submitted. In 1961 there was a backlog of over 500 grievances to be handled, and these formal grievances were occurring at a rate of 125 each month. [29] A 1964 analysis shows that the norm is about 25 grievances monthly and only about 70 were in process at that time. Company officials regard this decrease in grievances due to the fact that the employees are "interested" in Kaiser's well-being.

Early in January, 1968, the Kaiser employees voted (3,293 to 1,763) to extend the plan for four years (retroactive to October 1, 1967) and to make two changes in the rules. [30] Under the revised plan, the wage and benefit reserve fund was eliminated and management agreed to pay employees the increased cost of the 1968 settlement (this has been estimated to be 20 to 25 cents an hour). The other provision allows certain crews that were previously covered by the incentive program to return to unit performance measures (similar to incentive plans), if they prefer.

The ultimate question still remains, "Is Kaiser's sharing plan a success and is it a plan for use in future labor relations?" Only a subjective type answer can even be attempted when presented with this question. Up to this point, the Kaiser sharing plan seems to be a mutual success for both the United Steelworkers at Fontana and the Kaiser Steel Corporation. Only time will tell how successful. Kaiser is quite satisfied with the general results of the plan. However, as far as being an answer for the rest of the steel industry, the plan may have limited usefulness. The plan, as briefly presented in the preceding paragraph, is workable and useful only to the extent that capable management uses and modifies its provisions for its particular problems. This plan is not necessarily a prototype for future labor relations. However, it is a good example of what is to be demanded in future labor relations; that is, a mutual understanding and basic harmony between management and union officials in seeking long-range, lasting solutions to labor inequities.

---

[29]"Outsiders Keep Peace at Kaiser," *Business Week* (October 24, 1964), p. 105.
[30]"Kaiser Vote Retains Revised Sharing Plan," *AFL-CIO News* (Washington, D.C.), Vol. XIII, No. 5 (February 3, 1968), p. 3.

The Lincoln Electric Incentive Plan

The Lincoln Electric Company of Cleveland, Ohio, is one of the world's largest manufacturers of arc welding equipment and supplies and is well known as a producer of electric motors. Its company-wide bonus plan has been in effect since 1934. The plan is presently used also in their plants in France, Canada, and Australia. The company has never lost an hour of work due to a strike in over 70 years, and employee absenteeism and turnover (less than 1 percent) are far below the national averages. [31] Although the nonunionized firm pays wages that are said to be average for Cleveland, year-end cash bonuses raise the average annual earnings of its employees to about double the level for comparable work in other companies. [32]

The unusual effectiveness of the Lincoln plan (also referred to as incentive compensation) must be credited to the philosophy of the late James F. Lincoln, former president and chairman of the board of the Lincoln Electric Company. His writings regarding the structure of his organization and its creative incentive management [33] reflect his deep understanding of human nature. In his book, *Incentive Management*, Mr. Lincoln said that "The primary goal of any industry, to be successful continuously, must be to make a better and better product to be sold to more and more people at a lower and lower price." [34] Profit should not be the goal, but a by-product. If such a philosophy is carried out, there will be large profits which must be properly divided between the customer, the employee, and the stockholder. He believed that management could not obtain its goal alone but that there must be an incentive to create an active interest on the part of all employees to work toward the goal common to all — success.

According to Mr. Lincoln, one of the governing principles of a successful business lies in inspiring each member of the organization to develop the spirit of teamwork, just as each member of an amateur athletic team is inspired to win. He contends that the parallel between an effective incentive in industry and winning a game is close, although industrial intricacies make the former a more complex problem. A pertinent comparison by Mr. Lincoln is:

> What, then, is the incentive that causes people to strive so mightily for success in an amateur athletic game? The answer is *recognition of our abilities by our contemporaries and ourselves*. The gaining by our skills of the feeling that we are a man among men. . . . The feeling that we are different in some way or ways that others admire and wish to emulate . . . . That is the incentive that almost completely determines our efforts in life.[35]

---

[31]Allen Van Cranebrock, "Cost Cutting Ways of Lincoln Electric," *Traffic Management* (May, 1966).
[32]*Ibid.*
[33]James F. Lincoln, *Incentive Management* (Cleveland: The Lincoln Electric Company, 1951; 4th printing, 1957).
[34]*Ibid.*
[35]*Ibid.*

Mr. Lincoln defines incentive management as a philosophy of life translated into productivity. However, he repeatedly stresses: "*An enthusiastic organization should use the powers latent in all the individuals to a common end.*" This is important since each individual is essential to the business and all the individuals are complementary in their work. Therefore, all should be provided with full incentive opportunities.

Quoting Mr. Lincoln once again:

> The Lincoln bonus is the extra reward that can come from cooperation, skill, development of latent ability and desire to use these abilities for the best interests of those involved, i.e., consumer, worker and owner.[36]

Nature of the Lincoln Plan. At the heart of Lincoln Electric's operation there are three basic ideas that combine to create an intangible climate of self-interest and incentive:

1. To make better welding equipment to sell at lower prices. Profits will follow. Prices are established in relation to manufacturing cost, and as costs are reduced, prices are cut. Profits — after taxes, reserves, and dividend — are distributed to all employees in a year-end cash bonus.
2. Guaranteed employment. The company does not lay off workers. . . . It is policy to contract the number of hours of work — not to reduce employment.
3. Recognition of the individual in proportion to what he contributes.[37]

The incentive management program at Lincoln provides the foundation for the company's cost reduction program. This program, applied in every department of the company's operations, has reduced costs so that selling prices have been lowered in many cases. The firm has realized many economies by limiting costs to the essentials and getting along without a lot of trimmings. Its offices are plain and functional. There is no executive dining room. Expendable paper work is ruthlessly eliminated, as are time- and labor-consuming tasks that do not contribute to the final product. The plan has demonstrated that incentives, when properly applied, can solve many of industry's problems and bring higher wages to the worker, a steady return to the stockholder, and lower prices to the customer. From 1934 to 1967, employees received a total of $170 million in bonuses, or a little over $5 million a year. [38] The stockholders generally receive an annual dividend in excess of 6 percent of book value, while prices of some products are at 1934 levels. Such benefits result from the fact that each employee knows that his earnings are limited only by the extent of his contribution to the success of

---

[36]*Ibid.*, p. 111.

[37]A. N. Wecksler, "A Case Study of the Lincoln Electric Co.," *Incentive Management — The Lincoln Electric Company's Approach to Cutting Costs and Reduced Selling Prices*, CO-1 (Cleveland: Lincoln Electric Co., January, 1966), p. 2.

[38]Information received in a letter to the authors on August 28, 1968, from Charles G. Herbruck, assistant secretary of the Lincoln Electric Company.

the company as a whole. Cooperation between employees and management is so good that new machines and work changes are readily accepted because these mean increased production, which leads to larger bonuses.

In line with their policy of rewarding the individual in proportion to his contribution to the firm, most production employees are paid on straight piece-work. Basic wages rates are established by a committee of supervisors using a job evaluation procedure that measures each job according to the demands it makes upon the employee. Each employee's contribution (engineers, production workers, supervisors, etc.) is evaluated by a merit rating program that measures the employee's actual job performance. Each employee is rated twice a year on four equally weighted factors: workmanship (quality), ideas (improvements), output (quantity), and supervision (required). There is a separate rating card for each factor since the worker's foreman rates him on supervision. The production department rates output, the inspection department rates workmanship, and the methods department rates ideas and cooperation. The overall rating assists in determining an employee's cash bonus and his opportunities for promotion.

In addition to the motivation of employees through direct wages, there are several other incentives that play an important part in Lincoln's incentive management program. This program has a guaranteed continuous employment plan that guarantees every employee who has been with the firm for two years, continuous employment for 49 weeks each year with a minimum of 30 hours of work each week.[39] The remaining weeks are a paid vacation for those with proper tenure. Then, too, the firm makes all promotions from within the organization and strictly on the basis of merit. Seniority does not count. This shows a high regard for people and tends to develop respect, cooperation, and teamwork among all employees. This results in confidence and mutual trust between management and the employees, which is said to be one of the main reasons for the success of their incentive plan. No doubt, Mr. Lincoln's labor-management creed of "We do not distinguish between so-called management and labor. All management must labor and labor must manage"[40] had a great deal to do with developing this harmonious relationship. Other methods that Lincoln uses to motivate employees include a stock purchase plan, a chance to be elected to an advisory board, and a system of organizing work that lets many plant employees function almost as independent subcontractors.

The reader may wonder whether Lincoln's policy of promotion from within causes ingrown problems and dying incentives. Mr. Charles Herbruck, assistant secretary of Lincoln, says, "Since we are constantly cutting prices we make it impossible for employees to earn the same bonus with the same effort since the price cuts would reduce income. Thus we go beyond the ordinary concept of

[39]William Irrgang, "Incentive Management in Action," *Assembly Engineering* (March, 1967).

[40]Wecksler, *op. cit.*

profit sharing. We have a goal we never reach, a constant spur and a constant incentive." [41]

The Piece-Rate Plan. The individual incentive plan, as such, is a piece-rate plan with a guaranteed day rate. It has been satisfactory to workers and management since its installation in 1914. Certain jobs, generally considered as "unmeasurable," have been closely analyzed, standardized, and included in the piece-rate incentive system. Motion and time study experts have set time standards and the money units for piece rates. If a worker is not satisfied, he can challenge the piece rate. The challenge is handled by a special committee including the worker, the time-study man, the foreman, and the personnel director. If the operator is still not convinced, the time-study man runs the job himself for a day or two. His reestablished time — either as originally set, higher, or lower — is then accepted as standard.

Piece rates are never cut unless the method is legitimately changed, the parts are redesigned, retooling occurs, or the job is reevaluated. Strict inspection maintains quality. A worker guards against any lessening of quality and quantity of work since his annual bonus suffers accordingly.

The Year-End Bonus. The amount of money available for the year-end bonus is the balance of money remaining after provision for taxes and reserves, and after the regular 6 percent dividend to stockholders is deducted. The size of an employee's bonus is dependent upon three factors: his merit rating, his base wage or salary, and the amount of money in the bonus pool. Each person's actual bonus is arrived at by multiplying his base wage or salary by his merit rating and then multiplying this by the bonus factor. The bonus factor is the dollars of total bonus pool divided by dollars of total company payroll.

During the years 1935 to 1950, employee bonuses varied from a minimum 20 percent of the annual wages to a maximum of 128 percent each year. For the past several years it has ranged between 80–100 percent of the entire payroll. Table 18.2 on page 500 compares the average hourly earnings (bonuses included) of employees at Lincoln Electric with all manufacturing industries. In 1966 the bonus amounted to a total of $16,100,000, which when divided by some 1,976 employees, comes out to an average of $8,148 each. In 1967, $14,738,000 was divided by 1,912 employees for an average bonus of $7,708 per employee.

The Rucker Share-of-Production Plan

The Rucker share-of-production plan is based on the mathematically measurable relationship between production value added by manufacture and the total compensation of employees, direct and indirect labor combined. The

[41]John Fisher, "Lincoln Electric Price Reductions Attributed to Cost Cutting Program," *Lincguard/Multiguard Electric Motor News* (January 15, 1964).

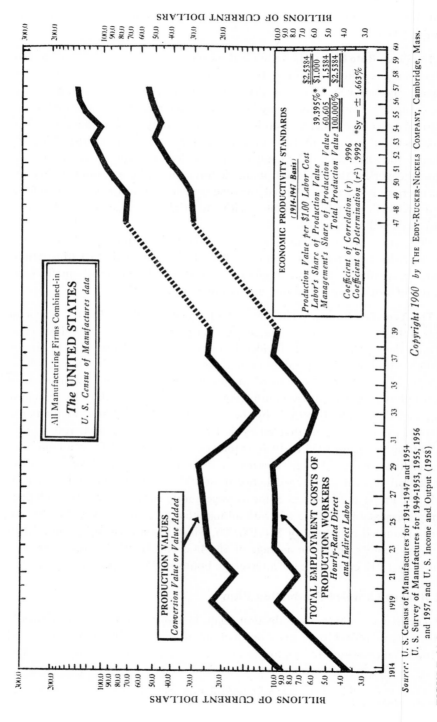

BILLIONS OF CURRENT DOLLARS

All Manufacturing Firms Combined—in
The **UNITED STATES**
U. S. Census of Manufactures data

PRODUCTION VALUES
Conversion Value or Value Added

**TOTAL EMPLOYMENT COSTS OF
PRODUCTION WORKERS**
*Hourly-Rated Direct
and Indirect Labor*

ECONOMIC PRODUCTIVITY STANDARDS
(1914-1947 Basis)

Production Value per $1.00 Labor Cost		$2.5384
Labor's Share of Production Value	39.395% *	$1.000
Management's Share of Production Value	60.605 *	1.5384
Total Production Value	100.000%	$2.5384
Coefficient of Correlation (r)	.9996	
Coefficient of Determination (r²)	.9992	*Sy = ± 1.663%

Source: U. S. Census of Manufactures for 1914-1947 and 1954
U. S. Survey of Manufactures for 1949-1953, 1955, 1956
and 1957, and U. S. Income and Output (1958)

Copyright 1960 by THE EDDY-RUCKER-NICKELS COMPANY, Cambridge, Mass.

FIGURE 20.2 RATIO CHART — THE RUCKER SHARE-OF-PRODUCTION PRINCIPLE. Annual production values and annual employment costs, 1914 to 1957.

principle is also equally as adaptable to incentives for salaried personnel, executive, professional, midmanagement, and sales teams. The economic productivity of each employee "team" is measured monthly against a predetermined standard; incentive payments of the "team" are prorated among individuals on the basis of their individual regular monthly earnings (including overtime premium). The plan integrates improvements in physical output per man-hour; savings in materials; improvement in quality; and reduction in rejects, rework, and absenteeism.

From his research based on the official records of the U. S. Census of Manufactures for the census years 1899 to 1929, Allen W. Rucker discovered in 1932 that:

> *Factory payrolls are directly proportionate to factory Production Value. Factory payrolls year after year are a near-constant simple percentage of Production Value.*[42]

This relationship is graphically shown in the ratio chart, Figure 20.2, based on the official data of the U.S. Census of Manufactures for the years 1914 to 1957. Note that "labor's" share of production value is consistently 39.4 percent within narrow limits of deviation for all years. The empirical data of the official census confirm the Rucker principle or "law" that labor's pay is proportionate to *economic* (money) productivity. This same principle operates in individual businesses, regardless of industry, geographical location, or currency used in a foreign country. Figure 20.3 illustrates three different industries of several hundred studied in the United States and other countries.

The Rucker plan is the individually engineered application of the "share-of-production" principle for each enterprise, mutually deliberated and approved by employer and employees. The standards for the plan in each plant are determined by an Economic-Engineering Audit that covers three to five years of operating experience, with at least two of the years on a monthly basis. The Audit establishes the standard economic productivity or productivity ratio, and the respective percentage shares for the employee team and for management of economic productivity as 100 percent. The standard ratio or economic productivity is the dollar amount of production value output per $1 of regular compensation input.

Assume that the standard ratio or economic productivity is $3.10 per $1 of regular pay, including fringe benefits. Assume that the actual payroll for a given month is $100,200; then that figure multiplied by the standard productivity ratio of $3.10 shows that the plant's required production value in that month must be $310,620 to earn the regular payroll, and in excess of that figure to earn incentive

---

[42]*Progress in Productivity and Pay, All Manufactures Combined* (Cambridge, Mass.: The Eddy-Rucker-Nickels Company, 1952; prior publications, 1934 and 1937). Also, *The Rucker Plan,* same source, 1957.

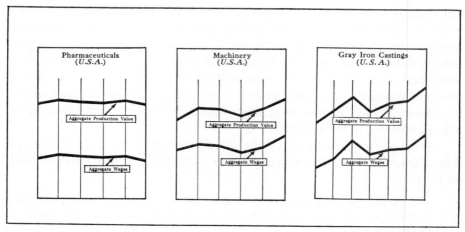

FIGURE 20.3   THE RUCKER SHARE-OF-PRODUCTION PRINCIPLE IN INDIVIDUAL COMPANIES (BEFORE INSTALLATION OF THE RUCKER PLAN). Shares of production value vary from industry to industry, but within each industry, production value is near constant.

pay. Assume that the actual production value is $400,700. Subtract from this figure the standard required production value: $400,700 — $310,620 = $90,080, the gain over standard. This gain is shared between the employee team according to its predetermined standard share of 32.26 percent and the company according to its predetermined standard share of 67.74 percent. The two percentage shares always total 100 percent of the improvement. In this example, the employee share of the gain is $29,060 and the company share is $61,020. The company share covers any *added* salaried compensation, noncompensation variable expenses other than materials and supplies, fixed charges such as depreciation, as well as property and income taxes, insurance, together with *added* profit.

The productivity earnings of the employee team, $29,060 in this example, are distributed to individual participants as follows: one fourth of the gain in any month is carried to a Reserve Account; the remaining three-fourths gain is distributed pro rata to each individual according to his own individual regular pay (including overtime and shift differential) in that month. At the end of the year, the Reserve Account is balanced by offsetting the credits as described above by any debits resulting from months (if any) in which economic productivity was below standard. At the year-end, the net balance is distributed pro rata to participants, thus assuring them of receiving their full standard percentage share of production value for the year.

The Rucker share-of-production plan has long been used in such companies as Reznor Manufacturing Company, Mercer, Pennsylvania; Lockwood Manufacturing Company, Cincinnati, Ohio; Pohlman Foundry Company, Incorporated, Buffalo, New York; Dusing & Hunt, Incorporated, Leroy, New York; Sealol Manufacturing Company, Providence, Rhode Island; Morton Manufacturing Company, Muskegon Heights; and many others, including firms in Canada, England, Germany, and Japan. The plan has more lately been applied by Mr. Rucker to multiplant operations such as American Can Company and Hewitt-Robins, Incorporated, as an executive and midmanagement incentive.

Models of group nonfinancial incentive plans

Within the last decade, several new types of group nonfinancial incentive plans have been developed. Two examples of these are described below.

Zero Defects

A very popular and country-wide program that has been adopted by over 800 companies as a nonfinancial incentive to spur employees on to improve the quality of goods and services produced is called the *Zero Defects plan.*[43] The Zero Defects concept attempts to reduce defective parts and products to its lowest point (zero). The plan is a motivational program aimed at developing a constant, conscious effort on the part of each employee to improve performance continually in accomplishing his job so that he will do it correctly the first time. Someone has described the program as the personal search for perfection by everyone. The program has a number of other labels or titles, including PRIDE, which stands for Personal Responsibility in Daily Effort; VIP, Value in Performance; COMPETE, Customer Orders Mean Protection of Earnings Through Efficiency; and AIM, Attack Individual Mistakes.[44] The Zero Defect (ZD) technique utilizes what the sociologists call group motivation to get individuals within the group to assign the same importance to their industrial activities as they do to their personal affairs. Through the ZD program, various nonmonetary rewards are established to convince each employee that his every effort toward excellence is needed for his own good and that of the firm's. In this concept a major effort is made to return to the old craftsman's concept of "pride in workmanship" with rewards for achievers, but no punishment for slackers.

According to the United States Army Material Command in Washington, D.C., the ZD program began in 1962 as a joint venture between the Martin Company and the United States Army Missile Command at Redstone Arsenal.[45] In 1963 the Martin Company at Orlando, Florida, was reported to have reduced hardware defects by 54 percent and in 1964 an additional 25 percent drop which has, in total, saved the firm $1,650,000.[46] The ZD program has spread to other defense and space firms where special emphasis has been placed on increased quality and reliability of their products. It has also been adopted by Ford and

---

[43]"More ZD Reports," *Quality Assurance* (August, 1965), p. 21.
[44]"How ZD Gets That Way," *Quality Assurance* (September, 1965), p. 24.
[45]*Ibid.*
[46]*Ibid.*

Chrysler and is especially helpful to those firms that are offering greater warranties on their products (Chrysler's 50,000 mile or five-year guarantee on cars, Motorola's full year on TV sets, etc.)

Glen A. Gray, Jr., the National ZD coordinator and an employee at the Firestone Tire and Rubber Company in Akron, Ohio, had this to say after his firm was well into their second year of the ZD program:

> "Everyone benefits from Zero Defects" is a slogan at Firestone. The customer gains in increased confidence in Firestone products; the company wins higher product quality and better motivated employees; the worker receives personal satisfaction from having done his job well and the management achieves both more economical and productive operations. . . . Tangible benefits . . . (at Firestone) include: reduction of waste, material handling and repair.[47]

Although there are a great number of different approaches as to how to conduct ZD programs, the following steps are suggested by Mazel as guides for planning, implementing, and following up a ZD program:[48]

> (1) Decide to go with a Zero Defects program, (2) Select a Zero Defects administrator, (3) Organize a Zero Defects committee, (4) Plan the Zero Defects program carefully, (5) Brief the management personnel first, (6) Indoctrinate the supervisors next, (7) Confide in Union officials (enlist their support), (8) Publicize Zero Defects (posters, dinners, teaser campaign), (9) Start with a bang on kick-off day, (10) Obtain employee support (voluntary stressed, pledge cards used), (11) Institute "error cause removal" (employee invited to point out sources of error), (12) Record and recognize achievements (awards, charts, plaques, trophies, pins, etc.), (13) Sustain the Zero Defects concept (follow-up, pep-up, competition).

Critics of the ZD program point out the following possible weaknesses:

1. It is difficult to try to motivate workers fully all the time by the use of a single program.
2. The program is based on the assumption that all defects are only *worker* oriented.
3. It is very difficult to establish a system of rating employees in nonproductive areas.
4. It is difficult to appraise the value of the program because of the many hidden costs in terms of time, staff, etc.

Like most other programs designed to motivate employees, ZD should be considered as only one of those tools that meet the needs of employees and a firm for a period of time. Like any other tool it eventually wears out and must be repaired or replaced. No single tool is ever a cure-all for all of management's

---

[47]"Zero Defects: Is It Just a Passing Fad?" *Factory* (now *Modern Management*) (January, 1967), p. 14.

[48]J. L. Mazel, "ZD: Countdown to Perfection," *Factory* (now *Modern Management*) (July, 1965), pp. 66–71.

problems. There is no reason why the ZD concept cannot be applied to all the employees in the firm and some analysis of its costs made to determine its value to the firm. If a ZD program leads to improved job performance, better motivated employees, and greater economical operations of the firm, it is serving a valuable purpose. However, each management will still need to determine whether the overall benefits are worth the costs.

Armstrong Cork PRIDE Program[49]

The Armstrong Cork PRIDE program is an application of the Zero Defects concept. It does not use any financial rewards but relies on social rather than economic motivation. The program may be considered a total systems motivational device having the following objectives: (1) to establish specific performance improvement goals, (2) to improve plant performance, and (3) to get 100 percent participation. The PRIDE program was initiated at the Pensacola plant in 1965. Introductory meetings, which all employees attended, were held on company time. At these meetings talks were given by the plant manager, sales manager, and assistant plant manager. Booklets, bulletins, posters, and other publicity on PRIDE, produced by a Pensacola consultant, were prominent throughout the company at this time. Several days after this meeting a plant open house was held for employees and their families. Posters, mobiles, cutouts, and giveaways, all centered on the PRIDE program, were widely used.

One week later the supervisors introduced the program to their individual crews. The supervisors held individual conferences with each employee to try to: (1) sell the employees on the program and get their support, (2) discuss their jobs with employees, (3) sell the employees on error-free performance, (4) tell them about the CARE program — (Cause and Removal of Errors), (5) ask them to set standards for themselves, (6) ask them to check on performance improvement, and (7) tell them their job will be reviewed again in three months.

Some of the publicity materials specially designed and used in the program were: a large roadway plant banner; billboards on the road to the plant and in parking lots; bulletin board posters; large easel posters throughout the plant; newspaper, radio, and television publicity; sound slide films on the PRIDE program; and special PRIDE key chains, coin purses, buttons, and puzzles distributed periodically to all employees.

The CARE program, an important part of PRIDE, involves the employee as follows:

1. When the employee identifies an error, he tells the supervisor.
2. The supervisor records it, corrects it if he can, and notifies the employee within three days.

---

[49]Information was obtained from the *Wisconsin Productivity Letter*, No. 2 (Madison, Wisconsin: Center for the Study of Productivity Motivation, University of Wisconsin, 1967), pp. 3–4. Permission has been granted to quote this material.

3. If the error cannot be corrected by the supervisor, the employee fills out a CARE form and submits it to the PRIDE committee.
4. If the committee can solve the problem, it notifies the employee through his supervisor.
5. If the committee cannot solve the problem, it sends the problem to the appropriate department and notifies the employee.
6. The department head takes action to correct the error.
7. The committee informs the employee's supervisor of the action.
8. The supervisor informs the employee of the action.
9. If the employee disagrees with the solution, he can notify the committee through his supervisor.

The company also uses a Suggestion for Progress program, a standard employee suggestion system. Keeping the PRIDE program "alive" is a major problem, and to sustain employees' interest, new ideas and continual publicity are needed.

Mr. R. W. Kievit, the Pensacola plant production planning manager, in commenting on the success of their program said, "In my opinion the most beneficial part of the program is the individual supervisor-employee contacts provided, particularly in departments where a foreman may supervise 30 or 40 men and have only infrequent personal contacts with some of them." [50]

REVIEW QUESTIONS

1. What factors appear to be responsible for the trend toward group incentive plans?
2. What advantages do group incentive plans have over individual incentive plans?
3. What are some of the limitations of group incentive plans?
4. What is the essence of the theory of group incentive plans?
5. Why would a company want to share profits with its employees?
6. Identify the various methods or plans for sharing profits and indicate the chief advantages of each.
7. (a) What advantages does a profit-sharing plan have over other group incentive plans? (b) What limitations does it have?
8. What prerequisites are necessary for a successful profit-sharing plan?
9. (a) What are the essential differences between the Rucker and the Scanlon plans? (b) between the Rucker and the Lincoln plans?
10. Is the philosophy of the Scanlon plan acceptable to you? Why? Why not?
11. (a) What do you like about the Kaiser Steel long-range sharing plan? (b) What do you dislike about it?

---

[50] In personal letter to authors on August 25, 1967.

12. State why you agree or disagree with James F. Lincoln's statement that "The primary goal of any industry, to be successful continuously, must be to make a better and better product to be sold to more and more people at a lower and lower price."

13. What are the main ideas behind the Lincoln Electric incentive plan?

RESEARCH OR SEMINAR QUESTIONS

1. Your company has just heard about a new office machine that can perform the work of three clerks more quickly, accurately, and economically. Top management has tentatively decided to purchase six of these machines because it believes they will be beneficial to the company. Your management has no intention of discharging any of the clerks that the machine might replace.

The president of your company has requested you to recommend the course of action that should be followed to make the change. Prepare an outline of the procedure to be followed and the reasons for each suggestion you make.

2. Gather whatever evidence you can to argue the point that employees have a "right" to share in the profits of a firm.

3. Of the various types of incentive plans you know, under which type would you prefer to work? Why?

4. What effect will union demands for a profit-sharing plan have upon management compensation?

5. Rising profits, accompanying increased productivity, are a sign of labor's working better and faster; and, as a result, labor should be given the difference in their pay envelopes. Discuss this concept in relation to a just return on capital investment, mechanical innovations, raw material costs, and improved working conditions (fringes).

6. Contrast the theory of group incentive plans to the theory of individual incentive plans.

7. Discuss the pros and cons of sharing profits with the stockholders versus the employees.

PRACTICAL EXPERIENCE ASSIGNMENTS

1. Your company has recently switched from individual to group incentives. Some employees are now receiving less incentive pay than they received under the old incentive program. You, as the department supervisor, are requested to prepare an explanation that will be directed in writing to all department employees.

2. Visit a business or industrial concern that is known to provide financial incentives for indirect labor. Learn what you can about the classes of employees covered, how their incentive standards are set, and what the company feels are the benefits being derived from the program. Be prepared to give a three-minute report to the class on the highlights of your visit.

3. Members of a production group in plant Q have been given the chance to work under a group incentive plan. There are 12 men in this group, each doing different work on the same project. One of the group members is "Pop" Daily, who is to retire in five years. He is opposed to this program because of the required speed-up. Members of the group say they will be penalized because of "Pop's" refusal to try to achieve maximum output. How could this situation be cleared up?

4. Contact a firm that has had experience with the Zero Defects program and learn what you can about its success and failures at this company. Be prepared to give a report to your classmates on the highlights of your plant contact.

5. For the past three years, Company L has been on a profit-sharing bonus payment plan. During this time, low profits have made only small bonuses available. The plan has increased production, but sales have dropped off slightly. The union is demanding a swing back to a straight-time wage payment plan. How would you as the director of wages handle this?

CASE PROBLEM

20–1. THE GREENLEAF MANUFACTURING COMPANY

Need of Indirect-Labor Incentives

The Greenleaf Manufacturing Company, established by Mr. Arthur Greenleaf in 1940, is located in the Middle West. It specializes in the manufacture of small tractors, gasoline motors, pumps, and a variety of other small machinery.

The company employs 800 shop workers. Of these, 75 percent comprise direct labor of semiskilled and unskilled operators who are paid on a wage-incentive plan. The 200 workers producing indirect labor consist of high-grade machinists, toolmakers, setup men, electricians, and maintenance men. While the wage-base rates of indirect-labor workers are higher than those for direct-labor workers, nevertheless, in many cases the "take-home" pay of indirect-labor workers does not equal that earned by the semiskilled workers paid on the incentive plan.

At a wage bargaining meeting, the union representatives claimed that the wage and salary structure is distorted. They argued that the take-home pay of indirect-labor workers should be in proportion to their wage-base rates, and should be considerably higher than that of direct-labor workers.

One recommendation made by union representatives is to pay the indirect-labor mechanics a bonus equivalent to the percentage of extra earnings by direct labor. That is, assume that the direct-labor workers earn 25 percent more than their total wage-base rate earnings. Then, the indirect-labor workers should be paid 25 percent of their wage-base rates in addition to the day-rate earnings.

Mr. George Knoll, the plant manager, opposes the recommendations in the belief that the additional cost of indirect labor will far exceed its contributions. Mr. John Herter, the personnel manager, also vigorously objected to such recommendations on the basis that it will bring endless grievances and complaints from the direct-labor personnel. He cited instances when direct-labor workers did not produce above standard, either because of incompetence or deliberate unwillingness to produce more than the average performance standard calls for.

Mr. Arthur Greenleaf, the president, agrees wholeheartedly with the plant and personnel managers. He feels that the actual performance of indirect-labor jobs should be measured, standards established, and the additional earnings of indirect labor based on increased output as established by some incentive plan. He insists that only then can the higher earnings be equitably distributed.

Problems:

As the wage and salary administrator, you are asked to study the pros and cons, and discuss the setting of standards to establish an incentive plan for about 200 indirect-labor workers. You are to report your findings and recommendations at the next union-management meeting. State the feasibility and the necessary conditions required to install a plan. Indicate the reasons why you recommend the plan you have selected and briefly explain how you propose to carry out the installation.

chapter 21

THE ADOPTION, INSTALLATION, AND MAINTENANCE OF INCENTIVE PLANS

The purpose of this chapter is to offer guidelines in the selection, installation, and continuance of whatever incentive plans that a firm may wish to use. Before adopting any kind of program, special consideration should be given to what the firm hopes to accomplish. Many questions are usually raised that call for careful consideration if a plan is to succeed. Questions like these are usually asked: What is the firm trying to achieve? Is this a short-range goal or a long-range goal? Should a ready-made plan be adopted or should an individualized plan be prepared? How will the employees react? Will the union favor the plan? Will management personnel back it and be able to administer it? Who should be charged with its installation and maintenance?

A discussion of these and similar questions will be brought into focus by a treatment of the following topics which may be used as guidelines in the adoption, installation, and maintenance of an incentive plan: (1) the decision to adopt a plan, (2) the selection of an incentive plan, (3) installing an incentive plan, and (4) maintaining an incentive plan.

The decision to adopt an incentive plan

If an incentive plan of compensation is ever to be established, someone must make a decision that a plan is needed. No plan is likely to succeed unless the decision is either made by, or backed by, top management and the union.

Why should a firm be interested in an incentive plan? Most sound managements today realize that employees are the major differences in the varying degrees of success of different firms. Therefore, most incentive plans attempt, in some way, to motivate employees to perform at greater efficiency so that the firm and its employees can look forward to greater security and rewards. Or an incentive system may be an attempt to correct or improve a weakness in the firm. More specifically, incentive plans have been adopted for such reasons as: (1) to increase competitiveness and profits through increased productivity, (2) to increase employee earnings, (3) to decrease material and labor unit costs, and (4) to correct a weak pay system, strengthen a firm's financial position, or improve employee-employer relations. In short, there must be some reason or need to adopt an incentive system, and the need must be recognized by all those who will have a hand in making it a success or a failure.

Once a tentative objective or reason has been established for accomplishment by an incentive system, some type of feasibility study should be made of the firm's conditions to determine the possible benefits and shortcomings that would result by a decision to adopt an incentive plan. The study should attempt to answer such questions as: How much will an incentive plan increase productivity, employee pay, and profits? What will it cost to establish and maintain an incentive program? How long will it take to become effective? How long is it likely to remain effective? Will it have a high chance of success? How will business conditions affect the plan? What will be the effect of an incentive plan on the following: the firm's image, employee morale, labor turnover, unit costs, product prices, and the firm's competitors, customers, and stockholders? What will be the total costs to achieve the objectives? Will the benefits gained be worth the total costs incurred?

Before deciding to adopt a plan to achieve one or more objectives, it should be made clear that no incentive plan can ever hope to work successfully for any length of time unless employees respect and trust management and vice versa. If employee-employer relations cannot meet this test, the incentive plan will fail unless the causes for the poor relationship are removed. If management has alienated employee cooperation for one reason or another or if management has been too dictatorial, there has to be a decided change in management thinking and a willingness on its part to establish a company environment that is conducive to employee cooperation. In some firms this has meant the sharing of decisions with employees as well as the sharing of responsibilities. No incentive can be a substitute for past poor management unless past poor management practices are eliminated or changed for the better.

Any decision to adopt incentives must have advantages to employees as well as to management. This means that employee needs and desires must be considered whenever they are expected to cooperate in any pay plan. If employees do not either see or believe that a plan is worthwhile to them, the plan has little chance of succeeding. If employees are to believe in the incentive system, it has to measure up to the goals and benefits established; otherwise the employees will not be convinced of its merits. Management cannot expect to get employee acceptance by edict.

In short, all the various factors that have a bearing on the healthy relationship between employees and management need to be appraised to determine whether any incentive plan has a reasonable chance of succeeding. It would appear that discussions with employees are required to learn their reactions and attitudes toward any contemplated incentive system. Unless employees show a strong desire for an incentive plan and a willingness to make it succeed, it has little chance of succeeding.

The selection of an incentive plan

After the decision has been made to adopt some kind of incentive system to accomplish some specific objective, it is necessary to review the various kinds of incentive systems available to determine which one comes the closest to fitting the firm's needs and circumstances. It is unlikely that any known incentive plan can perfectly fit another firm's needs. This means that there must be some modification or tailoring of a plan to fit another company.

In selecting an incentive plan there are two basic forms to consider — the individual type and the group or plant-wide type. It is possible to use both types since they are compatible with each other. Although individual incentives are treated in greater detail in Chapter 19 and group incentives in Chapter 20, Table 21.1 contains a summary of the basic characteristics, advantages, and limitations of each.

The reader should bear in mind that although an individual-type incentive plan pays a limited number of individual employees extra pay for their physical efforts that result in extra productivity, the plan is generally limited to this feature. On the other hand, the group incentive plans not only do what the individual incentive plan can do but also offer extra pay when any one of the following conditions takes place: when improved machines reduce labor costs; when red tape and administrative expenses are reduced; when quality is improved; when product prices are increased; when fewer or less costly raw materials or parts are needed; or when outside supplies and service costs are reduced. Conversely, because the group incentive plans offer extra opportunities to earn extra pay, they also provide a number of circumstances that can limit the earning of extra pay. For example, if any of the following circumstances were to take place, the employees would find their opportunities for earning extra pay curtailed: when competition forces product prices down; when basic labor costs (and fringes) are increased; when consumers or competitors force higher quality standards on company products; when plant equipment and technical progress

TABLE 21.1   **605**

A COMPARISON BETWEEN INDIVIDUAL INCENTIVES AND GROUP INCENTIVES

Items of Comparison	Incentives	
	Individual	Group and Plant Wide
BASIC CHARACTERISTICS	Rewards are based on individual performance in number of units produced per hour.	Rewards are based on group performance in number of dollars saved or increased (in profits, sales values, production value added by manufacturer, or prime costs).
	Performance (output) needs to be within the direct control of the individual.	Performance is often only indirectly controlled by employees.
	The industrial engineer usually determines performance standards.	A committee is most likely used to determine performance standards.
	Rewards are forthcoming every pay period.	Rewards are forthcoming on a monthly, quarterly, semiannual, or annual basis.
	Encourages individuality and competition.	Encourages teamwork and unity.
	Relies heavily on monetary rewards.	May have nonfinancial as well as financial rewards.
BASIC ADVANTAGES	Appeals to individualists. Rewards employees in direct proportion to their productivity. Provides fairly accurate cost data for estimating job costs.	Motivates large numbers of employees. Useful on a wide variety of tasks. Draws employee and firm goals together. Can include all employees in firm. Administrative costs are minimal. Does not resist technological change. Employees cooperate in solving problems that arise. Provides continuous opportunities for employees to be constructive and to satisfy many of their needs.
BASIC LIMITATIONS	Rarely includes all employees. Restricted to mass-produced, relatively simple operations. Causes a number of grievances. Has been limited to physical output. Not very adaptable to high-quality jobs. Difficult to get agreement on job standards. Employees do not cooperate in policing system. Extra records and costs are incurred. Difficult to maintain over the long run.	Does not reward each employee according to his exact productivity.

fall behind their competitors; or when raw materials and supplies or outside services go up in costs. The above sets of circumstances would not affect individual earnings under an individual piece-rate incentive plan. Under the individual incentive plan, the company would either absorb the increased costs or pocket any savings made.

In considering the basic group incentive plans that generally center around the sharing of costs, sales values or production values, or profit, the following summary pinpoints some of their main differences. The *cost-savings sharing plan* can be thought of as an extension of the usual individual piece-rate plan applied to a group, thus extending the employee coverage of the plan. The intent of this plan is to share those savings on costs that make up a job or a product. It often covers only the cost of labor (quantity of production) that is within the control of the employees. However, it can and often does include a sharing of costs that are saved on the reduced amounts of materials and supplies used in the plant. It is not usually related to product price changes, basic wage rates, the cost of raw materials outside the plant, or machine improvements. In the *sales-value sharing plan* employees attempt to reduce the percentage of labor costs (payroll) of the total value of sales. Savings under this plan can be made through quality improvements, better methods, and through equipment (machine) improvements, in addition to any increased savings made through greater quantities produced. Whatever savings are made through this plan are usually shared with the company. Sales-value sharing generally protects employees from material wastage and material price changes outside the plant but does not protect them from price changes of the product to be sold. In the *production-value sharing plan*, employees share with the company the value they add in manufacturing the product. Employees can add value (and thus make production savings) on all the items included in both the cost-savings sharing plan and the sales-value sharing plan (increasing the quantity of production; reducing costs of materials and supplies, within and outside the plant; and in improving product quality, methods, and equipment) and through increases in product price to the customer. In the *profit-sharing incentive plan*, employees share with the company a part of the firm's profits. A company's profits, of course, are based on an almost limitless number of factors within and outside the firm. Therefore, the profit-sharing plan offers the most comprehensive list of items in which to make savings that can ultimately affect profits. Profit sharing would include not only opportunities for savings through the various items that have previously been mentioned in the other three group incentive plans but also savings made in office costs and general administrative expenses for research, engineering, selling, depreciation, and interest, etc. There is really no limit as to what can be done within the firm to eliminate waste or the inefficiency of time, labor, materials, costs and the like in order to increase the profits to be shared.

Profit-sharing plans can be found in a very wide array of firms, large and small, and in different industries. They would appear to have a good chance of succeeding where union-management relations are at least satisfactory and where there is a reasonable expectation that profits will continue and can be increased. Profits would have a good chance of increasing in a firm having high labor costs and where employees are anxious to cut these costs through more efficient methods. Profit sharing would appear to have less of a chance of succeeding in a new firm with no record of profits or in a highly competitive industry where profits are generally slim or regulated by the government. Certainly a profit-sharing plan should not be considered in a closely held firm or in one where some of the members of the management team believed that employees have no rights to profits.

In the various sharing plans that are based primarily on labor cost sharing, it would appear that their best chances for success would be in firms where the work force can influence the labor cost. In other words, a value-added sharing plan should be installed where the direct and indirect labor groups can potentially do something to improve quality, reduce scrap, increase output, save time, save material, or save supplies. On the other hand, if the work force can do little about these elements by virtue, say, of a highly automated or a process-type industry, such a program should most likely not be used. Labor-cost sharing plans have been especially workable in some firms having financial troubles due partly to the high labor costs. Sharing plans would most likely be disappointing in firms where the labor costs are negligible.

Robert C. Scott, a vice-president of The Eddy-Rucker-Nickels Company, Cambridge, Massachusetts, has identified a number of considerations that he believes are important in the selection of an incentive plan. In Table 21.2, Mr. Scott shows how labor and material variances affect incentive payments, and, in Table 21.3, how material and product price changes affect incentives.[1] The data in Tables 21.1, 21.2, and 21.3 need to be studied very carefully before a specific incentive plan is selected. Each firm needs to identify its own set of circumstances to determine which type of incentive plan is most suitable for adoption in its plant. No matter which incentive plan is adopted, there should be ample evidence that the plan will be able to pay a regular bonus continually and a determination on the part of all employees involved that they will get behind the plan to do everything in their power to make it a success. If a group incentive plan is to be adopted, it is most important that a sense of partnership and trust be developed. When this is achieved, the type of incentive plan selected is probably of secondary importance.

---

[1]R. C. Scott, *Incentives in Manufacturing: Individual and Plant* (Cambridge, Mass.: The Eddy-Rucker-Nickels Co., 1966), Vol. 2, Parts 6–11; Table 21.2 is found on p. 16; Table 21.3 is found on p. 22. Reprinted with permission from Mr. Scott.

TABLE 21.2

HOW LABOR AND MATERIAL VARIANCES AFFECT INCENTIVE PAYMENTS

WHAT HAPPENS IF — ?	WITHOUT INCENTIVE	WITH INDIVIDUAL INCENTIVES	WITH PLANT-WIDE PROFIT SHARING	WITH PLANT-WIDE SALES VALUE SHARING	WITH PLANT-WIDE PRODUCTION VALUE SHARING	WITH PLANT-WIDE COST SAVINGS SHARING
A. Labor cost is HIGHER than normal or wage rates are increased.	Company absorbs all the excess.	Company absorbs all the excess.	Incentive pool is hurt by the profit-sharing formula percent (generally 10–20%). Company absorbs the remainder of the excess.	The entire excess labor cost comes out of the incentive pool built up on all other work in the plant.	The entire excess labor cost comes out of the incentive pool built up on all other work in the plant.	Incentive pool is hurt by the formula percent (generally 50%). Company absorbs the remainder of the excess.
B. Labor cost is LOWER than estimated or normal.	Company keeps all the gain.	After paying direct workers, usually ALL the savings on their time, the Company keeps any gain from Indirect Labor.	Incentive pool is helped by the profit-sharing formula percent (generally 10–20%). Company keeps the remainder of savings.	The entire payroll saving goes into the incentive pool, subject to possible losses from other work in the plant and to plant-wide wage or benefit increases.	The entire payroll saving goes into the incentive pool, subject to possible losses from other work in the plant and to plant-wide wage or benefit increases.	Incentive pool is helped by the formula percent (generally 50%). Company keeps the remainder of savings.
C. Material use or cost is HIGHER than estimated or normal.	Company absorbs all the excess.	Company absorbs all the excess.	Incentive pool is hurt by the profit-sharing formula percent (generally 10–20%). Company absorbs the remainder of the excess.	Company absorbs all the excess. (The use of Sales Value as the output measure eliminates material use from control by the incentive.)	Incentive pool is hurt by the formula percent (generally 30–50%). Company absorbs the remainder of the excess.	Incentive pool is hurt by the formula percent (generally 50%). Company absorbs the remainder of the excess.
D. Material use is LOWER than estimated or normal.	Company keeps all the gain.	Company keeps all the gain.	Incentive pool is helped by the profit-sharing formula percent (generally 10–20%). Company keeps the remainder of savings.	Company keeps all the gain.	Incentive pool is helped by the formula percent (generally 30–50%). Company keeps the remainder of savings.	Incentive pool is helped by the formula percent (generally 50%). Company keeps the remainder of savings.

Source: Copyright 1965 by Robert C. Scott of The Eddy-Rucker-Nickels Company, Cambridge, Massachusetts.

TABLE 21.3

HOW MATERIAL AND PRODUCT PRICE CHANGES AFFECT INCENTIVES

WHAT HAPPENS IF — ?	WITH INDIVIDUAL OR SMALL GROUP INCENTIVE	WITH PLANT-WIDE PROFIT SHARING	WITH PLANT-WIDE SALES VALUE SHARING	WITH PLANT-WIDE PRODUCTION VALUE SHARING	WITH PLANT-WIDE COST SAVINGS SHARING
A. Material prices rise.	Incentive payments are not affected. Company absorbs the entire cost increase.	Incentive pool is hurt by the profit-sharing formula percent (generally 10–20%). Company absorbs the remainder of cost increase.	Incentive payments are not affected. Company absorbs the entire cost increase.	Incentive pool is hurt by the formula percent (generally 30–50%). Company absorbs the remainder of cost increase.	Incentive pool is hurt by the sharing formula percent (generally 50%). Company absorbs the remainder of cost increase. HOWEVER, MANY PLANS OF THIS TYPE ADJUST COST STANDARDS TO INSULATE INCENTIVE FROM MARKET.
B. Material prices fall.	Incentive payments are not affected. Company keeps the entire cost decrease.	Incentive pool is helped by the profit-sharing formula percent (generally 10–20%). Company keeps the remainder of cost decrease.	Incentive payments are not affected. Company keeps the entire cost decrease.	Incentive pool is helped by the formula percent (generally 30–50%). Company keeps the remainder of the cost decrease.	Incentive pool is helped by the sharing formula percent (generally 50%). Company keeps the remainder of cost decrease. HOWEVER, MANY PLANS OF THIS TYPE ADJUST COST STANDARDS TO INSULATE INCENTIVE FROM MARKET.
C. Product prices rise.	Incentive payments are not affected. Company keeps the entire income increase.	Incentive pool is helped by the profit-sharing formula percent (generally 10–20%). Company keeps the remainder of the income increase.	Incentive pool is helped by the sales formula sharing percent (generally 15–30%). Company keeps the remainder of the income increase.	Incentive pool is helped by the formula percent (generally 30–50%). Company keeps the remainder of the income increase.	Incentive payments are not affected. Company keeps the entire income increase.
D. Product prices fall.	Incentive payments are not affected. Company absorbs the entire income loss.	Incentive pool is hurt by the profit-sharing formula percent (generally 10–20%). Company absorbs the remainder of the income loss.	Incentive pool is hurt by the sales sharing formula percent (generally 15–30%). Company absorbs the remainder of the income loss.	Incentive pool is hurt by the formula percent (generally 30–50%). Company absorbs the remainder of the income loss.	Incentive payments are not affected. Company absorbs the entire income loss.

Source: Copyright 1965 by Robert C. Scott of The Eddy-Rucker-Nickels Company, Cambridge, Massachusetts.

Installing an incentive plan

Almost any suitable plan can be readily prepared and installed, provided management and employees thoroughly understand how the standards are set and why a particular incentive plan was selected. If an incentive plan has been in existence and must be changed to another more desirable one, the new plan should be introduced judiciously to avoid obstacles, even though a labor-management committee may have decided on the change. It is advisable to implement one or several media of methodic communication to announce the reasons for the contemplated new installation, and to follow up on the communication with a simply worded explanation of the plan with concrete, easily understood examples of how the plan will be used.

The essential features of a successful incentive plan installation will vary according to the activity for which the plan is intended and the objectives involved. An arbitrarily selected plan may work favorably in one enterprise or plant, but this is no assurance that it will be effective in another plant or office. Hence, it is advisable to study the advantages and disadvantages of the plan selected in the light of its application to local conditions and the essentials of installation. The following characteristics — which are not listed sequentially — are considered essential for the installation of most incentive plans.

Incentive Plans Should Be Tailor-Made to Suit the Firm

Very few, if any, plans can be adopted in total as used in another firm, for some modifications are usually desirable. The plans should be simple and flexible in their design and administration so that employees can understand them and easily calculate their earnings without expert assistance. Whimsically designed, elaborate, and complicated plans should be avoided.

Equitable Base Wages and Salaries Must Exist Prior to Incentives

Equitable base wages and salaries must first exist as a sound foundation before incentive standards and supplementary rewards are established. This means that the incentive plan is not a substitute for paying low wages or salaries and that the firm already has valid methods of job evaluation and employee evaluation. The incentive plan should be built upon a minimum wage or salary guarantee to the employees.

Preliminary Preparation for Incentives

Preliminary preparations need to be made before incentive performance standards and rewards can be established. For individual incentives it may be necessary to first establish some form of motion and time study (or work simplification), quality control, and the elimination of waiting time (for tools, materials, maintenance, etc.). For group incentives it may be necessary to study past records and factors that affect performance standards.

Establishing Acceptable Performance Standards and Rewards

Incentive performance standards and rewards should be established that are acceptable to both management and the employees involved. Individual incentive performance standards should represent the work performed per unit of time by an average, qualified worker performing according to a "best" method under normal conditions. Accurate units of quantity, quality, and time are the standards upon which a fair day's work is based. Time standards and work methods (and how they were arrived at) should be known to the worker before the job is started in order to avoid future difficulties and misunderstandings. Group incentive performance standards and rewards are usually based upon objective past performance data that are factual and easily understood and accepted. In the final analysis, the incentive performance rewards are the critical issue because most compensation disagreements are caused by differences on how the economic pie should be divided. Early acceptance of incentive performance standards and rewards is achieved when respected and trusted employee representatives either participate in these decisions or are at least fully informed (and satisfied) on how they were determined. Chapter 15 treats in detail who should set job performance standards and identifies useful criteria for setting performance standards that pave the way for acceptance of them by the union and management. Any attempt by management to put a ceiling on earnings will be unpopular and more than likely rejected by the union. Once performance standards have been established and agreed upon, they should not be changed unless *absolutely necessary*. Changes should be considered necessary *only* if the job or work changes *substantially*, if employee earnings prove to be *way below* that expected, or if earnings are *above an amount* that the product or the firm can absorb. Guidelines on the need for changing performance standards should be established and agreed upon at the time the performance standards are established. No performance standard or reward should attempt to spur employees to exert abnormal effort that would be injurious to their health. Overexertion or overtaxing of employee energy should at all times be discouraged.

Separating Incentive Rewards from Wages and Salaries

Incentive rewards should be separated from basic wages and salaries to distinguish the amount of incentive earnings. Employee motivation is weakened by deferred payments when the time interval is so great that the employee fails to see the relationship between his extra efforts and his incentive earnings.

Informing Employees of the Plan

Sooner or later each employee who will be involved with the incentive plan will need to learn about it. In order that all employees learn of the plan first-hand and understand it in a similar sense, the plan needs to be put into writing and distributed to all concerned. There should be ample opportunity for employees to raise any questions they have about the plan or its administration.

Putting the plan in writing takes some time. However, when the plan is put into writing, it tends to clarify the firm's thinking on the plan; and if unforeseen questions arise, there is still time to reconcile them before it appears too late. The write-up should be in very simple, clear, and concise layman's language so that all who can read can easily understand the plan. Objectives or goals of the plan need to be especially spelled out because these give direction to the plan and later serve as the criteria in evaluating the success of the plan. Putting the plan in writing also serves as an invaluable teaching aid in the training of those employees who must administer the plan. Many firms prepare a booklet that contains various illustrations and examples to show how the plan works. A few firms even prepare a short filmstrip or a number of slides so as to leave nothing to the imagination. There is no substitute for having well-versed administrators and employees who have a written document that can combat rumors and serve as an authentic reference for the incentive plan.

A Trial Run on the Plan

Whenever or wherever the plan is started, it should be done on a trial or short-period indoctrination basis so that the installation procedures can be introduced and integrated gradually with only a minimum of inconveniences and changes. The initial installation should be looked upon as a trial period or "dry run" test period so that minor adjustments can be made as experience is gained in order that the plan will perform as close to its aims as is possible.

When it is impractical or impossible to introduce the plan all at once, it can be introduced in a piecemeal fashion, one department at a time. The department which has the greatest need for the plan, which realizes its need, and which is most anxious to get started should be chosen to begin the plan.

After the trial period, and as part of the installation of every incentive plan, there should be some vehicle or means of investigating and handling problems that might arise throughout the life of the incentive plan. Often participating employees meet periodically (monthly) to discuss ways and means of improving or keeping the incentive plan functioning effectively. Sometimes a special committee is appointed to handle suggestions and complaints. In other cases, grievances may be processed through the plant's grievance procedure. It does not appear to matter which method is used as long as there exists some satisfactory medium for handling the day-to-day and week-to-week problems that, if given no attention, have the potential for eventually destroying the plan.

When a special committee is appointed to administer the plan, it has the opportunity to recommend major revisions in the incentive plan if that becomes necessary. Business conditions often have an impact on incentives which may require modification of the plan so that it may continue to be generally acceptable. If it appears that there is little likelihood of the plan succeeding due to some circumstance beyond the control of the firm and its employees, there should be an opportunity for the employees and the management to drop the plan if either finds the plan becoming unacceptable. It should be part of every incentive plan to have periodic evaluation periods (maybe every year) in which the employees or management can decide whether to drop the plan, to modify it, or to continue it as is. There are too many instances on record where an incentive plan starts out on a very favorable note but later runs into an impasse in which there appears to be no way out of a dilemma. The periodic expiration of an incentive plan, unless there was mutual agreement to its continuance, would terminate a plan that had become unsatisfactory. Often an incentive plan becomes unsatisfactory because the plan has not been maintained properly, and this is discussed in the following section.

Maintaining an incentive plan

The initial successful results of an incentive plan may lull management into the erroneous belief that the plan will run itself or can be run with a minimum of staff. Nothing could be further from the truth. Maintaining an incentive plan requires top-notch management and may be thought of as a test of management's adequateness.

When a firm buys a new car for the company's operations, everyone knows that the car will not continue to perform efficiently for any length of time without supplying the car with gasoline, oil, and periodic adjustments and repairs. All incentive plans likewise require periodic maintenance if the plans are to be kept from becoming rusty and inoperative. Periodic checks or examinations of an incentive plan to determine if it is achieving the goals that were established for it are the starting place in the satisfactory maintenance of any incentive plan. When an audit of the plan is made and unsatisfactory progress is found, it is necessary to find the causes of poor performance so that satisfying solutions can be found to adjust the plan back to satisfactory performance. If this cannot be done, the plan may need scrapping just like a worn-out automobile.

A good example of what can happen to incentives and often does happen is the case of a large well-known national manufacturer. Sometime in late 1964, the firm, which had some 3,000 employees on individual incentive pay, finally came to grips with the fact that they had a 60-year old incentive program that no longer offered an incentive.[2] Incentive employees were said to be earning an average of $4.36 per hour while some 6,000 hourly paid employees were averaging $2.91.[3] The management of the enterprise believed that they had to get rid of the system because it had become a noose around the firm's neck and was slowly strangling the company. The amount of work that the firm got from their pieceworkers was said to bear little relationship to what they were paid.[4] Here was a good case where the situation became so acute that the union was willing to go out on strike to keep an obsolete incentive system. The firm indicated that it had no alternative but to close the plant if they were forced to continue as is because they could not be competitive in the customer market. The firm admitted that over the years they may have unwillingly compromised and capitulated in the wage rates and thus were partly responsible for getting the rates so far out of line.[5] Luckily, the union and management were able to work out a solution so that the firm could scrap its obsolete incentive system without severely penalizing its employees and thus remain in business. It was reported that the firm was willing to put $60 million into new and revised facilities in order to be able to drop their decayed incentive plan.[6]

Over the years, incentive plans have been known to wear out or become unsatisfactory for a number of reasons. The more common of these maintenance problems are described in the paragraphs that follow.

The Human Element

One of the most important reasons incentive plans fail or are not maintained is because of the human element. Management personnel too often fail to provide a competent person or committee to look after the maintenance of the program. Sometimes the people assigned to the administrative task lack authority or do not get the backing to do what needs to be done. In other cases, the human weaknesses of employees may cause them not to abide by the rules of the incentive plan. Workers have been known to pad the figures to gain added bonuses, and managers have been known to manipulate records to produce personal benefits. Unions have been known to restrict production. For an incentive plan to continue to perform satisfactorily, all employees need to consider their colleagues as equals, to have a strong desire to do what is right for the majority, to share information, and to keep everything aboveboard. Distrust, selfishness, and lack of cooperation among employees in the plan lead to decay of the plan. Employees who are not covered by incentives are many times jealous of the

[2]"Is Incentive Pay Headed for Shelf?" *Business Week* (June 27, 1964), p. 51.
[3]*Ibid.*
[4]*Ibid.*
[5]*Ibid.*
[6]"Production Wage Incentives at the Crossroads," *Industrial Relations News* (September, 1964).

employees who are covered, and this makes it difficult for such plans to succeed. For an incentive plan to be maintained properly, the human element needs to be kept in a healthy state of affairs. This can be done by being ever willing, ready, and able to discuss in a frank way the problems that arise in the incentive plan. Without an examination of the faults of an incentive system, any incentive system will eventually fail in time. In short, management and employees alike must be willing to devote time and energy to make the incentive plan work and continue to work. The maintenance of a plan does not take place automatically.

The Technical Element

Another facet of maintaining an incentive plan deals with technological change. In a dynamic industry, methods, materials, and machines may change rapidly. It may be very difficult to keep up-to-date on job performance standards. It may also appear to be costly. Firms generally experience some difficulty in being flexible enough to make the necessary changes on the jobs, their standards, and conditions to keep the employees satisfied. Then, too, when job standards remain the same for a prolonged period of time, there is a tendency for the standards to become loose and only the workers on those jobs remain happy. It is important that whenever conditions occur that would change the equitability of an incentive system, there must be corresponding changes in the incentive plan to maintain the equitability of the incentive, because the passage of time will not correct the inconsistencies that develop but will only compound them. To argue that it costs money to revise standards may be so; however, such a cost is negligible when compared with the cost of a complete overhaul at some future time when the whole incentive structure is out of line.

All this adds up to the fact that changing technology can cause an incentive plan to become obsolete if nothing is done to adjust to the technology. The employee charged with the administration of the incentive plan should be the one who should see that obsolescence does not overtake the plan. If he should fail in this responsibility, the committee that handles complaints and grievances should be able to detect trends by the nature and volume of the complaints. Sometimes a special rotating committee, composed of rank-and-file employees and management personnel, is set up to help maintain the incentive plan. This committee raises questions which its colleagues have about the plan, and the rotating nature of the committee means that new ideas and thoughts are continually being given to the plan to keep it effective. If one or the other of the committees fails to sense potential obsolescence difficulties, a yearly audit and evaluation of the plan should bring to the surface what the situation is and what remedial action is needed to keep the incentive plan current and effective. Incentive plan audits can be performed by the industrial engineering department in the company or by outside consultants who are known to be objective. If it appears that the pace of technology is outstripping the usefulness of the incentive plan, and nothing can be done to adjust for it effectively, the plan needs to be scrapped. When this happens, there must be a sensible way to scrap such a plan. One method to do this would be to have an incentive plan expire after a period of time, as is done with union-management contracts. Such a method would call for periodic appraisals of the plan and its problems and offer a chance for either the union or the management (or both) to reject continuance of the plan beyond its expiration date. Thus, if the employees were taking unfair advantage of the firm, the company could terminate the plan at its termination date, and vice versa. Such a method should force an incentive plan to keep pace with technology, or to go out of existence before it becomes ineffective and a burden on the firm.

The Communication Element

Another facet of maintaining an incentive plan is the need for prompt, clear, and adequate communications to all employees involved. It is not enough to merely inform the union officers, department heads, supervisors, and incentive committee members. Everyone participating in the incentive plans must periodically receive firsthand communications regarding the status, problems, and future outlook of the plan. This might be done by way of posters, the bulletin board, payroll envelopes, letters to employees and their families, and talks to the whole plant. Unless all employees are knowledgeable, there will be some misleading rumors and speculations made about the status of the incentive plan. Employees need the facts if they are to have confidence in the plan, to understand it, and to be able to offer constructive criticism and effort to make it succeed. In other words, communications is a two-way street and should provide for upward as well as downward communications. Too many plans fall by the wayside or are less effective than they should be because of poor communications or an information gap. The more educated the firm's employees, the more information they will expect and need if they are to be avid supporters of the plan, rather than a thorn in its side. Communication with employees should be on a continuing and regular basis; informing employees about significant points of the incentive plan only once is not enough. A certain amount of repetition is needed for the average person to understand fully and remember the facts. A certain amount of repetition is also needed because all firms have some labor turnover. If a plant had only 4 percent of its employees leaving each month, over a 12-month period it is possible that 48 percent of the plant's employees would never have had a chance to receive the company communications which are sent out only once a year.

This draws to a close the three chapters dealing with the use of various incentive plans as a means of compensating employees. We shall now turn to the relationship and place of fringe benefits in compensating employees.

REVIEW QUESTIONS

1. What factors need to be taken into consideration in making the decision to adopt an incentive plan?

2. Tell why you agree or disagree with the statement, "No incentive plan can ever hope to work successfully for any length of time unless employees respect and trust management and vice versa."

3. (a) Indicate what you consider to be the essentials of installing an incentive plan. (b) Which is the most important?

4. How should a firm evaluate the effectiveness of its incentive plan?

5. What is the basic difference among the following group incentive plans: the cost-savings sharing plan, the sales-value sharing plan, the production-value sharing plan, and the profit-sharing plan?

6. Is it really necessary to put into writing the fundamentals of an incentive plan that the firm wishes to use? Why?

7. Should an incentive plan have a periodic audit? Why?

8. How can a firm gracefully do away with an obsolete incentive plan?

RESEARCH OR SEMINAR QUESTIONS

1. How long can an incentive plan be expected to satisfy man's basic needs and wants?

2. Under what conditions could an incentive plan designed in 1970 be adequate for 1980?

3. What factors are necessary for the success of an individual incentive system? a group incentive system?

4. (a) Is it possible to have more than one type of incentive wage program in a company? (b) What are the advantages and disadvantages of installing more than one type?

5. Contact some firm that is considered to have a successful incentive plan. Try to get a story on it to report to the class. See if you can find out why the plan is used, who made the decision to go ahead with it, how its success is evaluated, how it is kept effective, etc.

PRACTICAL EXPERIENCE ASSIGNMENTS

1. Company ABC is considering inviting the union to participate in the development of a wage incentive plan. Select a group of four or five students to participate in an unguided conference. Act as the conference leader and discuss the following topics:

   (a) What are some of the problems that could result when the union is invited to assist in the formulation of a wage incentive plan?

   (b) How can the company avoid and/or solve these problems?

   Prepare a conference report summarizing the conference highlights and indicating the group decisions relative to the problems.

2. Discuss the pros and cons of whether one person or a committee should be given the responsibility to administer a company-wide incentive plan.

CASE PROBLEM

21–1.   THE HARROD MANUFACTURING COMPANY

Installing a Wage Payment System

The Harrod Manufacturing Company has a ferrous cast iron foundry which has traditionally had a piece-rate incentive plan for wage payments to molders. Rates are assigned to the different jobs through motion and time study which determines the standard production and allowances. Recently the company has installed new equipment and procedures, which in turn have required new studies and rates. After a "break-in" period during which the molders were allowed to become accustomed to the new equipment and procedures, sampling time studies were taken from which it was determined that all job rates could be reduced by 30 percent. With the reduction of piece-work rates, the guaranteed day rate was increased by 10 percent.

The union refused to accept these new terms on the basis that all time-study sampling had been taken on an exceptional employee. This employee's record revealed that he had continuously produced an average of 145 percent of normal capacity. Union records showed that 75 to 80 percent of the sampling was taken on this exceptional employee. The union contended that the rates were not set at a normal standard and offered as proof the fact that most of the molders could not attain normal production under the new rates. The union wanted the company to take actual time studies of each job as produced by five separate employees, excluding the slowest and the fastest men. They also wished a redetermination of the fatigue and personal allowances.

The company refused the union demands by stating that the molder wages were already above the area level and that the samplings taken of the fastest employee were correct and accurate because he was employing the most efficient individual production methods. The other molders could but would not attain the new production level because they were not fully utilizing the equipment and procedures correctly.

The median wage for the molders under the old system was $4 per hour. Since the installation of the new rates, the median had fallen to approximately $3.80 per hour. It was shown that most of the molders were presently only producing at the guaranteed day rate of $3.20 per hour. The exceptional molder, who was looked upon as a leader, refused to produce more than 110 percent according to the new rates. The normal rate is considered to be 100 percent. The Personnel Manager is in charge of wage and salary administration. It is his responsibility to see that the employees accept the new rates which evolved as the result of installing the new equipment and procedures.

Problems:

1. What cardinal points of good management did the company overlook when it installed the new pay system?

2. What plan or plans of action must now be instituted by the company to gain employee confidence and acceptance of the new system?

3. Write up a confidential proposal to the president of the company covering the answers to the above questions and any other pertinent material that you think should be included.

part six • Supplementary plans of
compensating employees

chapter **22**

SUPPLEMENTARY COMPENSATION:
THEORY AND EMPLOYEE BENEFITS

The objective of the next two chapters is to discuss the place of supplementary compensation in the compensation of employees. In this chapter we will develop the background and theory of supplementary compensation in general and identify those employee benefits that directly pay their way according to some predetermined relationship between savings and earnings. The next chapter will discuss those supplementary compensations (better known as fringe benefits) that indirectly pay their way, and their relationship to the total compensation system. The topics examined in this chapter will be discussed in the following order: (1) nature of supplementary compensations, (2) theory of supplementary compensations, (3) the vehicles of supplementary compensations, (4) determining supplementary compensations, and (5) supplementary compensations that directly pay their way.

Nature of supplementary compensations

Supplementary compensation has, since its inception, been identified by many different titles. A listing of the various names would include such terms as *employee benefits, employee services, hidden wages, hidden payroll, indirect payment plans, social wages, supplementary incentives, welfare plans,* and *fringe benefits* (the most commonly used term). None of these terms have been universally accepted, and each seems to present only a part of the entire supplementary compensation picture. None of these terms appear to be all-inclusive enough to cover some 200 or more different benefits that are known to exist. Therefore, there is a need for an appropriate term that includes all the supplemental benefits beyond the employee's regular base rate of compensation. The term *supplementary compensation* is more all-inclusive and appropriately descriptive than any of the others and thus should be used. In order for the student to be able to understand better the reasons for our recommending this term, rather than the term *fringe benefits*, it is necessary to present a brief background of the origin and development of supplemental benefits.

The term "fringe benefits" was unknown prior to World War II. It was an outgrowth of the federal government's effort to curb inflation during the war by preventing employers from granting wage raises, or from paying new employees high wage-base rates and salaries. Some employers attempted to attract workers with compensations that the national War Labor Board regarded as mere "trimmings" — at the periphery of direct wage and salary payments. These compensations were referred to as fringe benefits by the chairman of the War Labor Board because they were actually only on the fringe of real compensations. However, fringe payments soon expanded from a few items of insignificant amounts to numerous benefits and services totaling many billions of dollars each year, affecting the entire economy, and raising the cost of production.

After the war, the practice of granting fringe benefits grew more rapidly. The term "fringe benefits" continued to be loosely applied to anything and everything that was not considered a base-pay rate. As a result, such benefits have assumed many and varied meanings. To some industrial relations practitioners, "fringe" denotes higher cost without additional production. To others, "fringe" means procedures adopted to provide supplementary compensation that is over and above the agreed-upon wage or salary rate and for which no additional productivity is required. Or it may carry the false impression that there are extras added to the wage. Thus, the word "fringe" is an unfortunate one because it is ambiguous and subject to a variety of definitions.

The United States Department of Commerce adopted the term "Supplements to Wages and Salaries" for national income purposes, describing it as follows:

> Supplements to Wages and Salaries are the monetary compensation of employees not commonly regarded as wages and salaries. They consist of employer contributions for social insurance, employer contributions to private pension and welfare funds, compensation for injuries, pay of the military reserve, and a few other minor items of labor income.[1]

The term "Supplements to Wages and Salaries" is also used by the United States Bureau of Labor Statistics to cover all payments to employees that are not direct wages or salaries.

---

[1]Esther L. Becker, *Dictionary of Personnel and Industrial Relations* (New York: Philosophical Library, Inc., 1958), p. 306.

It is felt that the following is a more all-inclusive and appropriate definition: *Supplementary compensation* consists of all financial and nonfinancial payments made by the employer to, or for the benefit of, the employee which are over and above the agreed-upon base compensation rate due the employee for the minimum productive results expected on the job. Thus, supplementary compensation would include everything from paid holidays and vacations to overtime, travel time, and wash-up time. Figure 22.1 contains an alphabetical list of the more common items for which supplementary compensations have been known to be paid.

Supplementary compensations may be understood better and discussed if they are subdivided into two basic categories: (1) those that are expected to pay their way directly, and (2) those that are not expected to pay their way directly. This second category, which is more commonly referred to as "fringe benefits," will be the topic of the next chapter. The remainder of this chapter will discuss the theory of supplementary compensations and those forms of supplementary compensation that directly pay their way.

Theory of supplementary compensations

Although the use of supplementary compensations has been very widespread since World War II, very few businessmen have taken the time to determine what they are attempting to do through their use.

Why Offer Supplementary Compensations?

After analyzing the various types of benefits that are presently being given by employers, the authors have identified the following six key reasons that employers have used to justify their offering of supplementary compensations:

1. To attract and hold more desirable employees.
2. To assist the employees in better meeting their needs.
3. To prevent the unions from organizing the company employees.
4. To keep pace with the benefits being offered by other companies.
5. To assist in lowering the unit cost of production.
6. To fulfill requirements imposed by the federal and state governments.

To Attract and Hold More Desirable Employees. Generally, the primary purpose of supplementary compensations is to attract and to retain the best employees, thereby reducing labor turnover. Typical of our competitive system of free private enterprise, some employers offer more supplementary compensation than others, just as some employers offer more attractive wage-base rates and salaries than their competitors within the same community or industry. Other things being equal, employees naturally tend to gravitate toward employers who offer the most complete benefits and service programs. Such employers install supplementary compensation programs for the purpose of providing economic

Accident insurance
Anniversary awards
Annual report to employees
Athletic equipment
*Attendance bonuses

Baby bonus
Baby sitter pay
Baitcasting team
Barber shop (in plant)
Baseball teams
Basketball teams
Beauty parlors
Billiard tables
Blood bank
Bowling leagues
Business sabbatical leaves

*Cafeterias
Call-back pay
Call-in pay
Camera club
*Canteen service
Carpeted floors
Charm courses
Chauffeur service
Check-cashing time
*Christmas bonuses
Christmas parties
Clothes-changing time
Company airplane
Company car
Company housing
Company orchestra
Company picnics
*Company stores
Cooking schools
Cost-of-living bonus
Country club
Country club dues
Credit unions

Day nurseries
Death benefits
Dental care time
Dental surgery
Dietetic advice
Disability insurance
Downtime

Educational assistance
Emergency aid plan
Employee counseling
Employee discounts on purchases
Employee parties
Employee pleasure trips

Employee publications
Employees' loan associations
Employees' stock purchase plans
Employees' thrift plans
Enforced absences
Eye examinations
Eyeglasses

Family allowance
Financial advice
Fishing jamborees
Floating holiday
Flowers for ill and deceased
   (employee and family)
Football teams
Free beer
Free laundry
Free meals
Free services that company sells
Functions for retired employees

Glee clubs
Golf instruction and teams
Group hospitalization insurance
Group surgical insurance

Haircut time
Haircuts
Hairpieces (for bald salesmen)
Hazard pay
Health and welfare fund
Health education
*Holiday premium
Holidays paid for but not worked
Home financing
Horseshoe courts
House organ
Hospital facilities

Income extension aid plan
Income tax services
Individual hospitalization insurance
Individual surgical insurance
Information racks
Inside mutual funds

Jury duty pay

Keys to special lavatories

Layoff pay
Legal aid
Libraries
Life insurance
Lunch period entertainment

*Supplementary compensations that directly pay their way.

FIGURE 22.1 ITEMS FOR WHICH SUPPLEMENTARY COMPENSATIONS HAVE BEEN
KNOWN TO BE PAID

Machine setup time
Magazines
Matching gift programs
Maternity leaves
Medical exams (voluntary)
Medical time
Military induction bonuses
Movies
Moving expenses
Music at work
Music lessons
Mutual benefit associations

National Guard duty pay
Nursery
Nursing home care

Old-age, survivors, disability, and health
  insurance
On-call-pay
*Overtime premium

Paid club memberships
Paid death-in-family leave
Paid lunch periods
Paid magazine subscriptions
Paid sick leave
Parking space operation
Pensions
Portal-to-portal pay
Posthumous pay
Prescription drug program
*Profit sharing
Psychiatric care
Purchasing service

*Quality bonuses

Railroad retirement tax
Railroad unemployment insurance
Reading room facilities
Real estate purchases
Relief time
Religious holidays
Retiree benefits
Reporting pay
Reserve military pay
Rest periods
Restroom facilities
Rod and gun club
Room and board allowance

*Safety awards
Safety clothes
Safety goggles
Safety programs
Safety shoes

Savings bond administration
Scholarships (employee's children)
*Service bonuses
Severance pay
*Shift premium
Showers and locker rooms
Sick leaves

Sickness benefits insurance
Softball teams
Soundproof offices
Sportscar club
State disability insurance
Stock purchase options
Study club
*Suggestions awards
Supper money
Supplemental unemployment benefits (SUB)
Supplements to workmen's compensation

Table tennis
Tennis teams
Time and one-half vacation pay
Time spent on contract negotiation
Time spent on grievances
Trading stamps
Transportation
Trapshooting ranges
Travel allowance or expenses
Travel insurance
TV

Unemployment compensation
Uniform allowance

Vacation facilities
Vacation pay
Vaccination shots
Visitation with children's teachers
Visiting nurse
Vitamins and salt tablets
Volleyball teams
Voting time

Wash-up time
*Waste elimination bonuses
Wedding gifts
*Weekend premium
Witness time
Work clothes
Work clothes laundry
Workmen's compensation

*Year-end bonuses

*Supplementary compensations that directly pay their way.

FIGURE 22.1 ITEMS FOR WHICH SUPPLEMENTARY COMPENSATIONS HAVE BEEN
KNOWN TO BE PAID (*concluded*)

security for their employees and *hope* that the employees will in turn reciprocate with loyal support of the company and a continued interest in their jobs that leads to continuous increases in productivity. Some examples of supplementary compensation plans that are used for these reasons are stock purchase options, company pension plans, home financing, mutual benefit associations, and generous vacations.

To Assist the Employees in Better Meeting Their Needs. The rapid expansion and growth of supplementary benefits is, in part, a result of their ability to more completely fulfill the employees' needs. Employees have found that benefits provided by the company are better able to fulfill their needs than if they were given the money to provide the benefits for themselves. This is a result of two economies: First, the employee does not have to pay a federal income tax on many of the benefits, whereas he would on any income he would receive in lieu of the payments. Second, by taking advantage of the economies of larger numbers, companies, in most cases, can provide at a lower cost the same benefits the employees could buy on their own if they acted singly.

To Prevent the Unions from Organizing the Company Employees. Some companies give their employees supplementary benefits in order to keep their workers from becoming so dissatisfied that they would vote to unionize the company. The companies reason that the benefits gained by not having to deal with a union outweigh the costs of the supplementary compensations that they are giving the employees. The benefits given to the employees for this reason would have to be of at least the same kind and quality as those given to unionized employees or a company would fail to meet its objective of keeping the union out.

To Keep Pace with the Benefits Being Offered by Other Companies. It would appear that many companies have developed their supplementary compensation programs to keep up with those offered by other companies. This approach seems to be quite a common one based on the similarities that are found in many supplementary compensation plans. Although this is not necessarily bad in itself, it could be if the needs of one employee group differ greatly from those of another company. It also may result in compounding an original poor judgment on the part of the first company to adopt the benefit. A big objection to this policy is that the needs differ from one company to another and therefore the benefits to fill these needs should also differ. Many of the plans that are copies of others are wasting the company's money if they do not fulfill their employees' needs. The fact that some people's needs are common to all employees is not a good reason to believe that all needs are.

To Assist in Lowering the Unit Cost of Production. Although the majority of people think of supplementary compensation as added costs, this is not always the case. Some forms of supplementary compensation, such as overtime pay and weekend premiums, are designed to lower the unit cost of production. The reason such compensation can sometimes cause lower costs is that by having present employees work longer hours, the same fixed (overhead) costs can be spread over more units of production, thereby lowering the unit cost. Also, by using the same workers that are already experienced in doing the job, the company will save the extra costs that would be incurred in hiring and training additional employees. Then, too, by using the skilled employees who are already well acquainted with the job, there will be less scrap and consequently higher production.

To Fulfill Requirements Imposed by the Federal and State Governments. Many of the benefits that employees receive from their employers are a result of laws that have been passed by the federal or state governments for the protection and well-being of the employee. A good example of this is the Social Security Act of 1935. Since that time, amendments have been made to the original act, and additional laws have been passed that have increased the scope of the coverage as well as the number of persons enrolled. At present over 95 percent of the gainfully employed are protected by some legal program. Examples of this type of supplementary compensation are old-age, survivors, disability, and health insurance; state disability insurance; unemployment compensation; railroad retirement tax; and railroad unemployment insurance.

To sum up, we have identified a number of good reasons why a firm might wish to offer supplementary compensations. As a general rule, firms regard the costs connected with supplementary compensations and fringes as an investment. They expect a return in some form, either in a monetary or productive fashion, or in a stable or more effective labor force. The success of supplementary compensations depends to a great extent on whether there is a real need and desire for them and whether the employees understand and appreciate the value of the benefits provided.

Modern personnel management considers the employee as the most important factor in the success of a company. Employees are therefore treated with human dignity and not just as hired hands. Management is concerned with the general welfare of employees not only while on the job but off the job as well. When employees have problems that are likely to affect adversely their productivity and morale, it is to management's advantage as well as the employee's for management to provide whatever help it can to assist the employee to meet his personal problems. There appears to be no clear-cut line as to how far a company can or should go in assisting its employees. Offering supplementary compensations and a variety of fringe benefits is only one part of a company's total personnel program to assure that its employees are treated equitably and with human dignity.

When Should Supplementary Compensations Be Utilized?

Since the movement of supplementary compensations has increased in pace since World War II, little if any time has been taken by employers to determine the true value of supplementary compensations and under what conditions they should be offered. This practice, whether a result of the rapid expansion of supplementary compensations or for some other reason, if continued, could result in unsound management. In order to facilitate the adoption of sounder plans of supplementary compensation, the following guidelines should be considered before adopting or revising any plan of supplementary compensation.

In spite of management's insistence that objectives be determined for almost every other major undertaking, few companies have clearly defined and communicated the objectives of their supplementary compensation plan. In many cases, the failure to determine the objectives has resulted in the selection of plans that have not met the needs of the company nor those of its employees. By determining the objectives in advance of the plan's installation, management is better able to evaluate the plan's progress according to some objective standards.

Another consideration necessary in determining if a particular plan should be adopted is whether it benefits *both* the employee and the employer. Only if both parties benefit from the plan is it likely to be successful in the long run.

Supplementary compensation plans should not be installed as a substitute for an inadequate base rate. They should, as their name implies, be used to supplement an adequate wage-base rate. They should never be used as a replacement for wages.

Since most forms of supplementary compensation tend to be intangible as far as the average worker is concerned, they should be used only after the more direct means have been exhausted. The average worker has no idea how much is being spent on him in the forms of supplementary compensation and therefore it does little to motivate him.

Lastly, supplementary compensation, like all other forms of compensation, must be directly or indirectly earned if it is to be distributed to the workers. Any supplementary compensation that is given rather than earned will result in increased cost of the end product and/or reduce the profit for the owners. In the long run, both of these alternatives will hurt the company and therefore the employees.

Vehicles of supplementary compensations

Analysis of supplementary compensation plans in use today indicates that there are three vehicles or media mainly used to convey supplementary compensation benefits to the employees: (1) extra cash payments, (2) "paid for" gifts and services, and (3) present or deferred payments for employee security. This breakdown is useful since the first payment medium is, in most cases, reserved for those payments that directly pay their way. The second two are, in most cases, used to convey payments that are not expected to pay their way directly. Therefore, by checking on the medium which is used for payment, a person can quickly determine if the benefit is of the type that is supposed to pay its way directly. An examination of the composition of a company's plans may also indicate how much benefit the firm is getting from its supplementary compensation plans.

Extra Cash Payments

The payments that fall under this classification include premiums for overtime, shift differentials, and premiums for working weekend hours. It also covers Christmas bonuses, suggestion plan payments, waste reduction bonuses, and year-end bonuses.

The most important advantage of paying these supplementary benefits in cash is that it is easy for the employee to see the results of his work. He has a tangible reward for his effort and therefore may be more highly motivated to maintain or improve his productivity. In addition, paying cash benefits rather than granting other supplementary benefits normally reduces the high administrative costs associated with supplementary compensation.

An important drawback of using cash as the medium of payment of supplementary benefits is that employees may soon begin to take the payments for granted just as they expect their base rate. They plan their future expenditures including the extra payments which may not be forthcoming in the same magnitude as in the past. If the cash benefits have to be reduced, the employee will be more aware of this change than if a small noncash percentage benefit such as the company's contribution to the pension fund has to be reduced. Another limitation to paying supplementary benefits in cash is that the benefits become subject to an income tax for the employee. The effect is that the employee ends up with fewer net dollars worth of benefits than if the company had supplied them through a nontaxable supplemental benefit account.

"Paid For" Gifts and Services

Payments for such things as cafeterias, company athletic teams, recreational facilities, free meals, employee purchase discounts, scholarships, and working clothes all come under benefits known as "paid for" employee gifts or services.

The proponents of the use of this medium claim that an important advantage of this method is the unity and goodwill that it promotes among employees and between employees and employers. Another advantage of this type of benefit is the image of the company that is projected to potential future employees. If these benefits can make a company appear to be a good place to work, the firm will attract more job applicants, thereby giving the company an opportunity to select better employees.

A possible limitation on the use of employee gifts or services as a form of employee compensation is that too few employees may make use of the facilities to warrant the high cost. After all, the critics claim, only a very small percentage of the employees are members of the baseball team, few utilize the company library, and only a small percentage of the employees' children benefit from disability plans. Another disadvantage of the use of employee services as an employee benefit is that this may create a "country club atmosphere," thereby reducing the company's output. Thus, the "horseplay" that is promoted by the employee service benefits may be carried over to the employee's work.

Present or Deferred Payments for Employee Security

The employer's contributions to all types of employee security plans — insurance, pension, unemployment, and workmen's compensation — come under the classification of present or deferred payments for employee security.

For many years, two advantages of this form of supplementary compensation have been well known. First, because of the large numbers involved in company-wide insurance plans, the cost of the same protection is lower when it is provided by a group employee plan than if the employee provided it himself. Second, many of the payments for employee security plans help reduce the turnover that would be experienced without them. However, these benefits, as will be pointed out in the next chapter, may be lost if portable pension plans gain more general acceptance.

A disadvantage of using this medium for the payment of supplementary benefits is that the benefits that are derived are not always felt while the employee is working. The benefits may not be important from the employee's point of view until he starts to plan for his retirement. Therefore, until the employee begins to think seriously about his retirement, this medium will do little toward meeting its objective of reducing employee turnover.

Determining supplementary compensations

Someone needs to make a decision to determine who gets how much of what type of supplementary compensation. These decisions can be determined in one of three ways: by the employer alone, the employee (or union) alone, or by joint action of the employee (or union) and employer. A discussion of the advantages and disadvantages of each of these three methods of determining what supplementary compensations are to be offered will now follow.

Employer Determines the Supplementary Compensations to Be Offered

One of the advantages of having the employer determine what supplementary compensation is to be granted is that it makes administration of the supplementary benefit much easier. All employee groups get the same benefits within the group rather than several employees in the same group receiving one type of benefit while others get another. This cuts the cost of administration and makes possible lower rates for the benefits that are granted. Another advantage is that it makes comparison with other companies' supplementary compensations much easier. A prospective employee is able to see quickly the advantages of one company benefit over another. Another often-cited advantage of the employer alone making the selection is that it keeps the control of the plan with the employers. If the wrong benefits are given, it is management's responsibility to rectify the situation since it made the mistakes. However, if the employees had control and made a mistake, they would, in most cases, expect management to take the necessary action to correct the error that had been made. Therefore, since management is the one who has to pay for any mistakes that are made, management prefers, in most cases, to have the final say-so.

A disadvantage of having the employer alone determine the benefits is that he may not be close enough to the employees to know their needs and therefore he might select a plan that is either unsuitable or unacceptable to them. However, if he does have accurate information about the employees' needs, this may become one of the stronger advantages of having the employer select the plan. Another disadvantage of the employer selecting the plan without consulting the employees is that it may be difficult to get the employees to accept the plan even though it is able to meet their needs. In spite of generally fair treatment for many years, some older employees, and new ones, may think that management is trying to take advantage of them. They may see a supplementary compensation plan developed by management alone as an attempt to take advantage of them by giving them something that is not as advantageous to the employee as it should be.

Employees Determine the Supplementary Compensations to Be Offered

The second course of action available to management is to permit the employees (or their unions) their choice of having the supplementary compensations they prefer. One of the more important advantages of allowing employees to select supplementary compensations is that they will be more willing to accept them than if management had chosen them. The employee-employer relationship should improve as a result of the fewer disagreements that take place in trying to determine what supplementary compensations should be utilized. Another advantage of having employees select their own is that they should know their own needs much better than the employer. They should, therefore, be better able to select those benefits that will meet their needs better than anyone else. Although this is an advantage in one sense, it could also be one of the more important disadvantages as we will point out later. Lastly, by spending the time necessary to determine the appropriate supplementary compensations that should be used, the employees will become aware of the costs of the benefits that they receive from the company. This contact will, in many cases, make the employees aware that the company is spending a lot more money on them than they had ever thought possible. This experience may indirectly help to build better morale between the employees and their employers.

One of the disadvantages of allowing the employees to select the benefits they wish to receive is that the employees may be shortsighted and choose a plan which foregoes meeting some of their more important long-range needs in favor of the ones which are realized over the short term. Or they may select benefits that do not fulfill management's needs. Since long-term needs must be fulfilled, management may be thus forced by the employees or their unions to give additional benefits to fill the void left by the employees' poor judgment. These would, in most cases, be additional benefits because there is a very strong resistance on the part of the workers or their union to give up a benefit once it has become established. A second disadvantage often cited for the selection of supplementary compensation by employees is that a lack of agreement among workers can result in poor morale, thereby defeating one of the purposes of the benefits. Friction among the workers could be much worse than the type that results when the employer is left alone to select supplementary compensations for the employees. Another disadvantage connected with employee selection of supplementary compensations is the increased administrative costs that are normally associated with the increased number of supplementary compensations they would choose. There is also more paper work associated when a larger variety is chosen, since each has a somewhat fixed amount of clerical work involved to maintain it. In addition, a higher unit cost rate is incurred because the number of participants is smaller in each benefit when a variety of benefits is available.

Employer and Employees Jointly Determine the Supplementary Compensations to Be Offered

The third method for determining the choice of supplementary compensation calls for joint action by both the employee and the employer. There are two somewhat different variations that have developed within the framework of employee-employer joint action. The first variation gives the employees their choice between the alternatives that have been set up by management. This does away with many of the disadvantages of allowing the employees to make all the decisions. Because of the limited selection, the cost of administering such a program is normally lower than when employees are offered unlimited selection of benefits. The drawbacks of this concept are similar to those when the employer makes all of the decisions alone. Even with the increased scope, the employee may be unable to select a plan that will meet his needs as well as he could if other benefits were offered.

The second variation, which is known as the *cafeteria method,* is a compromise attempt to develop a plan that has as many of the advantages and as few of the disadvantages as possible. The employer selects several benefits that he thinks all employees need to have for themselves and their family's security and well-being. Each employee is allowed to select any other benefits whose cumulative cost does not exceed an agreed-upon amount. This allows each employee the opportunity to select certain benefits that especially meet his personal needs. In establishing such a cafeteria method, both management and the employee have a chance to see that their needs are met and that the objectives of supplementary compensation are also fulfilled. Although this method has not received much publicity or been given an adequate trial, it has very good potential if used under the following circumstances. First, both management and the employee must be reasonable and well informed as to the objectives of supplementary compensation in the company. Next, the employee must have adequate knowledge of the plans that are available. Finally, both the employee and the employer must be aware of the limit on the amount of money that can be spent on supplementary compensations.

Supplementary compensations that directly pay their way

The theory of supplementary compensations was discussed up to this point in order to acquaint the student with what can and cannot be expected from them. As pointed out previously, there are two types of supplementary compensations in use today: (a) those that directly pay their way, and (b) those that do not directly pay their way.

Figure 22.1 lists some of the supplementary compensations that directly pay their way as well as those that do not pay their way. The items that are listed in this figure are not intended to be, nor are they, exhaustive. The listing is designed to give a sampling of the types of benefits that are being used.

The rest of this chapter will deal with those individual benefits that directly pay their way. The following chapter will take up those benefits that produce intangible results which, although they contribute something to the company, are not expected to pay their way directly.

Supplementary compensations have been known to be paid for a variety of items that directly pay their way, that is, they give something tangible in return for the compensation received. Although there is no clear-cut or standard way of classifying such items, we might say that supplementary compensations have commonly been paid for the following:

1. Increased quantities of the product or service.
2. Improved quality of the product or service.
3. Method changes and improvements.
4. Increasing profits.

5. Continuous plant operation.
6. Length of service with company.
7. Punctuality and attendance.
8. Safety achievements.

Each of these categories will be explained so as to see the relationship between the supplementary compensation and what is directly gained in return for it.

Increased Quantities of the Product or Service

It is not our intent to elaborate further on this category as it has already been thoroughly treated in Chapters 17 through 21. There is a wealth of examples of incentive plans that are principally based on increased compensation for increased production. Usually there is a direct increase in compensation paid for a definite increase in production.

Improved Quality of the Product or Service

Traditionally there have been only a few examples of supplementary compensations paid for maintaining or improving the quality of a product or service. Chapter 19 describes how this has been done in retail work, factory inspection, and janitorial, housekeeping, and maintenance work. Some firms actually offer compensations for the elimination of waste or the prevention of low-quality products as described below.

Elimination of Waste. A bonus for eliminating waste is also known as an "economy bonus." It is paid for avoiding waste in handling and using the materials that go into a product. In some cases it is just as effective as a production efficiency bonus which is designed to save time and reduce cost by increasing the output.

Some manufacturers have found it advantageous to establish a financial incentive in the form of a bonus or piece-rate payment to the operator who notices flaws in the materials or finds defective parts while the product is in the process of manufacture. Thus, a high-quality product and the elimination of "seconds" is guaranteed. Depending on the nature of the product and the quality standards, 8 percent of the operator's earnings may be paid as an extra incentive if his work is completed without any defects. This is especially desirable with regard to items such as castings, in which "blow holes" cannot be detected until after several operations have been performed. It can also apply to the weaving of rugs and the manufacture of towels and clothing, where extra compensation can be paid to reduce the number of imperfect products.

Prevention of Low-Quality Products. Modern industries provide ways and means to maintain the desired quality of products through quality control in special inspection departments. However, it is often necessary to encourage workers with financial incentives in order to maintain a high-grade product. A worker generally realizes that low-quality work will not pass inspection. Nevertheless, he will take chances on overspeeding equipment and producing below-standard products. For that reason an additional "quality" bonus is advisable, particularly where a high-grade product is essential and where quantity production rewards may tend to lower quality. In certain manufacturing plants the production efficiency bonus is not paid unless the quality bonus is completely earned, thereby insuring the quality as well as the quantity. The quality bonus is usually based either on a quantity factor or on the maintenance of high-quality standards over a certain period.

A combination production piecework and quality-incentive is successfully maintained by some companies. The plan is nothing more than a differential piecework rate that increases with the percentage of perfect quality production. Hence, the piecework rate may be increased 4 to 8 percent when the completed job shows 100 percent perfect merchandise. Some companies pay production operators weekly quality bonuses above their regular piece-rate earnings. Other firms pay quality bonuses based on 100 percent quantity without spoilage or waste of materials, resulting in a combined waste elimination and quality-incentive plan.

The quality of a product becomes of increasing importance as automation and complicated machines become a reality. Space vehicles and interplanetary trips would be an impossibility without the highest degree of reliability and quality of the product. On the other hand, the speed of manufacturing a product becomes of less importance to the employee because the rate of output is controlled by the machine.

Method Changes and Improvements

In the past, opportunities to make changes or improvements in tools, methods, equipment, and the like were usually reserved to management personnel as it was believed to be a management prerogative. However, times have changed and today's employees are highly educated and capable of discovering new and better ways to increase plant efficiency. A well-managed firm should be interested in advantageous method changes and improvements no matter what their source. Management should promote this and pave the way for all employee innovations by establishing an industrial climate that encourages and rewards such performance. Generally, management establishes a suggestion system that equates method changes and improvements to compensations. Most suggestion systems leave much to be desired because they do not measure up to expectation. Some of the reasons employees do not take the suggestion system seriously are that the rewards are too meager and there is much delay in acting on or acknowledging a suggestion advanced. When a suggestion is not accepted, there is little or no reasonable explanation given why it was turned down. When these conditions exist in a suggestion system, it is doomed to failure because it does not really establish the conditions conducive to motivating the employee to come up with his good ideas. R. J. Gillespie of Sylvania Electric Products, Inc., estimates that the $200 million corporation may lose $13–$31 million annually because good ideas are allowed to die. [2]

Increasing Profits

A current trend is to pay supplementary compensations in some proportion to the part that employees play in increasing profits. Since an almost unlimited number of factors affect profits, the employee has an almost unlimited number of opportunities to perform in a manner that improves company efficiency and in turn increases profits. Profits might be increased through increased production, improved quality, new methods, product innovations, more efficient equipment, greater sales, lower overhead, less scrap, and product price changes. This supplementary compensation, more commonly called profit sharing, is described at length in Chapter 20.

Continuous Plant Operation

Because of the increased fixed investment necessary to compete successfully in business, it is becoming increasingly important to keep the high-cost equipment and plant in operation at all times. By running the equipment on all three shifts, seven days a week, the fixed costs can be spread over more units than if one shift were used, thereby reducing the unit cost of production. There are two requirements if the unit cost is to be reduced in this manner. The fixed investment should be high in relation to the variable cost of production; and the premiums paid to the workers, taken on the basis of units, cannot be higher than the fixed per unit saving. It is assumed, of course, that a firm would not use continuous plant operation unless there was a continuous market demand for the product that far outnumbered the plant's ability to produce the product.

Another saving resulting from the payment of premiums is that by keeping the plant in operation at all times, the company is able to avoid costly shutdowns. This saving is most significant in the steel and other metal processing industries.

Table 22.1 illustrates the effect that overtime, weekend, and shift premiums have on the unit cost of an item. The one-shift operation runs five days a week and eight hours a day. The three-shift operation runs seven days a week. Each shift is staggered in such a way that each worker gets 42 hours a week of work. The plant in this operation is run 168 hours a week. Holiday premiums are neglected in both examples.

---

[2]K. W. Bennett, "Unused Ideas Cost Companies Millions," *Iron Age* (November 4, 1965).

TABLE 22.1

EFFECT OF OVERTIME PREMIUMS ON THE UNIT COST OF PRODUCTION

No. of Shifts	Shift No.	Units Produced by the Shift	Base Rate of Pay	Shift Premium	Week-End Premium	Av. Unit Labor Cost	Weekly Shut-down Cost*	Weekly Dept. Cost	Unit Shut-down and Dept. Cost	Unit Cost
1	1	50,000	3.00	.00	.00	3.00	10,000	100,000	2.20	5.20
3	1	70,000	3.00	.00	.10	3.06	—	33,334	.48	3.54
	2	68,000	3.00	.15	.10	3.26	—	33,333	.49	3.75
	3	67,000	3.00	.30	.10	3.41	—	33,333	.50	3.91

*This applies only to the one-shift operation, since the other is run 7 days a week and 24 hours a day.

Workers should be educated to realize that overtime payments and shift and holiday premiums are not gifts or trimmings. By the same token, management personnel should realize that overtime and shift payments are not to be regarded as nonproductive supplementary compensations. They are production incentives that call for some sacrifice (working longer hours or nights) to produce at the standard rate. The employer should gain a profitable return from the extra large or overflow orders completed by the late afternoon or night shifts. A big order obtained on a low bid in competitive bidding shows poor business acumen if it involves paying 50 percent overtime over a certain period without increased productivity. Employers occasionally take on such work "to keep the crew busy" in order to retain skilled workers. Under these conditions, supervisors and workers should be informed of the circumstances in an effort to keep costs down. Operating second or third shifts on a shift-premium basis is equally impractical unless overhead is reduced to make it profitable.

Length of Service with Company

Companies that employ steady workers save on labor turnover and overhead costs. A worker employed for a number of years by the same company is usually capable of doing many jobs, and is well acquainted with shop or office routines and conditions. He is, therefore, invaluable in an emergency. He generally is a diligent and loyal employee, interested in his work. Although these qualities are not directly measurable, they contribute toward efficient productivity and the realization of larger profits. Therefore, a *length-of-service bonus* is paid as an extra reward. In most companies, the worker becomes eligible for such a bonus after a specific period of employment. This requirement is designed to exclude "floaters," and to avoid the costs incurred by the constant hiring and training of new employees.

One electrical supply company bases its bonus on the actual amount of pay drawn over a certain period rather than on the wage-base rate or salary rate. The bonus rate paid under this plan begins at 2 percent of each employee's actual earnings after the first year of service, and increases 1 percent each year until it reaches the tenth year. After that, the bonus is fixed at 10 percent of the employee's yearly earnings.

It is easy to see how a firm saves money when a competent employee remains with the company. If the cost of hiring a replacement for the employee were placed at only $500–$1,000 (a very conservative amount) and the company had to find a replacement each year for the 30 or more years that constitute an employee's career, the amount of money that the firm saves is at least $15,000 and more likely over $30,000. Therefore, this type of saving should be shared with an employee who remains with the same company long enough for such a saving to accrue to the company. Years ago some firms rewarded the long-term employee (at retirement) with a gold watch or some other appropriate token of their appreciation. Today, a number of firms are offering some supplementary compensation before retirement as an inducement to remain with the firm. The military establishment (Army, Navy, Air Force, and Marines) provides a bonus (called a foggie) which provides for a 5 percent raise in pay for each serviceman who agrees to reenlist or remain with the service for another tour of duty (usually four years). In this way, the supplementary compensation offered to the employee for the length of service he gives to the firm pays its way through the money saved in reduced labor turnover and hiring costs.

Punctuality and Attendance

While it is true that under ordinary conditions every employee should report on time, nevertheless, the fact remains that tardiness is a problem. Therefore, inducements for punctuality are advisable to maintain production requirements and to complete orders on specified or scheduled dates.

In a complex organization with production required on predetermined schedules, regular attendance is a prime necessity. Irregular attendance is responsible for losses because of idle machinery, interrupted schedules, and retarded departmental operations. Furthermore, dismissals of employees due to their records of tardiness and absenteeism incur a considerable loss because of the necessity to hire and train replacements. Besides financial losses to employer and employee, such conditions also are demoralizing to the steady and punctual employees.

The disagreeable old method of penalizing tardiness and absenteeism by using the "negative" incentive of docking the employee's pay is still prevalent. *Business Management* magazine reports that 74 percent of firms deduct pay when absenteeism is excessive among their clerical and white-collar workers. [3] Only 12 percent offer some positive incentive to minimize absenteeism and tardiness. Deductions for lost time vary from money value in minutes lost to severe penalties of 100 to 300 percent of the actual time value. Other negative incentives may include deferring the employee's wage increase and promotion, and transferring him to a less desirable job.

The loss in workers' wages, employer's profits, and customers' orders surpasses any gain made through penalties. Hence, negative incentives are giving way to "positive" incentives — in the form of a financial bonus — as a more effective means to encourage punctuality. Bonuses range from 2 to 10 percent of the employee's weekly earnings.

Some firms are granting employees one or two days off a year as an incentive and reward for keeping themselves in top physical condition and thus not having a need to be absent because they are physically ill. When a firm has a sick leave policy, it usually allows the employee one day of sick leave per month if he is so unfortunate as to become sick. This means that the employee does not lose any pay for a maximum of 12 days' absence from the job due to his illness. This policy, in many cases, has not worked well because employees tend to abuse the privilege by taking days off when they are not really sick. They may be "sick of work," but the policy and its costs are intended to cover only those employees who are really ill and unable to be up and around and on the job. To cope with this abuse of a sick leave privilege, a firm might gain valuable employee services when it can motivate the employee to be on the job whenever he is physically fit. The offering of one or two days off a year for those employees who have perfect attendance serves as a supplementary compensation for the employee and a cost savings for the firm when the employee does not abuse the sick leave privilege.

An alternate award that some firms make in place of the days off is to pay $10 for a quarter of a year of perfect attendance, while some others pay $50 for a perfect year. The Atlanta Envelope Company pays a bonus of two hours' extra pay if the employee is present every working day of the month. If the employee maintains perfect attendance for six consecutive months, he gets the two-hour bonus for each month plus an additional eight hours' pay (or a total of 20 hours pay). If the employee had perfect attendance for a full year, he receives a week's extra pay. Since this plan has gone into effect, the man-hours lost per month have dropped 50 percent and production with the same work force has increased 15 percent. [4] It is easy to conclude that this plan of supplementary compensation for attendance is directly paying its way.

---

[3]"The Nagging Problems of Absenteeism and Tardiness," *Business Management* (October, 1967), p. 12.

[4]*Notes and Quotes*, No. 330 (Hartford, Conn.: Connecticut General Life Insurance Co., November, 1966), p. 1. Reprinted from *Executive's Bulletin* (Waterford, Conn.: National Foremen's Institute, November 30, 1966).

Safety Achievements

To reduce losses in production and earnings, the personnel departments of many companies have designed successful financial incentive plans for safety achievements and accident prevention. However, it appears that rewards, such as prizes, contests, and various publicity measures, have been equally successful in getting beneficial results.

The National Safety Council, an organization most active in disseminating safety principles, makes the following suggestions:

> Competition, if properly organized, can do much to develop teamwork among the men. Some workers who apparently give no thought to their own safety can be influenced to cooperate with their fellows if they know that an injury will bring discredit upon their department or "team."
>
> In organizing safety competitions, many companies plan to award bonuses to the contest winners. Some managers, however, are of the opinion that when a worker accepts a job he automatically assumes an obligation to perform his work carefully and without causing injury to himself or to his fellow workers. ... It is often stated that "it is just as foolish to reward a man for being safe as it is to pay him for being honest."
>
> Those who favor safety prizes and bonuses are strongly opposed to the idea of bribery; they consider such awards just as harmless as other self-respecting citizens consider a cup to the winner of a tennis or a golf tournament ... a prize gives tangible evidence and a certain degree of permanence of a feat of winning.[5]

In hazardous industries where it is normal to have a reasonable number of accidents, supplementary compensations are one means of reducing accident costs and thus can pay their way. One of the authors worked for a transit company that had yearly accident costs in excess of $500,000. The firm began offering supplementary compensations in the form of cash, driver uniforms, and safe-driving pins, and found that these rewards for safe driving paid off in real savings. There is no reason why a firm plagued with accidents cannot save much time, money, and personal hardships if it is willing to share some of the reduced costs with the employees in the form of supplementary compensations or awards.

This chapter has attempted to show how those supplementary compensations that pay their way fit the wage structure. The next chapter will deal with the place of those supplementary compensations that are more commonly called fringe benefits.

REVIEW QUESTIONS

1. What is the essential difference between a supplementary compensation and a fringe benefit?

---

[5] *Safety Contests*, Pamphlet No. 74 (Chicago: National Safety Council, 425 N. Michigan Ave., 1951).

2. What valid reasons are there for a firm to offer supplementary compensations to its employees?

3. (a) What media are available for use in conveying supplementary compensations to employees? (b) What are the main advantages of each medium?

4. What criteria should management use to decide whether to offer supplementary compensations?

5. Who should decide what specific supplementary compensation is best for a certain group of employees? Why?

6. Should there be any limit on the number of supplementary compensations that an employer might offer his employees if the compensations directly pay their way? Why?

7. What is the essential difference between a supplementary compensation that pays money for an increase in production and a piece-rate system of compensation?

8. What is the justification for paying a premium for shift work? for overtime?

9. What considerations should the management of a firm give to supplementary compensations before deciding whether to adopt one or more of them?

RESEARCH OR SEMINAR QUESTIONS

1. What term could you coin that might better describe supplementary compensations?

2. What new forms of supplementary compensation can you think of which would pay their way and are presently not being utilized?

3. In what ways might a supplementary compensation which pays its way get out of hand?

PRACTICAL EXPERIENCE ASSIGNMENT

Contact some company which utilizes a supplementary compensation that is supposed to pay its way. Try to learn all you can about how it works, how it was selected and installed, and what results it has had in this firm. Be prepared to report to your class the highlights of your visit to the company and to answer any questions the students might have.

CASE PROBLEM

22–1. THE MERIT COMPANY

Cost of Living v. Supplementary Compensations

The Merit Company is a well-known manufacturer of steel products that has been highly successful for over 35 years. Its employees number close to ten thousand and they are said to be receiving above-average wages for their community. The employees have received annual wage increases every year since World War II. Most of the employees have the opportunity to earn supplementary compensations of 5 to 30 percent above their regular wages if they are willing to exert extra efforts.

During the past five years the firm has increased its productive efficiency on an average of 10 percent each year. Since the annual union-management labor contract will expire in another month, the negotiations are now in progress. The union is asking for a 10 percent across-the-board raise for all employees because it is their belief that everyone should share equally in the 10 percent increased efficiency and prosperity of the firm. The economic conditions in the United States at this time are such that most employees throughout the country are complaining bitterly about the high cost of living and that the rising costs of living tend to cancel out the wage increases so that employees are not being able to improve their financial status. Unemployment in the country is also on the increase.

The management of the firm acknowledges that the productive efficiency of the company has increased at an average of 10 percent each year and is very appreciative of this fact. However, the management team believes that the employees are not entitled to all the 10 percent increase in productive efficiency of the firm, since much of the increased efficiency has been due to the purchase and installation of more modern equipment that was financed by the firm's stockholders. Furthermore, the management team believes that the increasing costs of living are rising because employees are generally asking for, and receiving, higher wage raises than their productive efforts have made possible. In light of this, the management negotiators are recommending to the union that the employees be granted a 6 percent wage increase, the stockholders be given dividends of an extra 2 percent from the results of the new equipment efficiencies, and that the selling price of the firm's products be reduced 2 percent.

By doing this, management believes it is treating the union and stockholders fairly, and more importantly it is stemming the rising cost of living by lowering its prices 2 percent. If other firms were to follow suit, the company believes there would be a general trend toward lower prices and living costs and thus all employees and customers would benefit.

The union has scoffed at the management proposal. The union says it is looking out for itself and demands that its members receive the full 10 percent wage increase to which they are entitled.

Problem:

Since you have just joined the firm as a member of the personnel department in a supervisory capacity and the management team has learned that you have recently completed a high-caliber course in Wage and Salary Administration, they have called upon you to evaluate the positions of both the union and management and to make appropriate proposals or comments.

chapter 23

SUPPLEMENTARY COMPENSATION: FRINGE BENEFITS

In the last chapter, the general theory of supplementary compensation was developed, and one part of it — supplementary compensations that directly pay their way — was discussed. In this chapter, we shall deal with the other part of supplementary compensations — fringe benefits.

Nature of fringe benefits

Supplementary compensations have been defined as all financial and non-financial payments made by the employer to or for the benefit of the employee that are over and above the agreed-upon base compensation rate due the employee for the minimum results expected on the job. Some forms of supplementary compensation are expected to produce direct results, while others are not. Therefore, in order to differentiate between the two, *fringe benefits* may be thought of as a form of supplementary compensation given by the employer to the employee without expecting some direct tangible productive job results in return. However, the employer does *hope* that he will obtain some return from these in terms of lower turnover, higher morale, or some other advantages.

Despite the prevalence of the term "fringe benefit" in management literature, we are convinced that the term is outmoded. The term fringe benefit is a poor choice since it does not adequately describe the kinds of benefits that are being given. Besides, they are no longer a fringe, but an important part of the employer's payroll. A more appropriate name for these benefits would be *employment benefits* since it better describes the purpose for which they are given. The term fringe benefit is used in the rest of the chapter only to avoid confusion that might result if the term employment benefits were used.

Growth of fringe benefits

During the nineteenth century few fringe benefits were granted to the employees. However, two benefits that are very common today got their start in the last 25 years of that century. In 1875, the American Express Company established the first private pension plan in the United States. In 1886, the Westinghouse Corporation was one of the first to grant paid vacations to their workers. After the turn of the century, the pace at which new benefits were granted increased. In 1908, the first workmen's compensation law for federal government employees was enacted. In 1911, Wisconsin enacted the first state workmen's compensation law that was ruled to be constitutional by the courts. In 1920, the Civil Service Retirement Act for federal employees was enacted. Prior to 1920, some companies offered life insurance, pensions, and sick benefits to their employees. At that time, however, employees generally felt that fringes were management gratuities designed to undermine the union cause. In spite of employees' misgivings, many employers recognized that their employees should have a desirable place to work as well as some degree of job security and therefore provided various types of fringes on a more or less informal basis.

Through the late 1920's and the 1930's most of the additional benefits that were granted to employees came as a result of federal and state legislation. The real impetus to fringe benefits came about during World War II when the United States government froze wages to prevent employees from changing jobs and companies in order to gain pay increases. Offering fringe benefits appeared to be the answer to recruiting new employees to replace those called into the military. Although fringe benefits helped employers to obtain needed personnel during the war, most employers found themselves saddled with the payments of these benefits after the war because employees and their unions were unwilling to give them up. In 1948, the courts made a decision in the Inland Steel case that opened the "flood gates" for unions to demand more fringe benefits. The National Labor Relations Board ruled that the Taft-Hartley Act gave unions the right to bargain over wages, hours, and other conditions of employment which included fringe benefits and contributions made to pension plans.

In 1929, fringe benefits were costing the average employer about one penny per hour per employee. This amounted to about 3 percent of the total amount paid out for wages and salaries. By 1949, fringe benefits were averaging about 23.7 cents per hour per employee or 16 percent of the payroll. By 1959, fringes were averaging 54.8 cents per hour or 22.8 percent of the payroll.[1] By 1965, fringes were averaging 71.5 cents per hour or 24.7 percent of the payroll hour.[2] By 1967, fringes in some 1,150 companies were averaging 82.2 cents per hour or 26.6 percent of the payroll hour.[3] In short, since 1949 fringe benefits have risen some 58.5 cents per hour (or over $23 per week) and may range anywhere from 8 to over 60 percent of the payroll. Fringes are presently costing the average employer about $32.88 per employee per week, which amounts to over 26 percent of the average company's weekly payroll.[4] It has been said that fringe benefits such as stock options, pensions, profit sharing, and deferred compensation now account for nearly one half of the average company officer's total compensation.[5]

Impact of fringe benefits

The rapid growth of fringe benefits has had a marked impact on the employee, the employer, and the public. The effect of fringes upon each is examined in the following paragraphs.

Effect upon the Employee

Today, the average worker is receiving the following fringes that were not available to him in 1936: paid vacations and holidays; paid leave periods for illness and jury duty; insurances such as life, unemployment, and medical; and old-age benefits under social security and company pensions. These benefits have given the employee a much higher standard of living than ever before. They are very popular with most employees because (1) many of the benefits are exempt from income tax, (2) the employer can generally provide more benefits than the employee could purchase for himself if he were given the money, and (3) each employee is being helped to meet his basic needs.

On the other hand, there is a growing number of employees who feel that some of the so-called "benefits" are not really benefits for them but "detriments" because these employees cannot use (or do not want) all the fringes offered. As one employee has put it, "Please take it easy on any more fringe benefits; I'm already planning and spending so much for the future that I don't have enough left to really live today."[6] Another possible limitation of some fringes, such as pensions, is that they restrict the mobility of workers to go wherever job opportunities are greater.

---

[1] *Fringe Benefits, 1959* (Washington: Chamber of Commerce of the United States, 1960), p. 9.

[2] *Fringe Benefits, 1965* (Washington: Chamber of Commerce of the United States, 1966), p. 9.

[3] *Employee Benefits, 1967* (Washington: Chamber of Commerce of the United States, 1968), p. 5.

[4] *Ibid.*, p. 9.

[5] "Are Executives Paid Enough?" *U.S. News & World Report* (January 29, 1968), p. 64.

[6] *Digest of the Second Annual Industrial Relations Workshop of NAM* (October 6, 1960), p. 10.

In general, it would appear that most employees want and need fringe benefits. However, the question should be raised as to whether the money presently being spent on fringes is the best method of providing for the needs of each employee. It would also appear that fringes have become so involved that the average employee is not usually abreast of the benefit costs. In one survey it was revealed that the fringe costs were six times as much as the average worker thought they were.[7]

Effect upon the Employer

Many employers are beginning to wonder about the value to the company of all the fringe benefits presently being offered. Managements are questioning whether the increased productivity, job satisfaction, and lower labor turnover are worth the cost of the fringes. Some employers believe it may be socially healthier for employees to provide some of their own benefits to avoid socialism.

Other employers show concern over the fixed cost aspects of fringe benefits in that once fringes are granted they appear irrevocable. Of more concern are the uncontrollable, skyrocketing, almost automatic costs tied to some fringes. For example, Blue Cross and Blue Shield rates continue to rise each year because more people are using hospitals for minor treatments and because people are living longer and therefore receive more benefits. In the Milwaukee Breweries the yearly pay costs for time not worked such as vacations, holidays, and rest periods have risen from $659 per employee to over $1,700 (average cost increase of $101 per employee for each year over a 10-year period),[8] without the workers having to bargain specifically for them. In 1968, the average brewery worker was receiving $3,675 in fringe benefits.[9] It is estimated that he is now receiving over $4,000 in fringe benefits each year.

Today it is practically impossible to grant a wage increase without producing a compounding effect on fringe costs because wage increases are tied to overtime, sick leave, vacations, holidays, rest periods, and the like.

Another impact of fringes on employers concerns unemployment insurance. There are cases on record where a company's unemployment insurance benefits have actually helped to finance a strike against the company because the state paid unemployment compensation to strikers.

In summary, employers are realizing that fringe benefit costs have become a significant cost of production and that there must be a more direct relationship between productivity and benefits if fringes are to be kept from getting completely out of line. The *Progress Sharing Plan* of American Motors is a good example

---

[7]"The Wages that Nobody Counts," *U.S. News & World Report*, Vol. XLIX, No. 24 (December 13, 1960), p. 5.

[8]H. G. Zollitsch and Ralph Brownlee, *An Economic Study of the Milwaukee Brewing Industry* (Milwaukee: Milwaukee Brewery Proprietors, February, 1965), p. 35.

[9]Ralph Brownlee, *An Analysis of Economic Factors Affecting Milwaukee Breweries and Brewery Workers* (Milwaukee: Milwaukee Brewery Proprietors, May, 1969), p. 3.

of how benefits can be tied to productivity and profits. In American Motors' plan, certain fringes are paid for from profits the company shares with the union. Thus, if there are reduced profits, there are reduced fringes. The present and future impact of fringe benefit costs on the employer may be far more important than the cost of investments in new machines or in a new addition to the plant.[10]

Effect upon the Public

What has been the effect of fringe benefits on the public? Generally, various segments of the public look favorably upon fringes. The record shows that politicians have instigated a few fringes themselves, realizing that fringe benefits can be vote getters. Economists tend to say that fringes are not as inflationary as direct wage increases and that fringes provide a cushion of cash to pad jolts when the economy goes downward. Local social and welfare organizations feel that fringe benefits and services help reduce the community welfare burden. Most everyone knows that unions are in the "fringe benefit business."

The federal government could be one sector of the public that might feel that there are some abuses of fringes and that they constitute a tax dodge. The consumer appears to be gradually becoming aware that fringe benefit costs which have not been earned are partly responsible for higher prices. There is no easy way to hide a fringe cost that amounts to 27 percent of the payroll, nor to make it palatable to the customer who is compelled to pay the higher prices.

Categories and classifications of fringe benefits

The first division of supplementary compensations into categories and classifications should be credited to L. B. Michael, who divided the comprehensive subject into five general categories. Prophetically, Michael stated: "In making these individual classifications, the author realizes that his classification may be considered by some to be arbitrary and subject to controversy."[11] "Categories are still selected arbitrarily and, so far, have remained controversial.

In 1949, the Chamber of Commerce of the United States classified supplementary compensations into eight categories, and later condensed them to five, as shown in Table 23.1. Many companies have adopted various categories different from those of the Chamber. For proper comparison, however, we shall consider the Chamber's data and use some of the categories in Table 23.1 in our discussion.

By closely studying Table 23.1, the reader will realize that an explanation of each item would require considerable space. It is neither within the scope of

---

[10] *Digest of the Second Annual Industrial Relations Workshop of NAM, op. cit.*, p. 13.
[11] Lionel B. Michael, *Wage and Salary Fundamentals and Procedures* (New York: Mc-Graw-Hill Book Co., Inc., 1950), p. 156.

TABLE 23.1

AVERAGE SUPPLEMENTARY (FRINGE) PAYMENTS BY TYPE OF PAYMENT, 1967

Type of Payment	Total, All Companies	Total, All Manufacturing	Total, All Nonmanufacturing
Total employee benefits as percent of payroll	26.6%	25.6%	28.2%
1. Legally required payments (employer's share only)	5.9	6.4	5.3
a. Old-age, survivors, disability and health insurance	3.9	4.1	3.7
b. Unemployment compensation	1.0	1.1	0.8
c. Workmen's compensation (including estimated cost for self-insured)	0.8	1.1	0.5
d. Railroad retirement tax, railroad unemployment insurance, state sickness benefits insurance, etc.**	0.2	0.1	0.3
2. Pension and other agreed-upon payments (employer's share only)	8.0	7.0	9.1
a. Pension plan premiums and pension payments not covered by insurance-type plan (net)	4.0	3.2	5.4
b. Life insurance premiums, death benefits, sickness, accident and medical-care insurance premiums, hospitalization insurance, etc. (net)	3.2	3.5	2.6
c. Contributions to privately financed unemployment benefit funds	0.1	0.1	*
d. Separation or termination pay allowances	0.1	*	0.1
e. Discounts on goods and services purchased from company by employees	0.2	*	0.3
f. Employee meals furnished by company	0.2	*	0.5
g. Miscellaneous payments (compensation payments in excess of legal requirements, payments to needy employees, etc.)	0.2	0.2	0.2
3. Paid rest periods, lunch periods, wash-up time, travel time, clothes-change time, get-ready time, etc.	2.7	3.0	2.6
4. Payments for time not worked	7.9	7.3	8.7
a. Paid vacations and bonuses in lieu of vacation	4.2	4.2	4.1
b. Payments for holidays not worked	2.6	2.5	2.7
c. Paid sick leave	0.8	0.4	1.4
d. Payments for State or National Guard duty, jury, witness and voting pay allowances, payments for time lost due to death in family or other personal reasons, etc.	0.3	0.2	0.5
5. Other items	2.1	1.9	2.5
a. Profit-sharing payments	1.2	1.1	1.4
b. Contributions to employee thrift	0.1	0.1	0.2
c. Christmas or other special bonuses, service awards, suggestion awards, etc.	0.5	0.5	0.6
d. Employee education expenditures (tuition refunds, etc.)	0.1	*	0.1
e. Special wage payments ordered by courts, payments to union stewards, etc.	0.2	0.2	0.2
Total employee benefits as cents per payroll hour	82.2¢	78.3¢	88.6¢
Total employee benefits as dollars per year per employee	$1719	$1656	$1822

*Less than 0.05%.

**Figure shown is considerably less than legal rate, as most reporting companies had only a small proportion of employees covered by tax.

Source: Employee Benefits, 1967 (Washington: Chamber of Commerce of the United States, 1968), p. 9.

nor the purpose of this book to delve into the details of each item.[12]   Further-more, items of interest to one organization may be of little value to others. Therefore, we shall confine our discussion primarily to some of the main cate-gories and touch upon the often misinterpreted items.

Legally Required Payments for Compulsory Employee Benefits

Some supplementary compensations became mandatory by reason of the workmen's compensation laws and the Social Security Act.   These compensa-tions are known as *legally required payments* (category 1 in Table 23.1) for *com-pulsory employee benefits*. The mandatory payments supplement the daily and weekly wages or salaries of all employees covered under provisions of the legisla-tion.   In other words, anywhere a worker applies for employment in a covered occupation, he is entitled to the same supplementary compensations. These com-pulsory payments pertain to the national old-age, survivors, disability, and health insurance (OASDHI) program, and they are given a more detailed explanation in this chapter under "Pension Plans."

Payments for Time Not Worked

Some leading companies with a large number of personnel have classified all supplementary compensations into two main classes — "Pay for time not worked" and "Pay for time worked."[13]   All supplementary compensations are then classified into either one or the other of these two main divisions.

Note that "Payments for time worked" is not shown in the Chamber report (Table 23.1).   We believe that this is an important category, especially when sub-divided into three classifications on job features such as: (a) "Nonproductive time on the job," referring to machine breakdowns, personal time, grievances, rest periods, etc.; (b) "Working under special conditions on the job," referring to nights, overtime, holidays, safety awards, service bonuses, attendance bonuses, etc.; and (c) "Increased productivity on the job," referring to profit sharing, sug-gestion awards, and other bonuses supplemental to production incentives.

On the other hand, close analysis will reveal that a supplementary payment for time worked, in reality, is part of the production payments for work per-formed.   Similarly, some payments are outside the supplementary payment category.

---

[12]For a broad discussion of items in each field, we recommend Jay V. Strong, *Employee Benefit Plans in Operation* (Washington: The Bureau of National Affairs, Inc., 1951); Francis M. Wistert, *Fringe Benefits* (New York: Reinhold Publishing Corporation, 1959); Editorial Staff of Prentice-Hall, *Successful Employee Benefit Plans* (Englewood Cliffs, N.J.: Prentice-Hall, Inc., 1952).

[13]See Robert H. Hoge, "Pinning Down the Problematic Fringe," *The Personnel Function: A Progress Report*, AMA Management Report No. 24 (1958), pp. 112–117.

Payments for Items Pertaining to Employee Security Benefits

There was a time, especially during economic depressions, when the only security desired by workers was a steady job. Since World War II, however, jobs have become so plentiful that skilled workers are bypassing job steadiness in their quest for "what there is in it for the future." In other words, job steadiness concerns them only from the standpoint of future security for themselves and their dependents in the event of old age, illness, or death. Freedom from uncertainty regarding future economic security, and the assurance that dependents will be provided for in the event of illness, disability, death, or retirement, are reflected in better employer-employee relations and loyal adherence to company objectives. It is the wage and salary administrator's function to impress upon employees that the fringe benefits are possible because of solvent business conditions due to efficient productivity and minimum expenses.

Payments for Items Pertaining to Employee Service Benefits

Employee service benefits are differentiated from security benefits in that service benefits consist of financial aids to employees and their dependents to provide for emergencies, to alleviate temporary economic setbacks, to encourage thrift, to carry out certain insurance programs, and to help the employees and their dependents become established as desirable citizens in the community. The following items indicate the nature of employee services: cafeteria privileges and canteen services; free meals; company housing; home financing; health and welfare plans; hospital facilities; health and medical clinic services for dependents; sickness and hospitalization plans; visiting nurse service; thrift plans; scholarships; and items of a recreational nature.

Financial aid for items of a recreational nature should be regarded as effective compensations in the form of service benefits even though the employees are not recipients of monies. Compensational and incentive values are enhanced by broad programs offering athletics, various sports, social functions, education, and cultural activities to all the employees, sponsored wholly or partially by the employer. Such activities relieve mental and physical tensions, and develop a teamwork spirit that thrives in a climate of togetherness. The employees tend to be more favorably inclined toward the employer.

In all categories of supplementary compensations, employees should be cautioned against taking for granted — as an inconsequential fringe — items either provided by the employer or offered to the employee at a nominal fee. The employees should be made to realize that if they do not have to pay for such benefits outright, the company must absorb the expense. This means lower profits and, as frequently mentioned, profits and production must balance if the company is to survive. It is our firm conviction that *plans of a contributory nature,* in the long run, are more equitable for both the employer and employee. Under such plans, employees are made to realize that the benefits are costly and should not be misused.

Pension plans

Pension plans are established and maintained for the purpose of providing predetermined amounts of money to employees who are retired because of old age, illness, or disability. The plans are complex and require legal, financial, technical, and actuarial knowledge for their proper installation and administration. Insurance companies, banking institutions, as well as consultants specializing in pension and profit-sharing planning, can be of inestimable assistance. Therefore, we shall only touch upon the most important features of the subject to give the reader a general idea of what is involved.[14]

Older workers generally require considerably less for daily living than younger people. Their expenses for food, shelter, clothing, and recreation approximate one half the average expenditures of their earlier years, provided they are in reasonably good health. Nevertheless, after age 65 or 70 very few workers are self-supporting. To alleviate the hardships of old age, federal and state governments provide old-age, social security, and survivors' benefits which are supported by tax contributions from covered employees and employers, as well as from self-employed persons. Of all the workers in the labor force who reached age 65 during 1966, 95 percent were covered by one of the federal retirement systems (social security, civil service, or the railroad retirement). By 1985 it is expected that 98 percent of all workers will be covered by these federal retirement systems.[15] Pension plans are the most popular of all the supplementary compensations available to employees.

Legally Required Pensions and Other Benefits

Due to the collapse of our national economy in the 1930's, laws were enacted to protect the social and economic welfare of workers. The Social Security Act of 1935 with its subsequent amendments has had a far-reaching effect on the welfare of the average worker. The old-age and survivors insurance (OASI) portion of the Act, which is now in effect in all 50 states and United States territories, provides an income for the worker and his dependents upon retirement at age 65 (or at age 62 with reduced benefits); or, for the dependents if the worker dies. An amendment to the original law provides for the payment of disability insurance benefits to the disabled worker and his dependents, and

---

[14]For detailed discussions see: J. A. Melone and E. T. Allen, *Pension Planning* (Homewood, Ill.: Richard D. Irwin, 1966); M. C. Bernstein, *The Future of Private Pensions* (New York: The Free Press of Glencoe, 1964); Paul P. Harbrecht, S.J., *Pension Funds and Economic Power* (New York: Twentieth Century Fund, 1959); Dorrance C. Bronson, *Concepts of Actuarial Soundness in Pension Plans* (Homewood, Ill.: Richard D. Irwin, 1957).

[15]Bert Seidman, "The Case for Higher Social Security," *AFL-CIO American Federationist* (January, 1967), p. 1.

another amendment provides medical care for the aged and disabled in addition to the pension benefits.   The total program is known as the national old-age, survivors, disability, and health insurance (OASDHI) program.

In 1968 there were 89 million workers who were contributing to the social security plan.[16]   However, there were only 24 million workers who were qualified to receive some type of benefit.[17]   Social security is presently providing retirement benefits to more than 15 million workers and their dependents.[18]   It is also providing survivors' benefits to 5.6 million widows and orphans, and disability benefits to more than 2 million disabled workers and their dependents.[19]   It provides health benefits to over 19 million persons over age 65.[20]

The benefits of the OASDHI program are provided for by funds obtained from equal employer-employee contributions.   The tax rate as of January 1, 1970, on net annual earnings up to $7,800 is 4.8 percent paid by the employer and 4.8 percent paid by the employee.   Table 23.2 shows the schedule of future tax rate increases that have been planned under the 1967 amendments to the Social Security Act.

TABLE 23.2

SCHEDULE OF PLANNED TAX RATE INCREASES OF SOCIAL SECURITY

| | CONTRIBUTION PERCENT OF EACH EMPLOYEE AND EACH EMPLOYER | | |
CALENDAR YEARS	FOR OLD-AGE, SURVIVORS, AND DISABILITY INSURANCE	FOR HOSPITAL INSURANCE	TOTAL
1969–70	4.2%	0.6%	4.8%
1971–72	4.6	0.6	5.2
1973–75	5.0	0.65	5.65
1976–79	5.0	0.7	5.7
1980–86	5.0	0.8	5.8
1987 and after	5.0	0.9	5.9

Source: Social Security Administration, U.S. Department of Health, Education, and Welfare.

Retirement Benefits.   The amount that a worker who retires at age 65 is entitled to receive is based on his average yearly earnings.   It has been estimated that in 1968 the average monthly social security benefit for a single, retired male was $106 a month (or approximately $24 a week); and for a retired couple, the

---

[16]Robert M. Ball, "Your New Social Security," *This Week Magazine, Milwaukee Journal* (March 31, 1968), p. 13.
[17]*Ibid*, p. 10.
[18]Bert Seidman, "The Future Role of Social Security," *AFL-CIO American Federationist*, Vol. 75, No. 4 (April, 1968), p. 1.
[19]*Ibid.*
[20]*Ibid.*

average benefit was about $159 a month (or about $37 a week).[21]   A single male worker who retired in 1968 and was earning $6,600 at the time of retirement would receive a yearly retirement benefit of about 28 percent of this amount ($1,848); if married and with a wife eligible for benefits, the couple would receive about 42 percent of the $6,600 (or $2,772).[22]   A flat 15 percent increase in the social security primary insurance amount became effective in January, 1970. This raised the monthly minimum amount payable from $55 to $64.   It also raised the maximum amount payable at retirement in 1970 for males from $165 to $189.80; and the eventual maximum of $218 payable in the year 2006 will go to $250.70.   Table 23.3 lists the latest benefits of a retired worker and a couple, according to the average monthly wages earned.   If the worker elects to take benefits early (at age 62, 63, or 64), the amount that he receives is reduced accordingly.

Benefits of family members are related to the worker's benefits.   The monthly payment to the wife or dependent husband or child is equal to half the amount paid to the retired worker.   In 1970 the minimum family payment at retirement is $96 and the maximum family payment is $354.40.   Eventually the maximum family benefits will be $434.40 each month.[23]

TABLE 23.3

**PRESENT SOCIAL SECURITY MONTHLY RETIREMENT BENEFITS
OF RETIRED WORKER (AGE 65) AND COUPLE (AGE 65)**

	Monthly Benefits	
Average Monthly Wage	Retired Worker 1970*	Retired Couple 1970**
$ 67 or less	$ 64.00	$ 96.00
100	82.30	123.50
150	101.70	152.60
175	110.00	165.00
200	116.90	175.40
250	132.30	202.40
300	146.20	240.00
350	161.50	280.80
400	176.70	322.40
550	218.40	395.60
650	250.70	434.40

*Primary insurance amount.
**Maximum family benefits.

Source: *Medicare and Social Security Explained* (Chicago: Commerce Clearing House, Inc., 1970).

---

[21]*Ibid.*, p. 3.
[22]*Ibid.*, p. 4.
[23]*Medicare and Social Security Explained* (Chicago: Commerce Clearing House, Inc., 1970), p. 7.

Medical Care. The medical care amendment to the Social Security Act has two provisions. The first provision, which nearly all Americans receive at age 65, provides for the following services: (1) hospital care of up to 90 days for each period of illness and a lifetime reserve of 60 extra days of hospital care; (2) post-hospital care in qualified skilled nursing homes of up to 100 days for each period of illness; and (3) post-hospital care by nurses and technicians from home health agencies of up to 100 visits in the home each year. The cost for these services is included in the normal payments made while the employee is working.

The second provision of the medical care amendment provides additional medical care on a voluntary basis. In order to qualify, a person must be at least 65 years old and make a monthly payment of $5.30 to the special fund. (The amount of monthly payment is subject to change each year.) The government matches the amount out of general funds. The voluntary medical insurance covers 80 percent of the reasonable charges after the first $50 for: physicians' and surgeons' services, an additional 100 visits by a home health service nurse or technician, outpatient diagnostic hospital services, outpatient physical therapy services, and other medical and health services.

Unemployment Insurance. An essential but costly segment of the social security program is the Federal Unemployment Tax Act, now part of the Internal Revenue Code. This Act taxes employers in commerce and industry having four or more employees who work 20 weeks of the year. The Act gives each state an incentive to establish unemployment insurance and to tax the employers according to the state's needs. A state program has to meet certain federal requirements before employers can offset the federal tax and the state can receive federal grants for administration.

To stabilize employment, most states reduce the unemployment insurance tax, or the employer may be released from paying any taxes under the experience-rating provisions of the state law. In other words, an employer's contribution is reduced or discontinued if there is little or no unemployment among his workers.

Workmen's Compensation. Another item pertaining to legislated employee benefits is workmen's compensation. Like unemployment insurance, it is a state-regulated system that provides payments to workers or their dependents for occupational injuries or fatalities. All states now have such laws, with the usual state-to-state variations.

The entire cost of workmen's compensation insurance — which fluctuates according to the accident rate — is absorbed by the employer. For that reason, safety awards or bonuses are significant items of fringe benefits. They tend to lower the accident rate, thereby reducing or entirely eliminating workmen's compensation insurance premiums.

All contributions involved in the legislated employee benefits may be considered a tax expense for accounting purposes. But, they should not be written off as a forgotten wage trimming. The employer's payments are noteworthy contributions. They may be considered a direct part of the basic wage and applied to production costs.

Private Pension Plans

As stated before, under legally required pensions, when an employee retires upon reaching the qualifying age, he receives a certain amount under the OASI program; and the employer's responsibility ceases. Many companies, however, supplement the government payments by some funded pension plans of their own, known as *private pension plans.*

Prior to enactment of the Social Security Act in 1935, many employers with a sense of social responsibility and a genuine desire to promote goodwill among their employees, as well as to improve public relations, established pension plans for superannuated employees. By diverting a certain amount of the high corporate taxes, which included the 85 percent excess profits tax, the establishment of pension plans became relatively inexpensive.

William J. Howell, a Chicago management consultant, estimates there are about 82,000 pension plans in the United States.[24] Practically all large firms today have a company pension plan for all their full-time employees. At least half of the medium-size firms have private pension plans for their employees, but very few small firms have pension plans. The typical pension plan usually sets aside about 1 percent of an employee's pay for each year of his service with the company. Recently, the trend is shifting to a larger size payment based on a fixed percentage of the employee's annual earnings during his last few years with the company and multiplied by his total years of service. Most retirement plans that establish a fixed amount for the employee's retirement are tied to the social security benefits the employee will receive. And in many cases the social security payments will represent three fourths of the employee's pension. Thus, voluntary pension plans supplement the Social Security Act. In 1950, an estimated 6.2 million employees were covered by a pension plan of some type. The number covered had increased to approximately 16.5 million in 1959.[25] In 1966, the coverage of those under private pension plans had increased to 28 million. At the present time about 30 percent of the labor force are currently in jobs covered by private pension plans (and only 15 percent of persons over age 65 receive private pension payments.[26] Pension experts estimate it will be another 15 or 20 years before 30 percent of the retired workers can count on private pension income in addition to social security income.[27]

[24]William J. Howell, "A New Look at Profit Sharing, Pensions, Productivity Plans," *Business Management*, Vol. 33, No. 3 (December, 1967), p. 30.

[25]Paul P. Harbrecht, S.J., *Pension Funds and Economic Power* (New York: The Twentieth Century Fund, 1959), p. 7.

[26]Seidman, *op. cit.*, p. 3.

[27]*Ibid.*

An employer may sometimes question whether private pension plans, to supplement those established by law, are fully justified. Private plans are bound to cost the employer more as an incentive for the unskilled workers since their contribution to the profits is considerably less than that of the skilled workers, especially if the union negotiates a uniform amount for each member without considering the differential in jobs and hourly earnings. Nevertheless, the advantages accruing to the employer from a pension plan are manifold. The benefits are reflected in the orderly retirement of superannuated personnel as well as in the improvement of goodwill.

From the standpoint of taxes, an approved plan has many advantages for the employer, the employee, and the trust. The best procedure is to introduce a government-approved pension plan, that is, one that meets the provisions of the Internal Revenue Code and its accompanying regulations.

The first exemption in favor of pension trusts was incorporated in the Revenue Act of 1921. This Act declared the income from pension and profit-sharing trusts exempt from income tax and relieved employees of paying a tax on current contributions made to a trust fund. In 1928, contributions to a pension fund became tax deductible from gross income because they constituted a business expense, even though a company could at some future time revoke the plan and divert pension funds to other uses. The Revenue Act of 1938, however, allows an exemption only if the contents of the plan specify that the pension funds are to be used exclusively for the benefit of the employees.

Union Impact on Pension Plans

Union influence upon pension plans is evidenced by the fact that "approximately 60 percent of the workers who are covered for pension benefits and about 40 percent of those covered by various welfare programs have obtained them through collective bargaining."[28] Therefore, in a unionized plant, the wage and salary administrator is disposed to discuss the installation and administration of a pension program with union representatives before beginning to plan the pension. Unions invariably insist on the right to represent their membership in matters pertaining to pensions, even if the pensions are proposed solely by the employer. In fact, some unions demand a certain percentage of union representation on the management-appointed committees to administer the employer's plan.

Sections in collective bargaining agreements that relate to pensions are not a part of the actual plan. Nevertheless, there may be features in the plan that concern the union as well as the employer when contractual agreements are negotiated. In many cases, clauses are included in the collective bargaining agreement which render the contributory or noncontributory phases of the plan binding.

---

[28]Harbrecht, *op. cit.*, p. 39.

The union takes advantage of such an agreement even though a voluntary pension plan existed long before the union appeared on the scene.

Installation and Administration of Pension Plans

Numerous companies have installed and are administering their own pension plans. In 1966, 24 of the 28 million employees were covered by pension plans (mostly noncontributory) that were administered by a single employer. Management of the plan is usually vested in a pension committee or in a board consisting of representatives appointed by the employer. Generally, a committee composed of employees and management works out the installation and administration of the plan. Because of their participation, employees have full confidence in the success of the plan. The committee should have sole charge of administering the plan, that is, checking and deciding on retirements, making payments, transacting changes in beneficiaries, preparing statistical data, issuing communications to employees, and handling any correspondence or details regarding the pension plan. In some collectively bargained plans, provision is made for union-appointed representatives, usually to serve on grievance committees. Their activities are, however, restricted to such matters as eligibility, termination of benefits, and settlement of particular grievances.

In order to qualify for tax exemption and to comply with the Welfare and Pension Disclosure Act, a pension plan must have a complete description as indicated in the Act, namely: (1) Eligibility rules; (2) Description of the formula to determine the amount of benefits; (3) Provisions for early, compulsory, and disability retirement; (4) Data regarding the cost of the pension program; (5) Whether the plan shall be contributory or noncontributory; (6) Vesting provisions; and (7) Past service liability, future liability, etc.

Funding the Pension Plan

There are four possible methods of funding a pension plan: (1) payroll method, or the so-called pay-as-you-go method; (2) insured plan; (3) trusteed plan; and (4) profit-sharing pension plan.

Payroll Method. Of the four methods of funding a pension plan, the *payroll method* is the simplest since no special insurance or underwriting of funds is required. Upon retirement an employee receives certain amounts from some reserve fund or from cash on hand. This method has its disadvantages, however. In the first place, the aforementioned tax allowances are not applicable. Secondly, it is contrary to ethical principles or plain common sense human relations for an employee to work a number of years in the hope of gaining some benefits only to find that the cash or assets are not available. Therefore, the progressive methods of funded insurance or trusteed pension plans are more equitable. They have a sufficient deposit of reserve funds and current contributions to meet the already incurred and currently accruing liabilities. The funded pensions are usually determined actuarily on the basis of various predictions and assumptions such as mortality (mortality tables), financial security, and interest rates.

Insured Plan. *Insured plans,* as the term implies, are financed through an insurance company under one or more annuity or insurance contracts. The insurance company assumes all the responsibilities of keeping the plan structurally sound. Upon payment of premiums by the employer, the insurance company becomes obligated to fulfill all future pension liabilities. Thus, the employer is relieved of all pension management problems and responsibilities. This setup has tax advantages and, at the same time, assures the employees of receiving definite amounts upon retirement.

Trusteed Plan. Some large companies may act as their own insurance company or trust. Most *trusteed plans,* however, are administered by banks or trust companies who assume trusteeship under the terms of a trust indenture. These institutions have experienced actuaries and lawyers whose main functions are to save the employer as much as is compatible with the legal requirements and, at the same time, make it possible for the retired employee to receive all that he or his dependents are entitled to. Each year an actuarially determined amount is paid to the trustee, and pension payments are made from the fund as they become due.

An employee's pension is assured in both the insured and trusteed plans. The difference, however, is in the method of spreading the cost over the work years of the future annuitant. Due to the very conservative way in which insurance companies conduct their business, the insured fund generally costs more than the trusteed funds. The insurance company must be compensated for undertaking to guarantee a pension many years ahead. The trusteed fund, on the other hand, makes it possible for the trustee to invest the employer's contribution in lucrative stocks and bonds paying dividends and interest that can be reinvested or utilized to reimburse the expenses incurred in administering the plan.

Profit-Sharing Pension Plan. *Profit-sharing pension plans* are contingent upon fixed percentages of profits that are equitably distributed to employee accounts according to certain formulas. The profits from which a pension is purchased are cumulative. Of course, since profits fluctuate, the employer's contributions will vary yearly. As a matter of fact, in profitless years there are no contributions.

Instead of assuming the burden of distributing individual annuity premiums, many companies have decided upon the installation of profit-sharing plans that require no contributions when there are no profits. Nevertheless, numerous companies — large, medium-size, and small — such as Sears, Roebuck & Company, Kellogg Company, Schlumberger Oil Well Surveying Corporation, and Bell & Howell have successfully supplied adequate funds and paid substantial pensions to the retirees. The solvency of such plans is assured by investing the contributions in stocks and government bonds. This type of pension plan is discussed in more detail under the section "Profit Sharing" in Chapter 20.

Contributions to Costs of Pensions. Private pension plans are either *noncontributory* (the employer absorbs the entire cost) or *contributory* (the employee contributes part of the cost by agreement through payroll deduction). There are, however, arguments for and against the noncontributory plans.

For Noncontributory Plans. Those who favor the noncontributory pension plan believe that because the employer is in full control he can carry out his policies to the satisfaction of all concerned. Also, it has been affirmed that unions prefer this type of plan because the workers' earnings are not affected. The payroll department does not have to contend with collecting contributions from employees, and there is no need to sell the plan to the employees since they automatically become participants. Therefore, it costs less to administer this type of plan. Some claim that in appreciation of the employer's generosity in their behalf, the employees tend to reciprocate by increasing production and avoiding waste.

Against Noncontributory Plans. Those against the noncontributory pension plan — but for contributory — claim that the contributing employee develops a keen interest in the plan that leads to full realization of its value. Therefore, he appreciates his employer's contribution in his behalf, and willingly contributes his share. Further claims are that the extra contribution helps to provide a broader coverage and greater benefits; that the contribution encourages thrift; that it is a source of saving for the future; and that the periodic payroll deductions serve as a reminder for the employee that the future is secure.

Eligibility Rules

Before employees are covered by a pension plan, rules must be established regarding the objective and aim. The rules should encompass: the age limit for eligibility to join the plan; the employee groups that are eligible to receive pensions; the waiting period before an employee becomes eligible to join; the required length of service for eligibility to receive pension payments; and the amount of pension the employee will receive upon retirement. Published rules should be available to each prospective applicant.

Generally, the eligible age for joining the plan is between 25 and 35 years. This age limit has been chosen because of the claims that employees within this age group have a lower rate of turnover than younger people; and the cost of the plan is less than for an older age group. The latter condition has stirred up a great deal of controversy because some companies do not consider even highly skilled, healthy persons for employment when they are above 40 years of age.

It is a matter of policy in some enterprises to separate executives and certain salaried personnel under one rule of eligibility, and to group shop employees and clerical workers under another rule. In this respect the unions may demand certain conditions for eligibility of a specific group of employees. A definite waiting time, such as one to five years of service, is an almost universal requirement, mainly to eliminate labor turnover and to retain a steady, efficient crew.

The retirement age is contingent upon the employee's length of service in the company. Some companies have established a definite age, normally 65, for the retirement of an employee. Others are more liberal, permitting employees to retire as early as 45 years of age, or as late as age 70, depending upon the usefulness of the employee to the company.

The most important, and perhaps the most varied, part of the pension plan is the amount of compensation provided for retirement benefits. The benefits, upon retirement, usually comprise one third to one half of an employee's earnings. These payments may or may not be affected by social security benefits, age of retirement, and years of service.

In general, pension payments are based upon an employee's earnings per year and the number of years of service. The formula followed is the amount for each year of service, or a percentage of the employee's weekly wages, multiplied by the number of years of service. Payments also differ according to the type of plan. The noncontributory plans may pay from $60 to $410 per month, while the contributory plans may pay from $75 to $660 per month. However, the three most common methods of computing benefit payments are:

1. Number of years of service in relation to the earnings during those years. For example, 2 percent of pay is allowed for each year of service from the year employment started to retirement.
2. Pay a certain amount, say $2 to $5 per month, for each year of service to retirement.
3. Pay a certain percentage, say 30 or 40 percent, of wages or salary earned per month as an average prior to or at the time of retirement.

Problem of Vesting

Vesting means that, upon termination of employment, an employee is entitled to the pension payments made in his behalf. Whether the employee is entitled to the employer's contribution to the pension, in addition to the amount he has contributed, is often subject to controversy. The views vary. Some, like the union leaders, claim that private pension plans without vesting provisions are detrimental to the individual's freedom to choose an employer. Thus, there is a growing tendency to include vesting provisions in union-negotiated agreements. Others believe that since voluntary private pensions are funded for the common good of the whole group working together for future security, no vesting privileges should be granted to those who leave the team. Since effective teamwork is responsible for the extra payments made by the employer, the pension costs should revert to the fund either to decrease the overall costs or to increase the pension payments for those who remain in the company's employ until retirement. This arrangement may hold good where *noncontributory* plans exist.

On the other hand, one should realize that if the employee contributed his money and faithfully did his best, he should be worthy of the employer's contribution and is truly entitled to some equitable adjustment at the time of separation. The employee is unquestionably entitled to his own investment, less the expenses incurred in administration of the fund. One fair solution to the problem is that under contributory vesting, the employer's contribution should be made contingent upon the employee's leaving his contributions with the pension fund or the insurance company, to be applied toward the purchase of a paid-up deferred pension, and receipt of the benefit be delayed until the employee reaches retirement age. Let us be mindful of the fact that a pension is really one of the fringe benefits that should be regarded as a deferred wage; also, that pensions are paid out of funds the employee has earned. In these circumstances, even under a noncontributory plan, an employee should have a vested right in a certain portion of the fund, if for some good reason his employment must be terminated before retirement age.

The latest wrinkle in private pensions is for the unions to seek *portable pensions*. A portable pension has full, immediate vesting and is transferred and carried on by another employer should the employee move from one job to another within the same industry. Like the social security retirement benefits, the employee does not lose credits when he changes jobs. If private pensions become portable, employees will become more mobile and some employers may stand to lose employees while other employers may gain employees, because the private pension will no longer serve to motivate an employee to make a career with one firm.

Fringe benefit trends and implications

In the past there was some controversy and question as to whether companies should grant fringe benefits. Today, it would appear that there are very few employers who would strongly question the desirability of some fringes. In other words, fringe benefits are pretty well established and here to stay. The real problem at present is how to control them!

Trends and patterns that are developing are sometimes difficult to identify until they have been in existence for a number of years. The major trends that your authors see are as follows: (1) fringe benefit costs are continuing to increase

TABLE 23.4

COMPARISON OF EMPLOYEE BENEFITS FOR 79 COMPANIES, 1947–1967

Item	1947	1949	1951	1953	1955	1957	1959	1961	1963	1965	1967
All industries (79 companies)											
1. As percent of payroll, total	16.1	17.5	19.4	21.0	22.3	24.2	25.1	27.1	28.6	28.1	29.9
a. Legally required payments (employer's share only)	2.7	2.6	2.8	2.6	2.8	3.1	3.7	4.2	4.8	4.1	5.0
b. Pension and other agreed-upon payments (employer's share only)	4.8	5.7	6.0	7.0	7.6	8.2	8.6	9.2	9.8	10.1	10.4
c. Paid rest periods, lunch periods, etc.	1.6	1.6	1.8	2.1	2.5	2.5	2.2	2.5	2.5	2.4	2.5
d. Payments for time not worked	5.5	6.1	7.1	7.5	7.6	8.6	8.8	9.3	9.3	9.5	9.9
e. Profit-sharing payments, bonuses, etc.	1.5	1.5	1.7	1.8	1.8	1.8	1.8	1.9	2.2	2.0	2.1
2. As cents per payroll hour	22.1	27.1	35.0	43.2	48.3	54.9	63.5	73.9	86.2	88.3	103.1
3. As dollars per year per employee	450	551	718	893	999	1157	1287	1530	1794	1874	2132
All manufacturing (45 companies)											
1. As percent of payroll, total	14.3	16.0	17.3	19.3	20.9	23.4	24.0	26.3	27.8	27.7	28.7
a. Legally required payments (employer's share only)	2.9	2.7	2.8	2.6	3.1	3.2	3.9	4.3	4.9	4.2	5.2
b. Pension and other agreed-upon payments (employer's share only)	3.5	4.6	5.3	6.2	6.9	7.7	7.8	8.7	9.2	9.7	9.8
c. Paid rest periods, lunch periods, etc.	1.6	1.6	1.7	2.2	2.4	2.5	2.2	2.5	2.6	2.6	2.5
d. Payments for time not worked	4.8	5.5	6.1	6.7	6.9	8.1	8.4	9.2	9.1	9.5	9.8
e. Profit-sharing payments, bonuses, etc.	1.5	1.6	1.4	1.6	1.6	1.9	1.7	1.6	2.0	1.7	1.4
2. As cents per payroll hour	20.2	24.9	33.1	40.2	46.4	54.2	63.4	73.6	82.1	88.9	99.3
3. As dollars per year per employee	416	508	690	842	966	1165	1269	1533	1861	1896	2064
All nonmanufacturing (34 companies)											
1. As percent of payroll, total	18.8	20.3	22.4	23.5	24.5	25.0	26.8	28.2	29.8	28.4	30.8
a. Legally required payments (employer's share only)	2.5	2.5	2.8	2.7	2.6	3.0	3.5	4.0	4.6	4.0	4.8
b. Pension and other agreed-upon payments (employer's share only)	6.8	7.8	7.0	8.1	8.6	8.8	9.8	10.1	10.8	10.4	10.8
c. Paid rest periods, lunch periods, etc.	1.6	1.7	1.9	1.9	2.5	2.4	2.3	2.4	2.3	2.2	2.5
d. Payments for time not worked	6.5	7.0	8.7	8.8	8.7	9.0	9.2	9.5	9.5	9.5	10.1
e. Profit-sharing payments, bonuses, etc.	1.4	1.3	2.0	2.0	2.1	1.8	2.0	2.2	2.6	2.3	2.6
2. As cents per payroll hour	25.1	30.5	37.9	47.9	51.4	55.3	63.6	74.3	88.3	87.5	105.3
3. As dollars per year per employee	506	617	763	972	1056	1135	1316	1524	1751	1798	2165

Source: Employee Benefits, 1967 (Washington: Chamber of Commerce of the United States, 1968), p. 27.

at a steady pace, (2) there is an increase in the variety and liberalization of fringe benefits, and (3) the movement for more leisure time is gaining momentum. Let us look at each of these trends and their implications.

Fringe Benefit Costs Are Increasing

The United States Chamber of Commerce has collected data on a group of 79 companies every other year since 1947. This means that it is possible to trace the growth of fringe benefits for an identical group of companies. Table 23.4 tells the story of the increasing costs in this group of companies from 1947 through 1967. The table illustrates that fringe costs showed increases at practically every survey period. In 1947 the fringe costs were 22.1 cents per payroll hour and by 1967 the costs had soared to 103.1 cents per payroll hour, or a rise of 367 percent in the 20 years.[29]

Table 23.5 shows how various fringe benefit costs have increased over the years in the steel industry. It is interesting to note that the steel industry does not use the term fringe benefits but calls them wage supplements. The table shows how the total annual cost of wage supplements has risen from $123.8 million in 1946 to $1,106.8 million in 1967, or nearly a ninefold increase.

Since World War II, the biggest gains in fringe benefits have been designed to protect the employee and his family. At present, close to one third of all fringe costs goes for employee security. The National Industrial Conference Board reports that employee payments for employee security (social security, unemployment insurance, private pensions and welfare funds, and workers' compensation for injuries) have climbed from 4 percent of all compensation in 1949 to 8 percent in 1963.[30]

It should be mentioned that fringe benefit costs are increasing at a ratio of about three times as fast as wages. Fringe costs have been increasing in numerous ways. First, the trend has been for management to assume the full cost of fringes instead of on a contributory basis. Second, there are new fringes being introduced. Third, present fringes are being extended. Fourth, wage increases automatically increase fringes tied to wages. Fifth, the rates of present fringes increase as the cost of living goes up.

A common example to show the extent that fringe benefits have been increasing at a steady pace is the social security tax. Since the system was first established, there were ten increases in rates, from 1935 to 1968. From 1969 to 1987 there are six more raises in rates planned. This means the rate will have risen from 1 percent in 1935 to 5.9 percent for *both* the employee and the employer (or from a total tax of 2 percent to 11.8 percent) by 1987.

---

[29]*Employee Benefits, 1967* (Washington: Chamber of Commerce of the United States, 1968), p. 27.

[30]"Employer Payments for Employee Security," *FOCUS* (New York: National Conference Board, February, 1964).

TABLE 23.5
ANNUAL COST OF SELECTED WAGE SUPPLEMENTS, 1946–1967
(Millions of Dollars)

Year	Vacations and Holidays	Pensions, Insurance, Social Security, etc.	Shift Differential & Premiums for Overtime & Sundays	Total	Wage Supplements as Percent of Total Employment Costs
1967	$377.7	$564.2	$164.9	$1,106.8	28.4%
1966	384.0	548.1	199.0	1,131.1	27.5
1965	304.8	487.5	197.0	1,087.6	26.9
1964	358.5	485.7	173.7	1,017.9	26.9
1963	271.1	442.3	135.1	848.5	25.3
1962	248.6	409.5	115.6	773.7	24.2
1961	231.8	377.9	111.5	721.2	23.2
1960	240.5	396.2	118.0	754.7	23.5
1959	249.6	293.5	146.1	689.2	23.6
1958	212.5	251.6	82.6	546.7	20.6
1957	218.1	295.0	109.2	622.3	19.6
1956	184.4	261.5	112.3	558.2	18.4
1955	166.6	226.4	107.5	500.5	17.3
1954	146.4	161.6	54.0	362.0	16.0
1953	156.6	194.0	114.2	464.8	17.0
1952	95.6	162.5	116.3	374.4	16.7
1951	78.7	191.7	117.4	387.8	16.2
1950	65.2	165.7	79.8	310.7	15.9
1946	39.3	41.8	42.7	123.8	10.5

Source: American Iron and Steel Institute.

Ten years ago few employees had more than six paid holidays a year. Today, eight or more paid holidays are common. The trend indicates that even more days will be granted in the future. Holidays are coupled with so-called "floating" holidays to give the employees extended weekends. Holidays that fall on the weekends and therefore were not considered days off in the past are now being observed on weekdays as paid days off. Those who work on holidays now receive triple pay instead of the traditional double time. In addition to the regularly observed holidays that all employees receive off with pay, some companies are now granting "personal" holidays for such events as birthdays or other "holidays" of their choice.

The major implication of the steady increase of total fringe benefit costs is that costs are mounting so high that it appears impossible to continue to grant the benefits without some regard to employee productivity. This may mean that fringe benefits need to be considered more in the same light as wage and salary compensations in order to keep them from getting completely out of line. The granting of additional fringes will more likely have to be based on merit through increased productivity, or the costs will have to come out of profits or be passed along to the customer in terms of higher prices. This may unduly burden the American business enterprise, to say nothing of its adverse effect on foreign competition. This dilemma is easily appreciated when the question is asked, "How long will the United States be able to compete with foreign competitors when our unemployed insured workers already receive more compensation per week than the combined income of wages and fringes received by fully employed foreign workers?"

If and when employers begin to expect that new fringe benefits will have to be earned in some ways, such as through increased productivity, we can then expect that fringes will become a *right* rather than a *privilege*. They will then come under the same rights and privileges as cash pay and as such will give the workers a greater participation and voice on how benefits will be handled. If the employer does not voluntarily recognize this, sooner or later he will be faced with legal or government action to comply with the rights of the employees. The fringes may then also become subject to income taxes in the same light as other income.

A recent reaction to the increasing fringe benefit costs is related to overtime. Some employers prefer to pay present employees overtime rates in order to avoid hiring a new employee and being committed to paying the cost of yearly fringes. Several years ago Andrew Biemiller testified for the AFL-CIO before a House Labor Subcommittee that "the revolution in fringe benefits has made it cheaper to schedule overtime than to add new workers in many cases."[31]

An employer can pay a great deal of overtime pay before it comes close to equaling the cost of a new and less efficient employee. In fact, paying overtime rates may offer much more flexibility and job security to present employees as well as the likelihood of the employer having fewer grievances to handle.

If the steady increase in fringe benefit costs continues, without being earned in some way, we are likely to see more employers turning to automation to reduce the total fringe costs and the problems that go with them.

The cost of fringe benefits depends, of course, upon how fringes are defined and who is adding up the bill. Although a fringe is usually considered as any benefit or service or compensation (other than wages), most employers do not include in their fringe costs the floor space used by the credit union, the parking

---

[31]"Labor Urges Double-Time for Overtime Assignments," *IUD Bulletin*, Vol. 9, No. 3 (March, 1964), p. 10.

lot, employee discounts, and many similar items which if included would really raise the cost of fringes to an astounding figure far beyond what has already been previously mentioned.

An Increase in the Variety and Liberalization of Fringe Benefits

The trend in fringe benefits seems to be one of adding to the number, kind, and coverage of fringe benefits. The major fringe benefits that have been liberalized and extended from their original form include social security, vacations, holidays, pensions, retiree benefits, and various forms of insurance such as health and unemployment insurance.

A few examples should suffice to convey this trend. Unemployment insurance started in the early thirties giving the employee 13 weeks of coverage. Since then it has generally been extended to 26 weeks of coverage. In 1958 it was temporarily extended to 39 weeks. The need to provide more than the 50 percent of pay benefit of unemployment insurance brought about Supplementary Unemployment Benefits (SUB) in 1955. SUB was intended to raise the total unemployment benefits from 50 percent of regular pay to 65 percent of regular pay. Some employers feel that benefits of 65 percent create some difficulty in getting unskilled workers to return to a job until the benefits are exhausted. If an unemployed worker can get 65 percent of his pay without working, is there enough incentive for him to return to full-time work to collect the other 35 percent? The authors were informed recently of the story of a secretary being laid off in a local manufacturing plant. The personnel director mentioned to the employee that he could find a place for her before long. She responded, "Please don't do me any favor. I have been looking forward to this for a long time," meaning that she was going to enjoy living on unemployment insurance payments for an extended period of time.

Vacations have also been receiving considerable liberalization in recent years. In the early 1920's paid vacations were usually available only to salaried employees. By 1925 only 18 percent of employers gave vacations with pay to production workers.[32] Today, most workers under major collective bargaining agreements receive one week's vacation after one year of service, two weeks after two years, three weeks after ten years, and four weeks after 20 years.[33] Some employees (St. Louis Brewery workers) now enjoy up to eight weeks of paid vacation each year. In many new contracts, there is a provision that states the circumstances under which employees can take pay in lieu of vacation. The steel industry is now offering 13 weeks' sabbatical vacations every fifth year to employees who have been with the company for 15 or more years. In spite of these large gains, the trend indicates that even more vacation benefits will be

---

[32]*Monthly Labor Review* (March, 1963).

[33]Rudolph Oswald, "The Growth of Longer Vacations," ¦*AFL-CIO American Federationist* (November, 1967), p. 19.

granted in the future. Within the next ten years, the five- and six-week vacation plans may become as common as the four-week plan of today.

Some persons are advocating increased vacations as a means of creating jobs for unemployed workers. This proposal is bound to further increase the unit cost of a product or service. It might work out well where there are un-limited sales or services to be rendered, or where the employer or the customer is willing to foot the increased costs. It is doubtful whether this proposal could work satisfactorily in an industry that already has difficulty offering job security to its present employees. Spreading the work and hiring more people would only aggravate the job security problem.

Since the early 1960's there has been an intensified effort directed toward an increasing coverage of pensions. The amounts paid to workers have been steadily increasing over the entire period. Although with the increased payments, the retirement age has tended to decline from the traditional 65 to 62 or lower. Many of the gains that are being made for present employees are also being applied to those workers who have already retired. Finally, there is increasing pressure by unions and Congress for pensions to be made "portable," that is, to follow an employee until he reaches retirement age, no matter how many differ-ent companies he may work for (very similar to social security pensions). The number of persons covered by portable pensions has increased from 3.3 million in 1960 to 40 million in 1966.

Some of the recent fringe innovations that further illustrate the liberalization of an already large variety of fringes are as follows: travel insurance policies, businessmen's sabbatical leaves, the longshoremen's automation agreement on job security, medical and dental benefits for the worker's family, employee edu-cation expenses (tuition refunds), savings plans, and progress sharing. If a com-plete list of fringes were available, it probably would include over 200 types and varieties. It seems that the only limitation to new fringe benefits is the imagina-tion. Sometimes requests for fringes can become pretty amusing as in the case of the retail clerks in a western state who were seeking free psychiatric treatment for store clerks who crack up under the pressure of keeping the shelves stocked.

As the variety of fringes increases, it becomes more of a problem for an employer to control them. At the same time there is some danger of the duplica-tion of fringe benefits if both husband and wife are working. Abuse of fringes also becomes easier. Employees may call in "sick" in order to "use up" the sick leave they feel they are entitled to, in spite of the fact they may be only "sick of work" rather than physically ill.

The implications of this trend toward the increased variety and the extension of present fringe benefits point to the need for both managements and unions to take a closer look at the purposes of fringes and the needs of the employees. Managements must better identify what they hope to accomplish through fringes and develop better ways and means of accomplishing these goals. Unions and managements should realize that the higher the percentage of wages that fringes become, the more fringes tend to destroy whatever equitable pay relationships previously existed.

The authors have always found it difficult to see how union demands for excessive increased vacation time or some other nonessential benefits can help employees obtain job security, especially when these employees are already getting four weeks' vacation time. It would appear that, perhaps, some of the present nonessential fringes should be traded in for some kind of reserve or security fund that would offer the real protection the worker needs. Or the funds could be used as a "floating reserve" to meet whatever pressing needs the employees have at the time.

We have also been puzzled by the lack of management initiative and imagination in trying to solve more of the real employee problems. Too many employers are content to go along with whatever fringe benefits another company is offering without checking to see whether these benefits would meet the needs of their employees. More research studies are needed to find out what minimum fringes all employees need and to determine how to establish a flexible system of fringe offerings to meet the changing employee needs.

Maybe an employer should provide the bare minimum fringe benefits essential for all employees and then make a reserve fund available that would allow each employee an amount of money to be used on additional fringes that the employee selects that best meet his individual needs at the time. As an employee's needs change during his career, the employee could shift his allotment of the fund to the most appropriate fringes he needs. Thus, as employees find their needs changing, they could increase or decrease their benefits. In this way fringes would always be a benefit and never a detriment to anyone. Such a plan would offer a great deal of flexibility and tend to reduce fringe abuses. It would encourage the employee to take a greater interest in his future since he would have more control over it. Active participation and contribution by the employee would prevent him from abusing or taking fringes for granted. This plan would be more in keeping with the American way of allowing the employee the chance to make more of his own decisions according to his needs and desires.

Society needs to teach workers how to determine what fringe benefits they need and how to secure and manage them. Too many workers are living for today only and have never been taught to plan for tomorrow.

The Movement for More Leisure Time

Various fringe benefits such as sabbatical leaves, longer vacations, increased holidays, shorter work weeks, and early retirements are tending to give employees more leisure time. The Chase Manhattan Bank in New York City has indicated that the average employee has gained the equivalent of 19 days off a year (almost four weeks of working days) since World War II, due to more holidays, longer vacations, and shorter working hours.[34] Today's employees already have about 1,000 more hours of leisure time each year than their grandfathers had. The 30-hour week has been predicted for sometime in the 1970's. If this should materialize, it would give the employee another 500 hours of leisure time each year. The electrical workers in New York City are already on a 25-hour week.

Leisure time is something that Americans have never had in great quantity. Little appears to have been done to educate people to use leisure time wisely and enjoyably. Our society has not been able to teach employees how to retire gracefully or gradually. An employee working steadily for 30 or more years is suddenly expected to live a completely different type of life the day after retirement. This is a severe adjustment to make and calls for some planning and study. Most employees fail to think enough about retirement until it arrives, and then it is too late to prepare for it.

One further problem of added leisure time is that it usually requires a reasonable amount of money to spend to enjoy the leisure. As yet, our country has not learned to strike a favorable balance between the leisure time available and an adequate monetary benefit to enjoy the leisure time with respectability.

Guidelines in establishing supplementary compensations

If after due deliberation, a firm has decided to offer one or more supplementary compensations to their employees, the following guidelines represent a brief summary of suggestions that the wage and salary administrator and his firm should consider in establishing each supplementary compensation.

1. Determine clearly defined aims and objectives long before a supplementary compensation program is introduced. A clear-cut program depicting all the benefits and services should be explicitly presented to all employees.
2. Avoid imitating a competitor's program — that may have been established unilaterally — without first appraising its adaptability to your own conditions. Supplementary compensations must be custom tailored.
3. Make certain that the supplementary compensations are actually in accord with the needs and desires of employees, as expressed either by them or their representatives.
4. Strive for the best joint (bilateral) program by selecting the most competent and fair-minded employees to represent management and labor on the committee for preparing, installing, and administering the compensation program.

---

[34]*Notes and Quotes*, No. 306 (Hartford, Conn.: Connecticut General Life Insurance Co., November, 1964), p. 1.

5. Be sure that employees will support the program willingly, sharing part of the expense, if necessary.

6. Employ reliable consultants to assist in carrying out the legal, financial, and actuarial matters to the satisfaction of all concerned.

7. The employer should contribute part of, or in some cases, the full cost of welfare benefits and compensation for the protection of the employees and their dependents.

8. Every supplementary compensation should have a time table for an evaluation and review to determine whether it should be retained, dropped, or altered in light of today's needs and conditions.

This draws to a close the two chapters that have attempted to present the relationship between supplementary compensations and the total compensation structure of the firm. The next few chapters will deal with the application of compensation principles to managerial personnel.

REVIEW QUESTIONS

1. Should fringe benefits in some way be expected to pay their way? Why?
2. What has been the impact of fringe benefits on the employee, the employer, and the public?
3. Since the Internal Revenue Service allows legislated supplementary compensations to be deducted as a tax expense, can a firm claim that it is paying for these employee benefits? Why?
4. Cite an example of a fringe benefit that is really not a benefit but a detriment to an employee.
5. What advantages are there to an employee when he is asked by his employer to support a fringe benefit on a contributing or joint basis?
6. Discuss the possible disadvantages to employees that are associated with some fringe benefits that when critically and objectively analyzed tend to be a hindrance rather than a benefit.
7. Under what circumstances would an increase in fringe benefits tend to destroy whatever equitable pay relationships previously existed?
8. Draw up a list of recommendations that you would offer to management in its attempt to establish a sound supplementary compensation.
9. Should the same pension benefits be granted to all employees on an equal basis or should they be allocated by some other criteria?
10. Should employee benefit payments which the government requires of every employer (like disability insurance and unemployment insurance) be considered supplementary compensation? Why?

RESEARCH OR SEMINAR QUESTIONS

1. (a) Cite the pros and cons of management furnishing the supplementary compensations v. paying the employees the money spent on fringes to purchase their own benefits. (b) Which plan do you prefer? Why?

2. Should supplementary compensations be considered part of an employee's wages? If so, should the employee have any choice of which benefits will be granted?

3. How can the supplementary compensations of one company be compared with those of another firm when they vary so much?

4. (a) Is severance pay sound wage policy? Why? (b) On what basis should the awards be made?

5. (a) What are the advantages and disadvantages of the contributory and non-contributory types of financing supplementary compensations? (b) Which is considered the better plan? Why?

6. Is it fair to the consumer for a firm to offer above-average supplementary compensations and pass the cost of them on to the customer? Why?

7. How should supplemental benefits relate to total compensation?

8. When does a firm reach the point that fringe benefits are considered out of line or beyond what a company can handle?

9. How can management determine whether a fringe benefit is really essential to its employees?

10. Should fringe benefits be considered as wages or social obligations?

11. Should companies help employees become stockholders? Why?

PRACTICAL EXPERIENCE ASSIGNMENTS

1. Draw up arguments to favor the proposition that an employer should not have to support a fringe benefit, such as unemployment compensation, whenever these funds would be used to support an employee labor strike against the employer.

2. Suggest some practical ways and means that an employer might use to control fringe benefits so they will not get out of line.

CASE PROBLEM

23—1. ELECTRIC MOTOR CAR COMPANY

The Fringe Benefit Snowball

The Electric Motor Car Company is a newly established firm that manufactures electric automobiles in competition with the auto makers of gasoline cars. As a new firm, Electric Motor Car Company is having financial difficulties, and it has barely managed to remain in business. However, the forecast for the coming year appears promising, and all indications point to a 5 percent profit for the current year.

The firm's 10,000 employees have recently voted to have a union represent them. The union officers are preparing a list of wage demands along with the first union-management contract. The employees are asking for a wage raise and fringe benefits comparable to those offered by the other auto manufacturers. The Electric Motor Car Company believes it can grant the wage increase if business is good, but it does not see how it can grant the same fringe benefits as its competitors at this time. In fact, the Electric Motor Car management has a different idea on fringes than the competing auto firms. The other auto firms have granted the fringe benefits with no strings attached. As a result, their fringes are close to 30 percent of the employees' wages and they appear to be rising continually. The management of the Electric Motor Car Company believes that it can grant some basic fringes such as pensions, life insurance, holidays, and vacations but that further fringe benefits must be tied to the profitability of the firm. In other words, the company is willing to put a certain portion of all profits beyond 5 percent into fringe benefits that the employees elect. Thus, if the employees want hospitalization benefits, the amount of benefits will be determined according to the percentage of money that can be used from all the profits over 5 percent. If there are no profits over 5 percent, there are no hospitalization benefits for that year.

Management believes that such a system of supplementary fringe benefits tends to pay its way partially and, because it is related to company profits, all employees will be motivated to do their best to earn whatever benefits they desire. In this way the firm is not unconditionally committed to a gamut of fringes that could easily put the new firm out of business or make it noncompetitive.

The union and its employees have discussed management's proposal, and although they realize that the firm is not financially secure, they have decided that they are entitled to the same fringes as the employees of the other car manufacturers.

Problem:

As a student of wage and salary administration, you are asked to appraise the concept that management has, which ties fringes to the profitability of the firm. You should comment on their proposal from the viewpoint of an employee and an employer as well as any other interested party.

chapter 24

COMPENSATING FOREMEN
AND SUPERVISORS

The subjects in the preceding six parts of the book pertain primarily to personnel below the managerial rank. Part Seven will be confined to a discussion of how managerial personnel are compensated and how many of the principles previously cited are applicable to managerial employees. Chapter 24 deals with compensating the first-line members of management, commonly called managerial supervisors, while Chapter 25 treats the higher levels of management compensation from the supervisor's immediate superior to the chief executive of the company.

In this chapter we shall treat the following topics:

1. Concept of the supervisory position.
2. The need for evaluating supervisory positions.
3. Basic tests of management compensation.
4. The theory of compensating supervisors.
5. Supervisory compensation practices.
6. Incentives for supervisors.
7. A summary of suggestions to consider in compensating supervisors.

Concept of the supervisory position

Before beginning the discussion of the need for an evaluation of supervisory positions, it may be well to clarify who is considered a supervisor. *Supervisor* appears to be the broad term used to indicate the man or woman in management who deals directly with the rank-and-file workers. The major part of the job requires 50 to 80 percent of the supervisor's time in performing work related to management policies or general operations. This means that the supervisor generally directs and supervises two or more employees and that he has the authority to recommend the hiring and discharge of employees. In an office, the first-line supervisor is likely to be called the office manager, while in the shop or factory he is more commonly referred to as the foreman. This chapter refers specifically to all first-line members of the management team (both staff and line) who are charged with the duty of representing the company to the worker. They are considered to be the personnel who are *exempt* from overtime payments according to the Fair Labor Standards Act. Reference is *not* intended to include assistant foremen, group leaders, straw bosses, section leaders, lead or key men, or other personnel who may assist the office supervisor or foreman; these persons are regarded as *nonexempt*. Such nonexempt employees are usually motivated and receive incentive wages based on individual or group plans as discussed in Chapters 17 through 21. If a department is rather large, requiring specialized assistance, then the specialists are recognized to be in the same category as the "chief foremen." Such assistants usually are granted the privileges and benefits accorded their "chief."[1] In various departments such as large stock rooms, shipping and receiving rooms, and other similar activities, where groups of people have to be guided and supervised, the terms foreman and supervisor are used interchangeably.

Supervisory Status

If there is one general source of supervisory complaints, it is that too many managements have not fully accepted the supervisor as a legitimate member of the management team. In the early days of commerce and industry, a foreman was chosen from among the workers and was expected to serve as a buffer or wedge between the workers and the firm's owner. A foreman who could get the work out, regardless of the methods or tactics used, was considered a success. Many foremen were untrained and got results by instilling fear and even threatening the workers. Many such foremen actually caused the workers to resist top management whenever they could. Top management failed to realize that the foremen were their representatives and that lasting results are better achieved through friendly inspiration rather than by means of negative motivation. Thus, the supervisor found himself all alone. He was not fully accepted by the owner as part of the management team and the workers disliked his driving methods. This undesirable situation was eventually remedied when foremen began attempt-

---

[1]The title of "chief foreman" is applied by some large companies to a foreman whose duties and responsibilities are of an executive nature. This title and position is not to be confused or compared with the position of general foreman on the *middle management* level.

ing to organize foremen unions and the supreme court made the decision that foremen could not join a union because they belonged to the managerial class.

Some top managements today are still of the old school as described above. They are not selective in choosing their supervisors nor do they provide them with any management training to represent the company properly. In fact, some firms appear to just tolerate the supervisor since they do not realize that to many workers, the foreman *is* management. To the workers he represents the only management they will come in contact with and will ever know. In one company, well known to the authors, the supervisors were paid the same rate of pay as their subordinates. Top management wondered why the supervisors did not represent them very well. This management tried to justify the supervisor's pay rate on the basis that the supervisor was getting greater compensation because he was given the chance to earn more money by working more hours a day. What this management failed to realize was that they were giving the impression that the supervisor was not any more important than the workers. The supervisor had no status as shown by management's action.

In this discussion on supervisory remuneration, the basic assumption is that the position held by the supervisor is needed and is of greater importance than the jobs of those employees he supervises. Consideration is not given to supervisory positions which management has created to make way for a pensioner or a friend of the boss. Such jobs generally could not stand a fair appraisal and still be found to be worth more than some rank-and-file jobs.

Importance of Selecting Qualified Supervisors

If management is staffed with inefficient supervisors because higher management has selected them on the basis of politics, religion, or family relationship, rather than on the qualifications which relate to the position, then the effectiveness of first-line management is questionable. A company must eliminate methods of selection that bring forth inefficient supervisory personnel if it hopes to attract good potential first-line managers. The present capable supervisors should be given the necessary status that they deserve and need to perform their positions well. Without regard for proper status, management cannot expect to draw supervisory talent from the ranks of the workers on the basis of either salary or "prestige" because the workers know that the prestige and salary differential is negligible.

Change of Attitude Toward Foremen

During the last few decades, progressive companies have realized that foremen are not to be recognized as "unknown quantities." Many of the well-managed companies referred to in this book, such as the American Seating Company, Armstrong Cork Company, Bell and Howell Company, Eastman Kodak

Company, and Owens-Illinois Company, place as much emphasis on the training and development of foremen and supervisors as they do on the development of executives. It should be remembered that many outstanding executives or company officers have their roots in the shops or offices because they have succeeded through the opportunity of receiving a well-planned training program.

The need for evaluating supervisory positions

Supervisors, like any other employees in an organization, are human beings and have much the same basic needs, desires, likenesses, and differences as those under their supervision. This means that the supervisory positions as a group, as well as in comparison with the rank and file, need to be evaluated in order to determine the compensation to which they are entitled. It may be reemphasized that jobs requiring more mental agility than physical prowess are more commonly referred to as positions.

If a supervisor's position is not considered more valuable to the company than that of any of the subordinates, the supervisor does not warrant more pay than his subordinate. It is apparent that either an improper selection of supervisor has been made for the position, or the position is superfluous. Only by a systematic and consistent method of evaluation can an equitable salary be determined. A fair evaluation of a supervisor's position should leave no doubt in the minds of management as well as the workers that the supervisor earns his higher salary, and that he is entitled to any special consideration in the line of management. The evaluation also gives the supervisor self-assurance and raises his prestige, which helps to satisfy part of his basic needs. In short, the proper evaluation of supervisory positions should prevent wage inequities among supervisors just as it should do so among their subordinates, proving that the company is being fair with all employees according to their status, jobs, or positions. The company sets an excellent example by evaluating also the members of its management team.

One company had never made a formal evaluation of its employees' jobs. When, however, the jobs were evaluated, it was found that the wages of many subordinates exceeded the salaries of their supervisors. Obviously it was unfair to the supervisors and to the rank-and-file workers. Such a condition neither helps to raise the morale, nor does it motivate the management personnel to do their best, nor to strive for advancement. This striking example points up the need for evaluating supervisory positions as well as the rank-and-file jobs. Compensation proportioned according to the worth of the job and of the individual assures the supervisor of his important status as an accepted member of the management team. It is one of the standards by which he measures his value and his success in the company.

Basic tests of management compensation

Every company has some compensation plan for its managerial personnel whether the management has formalized it or not. Those companies which have not put the plan in writing may experience difficulty in communicating it to the personnel involved and in having them understand and accept it. Likewise, it will be difficult to evaluate the plan to determine how well it is succeeding and to know what measures to take to improve the plan.

Sibson outlines some basic considerations that have to be met if managerial compensation is to succeed. He states:

> Any salary administration program for managerial, administrative, and professional personnel, either present or proposed, should be examined against the criteria by which those affected will judge it. There are four basic tests. Does the company's plan:
>
> 1. Establish logical and justifiable relations between jobs?
> 2. Provide a prudent man with enough to establish and maintain a standard of living in line with his business position and his community standing?
> 3. Set salaries which are reasonably comparable to those paid people holding similar positions in other companies?
> 4. Reward the individual in a manner that is consistent with his contribution to the success of the enterprise?

Similarly, the company has four tests which it can apply in evaluating the success of a salary administration program. Some of these may seem simple and self-evident, but they rest on basic principles and should never be forgotten or submerged in the confusing welter of details.

> Does the system:
>
> 1. Effectively communicate to management personnel a sense of the company's intention to be fair?
> 2. Attract and retain the number and type of managers needed?
> 3. Induce optimum effort and performance, and provide incentive for improvement?
> 4. Effect the best utilization of the company's financial resources (i.e., economizing in the true sense of the term — not paying the least possible but getting the most in return for payments made)?[2]

These considerations must be found acceptable to both employees and management if the compensation program is to be effective and help develop and maintain a high state of morale.

---

[2]Robert E. Sibson, "Plan for Management Salary Administration," *Harvard Business Review*, Vol. XXXIV, No. 6 (November–December, 1956), p. 102.

The theory of compensating supervisors

Supervisory compensation, like any other employee compensation, should be adequate and equitable not only to attract first-class supervisors but also to retain them once they are hired. When a company has an attractive starting salary but lags on pay increases, failure to keep pace with the salary rates of other companies may invite "pirating." In other words, competitive companies may begin to entice personnel away from the lower paying company.

Compensation Formula

The salary of a supervisor should be based upon the same "formula" used for all employees, that is, (1) the value of the job, plus (2) the value of the individual, plus (3) any other pertinent pay considerations. Again, it should be pointed out that the overall weight or value of the job and the individual changes as the jobs or positions in a company become more complex. That is to say, that as the supervisor advances in rank in a company, his total compensation should be based more on the individual than on the job. Figure 5.2, page 143, graphically emphasizes the contrast in jobs by comparing an unskilled job with a first-line supervisory position. Note that the bigger and more complex a job becomes, the greater is the challenge for the individual to make a success of it. It could be said that at the managerial levels the "man makes the job," while at the lower level of the jobs in an enterprise, the "job makes the man." The reasoning behind this philosophy is that at the unskilled job levels the job duties are less difficult to perform. Almost anyone not physically handicapped can perform them satisfactorily, and there is very little difference in the performance of one worker or another. Unskilled jobs are mostly of a routine nature and very few of them require the exercise of a person's individuality. Thus, the "job makes the man" since it is the predominant element when comparing the job with the individual performing it. The primary goal of managerial compensation should be to motivate management personnel to perform to their maximum effort rather than simply to pay them for their jobs.

On the other hand, when an employee joins the supervisory ranks, the job (more appropriately referred to as a position) has comparatively little of the repetitive routine. The tasks, duties, and responsibilities are more diversified and far less predictable. Not everyone can always perform with satisfactory results. The results achieved by those who can perform effectively vary to a greater or lesser degree because there are ample opportunities for performing the position in many different ways, depending upon the individual element. This means that the outcome depends to a greater degree on the person performing and his individual abilities. In fact, his individual talents can be more fully exercised. Whether he makes a success of the position rests more on his individual abilities than on the job as such. Thus, it is said that the "man makes the job," meaning, of course, that the individual plays a larger part in the success of the job than the job duties themselves.   For this reason, the wage and salary compensation formula should place greater emphasis and importance on the individual as the job or position becomes more complicated.   Such individual achievements should be rewarded in the form of more money in the pay envelope.

Just how much value or weight should be placed on either the job or the individual is for management to appraise and decide. Chapters 6 through 10 discuss the methodology for arriving at the relative value of a job. The evaluation of individuals is discussed in Chapters 14 through 16.

Salary Differential

It is generally agreed as a matter of principle — and carried out by well-managed companies — that supervisors are entitled to salaries greater than the weekly earnings of their subordinates. Some companies pay a flat salary amount above a specified number (usually five) of the highest paid subordinates, while most companies maintain a higher salary based on a percent basis.   Just how much more compensation a company should pay is a difficult question to answer because it depends upon such conditions as the complexity of the work supervised, the profitability of the industry, management's philosophy on the value of supervisors, and the capabilities of the individuals themselves. There seems to be a tendency in many companies to regard a differential of 10 percent above the highest income of the supervisor's subordinates as an adequate and equitable compensation for a supervisor. If a foreman or supervisory position is considered a managerial function, it must be realized that such compensation is out of line with managerial duties and responsibilities.   If the union were to win a wage increase, it could easily embarrass management because some workers could then be earning more than their supervisors. To avoid such possibilities and to give the supervisor prestige, he should be paid at least 20 percent more than his highest paid subordinates.   Some companies pay as much as 40 percent more. Torrence says that most companies try to maintain at least a 25 percent differential between the earnings of production and their supervisors.[3] It is important that the salary differential in each organization should be such that it gives managerial status to the supervisor.

Supervisory compensation practices

As can be readily appreciated, there are numerous methods of compensating supervisors. However, in order to assist the wage and salary administrator in evaluating supervisory compensation and to offer some ideas for improvement

---

[3]George W. Torrence, *The Motivation and Measurement of Performance* (Washington: The Bureau of National Affairs, 1967), p. 36.

where a certain method already exists, the common supervisory compensation practices in commerce and industry will be briefly cited.

Salary Method of Compensation

By far the most common method of compensating supervisors is on a straight salary basis, that is, a set amount of money quoted per month or per year. The salary is paid in weekly, biweekly, semimonthly, or monthly installments. Shop supervisors are more likely to receive pay checks weekly while office supervisors usually receive their checks every two weeks (biweekly) or twice a month (semimonthly). The salary is usually determined by first appraising the worth of the position by a method of job evaluation and then pricing the position (setting a starting wage) in accordance with some consistent or systematic plan. The plan may involve a comparison of similar supervisory salaries in the community or the particular industry, then paying either the average or a percentage above or below the median salary in the community or within the industry. Salaries are usually enhanced because of "seniority" on the job or because of efforts of the supervisor using periodic employee evaluations.

Every company has to make the decision whether its supervisory employees shall be compensated at a flat salary with no opportunity for advancement in pay or be compensated according to a salary range having a minimum starting salary with the opportunity to receive pay increases to a maximum amount. The vast majority of companies compensate managerial personnel according to a salary schedule system which permits periodic pay raises or increments.

One of the major differences between compensating rank-and-file employees and management personnel is the basis used to determine pay increases. Nonmanagerial personnel are generally given pay raises based on seniority or merit, with the emphasis on seniority. Management personnel are almost always given pay raises based on merit rather than seniority. A second major difference between nonmanagerial and managerial compensation is the wage-base rate and the salary range, that is, the amount of spread between the minimum and the maximum wage or salary rates. It has been previously suggested that any rate range spread that is to serve as an incentive should be at least 20 percent, which is generally the nonmanagerial wage spread among most jobs. First-line supervisory salary ranges should be higher than for rank-and-file jobs. Occasionally supervisors have the opportunity to increase their starting salaries as much as 50 percent through their individual efforts. The usual spread between the minimum and maximum salary, however, is about 33 percent.

Job Evaluation Factors Involved in Supervisory Positions

One of the questions that arises in the minds of employees is, "What are the job factors for which the supervisors are paid?" Some uninformed workers assume that supervisors have "soft" jobs and are overpaid. In reality, however, the front-line supervisor has specific duties and responsibilities that are of a weighty nature. An honest inspection and appraisal of supervisory position factors will substantiate this. A long list of job factors for which companies pay their supervisors could be compiled since supervisors in different industries may be paid for various activities. However, a representative list of the factors used in many companies might be like the one used by Revere Copper and Brass Incorporated (See Figure 10.4, pages 264 to 269). The job factors they use are:

1. Elemental factor value.
2. Technical knowledge required.
3. Practical knowledge required.
4. Exercise of judgment.
5. Demand for leadership.
6. Planning.
7. Number of employees.
8. Conditions of work.
9. Liability of damage to product.

Other companies indicate that they pay their supervisors for similar factors, such as:

Complexity and difficulty of the work supervised.
Number of employees supervised.
Previous experience required.
Responsibility for safety of others.
Ability to deal with people.
Initiative and creativeness.
Responsibility for equipment, product, or money.
Ability to withstand pressure and handle emergencies.
Educational preparation required.
Making decisions.
Ability to solve problems.
Accountability for material and supplies.

It can be readily seen that each company may place a different weight or value on the various factors used because of the particular conditions within the company or industry. In other words, the elimination of a certain percent of scrap may be of vital concern to one company and negligible to another. Other factors likewise may vary in importance or degree of value. Each company has to decide for itself what factors are common to the supervisory positions that are to be evaluated. Once the list of factors has been decided upon, the weightings can be assigned to the factors as described in Chapter 9. The total point value of the supervisory position can then be determined by applying the procedures described in Chapter 10.

From the preceding list of job factors it is apparent that a supervisory position deals basically with the actions and reactions of people, while the factors of a worker's job deal basically with tangibles such as machines, tools, and materials. Because tangibles remain fairly stable, they are easier to cope with than people with their varying and unpredictable characteristics. Thus, a supervisory position is much more difficult to perform than a nonsupervisory job since it calls for more vision, ability, and leadership to deal with the changing elements effectively.

Job Pricing

After supervisory positions have been evaluated by some method of job evaluation, they are assigned a definite salary. This amount of money is determined by many factors such as: what the labor supply and demand are; what competitors are paying; the profitability of the business; geographical location; how important the job is; and what compensation is being received for jobs above and below the supervisor's level. The assurance that compensation relationships within the company are equitable is considered more important than external compensation relationships with other companies and areas. With this in mind, the main consideration becomes one of determining what amount or percentage the supervisor should receive above the pay of his subordinates. It is common practice to pay 25 percent above a subordinate's highest pay.

Merit Increases

Once the correct starting salary has been decided upon and found acceptable by the person holding the job, the question may be raised as to how often the salary should be reviewed for merit increases. In an AMA study, Rosensteel reported that of over 110 companies, two thirds reviewed supervisory salaries for merit increases every 12 months. [4] One fifth of the companies reviewed supervisory salaries every 6 months, while the remaining companies did so every 18 to 24 months.

Overtime Pay

Although companies are not legally obliged to pay exempt employees for working beyond regular working hours, the National Industrial Conference Board, in a study of 673 companies, found that 52 percent of the manufacturers pay supervisors for overtime while less than a third of the nonmanufacturing companies are paying supervisors for overtime. [5] More of the larger companies pay overtime than do the smaller companies. Overtime remuneration may consist of straight time, time and one half, or equivalent time off. Higher paid supervisors are more likely to receive straight time for the extra hours they work, while lower paid supervisors usually receive time and one half for their overtime.

It is evident that some companies fail to appreciate the value of the time that a supervisor may work over and above a 40-hour week. If a supervisor were

---

[4]D. H. Rosensteel, "Supervisory Compensation: An Interim Report," *Personnel*, Vol. XXXIII, No. 1 (January, 1957), p. 357.
[5]"Overtime Pay for Exempt Employees," *Studies in Personnel Policy*, No. 208 (National Industrial Conference Board, 1967), p. 2.

to average only an hour's overtime each day, he may be working at a lower rate of pay than his subordinates. For example, if his subordinates average $10,000 per year for fifty 40-hour weeks, they are earning about $5 per hour. If the foreman is to receive $5.50 per hour for 40 hours per week, he would receive $11,000 per year. The $1,000 per year the supervisor receives over and above his subordinates may appear large. In fact, it is 10 percent more than the pay of his subordinates — other things being equal. On the other hand, if part of the supervisor's $11,000 job is to work additional hours as needed and this calls for one hour a day of overtime, the supervisor is really earning $4.88 per hour (less than his subordinates) because he is working overtime 250 hours a year (over six weeks) without additional pay. If the foreman were paid for this 250 hours of overtime at time and one half (the same rate the worker would receive), the foreman would receive an additional $2,062 more per year, or a total yearly salary of $13,062. Is it any wonder then that a qualified and intelligent worker, after seeing his supervisor put in all this free overtime, is quick to decide that he is not interested in a supervisory position? This example illustrates an inequity that can occur when management sincerely believes that the supervisor is fully compensated because he is earning $1,000 (10 percent) more than his subordinates. Had the worker put in 250 hours of overtime, he would have earned an extra $1,875 or a total of $11,875, which is $875 more than the supervisor for the same number of hours. This illustration indicates why a minimum 20 percent pay differential between the first-line supervisor and his subordinates is recommended. The supervisor's compensation should be such that it adequately compensates for possible overtime and that it reflects the importance that top management attaches to the position. When workers and supervisors regularly work overtime, it is a sign of mismanagement because costs go up. Overtime compensation for supervisors is to be discouraged and salaries should be high enough to more than allow for an emergency or an occasional need to work overtime.

The Guignard Brick Works of Cayce, South Carolina, has a unique method of paying its mining foremen so that overtime pay does not become a problem.

> The foreman is paid on the "fluctuating work week" principle. This means his base pay is divided by the number of hours he worked in the week to determine the average hourly rate. Half of this rate is paid for hours beyond 40. Thus, if the foreman's base pay is $90 a week, he receives this $90 whether he works 1 hour or 40. If he works 45 hours, his rate is $90/45 or $2/hr.; so, in addition to his $90, he would receive $2/2 × 5 or $5, for a total of $95. If he works 60 hours, his rate is $90/60 or $1.50/hr.; so, in addition to his $90, he would be paid $1.50/2 × 20 or $15, for a total of $105.

> This procedure gives the foreman something extra when he works overtime, but not enough for him to GENERATE overtime. One of the disadvantages of paying a foreman time-and-a-half for overtime is that although a foreman should be free to work as many hours as required by

his job, a foreman who wants to earn extra money may be tempted to work unnecessary overtime. Worse yet, in order to justify his own overtime, such a foreman will in all probability have his whole crew work overtime.[6]

Supplemental Benefits

Supervisors generally receive the same supplemental benefits that are accorded the rank-and-file employees. However, many companies grant their supervisors additional benefits, such as supper allowances, jury duty fees, club memberships, expense accounts, dues and expenses in professional societies, and fees as well as tuition in attending universities, colleges, and seminars for professional development on company time. Although the benefits generally are not considered as a direct part of wages and salaries, they are accepted as a significant indirect compensation inasmuch as such benefits often are influential when a supervisory job applicant is confronted with a choice between two jobs. Salaries sometimes are enhanced by additional amounts of money given as a reward or earned for various other reasons.

Incentives for supervisors

Various attempts have been made to spur managerial employees on to greater effort to achieve managerial goals. The National Industrial Conference Board found that more than half the firms it studied offer first-line supervisors some kind of incentive by paying them some sort of bonus or extra compensation in addition to base salary.[7] These incentives, like those for nonmanagerial employees, are intended to improve morale and to lower operating costs, as well as to reward supervisors for their greater efforts. Supervisory incentives differ from nonmanagerial incentives in scope. There appears to be a great variety of incentives at the first-line supervisory level. In one company, the goal may be increased productivity or profits, while in another firm it may be lower costs based on reducing scrap.

Lundgren and Myers, in a recent survey of foremen incentive systems, reported the following:

> The number of factors usually ranges from three to seven. . . .factors usually include some form of direct labor cost . . . and many include schedule maintenance, budget performance, methods improvement, housekeeping, safety, tardiness, and labor turnover. The range of bonus is still usually based on the foreman's salary and may range up to 40% of his base. The most common range is 10% to 30%.[8]

---

[6]Richard Winchell, "Incentives for Brickyard Supervisors," *Ceramic Age* (July, 1967), p. 34.
[7]"Overtime Pay for Exempt Employees," *op. cit.*, p. 56.
[8]Earl F. Lundgren and Dayle F. Myers, "A Survey of Foremen Incentive Systems in Wisconsin," *Marquette Business Review* (Spring, 1969), p. 8.

Other factors that have been used include economy in the use of materials and services, and cooperation between supervisors and top management. Another difference between supervisory and nonsupervisory incentives is that of control. The supervisor has greater authority in the company than nonmanagerial employees and he may be tempted to take unfair advantage of his subordinates to get results favorable only to himself. If such a condition is encouraged through incentive plans, the overall effects are more harmful to the company than the good that an incentive plan may produce.

Fundamentals of an Incentive Plan for Supervisors

In designing an incentive plan for supervisors, it is well to keep in mind that there is no ideal single plan that will fit all organizations. Each plan should be tailored to the specific requirements of the company concerned. Each plan needs to be integrated into the total compensation picture as it is only one of all the aspects of wage and salary administration. Every plan needs to be reviewed and evaluated periodically so that it may be adjusted to changing conditions, thereby maintaining its effectiveness in the long run.

Walley suggests seven fundamentals of a sound foreman's incentive plan. These seven fundamentals, which are equally applicable to other supervisors, are:

1. Establish plan to encourage foremen to reduce operating expenses over which they exercise a degree of control, such as labor, materials, supplies, utilities, and scrap.

2. Establish variable expense standards using measured hours produced by direct labor as the control.

3. Use moving averages to smooth out highly fluctuating expenses which, if charged out in one month, would erase any possible incentive earnings and discourage foremen from attempting to control other expenses at a critical time.

4. Describe plan fully in writing, covering such aspects as addition of new participants, changes in expense standards, life of plan, effect on expense standards when management authorizes new equipment which was not suggested by the foremen, an example of how the bonus is calculated, and an explanation of when and under which circumstances a bonus will be paid.

5. Hold regular meetings with the foremen, discussing variances above expense standards, and attempt to work out solutions — keeping minutes of the meeting — that will get and hold costs below the budget for volume of hours produced.

6. Pay the bonus each month — by separate check — so that the foremen will definitely relate the bonus check to periods when they exercised their managerial skills in a manner that the company rewards.

7. Give the foremen instruction and information needed to use expense standards for planning ahead — so that they are shooting at a definite

target — and can achieve maximum benefits for themselves and their company.[9]

Incentive plans are known under different names such as bonus, profit sharing, and commission. Since most supervisory incentive plans are referred to as bonuses, we shall restrict our discussion to bonus plans. The reader should bear in mind, however, that no matter what the incentive plan is called, the basic objectives and principles are the same.

Bonuses

Bonuses are one of the older forms of compensating supervisors beyond their regular salaries, and have been a long time favorite of some companies in rewarding the supervisors for a job well done. Bonuses for supervisors usually are determined as a percentage of the incentive earnings of their subordinates. The amount of bonus which the supervisor receives may also be based on a percentage (usually 25 to $33\frac{1}{3}$ percent) of the total time saved in performing departmental work. Commonly the amount of money earned through a bonus is calculated so that the supervisor will receive the equivalent of about 20 to 25 percent of his base salary as a bonus. (See Chapters 17 through 21 for a discussion of different bonus plans.)

Of the 163 companies surveyed by Lundgren and Myers, 55 percent included their foremen in some kind of bonus plan.[10] Some companies believe that the inclusion of supervisors in a bonus plan in which higher management participates is an excellent practice because it definitely identifies supervisors with the management group. However, this is not sound practice if the plan is primarily based on factors over which the supervisor has no control. Higher management bonuses may have other considerations such as deferred payments and discretionary awards, which may be unacceptable to supervisors. Then, too, such bonuses may lead supervisors to drive their workers unreasonably hard or otherwise take advantage of them. Such pressure is naturally resented by the non-managerial personnel who are not included in managerial bonuses.

Bonuses are commonly based on group or departmental production or sales beyond a standard quota. In these plans, there is a close relationship between increased production (efficiency) and the supervisor's bonus. If such bonus plans are to succeed, the supervisor must be made aware of this relationship or he may slacken his efforts in seeing that his employees are productive and effective. When supervisors are not fully informed of the base upon which a bonus is determined, the bonus tends to become a disappointing or meaningless amount.

---

[9]John R. Walley, "Incentive Plans for Foremen Needn't Fail," *Mill and Factory*, Vol. LXV, No. 5 (November, 1959), p. 103.
[10]Lundgren and Myers, *ibid.*, p. 4.

A bonus plan then becomes ineffective and usually elicits a negative reaction from supervisors. In order to make bonuses more attractive, some companies issue special bonus checks so that the supervisor can readily comprehend the base upon which the bonus is determined. This practice also helps to overcome any tendency for the supervisor to take a bonus for granted, which would result in a drop of earnings.

Bonus practices differ widely. Before adopting a bonus plan, therefore, each company has to consider such factors as: the salaries already established to compensate supervisors; the profitability of the company; the acceptability of the bonus plan by the supervisors; whether the industry lends itself to such plans; and whether all activities are standardized to govern the permanency and administration of a bonus plan. It is well to be mindful, as stressed above, that in offering any production or efficiency bonus payment, the plan must clearly indicate the relationship between the supervisor's extra effort and the amount of the bonus that must be considered a reasonable reward for expending the additional effort. A plan is more likely to be successful when it clearly outlines the fundamental responsibility of the supervisor in guiding his workers to make their efforts more effective and economical.

A Sample Incentive Plan for Managerial Supervisors[11]

In order to acquaint the reader with the practical application of an incentive plan for supervisors, an incentive plan that is applicable to first-line supervisors will be presented. The Management Effectiveness Plan was installed at the Wehr Steel Company, Milwaukee, Wisconsin, in 1965, and has been in operation ever since that date. [12]

Philosophy of the Wehr Management Effectiveness Plan. The Wehr Steel Company believes that a good management team is largely responsible for the success of any enterprise. Therefore, the members of management should have the opportunity to share in the success of the company. Financial rewards are based on the results of the performance of the plant in certain key areas.

The aim of the plan is to produce extra compensation through effective job performance, and in no way is this to be regarded as a substitute for proper salary administration or for any fringe benefit which the company currently has or may add in the future. In short, the plan provides income, beyond salary, for management effectiveness in certain key areas.

---

[11]For various other examples of supervisory incentive plans for different industries, see Appendix A of "Compensating First-Line Supervisors in Factory and Office," *Studies in Personnel Policy*, No. 177 (National Industrial Conference Board, 1960), pp. 68–83.

[12]We are indebted to Chester Niles, Director of Industrial Relations, and Nicholas Serio, Standards and Cost Manager, at the Wehr Steel Company, for supplying us with the information described in the plan.

General Provisions of the Plan. The Management Effectiveness Plan involves the use of the following four factors which are well within the sphere of management responsibilities: (1) indirect labor budget costs, (2) shop scrap, (3) customer returns, and (4) lost time accidents. For each of these factors, standards of effectiveness are established and financial rewards are related to a comparison of actual job performance with budgeted standards.

A calendar year, which begins in January, is divided into four segments of three months each. These three-month periods constitute the performance periods upon which the incentive awards are based. Each period stands on its own; and at the completion of the January through March period, the job performance results are tabulated. If additional compensation is earned, it is paid about the middle of the following month (April). Results are not accumulative. Compensation might be paid in one period based on favorable results, and not paid in another period, based on failure to meet the established standards.

The eligibility requirements for the plan are simple. All members of management who have the status of an "exempt employee," as defined by the Fair Labor Standards Act, are eligible to participate in the plan. However, company officials are excluded from the plan. New employees who are promoted into the exempt category are eligible to participate in the plan after six months of service in their new positions. Employees who terminate their association with the company are not eligible for any compensation beyond that which was paid prior to their termination.

Periodic meetings are held in order to appraise the effectiveness of the plan, supply information to the participants, and discuss possible areas of improvement. The company reserves the right to alter, amend, or discontinue the plan, and the Personnel Department administers the plan and answers any questions which arise about its provisions.

How the Plan Works. The Management Effectiveness Plan contains a number of cost standards which need to be developed by each firm to serve as guideposts for the operation of the plan. For example, it is necessary to determine:

1. The average scrap cost charge for each ton of steel molded in the shop. (for example, $6)
2. The average customer return cost charge for each ton of steel molded. (for example, $7)
3. The average employee lost time cost charge for each man-hour worked in the plant. (for example, $.01)
4. The average cost for each ton of steel that has to be scrapped in the shop. (for example, $200)
5. The average cost for each ton of steel that the customer returns that has to be reworked. (for example, $300)
6. The average cost for each case in which an employee loses time on his job. (for example, $800)

Figure 24.1 shows some hypothetical figures (which are considered as constants) entered on the monthly reporting form that Wehr Steel uses.

REPORT FORM — MANAGEMENT EFFECTIVENESS PLAN WEHR STEEL COMPANY						
Mo. April	Act./Std. =		% Achievement		=	% **Pay**
MEASURE	COST	STANDARD	FACTOR	MEASURE	COST	ACTUAL
Tons Molded	$ 6	$	Scrap	Tons Scr.	$ 200	$
Tons Molded	$ 7		Cust. Ret.	Tons Ret.	$ 300	
No. Man Hrs.	$ 0.01		L. T. Cases	No. Cases	$ 800	
Budget			Ind. Labor	Actual		
Total Standard Cost	$		Total Actual Cost			$

FIGURE 24.1 FIXED STANDARD PERFORMANCE COSTS OF EACH UNIT
(Columns 2 and 6)

Figure 24.2 shows the type of additional data that are also entered and which *vary* from month to month.

Mo. ·April	Act./Std. =		97 % Achievement		=	111.0 % **Pay**
MEASURE	COST	STANDARD	FACTOR	MEASURE	COST	ACTUAL
Tons Molded 1,600	$ 6	$ 9,600	Scrap	Tons Scr. 45	$ 200	$ 9,000
Tons Molded 1,600	$ 7	11,200	Cust. Ret.	Tons Ret. 30	$ 300	9,000
No. Man Hrs. 67,000	$ 0.01	670	L. T. Cases	No. Cases 0	$ 800	– 0 –
Budget 140,000	.90	126,000	Ind. Labor	Actual		125,000
Total Standard Cost	$ 147,470		Total Actual Cost			$ 143,000

FIGURE 24.2 DATA THAT VARY FROM MONTH TO MONTH
(unshaded areas)

In short, a company should be interested in comparing the total actual cost with the budgeted standard cost (which is the target to beat). Whenever the actual costs for the three-month reporting period are lower than the standard costs, there is a bonus or additional compensation earned. If the total *actual* cost ($143,000 for April) is divided by the total *standard* cost ($147,470 for April), the resulting figure represents the percent (97 percent for April) of achievement. This percent of achievement can be converted into the percent of pay that an individual employee earns by use of the conversion chart in Table 24.1. (The 97 percent of achievement would convert into 111.0 percent of pay.)

TABLE 24.1

CONVERSION CHART FOR CONVERTING PERCENT OF BUDGET ACHIEVEMENT INTO PERCENT OF PAY

	PAY PERCENT									
% BUDGET ACHIEVED	0.0	0.1	0.2	0.3	0.4	0.5	0.6	0.7	0.8	0.9
90.	115.0					114.9				
91.	114.8					114.7				
92.	114.6			114.5				114.4		
93.	114.3		114.2		114.1		114.0		113.9	
94.	113.8		113.7		113.6		113.5	113.4	113.3	113.2
95.	113.1		113.0	112.9	112.8	112.7	112.6	112.5	112.4	112.3
96.	112.2	112.1	112.0	111.8	111.7	111.5	111.4	111.3	111.2	111.1
97.	111.0	110.8	110.6	110.4	110.2	110.0	109.8	109.6	109.4	109.2
98.	109.0	108.8	108.6	108.4	108.2	108.0	107.8	107.6	107.4	107.2
99.	107.0	106.8	106.6	106.4	106.2	106.0	105.8	105.6	105.4	105.2
100.	105.0	104.8	104.6	104.4	104.2	104.0	103.8	103.6	103.4	103.2
101.	103.0	102.8	102.6	102.4	102.2	102.0	101.8	101.6	101.4	101.2
102.	101.0	100.8	100.6	100.4	100.2	100.0	99.8	99.6	99.4	99.2
103.	99.0	98.8	98.6	98.4	98.2	98.0	97.8	97.6	97.4	97.2
104.	97.0	96.8	96.6	96.4	96.2	96.0	95.8	95.6	95.4	95.2
105.	95.0	94.8	94.6	94.4	94.2	94.0	93.8	93.6	93.4	93.2
106.	93.0	92.8	92.6	92.4	92.2	92.0	91.8	91.6	91.4	91.2
107.	91.0	90.8	90.6	90.4	90.2	90.0	89.8	89.6	89.4	89.2
108.	89.0	88.8	88.6	88.4	88.2	88.0	87.8	87.6	87.4	87.2
109.	87.8	87.7	87.6	87.5	87.4	87.3	87.2	87.1	87.0	
110.	86.9	86.8	86.7	86.6	86.5		86.4		86.3	
111.	86.2		86.1		86.0		85.9		85.8	
112.	85.7			85.6				85.5		
113.	85.4					85.3				
114.	85.2					85.1				
115.	85.0									

Table 24.2 shows a summary of some data for a three-month reporting period. It shows that 98.19 percent of the budget was achieved; and when this is translated into pay (from Table 24.1), 108.6 percent of pay has been achieved. This means that each eligible employee would receive as a bonus 8.6 percent over his regular salary.

TABLE 24.2

SUMMARY DATA FOR THE THREE-MONTH REPORTING PERIOD

RECORD TO DATE		1st. Mo. (APRIL)	2d. Mo. (MAY)	3d. Mo. (JUNE)	FINAL (TOTAL)
Standard Cost $		155,243	165,626	151,454	472,323
Actual Cost $		149,111	161,023	153,655	463,789
Achievement	%	96.05	97.22	101.45	98.19
Pay	%	112.1	110.6	102.0	108.6

The specific financial reward for each three-month evaluation period for each eligible employee is calculated by averaging the employee's performance rating, subtracting 100, and multiplying by the employee's base salary for the three months. For example, if the employee's average performance rating was 108 percent and his monthly salary was $800, the calculations would be:

$$(108\% - 100\%) \times \$800 \times 3 \text{ months}$$

Thus, 8 percent of $2,400 results in a financial reward of $192 of additional compensation.

The performance standards which are established, if applied to the previous year's operations, would result in an appraisal of 105 percent of "normal." In other words, obtaining last year's peak operations would increase one's salary 5 percent. It is believed that a well-managed operation can achieve up to a rating of 115 percent, which would mean a 15 percent financial reward beyond one's present salary.

Results of the Management Effectiveness Plan. Since the plan was first installed in 1965, extra compensation beyond salary for a reporting period has ranged from a low of 3 percent to a high of 14 percent. Originally, the reporting period was for a period of four months. However, this was later changed to a three-month reporting period so that financial rewards would be forthcoming more often and thus the relationship between job performance and reward would more easily be seen. Like all management incentive plans, various changes need to be made from time to time to keep any plan current and attractive as well as effective.

Nonfinancial Incentives

Many social scientists today hold that nonfinancial incentives can be strong incentives if supervisors are paid fair and equitable base salaries and are assured of some degree of job security. Nonfinancial incentives that motivate employees and should be considered because they often appeal to the supervisor would include: (1) giving due recognition of him and his achievements; (2) giving him a sense of responsibility and assigning him commensurate authority; (3) placing him in the position that gives him great job satisfaction; (4) providing the climate in which he can gain experience working under fair and skillful leadership; and (5) giving him the opportunity to be a full-fledged member of the management team. For a comprehensive treatment on how employees are affected by various incentives, see Chapter 18 which discusses the influence of the behavior sciences on compensation incentives.

Summary

In order to bring together some of the more important points stressed throughout this chapter, the following suggestions represent a summary of items to be considered when planning compensations for supervisors:

1. Supervisors should earn more than their subordinates. Present pay ranges are between 10–40 percent above that of subordinates. The average rate differential between managerial supervisors and highest paid subordinates is about 30 percent.

2. The salary range (or spread) between the minimum and the maximum salary of a first-line supervisor's pay grade should not be less than 25 percent.

3. A plan for compensation should be tailor-made to fit the company conditions, which include management philosophy, ability to pay, profitability of business, labor market, existing salaries in the community, geographical location, etc.

4. Every compensation plan should include some type of incentive which will motivate the supervisor to show initiative, to keep up-to-date, and to work progressively toward his maximum capacity. Incentives should closely relate to individual performance whenever possible. In turn, the plan should reward each supervisor in relation to his individual merits and the results he achieves. Incentive or bonus earnings should be paid monthly (or at regular pay periods) by separate check so that the relationship between regular pay and incentive efforts is easily recognizable.

5. Supervisors should understand the company compensation plan and feel that it is fair and consistent.

6. The program should be efficiently and continually administered by a permanent committee, preferably composed of a few members of middle management, and a top executive. The committee should periodically review the supervisors' evaluations, rate their value to the company, and establish their status with regard to salary increases and promotion.

Chapter 25 will continue the discussion of managerial compensation as it applies to the remaining levels of management above the first-line supervisor.

REVIEW QUESTIONS

1. Should supervisory positions be evaluated with the same job evaluation plan that is used for clerical positions? Why?
2. How should management attempt to determine the worth of each supervisory position within a company?
3. Explain why you believe supervisory personnel should or should not be compensated for all hours worked beyond the normal work week of the company.
4. Should the salary spread between the minimum and maximum amount for the supervisor be greater than the wage spread for rank-and-file workers? Why?
5. Some managers believe that supervisory personnel should receive the same salary increases that are granted to unionized workers. Give your reasons for agreeing or disagreeing with such a policy.
6. Would it be a good idea to compensate each supervisor a fair and definite percentage of money above the pay of his subordinates and eliminate the need and expense of supervisory job evaluation? Explain your preference.
7. How much more compensation do you think a supervisor should receive than the workers he supervises? Justify your answer.
8. Who should assist the wage and salary administrator in maintaining an incentive plan for supervisors?
9. Explain the advantages and the disadvantages of the group incentive plan cited as a sample case in the text.

RESEARCH OR SEMINAR QUESTIONS

1. What should be done with a veteran supervisor who is failing to perform his duties and is no longer earning his salary? Explain in detail.
2. Should supervisory salaries be kept confidential? Express your opinion fully.
3. The record shows that a few companies have reduced the earnings of supervisory and other management personnel during the time the union is on strike against the company. (a) What are your pros or cons of such a policy? (b) Do you think the policy is justified? Why?
4. Do you think that the typical wage surveys for rank-and-file workers are applicable to salary surveys for supervisors? Explain your reasons.
5. If incentive plans are established for foremen or for office supervisors, what should the maximum payments be in percentage of their base salaries?
6. What nonfinancial forms of incentives have popular appeal today to supervisors?
7. When should pay raises be granted to supervisors — before or after the union has received a raise? Why?

PRACTICAL EXPERIENCE ASSIGNMENTS

1. (a) Choose some supervisory position that you have held (or know of) and indicate the factors that should be used in evaluating this position. Assign points to each factor.

   (b) List the personal factors that you believe the supervisor should be rated on periodically. Assign weights to each of these evaluation factors.

2. The president of a successful manufacturing company of 1,000 employees is considering hiring you as the wage and salary administrator. You have found out that the president has a young son who is a mediocre college student who expects to graduate in a year. The president wants to employ his son as soon as he graduates as an executive at a salary of $20,000 per year. (a) What would your procedure be to convince the president that the position and salary are or are not justified? (b) What is your reaction to the president's idea?

3. Explain how a company can prevent its supervisors from taking unfair advantage of their men in order to earn a big bonus for themselves.

4. What would you, as the new wage and salary administrator, do when you discover several supervisors who got their positions through influence are not really earning their salaries?

5. What should be done when it is discovered that some workers consistently earn more compensation than their supervisors? Prepare a plan that can be presented to the class in about five minutes.

CASE PROBLEM

24–1. A. B. SEA CORPORATION

Supervisory Wage Grievance

Bob Thomas and Ron Jones attended Ivy Tower High School in western Pennsylvania. They were born in the same neighborhood, lived within a block of each other, and attended the same grade school and high school. Both were members of the high school's football and basketball teams and both carried "B" averages in their studies.

Upon graduation, Ron went to work as a file clerk for the A. B. Sea Corporation in upstate New York. After four years of satisfactory work, Ron was rewarded by being named as one of the two assistant training directors needed by A. B. Sea. The other position had not yet been filled. It happened that Ron's old friend, Bob Thomas, was applying for the vacant position of assistant training director.

Bob, an athletic hero, had been given a scholarship to Scholar University, where he majored in Management and specialized in Industrial Training. Four years later these two old friends met when Bob was applying for the position of assistant training director. The company had two reasons for hiring Bob: he had the qualifications necessary for the job, and he could help their basketball team, which was in dire need of help at the time. Ron was glad to see his old friend since he thought that they could again be teammates on A. B. Sea's management team, as they had been on the teams in high school.

All went well for a few weeks while Bob was becoming accustomed to his new job. Soon, though, Ron noticed that he was performing his own duties and many of Bob's without any recognition either in pay or "slaps on the back." He therefore cornered Bob one day and asked him if he knew which duties he was expected to perform. The answer to his question came like an "uppercut" to the jaw when Bob stated that the only duty he had to perform was to play a good game of basketball on Saturdays, when there were Industrial League games. Ron was even further disillusioned when he learned that Bob was earning nearly $50 a month more than he was. Ron inquired about the pay difference and the manager told him that Bob was getting more money because he had a college education.

Problems:

1. What are the management problems involved in this case?
2. Which of these problems concern the wage and salary administrator?
3. What can be done to correct the salary problem?
4. What is your recommendation as to the best way of handling the compensation problem?
5. How could the salary problem have been avoided?

chapter 25

COMPENSATING EXECUTIVES

This chapter deals with the compensation of all levels of management above the first-line supervisor. In a manufacturing concern, this would include the general foreman, superintendents, professional department heads, plant managers, vice-presidents, and the president. The intent is not to spell out in detail the exact amount of pay that every member of management should receive, but to treat the principles and methodology involved so that managerial personnel, both line and staff, can be adequately compensated.

The objectives of executive compensation are similar to those of compensating supervisors and nonmanagerial employees, that is, to pay an adequate and equitable salary that will not only attract and hold competent employees, but that will also motivate them to perform according to their capabilities and in turn to reward them accordingly.

The topics treated include:

1. The need for adopting a formal compensation plan for executives.
2. Theory of compensating executives.
3. Areas where executive compensation may differ from other levels of compensation.
4. Some research conclusions on management compensation.
5. Summary of recommendations for compensating executives.

The need for adopting a formal compensation plan for executives

The formalized evaluation of executive positions has lagged far behind that of nonmanagerial jobs. Union pressures and complaints have forced companies to devote greater attention to nonmanagerial jobs than to managerial positions. Many job evaluation methods have stopped just short of the middle and top levels because of both real and imagined difficulties in evaluating executive functions. However, there is a growing awareness on the part of management of the need for systematically evaluating all jobs from the first-line supervisor to the president. Some companies have either formalized or systematic plans for evaluating their executive jobs, but at present these companies are still in the minority.

Sibson lists several reasons why a company should adopt a formal executive compensation plan:

1. To insure consistent salary treatment for all management personnel.
2. To instill confidence among executives by having policies that are not only consistent but also spell out explicitly so that those affected can know and understand the system.
3. To obtain more logical and justifiable internal relationships among jobs, both through the refinement of techniques and through the concentration on problems which ensue.
4. To help set salary schedules for management jobs on a competitive basis.
5. To obtain better control of individual bargaining over salaries.
6. To aid in organizing and manpower planning by focusing attention on duties and responsibilities.[1]

The need for a formal executive compensation plan becomes apparent when the number of executive positions gets so large that the executives and their records of performance are no longer ready knowledge of the company president. This number of positions is estimated to be between 15 and 25.

Even though the accuracy of the executive compensation method chosen may not be so precise as for nonmanagerial employees, it is important that some consistent and "above-the-board" method be used to show the fairness of the company and to pave the way for developing more highly accurate methods. Company personnel, stockholders, customers, and even some members of management, will never be convinced that executive compensation is fair and equitable without a formal plan. Granted that the evaluation of high-level positions is difficult and that the more complex a job becomes the more difficult it is to evaluate, the fact remains that no first-rate or reliable method will ever be developed unless continued honest attempts are made to tackle the task. In this

---

[1]Robert E. Sibson, "Plan for Management Salary Administration," *Harvard Business Review*, Vol. XXXIV, No. 6 (November–December, 1956), p. 103.

chapter are cited some of the attempts that have been made and are being made to solve the executive evaluation problem. Suggestions are also offered that may help some companies meet this problem.

Theory of compensating executives

Thus far throughout the book, it has been stressed that the total compensation of every employee should be based on the same pay formula — job worth, plus individual worth, plus any other pertinent pay considerations. However, it has also been stressed that the pay formula places greater emphasis on the job worth at the first level, and on individual worth at the executive level. It is felt that this concept is sound and flexible enough to meet the changes that occur in every enterprise.

To compensate executives equitably is a much more difficult task than to compensate other levels of employees in the organization. As an employee advances in an organization, the job becomes more complex and less routine; that is, the part that the individual plays becomes greater and more important (see Figure 5.2, page 143). This is especially true of executives! There is no fixed way to perform the various tasks of their positions. No two positions are identical and performance varies greatly. So much depends on how well executives perform that it has been stated that they "make" the job. Woodrow Wilson illustrated this point very well when he said of the Presidency of the United States that . . . "The rules of the job permit the holder of it to be as big a man as he can." In other words, the job of a company executive varies with the personality of the man who holds it, and — as a corollary — his greatness or smallness, as the case may be, is reflected in the image of the corporation.

Since managerial pay becomes based increasingly more on the man as he moves up the managerial ladder, it is very important that the compensation for the man be based on some meaningful job performance standards. This means that each firm has to identify clearly for each managerial job at least three categories of job performance: what is unsatisfactory; what is satisfactory; and what is outstanding. If four or more levels of performance (unsatisfactory, satisfactory, above average, outstanding) can be identified, so much the better. It is then possible to reward executive performance commensurate with results and in a fair and consistent manner.

For a company to receive real value from its executive compensation plan, that is, to get what it pays for, the firm must first identify what it wants to achieve. This means reverting back to the aims and goals of the business and setting performance standards according to the degrees of results obtainable. This will probably vary as each firm is a unique economic and sociological entity that has many variables to consider, such as its products, markets, competition, strengths, limitations, personnel, and company philosophy. This is a sound approach to executive compensation that works. It is a program tailored to the firm and is as individual as the company itself and its executives.

At General Motors, the management policy and belief is that the most effective results and the maximum progress and stability of the business are achieved by placing executives in the same relative position, as far as possible, that they would occupy if they were conducting a business of their own.[2] In this way there is opportunity for accomplishment through the exercise of individual initiative, and the opportunity for economic progress is commensurate with performance. Each individual should then be rewarded in proportion to his contribution to the profit of his own division and of the corporation as a whole.

In short, executives should be compensated mainly for whatever they personally bring to the job and for the results they obtain rather than for what the minimum duties call for on the job. Executive compensation should attempt to motivate the executive to perform at his maximum effort rather than to simply pay him for his job. This is especially true today where a firm's survival depends on innovation, growth, and executives who are not only dissatisfied with the status quo but who are also capable of changing it. The following are some of the yardsticks that often serve as guidelines in determining executive pay:

According to the existing internal salary relationships
Accountability for profit or loss on budget
Additional business brought into the company
Authority assumed
Cost of living
Demonstrated ability to develop potentialities of assistants
Dollar volume of business
Executives' success on overall manpower management

Geographical location
Ideas for improvement
Income tax rates
Job skills required
Net profits
Number of employees supervised
Overtime
Reputation
Responsibilities and difficulties of job
Risk assumed (insecurity)
Value of managerial ability
What competition pays
Years of service to company

These yardsticks may be important depending upon their wise selection and use. It is felt, however, that whatever yardsticks are used, they should be integrated as definite parts of a formula for determining total compensation.

Areas where executive compensation may differ from other levels of compensation

Throughout the previous chapters of this book the governing principles and techniques of employee compensation have been treated. In the main these are

---

[2]Alfred P. Sloan, Jr., *My Years with General Motors* (New York: Doubleday & Company, 1964), p. 407.

applicable to managerial compensation. However, executive managerial positions are more complex, they are fewer in number, and there is greater competition for them. Thus, a different emphasis is placed on them during evaluation. The main areas in which executive compensation differs from other levels of compensation will now be discussed so that current managerial compensation will be better understood.

Job Evaluation Factors

When using the point method of job evaluation, there is a tendency to use more factors in appraising managerial positions than nonmanagerial jobs. This is understandable since more complicated jobs would normally involve more factors. A composite list of the factors that companies use to evaluate executive positions would include the following:

Ability to deal with people
Accountability (for errors, performance costs, standards, etc.)
Analysis
Contacts required
Counseling skill
Creativeness
Decision making
Initiative
Judgment
Knowledge and experience needed
Mental application
Organizing and planning skill
Persuasive skill
Physical effort
Policy making
Pressure and tension
Problem-solving ability
Responsibility assumed
Supervision given
Supervision received

Many of these factors obviously overlap and need to be chosen carefully by the company using them. The weights assigned to each factor generally differ since each company has its own ideas and values.

Job Evaluation Methods

It must be recognized that an executive position depends on the person holding the job because he makes the job. Any two executives supposedly performing the "same" job would perform it so differently that there would really be two different positions. Thus, when evaluating the position, one should concentrate on how the executive functions. Evaluating the position as the executive performs is an approach that applies only to executive positions.

Most of the formal methods of job evaluation being used for executive positions are modifications of the four basic methods described in Chapter 7. The name of the method may be that of the person doing the modifying or the name may have assumed that of the modifying technique. Two of these modifications which have come to the attention of the authors will now be discussed briefly.

Guide Chart-Profile Method.[3] In 1951, the *profile method of job evaluation* was developed by the management consulting firm, Edward N. Hay & Associates, in response to the demand of a large client company for an explanation, or "rationalization," of the salary structure established for one of that company's divisions. In 1954, formal guide charts were added to the profile method to explain the assignment of evaluation points. Since that time, this method of position evaluation has become known as the *guide chart-profile method*. Although this method had its origins in aspects of both the factor comparison method (discussed in Chapter 7) and certain point plans, in its present sophisticated form it is separate and distinct from both origins.

The guide chart-profile method is currently being used in more than 700 companies, nonprofit organizations, and government jurisdictions in the United States, Canada, Mexico, the United Kingdom, and Australia. Originally designed to evaluate clerical and low-level managerial positions, the method is most frequently used today in the evaluation of middle- and top-management positions. The resulting evaluations are utilized as the basis for both base salary and incentive compensation programs.[4]

How the Method Works. Using complete, well-designed job descriptions as the basis for evaluations, the guide chart-profile method involves the evaluation of each position twice; once via the guide charts and again by "profiling." The Hay technique measures the job content of all positions in the organization hierarchy, from the lowest to the highest and across all functional lines, against the following identical criteria: *know-how, problem-solving,* and *accountability*. These three factors consider the value of a position in terms of (1) the knowledge and skills that are required of the job (*know-how*), (2) the thinking required to solve the problems that are normal to the job (*problem-solving*), and (3) the results that can be expected (*accountability*). Each of these criteria, as shown in Figures 25.2, 25.3, and 25.4, has two or three elements. Each element, in turn, is divided into ascending, defined levels of importance. The charts are designed in a form of "grid" scale so that the ratings of all elements can be considered separately but be fitted into a single numbered slot that provides the measure or "weight" for that criterion.

---

[3] We are indebted to Mr. Leonard M. Lewis, Director of Communications of Edward N. Hay & Associates, Management Consultants, Philadelphia, Pennsylvania, for supplying the guide-chart illustrations and for assisting in the description of this method.

[4] Jeremy Main, "An Expanding Executive Pay Package," *Fortune*, Vol. LXXVII, No. 7 (June 15, 1968), p. 166.

Guide charts are specifically tailored to the size and needs of the individual company or organization to assure the internal equity of evaluations. The charts are both the medium and the mechanism for measuring job content on a standard scale.

Initially, the profile evaluation was the more important of the two means of evaluation. However, in the course of its evolution, the guide chart evaluation became more sophisticated and today is the dominating evaluation. Profiling is presently used to check the guide chart evaluations.

Guide Chart Evaluation. Figure 25.1 illustrates the evaluation of a typical management job. Let us consider the first of the three hypothetical cases to see how the guide charts work to arrive at a total point value of 143 points for the position of keypunch supervisor.

POSITIONS	1. KH (KNOW-HOW)		2. PS (PROBLEM-SOLVING)		3. AC (ACCOUNT-ABILITY)		TOTAL POINTS
	Rating Code	Slot Points	Rating Code	Slot Points	Rating Code	Slot Points	
1. Supervisor Keypunch	DI3	66	D3 (33%)	22	C1p	55	143
2. Research Associate	GI1	70	F5 (80%)	56	D3s	130	256
3. Division Manager	GIII3	98	G4 (70%)	68	G3p	550	716

FIGURE 25.1 Guide Chart Criteria or Factors

Guide Chart for Know-How. Every company requires some minimum amount of knowledge that accompanies the skill that is required for acceptable job performance. The "know-how" comprises technical depth, managerial knowledge, and human relations skills. To measure the breadth and depth of these considerations, the guide chart in Figure 25.2 allots points according to the know-how that the job requires. The know-how of the keypunch supervisor was evaluated at "DI3" from Figure 25.2; the "D" refers to the fourth level of know-how (advanced vocational); the "I" places the job in the first vertical section of managerial know-how (limited — within a single function with operational regard for related fields); and the "3" recognizes that, as a supervisor of a group, an incumbent must have a high degree of human relations skills in order to understand and motivate his people. Thus, the DI3 rating on the know-how chart is evaluated at 66 points.

Hay Guide Charts are custom designed for each installation.
The wording and the numbering pattern here is illustrative only.

HAY GUIDE CHART

KNOW-HOW

Know-How is the sum total of every kind of skill, however acquired, required for acceptable job performance. It comprises:

- Technical Depth
- •• Managerial Know-How
- ••• Human Relations Skills

•• MANAGERIAL KNOW-HOW

Know-How of integrating and harmonizing the diversified functions involved in managerial situations (operating, supporting and administrative). This Know-How may be exercised consultatively as well as executively and involves in some combinations the areas of organizing, planning, executing, controlling and evaluating.

		I. LIMITED — Within a single function with operational regard for related fields.			II. RELATED — Primarily within a single field with some integration with related fields.			III. DIVERSE — Integration and coordination of diversified activities in a broad management area or consulting field...(defined)			IV. BROAD — Comprehensive integration and coordination in a major management area...(defined)		
		1.	2.	3.	1.	2.	3.	1.	2.	3.	1.	2.	3.
A. PRIMARY: Some secondary (or equivalent) education; plus work indoctrination.		50	53	57	60	64	68	70	75	79	80	86	90
		51	54	58	61	65	69	71	76	80	81	87	91
		52	55	59	62	66	70	72	77	81	82	88	92
B. ELEMENTARY VOCATIONAL: Uninvolved, standardized work routines and/or use of simple equipment and machines.		53	56	60	63	67	71	73	78	82	83	89	93
		54	57	61	64	68	72	74	79	83	84	90	94
		55	58	62	65	69	73	75	80	84	85	91	95
C. VOCATIONAL: Procedural or systematic proficiency, and/or use of specialized equipment.		56	59	63	66	70	74	76	81	85	86	92	96
		57	60	64	67	71	75	77	82	86	87	93	97
		58	61	65	68	72	76	78	83	87	88	94	98
D. ADVANCED VOCATIONAL: Some specialized (generally nontechnical skill(s); giving additional scope to a generally single function.		59	62	66	69	73	77	79	84	88	89	95	99
		60	63	67	70	74	78	80	85	89	90	96	100
		61	64	68	71	75	79	81	86	90	91	97	101
E. BASIC TECHNICAL-SPECIALIZED: Sufficiency in a technique requiring a grasp of involved practices and precedents; or of scientific theory.		62	65	69	72	76	80	82	87	91	92	98	102
		63	66	70	73	77	81	83	88	92	93	99	103
		64	67	71	74	78	82	84	89	93	94	100	104
F. SEASONED TECHNICAL-SPECIALIZED: Proficiency, gained through wide experiences in the specialized or technical field.		65	68	72	75	79	83	85	90	94	95	101	105
		66	69	73	76	80	84	86	91	95	96	102	106
		67	70	74	77	81	85	87	92	96	97	103	107
G. TECHNICAL-SPECIALIZED MASTERY: Mastery of techniques, practices and theories gained through wide seasoning and/or special development.		68	71	75	78	82	86	88	93	97	98	104	108
		69	72	76	79	83	87	89	94	98	99	105	109
		70	73	77	80	84	88	90	95	99	100	106	110
H. PROFESSIONAL MASTERY: Unique mastery in scientific or other learned disciplines.		71	74	78	81	85	89	91	96	100	101	107	111
		72	75	79	82	86	90	92	97	101	102	108	112
		73	76	80	82	87	91	93	98	102	103	109	113

PRACTICAL PROCEDURES — SPECIALIZED TECHNIQUES — SCIENTIFIC DISCIPLINES

EDWARD N. HAY & ASSOCIATES
COPYRIGHT 1968

••• HUMAN RELATIONS SKILLS

1. BASIC: Ordinary courtesy and effectiveness in dealing with others.
2. IMPORTANT: Understanding influencing people are important, but not critical considerations.
3. CRITICAL: Skills in understanding and motivating people are critical.

FIGURE 25.2   **GUIDE CHART FOR EVALUATING KNOW-HOW**

HAY GUIDE CHART
PROBLEM-SOLVING

Problem Solving is the original, "self-starting" thinking required by the job to: (1) identify, (2) resolve a problem. Ideas are put together from something already there. Therefore, Problem Solving is treated as a percentage utilization of Know-How.

Hay Guide Charts are custom designed for each installation. The wording and the numbering pattern here is illustrative only.

THINKING CHALLENGE

Thinking Within: (Thinking Environment)	1. REPETITIVE — Identical situations requiring solution by simple choice of learned things.	2. PATTERNED — Similar situations requiring solution by discriminating choice of learned things.	3. INTERPOLATIVE — Differing situations requiring search for solutions within area of learned things.	4. ADAPTIVE — Variable situations requiring analytical, interpretative, evaluative, and/or constructive thinking.	5. CREATIVE — Novel or nonrecurring pathfinding situations requiring the development of new concepts and imaginative approaches.	
A. STRICT ROUTINE: Simple rules and detailed instructions.	10%	15%	20%	25%	30%	A.
B. ROUTINE: Established routines and standing instructions.	12%	18%	24%	30%	40%	B
C. SEMI-ROUTINE: Somewhat diversified procedures and precedents.	14%	21%	28%	36%	50%	C
D. STANDARDIZED: Substantially diversified procedures and specialized standards.	16%	24%	33%	44%	60%	D
E. CLEARLY DEFINED: Clearly defined policies and principles.	18%	28%	38%	52%	70%	E
F. BROADLY DEFINED: Broad policies and specific objectives.	21%	32%	44%	60%	80%	F
G. GENERALLY DEFINED: General policies and ultimate goals.	24%	36%	50%	70%	90%	G

EDWARD N. HAY & ASSOCIATES
COPYRIGHT 1968

FIGURE 25.3   GUIDE CHART FOR EVALUATING PROBLEM-SOLVING

Guide Chart for Problem-Solving. This factor indicates the nature and control that the executive may have over his job decision as well as the conditions under which the decisions are made. The problem-solving guide chart in Figure 25.3 shows the percentage of know-how that is needed for solving problems. Thus, the evaluation points awarded for the problem-solving factor are a percentage of the points already obtained in the first factor of know-how. According to Figure 25.3, the hypothetical evaluating committee rated the problem-solving ability of the keypunch supervisor as "D3," i.e., a "D. Standardized" environment of "substantially diversified procedures and specialized standards," and with a thinking challenge of "3 — Interpolative — differing situations requiring search for solutions within area of learned things," resulting in a score of 33 percent. Since this 33 percent represents the percentage of the know-how that is needed for solving problems, 22 points are awarded for the problem-solving factor (33 percent of the 66 know-how points).

Guide Chart for Accountability. This factor measures the actions that must be taken to get job results. These actions are evaluated according to: the degree of freedom the executive has to act; the magnitude or size of the action; and the impact or strength of the action. Figure 25.4 is a guide for the evaluation of the factor of accountability. For accountability, the keypunch supervisor was viewed as "C1p"; i.e., a "C" Freedom to Act — standardized practices and procedures; in the magnitude "1" — Very Small (as compared with the entire company), and with a "p" or "Primary" impact. The resulting accountability evaluation shows 55 points. The total evaluation is therefore 143 points.

Profiling Positions. *Profiling* is the process of considering each position in terms of the three basic criteria (know-how, problem-solving, and accountability), and assigning a percentage to each criterion so that the three percentages total 100. The assigned percentages are the managerial judgments of the experienced evaluator or evaluation committee as each position is trisected into relative weights or values. "Is it primarily a high know-how and problem-solving position?" as is the job of the research chemist, or "Is it a heavy accountability job?" as are the positions of the division vice-president or the chief executive.

These *profiles* are then checked against the *actual profiles* that resulted from the guide chart evaluations. Where there is a substantial variance between the two, the position must be reexamined and the evaluations reconciled. The *actual profiles* are the percentages of the points for each major criterion against the total evaluation points. Profiles not only assure the validity of internal evaluations but also the consistency of evaluations between companies as there is a characteristic profile for each *kind* of job, regardless of its size.

Other Uses of Guide Charts. Through the process of correlation, each organization's evaluations can be converted to the Hay control standards, thus

HAY GUIDE CHART

ACCOUNTABILITY

Accountability is the answerability for action and for its consequences. It is the measured effect of the job on end results. It comprises:

- Freedom to Act.
- • Job Impact on End Results — as defined below.
- • • Magnitude — of area most clearly affected by the job.

Hay Guide Charts are custom designed for each installation.
The wording and the numbering pattern here is illustrative only.

• IMPACT

• • IMPACT OF JOB ON END RESULTS

1. REMOTE: Recording or incidental services.
2. CONTRIBUTORY: Advisory or facilitating services for use by others.
3. SHARED: Participating with others in taking action.
4. PRIMARY: Controlling impact on end results.

		MAGNITUDE (ANNUAL DOLLARS)															
	1. VERY SMALL OR INDETERMINATE Under $			**2. SMALL** $ – $				**3. MEDIUM** $ – $				**4. LARGE** $ – $				
	Remote	Contrib	Shared	Primary	Remote	Contrib	Shared	Primary	Remote	Contrib	Shared	Primary	Remote	Contrib	Shared	Primary	
A. PRESCRIBED: Detailed instructions under close supervision.	10	15	20	25	14	19	22	29	20	27	33	44	25	38	52	66	A
B. CONTROLLED: Established work routines. Close supervision.	15	20	25	30	22	33	44	55	30	40	50	66	50	68	77	99	B
C. STANDARDIZED: Standardized practices and procedures. Supervision of progress and results.	22	33	44	55	30	44	66	88	40	55	75	100	75	90	110	140	C
D. GENERALLY REGULATED: Practices covered by well defined policy. Supervisory review.	40	50	66	80	40	66	90	120	60	88	130	190	100	120	145	220	D
E. DIRECTED: Broad practice covered by functional precedents and policies.	50	70	100	130	66	99	133	200	100	125	200	300	150	180	230	330	E
F. ORIENTED DIRECTION: Functional policies and goals.	80	120	160	200	110	144	200	300	150	185	300	400	210	260	360	440	F
G. GUIDANCE:	120	170	220	300	160	200	300	400	220	330	440	550	310	420	540	700	G

F R E E D O M   T O   A C T

EDWARD N. HAY & ASSOCIATES
COPYRIGHT 1968

FIGURE 25.4 GUIDE CHART FOR EVALUATING ACCOUNTABILITY

permitting direct comparisons of the salary and evaluation practices of any organization with the practices of selected groups in an industry or in a geographical area. Edward N. Hay & Associates, the developer of the method, publishes annual surveys showing the compensation practices of selected groups of companies. As all of these organizations use the same evaluation method, participants in the surveys may make comparisons of how their salary or compensation "lines" relate to the group, as well as to how specific total job content weights are compensated by the participating companies. One example of the Hay comparisons is shown in Figure 25.5.

A unique advantage of this method is that the criteria of the guide charts not only have application to base salary and incentive compensation but also they are being used widely, either directly or in some adapted fashion, as the basis for organizational analysis, performance appraisal, management development, and to meet other managerial needs.

Linear Programming. The *linear programming* method utilizes ranking and point method procedures. This technique is used to indicate which of the job evaluation factors that have been suggested are important and assigns weights to these factors.[5] Thus, linear programming converts simple rankings of suggested job factors into an overall, final, and more meaningful ranking by systematically and objectively assigning values to each of the job ranks so that the distance between final job ranks is then known in terms of points. Usually, in the ranking system everyone knows which job is first, second, etc., but few ever know how much more important one job is than another. The simplex method of linear programming supplies the answer to how far apart the various jobs are in their rankings by assigning a definite point value for each rank. The final results are much the same as the point system in that all jobs are valued or appraised in terms of points.

The main advantage that this plan appears to have over other methods is that an objective mathematical means is used to establish the final factors and their weights — as opposed to the more subjective means usually employed in salaried plans. The linear programming method also rejects the unimportant factors that have been suggested. In addition, *in one set of computations it is possible to determine factors and factor weights.* The chief disadvantages appear to be the complicated mathematics involved and the reluctance of employees to accept a method which they may not fully understand.

Job Pricing

The *pricing* of positions means the establishment of minimum starting salaries for all the positions that are under consideration. The pricing of

---

[5]R. O. Ferguson, L. F. Sargent, and N. V. Reinfeld, "Pay Plan for Management," *Factory Management and Maintenance*, Vol. CXII, No. 3 (March, 1954), p. 2.

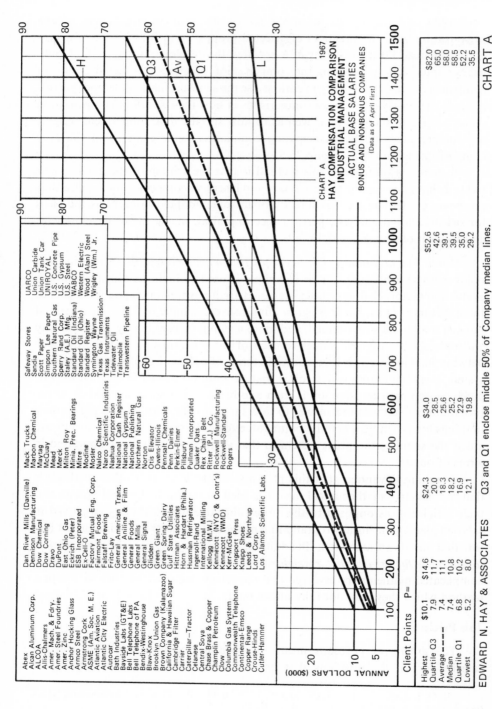

EDWARD N. HAY & ASSOCIATES   Q3 and Q1 enclose middle 50% of Company median lines.

FIGURE 25.5 COMPARING SALARIES WITH TOTAL JOB POINT EVALUATIONS

managerial positions is a difficult task since there is not, as yet, a wealth of information nor established "going rates" to support very strongly the decisions made. Wage surveys of nonmanagerial jobs are more plentiful and can be used to assist the pricing of those jobs, but managerial pricing of jobs still has a long way to go. Compensation data for top-level positions may be secured through the American Management Association (AMA), company reports to the Security and Exchange Commission (SEC), proxy statements, and cooperative company salary surveys. Since 1966, R. E. Sibson has been making an annual study of executive compensation, and the results are published in the January issue of the *Business Magazine*. Every year other magazines, such as *Business Week, U.S. News & World Report*, and the *Harvard Business Review*, usually report on salaries of top executives. The AMA, the Dartnell Corporation, and the National Industrial Conference Board have been making wage surveys of managerial positions, too. However, at this level the technique has not as yet secured the wide usage as at the nonmanagerial level. Pricing, therefore, becomes a matter of judgment as to what relationship there should be among the managerial positions and between nonmanagerial jobs. Much research and time will be needed to provide adequate and ample data to price executive positions with more certainty. In the meantime, whatever wage surveys are available can be used as a starting point in helping to make one's judgment as objective as possible. Some of the different approaches that could be used to price positions are described below.

Top Down Approach. The *top down method* prices positions by first deciding what the minimum salary should be for the president, or top executive of the company, and then determining what amount subordinate executives should get in relationship to the top executive. Robert E. Sibson, an authority on management compensation, believes the chief executive's salary is the correct starting place in evaluating a company's compensation set-up because the top executive's salary is the yardstick by which all other salaries should be set.[6] When the top salary is not correct, the following often happen: other forms of compensation related to salary (bonuses, pensions, etc.) present problems; other firms lure executives who are underpaid; when executives are overpaid, there is criticism from stockholders and unions and this can lower employee morale. The minimum salary for the company president might be determined by looking over the salary figures paid top executives in other companies and then by making whatever adjustments need to be made because of the particular circumstances of the company being considered. Such considerations may include the company's basic philosophy to be a high-, low-, or medium-paying company. It may include the ability of the company to pay according to its profits. It may include such other factors as kind of business, geographical location, kinds and number of competitors, supply and demand for such executives, and income tax bracket.

---

[6]R. E. Sibson, "How Much Chief Executives Are Paid," *Business Management* (January, 1968), p. 29.

TABLE 25.1

AVERAGE ANNUAL SALARIES OF CHIEF EXECUTIVE OFFICERS FOR VARIOUS SIZE FIRMS AND INDUSTRIES (1967)

Size of Firm by Sales Volume (Millions of Dollars)		Annual Salary of Chief Executive in a Firm Which Pays:				
		Low — Casualty Ins., Education, Government, Hospitals, Utilities, Wholesale & Retail	Low Average — Chemicals, Food, Instruments, Machinery, Rubber, Transportation	Average — Banks, Beverage, Bus. Supp. & Equip., Construction, Fab. Metal Products, Furniture, Glass, Leather, Paper, Pharmaceutical, Tools & Hardware	High Average — Auto & Truck, Life & Group Insurance, Metals, Textiles, Tobacco	High — Aerospace, Auto Supplier, Bus. Mach. & Equip., Elec. & Electronics, Petroleum & Gas Utilities, Printing & Pub.
SMALL	Under .5	$ 17,000	$ 23,000	$ 30,000	$ 35,000	$ 40,000
	.5–1	18,000	24,000	32,000	37,000	41,000
	1–5	22,000	27,000	33,000	39,000	42,000
	5–15	33,000	40,000	44,000	48,000	49,000
MODER-ATE	15–25	$ 36,000	$ 43,000	$ 49,000	$ 57,000	$ 64,000
	25–35	46,000	53,000	60,000	65,000	72,000
	35–50	55,000	59,000	64,000	70,000	76,000
	50–75	60,000	66,000	72,000	77,000	81,000
INTER-MEDIATE	75–175	$ 75,000	$ 83,000	$ 90,000	$ 98,000	$105,000
	175–250	90,000	95,000	107,000	115,000	126,000
	250–500	97,000	110,000	122,000	132,000	145,000
LARGE	500–1000	$110,000	$125,000	$144,000	$159,000	$180,000
	1000–2000	145,000	175,000	200,000	220,000	250,000
	Over 2000	Insufficient Data	Insufficient Data	230,000	Insufficient Data	Insufficient Data

Source: Business Management (January, 1968), pp. 28–32.

Table 25.1 shows the average salary received by the chief executive in some 600 companies of various sizes in the United States. This type of data would be an excellent starting point to use the top down approach because the table gives the salaries received in low- and high-paying industries as well as the size of the firm according to sales volume. It is interesting to note that the presidents in low-paying industries get less than half the salary of presidents in high-paying industries. In a recent study of over 1,200 companies the National Industrial Conference Board found that the amount of executive compensation increases with company size.[7] Numerous studies have shown that when the average company doubles in size, top-level compensation increases 20 percent or more.[8]

Sibson says that, as a rule of thumb, any salary less than 85 percent (of those reported in Table 25.1) is too low (barring unusual or extraordinary circumstances) and any salary more than 115 percent of those in the table could invite trouble from stockholders or regulatory bodies (unless unusual circumstances justify the amounts).[9] Senior executives do not generally receive salary increases every year. Every two years seems to be the norm, although every third year is not unusual.[10] This means that adjustments have to be made in pricing salaries according to the percent that salaries have increased since the last salary increase.

Table 25.2 shows the average relationship of the chief executive's salary to the salary of the next nine highest salaried personnel in the firm. The table shows these relationships for three different kinds of companies. Generally, small firms tend to have a steep compensation slope and large firms, a flat slope. This table may assist a company in determining whether its internal salary relationship among the top salaried officers is reasonably correct or needs to be adjusted. However, the use of the table is valuable only when the chief executive officer's salary is correct. If his salary is not correctly priced, the others will likewise be out of line.

Peter Drucker, in his book, *The Practice of Management*, reported that researchers had discovered that when the salary levels of the top four or five men who head the firm are close together (75 to 90 percent as much as the president), the performance and morale of the management group are likely to be high.[11] However, when the president's main subordinates get only 25 to 50 percent of what he gets, then it is time to look for trouble as the firm is likely to be badly managed since it has to depend too much on one strong man for its success.

From time to time there are many critics of the salary that a chief executive of a firm receives. Stockholders, unions, employees, other executives, and the

---

[7]*Focus*, Vol. II, No. 1 (January 1, 1965), p. 2.

[8]Arch Patton, "Top Executive Pay: New Facts and Figures," *Harvard Business Review* (September–October, 1966), p. 94.

[9]Sibson, *loc. cit.*

[10]*Ibid.*, p. 26.

[11]Peter Drucker, *The Practice of Management* (New York: Harper & Brothers, 1954), p. 175.

TABLE 25.2

**THE RELATIONSHIP OF THE ANNUAL SALARIES
OF THE TOP TEN EXECUTIVES**

RANK ORDER OF ANNUAL SALARY	ANNUAL SALARY AS A PERCENT OF THE CHIEF EXECUTIVE'S ANNUAL SALARY IN A FIRM WHOSE SALARY SLOPE IS		
	STEEP	AVERAGE	FLAT
Chief Executive Officer	100%	100%	100%
2d highest	65	70	75
3d highest	55	60	65
4th highest	55	55	65
5th highest	45	50	55
6th highest	40	42	45
7th highest	35	38	42
8th highest	30	35	40
9th highest	29	32	34
10th highest	29	30	32

Source: Business Management (January, 1968), p. 36.

public often wonder whether his salary is justifiable or not.   Clarence B. Randall,[12] past president of the Inland Steel Company, has implied the following questions that might be used as benchmarks in determining whether the chief executive's salary is appropriate: (1) Has the salary been approved only by an inside board of directors made up entirely of men who work for him? (2) Is his salary the largest in the industry? (3) Is his compensation out of line with other men bearing similar responsibilities in other industries? (4) Does he pay himself 50 percent more than the next officer in line in his own company? If there is a yes answer to any one of the above questions, a very careful reappraisal should be made to determine whether the compensation is really justified and whether the criticisms are not correct.

A few years ago, the chairman of the board of one of the major firms in the United States was asked by a stockholder what made him worth $650,000 a year. The chairman was reported to have replied, "I don't know. I'm probably not worth it, but that's what I get paid."[13] In another case, the president of a union

---

[12]For an interesting viewpoint on executive compensation, see Clarence B. Randall, "The Myth of the Almighty Dollar," *The Folklore of Management*, (New York: The New American Library of World Literature, Inc., 1961), chap. 5.

[13]*The Milwaukee Journal*, May 22, 1966.

had his salary raised from $25,000 a year to $75,000 a year. Such examples of executive compensation draw suspicions, and without sound and valid justifications, only lead to distrust and a lack of respect for those executives in charge.

Bottom Up Approach. The *bottom up method* prices positions using nonmanagerial jobs as its starting point. The assumption is that the nonmanagerial jobs are priced correctly and that the managerial positions should be priced according to some fixed percentage relationship above the nonmanagerial jobs. In principle, the bottom up approach is the reverse of the top down approach. The major difference is that the top down approach uses present top executive salaries as its starting point working downward through the position hierarchy, while the *bottom up approach uses the highest nonmanagerial job pay as its starting point and proceeds upward through the managerial position hierarchy.* In either approach, management has to decide on some percentage relationships among all jobs. Formal job evaluation plans can, of course, help to establish the relative values of the various positions. It has already been indicated in Chapter 24 that first-line supervisors receive between 10 to 40 percent more than the highest pay received by nonmanagerial personnel.

Budget Approach. The *budget approach* prices positions by allocating a percentage of the total payroll to executives. In two studies of large companies, Patton suggested the use of a proportional theory to compensate executives.[14] He found that in companies of 20,000 employees or more, the top and middle-management executives represent 1 percent of the company employees (top executives represented .1 percent, while middle-management executives totaled .9 percent). Table 25.3 shows the percent of total payroll the executives received in large companies in four different years. Thus, the determination of what percentage of total payroll executives should receive could serve as a starting point in pricing these positions. Consideration should also be given to what the trend

TABLE 25.3

THE PERCENT OF TOTAL PAYROLL RECEIVED BY EXECUTIVES

EXECUTIVES	PERCENT OF TOTAL PAYROLL RECEIVED IN:			
	1939	1945	1952	1956
ALL (Top and Middle) . . . = 1.0%	5.8%	4.3%	4.1%	4.3%
TOP. . . . . = .1	1.9	1.2	1.1	1.1
MIDDLE. . . . . = .9	3.9	3.1	3.0	3.2

[14]Arch Patton, "Top Management's Share of the Payroll," *Fortune*, Vol. XLVI, No. 1 (January, 1953), p. 106, and "Does High Executive Pay Mean High Profits?" *The Controller*, Vol. XXVI, No. 2 (February, 1958), p. 61.

is in the percentage the executives receive of the total payroll. Foote[15] found that in 1963 the top .1 percent of executives were receiving only .9 percent of the total payroll; thus, from 1939 to 1963 there had been a decrease from 1.9 percent to .9 percent. In a recent study of an 11-year pay period, the average pay of chief executives rose only 25 percent, while the compensation of hourly production workers increased 46 percent;[16] thus, the trend to narrow the percentage compensation gap continues.

Once the total executive payroll has been decided, budgets are prepared for departments and subdivided according to the managerial personnel making up the departmental team. This could be looked upon as the team concept of executive compensation and the various members of each department could be compensated according to some percentage plan similar to the one illustrated in Table 25.2.

The position pricing concepts described show that there are at least three approaches available for determining basic salary in a consistent and equitable manner. To make allowances for those executives who perform far beyond what is normally expected for the position and who would thus tend to destroy the equitability of the position relationships, the company has at least two methods of adequately compensating these outstanding executives. One method is to supplement their base salary with additional income through bonuses and deferred compensation such as stock options, profit sharing, pensions, fringes, and other allowances. The other method is to promote them to higher positions that have the base salary that these executives appear to be deserving. The total amount of compensation received through the former method can be and oftentimes is more than the basic salary itself. In other words, flexibility in the compensation plan is needed to cope with the varying results that are bound to occur. Flexibility can be achieved through the various means of increasing income beyond the basic minimum salary. Sibson has indicated that the amount of extra compensation typically averages from 10 to 15 percent of the base compensation for middle management, and as much as 100 percent or more of the base compensation for top management.[17]

Maturity Curve Approach. A relatively recent technique for pricing professional and scientific jobs and in determining equitable salaries is through the device commonly referred to as a *maturity curve* (it sometimes is also referred to as a *career curve* or an *experience curve*). The maturity curve is simply a graph that plots salaries against age or against years of job experience. Generally, it shows a relationship between salary and job experience, usually measured in the

[15]George H. Foote, "A New Era in Executive Compensation," *Personnel Journal*, Vol. 44, No. 8 (1965), p. 406.
[16]"Executive Pay — Perplexity in Taxes, Deferrals, Pension," *The Employment Counselor*, Vol. 25, No. 11 (March, 1969), p. 1.
[17]Sibson, "Plan for Management Salary Administration," *op. cit.*, p. 104.

number of years since the professional employee received his college degree. The curves are established from data obtained in salary surveys, and their effectiveness depends upon the validity of the data. The maturity curves have been most useful for special groups of employees, such as engineers and researchers, where a comparison with other groups would not be applicable or fair because of significant job differences or because of a tight labor market supply. Maturity curves were developed to identify the pay received by recent graduates and those professionals who have been employed several years. The curves also indicate what the going rates are for transient classes of employees in an unstable labor market.

Maturity curves can be developed according to whatever data are available or desired. Figure 25.6 shows the weekly salary paid to five levels of engineers according to their birth years and relative position (percentile) within a pay distribution. From this figure an employee can compare his weekly salary against his age group to ascertain his presumed "quality" within his age group. To do this, an employee locates the year of his birth (along the horizontal axis) and then reads (along the vertical axis) the weekly salary received by the typical em-employee (median), the top 10 percent, the top 25 percent, the lower 25 percent, and the bottom 10 percent. In this way, an employee knows how he stands in relation to most other employees born in the same year as he. The data in Figure 25.6 are anonymous and cover some 13,500 people represented by the Seattle Professional Engineering Employees Association (SPEEA).[18]

Maturity curves are especially useful to an employment recruiter in equating the salaries of recent college graduates and professional employees who have several years of experience. In a floating labor market, the curves assist the salary administrator in determining a more equitable salary based on the employee's maturity level and the demand-supply level of the labor market. When maturity curves are related to both employee experience and job performance, they provide an equitable means of justifying salaries in the professional labor market. They are also useful in establishing salary progressions for employees. They have sometimes been used as a substitute for job evaluation, pay grades, and pay raises.

We believe that maturity curves are most useful when used as a guideline for pricing positions and determining equitable salary levels. They should be used to supplement job evaluation and employee evaluation and never as a substitute for these basic appraisal methods. Jobs within a profession will usually vary in difficulty and responsibility. Employees holding similar jobs will likewise vary in their abilities and job performances; thus, employee age or years of job experience should not be the sole criteria for the determination an employee's compensation.

---

[18]*Incentive Com, ·tion and Salary Data, 1967–1968* (Seattle: Seattle Professional Engineering Employees ɔciation [SPEEA], August, 1968), p. 1.

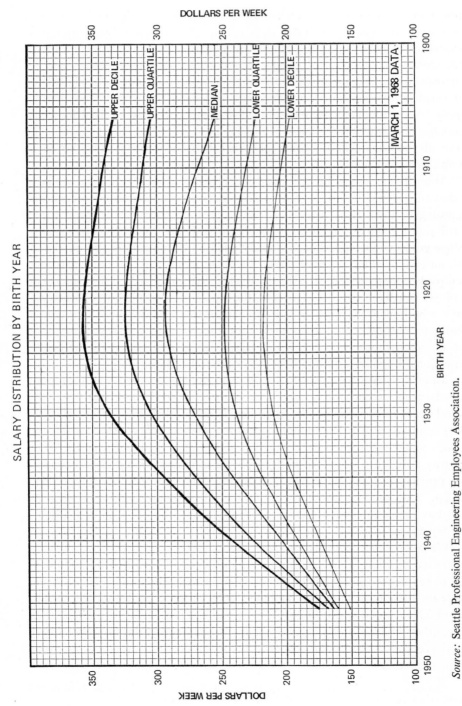

DOLLARS PER WEEK

SALARY DISTRIBUTION BY BIRTH YEAR

UPPER DECILE

UPPER QUARTILE

MEDIAN

LOWER QUARTILE

LOWER DECILE

MARCH 1, 1968 DATA

BIRTH YEAR

DOLLARS PER WEEK

Source: Seattle Professional Engineering Employees Association.

FIGURE 25.6 MATURITY CURVE SHOWING SALARIES PAID TO FIVE LEVELS OF ENGINEERS ACCORDING TO BIRTH YEAR AND POSITION WITHIN A PAY DISTRIBUTION

Salary Ranges

It has been previously pointed out that first-line supervisors have salary range spreads which average 33⅓ percent. Executive positions should have a greater salary range spread than all other levels because the positions can be as big as the executives make them. Executive positions generally have a salary range spread of 50 percent. However, some companies which feel that 50 percent is not a large enough incentive have 70 percent salary spreads. In a number of large companies, the "ideal" spread is considered to be from 80 to 100 percent near the top.[19] Employee evaluation is the basis for determining what amount of the salary spread the executive is to receive.

Managerial Employee Evaluation

Recent trends in appraising managerial employees have tended to seek two goals: (1) to measure job performance, and (2) to assist the executive in self-development. The purpose of measuring job performance is for pay purposes, that is, to reward the executive commensurate with the results he has achieved. Factors that have been used to measure job performance results include the following:

Fewer customer complaints	Increased profits
Decreased costs and expenses	Improved quality
Improved goodwill	Increased sales
Number of innovations	Decreased scrap
Number of new accounts	Improved services
Fewer returns	

The task of developing a reasonable standard or basis for judging the performance of an executive presents a real problem, especially for incentive payments. However, each company has to solve this problem in light of its own circumstances. Without adequate performance standards as a basis for pay raises and supplementary incentive compensations, straight salary may be the better form of compensation.

To assist executives in their self-development and in improving their job results, it is necessary to identify and rate those factors that either cause or relate to job performance. These factors are usually of a personal nature. They should not be used as a prime base for monetary rewards since having them does not assure results. Those factors that have often been used to identify the strengths and weaknesses of executives, as a basis for job improvement, would include the following:

---

[19]George W. Torrence, *The Motivation and Measurement of Performance* (Washington, D.C.: The Bureau of National Affairs, Inc., 1967), p. 36.

Ambition or drive	Job knowledge
Analytical ability	Judgment
Appearance and habits	Integrity
Attitude	Initiative
Creativeness	Persuasiveness
Emotional stability	Sociability
Experience	Teamwork
Health	Vision

It is easy to see that many of these factors overlap each other. Some companies use precise factors while others use general ones. To avoid possible confusion, each factor needs an accurate definition to identify what is covered by it and an assigned weight determined by each company according to the value that the company places on the factor.

Executive Expenses

Until 1968, there was little available information on how highly paid executives spent their money. The need for a Management Expenditure Index (MEI) was recognized by the editors of *Business Management* magazine and the research staff of Sibson and Company, New York City management consultants, who developed the MEI and conducted a survey to gather data for the index. The MEI is a statistical compilation of expenditure patterns of nearly 500 managers who earn more than $20,000 a year. It is an index of changes in prices of the things a management-level family typically buys.[20] This index should be helpful in planning and analyzing executive compensation programs.

Table 25.4 shows the various percentages of their compensation that executives spend on their families (which averaged four in number). The table tends to show the following:

1. The percent of income spent on food and housing decreases as income rises, while taxes increase directly with income.

2. Housing is one of the largest items in the budget.

3. Taxes, savings, and transportation take more of the budget than food and clothing.

4. Expenditures change markedly as income rises.

5. Expenditures for savings, recreation, and apparel remain relatively constant. This is another way of saying that executive families simply trade up in quality as they grow richer, buying fur coats instead of cloth, and purchasing yachts instead of outboard motor boats.[21]

---

[20]R. E. Sibson, "How Top Managers Spend Their Money," *Business Management* (January, 1968), p. 48.

[21]*Ibid.*, pp. 50–56.

TABLE 25.4

HOW VARIOUS LEVEL EXECUTIVES SPENT
THEIR COMPENSATION ON THEIR FAMILIES
(Which Averaged Four in Number)

EXPENSE ITEM	THE PERCENT OF ANNUAL INCOME SPENT						CONSENSUS
	UNDER $20,000	$20,000–25,000	$25,000–30,000	$30,000–37,500	$37,500–50,000	$50,000 PLUS	
Food........	13%	12%	10%	9%	7%	5%	9%
Housing......	26	23	19	22	12	17	20
Apparel......	4	6	5	5	4	4	5
Transportation	11	9	9	9	8	7	9
Education....	4	4	5	7	7	11	6
Health.......	4	3	3	3	2	2	3
Recreation....	7	7	6	5	5	7	6
Life insurance.	2	3	3	4	4	2	3
Savings......	6	9	10	10	17	10	10
Miscellaneous.	10	7	10	7	10	3	8
Tax..........	13	17	20	19	24	32	21
Total......	100%	100%	100%	100%	100%	100%	100%

Source: Business Management (January, 1968), p. 50.

Table 25.5 shows a comparison of expenditure patterns for the average city worker's family and the average manager's family. In comparing the two types of families, it is apparent that there are great differences in expenditures and that there is little relationship to each other. It also would appear to indicate that the consumer price index is not a valid basis for measuring the changes in real earnings of executives. The data in the table should also serve to indicate where each of the families' needs is in terms of the expenditures they are making in the various categories. These data should be considered in motivating employees and in establishing the total compensation package for these various employee categories.

In short, the study of management expenditures tended to bring out these major conclusions and implications:[22]

1. The manager's standard of living does not rise in the same way that the average city worker's does; therefore, it is unrealistic to base executive raises on the "cost of living" increases published by the Bureau of Labor Statistics.

---

[22]*Ibid.*

TABLE 25.5

COMPARISON OF EXPENDITURE PATTERNS
For the Average City Worker's Family[a]
and the Average Manager's Family[b]

ITEM	CPI[c]	MEI[d]
Food	23%	9%
Housing	24	20
Transportation	9	9
Clothing and personal care	10	6
Medical care	5	3
Education	(e)	6
Recreation	(e)	6
Life insurance	2	3
Savings	(e)	10
Gifts and contributions	3	3
Miscellaneous	12	4
Taxes	12	21
Total	100%	100%

(a) Family of four with income of $9,191 (*Source:* Bureau of Labor Statistics, Consumer Price Index).
(b) Family of four with average income of $32,000 (*Source: Business Management,* Management Expenditure Index Survey).
(c) Consumer Price Index.
(d) Management Expenditure Index.
(e) Not shown in Consumer Price Index. Assumed to be included under miscellaneous.

Source: Business Management (January, 1968), p. 52.

2. Savings, life insurance, and education tend to consume a larger portion of an executive's income as his salary increases until he reaches the highest salary levels. This means that these items are important to him and if management wishes to motivate the executive, consideration should be given to supplying the executive with rewards that will make more of these things possible.

3. There is a growing number of executives who have a good deal of personal income to rely upon. Some have inherited wealth while others have outside sources of income. This means that more and more executives have less fear about losing their jobs. It also means that many executives are interested in capital gains programs because they do have the capital to take advantage of such programs. Finally, it means that some executives may prefer to choose a job whose work they enjoy and find a challenge, rather than to choose a job which pays the most.

Executive Motivation[23]

Recent studies reaffirm that for the overwhelming majority of executives, money remains the number one motivator.[24] This may be in the form of pay raises, cash bonuses, or a combination of these. However, many people are beginning to wonder whether pay is beginning to lose some of its motivational power. As the younger generation of executives moves into middle and top management levels, they appear to have a different set of motivational values.

The younger generation of executives has grown up in an increasingly prosperous economy that has had few setbacks and no major depressions. Thus, they are better educated, aggressive, confident, and unwilling to go along with the traditional conservatism of the older generation of executives. They are optimistic about the future and tend to look upon the technological explosion that is taking place as an opportunity to get involved and to accomplish something. Such accomplishments are very satisfying as well as rewarding to the younger generation. Company organizational changes that are needed to meet changing technology and a firm's growth mean more job promotions and the challenge to do something new. Thus, the up-and-coming generation of executives is more likely to be motivated by nonmonetary incentives than by money. This is also true of the older generation of senior executives when they believe they are already well paid. In short, there is a growing number of executives who are more strongly motivated by nonmonetary incentives than by monetary ones. These executives may be motivated by more challenging assignments, longer vacations, more time off for personal reasons, and working on special projects. It is therefore necessary that the compensation program be designed according to the needs and desires of the employees as well as of the firm.

Compensation Beyond a Salary Schedule

At the present time, the most popular method of compensating executives is through a fixed annual salary. About half of all companies rely primarily upon this method. Thus, salary is most often the measure of how well an executive is doing in his job. However, salary alone provides only a limited insight into what executives can earn. A salary by itself is generally not a true measure of an executive's worth nor an appropriate compensation for him. Salary is only a part of what might be thought of as a total systems compensation approach. We have previously pointed out that a starting salary represents primarily what the job is worth and anything beyond this amount is what the individual is worth. It is therefore common practice for many firms to offer inducements beyond salary

---

[23]For a more detailed analysis of executive motivation and how it is changing, read the article by Arch Patton appearing in the January, 1968, issue of *Management Review*.

[24]R. E. Sibson, "How to Increase Executive Effectiveness," *Business Management*, (January, 1968), p. 66.

so as to motivate executives as fully as possible and to serve as a reward for performance beyond the minimum requirements of the job. However, it should be pointed out that, as yet, only a small number of firms are providing some form of extra compensation to their professional and technical employees.

Table 25.6 shows the range of total compensation that executives often receive at various salary levels. This table tends to confirm the theory that the man often makes the job at the executive level since compensations beyond a basic starting salary often exceed this amount and thus the executive is paid more for his individual performance than for the minimum job requirements. The table indicates that executives often receive as little as 7 percent and as much as 207 percent beyond salary as an inducement for greater effort or as a reward for demonstrated performance. Thus, the various means of compensating an executive beyond a salary schedule can offer the flexibility needed to motivate him to greater performance and to reward him in proportion to his increased performance contributions.

TABLE 25.6

THE RANGE OF TOTAL COMPENSATION* THAT EXECUTIVES RECEIVE

If an Executive's Annual Salary Is	The Total Annual Compensation That an Executive Might Receive Is:	
	From	To As Much As
$200,000	$375,000	$615,000
150,000	270,000	410,000
100,000	165,000	260,000
75,000	119,000	167,000
50,000	75,000	105,000
40,000	56,000	79,000
30,000	40,000	52,000
25,000	32,000	40,000
20,000	23,000	29,000
15,000	16,000	20,000

*Total compensation means monetary amounts derived from salary, bonuses, stock options, profit sharing, and savings plans.

Source: Business Management (January, 1968), p. 44.

Compensation beyond a straight salary schedule may be of a financial or nonfinancial form or both. Financial incentives may include any form of payment such as cash bonuses, stock options, and other deferred payments. Nonfinancial incentives include some form of benefit or service provided for the executive by the company. Benefits and services are better known as fringes and typically include insurance, vacations, memberships, educational conferences, conventions, and other forms of conveniences which are not paid for by the executive. Due to limited space nonfinancial incentives will not be discussed. However, a brief discussion of the more common financial incentives — bonuses, deferred compensation, expense accounts, and stock options — follows.

Bonuses. *Bonuses* are awards in the form of cash, stock, or deferred payments made to executives as a reward for their performance. Bonuses are one of the older and more varied forms of stimulating executive performance. The duPont Company and the General Motors Corporation have been two of the most prominent exponents of the bonus plan, and they have likewise been very successful with its use. Alfred P. Sloan, Jr., in his book, *My Years with General Motors,* had this to say about bonuses:

> I believe that the Bonus Plan has been, and continues to be, a major factor in the remarkable success of the General Motors Corporation. . . . The Bonus Plan creates different kinds of incentives at different levels in the corporation. It creates a tremendous incentive among employees not yet eligible for bonus awards to become eligible. . . . Since bonuses are awarded annually, the incentive continues as long as the man stays with the corporation. The stimulus . . . becomes increasingly effective as a man advances in the organization, for the bonus is generally larger . . . at high-salary brackets than it is at low brackets.
>
> The incentives and rewards are not solely financial. . . . The potential rewards of the Bonus Plan to ego satisfaction generate a tremendous driving force within the corporation. . . . To the recipient it is also an evaluation of his personal contribution to the success of the business. . . . It makes each participant acutely aware of his relation to his job and his superiors; . . . . The Bonus Plan also provides much more flexibility . . . than is possible under a salary system. . . . The bonus makes it possible to tailor the reward to the period in which performance was unusual. And so the Bonus Plan makes it possible for the exceptional individual to break out of the over-all salary schedule without at the same time upsetting the schedule.
>
> The Bonus Plan, moreover, tends to keep executives with the corporation. . . . To abolish or seriously modify the Bonus Plan after forty-five years of successful operation might very well destroy the spirit and organization of the corporation's management.[25]

The amount of bonus award may be geared to a percent of the executive's salary or to some formula based on profits, sales, or other criteria. In some cases a bonus may merely be an arbitrary amount awarded because the company had a profitable year, or because of some outstanding performance by an individual. Usually a bonus committee is formed to make recommendations to the board of directors on the bonus plan to be used and on how it is to be administered. The board makes the decisions on all bonus matters. Bonuses, like wage incentives

---

[25]Alfred P. Sloan, Jr., *My Years with General Motors* (New York: Doubleday & Company, 1964), pp. 425–428. Reprinted by permission of Harold Matson Company, Inc.

for production operators, can be of the group or individual type. The individual type predominates. It would appear that this type allows flexibility to the company and is more equitable to the individual.

For a bonus to be an effective motivator, standards of performance must first be established, and the amount of the bonus award must be considered by the executive to be a sufficient reward for his performance. In the past, many bonus plans were similar to profit-sharing arrangements in which each executive received a more or less fixed percentage of the bonus pool. The present trend, in order to make bonus awards truly incentives, is to determine each executive's impact on profits and reward him accordingly. Table 25.7 shows what bonuses executives could expect at different salary levels based on 1967 performance. It should be noted that there are different bonus amounts that are associated with staff positions, line positions, and entrepreneurial positions. Bonuses that are related to the profitability of the firm will thus vary each year according to the firm's profitability. The size of bonuses is becoming increasingly linked to and dependent upon the firm's profitability. Some profit formula that is approved by the firm's stockholders sets the limit on what percentage of profits can be paid in bonuses. Table 25.8 shows the average bonus as a percent of base pay for middle managers holding various kinds of jobs. It also indicates that only one third of the middle managers gets a bonus.

TABLE 25.7

VARIOUS EXECUTIVE BONUSES EXPECTED AT DIFFERENT ANNUAL SALARY LEVELS FOR 1967 PERFORMANCE

ANNUAL EXECUTIVE SALARY LEVEL	EXPECTED BONUSES FOR VARIOUS EXECUTIVE POSITIONS		
	STAFF AND SUPPORT — PERSONNEL ADMINISTRATIVE FINANCIAL	TYPICAL LINE — DIVISION MGRS. SALES EXECUTIVES MANUFACTURING	ENTREPRENEURIAL
$200,000	$75,000	$125,000	$175,000
150,000	50,000	75,000	100,000
100,000	25,000	40,000	60,000
75,000	14,000	26,000	32,000
50,000	10,000	15,000	20,000
40,000	6,000	10,000	13,000
30,000	4,000	6,000	8,000
25,000	3,000	4,000	5,000
20,000	1,000	2,000	3,000
15,000	0	1,000	2,000

Source: Business Management (January, 1968), p. 40.

TABLE 25.8

**AVERAGE BONUS AS A PERCENT OF BASE PAY
FOR MIDDLE MANAGERS**

ONE OUT OF THREE MIDDLE MANAGERS GETS A BONUS

AVERAGE BONUS AS PERCENT OF BASE PAY	PERCENT OF MANAGERS SURVEYED				
	MARKETING	MANUFAC-TURING	FINANCE, LEGAL	RESEARCH AND ENGINEERING	INDUSTRIAL AND PUBLIC RELATIONS
Less than 5%	4.4%	4.6%	1.6%	2.9%	3.4%
5–10%	10.0	10.3	6.0	9.2	8.0
11–15%	10.5	6.2	4.3	4.8	3.1
16–25%	8.1	7.6	4.9	6.3	3.9
26–35%	3.4	3.7	1.9	2.2	1.5
36–50%	1.9	2.3	1.1	2.4	.7
Over 50%	1.9	1.1	.9	.8	.4
% not shown	6.4	4.6	4.8	5.3	2.9
Total managers receiving bonus	46.6%	40.4%	25.5%	33.9%	23.9%

Source: American Management Association.

Torrence believes that a bonus should provide an opportunity to earn a minimum of 25 percent of base earnings and that this figure is sound because it has been developed over long periods of experience and observation.[26]

Sibson suggests five tests that a sound incentive compensation plan for executives should be able to meet:

> First, it should restrict eligibility to those who, by the nature of their responsibilities, genuinely make decisions and judgments that affect the profit results of the business.
> Second, the plan should contain some reasonable eligibility guides — reasonable in the sense that they first help management make decisions as to who should be eligible. They should also help clarify participation or nonparticipation in the plan to key persons.
> Third, the plan should include a bonus fund formula that is geared to the financial goals of the business.
> Fourth, there should be a method of determining individual payments that is geared to your normal management practices. The size of these payments should be related to what each manager accomplished in that year, or contributed in that year, to the results of the business.
> Fifth, the program should provide, wherever possible, reasonable alternatives for managers. For example, an executive might be given a choice

---

[26]Torrence, *loc. cit.*

between cash or stock, or current or deferred income. The incentive value of the bonus increases when a man has the opportunity to slice the cake his own way.[27]

Deferred Compensation. *Deferred compensation* refers to a portion of an executive's salary which is paid at some date later than his regular monthly paycheck. Usually deferred compensation is paid at retirement or thereafter. Deferred compensation may be in the form of cash or stock, given in a lump sum or in a series of payments over a period of years. Deferred compensation serves to reduce the high income tax bite on the earnings of senior executives and at the same time provides them with some financial security during their retirement. Junior executives generally are not as enthusiastic about deferring their compensation at their younger age because they want all the cash they can get at a time when they need it the most, that is, when their family expenses are greatest during the middle of their working careers. Then, too, junior executives are not so sure that they will still be employed by the same company when they reach retirement age.

Deferred compensation appears to be especially useful in small companies which find it more difficult to attract and hold competent executives. Smaller companies cannot pay the higher salaries that large companies can, but they can partly make up this differential by means of deferred payments which are not due for a period of years. This gives the smaller company a chance to better utilize its funds during its growing stages. It should not be implied, however, that deferred compensation is only for small companies. In fact, more large companies have such plans. In the large company such a plan provides an additional means of making executive compensation more flexible. In both large and small companies, protection for the company can be built into the deferred compensation plan to make sure that the retired executive does not give away trade secrets or start a competing organization.

Deferred compensation plans vary from company to company but not as much as bonuses or stock options. The plan which pays a fixed sum for a period of time, as noted in Chapter 23, is known as a pension. The amounts of such pensions may be determined during the initial employment and included in an employment contract. However, the sum varies according to the salary of the executive, length of service, age at retirement, and contributory provisions. In a study of some forty well-known companies in different businesses and industries, the NICB reported:

> On the average, an executive with thirty years' service at retirement would receive a pension that is 44% to 48% of his average salary over the period. If the pension is based on his salary during the five or ten years just prior to retirement, his annual check will represent about 30% to 35%

---

[27]R. E. Sibson, "A Top Manager's Guide to Compensation Planning," *Business Management* (January, 1967), p. 25. (Permission received.)

of his average salary in these last years of his career. About two-thirds of the companies require the executive to contribute to some or all of the plans that provide his retirement income. His contributions are 3.5% to 4% of his pay, on the average.[28]

Company deferred compensation in the form of pensions is, of course, usually over and above any benefits the executive gets under social security, or in the case of the railroads, the Railroad Retirement Act. Generally, deferred compensation plans provide for payment after retirement. However, payments are made earlier in the event of disability or death. In the case of death, the executive's widow or heirs receive the payments.

A few deferred compensation plans are part of employment contracts offered key executives to engage their services as company consultants for a period of years after retirement. This is sometimes a device for retaining the more competent executives after retirement. In any event, this type of plan does provide a way of giving additional compensation to key executives at a time when they will be in a much lower tax bracket. It also can serve to fill the manpower gap in time of a tight or short labor market.

Expense Accounts. *Expense accounts* refer to monies allowed an executive to perform his job properly. Though this normally may not seem a part of executive compensation, Smith and Weiss have observed that an expense account is one of the most widely used supplements to an executive's income.[29]

From a strict point of view, it would appear that expense accounts, if used prudently, would involve only a reimbursement for the necessary expenses incurred for proper job performance and therefore would not be considered supplementary income. Difficulty arises as to what expenses are necessary for job performance. This is not an easily answered question. Tradition and good judgment count heavily in deciding job requirements.

It would appear that a liberal expense account would give the executive some relief from high taxes. Some executives are allowed wide latitude in expenses for travel, housing, recreation, education, and entertainment. Under such conditions and when an executive's expense account includes the cost of club memberships, company cars and planes, social functions, and the like, it could be considered as supplementary income, especially when it saves the executive money he would normally spend anyway. Recent income tax rulings have made it more difficult to "make money" on expense accounts without paying a tax on such income. This area of supplementary income will probably remain controversial until such time as essential job expenses have been determined and have the approval of the Internal Revenue Service.

---

[28]Harland Fox, "Executive Retirement Programs," *Management Record*, Vol. XX, No. 9 (National Industrial Conference Board, September, 1958), p. 294.
[29]L. J. Smith and C. H. Weiss, "Executive Compensation Programs," *Personnel Journal*, Vol. XXXVII, No. 4 (September, 1958), p. 128.

In short, expense accounts may be instrumental in attracting and holding competent executives because of their prestige value, but such accounts are difficult to evaluate monetarily. It is even more difficult to determine the relationship or place of expense accounts in the overall compensation formula.

Stock Options. A *stock option* is a plan under which a company grants an employee permission to buy a certain number of shares of company stock at a set discount price which is usually below the market price. In most cases the stock option is restricted to top executives whose salaries are large enough to benefit by such options. It has been said that stock options have been the biggest boon to company officials in recent years, and may account for more than a third of a chief executive's total pay.[30] Some companies extend the option to members of middle management and first-line employees. The stock option privilege practically assures the executive of additional compensation since he can defer buying any or all the shares to which he is entitled for a number of years. Thus, he has ample time to observe the stock values and to buy and sell at an opportune time for profitable returns. Should the stock increase in value before he finally decides to make the actual purchase, he pays no more than the original price set when the option was granted him. If the stock should drop below the cost price offered to him, the executive simply declines to exercise the option. In some plans the option price is then either reduced or the old option cancelled and a new one substituted.

Stock options have become very popular since 1950 when Congress changed the tax laws. The high tax rate on profits made from the sale of stocks was greatly reduced. The stock options thus help to compensate for the loss of salary due to the high taxes on salaries at the executive level. They tend to restore the unlimited compensation ceilings which were open to executives before the progressive taxation rates on large incomes came into being. However, recent federal statutes have placed considerable restrictions on the terms of plans so that in general these are two basic types of plans now being offered: (1) a qualified plan, and (2) a nonqualified plan.

The *qualified plan* is one that grants options only to key employees and qualifies for capital gains tax advantage. Such a plan must be approved by the firm's stockholders within one year before or after the plan is established. There is a maximum ten-year life span for the plan and an option has a five-year life span from the date it is granted. After an option has been exercised, the stock must be held for three years to receive the capital gains tax advantage. In general, a stock option may not be granted for less than the market price nor may the options be taken out of sequence; that is, prior options must be exercised before later options. Then, too, there is a 5 percent limit on the stock the employee can own. This means that a stock option cannot be granted when, after exercise, together

---

[30]"Are Executives Paid Enough?" *U.S. News & World Report* (January 29, 1968), p. 65.

with prior shares, the optionee would own stock possessing more than 5 percent of the total combined voting power or value of all types of stock. Finally, options are not transferable except in the event of death and then only by will or the laws of descent.

In the *nonqualified plan* the individual does not qualify for the capital gains tax advantage. This means the executive must not only pay income taxes on any income he obtains as a result of the option, but also he has to be concerned about the timeliness of his decisions in exercising his options as well as keeping adequate records on his transactions. There is a tax advantage for the firm on the nonqualified plan. Stock option plans are used more often in manufacturing and retailing than in any other type of business.[31] Patton believes that stock options remain the most popular supplementary compensation device after pension plans.[32]

Stock option plans and policies vary a great deal in the different companies. Some plans offer the stock purchase as a form of bonus or profit sharing. Some base the number of shares of stock an executive may purchase on the size of his base salary. Others agree on the number of shares as part of the employment agreement or executive contract. Still others base the size of the stock purchase on the executive's performance. In some close corporations, the executive may be allowed to hold the stock only as long as he is with the corporation. Should he leave, he is required to sell the stock to the company.

Other close corporations offer a certain amount of their stock as profit shares to supervisors and executives in lieu of cash. Under "profit sharing," however, the supervisors and executives enter into a contractual agreement not to accept employment with a competitor within a stipulated period after severing connections with the company. During this interval, dividends are paid regularly, but the stock is held in escrow until the agreement expires, at which time the stock is turned over to the executive. Should the supervisor or executive accept a position with a competitor before the expiration date, however, he forfeits the stock and the dividends terminate.

Occasionally an executive is given some or all the financial benefits of stock ownership without actually receiving the stock from the company. Such a plan calls for a written transaction or record of the shares or stock units applied to his account. In this phantom stock plan, the executive receives cash dividends as actual stock shareholders do.[33] Stock option decisions, like the determination of bonuses, may be made by the board of directors upon the recommendations of a stock option committee.

Stock options generally have been assumed to benefit the company as well as the employee, although this has not been definitely established. A report of the

---

[31]*Focus*, Vol. II, No. 1 (January, 1965), p. 2.
[32]Patton, *op. cit.*, p. 97.
[33]Torrence, *op. cit.*, p. 55.

Securities and Exchange Commission has cast some doubt on this basic assumption. For example, a public utility company applied to the Securities and Exchange Commission (SEC) for approval of a stock option plan. The SEC report, as published by *U. S. News & World Report,* said in part:

> The record, says the SEC report, fails to show that utilities that grant stock options "have fared significantly better than the utility industry as a whole or the electric holding companies — which have not issued stock options. The contrary, in fact, appears to be true" . . . . the "compensation" given the employee by way of stock options does not necessarily produce anything of value to the stockholders.[34]

Holland and Lewellen of MIT, in a study of stock options, concluded that to give stock options to employees making less than $103,500 gross salary would cost the company more than an increase in salary (to provide the same take-home reward that might result from the stock option).[35] If salary is tax deductible within the 52 percent corporate income tax rate, a company could give $2.08 of salary increase for each $1 of gain realized from a stock option.

If managements hope to more closely relate pay to performance, they might wish to consider the elimination of stock options and other deferred payment plans that do not pay off soon enough to show how pay relates to performance. Furthermore, such plans may actually destroy the belief that pay is related to performance when the size of the reward is independent of or not in relation to the performance attained by the executive.

Some objectors to stock options claim that many corporation executives, aided by favorable tax laws, had made fortunes overnight at virtually no risk. The objectors are against stock options because of stock manipulations and the special privileges being granted to only a few who place their own interests above the interests of stockholders, customers, and the public.[36]

More time and some research will be needed to determine accurately the real advantages and limitations regarding stock options. At present, it would appear that the advantages and disadvantages of stock options as claimed by their advocates and critics are as follows:

Stock Option Advantages:

1. Stock options offer executives an opportunity to increase their incomes within a short time at virtually no risk.

2. As supplemental compensation, stock options can be instrumental in eliminating executive turnover.

---

[34]"The Stock Option Comes Under Fire," *U.S. News & World Report* (July 11, 1960), pp. 105–107.
[35]*The Milwaukee Journal* (April 22, 1962), Part IV, p. 21.
[36]*Ibid.* (August 9, 1959), Part I.

3. Stock options serve as a new and additional strong incentive for the executive who is motivated to raise the value of the company stock by virtue of being a part owner of the business.
4. The company has greater working capital because it does not have to spend actual cash when the necessity to increase salaries arises.
5. Stock options are one of the few forms of compensation that gear an executive's long-term income to the long-term results of the company.[37]

Stock Option Disadvantages:

1. Under some plans the executive may not be in a financial position to take full advantage of all the stock that he is eligible to purchase.
2. In a bear market, when stock prices are falling, or when the company is having financial difficulties, an option may be ineffective.
3. The executive has no assurance that his increased efforts will directly or consistently influence the value of the stock proportionately. Under certain conditions, hard work may have little effect on stock values.
4. If the options appear unreasonable, or if they are granted only to a privileged few, hard feelings and opposition may be incurred.

Some research conclusions on management compensation

Recent research on the psychological aspects of compensation practices has led Lawler to conclude:

> Even at the higher paid levels of management, pay is important enough to be a significant motivator of good job performance. However, it will be a motivator only when it is seen by the managers themselves to be tied to their performance.
>
> Managers can be, and in fact frequently are, satisfied with their pay when it compares favorably with the pay of other managers holding similar positions.
>
> Secrecy policies have significant hidden costs attached to them. The evidence indicates that secrecy may lead to lower satisfaction with pay and to a decreased motivation for promotion.
>
> In order to get the maximum value for money spent on compensation, organizations may have to institute "cafeteria" wage payment systems. Such a system would allow each manager to select the benefits that have the greatest value to him.[38]

The General Radio Company of West Concord, Massachusetts, has created a fluctuating monthly paycheck that may prove to be suitable for managers, professionals, and technicians. The paycheck is tied to performance and has four chief features: (1) a fluctuating monthly salary tied to orders and shipments;

---

[37]Sibson, *loc. cit.*

[38]Edward E. Lawler, III, "The Mythology of Management Compensation," *California Management Review*, Vol. IX, No. 1 (Fall, 1966). Copyright 1966 by the Regents of the University of California.

(2) a semiannual cash bonus pegged to a performance appraisal every six months; (3) tax-free stock offered as a bonus each year (based on employee contribution to the firm's success); and (4) deferred profit sharing for emergencies and retirement income.[39]   An interesting part of this plan is that managers have a choice as to whether they wish to accept it or not. No manager is forced into the plan. If a manager does not wish to take the risks, he can accept a fixed monthly salary based on the going community and industry rates. It will be interesting to follow the progress of this plan to determine its usefulness as a guide to be used by other companies.

Summary of recommendations for compensating executives

In conclusion, it may be well to offer some general recommendations that can greatly influence the effects of the total compensation program. If such a program is to be effective, fair, and acceptable, top management should take the following recommendations into consideration:

1. Select a competent and highly respected executive to be responsible for all executive compensation matters. This executive should be the chairman of a compensation committee composed of three to five other high-level executives. The committee should have an understanding of the principles of compensation. They should be responsible for seeing that a systematic and integrated plan of compensation is developed which will not only attract, but also hold, motivate, and reward executives in an equitable manner. The committee can serve as a board to handle compensation matters such as salary increases, complaints, supplemental income beyond base salary, and the like. The committee may be given the authority to make "final decisions" or to make only recommendations to the company president or the board of directors. Unless some one person or group of persons is directly responsible for coordinating all the facets of this dynamic and ever-changing activity, executive compensation will never amount to anything more than an admixture of unrelated acts. Such a situation rarely inspires executives to perform their best or to work together as a team.

2. Communicate the plan of executive compensation to the personnel concerned. Secrecy can create suspicion, dissatisfaction, and mediocre performance. Executives must have some assurance that the company is fair and the salary equitable if they are to wholeheartedly accept the compensation plan and to perform to their capacities. Will anyone be enthusiastic about accepting something as important as salary without an understanding of it? We think not! It should not be implied, however, that executives have to know the specific amounts of compensation received by other executives, but each executive is entitled to know at

---

[39]"A Fluctuating Paycheck for Managers," *The Conference Board Record* (National Industrial Conference Board, April, 1968).

least where he personally fits in the total compensation structure and what his salary potential is for his present position. The majority of executives that the authors have interviewed do not even know what the minimum or possible maximum is for their positions — much less where their present salaries fit. And furthermore, they are afraid to ask their superiors about their own status. They express disappointment and indicate that they probably would not get an answer if they did inquire. This is not a healthy or happy situation, nor is it good for morale and productivity.

3. Conduct periodic performance reviews. Every sound wage and salary program must have some method of appraising the progress of its employees. Since at the executive level, the man makes the job, executive evaluation is especially important. Common practice is to conduct these at yearly intervals. These confidential interviews and reviews of performance help to answer the questions of how am I doing? What are my strengths and weaknesses? What can I do to improve performance? Needless to say, an executive without periodic appraisals and guidance is like a ship without a rudder.

4. Provide for adequate administration and maintenance of the compensation plan. Not even the most carefully worked out plan of compensation will run itself. Some people believe that executive compensation is so dynamic that as soon as compensation decisions are made, it is already time to reconsider the problem. Adequate administration includes the day-to-day operation and keeping up-to-date on personnel, wages, techniques, progress, and the like. Once a plan of compensation has removed wage inequities, maintenance keeps it that way. Maintenance procedures call for a time table of periodic review of all activities — position descriptions, employee evaluations, control techniques, pay trends, company financial position, the labor market, executive turnover, and general business conditions.

Up to this point all the activities needed to set up both managerial and non-managerial wage and salary programs have been examined. Ways and means of maintaining a sound wage and salary program will be discussed next.

REVIEW QUESTIONS

1. What factors would you consider in determining what a fair salary is for the president of a company?
2. Should the salaries of top executives be kept confidential? Why?
3. (a) In your opinion, would executives object to a job evaluation of their own positions? Why? (b) What method of job evaluation should you use for executives?
4. Is there a justification for having a formal executive compensation plan for executives when they only constitute a percent or two of all employees? Why?
5. Who should handle the criticisms and problems involved in compensating executives? Why?

6. Which approach (top down, bottom up, or budget) to the pricing of the president's salary do you recommend? Why?

7. Is it realistic to base executive salary raises on the Bureau of Labor Statistics "cost of living" index? Why?

8. What are the elements of a yardstick by which executive compensation can be measured?

9. Can an executive incentive bonus plan be set up in a company in which the work is never routine? If not, why? If yes, how?

10. What are the advantages of supplementing an executive's salary with a bonus plan?

11. Should the same principles of job evaluation used for nonmanagerial employees be used to evaluate managerial positions? Why?

12. How can an incentive system be used to improve an executive's effectiveness?

13. Is the stock option a good incentive for the executive who is not well versed on either the income tax laws or on stock market conditions? Why?

14. Should a salary program for executives be geared to base salary or to total compensation?

15. How would the factors used in evaluating management positions differ from those used in evaluating clerical positions?

RESEARCH OR SEMINAR QUESTIONS

1. What compensation problems will probably have to be faced if the $15,000 man today will be making $70,000 by the year 2000?

2. Some persons believe that in the future money will diminish as a motivator of executives. Research this idea and be prepared to state why your findings agree or disagree with it. If you agree, what kinds of compensation will be substituted for money as it loses its motivational force?

3. Be prepared to defend why you do or do not believe that employees should share in the profits of a company when they have no financial interest in that company.

4. What qualifications should the individual have who is in charge of executive compensation?

5. (a) What criticism have you heard of the manner in which executives are compensated? (b) Do you feel this is justified? Why?

PRACTICAL EXPERIENCE ASSIGNMENTS

1. The president of a small, very profitable, and closely held corporation bears sole responsibility for determining wages and salaries of all personnel. His efforts are the dominant reason for the success of the company, and without him it would probably be forced to liquidate. He is not responsible to anyone for his wage and salary decisions. (a) What criteria or plan should the president use in determining his own salary? (b) What considerations, if any, should be given by the president to the compensation of other personnel and to the shareholder return?

2. Your company's traveling salesmen and executives on business trips have, judging from the expense reports filed, been living "pretty high on the hog." When questioned about the $15 steaks and $30 hotel rooms, several of the men state that the representative of a high-prestige company must live suitably, and that they regard the gracious living as a form of tax-free compensation rewarding them for the inconvenience of travel. Who should have the responsibility for investigating this matter? If the story is found to be true, what should be done?

3. Some executives have been known to be justly unhappy about their positions when their bosses fail to reward them, in the form of salary raises, for continued progress in their work. These "underpaid" men do not feel that they should have to "pressure" their bosses into salary raises by bringing to them offers received from other companies. What appears to be the problem here? What do you recommend to correct the situation? How could this type of problem be prevented from happening? If you were one of these "unhappy and underpaid" executives, what would be your approach to solving your unhappiness? Why?

CASE PROBLEM

25 — 1. ECONOMY UNIVERSITY

Preventing a Salary Inequity

Assistant Professors Bucks and Loyal were both employed by Economy University at the same time and for the same department. Professor Loyal received $200 per year more salary than his colleague Mr. Bucks.

At the end of his first year of teaching at Economy University, Professor Bucks found that teaching opportunities throughout the country were good so he decided to leave E. U. because of a more lucrative opportunity elsewhere. Mr. Loyal stayed at the university and after another year he was promoted to director of the department.

Four years after leaving E. U., Professor Bucks wanted to return. If he did so, he would be under the direction of Mr. Loyal, his former colleague, who was still head of the department. Professor Bucks was presently earning $800 per year more than Mr. Loyal. He was very desirous of returning to E. U. He expected to be offered at least the salary he was presently making and was hoping he would be offered more.

Although Economy University had several candidates for a teaching opening, the dean wanted to rehire Mr. Bucks at a salary that was $800 more than Mr. Loyal. Professor Loyal was unwilling to rehire Mr. Bucks unless the University paid him more than it offered to Mr. Bucks.

Problems:

1. What kind of salary policy can you recommend that would handle this situation equitably?

2. What salary problem might arise if Mr. Bucks were rehired at a higher salary than his boss?

chapter **26**

MAINTAINING A COMPENSATION PROGRAM

The closing chapter of this textbook is devoted to a discussion of the activities required to effectively support a previously established sound wage and salary program. It is assumed that time, effort, and expense have not been previously spared to plan, organize, and install a compensation program that is equitable, valid, and efficient. The only basic phase of good management that remains for discussion is control. Compensation programs, no matter how well designed, cannot run themselves; like new automobiles, they need proper upkeep if they are to continue to serve their purposes well.

What is involved in maintaining a compensation program?

A compensation program is never static but is a constantly changing activity which requires repeated adjustments. Duties and responsibilities of jobs frequently change. Sometimes new methods of performing work are evolved. New jobs may be added while old ones disappear. New employees may be hired and regular employees may be promoted, transferred, laid off, or pensioned. All of these changes affect compensation and must therefore be integrated into the total wage structure. Maintaining a compensation program not only includes the management of the new activities and changes that occur but also includes the supervision of established procedures to prevent them from becoming ineffective. In short, maintaining a compensation program involves the constant adjusting and controlling of programs so that they will continue to be efficient in serving their purposes. Periodic evaluations of programs to determine whether objectives are being met can indicate how efficient the programs are. Where actual results do not conform to desired goals, adjustments and controls are the corrective actions required.

To assist the reader in understanding how the maintenance of a sound compensation program can be accomplished, this chapter will elaborate on the following topics:

1. The goal of maintenance.
2. The importance of maintenance.
3. Major maintenance and control centers.
4. Fundamental guideposts for maintaining a compensation plan.
5. Techniques and methods that implement control.
6. Union-management relations in wage and salary administration.

The goal of maintenance

The primary goal of wage and salary maintenance is to support a compensation structure that top management can afford and to assure all employees of continual equitable compensation. Unless the compensation program is kept up-to-date and administered in an efficient manner that is prompt, consistent, and fair, there will be grumbling and dissatisfaction by the employees because today employees are more informed than in the past and can more easily detect any wage inequities.

Almost any activity can be controlled through a rigid set of rules. However, in as rapidly a changing activity as compensation, rules have to be flexible to allow for change. What is an acceptable standard today might not be acceptable tomorrow. Thus, control procedures have to be adaptable to progress without appearing inconsistent. On the other hand, if the procedures are inflexible, exceptions become commonplace; the rules then need tightening because control has been lost. Effective maintenance of the compensation program necessitates scheduled evaluations to keep in tempo with the times. Keeping up-to-date is a continuous process. Periodic evaluations may be looked upon as a form of preventive maintenance in which potential problems are avoided.

Importance of maintenance

Maintaining a sound compensation program is important to both non-managerial and managerial employees. To nonmanagerial employees, maintenance of a sound compensation plan assures them that compensation will continue to be equitable. Proper maintenance serves as an incentive for employees to perform to capacity because they are confident that the company will reward them according to their merits. It is important to the employees also since it demonstrates by actions that management is sincerely interested in treating employees fairly. This tends to promote company loyalty since, as a result, employees will trust and respect management. Thus, greater job satisfaction and higher morale develop.

To managerial personnel, the proper maintenance of a sound compensation plan assists management in attracting competent employees and in offering them job security. It should promote greater harmony and friendliness between management and employees. Grievances become fewer in number. Job turnover is reduced. Employee attitudes toward the company are more favorable. Thus, greater efficiency and productivity result. In addition, proper maintenance protects the investment that the company has made to install and develop a sound method of compensation. Poor maintenance is one of the consequences of mismanagement. With poor maintenance, the total payroll costs might rise higher than could be afforded. The company may be unable to compete in the field and might eventually go bankrupt. The best compensation plan available is hardly worth the effort and expense unless management intends to maintain it.

In summary, the proper maintenance of the compensation program helps the firm economically to attract, retain, motivate, and reward its employees. This accomplishment in turn helps satisfy some of the employee's basic needs, such as opportunity, recognition, and job security.

Major maintenance and control centers

Adequate administration of a sound wage and salary program is an important phase of the program. Complaints are sometimes erroneously made about compensation techniques such as job evaluation and employee evaluation when in reality the failure is due to poor administration rather than to the techniques. On the surface, administration appears to be involved because the maintenance activities have not been coordinated. For this reason, the majority of small and medium-size companies rarely have a complete set of controls.

The whole subject of maintenance, control, and general administration of compensation is so interwoven with general management, personnel administration, industrial engineering, and the other phases of a business that it is practically impossible to isolate matters that pertain strictly to compensation. Thus, the discussion which follows will emphasize (1) the major areas where wage and salary activities predominate, and (2) the related control points for these activities. Exact standards for each control center should be decided according to each company's experiences. For this reason, the standards may vary a great deal. Much research is needed in all areas to formulate standards and to improve the techniques of control. The major compensation centers that lend themselves to maintenance and control are as follows: (1) job analysis, (2) job evaluation, (3) job pricing, (4) employee evaluation, (5) incentives, (6) supplementary compensation, and (7) payroll costs.

Job Analysis Maintenance

Since the study of jobs and positions serves as a basis for such activities as personnel selection, hiring, training, compensation, and the like, the effectiveness of these personnel activities will be governed by the accuracy and recency of the job analysis data. Every enterprise has a surprising number of changes continually occurring. Some changes develop rapidly while others are so gradual that they are hardly noticeable. New jobs are created and old jobs disappear as the result of technology and progress. Even job titles change throughout the years. For these reasons, every member of management should be responsible for notifying the director of wage and salary administration when any changes take place or are contemplated. In addition, all jobs should be audited and their titles, descriptions, and specifications reviewed and amended, if necessary, at least every two years whether or not such reviews and amendments have been requested. In large companies there are so many job and position descriptions that the reviewing must be done on a continuing basis each day or each week. In this way, at the end of a certain period, all descriptions will have been reviewed and many will have been improved. Employees should be encouraged to appeal to their supervisors or to the wage and salary administrator whenever they believe their present job data are incorrect. If competent employees are to be selected, trained, compensated, and retained, job analysis activities must be kept up-to-date. The consequences of failing to maintain these activities are misplacements, waste and inefficiencies, lower morale, more grievances, job dissatisfaction, and higher costs through eventual labor turnover.

Job Evaluation Maintenance

One of the most common causes of the failure of job evaluation programs is faulty maintenance. As previously mentioned, jobs have a tendency to change with the passage of time. Small changes may appear insignificant, but over a period of time such changes have a cumulative effect. For this reason, job specification sheets, job descriptions, and job evaluation manuals should be reviewed at least once every two years to determine whether they are up-to-date or in need of improvement. If proper maintenance, as suggested under job analysis control, is conducted, new job descriptions will be prepared when the job changes and the jobs are reevaluated. Thus, job evaluation maintenance is crosschecked by the job analysis control area.

Once the correct evaluation of a job has been determined and accepted by all parties concerned, the evaluation should remain unchanged as long as the job remains unchanged. After the union has accepted the job evaluation, it should not be subject to collective bargaining unless there is a change in job conditions. If, through error, the job has been incorrectly evaluated, the evaluation should be corrected as soon as the error is discovered.

Sometimes the modernization of a plant or job improvements will change the working conditions. When this happens and jobs are reevaluated, they are usually found to have lower point ratings because working conditions are either less hazardous or more pleasant. Considering the seniority factor, management will usually allow present employees to retain their current rates of pay. But new employees should start on a particular job at the corrected lower rate of pay since the value of the job has been reduced.

Job Pricing Maintenance

It will be recalled that placing a price tag on each job is dependent mainly upon whether the policy of top management reflects that of a low-, high-, or medium-paying firm. Sometimes management's philosophy may be altered because of labor market conditions or other business reasons. The wage and salary administrator and all personnel who help administer compensation must be fully aware at all times of top management's policy. Proper maintenance calls for adequate wage surveys to obtain the going wage rates and trends. Every company should participate in at least one compensation survey each year and be in constant contact with employer associations, governmental agencies, chambers of commerce, research organizations, and other concerns who have wage data available.

In a tight labor market, top management has to be especially careful that it is not pressured into raising the starting wage of a job to the same level that is being earned by present employees. The regular employees will look upon such a condition as a wage inequity unless the qualifications and experiences of new employees are equal to those of present employees. Some companies who have overlooked this precaution have later found that the inequity has resulted in higher labor turnover and a loss of many reliable employees who have accepted jobs with other enterprises. When an enterprise employs untested personnel and compensates them at the same wage as the company's loyal and experienced employees, the compensation program is no longer equitable. Proper maintenance has failed when such wage inequities are allowed to develop.

If an enterprise is faced with the dilemma of having market pressure create wage inequities, the company should find ways and means to avoid that market influence.[1] It is recommended that one of the following solutions be utilized:

1. Add responsibilities to the job so that the employee is not overpaid.
2. Upgrade enough present employees into the jobs where market pressure exists and hire their replacements from noncritical market areas.
3. Ignore temporary market price and concentrate on convincing the prospective employee of the other compensating benefits offered by the com-

---

[1] Preston P. Breton, "Must Market Pressure Wreck the Company's Salary Structure?" *Personnel*, Vol. XXXVI, No. 4 (July–August, 1959), p. 35.

pany. Also emphasize the importance of maintaining internal wage consistency to protect the individual employee.
4. Employ new workers at the market price and limit their wage increases until the inequities of the other employees have been corrected.
5. Have the work performed by other manufacturers until the market pressure has receded.

Employee Evaluation Maintenance

Employee evaluation is an area where wage inequities are easily created. Persuasive employees may obtain merit increases on some basis other than performance. When this occurs, the wage structure becomes inequitable and corrections are not easily accomplished. Eliminating such wage inequities may take as much time as the elimination of red-circle rates. Employee evaluations should be periodically conducted at six- or twelve-month intervals and raises granted only to those employees who have merited them. The lower half of Figure 26.1 shows a daily performance record that would be useful in substantiating evaluations. Employees with less than two years of service with the company are more likely to be evaluated at the six-month intervals while employees with two years' seniority and more are usually evaluated at longer intervals of one year.

Most companies control individual raises by requiring a minimum amount of time to be spent in a job grade. If an employee has to undergo a waiting period of six to twelve months between raises, then the company is justified in granting the raise because performance is of a permanent nature. Employees normally have the opportunity to receive pay increases and to advance to the middle of the rate range within a certain period. Once the midpoint is reached, raises should be based more on superior performance, and the waiting period between raises may be lengthened. An employee who fails to qualify for the midrate of a job after a reasonable period of time should be transferred to a job for which he is better qualified.

Firms can also control raises by placing a limit on the amount of the raise. This limit might be a fixed amount per labor grade or a percentage limit, such as five, seven, or ten percent of the current salary. In devising controls for compensation, caution has to be exercised that the controls do not either discourage employee ambition or fail to reward outstanding performance adequately. When exceptional employees are discovered, exceptions to the usual control guides should be made. However, in exceptional cases the supervisor should be asked to justify the raise in writing and have it approved by his superior. Many times a salary review committee is asked to pass on all such recommendations for raises to assure that exceptions are not all coming from the same department and that there is a uniform processing of the recommendations in the company. Borderline cases should never be considered nor recommended for such raises.

Reprinted by permission, © 1954 by International Business Machines Corporation.

FIGURE 26.1   PERFORMANCE DATA AND CONTROL OF INCENTIVE RATES

Otherwise, a firm may later find that it is saddled with higher price employees who are not high producers.

Another instance where wages can become inequitable is when a competent employee is at the maximum wage bracket and the company wants to retain him but believes the employee will resign if a raise is not forthcoming. Normally the employee should be promoted to a higher classified job and his compensation increased accordingly. This gives the employee the opportunity to secure higher earnings while making a greater contribution. To grant him a raise beyond the rate range without an increase in performance can establish a precedent that may later become the rule and result in hard feelings among other workers and excessive costs for the work produced. As long as the wage spreads are adequate to motivate individuals, employees should not become restless for years. Some few companies do have a special rate beyond the maximum for employees with long service, such as fifteen years or more. To be granted a raise beyond the normal maximum requires outstanding performance and justification in writing by the supervisor. Continuance of compensation above the normal maximum should be dependent upon continuance of outstanding performance by the employee. The employee evaluation form, which is the record basis for remuneration increments, should be inspected periodically to determine whether it should be modified or whether it is in need of improvement.

Incentive Maintenance

As an area of control, incentive maintenance should be carefully observed since it is more costly to administer a piece-rate compensation plan than a straight time plan. In addition, there is a tendency for continual changes to occur because of technological innovations and progress. When job conditions are standardized, everything may appear to be proper. However, there is a tendency for changes to creep in without anyone noticing them. For example, an operator may find a short cut or fashion a new tool that will increase production. If administration is lax, the job rate becomes loose and other deviations are encouraged. Thus, methods, equipment, earnings, and conditions should be analyzed regularly to discover any irregularities that would cause wage inequities. The upper half of Figure 26.1 shows an analysis and comparison of actual performance earnings realized under specific incentive rates. Such data are useful for evaluating incentive wage rates and for establishing control policies.

In today's technological age, management cannot expect this year's standards to be next year's standards. If a company is to progress, standards will change as new and improved methods are devised, if management has engendered such a climate. Production operators should be encouraged to make suggestions on how to increase production and then be amply rewarded for those changes that save money or increase efficiency. If this climate is not present, operators will limit their production and full efficiency will never be obtained.

If, through excessive production resulting from loose standards, operators are allowed to earn exceptionally high wages, animosity between the inventive operator and his colleagues may develop. In addition, his supervisor may become dissatisfied when he learns that a subordinate is receiving greater compensation than he is.

With the level of education of the average employee constantly rising, management is not utilizing its employees to the best advantage unless the employees are encouraged to use their education to raise productivity. By offering employees ample opportunity for development, both the worker and the company can profit by suggested improvements. The foreman, the motion and time study engineer, along with the wage and salary administrator, should constantly seek to reward improvements as soon as they are proven sound and to readjust the incentive rates in line with the improvements. In a small company an incentive plan often creates ill will because an operator must use a different machine than that specified for the job standard. If one machine is not properly maintained or is more difficult to operate than another, a worker's production is not as high as he is capable of performing; the result is low earnings and justified irritation on his part. On the other hand, if the employee is operating a machine which for some reason is easier to operate than another, unusually high wages may result and the supervisor will probably cut the rate. In either case, the situation is not desirable. Management should therefore be alert and provide for regular inspections without appearing to be distrustful of employees, but rather be sincerely interested in assuring employees that all are receiving fair treatment. A study and analysis of past grievances can reveal the observations or inspections that are necessary and how often they should be required. Areas that can prove costly and hinder administration center around the procedures dealing with acceptable quality, discipline for low productivity, changes in standards, guaranteed average earnings, negotiation and verification of standards, and arbitration.[2] These troublesome areas should all have clearly specified clauses in the collective bargaining contract.

When incentive conditions are not properly maintained, dissatisfactions spread quickly; and if management fails to correct the situation in time, production may be restricted or limited. Every incentive plan, therefore, should be reviewed and evaluated periodically to adjust it to changing conditions and to maintain its effectiveness over the long run. One sure way that this can be accomplished is to have a termination date on every incentive plan established. The plan automatically expires at the termination date *unless both* the union and management agree to renew or modify it. This prevents *either* the union or management from taking any unfair advantage of each other if the plan has not worked out as originally intended.

---

[2]Irving A. Delloff, "Incentive Clauses: The Costly Clinkers," *Personnel*, Vol. XXXVI, No. 3 (May–June, 1959), p. 52.

Supplementary Compensations Maintenance

As emphasized in Chapter 23, one of the most significant compensation trends in the past fifteen years has been the growth of supplementary compensations. The majority of these compensations are primarily of the type in which remuneration is granted without requiring increased productivity. Failure to control supplementary compensations is tantamount to ignoring between one fourth and one third the total wages and salaries paid by industry. It is surprising how many companies are not fully cognizant of the importance of supplementary compensations and therefore have not integrated them into the total wage and salary structure.

The administration and control of supplementary compensations involves rendering adequate services and benefits and keeping the costs thereof in balance with the total payroll costs. Basic to both of these goals is the prerequisite of maintaining accurate records. Although most firms have the necessary records to indicate the services rendered, not all companies realize how much their supplementary compensations really cost.

The administration of supplementary compensations is primarily concerned with disseminating information about the kinds of benefits and services that are provided the employees. Many benefits are rendered employees when they are under the stress and strain of their daily work. Under such conditions, employees are not likely to be fully informed about the benefits. For this reason, the various personnel responsible for administering the benefits should take the initiative to make sure that each employee is well informed of his rights and privileges and to assist him in obtaining the benefits that are available. Periodic interviews and attitude surveys, plus searching investigations, can reveal administrative effectiveness and weakness.

To control employee services and benefits so that the costs thereof are kept in balance with other segments of compensation requires the accumulation of cost data per benefit and per employee. Large companies gather such data and are amply supplied with information to maintain such a balance. Most small companies and some medium-size companies apparently fail to compile records in order to determine costs and trends; therefore, these companies experience difficulties. In Chapter 23 it was shown that supplementary compensation costs may be expressed in total amounts per year per employee, or in amounts per hour per employee. As recorded on page 646, during the year 1967 industry spent an average of $1,719 per employee as supplementary compensation for such "fringe benefits" as pensions, vacations, and insurance protection. It was also noted that benefit costs are quoted as a percentage of total payroll costs. Precautionary measures have to be exercised, however, when making comparisons percentage-wise because incorrect interpretations can be misleading. For example, if two firms offer identical benefits, the company paying the lower basic wages will appear to offer the greater compensation to its employees because it offers the greater percentage of benefits; in reality, however, it offers less total compensation. For this reason, it is recommended that supplementary compensation controls be based on yearly amounts per employee, on hourly amounts per employee, or on costs per unit of output.

Supplementary compensations which grant remuneration based on increased productivity can be controlled more easily than the purely service or benefit type of payments because in the former situation the labor cost of the product can be ascertained more readily than in the latter. Supplementary compensations based on increased productivity may be controlled by periodic evaluations to determine whether objectives are being accomplished. The benefit type of payments, however, is inflexible and difficult to control. Once payments for benefits like hospitalization and insurance have been granted, the costs are not usually within the control of the company, but are based on experience tables. Over the years these costs have skyrocketed along with the cost of living. It is almost impossible for a company to control costs by either dropping the benefits or refusing to pay for additional rate increases. Therefore, the benefit payments become better controlled when the costs are on a contributory basis. If an employee has to increase his contribution because of rising costs, he is very conscious of keeping the benefit payments in check and does not take them for granted.

Frequently wage structures become unwieldy because supplementary compensation awards are not incorporated in the basic hourly rate but are treated as additions to the hourly rate. If top management expects to gain better control over supplemental benefits, such benefits must at all times be considered as an integral part of total compensation, and comparisons must be made on that basis. In this way comparisons can be made more accurately.

Overall Payroll Maintenance

The area of payroll maintenance really includes the total costs of all the other control areas previously mentioned and was for this reason purposely left to the last. If a firm is to remain financially sound and make arrangements for the future, it should utilize company forecasts to prepare company and departmental budgets. Expenses can be controlled through budgets and by the analysis and comparison of various operating expense factor ratios (see Figure 26.2). For example, a company may prefer to control compensation by comparing the cost ratios of sales to direct labor, or of indirect labor to direct labor (see top half of Figure 26.2), or of managerial to nonmanagerial, or of payroll to output. Sometimes records of overtime payments reveal excessive costs. Total payroll costs or unit costs can also be compared with the community, industry, or national costs to determine whether or not they are in keeping with top management's intentions.

DEPARTMENTAL EXPENSE RATIO REPORT

ACCOUNT BY DEPARTMENT

DEPT. NO.	ACCOUNT NUMBER	ACCOUNT NAME	CURRENT PERIOD		YEAR TO DATE	
			EXPENSE AMOUNT	% TO DIRECT LABOR	EXPENSE AMOUNT	% TO DIRECT LABOR
	1200	INDIRECT LABOR				
1	1201	SUPERVISION	150 00	5 2 2	1800 00	5 1 3
2	1201	SUPERVISION	200 00	5 3 9	2400 00	5 3 8
3	1201	SUPERVISION	175 00	4 4 7	1850 00	4 4 5
4	1201	SUPERVISIO				
5	1201	SUPERVISIO				
6	1201	SUPERVISIO				
7	1201	SUPERVISIO				
8	1201	SUPERVISIO				
9	1201	SUPERVISIO				
10	1201	SUPERVISIO				
1	1202	INSPECTION				
2	1202	INSPECTION				
3	1202	INSPECTION				
4	1202	INSPECTION				
5	1202	INSPECTION				

DEPARTMENTAL EXPENSE RATIO REPORT

DEPARTMENT BY ACCOUNT

DEPT. NO.	ACCOUNT NUMBER	ACCOUNT NAME	CURRENT PERIOD		YEAR TO DATE	
			EXPENSE AMOUNT	% TO DIRECT LABOR	EXPENSE AMOUNT	% TO DIRECT LABOR
1	1200	INDIRECT LABOR				
1	1201	SUPERVISION	150 00	5 2 2	1800 00	5 1 3
1	1202	INSPECTION	43 20	1 5 0	536 09	1 5 3
1	1203	TIMEKEEPING	62 83	2 1 8	756 10	2 1 5
1	1204	HAULING	65 24	2 2 7	792 35	2 2 6
1	1205	STOREKEEPING	47 71	1 6 6	576 82	1 6 4
						8 6
						1 6 1
						1 1 8
						1 6 3 6 ✲

DEPARTMENTAL EXPENSE BUDGET REPORT

ACCOUNT BY DEPARTMENT

DEPT. NO.	ACCOUNT NUMBER	ACCOUNT NAME	CURRENT PERIOD			YEAR TO DATE		
			EXPENSE AMOUNT	BUDGET AMOUNT	*OVER BUDGET	EXPENSE AMOUNT	BUDGET AMOUNT	*OVER BUDGET
	1200	INDIRECT LABOR						
1	1201	SUPERVISION	150 00	150 00		1800 00	1800 00	
2	1201	SUPERVISION	200 00	200 00		2400 00	2400 00	
3	1201	SUPERVISION	175 00	175 00		1850 00	1800 00	50 00 ✲
4	12							3 7
5	12							9 7
6	12							2 4
7	12							5 2
8	12							2 9
9	12							4 7
10	12							

DEPARTMENTAL EXPENSE BUDGET REPORT

DEPARTMENT BY ACCOUNT

DEPT. NO.	ACCOUNT NUMBER	ACCOUNT NAME	CURRENT PERIOD			YEAR TO DATE		
			EXPENSE AMOUNT	BUDGET AMOUNT	*OVER BUDGET	EXPENSE AMOUNT	BUDGET AMOUNT	*OVER BUDGET
1	1200	INDIRECT LABOR						
1	1201	SUPERVISION	150 00	150 00		1800 00	1800 00	
1	1202	INSPECTION	43 20	50 00	6 8 0	600 00	600 00	63 91
1	1203	TIMEKEEPING	62 83	65 00	2 1 7	756 10	780 00	23 90
1	1204	HAULING	65 24	70 00	4 7 6	792 35	840 00	47 65
1	1205	STOREKEEPING	47 71	50 00	2 2 9	576 82	600 00	23 18
1	1206	CLEANING	24 28	25 00	7 2	300 50	300 00	50 ✲
1	1207	GENERAL LABOR	46 20	50 00	3 8 0	566 35	600 00	33 65
1	1208	OVERTIME PREMIUM	36 10	50 00	13 90	415 16	600 00	184 84
			475 56 ✲	510 00	34 44	5743 37 ✲	6120 00	376 63
1	1300	SUPPLIES						
1	1301	ABRASIVES	10 15	10 00	1 5 ✲	129 18	120 00	9 18 ✲
1	1302	CUTTING OILS	26 10	25 00	1 10 ✲	340 75	300 00	40 75 ✲
1	1303	MACHINE LUBRICANTS	8 75	10 00	1 25	83 15	120 00	36 85
1	1304	SMALL TOOLS	41 20	50 00	8 80	532 48	600 00	67 52
1	1305	WASTE AND RAGS	7 50	10 00	2 50	103 10	120 00	16 90
1	1306	STATIONERY SUPPLIES	12 75	15 00	2 25	163 71	180 00	16 29
1	1307	GENERAL SUPPLIES	18 20	15 00	3 20 ✲	230 44	180 00	50 44 ✲
			124 65 ✲	135 00 ✲	10 35	1582 81 ✲	1620 00 ✲	37 19
1	1400	MAINTENANCE						
1	1401	BUILDINGS	12 52	15 00	2 48	172 24	180 00	7 76
1	1402	ELEC EQUIPMENT	13 22	10 00	3 22 ✲	168 28	120 00	48 28 ✲
1	1403	MACH EQUIPMENT	76 53	75 00	1 53 ✲	912 15	900 00	12 15 ✲
1	1404	TOOLS AND DIES	77 89	75 00	2 89 ✲	960 30	900 00	60 30 ✲
			180 16 ✲	175 00 ✲	5 16 ✲	2212 97 ✲	2100 00 ✲	112 97 ✲

Reprinted by permission, © 1954 by International Business Machines Corporation.

FIGURE 26.2   Control of Expenses by Ratio and Budget Comparisons

Total payrolls are greatly affected by general wage raises that are granted to the employees. It should be stressed that across-the-board raises create wage inequities and should be discouraged. The only time such raises are defensible is when the wage structure is already out of line and the across-the-board raise is used for correction purposes. Such a situation should rarely happen. Percentage increments are the only kind of raises that can maintain a structure that is already equitable. Management should take precautions against being pressured into an across-the-board raise one year so that the next year some raises must be granted to correct the inequities caused thereby. Collective bargaining on any other than a percentage basis would be either an admission that present rates are not in line and that they need correcting or that the company and the union are not interested in maintaining status or fair treatment for all employees.

There is a wealth of governmental statistics available to assist in evaluating and controlling costs. There are also successful industrial cost-control plans to emulate. In Chapter 20, we mentioned the Rucker and the Scanlon plans in which an agreement is reached between the company and the union on what is considered to be a reasonable cost for labor. These methods of controlling costs have proved very effective and at the same time have raised employee morale. Another point of control is overtime payments, which should be limited because the total payroll increases rapidly when premium wages are earned.

Labor turnover costs which are the direct result of wage inequities may legitimately be considered a point where more control could be exercised. Since sound wage and salary administration seeks to attract and retain employees, every means should be employed to reduce such turnover to a minimum. A study of resignations may reveal administrative weaknesses as well as cost-saving possibilities.

Improvement factor raises granted by General Motors and other companies represent an automatic type of control which assists in keeping wage raises equitable in relation to productivity. Any wage raise, like the cost-of-living type, which is not earned in some way tends to create wage inequities and their resulting consequences.

Fundamental guideposts for maintaining a compensation plan

If each of the major control centers of wage and salary administration is to be effective in the administering and maintaining of a compensation plan, there are some fundamental guideposts that should be followed. These guides are a necessity if a firm is serious about having employees accept the compensation program as fair over the long run. The guideposts are as follows:

1. Issue written policies to all concerned.
2. Centralize control of wage and salary matters.
3. Train managerial personnel for compensation activities.
4. Keep abreast of compensation activities.

Issue Written Policies to All Concerned

A survey on compensation for scientific personnel, made by a group of management consultants, shows that 80 percent of the American corporations polled did not have written salary policies available to their technical group.[3]

---

[3]James L. Watt, "Are Creative People Different?" *The Management Review*, Vol. XLIII, No. 7 (July, 1959), p. 21.

If a compensation program is to be controlled and maintained in an acceptable manner, the employees affected must understand what the objectives and the anticipated accomplishments are. Nonmanagerial employees expect more than promises of equitable wages from management. They want to be assured that management is sincere. Published policies not only inform employees of the company's aims but they also present the genuine intent of management to be fair — which is as important as the policies themselves. The company can further show its good faith by encouraging employees to report cases where they believe the company is not being fair. Of course, the firm must demonstrate its sincerity by a follow-up on cases reported. To do otherwise is acknowledgement that the policies are "window dressing."

Managerial employees are more anxious than rank-and-file employees about having published policies because they have to administer the policies. Written policies are also useful for reference, for study, and in answering questions. Published policies and interpretations are prerequisites to cooperation and uniform managing of administrative activities. They likewise contain the subject matter which is instrumental in training managerial personnel to administer the program. Another important reason for publishing policies is that it forces management to give more careful consideration to the objectives and goals of the plan. Unless goals are clear, understandable, and reasonable, they will not be acceptable to employees.

Centralize Control of Wage and Salary Matters

Frequently the question arises whether the control of all compensation matters should be centralized or decentralized. The advantages and disadvantages of centralized or decentralized activities should be determined by the type of enterprise, its products or services, and its personnel. Research and experience will dictate which one or, perhaps, a combination of both is to be adopted. Much depends upon which of the specialized functions and activities of the enterprises carries the most weight.

Control of compensation methods evolves into grouping the most closely related activities in the respective field. Here, reference is made to those phases which over many years have developed into a "must" in the wage and salary structure. Activities pertaining to job and employee evaluation; setting standards and establishing wage incentives; organizing and maintaining supplementary compensations, some requiring actuarial and financial experience, others necessitating knowledge pertaining to insurance; and the solving of problems concerning managerial and executive compensations — all require concentration on how they should be centralized or decentralized for good maintenance and control.

In numerous small and medium-size organizations, as well as in some large companies, compensation matters and various allied activities are so closely related that centralization of direction and control is just as important as centralization of business policy-making. Decentralization of wage and salary administration in small and in most medium-size enterprises has proven cumbersome, impractical, and expensive.

The functions of centralized wage and salary administration are depicted in the factors and guidelines for a compensation administrator, Figure 3.7, page 75, and are well presented in the actual organizational setups of two outstanding companies illustrated in Figure 3.2 (page 58) and 3.3 (page 59).

The activities of compensation may be compared with the special considerations or requirements involved in centralized or decentralized planning. It is natural to assume that in order to obtain desired results, to reduce expenditures, to minimize grievances, and to avoid personnel problems, centralized planning is essential to coordinate and synchronize departments as well as departmental activities. Only centralized supervision can effect proper coordination. These conditions hold good in all activities of compensation in general and in wage and salary administration in particular.

The primary advantage of centralized control is that the responsibility for administering all activities is concentrated at one source. Problems are channeled to one clearing point where they can be more efficiently solved according to company policies. Thus, unified administration is assured, and costly, confusing overlapping — duplication of effort — is avoided. Responsibility is more readily pinpointed when control is centralized. Administrative weaknesses are likewise more aptly discovered, easily analyzed, and corrected. A good centralized control system includes a reporting procedure that directs pertinent information to the proper source for necessary action, thereby maintaining an effective program.

It was previously indicated that most of the wage and salary activities may be successfully carried out by specific employees in several different departments, provided the control is centralized. It will be found, however, that wage and salary compensation activities in some companies never have been coordinated under centralized control. They are therefore not administered systematically in accordance with uniform methods. In these companies the compensation program is often criticized because it is inequitable and inefficient. Investigations have brought to light that middle-level managers and supervisors have had different points of view regarding top management policies. Yet the fact that supervisors should have specific authority and responsibilities within the field of compensation must also be considered. Clearly defined responsibility and authority at the lower supervisory level have to be maintained even under the most satisfactory centralized setup.

The wage and salary administrator can anticipate certain problems and important phases of compensation that must be adhered to and maintained according to policies, principles, and regulations. But, there are times when lower level management or the supervisor, being on the spot, is better able to cope with emergency conditions than the wage and salary administrator. The training of managerial personnel and supervisors in compensation matters is, therefore, not only advisable but also highly practical.

Train Managerial Personnel for Compensation Activities

Behind every successful compensation program are highly trained personnel. Training is especially necessary for first-line supervisors so that they understand the program thoroughly in order to answer promptly employee questions on compensation. Managerial personnel need to be conversant with top management's policies, and sold on all phases of the program as well as on the importance of their role. Only then can the administrators act in unison to represent management truly and to perform their roles effectively. It should be remembered that administrative methods and procedures are no better than the competency of the personnel selected to execute them.

Keep Abreast of Compensation Activities

A compensation plan designed to survive continual progressive changes requires periodic modifications to adjust to trends and improvements as they occur. The standards of success today may be antiquated, ineffective, and unacceptable in the near future. The need to realign wages to changed circumstances involves the reappraisal of the relative importance of the different wage-policy objectives. Compensation research in terms of wage surveys, governmental statistics, legislation, and the like provides much of the substantiation for important decisions that will prevent the program from deteriorating. The well-informed employee of today quickly becomes aware of trends and events which may affect his wages. The company therefore has to be alert especially about community wage rates and collective bargaining patterns. A review of present company grievances may enlighten wage administrators about the attitudes of employees and their expectations. A study of past grievances can reveal basic problems, their causes, and possible clues to improve controversial company practices. All company records that have a direct bearing on compensation matters should be examined for trends and guides in evaluating and improving present practices.

There are numerous organizations that render compensation services. Every company should be affiliated with one or more of these organizations to avail itself of the facilities offered. Among the prominent organizations that conduct research in the compensation field are: United States Department of Labor (Bureau of Statistics), American Management Association (AMA), National Industrial Conference ¡Board (NICB), Administrative Management Society (AMS), Society for the Advancement of Management (SAM), employer associations, and chambers of commerce. The majority of universities, especially in the colleges of business administration, have bureaus of research which conduct studies and research on the various wage and salary activities. A company that is represented in several of these research organizations is generally amply informed of the latest research activities.

Techniques and methods that implement control

The techniques and methods that implement control represent ways and means of accomplishing top management's intent to be fair in compensating its employees. The suggested guideposts previously recommended for maintaining and controlling a compensation plan can be more effective and more easily executed if they are implemented through preconceived techniques and well-informed personnel. Generally, an important segment of compensation administration is delegated to supervisors who should be adequately prepared for the task. Supervisors can be counseled and assisted by a compensation committee and by the director of wages and salaries. A brief discussion on the more important techniques and methods that implement administrative control is pertinent at this point.

Wage and Salary Committees

Every company large enough to require a formal wage and salary plan should appoint a committee to assist in its administration. One of the chief values of a wage and salary committee is its influence in securing employee acceptance of compensation decisions. To accomplish this important result, the committee should be composed of members from different departments who are free from local pressures and who have earned the respect and confidence of all employees through their record of impartiality and objectiveness in dealing with people. The compensation director is usually the chairman of the committee and the remaining members may be composed of an equal number of management and nonmanagement personnel who are thoroughly acquainted with compensation practices. If the chosen members lack such experience, they must first be trained in policies and the details involved.

The committee may function as the coordinating agent between departments in wage and salary matters such as: policy determination and modification, communications, compensation grievances, administrative routines, research, and establishment of standards and evaluation measures. Generally, committees serve in an advisory capacity on major decisions such as general wage increases and have delegated authority to rule on minor decisions such as rates on new jobs and rate changes on old jobs. It must be remembered that the maintenance of a compensation plan cannot be accomplished solely through a committee and the wage and salary administrator. Proper maintenance needs the assistance of all members of management, especially the first-line supervisors.

Administrative Role of Supervisors

First-line supervisors carry the burden of most administrative activities involved in maintaining an equitable wage and salary plan. Employees look to their supervisors to provide straightforward answers to their wage questions; employees are not satisfied with alibis or buck-passing. If the supervisor is to maintain his status and assist the company in maintaining equitable wages, he must be prepared to offer straightforward information. If the supervisor is well informed and follows the suggestions outlined by the director of compensation and his committee, most matters that need to be handled will become mere routine. Generally, however, it is not uncommon to find the supervisor ill equipped to fulfill his role in wage administration. He can then only function as a messenger instead of as an administrator.

An alert wage and salary administrator usually delegates as much administration as possible to the first-line supervisor and prepares him to perform well. Adequate preparation requires a formal course of at least six or eight group training conferences of two hours each on the fundamentals of compensation. Several follow-up seminars should likewise be conducted every three to six months to clarify questions which have arisen and to brief the supervisors on future activities. In all sessions the supervisors should be encouraged to discuss freely their problems so that effective solutions and preventive measures can be established by the collective thinking of the supervisors.

When nonroutine compensation policy changes are to be proposed by higher management, the supervisors should be assembled in conference to learn of the policy modifications and the philosophy behind them. Ample opportunity should be given for discussion on the proposed modifications. Group conferences have a tendency to engender teamwork and to improve administration because the opportunity is presented for the supervisors to solve their problems together. A more important advantage lies in that whatever decisions and solutions are decided on, they are thoroughly understood by the personnel who have to administer them. And since the supervisors participate in developing the solutions, they are not only sold on them but will also tend to administer the remedies in a more efficient and uniform manner than if higher management alone had suggested them. This is administration at its best.

Supervisors should have readily available all the job descriptions of the jobs under their jurisdiction. They should be responsible for maintenance of these descriptions by reporting job changes to the wage and salary administrator. The supervisor is expected to request reevaluations of jobs when needed and to coordinate the important phases of job evaluation and employee evaluation. Using his department budget and wage ranges as a guide, he can reward subordinates in accordance with the degree of merit they exhibit. Effective supervisory control over wages is aided by daily performance records (Figure 26.1) and

ANALYSIS OF PAYROLL
BY DEPARTMENT

DEPT. NO.	DEPARTMENT	DAY WORK HOURS WORKED	DAY WORK O.T. PREM.	DAY WORK AMOUNT REGULAR	AMOUNT PREMIUM	AMOUNT TOTAL	INCENTIVE HOURS WORKED	INCENTIVE O.T. PREM.	INCENTIVE AMOUNT REGULAR	AMOUNT PREMIUM	AMOUNT BONUS	AMOUNT TOTAL	DEPARTMENT TOTAL
1	ASSEMBLY A	1262	280	14625	3510	18135	18165	120	217945	1500	23618	243063	261198
2	ASSEMBLY B												
3	ASSEMBLY C												
4	CUTTING												

ANALYSIS OF PAYROLL
BY EMPLOYEE

DEPT. NO.	EMPLOYEE NUMBER	NAME OF EMPLOYEE	HOURS REGULAR	HOURS OVERTIME PREMIUM	EARNED	EARNINGS REGULAR	EARNINGS OVERTIME PREMIUM	EARNINGS BONUS	EARNINGS TOTAL	RATES BASE HOURLY	RATES AVERAGE EARNED
11	105	FRED ACKERLY	44	2	117	7920	408	1053	9381	1800	2039
11	145	MILTON CARGIN	40		8	6900		690	7590	1725	1897
11	170	GERALD DRISCOLL	40		11	6600		908	7508	1650	1877
11	245	JAMES DUHLMEIER	42	1	6	10500	268	750	11518	2500	2679
11	345	CLEMEN EDWARDS	40		92	9600		1200	10800	2400	2700
11	285	JOHN EGGLESTON	44	2	6	11000	552	1150	12702	2500	2761
11	2115	BARRY ENGELS	40		5	7200		540	7740	1800	1935
11	397	FRANK FARRELL	40	2		8250	396	469	9115	1875	1982
11	580	M J FOSTER	40			7500			7500	1875	1875
11	600	BARNEY GRAHAM	40			8000			8000	2000	2000
11	621	EDWARD GRESHAM	32		13	8000		1625	9625	2500	3008
11	645	LAWRENCE HENDERSON	40			10400			10400	2600	2600
11	711	JOHN HOWELLS	42	1	6	7560	193	540	8293	1800	1926
11	750	MICHAEL JAMES	40		6	7500		563	8063	1875	2016
11	782	RICHARD JAMES	40		8	7500		469	7969	1875	1992
11	806	PERCY JONES	40		7	8800		880	9680	2200	2420
11	872	QUINCY JONES	40		106	8000		700	8700	2000	2175
11	872	RADCLIFFE KIRK	40		81	9200		1219	10419	2300	2605
11	980	GERALD LOAFINGER	40		125	7200		729	7929	1800	1982
11	1032	AINSLEY MURDOCK	44	2	60	7260	377	1031	8668	1665	1884
11	1061	BOGART J SIMS	40		75	7200		540	7740	1800	1935
11		PETER TZYNSKI	40			7500		703	8203	1875	2051
			892	10	1516	179590	2194	15759	197543		

Reprinted by permission, © 1954 by International Business Machines Corporation.

FIGURE 26.3   ANALYSIS OF PAYROLL EXPENDITURES FOR MANAGEMENT CONTROL

payroll analyses (Figure 26.3) which reveal the worker's efficiency, hours earned, excessive overtime, and earnings. Employee evaluation serves as the justification for distribution of the wage dollar. Supervisors know better than anyone else which employees in their departments are productive and, through employee evaluation, are the best qualified to reward subordinates in accordance with their merits. As long as a supervisor remains within the established wage ranges and administrative controls, he should have a relatively free hand in deciding who is to be granted an increase in wages. If this procedure is followed, the supervisor will have a strong influence on productivity, morale, and motivation. In summary, the supervisor plays an important administrative role in compensation matters by being a source of information, by preparing employees to accept program activities and changes, by reporting changes, and by evaluating and rewarding subordinates according to their merits.

Schedule of Periodic Reviews

Sooner or later every phase of a compensation program has to be appraised. A well-managed company will usually complete all evaluations in from one to five years. There are so many details involved in maintaining a wage and salary program that it is practically impossible to remember all of them without some kind of aid. To help assure the efficient maintenance of a wage and salary plan, periodic compensation reviews as shown in Figure 26.4 are suggested. Figure 26.4 not only serves to give an overall picture of maintenance but can also be easily adapted to the daily calendar of those personnel involved in the maintenance activities. The schedule is invaluable as a checklist and serves as an aid in assigning the responsibility to those who have to carry out certain duties. It can assist management at any time in determining the progress or status of evaluations. Of course, the schedule is only suggestive and can be modified to suit the conditions of every company.

Records and Forms

Although it should be clear that wage and salary administration does not involve either inserting money in the pay envelope nor payroll accounting, it is advisable to be thoroughly informed of, and to utilize the records that are available in the payroll and accounting departments. All too often valuable data are available but not utilized because communication is lacking or friction exists between departments. Figures 26.1 through 26.3 illustrate the type of data that are — or should be — available for controlling compensation and for preparing reports for top management. Without records, remuneration decisions have to be reached without the facts. Every record which is maintained should not cost more than it is worth. To be most effective, all records and report forms should be reappraised once a year to determine those which no longer are worth their cost and should be discontinued.

COMPENSATION ITEMS SHOULD BE REVIEWED:

CONTINUALLY	MONTHLY	EVERY 3 MONTHS	EVERY 6 MONTHS	YEARLY	EVERY 2 YEARS	AS NEEDED
Business Forecasts	Company Budgets	Job Classification	Competitive Rates	Contract Provisions	Job Descriptions	Incentive Rates
Compensation Forecasts	Cost-of-Living Index	Job Standards	Employee Evaluation	Internal Communications	Job Evaluation Forms	Reevaluation of Jobs
Legislation	Departmental Budgets	Job Training Costs	Going Rates	Policies	Job Evaluation Manuals	
Overtime Payments	Government Statistics	Hiring Rates	Grievances	Routine Records	Job Titles	
	Improvement Factor	Internal Wage Structure	Internal v. External Wage Structure	Supervisor's Training	Reporting Forms	
	Labor Turnover	Labor Costs	Merit Increases	National Wage Surveys		
	Labor Turnover Costs	Labor Market	Ratios: (Cost) Direct v. Indirect Labor Fringe v. Total Payroll Management v. Total Payroll			
	Rate Ranges (Spreads)	Promoted Employees	Red-Circle Rates			
	Probationary Employees	Wage and Salary Briefing Seminar	Total Payroll			
			Wage Trends			

FIGURE 26.4 CHECKLIST OF PERIODIC COMPENSATION REVIEWS

Union-management relations in wage and salary administration

Responsibility for the administration of a wage and salary program is, of course, the obligation of top management. Administration is generally more effective and acceptable to the employees when they have a voice in it. In instances where a company does not have a union, it is good policy to invite employees from different departments to participate as the employees' representatives. However, most companies have unions which are the elected representatives of the employees. We strongly recommend employer-employee cooperation and joint action in compensation matters involving work simplification, wage determination, job evaluation, employee evaluation, and stabilization of financial incentives. Throughout the previous chapters of this book we have cited numerous successful companies in which management and the union share in administering the above activities. We believe that to maintain a successful compensation plan, both management and the union must agree to the following:

1. The company must operate at a fair profit.
2. The union must be allowed to bargain over matters pertaining to wages, hours, and working conditions.
3. Management must be responsible for running the business.
4. Both management and the union must subordinate their drives for power and seek a way to accommodate their differences.
5. Both management and the union must settle all problems on the basis of what is right and fair for the common good of the employer, the employee, and the public at large.
6. Both management and the union must keep communication lines open and be ready to discuss nearly anything, anytime, anywhere.

If both the union and management can agree to the above tenets, they can then spend their time and energy solving their mutual problems instead of wasting their energies disagreeing with each other.[4] The benefits to be derived are numerous. There would be few, if any, wage grievances that could not be satisfactorily solved without a strike. The atmosphere between the company and its employees would be one of friendliness and cooperative spirit with management taking the initiative in accepting employees as members of the company team. The union would realize that its prosperity is based on employees giving a fair day's work for a fair day's pay and that the union could not benefit if the company did not prosper. Because the union would feel secure, it would have confidence that it is the duty of management, not the union, to manage the business. The union would not therefore demand or try to force management to grant wage increases not justified by gains in efficiency or in increased production.

---

[4] See Stuart Chase, "Why Some Companies Have No Labor Trouble," *Reader's Digest*, Vol. LX, No. 362 (June, 1952), p. 16.

The natural problems that usually arise would be settled in an atmosphere of teamwork and friendliness and on their merits, not on the basis of selfish or fictitious reasons.

In short, a climate would so permeate the employer-employee relationships that the collective bargaining contract or agreement would embody those tenets that would permanently preserve the success of the wage and salary program and assure industrial peace.

REVIEW QUESTIONS

1. What should a company do when employees demand wages based on a pattern that a company genuinely cannot afford to match?
2. What are the symptoms which indicate an inadequate or weak wage and salary administration program?
3. A compensation manager must properly evaluate short-run and long-run influences if he is to help his company reach correct wage decisions. What aids should he use to help him evaluate these influences?
4. Should the immediate supervisor have sole authority to increase his subordinates' wages within a rate range? Why?
5. Participation and communications within the ranks of management play an important part in controlling a wage and salary program. Explain why.
6. Why does the administration of a wage program of proper job values and corresponding equitable rates of pay involve something more than just job evaluation and salary standardization?
7. After wages have been equitably established, how can management keep them equitable when the union has stronger bargaining power than the company?
8. What role should the union have in connection with the various phases of the wage and salary administration program?
9. If an employee asks to have his job revalued, is the value always raised? If not, in what way would you attempt to satisfy the employee?

RESEARCH OR SEMINAR QUESTIONS

1. When technological progress reduces the skills needed by the worker on his job, what should a company do regarding the worker's wages?
2. Should wage grievances be first brought to the wage and salary administrator's attention or be processed through the company grievance procedure?
3. Does collective bargaining make wage and salary administration unnecessary? Why or why not?
4. (a) How can management as a whole justify its union appeasement in granting high wages and other benefits over and above production? (b) Has not this been brought about by looking at the benefits of industrial peace without due regard for the costs?

5. Any good job evaluation method finds its ultimate justification in pricing jobs according to their respective worth. However, collective bargaining so often results in across-the-board wage increases and in effect nullifies the relative job worth relationships so painstakingly prepared. How can such inequities be minimized?

6. What tests can be applied in evaluating the success of a wage and salary administration program (a) from the standpoint of the employees? (b) from the standpoint of the company?

PRACTICAL EXPERIENCE ASSIGNMENTS

1. An employee in one job class is being trained as an emergency relief man in a higher class job. At the present he is performing the functions of this higher class job adequately. Since he will work in neither class exclusively, at which rate should he be paid and why?

2. A small-group manager promises a raise to a worker in order to keep him. After six weeks no raise comes through from the head office. The manager had no authority to increase pay. The employee becomes angry and threatens to quit. What can be done to remedy the immediate situation and to prevent similar occurrences in the future?

3. As a wage administrator you are negotiating with the union in setting a rate structure for your plant. The company wishes to use the community average as a basis for establishing the rate structure. The union wants you to pattern the structure after the industry average, which is thirty to fifty cents per hour higher than that of the community. Equal jobs in the companies in this community and in surrounding areas are comparable to the community average. How would you argue in deciding whether to use the industry or the community rates?

4. By union contract, laboratory helpers for a paint plant are hired at $450 per month. If they prove to be capable workers after three months, their salaries are increased to $500 per month.

   Warren Cramer is hired as a laboratory helper at $450 per month. Prior to military service, Warren had experience with another paint company and after one week it is obvious that he is worth more than $450 per month. The company is afraid they will lose a good man if they do not increase his salary to $500 immediately. They also fear, however, that they will set a union precedent for all new laboratory helpers if they do increase his rate immediately. Should the company increase Warren's pay after one week or wait three months? Explain the reasoning behind your answer.

5. As the head of a department you have transferred under your supervision two inexperienced employees to fill job openings in your department. These new employees both have over 20 years' seniority with the company in other departments and, through annual wage increases, are drawing salaries and other benefits exceeding the salaries of the experienced personnel in the department holding the same type of job. The present employees question this policy. How do you justify this situation?

6. John Bee, a chief photographer at X-Ray Company, asked his supervisor for a raise. His supervisor told him that he thought John deserved one but that

he was at the top of his pay bracket, and there was no place to promote him. John said he would leave if he did not get a raise. How could this problem be solved?

7. The husband of a woman employee died. She was therefore entitled to a widow's pension if her yearly salary was below a specified sum; however, her salary was not below that sum. The problem arose when she asked for a reduction in working hours which would reduce her earnings and enable her to qualify for the pension. Should management comply with her request? Explain the reasoning behind your answer.

CASE PROBLEM

26–1. E-Z CREDIT COMPANY

Administration Problems

James Smith started as a Credit Correspondent with the E-Z Credit Company five years ago at a salary of $650 per month. His background consisted of a BA degree in Economics. After five years of hard work and extremely conscientious effort, his salary has been increased to $850 per month. During this time there had been no change in the regular duties assigned to correspondents. At the present time, there are nine men employed in such a capacity.

Recently an opening occurred in the Credit Department for a new correspondent with the only requirement that he have a college degree. The starting rate for this position was quoted at $845 per month. Mr. Smith learned of the new starting rate and could not understand why he was only earning about the same salary as a new employee. However, since he had a deep faith in the company, he did not voice his concern about this situation to anyone except his close coworkers.

Problems:

1. Cite any weaknesses you believe exist in the E-Z Credit Company and in James Smith.
2. If, as the wage administrator, you overheard Mr. Smith's coworkers discussing the case, what should you do?
3. What administrative practices do you recommend to prevent a reoccurrence of this situation?

selected bibliography

part one • *Introduction and background*

Anderson, H. J. *The New Wage and Hour Law*, Rev. ed. Washington: Bureau of National Affairs, 1967.

Keyserling, Leon H. *The Role of Wages in a Great Society*. Washington: Conference on Economic Progress, February, 1966.

Lanham, Elizabeth. *Administration of Wages and Salaries*. New York: Harper & Row, Publishers, 1963.

McFarland, Dalton E. *Personnel Management: Theory and Practice*. New York: The Macmillan Company, 1968.

Merrill, Harwood (ed.). *Classics in Management: Selections from the Historic Literature of Management*. New York: American Management Association, 1960.

U.S. Department of Labor. *Minimum Wage Legislation*. Washington: U.S. Government Printing Office, 1967.

——————. *State Minimum-Wage Laws*. Washington: U.S. Government Printing Office, 1963.

part two • *The framework of wage and salary administration*

Burgess, Leonard R. *Wage and Salary Administration in a Dynamic Economy*. New York: Harcourt, Brace & World, Inc., 1968.

Dempsey, Bernard W., S.J. *The Frontier Wage*. Chicago: Loyola University Press, 1960.

Dunn, J. D., and Frank M. Rachel. *Wage and Salary Administration: A Systems Approach*. New York: McGraw-Hill Book Company, 1970.

Heneman, Herbert G., Jr., and Dale Yoder. *Labor Economics*, 2d ed. Cincinnati: South-Western Publishing Co., 1965.

Hicks, J. R. *The Theory of Wages*, 2d ed. New York: St. Martin's Press, Inc., 1963.

Hutchinson, John G. *Managing a Fair Day's Work*, Report No. 15. Ann Arbor: University of Michigan, Bureau of Industrial Relations, 1963.

Jaques, Elliott. *Equitable Payment*. New York: John Wiley & Sons, Inc., 1961.

Keyserling, Leon H. *The Role of Wages in a Great Society*. Washington: Conference on Economic Progress, February, 1966.

Lewis, H. G. *Unionism and Relative Wages in United States*. Chicago: University of Chicago Press, 1964.

Lincoln, James F. *A New Approach to Industrial Economics.* New York: The Devin-Adair Co., 1961.

McConnell, Campbell R. *Perspectives on Wage Determination: A Book of Readings.* New York: McGraw-Hill Book Company, 1970.

Ozonne, Robert. *Wages in Practice and Theory.* Madison, Wis.: University of Wisconsin Press, 1968.

Perlman, Richard (ed.). *Wage Determination: Market or Power Forces?* Boston: D. C. Heath & Company (Division of Raytheon Education Company), 1968.

Sibson, Robert E. *Wages and Salaries: A Handbook for Line Managers,* Rev. ed. New York: American Management Association, 1967.

Sutermeister, Robert A. *People and Productivity.* New York: McGraw-Hill Book Company, 1963.

Tolles, Arnold N. *Origins of Modern Wage Theories.* Englewood Cliffs, N.J.: Prentice-Hall, Inc., 1964.

Weintraub, Sidney. *Some Aspects of Wage Theory and Policy.* Philadelphia: Chilton Book Company, 1963.

part three • *Fundamentals of job evaluation*

Baer, Max F., and Edward C. Rober. *Occupational Information: The Dynamics of Its Nature and Use.* Chicago: Science Research Associates, Inc., 1964.

Belcher, David W. *Wage and Salary Administration,* 2d ed. Englewood Cliffs, N.J.: Prentice-Hall, Inc., 1962.

Brennan, Charles W. *Wage Administration: Plans, Practices, and Principles,* Rev. ed. Homewood, Ill.: Richard D. Irwin, Inc., 1963.

Chruden, Herbert J., and Arthur W. Sherman, Jr. *Readings in Personnel Management,* 3d ed. Cincinnati: South-Western Publishing Co., 1968.

CWS Salaried C & T Job Classification. New York: American Associated Consultants, Inc., 1968.

Evans, Gordon H. *Managerial Job Descriptions in Manufacturing.* New York: American Management Association, 1964.

Jaques, Elliott. *Progression Handbook.* Carbondale, Ill.: Southern Illinois University Press, 1968.

——————. *Time Span Handbook.* London: Heinemann, 1964.

Lanham, Elizabeth. *Administration of Wages and Salaries.* New York: Harper & Row, Publishers, 1963.

Lydall, Harold F. *The Structure of Earnings.* Oxford, England: Clarendon Press, 1968.

Moore, Franklin G. *Manufacturing Management,* 5th ed. Homewood, Ill.: Richard D. Irwin, Inc., 1969.

Patton, J. A., and C. L. Littlefield. *Job Evaluation,* 3d ed. Homewood, Ill.: Richard D. Irwin, Inc., 1964.

Ross, Edwin E. *Encyclopedia of Job Descriptions in Manufacturing.* Milwaukee: Sextant Systems, Inc., 1969.

U.S. Civil Service Commission. *Pay Structure of the Federal Civil Service.* Washington: U.S. Government Printing Office, 1969.

U.S. Department of Labor. *Training and Reference Manual for Job Analysis.* Washington: U.S. Government Printing Office, 1965.

U.S. Department of Labor, Bureau of Employment Security. *Dictionary of Occupational Titles*, 3d ed. 2 vols. Washington: U.S. Government Printing Office, 1965.

U.S. Department of Labor, Bureau of Labor Statistics. *Occupational Outlook Handbook*, 1968–69 Biennial ed. Washington: U.S. Government Printing Office, 1969.

part four • *Fundamentals of employee evaluation*

Barrett, Richard. *Performance Rating*. Chicago: Science Research Assocs., 1966.

Crossan, Richard M., and Harold W. Nance. *Master Standard Data: The Economic Approach to Work Measurement*. New York: McGraw-Hill Book Company, 1962.

Doulton, Joan, and David Hay. *Managerial and Professional Staff Grading*. London: Royal Institute of Public Administration, 1962.

Enell, John W., and George H. Haas (eds.). *Setting Standards for Executive Performance*, AMA Research Study No. 42. New York: American Management Association, 1960.

Hulin, Charles L. *Relevance and Equivalence in Criterion Measures of Executive Success*, Reprint Series No. 142. Champaign: University of Illinois, Institute of Labor and Industrial Relations, 1964.

Jackson, D. N., and S. Messick (eds.). *Problems in Human Assessment*. New York: McGraw-Hill Book Company, 1967.

Jurgensen, Clifford E., *et al*. *Employee Performance Appraisal Re-Examined*. Chicago: Public Personnel Association, 1961.

Kellogg, Marion S. *What To Do About Performance Appraisal*. New York: American Management Association, 1965.

Lopez, Felix M. *Evaluating Employee Performance*. Chicago: Public Personnel Association, 1968.

Managerial Appraisal Programs, BNA Personnel Policies Forum Survey No. 74. Washington: Bureau of National Affairs, September, 1964.

Niebel, Benjamin W. *Motion and Time Study*, 3d ed. Homewood, Ill.: Richard D. Irwin, Inc., 1962.

Pappas, Frank G., and Robert A. Dimberg. *Practical Work Standards*. New York: McGraw-Hill Book Company, 1962.

Performance Appraisals: Effects on Employees and Their Performance. Ann Arbor: Foundation for Research on Human Behavior, 1963.

Porter, Lyman W., and Edward E. Lawler. *Managerial Attitudes and Performance*. Homewood, Ill.: Richard D. Irwin, Inc., 1968.

Quick, Joseph H., *et al*. *Work-Factor Time Standards: Measurement of Manual and Mental Work*. New York: McGraw-Hill Book Company, 1962.

Torrence, George. *The Motivation and Measurement of Performance*. Washington: Bureau of National Affairs, 1967.

Valentine, Raymond F. *Performance Objectives for Managers*. New York: American Management Association, 1966.

Whisler, Thomas L., and S. F. Harper. *Performance Appraisal*. New York: Holt, Rinehart & Winston, Inc., 1962.

Wickert, Frederic R., and Dalton E. McFarland (eds.). *Measuring Executive Effectiveness*. New York: Appleton-Century-Crofts, 1967.

part five • Basic systems and plans of compensating employees

Argyris, Chris. *Integrating the Individual and the Organization.* New York: John Wiley & Sons, Inc., 1964.

Beach, Dale S. *Personnel: The Management of People at Work*, 2d ed. New York: The Macmillan Company, 1970.

Belcher, David W. *Wage and Salary Administration*, 2d ed. Englewood Cliffs, N.J.: Prentice-Hall, Inc., 1962.

Brennan, Charles W. *Wage Administration: Plans, Practices, and Principles*, Rev. ed. Homewood, Ill.: Richard D. Irwin, Inc., 1963.

Danielson, Lee E. *Characteristics of Engineers and Scientists*, Report No. 11. Ann Arbor: University of Michigan, Bureau of Industrial Relations, 1960.

Ewing, David W., and Dan H. Fenn (eds.). *Incentives for Executives.* New York: McGraw-Hill Book Company, 1962.

Gardner, John W. *Self Renewal: The Individual and the Innovative Society.* New York: Harper & Row, Publishers, 1964.

Gellerman, Saul. *Motivation and Production.* New York: American Management Association, 1963.

Huneryager, S. G., and I. L. Heckmann. *Human Relations in Management*, 2d ed. Cincinnati: South-Western Publishing Co., 1967.

Indik, Bernard. *The Motivation to Work.* New Brunswick, N.J.: Rutgers University, Institute of Management and Labor Relations Research Program, 1966.

Lincoln, James F. *A New Approach to Industrial Economics.* New York: The Devin-Adair Co., 1961.

Mangum, Garth L. *Wage Incentive Systems.* Berkeley: University of California, Institute of Industrial Relations, 1964.

McGregor, Douglas. *Leadership and Motivation.* Cambridge: Massachusetts Institute of Technology, 1966.

McQuaig, J. H. *How to Motivate Men.* New York: Frederick Fell, Inc., 1967.

Metzger, Bertram L. *Profit Sharing in Perspective*, 2d ed. Evanston, Ill.: Profit Sharing Research Foundation, 1966.

——————. *Investment Practices, Performance, and Management of Profit Sharing Trust Funds.* Evanston, Ill.: Profit Sharing Research Foundation, 1969.

Moore, Franklin G. *Manufacturing Management*, 5th ed. Homewood, Ill.: Richard D. Irwin, Inc., 1969.

Opsahl, Robert L., and Marvin D. Dunnette. "The Role of Financial Compensation in Industrial Motivation," *Psychological Bulletin*, Reprint No. 46. (Minneapolis: University of Minnesota, 1966), Vol. 66, No. 2.

Patton, Arch. *Man, Money and Motivation.* New York: McGraw-Hill Book Company, 1961.

Porter, Lyman W. *Job Attitudes in Management: Perceived Satisfaction and Importance of Needs*, Reprint No. 229. Berkeley: University of California, Institute of Industrial Relations, 1964.

Scott, R. C. *Incentives in Manufacturing.* Cambridge, Mass.: The Eddy-Rucker-Nickels Co. Vol. 1, 1966; Vol. 2, 1967; Vol. 3, 1968.

Sutermeister, Robert A. *People and Productivity.* New York: McGraw-Hill Book Company, 1963.

Vroom, Victor H. *Work and Motivation.* New York: John Wiley & Sons, Inc., 1964.

part six • *Supplementary plans of compensating employees*

Allen, Donna. *Fringe Benefits: Wages or Social Obligation,* Rev. ed. New York: New York State School of Industrial and Labor Relations, 1969.

Bankers Trust Company. *1965 Study of Industrial Retirement Plans.* New York, 1965.

Bankers Trust Company. *1967 Study of Employee Savings Plans.* New York, 1967.

Bernstein, Merton C. *The Future of Private Pensions.* New York: The Free Press of Glencoe, Inc., 1964.

Buckley, Joseph C. *The Retirement Handbook,* 2d ed. New York: Harper & Row, Publishers, 1962.

Burgess, Leonard R. *Wage and Salary Administration in a Dynamic Economy.* New York: Harcourt, Brace & World, Inc., 1968.

Chruden, Herbert J., and Arthur W. Sherman, Jr. *Readings in Personnel Management,* 3d ed. Cincinnati: South-Western Publishing Co., 1968.

Deric, A. J. (ed.). *The Total Approach to Employee Benefits.* New York: American Management Association, 1967.

Dietz, P. O. *Pension Funds: Measuring Investment Performance.* New York: The Free Press, 1966.

Employee Benefit and Pension Management, AMA Bulletin No. 59. New York: American Management Association, 1965.

Employee Benefits, 1967. Washington: Chamber of Commerce of the United States, 1968.

Employee Stock Purchase Plans, NICB Studies in Personnel Policy No. 206. New York: National Industrial Conference Board, 1967.

Fringe Benefit Practices, BNA Personnel Policies Forum Survey No. 87. Washington: Bureau of National Affairs, 1969.

Gottlieb, E. M. *Overtime Compensation for Exempt Employees,* AMA Research Study No. 40. New York: American Management Association, 1960.

Greene, Mark R. *The Role of Employee Benefit Structures in Manufacturing Industry.* Eugene, Ore.: University of Oregon, 1964.

Ingraham, Mark H., and F. P. King. *The Outer Fringe.* New York: Association of American Colleges, 1965.

McGill, Dan M. *Fulfilling Pension Expectations.* Homewood, Ill.: Richard D. Irwin, Inc., 1962.

—————. *Fundamentals of Private Pensions,* Rev. ed. Homewood, Ill.: Richard D. Irwin, Inc., 1964.

McNulty, James E., Jr. *Decision and Influence Processes in Private Pension Plans.* Homewood, Ill.: Richard D. Irwin, Inc., 1961.

Melone, Joseph J., and Everette T. Allen, Jr. *Pension Planning.* Homewood, Ill.: Richard D. Irwin, Inc., 1966.

National Foundation of Health, Welfare, and Pension Plans, Inc. *Textbook for Welfare, Pension Trustees, and Administrators.* Elm Grove, Wis.: 1969 Conference Proceedings, 1970.

Patterson, Edwin W. *Legal Protection of Private Pension Expectations.* Homewood, Ill.: Richard D. Irwin, Inc., 1960.

Reid, G. L., and D. J. Robertson (eds.). *Fringe Benefits, Labour Costs and Social Security.* London: George Allen & Unwin, Ltd., 1965.

Social Security and Private Pensions at the Crossroads: Crisis or Compromise? Washington: Machinery and Allied Products Institute, 1967.

U.S. Department of Health, Education, and Welfare, Social Security Administration. *Social Security Programs in the United States.* Washington: U.S. Government Printing Office, 1966.

U.S. Department of Labor, Bureau of Labor Statistics. *Digest of 100 Selected Pension Plans Under Collective Bargaining, Spring, 1968.* Washington: U.S. Government Printing Office, 1968.

part seven • *Managerial Compensation*

Andrews, Robert (ed.). *Managerial Compensation.* Ann Arbor: Foundation for Research on Human Behavior, 1965.

Belcher, David W. *Wage and Salary Administration.* Englewood Cliffs, N.J.: Prentice-Hall, Inc., 1962.

Compensation of Overseas Managers: Trends and Guidelines, Managing International Business No. 5. New York: National Industrial Conference Board, 1969.

Employee Stock Purchase Plans, NICB Studies in Personnel Policy, No. 206. New York: National Industrial Conference Board, 1967.

Ewing, David W., and Dan H. Fenn (eds.). *Incentives for Executives.* New York: McGraw-Hill Book Company, 1962.

Gottlieb, E. M. *Overtime Compensation for Exempt Employees,* AMA Research Study No. 40. New York: American Management Associstion, 1960.

Hulin, Charles L. *Relevance and Equivalence in Criterion Measures of Executive Success,* Reprint Series No. 142. Champaign: University of Illinois, Institute of Labor and Industrial Relations, 1964.

Lewellen, Wilbur G. *Executive Compensation in Large Industrial Corporations.* New York: National Bureau of Economic Research, 1968.

Managerial Appraisal Programs, BNA Personnel Policies Forum Survey No. 74. Washington: Bureau of National Affairs, September, 1964.

Moore, Franklin G. *Management: Organization and Practice.* New York: Harper & Row, Publishers, 1964.

Moore, Russell F. (ed.). *Compensating Executive Worth.* New York: American Management Association, 1968.

Roberts, David. *Executive Compensation.* New York: The Free Press of Glencoe, 1959.

Sibson, Robert E. *Wages and Salaries: A Handbook for Line Managers,* Rev. ed. New York: American Management Association, 1967.

Torrence, George. *Prevalence of Bonus Plans in Manufacturing,* NICB Studies in Personnel Policy, No. 185. New York: National Industrial Conference Board, 1962.

Top Executive Compensation, NICB Studies in Personnel Policy, No. 213. New York: National Industrial Conference Board, 1969.

part eight • *Wage and salary administrative controls*

Belcher, David W. *Wage and Salary Administration*, 2d ed. Englewood Cliffs, N.J.: Prentice-Hall, Inc., 1962.

Brennan, Charles W. *Wage Administration: Plans, Practices, and Principles*, Rev. ed. Homewood, Ill.: Richard D. Irwin, Inc., 1963.

Lanham, Elizabeth. *Administration of Wages and Salaries*. New York: Harper & Row, Publishers, 1963.

Patton, J. A., and C. L. Littlefield. *Job Evaluation*, 3d ed. Homewood, Ill.: Richard D. Irwin, Inc., 1964.

index